Communication Yearbook

2₄

WILLIAM B. GUDYKUNST, Editor

Communication
Yearbook
2_4

Published Annually for the
International Communication Association

Sage Publications, Inc.
International Educational and Professional Publisher
Thousand Oaks ▪ London ▪ New Delhi

P
87
.C5974
V 24
Dec., 2000

For information:

Sage Publications, Inc.
2455 Teller Road
Thousand Oaks, California 91320
E-mail: order@sagepub.com

Sage Publications Ltd.
6 Bonhill Street
London EC2A 4PU
United Kingdom

Sage Publications India Pvt. Ltd.
M-32 Market
Greater Kailash I
New Delhi 110 048 India

Printed in the United States of America

Library of Congress Cataloging-in-Publication Data

Library of Congress:
ISSN: 0-7619-2246-6 (hardcover)

01   02   03   04   10   9   8   7   6   5   4   3   2   1

Acquiring Editor:	Margaret H. Seawell
Editorial Assistant:	Heidi Van Middlesworth
Production Editor:	Diana E. Axelsen
Editorial Assistant:	Cindy J. Bear
Typesetter/Designer:	Barbara Burkholder
Indexer:	Kathy Paparchontis

CONTENTS

THE INTERNATIONAL COMMUNICATION ASSOCIATION

The International Communication Association (ICA) was formed in 1950, bringing together academicians and other professionals whose interests focus on human communication. The Association maintains an active membership of more than 3,300 individuals, of whom some two-thirds are teaching and conducting research in colleges, universities, and schools around the world. Other members are in government, the media, communication technology, business, law, medicine, and other professions. The wide professional and geographic distribution of the membership provides the basic strength of the ICA. The Association is a meeting ground for sharing research and useful dialogue about communication interests.

Through its Divisions and Interest Groups, publications, annual conferences, and relations with other associations around the world, the ICA promotes the systematic study of communication theories, processes, and skills.

In addition to *Communication Yearbook,* the Association publishes the *Journal of Communication, Human Communication Research, Communication Theory, A Guide to Publishing in Scholarly Communication Journals, ICA Newsletter,* and the *ICA Membership Directory.*

For additional information about the ICA and its activities, contact Robert L. Cox, Executive Director, International Communication Association, P.O. Box 9589, Austin, TX 78766 USA; phone (512) 454-8299; fax (512) 451-6270; e-mail icahdq@uts.cc.utexas.edu

Editors of the *Communication Yearbook* series:

Volumes 1 and 2, Brent D. Ruben
Volumes 3 and 4, Dan Nimmo
Volumes 5 and 6, Michael Burgoon
Volumes 7 and 8, Robert N. Bostrom
Volumes 9 and 10, Margaret L. McLaughlin
Volumes 11, 12, 13, and 14, James A. Anderson
Volumes 15, 16, and 17, Stanley A. Deetz
Volumes 18, 19, and 20, Brant R. Burleson
Volumes 21, 22, and 23, Michael E. Roloff
Volumes 24, 25, and 26, William B. Gudykunst

INTERNATIONAL COMMUNICATION ASSOCIATION
EXECUTIVE COMMITTEE

President and Chair
Joseph Cappella,
University of Pennsylvania

President-Elect
Cynthia Gallois,
University of Queensland

Immediate Past-President
Linda Putnam,
Texas A&M University

Finance Chair
Peter Monge (ex officio),
University of Southern California

Executive Director
Robert L. Cox (ex officio),
ICA Headquarters

BOARD OF DIRECTORS

Members-at-Large
Barbara O'Keefe, *University of Michigan*
S. J. Ball-Rokeach, *University of
    Southern California*
Daniel Hallin, *University of California,
    San Diego*

Student Members

Sarah J. Tracy, *University of Colorado
    at Boulder*
Kristine Nowak, *Michigan State University*

Division Chairs and Vice Presidents

Information Systems
Michael Shapiro, *Cornell University*

Interpersonal Communication
Steven R. Wilson, *Northwestern University*

Mass Communication
Sharon Strover, *University of Texas
    at Austin*

Organizational Communication
David Seibold, *University of California,
    Santa Barbara*

Intercultural/Development Communication
Bella Mody, *Michigan State University*

Political Communication
Steve Reese, *University of Texas
    at Austin*

Instructional/Developmental
    Communication
Jake Harwood, *University of Kansas*

Health Communication
Kim Witte, *Michigan State University*

Philosophy of Communication
J. Macgregor Wise, *Arizona State
    University West*

Communication and Technology
Joseph Schmitz, *University of Tulsa*

Popular Communication
Sharon Mazzarella, *Ithaca College*

Public Relations
Dean Kruckeberg, *University of
    Northern Iowa*

Feminist Scholarship
Dafna Lemish, *Tel Aviv University*

Language and Social Interaction
Robert E. Sanders, *University at
    Albany, SUNY*

Communication Law and Policy
Louise Benjamin, *University of
    Georgia*

Special Interest Group Chairs

Visual Communication
Ann Marie Barry, *Boston College*

Gay, Lesbian, Bisexual, and
Transgender Studies
John Nguyet Erni, *Columbia University
    School of Public Health*
Sue Lafky, *University of Iowa*

EDITOR'S INTRODUCTION

THE editorial policy of *Communication Yearbook* has been to publish competitively selected state-of-the-art reviews of communication research since Volume 19 under the editorship of Brant Burleson. Volumes 19 through 23, published under Brant Burleson's and Michael Roloff's editorships, contain in-depth analyses of specific lines of research (e.g., harmful speech, communication and customer service) representing wide cross sections of the scholarship conducted in the discipline of communication.

When I applied for the editorship of *Communication Yearbook,* I pointed out to the International Communication Association's Publication Committee that if I was selected, I planned to continue to publish review essays like those in the volumes that Burleson and Roloff edited. I also indicated that I wanted to include state-of-the-art review essays of research published in languages other than English and state-of-the-art reviews of senior scholars' lines of research in the volumes I edited. In addition, I specified that I wanted to devote one volume under my editorship to essays summarizing the state of the art of research and theory in the ICA's various divisions and interest groups. This is that volume. Volumes 25 and 26 under my editorship will return to the format of Volumes 19-23. These volumes also will include reviews of research published in languages other than English, as well as reviews of senior scholars' lines of research.

Communication Yearbook 24 is devoted to essays that address the current status of theory and research in each of the ICA's divisions and interest groups. When I applied to edit the *Communication Yearbook,* I saw this volume as making an important contribution to the discipline of communication, and one that could not be made by the traditional format. My goal was to include in the volume one chapter for each ICA division and interest group. The call for papers requested that authors submit proposals for review essays. The proposals that were submitted were reviewed by members of the editorial board. When there were multiple submissions for a specific division or interest group, the consulting editors were asked to recommend one of the proposals for publication in this volume.

After the initial proposals were reviewed, three things were evident. First, not all of the divisions and interest groups were represented. Second, not all of the proposal writers understood the task they were being asked to undertake (see the four questions included in the call for papers, noted on the next page). Third, the proposal that was accepted for one division (Intercultural and Development) did not represent the complete range of scholarship conducted in that division (i.e., it did not cover international or development communication). Publishing a volume that would not represent the full range of scholarship within the ICA and its divisions and interest groups, however, was not an option.

I was faced with two choices when I found that the proposals did not cover all ICA divisions and interest groups. I could drop the idea of doing a volume containing state-of-the-art essays about the ICA's divisions and interest groups or I could invite authors to write chapters for those divisions and interest groups or subareas for which I did not receive proposals. Dropping the idea for this volume was a potential problem because of the publication deadline. Inviting authors to write chapters also was a potential problem because recent volumes of the *Communication Yearbook* have all contained competitively selected chapters. I thought that the idea behind this volume was too important to drop, and so invited authors to write essays to fill in the gaps left by the proposals I had received. In most cases, I consulted with members of the editorial board or colleagues I know who are conducting research in the divisions or interest groups to find suitable authors. In the case of the Intercultural and Development Division, the person I invited to write the essay on international and development communication (Bella Mody) did not have time to write the chapter. She, nevertheless, found individuals to write essays on the two disparate areas of scholarship embraced by the division and integrated their contributions without taking credit as an author.

Authors submitted drafts of their chapters, which were then reviewed by members of the editorial board. My goal was for all authors to receive feedback from two colleagues. This was not always possible (e.g., in some cases only one reviewer returned the review). The review process led to a change in the coverage for one division. Both reviewers for the Language and Social Interaction Division suggested that the essay they reviewed did not cover the full range of scholarship conducted in the division (i.e., there are two very different lines of work within this division and the essay focused on only one line of work). I, therefore, asked one of the reviewers to write an essay representing the work not covered in the original essay. The companion essays now complement one another and reflect the work conducted in this division.

I posed four questions in the call for papers and in my instructions to the authors:

1. What are the parameters of the division/interest group, and what is the relationship of the division/interest group to other divisions/interest groups?
2. What are the major theories used in the division/interest group, and what research is there to support these theories?
3. What are the major lines of research in the division/interest group?
4. What are the major issues with which scholars in the division/interest group must cope in the next century?

I asked the authors to take positions regarding these four questions (e.g., to take positions regarding what the major theories and lines of research are), not to be all-inclusive in their coverage.

Given the space constraints of the volume, all authors were limited to 35 double-spaced manuscript pages. The authors of the various essays, therefore, had to make choices about the scholarship they discussed and the depth of their coverage. Because of the choices the authors made, the present volume does not include all theories and/or all lines of research conducted in each division or interest group.

Rather, the present volume contains reviews of what the authors consider to be the major theories and lines of research.

The authors addressed the four questions to various degrees in the first drafts of their essays. The reviewers did an excellent job of refocusing those authors who did not address the four questions in their initial drafts. Even though the final chapters are not necessarily organized using the four questions, all authors address the questions in some way. I believe the final chapters represent the state of the art of scholarship conducted within the ICA's divisions and interest groups.

To complement the essays covering the scholarship in the divisions and interest groups, I asked Linda Putnam, president-elect of the International Communication Association at the time editing of the volume began, to write an overview essay focusing on the discipline as a whole. Linda agreed to do this, and she asked Stan Deetz to coauthor the essay with her.

When all of the essays in this volume are combined, *Communication Yearbook 24* provides a state-of-the-discipline review as represented by the International Communication Association at the end of the 20th century. It is important, however, to keep in mind that the essays in this volume reflect only the discipline of communication as represented by the ICA. A slightly different view of the state of the discipline would emerge if a volume were published including essays regarding the state of the art of scholarship in the various divisions and commissions of the National Communication Association (NCA). Many of the divisions, interest groups, and commissions of the ICA and NCA have tremendous overlap in terms of membership and scholarly concerns. There are, nevertheless, areas of scholarly concern in the discipline of communication represented in the NCA but not in the ICA, and vice versa.

I could have chosen to expand this volume to include the areas of scholarship covered in the NCA but not in the ICA. I did not do this for three reasons. First, *Communication Yearbook* is a publication of the International Communication Association. Second, the original call for papers was limited to ICA divisions and interest groups. Third, space limitations precluded adding other chapters. As indicated earlier, the authors were limited to 35 manuscript pages. To include the additional chapters that would be necessary for full coverage of the discipline would have required such severe page limitations that it would not have been possible for authors to cover the major theories and lines of research in a meaningful way.

Even though the coverage is limited to ICA divisions and interest groups, this volume provides a solid summary of the state of the discipline at the end of the 20th century. It also provides an agenda for theorizing and conducting research into the 21st century. It should be extremely useful to scholars and graduate students in the discipline of communication.

Before concluding, I want to acknowledge the assistance I have received in preparing this volume. To begin, I want to thank the authors and reviewers. This volume would not have been possible without their contributions. Carrie Caudill, my editorial assistant for this volume, helped to set up the review system and helped to process the manuscripts. Rick Pullen, dean of the College of Communications, and Robert Emry, chair of the Department of Speech Communication at California State University, Fullerton, provided release time for me to work on the *Communication Yearbook* and funding for my editorial assistant. Michael Roloff, the previous editor, provided me with copies of the form letters he used and encouragement when I needed it. He made my job a lot easier. Finally, I want to thank Margaret Seawell, the communication editor at Sage Publications, for her invaluable assistance and support throughout the process of putting the volume together.

William B. Gudykunst

CHAPTER CONTENTS

1 Thinking About the Future of Communication Studies

STANLEY A. DEETZ
ICA President, 1996-1997
University of Colorado at Boulder

LINDA L. PUTNAM
ICA President, 1999-2000
Texas A&M University

This chapter presents the authors' thoughts on the future of communication studies. They argue that communication scholars and teachers should direct their attention to significant problems of our times (e.g., people making choices together). The authors assert that adequate conceptions of communication and negotiation can facilitate democratic processes and better joint decisions.

O THER writers in this volume have been asked to reflect on the past of communication studies; we have been asked to look to the future. Both projects are difficult, and the results of both are fundamentally contestable. Our goal is to initiate good discussions and evoke interesting ways of attending to communication. But looking to the future is different from looking to the past, in that the future is not simply to be described or predicted, but to be constructed. Furthermore, the most fundamental changes in society, and probably our discipline, are the least predictable. For example, who would have predicted in 1988 the fall of the Soviet bloc within a year or that the Dow Jones would hit 10,000 in 10 years? In this chapter, we address what may happen in our discipline as well as express our hopes for what could happen, if we work together. Although

AUTHORS' NOTE: This chapter draws on ideas presented in Stanley A. Deetz, "The Contribution of Communication Studies to the Emerging Age of Negotiation." *Florida Communication Journal*, 1997, vol. 25, pp. 11-23.

Correspondence: Stanley A. Deetz, Department of Communication, University of Colorado, Boulder, CO 80309-4120; e-mail stanley.deetz@colorado.edu responses to chance events may be more important than our visions for the future, clearly, we need to be prepared to address potential changes.

THE ECONOMICS OF THE MATTER

As we have seen in the past, economic matters will influence the future of the academy in major ways. Even in the face of a strong economy, we anticipate that state support of higher education will continue to decline in the United States, and perhaps elsewhere as well. This trend will have its greatest impact on enroll-ment-driven programs such as communication. Similar to the sciences, communi-cation departments will be forced to go to sources outside the university for greater percentages of their funding. Increasingly, communication programs will turn to corporate sponsors, federal and state grants, and foundation funding to support re-search and teaching.

This practice potentially leads to two related concerns. First, social conditions and practical issues, rather than faculty and departmental priorities, will have greater influence on the direction of instructional and research activities. This has been the case outside of the United States for some time. Gradually, we might expect greater convergence between U.S. and non-U.S. programs as non-U.S. pro-grams respond to enrollment and occupational pressures and U.S. programs respond more to corporate and social policy initiatives. Both will lead to less fac-ulty isolation and control. Multiple stakeholders will influence program develop-ment. Second, research will become increasingly more "pragmatic" in form. Rather than relying on our own theories and agendas, communication faculty will pose questions and solve problems that other groups have conceptualized.

To elaborate, we expect research opportunities to grow in those areas that have a close connection to regional and national priorities, specifically in domains linked to well-funded institutions removed from the academy. This trend has been clear-est in new funding initiatives in communication/information technologies, health, environment, and globalization. And in these areas, much of the funding, and hence the research, will assume a pragmatic or administrative form. Clearly, this trend has characterized new initiatives in mass communication and organizational communication for some time and is now developing in public relations, health communication, and communication and technology.

This move to pragmatic agendas will not go uncontested as academic disci-plines wrestle with the role of research and the nature of a "service" university. And, if this trend continues, these changes and the responses to them will engender conflicts in the field, conflicts such as those that have been productive in the past. For example, in the areas of mass communication and organizational communica-tion, the focus on pragmatic and administrative-based research has contributed to the development of critical alternatives and to options for including less powerful groups in research agendas. Looking back, we can see that these tensions have created socially relevant research that moves us away from sterile academic topics. The tricky question for the future is how these tensions will be managed in an economic arena that favors the priorities of funding agencies. If it is managed effectively, the struggle will be less about the nature of a service university and more about who is being served and for what purpose.

If our research becomes too critical of these pragmatic interests, we run the risk of elitism and perceived irrelevance. If, however, we become too pragmatic and administrative, the field runs the risk of duplicating what other organizations already do and thus adding little unique value to a knowledge-production chain. To contribute to our own future, communication scholars need to realize that dependence on external funding can enable our influence as well as narrow our domain; hence we must take risks to make this process a two-way interaction. Implicit in this concern is a belief that communication scholarship should reach out to broad-based publics rather than merely serve our own disciplinary and university agendas. In the future, our works rather than our words are likely to become increasingly important.

SOCIAL NEEDS

Logically, a social science discipline makes its most distinctive contributions in response to emerging salient problems, as is evident in the role of economics in understanding the marketplace and the role of sociology in addressing issues of urbanization (Deetz, 1994). The success of a new discipline often rests on its ability to display a fresh and useful way for the public to understand how a field conceptualizes its problems rather than how it conducts programmatic research. Its theories first and foremost have to be generative—that is, they must question and reconstitute social experience (Gergen, 1994).

In the future, our field needs to crystallize the link between our scholarly activities and the wider human community. The conceptualization of communication studies needs to respond to a set of social conditions rather than to an area of academic interest. Our publications, professional associations, and classroom teachings are not the ends of our work; rather, they are the means by which we address these social conditions. In the future, communication studies needs to provide a more fruitful way of thinking, talking, and enhancing the capacity to act on social problems. Only recently has the field turned its attention to social contributions, and this work has not gained the academic credence needed to sustain it. For example, research in health communication is just beginning to address the large-scale problems arising from managed care (Miller, Joseph, & Apker, in press). This work entails an integration of the knowledge and expertise across multiple divisions of the International Communication Association—namely, the Health Communication, Organizational Communication, and Political Communication Divisions and the Communication Law and Policy Interest Group—a difficult task to undertake because of our idiosyncratic domains of theory and research.

Moreover, individuals in our field have spent considerable time in recent years debating the status of the discipline (Deetz, 1994; Reeves, 1992; Shepherd, 1993; Sholle, 1995; Streeter, 1995; Swanson, 1993). These deliberations have resulted in the development of good advice about keeping our programs healthy, generating ways to connect them to the university's mission, and promoting the field to key constituents. Although these goals are necessary and valuable, the discipline continues to confound outcomes with the by-products of our work. That is, we resemble students who treat grades as the product of their labors and regard learning as an occasional by-product. In contrast, teachers typically believe that students should pursue learning as the product and make "getting good grades" a by-product of this process. In like manner, we need to center on the direction the field is taking and on the quality of our contributions, not simply on how to promote the discipline. Focusing our efforts on doing good works rather than on making our work look good is clearly a way to enhance the field. But what is good work? Good work, in our view, should engage the central intellectual and social issues of our time through addressing social problems and participating in intellectual debates.

But have we participated fully in the intellectual debates of our time? Although our field is clearly involved in academic debates, we have been slow to enter into the emergent intellectual deliberations in the social sciences. As a case in point, in the early stages of text theory and postmodern philosophy, communication scholars were generally absent from the scene. Similarly, many theorists stood by, focused mostly on general semantics, humanistic psychology, and behaviorism, while psychologists, sociologists, and family therapists made the earliest contributions to social construction (see Pearce, 1989, 1993; Peters, 1994; Shotter, 1993; Shotter & Gergen, 1994). In general, our field has been slow to embrace and slow to initiate major changes in the social sciences, including the recent linguistic turn in philosophy and social theory (Bakhtin, 1981; Lyotard, 1984).

We are not advocating blind acceptance of these alternatives, nor do we recommend that the field pursue them uncritically. We do contend, however, that the rank and file of our discipline need to move to center stage in these intellectual debates rather than sitting on the sidelines unable or unwilling to participate. Scholars need to understand emergent changes in social theory and their potential impacts on communication studies. More important, communication theorists need to be key players in these intellectual debates.

This indictment also applies to our field's efforts to address the social conditions of our time. Our conferences and our classrooms are typically organized around topics rather than around social problems. In our professional meetings, we present topical papers, often without integrating or pursuing the broader implications of these studies. As an illustration, many ICA members recall the Berlin conference held 25 years ago. As members emerged from their sessions, reporters with microphones inquired of them what communication scholars had determined. The members responded that they had heard papers on a variety of topics. "But what did you decide?" the reporters asked. In most cases, the attendees could not answer, because the academic discussions they had heard centered on topics unrelated to the implications of the work for social conditions.

Clearly, some arenas of communication scholarship, such as those addressing TV violence, freedom of speech, copyright issues on the Internet, satellite communications policy, and ethical dilemmas in public relations, focus on social problems. For the most part, in our interactions that cross disparate divisions, we rarely engage in dialogues about social concerns. By articulating the relevance of particular societal problems to the field as a whole, we as a discipline can root communication in social relevance. This step, in turn, will enhance our applications for research funding and aid in keeping communication research alive.

Similarly, our teaching continues to focus on what we know rather than on what students need to know or need to be able to do. Social relevance is more than getting a job. Communication studies should help students understand the central problems that society faces and the ways in which communication scholars can respond to them. As teachers, it is our responsibility to train students to assess communication principles and to apply those principles to society's problems.

THE ROLE OF SOCIAL SITUATIONS

Clearly, the 21st century is a significant time for communication scholars. As globalization takes shape, people throughout the world are responding to fundamental social, economic, and political issues (Monge, 1998). Old political boundaries are weakening, and people are becoming public consumers rather than "citizens" in the traditional sense of the term (Hart, 1994; Jamieson, 1988). That is, individual marketplace choices are replacing political discussion as the primary way social decisions are made (Deetz, 1992).

Not surprisingly, public decisions that influence our everyday lives appear increasingly beyond our reach and outside the realm of the democratic process. The resultant political apathy, cynicism, and self-centered opportunism are understandable and reflect the dangerously dominant attitudes of our times. If we are to rekindle a faith in our capacity to work together to produce the future we want, we must ask fundamental questions about where significant decisions are made and how the processes of making these decisions could be made effective and democratic. Although these concerns are at the root of communication questions, the field needs to address them in different ways. Several developments make it difficult to engage these concerns directly.

First, many scholars have become enamored of the rapid technological advances in information and mediated communication (see the reviews in this volume on information systems and communication and technology). Certainly these developments should not be left to vendors, engineers, and cognitive psychologists. The challenges that society faces today are clearly more fundamental and difficult than any anticipated by early proponents of the information revolution. Second, the loss of stable communities, shared values, and spaces for public deliberation has been a hidden side effect of rapid advances in transportation, data transmission, globalization of business, and a mass-mediated world. For the most part, proponents of information technologies focus on such issues as adoption, electronic connectedness, and data-sharing capacity, with no concomitant concern for the development of new social relations and communities. Even worse, rapidly reproduced information may replace public discussion by reducing society's capacity to engage in deliberation and to make collective decisions in the public sphere. Similarly, commercial artifacts may substitute for knowledge that arises from deliberation and conflicting experiences. In this era, information is often transformed into a neutral commodity, and communication is reduced to acts of transmission. The human problems that communication scholars must address today are not easily resolved through additional information; rather, they arise from providing people with the means for productively managing conflicts and making choices together.

THE AGE OF NEGOTIATION

What is radical about our new social context is not the rapid expansion of global information but the breakdown of the fabric of consensus and the walls of homogeneous communities in which decisions have traditionally been made. The presence of unexpected and often undesired diversity creates a problem for the traditional world, but it also offers a tremendous opportunity. In a diverse social context, the traditional cultural assumptions become only one type of social arrangement—one that can be maintained through control or changed through negotiation.

Today our most basic question is, How are we to make satisfying and just decisions collectively in circumstances in which most of the things we once took for granted are now open to constant renegotiation? The corpus of knowledge from communication studies should enable us to address this question. Unfortunately, our beliefs about quality communication are linked to social conceptions rooted in the ideals of free speech and the open marketplace (see Barber, 1984). Such ideals, once supported through relationships among people, language, and social situations, are no longer tenable. By characterizing our time as "an age of negotiation" rather than "the information era," we can increase our awareness of the social problems and opportunities we face and develop more robust communication concepts to address these problems.

Our current situation reflects an erosion of fundamental social consensus, the very consensus that is necessary for society and communication to work. New freedoms and opportunities come along with this erosion, but also new fears, insecurities, and dangers of colonization and domination. Within this context, traditional values and responsibilities decline, authority relations and social order become tenuous, crime and drug use often increase, and social conflict escalates. Contemporary societies often give rise to competing groups who handle these problems differently. Amid this conflict, four strategies are likely to emerge:

1. A return to traditionalism (even tribalism) in which community values and ethnocentrism prevail in the face of growing secularization, indeterminacy, and multiculturalism
2. A continued faith in modernity, particularly in the way that technological development and market economy provide a passive but commercially sponsored mode of integration
3. The development of a postmodern opportunism in which manufactured images substitute for identities and in which the most clever but least committed people seize momentary advantages
4. The search for a new and more powerful means to deliberate and negotiate, to maintain creativity and diversity and still make tough decisions together

Each of these positions has its theories of communication, but the first three create social dislocations; only the fourth can realize the potential in our current situation.

Traditionalism, commercial scientism, and personal opportunity have become strange bedfellows today. They are oddly compatible in outcome, and an attack on one seems to support the others. Each one precludes a robust social space and an opportunity to build a world together. They are best held together in their happy cynicism and implicit controlling moves. Cynicism and control are self-reproducing and toxic to all discussions. As discussion weakens, strategy and calculation become primary social determinants. Communication teachers and scholars should be especially concerned with the gradual replacement of discussion in contemporary society, whether it be with voting rather than deliberation, market economy rather than a public sphere, or opinion polls rather than the pursuit of joint commitment. A low regard for discussion is professionally costly as well as destructive to the invention of mutually satisfying decisions and personal commitments.

Although we sometimes fail to address our social condition adequately, recent work in communication theory provides an opening for a positive transformation. Actualizing the opportunities for negotiation requires a new conception of communication, one that is appropriate for the situation within new sites of public decision making. The need for public involvement in corporate decision processes has been clearly shown (Deetz, 1992, 1995), but equally important work is being done in many contexts. Unfortunately, the field has been a bit slow to embrace this work.

TOWARD A NEW WORLDVIEW OF COMMUNICATION

The possibility of a new way of thinking about communication requires a new way of thinking about human experience and society (Deetz, 1990, 1992, 1994). That is, our conception of liberal democracy purports that experience is first private and then becomes public; that is, one is first alone and then social. Our thinking about good communication, argumentation, free speech, and social contracts flows from this movement of private to public. New conceptions of this process suggest that experience is a social product and that we are first social before we are private. Therefore, the politics of the personal and the social/cultural grounds of experience present a wide array of issues that show inherent weaknesses in a liberal democracy. This view of the personal-social identity indicates why our popular conceptions of liberal democracy cannot deal with the fundamental negotiations required in this contemporary context.

Globalization and the awareness of genuine diversity, even if weakly formed, have demonstrated the inadequacy of previous assumptions and helped us understand the constructed and negotiated character of personal identity, social order, and visions for the future. Conceptions of human interaction based on objective facts should be replaced with theories of communication rooted in social interaction. In this move, communication surfaces as the means of producing and contesting temporary structures and orders. This rethinking has increased our understanding of the social-linguistic structuring of society, the politics of representation, the dialogic roots of existence.

The presumption that experience is located in the person and separate from the social hampers our development of a dialogic existence (Boland, 1987; Henriques, Hallway, Urwin, Venn, & Walkerdine, 1984). In contrast, new communication perspectives cast the individual as an abstraction from a set of interactions within complex, competing social systems rather than as a bundle of needs, personality, emotions, and motivations (Shotter & Gergen, 1994). These characteristics exert influence in being produced and reproduced in specific situations.

WHAT WE COULD DO IN THE FUTURE

The difficulty of articulating a radically new communication theory is probably as great as the difficulty faced by early revolutionary writers in generating concepts of liberal democracy. A carefully crafted contemporary theory of communication is as important for the next century as notions of free speech and natural rights were for past decades. If communication teachers and scholars are to contribute to the development of such a theory, our work needs to address four main goals: We must develop a unique model of explanation, rethink notions of mutual decision making, generate a new model of negotiation, and attend to issues of voice.

Developing a Unique Mode of Explanation

For the most part, scholars treat communication as an object to be studied rather than as the foundation of our discipline. What holds us together is that we study similar phenomena. Other social science disciplines are more organized around unique modes of explanation. Researchers in psychology, sociology, and economics do not simply study individual behavior, societies, or economies, respectively; they bring to their research particular lenses that help them to form explanations for how to view the world. Our inability to articulate a clearly developed "communicative" explanation for social life has not only hurt us professionally, it has kept society from understanding experience in this important way.

Moreover, the explanations and concepts produced by psychologists, sociologists, and economists (for example, affective or cognitive structures, social structure, market economy, and grand narratives) reify these abstractions and provide them with explanatory power. A communication lens centers on the processes of constructing and reproducing these concepts and on the ways that they influence collective decisions. That is, constructs such as *personality* and *social structures* exist as abstractions produced from patterned interactions, and their explanatory force emanates from the way they are produced and reproduced in ongoing interactions. Even to contribute effectively to interdisciplinary research, our field needs to articulate a unique explanation of social phenomena, one that positions us as pivotal to addressing social problems. Although the field is moving in this direction, the issue of a unique explanation needs to be at the top of our list of priorities.

Rethinking Practices of Mutual Decision Making

In our research, the autonomous individual is often treated as the site of decision making and the origin of perceptions, thoughts, and feelings. The possession and distribution of information, in this view, are critical for people to make quality decisions. These assumptions underlie our focus on expression skills, information dissemination, and information technologies. For example, the study of mass media has located its conceptual space in the development of information dissemination necessary for a liberal democracy. In this approach, democracy is reduced to such concepts as *freedom of expression* and *free markets,* often void of attention to deliberation and negotiation. Even though freedom of expression is essential to good decision making, free speech advocates often fail to examine access to speaking and differences in "megaphone" size that produce inequalities among constituents. Freedom of expression is meaningless if people are not present to state their positions or if the person with the biggest megaphone drowns out the chorus of free voices. In effect, freedom of expression neither specifies the right to be heard nor guarantees the expression of all positions.

The goal of engendering representation requires that alternative perspectives play equal roles in influencing decisions. This process is difficult because of the unobtrusive and subtle ways in which control systems operate to restrict representation and produce unwarranted consent. Ironically, the pursuit of self-interest often benefits particular individuals through the making of decisions that have long-term negative consequences for society as a whole. Until we change our belief in the nature of individuals, conceptions of negotiation will remain limited, important forms of domination will go undetected, and democracy will be weak.

This belief in the autonomous individual also influences the forums in which freedom of expression functions. In the United States, debate is the preferred political forum. The candidate who advocates effectively and persuades others to his or her position typically wins. An alternative forum might be one in which we watch intelligent candidates generate ways to meet society's diverse needs and values. The candidate who is most creative in finding mutually satisfying solutions might emerge victorious. This alternative, however, requires a different model of communication.

Scheduling more meetings, as small group scholars have pointed out, is not necessarily the answer (Seibold & Krikorian, 1997). More meetings and more chances for expression do not mean better decisions. The critical function of communication is to promote better decisions. In our attention to information and persuasion, we have often forgotten that the primary function of expression is to make sure the community does not neglect valuable positions. Rather than enhancing participation in decision making, our approaches have treated the goals of informing and persuading as ends in themselves. From the view of participation, rhetoric should facilitate discussions in times when deliberation may not seem needed (Deetz, 1983). Rarely do we highlight the critical functions of deliberation in uncovering neglected positions. For instance, in media studies scholars often attend to mass media's role in informing the public but typically remain mute regarding the media's influence on deliberation.

Generating a New Model of Negotiation

In like manner, the autonomous individual is central to traditional models of negotiation. Even win-win approaches that aim for mutual gain treat bargaining as a process rooted in self-interest, exchanges, and reciprocity of offers (Fisher, Ury, & Patton, 1991). In our society, negotiation takes the form of scripted behaviors with a prototypical set of activities, including exchanging offers, defending positions, making compromises, and formulating agreements (O'Connor & Adams, 1999). By focusing on exchanges and compromises, negotiation centers on reaching settlements (Putnam & Kolb, 2000). Communication in this model serves as information exchange and tactical maneuvers.

In many ways, reaching a settlement confounds the product with the by-products of negotiation. The product or general aim of negotiation should be effective conflict management and the development of relationships to foster future interdependence. Agreements in this perspective are actually by-products of the process and stepping-stones to the ultimate goal of managing the conflict effectively. However, in striving for a settlement, negotiators equate getting a settlement with effective conflict management.

A model of negotiation rooted in co-construction instead of exchange centers on mutual inquiry and collaboration. Rather than using trades to generate joint gain, mutual inquiry encourages expansive thinking and joint learning. Proposals in this model are blended through open deliberations instead of offers and counteroffers. This model engenders collaboration through ongoing dialogue rather than through debate and strategic moves.

This alternative shifts negotiation away from a commodity metaphor toward communal goals. Rather than aiming for equitable distribution of resources, negotiators respond to emergent voices and legitimate discussions of new vistas and directions. Whereas exchange and settlements function as the foci of traditional models, relationships and process move to center stage in this alternative. In this shift, interdependence is not predetermined or instrumental, as in traditional views. It is codeveloped through the emergent process of interaction. In traditional models, negotiated relationships are instrumental, rooted in the dilemma of trust/distrust and cooperation/competition. In the alternative model, building trust occurs from coming together, discovering new understandings, and finding common ground (LeBaron & Carstarphen, 1997). Negotiators form a connected relationship and a shared reality rather than oscillating between cooperation and competition. A new model of communication rooted in the emergent process of interaction is essential to the development of an alternative perspective for negotiation—one aimed at collaboration rather than concerned with winning and losing.

Although negotiation is often viewed as a skill or a particular kind of communicative event, it is actually a mode of deliberation, one that can serve as an antidote to control and a way of making communicative processes more democratic. Negotiation, particularly as a joint construction, is a way of capturing creativity through diversity. This joint construction not only aids in discovery, it facilitates reframing issues, embracing differences, and acting on social problems. In the alternative model, negotiation can provide a forum for testing consent and assuring the right to be heard. As we enter the "age of negotiation," we need to generate a new model for deliberating and for understanding the assumptions embedded in this vital communicative process.

Attending to Issues of Voice

As a consequence of focusing on information and expression, our society has increased the number of forums in which speaking occurs and decreased our attention to voice. *Forums* refers to the locations, times, and places for expression, whereas *voice* centers on individuals' ability to express their own meanings freely.

Clearly, a liberal democracy needs speaking opportunities, and thus scholars highlight the role of debates, mass media, and the Internet in providing free expression. However, because of contrived and flawed understandings, people can speak out but not be heard. That is, prior social constructions or images substitute for authentic situations (Baudrillard, 1983). These constructions contain embedded values that are not disclosed. Because these constructions are treated as reality, they are not open to negotiation or to discussion of alternative value premises. Attention is directed away from the embedded values to the shared "neutral" ones. For example, cyberspace advocates often refer to the Internet as a neutral medium. In popular opinion, the World Wide Web appears open to anyone, irrespective of age, race, gender, or income. Thus proponents express concerns about censorship and "free" speech on the Internet. But their issues of concern might be quite different if the focus were on group differences in access and usage, or ease of different groups in presenting their thoughts and feeling through this medium. Particular reasoning processes, forms of evidence, references to authority, and concepts of decision making may be different on the Internet compared to other forms of communication. The greatest restriction on the Internet is not governmental censorship, but the representation of voice in the medium itself. The literature on information systems rarely addresses implicit forms of representation that restrict voice. The ways in which the Internet fosters some voices and restricts others need to be a central concern in our studies. As Boland (1987) notes:

> At issue is the nature of language and human communication, and their role in our social construction of the everyday world. The problem that concerns us here is the way our images of information without in-formation lead to an ignorance of language and our human search for meaning which together deny the very possibility of human communication. The process of constructing the social world is a process of language and communication. Our distorted images of information and communication, and their widespread use to understand our everyday world, threaten our ability to construct and reconstruct it in humanly satisfying ways. (p. 366)

IN SUMMARY

Communication scholars and teachers should direct their attention to the significant problems of our time. One important issue that scholars should examine is how to increase the capacity of people to make choices together. Unfortunately, many of our commonsense conceptions of communication and democracy hamper our contributions. Common sense as a social historical product incorporates these taken-for-granted perceptions. Moreover, it retains conceptions that distort choices and fail to stand up to scrutiny. Perhaps the greatest shortcomings of common sense are received views of individual autonomy, information, and decision making. To the extent that we recognize and respect the heterogeneity of the world, we acknowledge that meanings are constructed and open to negotiation.

Our field can advance "good" communication either as a way to open considerations of voice or as a way to close off discussions and produce systematically distorted decisions. To aid in opening considerations to voice, scholars need to focus on social meanings rather than on influence-centered or expression-based views of liberal democracy. Our concern with the effective use of language has to question whose language it is, in what way it is partial, and how we can reclaim alternatives for understanding the world. A growing number of scholars take the issue of constructionism seriously and show how open interactions are foreclosed and how conflicting positions contribute to conditions of indeterminacy (Calás &

Smircich, 1991; Deetz, 1990; Martin, 1990). They show how interacting in this state of indeterminacy generates temporary moves aimed at providing additional options for the future.

Adequate conceptions of communication and negotiation can facilitate democratic practices and better joint decisions. Communication scholars can contribute to this process by employing research designs and pedagogy that respond to social conditions, by contributing to the central intellectual debates of our time, and by investigating where significant decisions are made and how they can be made democratically. Moreover, with a unique explanation of communication and an alternative model of negotiation, communication scholars can develop modes of deliberation that embrace diversity and increase creativity. Researchers can also contribute to this goal by critiquing forms of asymmetry and by showing how communication becomes distorted. Such work will help produce forums in which conflict and voice can be reclaimed, issues can be discussed openly, and decisions can be made with fairness and justice.

REFERENCES

Bakhtin, M. M. (1981). *The dialogic imagination: Four essays* (M. Holquist, Ed.; M. Holquist & C. Emerson, Trans.). Austin: University of Texas Press.

Barber, B. (1984). *Strong democracy*. Berkeley: University of California Press.

Baudrillard, J. (1983). *Simulations*. New York: Semiotext(e).

Boland, R. (1987). The in-formation of information systems. In R. Boland & R. Hirschheim (Eds.), *Critical issues in information systems research* (pp. 363-379). New York: John Wiley.

Calás, M., & Smircich, L. (1991). Voicing seduction to silence leadership. *Organization Studies, 12,* 567-602.

Deetz, S. A. (1983). Negation and the political function of rhetoric: A review essay. *Quarterly Journal of Speech, 69,* 434-441.

Deetz, S. A. (1990). Reclaiming the subject matter as a guide to mutual understanding: Effectiveness and ethics in interpersonal interaction. *Communication Quarterly, 38,* 226-243.

Deetz, S. A. (1992). *Democracy in the age of corporate colonization: Developments in communication and the politics of everyday life.* Albany: State University of New York Press.

Deetz, S. A. (1994). Future of the discipline: The challenges, the research, and the social contribution. In S. A. Deetz (Ed.), *Communication yearbook 17* (pp. 565-600). Thousand Oaks, CA: Sage.

Deetz, S. A. (1995). *Transforming communication, transforming business: Building responsive and responsible workplaces.* Cresskill, NJ: Hampton.

Fisher, R., Ury, W., & Patton, B. (1991). *Getting to yes* (2nd ed.). Boston: Houghton Mifflin.

Gergen, K. J. (1994). *Realities and relationships: Soundings in social construction.* Cambridge, MA: Harvard University Press.

Hart, R. P. (1994). *Seducing America: How television charms the modern voter.* New York: Oxford University Press.

Henriques, J., Hallway, W., Urwin, C., Venn, C., & Walkerdine, V. (Eds.). (1984). *Changing the subject.* New York: Methuen.

Jamieson, K. (1988). *Eloquence in an electronic age: The transformation of political speechmaking.* New York: Oxford University Press.

LeBaron, M., & Carstarphen, N. (1997). Negotiating intractable conflict: The common ground dialogue process and abortion. *Negotiation Journal, 13,* 341-361.

Lyotard, J.-F. (1984). *The postmodern condition: A report on knowledge* (G. Bennington & B. Massumi, Trans.). Minneapolis: University of Minnesota Press.

Martin, J. (1990). Deconstructing organizational taboos: The suppression of gender conflict in organizations. *Organization Science, 11,* 339-359.

Miller, K., Joseph, L., & Apker, J. (in press). Strategic ambiguity and the role of the development process. *Journal of Applied Communication Research.*

Monge, P. R. (1998). Communication structures and processes in globalization. *Journal of Communication, 48*(1), 142-153.

O'Connor, K. M., & Adams, A. A. (1999). What novices think about negotiation: A content analysis of scripts. *Negotiation Journal, 15,* 135-147.

Pearce, W. B. (1989). *Communication and the human condition.* Carbondale: Southern Illinois University Press.

Pearce, W. B. (1993). Achieving dialogue with "the other" in the postmodern world. In P. Guant (Ed.), *Beyond agendas: New directions in communication research.* Westport, CT: Greenwood.

Peters, J. (1994). The gaps of which communication is made. *Critical Studies in Mass Communication, 11,* 117-140.

Putnam, L. L., & Kolb, D. M. (2000). Rethinking negotiation: Feminist views of communication and exchange. In P. Buzzanell (Ed.), *Rethinking organizational managerial communication from feminist perspectives* (pp. 74-106). Thousand Oaks, CA: Sage.

Reeves, B. (1992). Standpoint: On how we study and what we study. *Journal of Broadcasting and Electronic Media, 36,* 235-238.

Seibold, D. R., & Krikorian, D. H. (1997). Planning and facilitating group meetings. In L. R. Frey & J. K. Barge (Eds.), *Managing group life: Communicating in decision-making groups* (pp. 270-305). Boston: Houghton Mifflin.

Shepherd, G. J. (1993). Building a discipline of communication. *Journal of Communication, 43,* 83-91.

Sholle, D. (1995). Resisting disciplines: Repositioning media studies in the university. *Communication Theory, 5,* 130-143.

Shotter, J. (1993). *Conversational realities: The construction of life through language.* Newbury Park, CA: Sage.

Shotter, J., & Gergen, K. J. (1994). Social construction: Knowledge, self, others, and continuing the conversation. In S. A. Deetz (Ed.), *Communication yearbook 17* (pp. 3-33). Thousand Oaks, CA: Sage.

Streeter, T. (1995). Introduction: For the study of communication and against the discipline of communication. *Communication Theory, 5,* 117-129.

Swanson, D. L. (1993). Fragmentation, the field, and the future. *Journal of Communication, 43*(4), 163-172.

CHAPTER CONTENTS

2 Information Systems Division: Intrapersonal, Meaning, Attitude, and Social Systems

MICHAEL A. SHAPIRO
Cornell University

MARK A. HAMILTON
University of Connecticut

ANNIE LANG
Indiana University

NOSHIR S. CONTRACTOR
University of Illinois

The Information Systems Division of the International Communication Association is concerned with the systems that make communication work, ranging from the intrapersonal (e.g., emotional and cognitive systems) to interpersonal, organizational, and societal systems. Over the past two decades, the interests of the division have focused increasingly on systems of mental processes in communication, but underlying mechanisms explored in information systems research range from reflexive processing of an advertisement's formal features to concepts of self-organizing systems used to model the behavior of large organizations. This review looks at four major areas of recent interest to scholars in the Information Systems Division. The first two sections examine systems of mental processing of media from reflexive attentional and emotional responses to the conscious interpretations made by viewers. The third section examines the workings of belief systems, particularly as they apply to attitude change. The final section moves away from the individual to the use of systems theory to understand complex social phenomena, including social organizations.

WHAT is the Information Systems Division? We get asked that a lot. Some confusion is understandable. Recent papers presented in the division appear to be about almost anything connected to communication: political communication, Internet advertising, television fiction, jury decision making, fund-raising letters, verbal aggressiveness, and more. Methods could be characterized as basically empirical, but otherwise they run the gamut from social observation to pushing reaction-time buttons and measuring heart rate. Experiments are popular, but so are surveys and other methods.

AUTHORS' NOTE: In addition to one of the sections, the first author wrote most of the introductory pages of this chapter and coordinated the overall effort. Otherwise, all authors contributed equally, and authorship is in order of the sections of the chapter. Michael A. Shapiro is currently chair of the Information Systems Division of the International Communication Association, Annie Lang is a past chair of the division, Mark A. Hamilton is currently vice chair of the division, and Noshir S. Contractor is a member of the division. Our thanks to Rebecca Polakow for her assistance with the manuscript.

Correspondence: Michael A. Shapiro, Department of Communication, 319 Kennedy Hall, Cornell University, Ithaca, NY 14853; e-mail mas29@cornell.edu

Communication Yearbook 24, pp. 17-49

Traditional categories don't help. Information systems research seems to include mass communication, interpersonal communication, organizational communication, new communication technologies, persuasion, and more. In fact, most of our division members are also members of other divisions, most commonly the Interpersonal Communication, Communication and Technology, and Mass Communication Divisions. We think this is true because information systems are central to making communication work, ranging from the intrapersonal (e.g., emotional and cognitive systems) to interpersonal, organizational, and societal systems. We study the processing of information within systems—all kinds of information processed by all kinds of systems related to communication. To an information systems scholar, information could be a pattern of light and shadow, the onset of sound, grief, joy, embarrassment, narrative structure, scary movies, background television, marital interactions, sitcoms, advertisements, Web sites, faces, posture, and more. Information is the stuff that's being communicated and processed in a system.

One way of looking at a system is as a system of nodes between which information passes. A node could be a mental process, a person, a department, a company, a country, or a group. It is a place where information is received, sent, altered, changed, or processed.

Over the past two decades, the interests of the Information Systems Division have focused increasingly on systems of mental processes in communication, but underlying mechanisms explored in information systems research range from reflexive processing of an advertisement's formal features to concepts of self-organizing systems used to model the behavior of large organizations. Information systems scholars are less interested in the effects of television than in how and why those effects occur. We are less interested in whether an interpersonal argument is persuasive than in the mental processes involved in constructing a persuasive message.

Trying to capture the range of theories and methods used in information systems research is like trying to capture all the theories and methods used in social science. A library, not a book chapter, is required. In this chapter we focus on four major areas within the many areas of scholarship in information systems. We first examine systems of mental processing of media, from reflexive attentional and emotional responses (in a section written by Annie Lang) to the conscious interpretations of messages made by viewers (in a section written by Michael A. Shapiro). In many ways those interpretations depend on how people mentally use belief systems. In a section written by Mark A. Hamilton, we examine the workings of those belief systems, particularly as they apply to attitude change. Finally, in a section written by Noshir S. Contractor, we move away from the individual to the use of systems theory to understand complex social phenomena, including social organizations.

INFORMATION PROCESSING AT THE INTRAPERSONAL LEVEL:
PASSING THE STUFF OF COMMUNICATION
AROUND INSIDE OUR OWN HEADS

What happens when you hear or see a message? Whether the message is from television or from a friend, it has to be processed by your brain. Information systems scholars have been in the vanguard of those looking at what the brain does with messages, particularly televised and other mediated messages. This work has redefined the way we think about media. Information systems researchers have conceptualized media not in terms of content but in terms of their impact on cognitive processing, using dependent variables such as attention, arousal, emotional response, allocation of processing resources, and memory. These dependent variables are then conceptualized and operationalized as parts of an information-processing system whose mechanisms can be studied and understood. This research has often led to the conclusion that the brain treats media messages pretty much the same way it treats other environmental stimuli.

Generally, information systems researchers who take this approach have conceptualized media (often television) in psychological terms (Singer, 1980). This means that mediated messages are defined not in terms of content (e.g., violence, commercials, news) but in terms of psychologically important variables, such as arousal (Bolls, Yoon, Dent, Potter, & Lang, 1997; Detenber, 1996; Kawahara, Bolls, Hansell, & Lang, 1996; Mendelson & Ognianova, 1998; Zillmann, 1982), structural features (Anderson & Levin, 1976; Ditton, Lombard, Kaynak, Linder, & Pemrick, 1998; Geiger & Reeves, 1993; Reeves, Lang, Kim, & Tatar, 1997), movement (Detenber, Simons, & Bennett, 1997), rate of production (Anderson, Levin, & Lorch, 1977; Bolls et al., 1997; Hitchon, Thorson, & Duckler, 1994; Kawahara et al., 1996; Thorson, Reeves, & Schleuder, 1985, 1987), and cognitive load (Armstrong, 1997; Kawahara et al. 1996; King & Behnke, 1998; Lang & Basil, 1996, 1998; Vaughn, 1996). One of the first things researchers have looked at in this new psychological conceptualization of media—particularly television—is the impact of structural features on the mental processing of messages.

The Role of Structural Features

Many information systems researchers have defined television in terms of structural features. For example, Lombard et al. (1996) conducted an ambitious content analysis of television content to describe and categorize all the structural features involved in the television medium. Other researchers have studied the effects of specific structural features on various processing and emotional response variables. Detenber et al. (1997) examined the effects of movement on attention and arousal responses to emotional pictures. Ditton et al. (1998) investigated the effects of structural features on the concept of presence. Reeves et al.

(1997, 1999) looked at the effect of screen size on emotional response and memory. Bolls et al. (1997) and Kawahara et al. (1996) examined the effects of rate of structural features on arousal, attention, allocation of processing resources, and memory.

Virtually all of these studies show that the structural features of a medium have important effects on the information processing of mediated messages. At a basic level, most of these structural features have been shown to elicit an orienting response in attentive television viewers. The orienting response is an automatic physiological attention response that causes a momentary increase in resources allocated to a task (Lang, 1990; Lang & Basil, 1996; Reeves et al., 1985, 1997). This research has substantiated theoretical conceptualizations of the orienting response as a mechanism for the automatic allocation of processing resources to the processing of mediated messages (Lang, 1997; Reeves et al., 1985; Reeves & Nass, 1996).

Limited-Capacity Models

Related to this, a major conceptualization of attention used by information systems scholars is that of the limited-resource or limited-capacity model (Armstrong, 1997; Basil, 1994a, 1994b; Bolls et al., 1997; Kawahara et al., 1996; King & Behnke, 1998; Lang, 1995, 1997; Lang & Basil, 1998; Vaughn, 1996). In such a model, media users are conceptualized as having limited processing resources available to allocate to the processing of mediated messages. Resources are allocated through a combination of automatic and controlled processes. Messages vary in the levels of resources required to process them. As a result, different messages are perceived as having various cognitive loads. The cognitive load imposed by a message is a major factor in determining how well that message will be processed (Armstrong, 1997; Hibbs, Bolls, & Lang, 1995; Thorson & Lang, 1992).

A great deal of information systems research has focused on how various features or characteristics of messages increase or decrease the messages' cognitive loads. Several researchers have shown that the processing of emotion requires additional resources (King & Behnke, 1998; Lang & Basil, 1996; Lang, Newhagen, & Reeves, 1996; Newhagen & Reeves, 1992). Complexity and fast pacing have also been shown to increase the resources required to process a message (Bolls et al., 1997; Kawahara et al., 1996; Lang, Bolls, Potter, & Kawahara, in press). Semantic redundancy between the audio and video channels is another structural feature that plays an important role in determining a message's cognitive load. Messages with high redundancy require fewer resources, whereas those with low redundancy may require greater resources (David & King, 1996; Fox, 1996; Grimes, 1991; Lang, 1995). Variations in the designs of human-computer interfaces have been shown to alter the cognitive load of computer programs (Vaughn, 1996). Finally, imagery (Viser & Gordon, 1996), movement (Detenber, 1996), screen size (Reeves et al., 1997), and the presence of background media

(Armstrong, 1997) have all been shown to increase the resources required to process a message.

In addition, controlled processing resources—that is, the resources intentionally allocated by the viewer—also play an important role in how thoroughly a message is processed. Less work has been done to investigate variables that increase and decrease controlled processing allocation. Among those investigated so far are emotion (Lang, Dhillon, & Dong, 1995), previous knowledge (Thorson & Lang, 1992), education (Grabe, Lang, Zhou, & Bolls, 1999), and age of viewer (Lang, Schwartz, & Snyder, 1999). Obviously, many individual-difference variables, such as interest, previous knowledge, goals, and motivations, play a role here.

Emotional Messages

Another focus of the research being conducted by members of the Information Systems Division is on the effects of emotion-eliciting messages on information processing (Bryant, 1997; Nabi, 1998; Viser & Gordon, 1996; Weaver, 1997). As mentioned above, emotion has been shown to increase both the automatic and controlled allocation of resources to a message. In addition, research shows that emotion affects processing in many other ways. Researchers have taken several different theoretical approaches to the study of emotion. One common approach has been to look at negative and positive messages and determine how the valence of a message alters processing. Research suggests that negative messages compel attention and that both positive and negative messages receive greater attention than neutral messages (Lang & Bolls, 1995; Lang et al., 1995; Newhagen & Reeves, 1992). Further, the research clearly shows that emotional messages are better remembered than neutral messages.

The second important component of emotion that has received significant research attention is arousal. Research has shown that arousing messages and calm messages are processed differently. The presence of arousing content in a message increases viewers' self-reported and physiological arousal (Bolls et al., 1997; Kawahara et al., 1996; Lang et al., in press). In turn, the elicitation of arousal in viewers leads to increased cognitive load and better memory for messages (Bolls et al., 1997; King & Behnke, 1998; Lang & Bolls, 1995).

Other studies have focused on how the use of emotion in messages alters other cognitive processes. For example, Nabi (1999) has developed a persuasion model that details how negative emotion alters the processing of persuasive messages.

Processing Pictures

Another major focus of research among members of the Information Systems Division concerns how people process video images as well as combined audio and video stimuli (e.g., audio-video redundancy). Many researchers have approached this problem using Pavio's dual coding theory (David & King, 1996;

David & Peay, 1998; Preston, 1996, 1997). This research suggests that video encoding is virtually an automatic process (Lang, Potter, & Bolls, 1999); that when pictures and words are redundant, memory improves (Grimes, 1991; Lang, 1995); and that concrete words that elicit visual imagery are remembered better than words that do not elicit imagery (David & King, 1996; David & Peay, 1998).

Presence

Recently, some information systems researchers have begun to focus on questions concerning the processing of new media and new media forms such as virtual reality, home theater systems, and computer-related media (agents, the Web, 3-D gaming, and so on). Questions about how information presented in these media is processed are receiving some attention (Nass & Steuer, 1993; Reeves et al., 1999; Reeves & Nass, 1996).

In addition, several information systems researchers have begun to examine the concept of presence or telepresence (Kim & Biocca, 1997; Lombard & Ditton, 1997). This concept is related to the notion that new media may blur the boundaries between reality and fantasy even more than other media do. To date, research has focused on attempts to conceptualize presence (Lombard & Ditton, 1997) and attempts to determine how structural characteristics of media and messages may alter users' sense of presence (Kim & Biocca, 1997). Studies suggest that structural features such as larger screens, point-of-view camera movement, and affective computer agents alter viewers' sense of being there (Deitz & Lang, 1999; Orton, Reeves, Leshner, & Nass, 1994). Recent research also suggests that presence may mediate viewers' physiological and emotional responses to some media (Lang, Schneider, & Deitz, 1999).

How Do We Do It?

In addition to studying interesting theoretical problems, information systems researchers are constantly searching for new methods to illuminate thorny research problems. The intraindividual focus of this area of research has led to a number of interesting methodological developments that have spread outward from the Information Systems Division into general usage in the field of communication. The focus on cognitive processes and mechanisms, many of which are automatic or unconscious, has led information systems researchers to search for covert measures of cognitive activity. Among the measures often used are (a) the recording of real-time physiological responses, including heart rate (as a measure of attention), skin conductance (as a measure of arousal), and facial EMG (as a measure of valence) (Bolls, Lang, Potter, & Snyder, 1999; Lang, 1994); (b) secondary task reaction times as a measure of resources allocated to media use (Lang & Basil, 1996, 1998); (c) latency to recognition as a measure of memory or judgment accessibility (David & Peay, 1998; Shrum, 1999); (d) signal detection analysis (Fox, 1996; Shapiro, 1994; Shapiro & Fox, 1995, 1996); and (e) a plethora of the more common self-report measures and paper-and-pencil memory tests.

What Does It All Mean?

Research conducted by members of the Information Systems Division suggests that the human information-processing system is a limited-capacity system (Geiger & Newhagen, 1993; Lang & Basil, 1996; Reeves & Nass, 1996). Many characteristics of mediated messages can trigger an increase in the automatic allocation of processing resources (i.e., attention; see Basil, 1994; Geiger & Reeves, 1993; Lang, 1990, 1997). Depending on the cognitive load of the situation, this increase in resources can lead to an increase or decrease in memory for messages (Thorson & Lang, 1992). Thus when cognitive load is high, additional calls for resources overload the processing system and memory for the messages decreases (Grimes, 1991). On the other hand, when cognitive load is low, additional calls for resources increase message processing and result in an increase in memory.

Emotion is an important variable in this system. Emotion alters the way in which information is processed (Newhagen & Reeves, 1992). Emotion-eliciting messages increase arousal. This means that viewers rate themselves as being more aroused, and the physiological measures of sympathetic nervous system activation increase. When viewers are more aroused, resources allocated to the message are increased, attention to messages is increased, liking for messages is increased, and memory for messages is increased (Lang et al., 1995).

The processing of pictures is an important focus of information systems research. Division researchers have clearly shown that pictures are frequently remembered better than words. In addition, research has shown that the encoding of visuals requires fewer processing resources than the encoding of text and audio stimuli. Further, when the visual track of an audiovisual presentation is produced in such a way as to compel attention (either through the addition of emotional images or through the use of visual production techniques to draw automatic attention), memory for the accompanying audio track decreases. This is particularly true when the redundancy between audio and visual stimuli is not high.

MESSAGES AND MEANING

Obviously, the brain also processes the meaning of a message. Although meaning is an element of the discussion in the preceding section, it is not the main focus. Information systems investigators have looked in detail at the mental systems involved in creating interpretations of a message. These systems can be relatively automatic or more thoughtful and less subject to the limited capacity of reflexive processing.

Until recently, the goal of most television-related communication research has been to discover when particular television effects occurred. Information systems investigators focus not just on when particular interpretations occur, but on what mental contents and procedures people use in making interpretations. Here, too, there has been a shift away from thinking of these meanings as a function of media content toward a more balanced view of meaning as a complex interaction among message content, prior experience, and the viewer's ongoing mental processes. By focusing on the systems of mental processes that create meaning, information systems investigators attempt to capture the complex ways people create meanings across a broad spectrum of media sources and media content, including entertainment, news, and advertising.

Meaning and Content

The challenge is to create a theory of meaning creation that accommodates viewers' real abilities. We know that viewers can share social meanings while simultaneously creating unique meanings. A systems approach accounts for subjective reactions to objective messages while at the same time permitting intersubjectivity (Hewes & Planalp, 1987).

Messages place at least some loose limits on possible interpretations if even approximate social meanings are to be transmitted. For example, if the writer of a television drama does not correctly anticipate at least some of the interpretations likely to be attached to a message, the message may become unintelligible. In such a television drama a police officer's questioning of a suspect may make sense only if the writer has correctly anticipated the viewer's understanding of earlier plot elements and the viewer has understood those plot elements in at least somewhat the same way as the writer. Of course, the viewer brings something to the interaction as well—his or her own prior experience. That experience can dramatically influence the viewer's interpretation of the police officer's questioning (as fair or unfair, for example). Such multiple interpretations can take place without threatening the writer's and viewer's shared sense of the basic elements of the story. Thus the meaning of a television message is a combination of the writer's skill in producing specific responses and the viewer's experiences and social and cultural interpretations (Livingstone, 1992).

Another factor is that a person's experiences, beliefs, attitudes, and goals are in part consequences of his or her social and cultural milieu. To the extent that those in a culture share mental contents, they are likely to produce similar interpretations. A corollary is that people from different value systems may interpret the same stimulus very differently (Liebes & Katz, 1986). However, information systems scholars are likely to focus on the fact that it is the similarity of mental contents, not mere membership in a social category, that leads to similar interpretations (Berkowitz & Donnerstein, 1982).

Some scholars have claimed that the mass production of television messages creates dominant cultural messages that tend to reduce some belief differences among viewers—particularly if they are heavy viewers (Gerbner, Gross, Morgan, & Signorielli, 1986). Although the debate over this claim is beyond the scope of this chapter, it is clear that two people can and often do interpret the same media message in very different ways (e.g., Cooper & Jahoda, 1947; Hoijer, 1992; Liebes & Katz, 1986; Vidmar & Rokeach, 1974). Considerable evidence shows that increasing television viewing does not change beliefs and attitudes in any one direction (Hirsch, 1980; Potter, 1991). The meaning of a message is the interpretation a person gives that message (Dervin, 1981, 1989).

A variety of content and audience factors can affect both the amount and the direction of influence. These include type of program (Potter & Chang, 1990), outcome of plot elements (Bryant, Carveth, & Brown, 1981; Tamborini, Zillmann, & Bryant, 1984; Weaver & Wakshlag, 1986), identification with characters (Reep & Dambrot, 1989; Turner & Berkowitz, 1972), audience perceptions of television (Adoni, Cohen, & Mane, 1984; Adoni & Mane, 1984; Cohen, Adoni, & Drori, 1983; Potter, 1986, 1988), prior experience (Austin, Roberts, & Nass, 1990; Ball-Rokeach & DeFleur, 1976; Fazio, 1986; Perry, 1987), attention (Anderson & Lorch, 1983; Chaffee & Schleuder, 1986), and audience goals (Meadowcroft & Zillmann, 1987; West, 1993; Zillmann, 1991).

The Process of Interpretation

Interpretive processes occur both while an individual is processing a message and later, when he or she may retrieve memories, beliefs, and attitudes. Mental elaborations that take place during viewing are sometimes called on-line processing (Hastie & Park, 1986). Few media studies have investigated this directly, but considerable research has shown that people often generate evaluative thoughts while processing persuasive messages (Greenwald, 1968; Petty & Cacioppo, 1981). These evaluative thoughts are used to change attitude during the processing of the message and are better predictors of later attitude change than memory for the message arguments or even memory of the evaluative thoughts (Greenwald, 1968).

Evaluative thoughts are only one element in the on-line interpretation of messages. For example, considerable on-line processing of a television situation comedy is needed to understand the social situation, the motives of the characters, and the consequences of various actions. (For a thorough treatment of how people create meaning while viewing television, see Biocca, 1991.) People may also be making on-line judgments about the reality of what they are seeing (Adoni & Mane, 1984; Shapiro & Chock, 1998; Shapiro & Lang, 1991). As Hoijer (1992) notes, audience interpretation of media is a "dynamic interaction" among "content, structure and presentation, and the realms of social experience of the viewers" (p. 599).

On the other hand, many decisions influenced by media content are made sometime after viewing. These depend on memory for bits and pieces of experience, including mediated presentations, to reconstruct a view of what the real world is like. Such reconstruction can be as uncomplicated as retrieving a memory or using a simple heuristic (Chaiken, Liberman, & Eagly, 1989), but more thoughtful reconstructions can be quite complex. For example, social reality estimates may involve a complex assembly of direct and indirect experience, possibly influenced by attitudes, preferences, and social pressures (Shapiro, 1995).

Finally, construction and reconstruction influence each other. Reconstruction depends in part on information stored in memory from previous on-line interpretations of television. On-line interpretations may be influenced by previous reconstructions stored in memory.

The Special Role of Direct Experience

Direct experience seems to have somewhat special potency in informing a wide range of interpretations of media. Experience with a topic may confer some immunity to media influence (Adoni et al., 1984; Cohen et al., 1983; Perry, 1987). Even children are more likely to think for themselves when they have some direct experience with a topic (Austin et al., 1990).

Direct experience influences interpretation of media for a number of topics, including crime (Doob & MacDonald, 1979; Elliott & Slater, 1980; Gerbner, Gross, Morgan, & Signorielli, 1980; O'Keefe, 1984; Schlesinger, Dobash, Dobash, & Weaver, 1992; Weaver & Wakshlag, 1986) and judgments about health risk (Flora & Maibach, 1990; Shapiro & Han, 1994; Snyder & Rouse, 1992; Tyler, 1980).

Although there is considerable evidence that direct experience is especially potent, we know little about its relationship to television experience. It seems possible that some television experiences can approach the status of direct experience (Shapiro & McDonald, 1992), but we have only begun to scratch the surface of when, how, and why. This seems like a fruitful area for future research.

Conscious and Unconscious Processes

People are not always thoughtful when they assign meaning to media messages. Meaning processing can range from intentional and controlled (the individual is highly aware of what is passing through his or her thoughts) to automatic (an environmental stimulus automatically causes a mental procedure to occur without the individual's being consciously aware of the event; see, e.g., Fazio, 1990; Hansen, 1989; Hansen & Hansen, 1988). Automatic processing does not require an explicit goal to occur (Sanders, Gonzalez, Murphy, Liddle, & Vitina, 1987; Schneider, Dumais, & Shiffrin, 1984; Shiffrin & Schneider, 1977). Most mental processing of television is a combination of automatic and controlled processing.

A large number of studies have shown that unconscious activation can influence interpretation of an ambiguous social stimulus (Higgins, 1989; Higgins & King, 1981). One suggestion is that relatively short-term priming effects may explain a number of television effects, including effects on estimates of social reality and on aggressive behavior (Berkowitz, 1984; Berkowitz & Rogers, 1986). For example, in political communication there is some evidence that exposure to a topic on television news may increase perceptions of that topic's importance and may make it more likely to influence later political decisions (Iyengar, 1990).

Construct activation may also prime social reality estimates by heavy television viewers (Shrum & O'Guinn, 1993). The subtle nature of these psychological effects may make some of them difficult to detect using a complex stimulus like television. Overall priming is a largely unexplored but potentially important explanation for television effects (Shrum, Wyer, & O'Guinn, 1998).

Another way in which relatively unconscious processes may influence reconstruction is through automatic processes that draw on episodic memories of specific television events and the contextual information stored with those memories to determine which memories are relevant to a social reality decision. The contextual information stored with memories may include the perceived source of the memory as well as psychophysiological responses to television. This contextual information acts as a sort of filter in various automatic processes that weighs and balances which memories are relevant (Mares, 1996; Shapiro & Lang, 1991; Shrum, 1997).

The distinction between automatic and controlled processing is an important one for media studies. Methods that are appropriate for the study of automatic processing are different from those that are appropriate for the study of controlled processing. Methods used to study automatic processing must assume that the processes involved are covert and not available to be reported directly by subjects. On the other hand, techniques such as thought listing can be appropriate for investigating more thoughtful processing (Shapiro, 1994). Interpretations based on automatic processing are not necessarily inferior to those based on more thoughtful processing. In fact, automatic mental procedures are that way because we are very good at them. Nonetheless, they may influence our interpretations in ways that might not stand up if given more thought. For example, sex-stereotyped music videos seem to have some unconscious influence on viewers' later judgments about women (Hansen, 1989; Hansen & Hansen, 1988).

Conclusions

The mental processing of media such as television is a complex psychological task, even when individuals are viewing ritualistically, to be relaxed or distracted. Viewers must keep track of plots, characters, and motivations to understand even the most mindless programs. Using television memories to make later decisions is equally complex. In both cases, the result is active interpretation of the television stimulus, not passive reception of content. This interpretation depends on both the content of television and an individual's prior experience and goals. The effect of television depends on the interpretation. Any consistency in interpretation across individuals exists because people who share cultural and social experiences also share prior experiences and goals. In addition, one goal of any communication is to share social meanings.

Related to this is the work of some information systems scholars who look in detail at the processing and interpretation of messages of one specific type: persuasive messages.

INFORMATION SYSTEMS AND PERSUASION

The two preceding sections have dealt with systems of mental processing of both the structure and meaning of messages. One common goal of messages is persuasion. Information systems scholars have made a significant contribution to our understanding of how persuasive messages work (and don't work).

Considerable research by Information Systems Division members has focused on the processes that mediate the impact of message exposure on belief change. Most of these researchers have investigated source (e.g., Basil, 1995), message (e.g., Crano & Chen, 1997), channel (e.g., Boster & Levine, 1997), or receiver (e.g., Tyson & Hamilton, 1996) variables that facilitate persuasion. Some researchers have also been developing models to explain resistance to persuasion (Nabi, 1995; Pfau et al., 1996).

This section explores two main themes of information systems research related to persuasion. The first involves the influence that knowledge structures exert on the communication process (Ritchie, 1995, 1997; Ritchie & Good, 1996). Knowledge structures link beliefs together and determine beliefs' centrality. Belief systems theory (Hamilton & Mineo, 1996, 1999; Rokeach, 1960, 1969) defines the centrality of a belief as the number of functional connections it has with other beliefs in a given knowledge structure.

A second theme has been how receivers process messages and the impact that message-processing variables have on receiver beliefs and behaviors (Basil, 1996; Meyer, 1996; Mongeau, 1996; Reynolds, 1996; Roskos-Ewoldsen, 1996; Tremain Koch & Crano, 1996). The discussion in this section will concentrate on the impact that certain message features have on receiver evaluations of source, message, and topic—an area often referred to as *message effects research.*

Information Systems Division members typically use multivariate statistics that reflect the complexity of message-processing phenomena. This research is characterized by a striving for methodological rigor, with an emphasis on accurate estimation of effect size, effort to control potential confounding variables, and the reporting of effect size estimates in conjunction with significance tests and estimates of the reliability of measurement devices.

Belief Structures as Information Systems

Although information systems research on belief structure often draws on a variety of theories, belief systems theory (Rokeach, 1960, 1969) holds promise as a means of synthesizing these diverse findings. Beliefs are more or less connected within knowledge structures, where the flow of information organizes the belief system along a central-peripheral dimension (Rokeach, 1960). Consequently, the belief system can be divided into the three major sections shown in Figure 2.1. The central region contains three types of primitive beliefs: the primary primitives related to cognitive competence, the secondary primitives related to the self-concept, and the tertiary primitives related to the generalized other (Hamilton & Mineo, 1999). The peripheral region contains beliefs derived from the central region. Peripheral beliefs can concern individuals, groups, or cultures. The intermediate region contains the processes that justify the derivation of peripheral beliefs from central beliefs. The three main justification processes are authoritarianism, rationalism, and emotionalism.

The intermediate region shown in Figure 2.1 contains ethnologics that represent three different ways of justifying beliefs. Ethnologics are the informal, personal logics that people use to justify their beliefs. Authoritarianism involves reliance on the opinions of experts. Receivers who derive their beliefs through authoritarianism will focus on the credibility of the source as a justification for belief change.

One recurrent topic for persuasion research under the information systems banner has been the conditions under which people doubt their own ability to render accurate judgments and turn instead to authoritative sources. Rational justification, also known as *criticalness,* involves reliance on reason and informal logic. Receivers who derive their beliefs through rationalism will elaborate on the issue as a justification for belief change. Information systems research has explored systematic reasoning processes (Mineo, 1995, 1996) and heuristic thought processes (Shapiro & Han, 1996; Stiff, 1995), with special attention to the types of arguments that people find more or less convincing (Allen & Preiss, 1996; Berkowitz, 1984; Slater & Rouner, 1995; Sopory & Dillard, 1996; Whaley & Weber, 1996). Receivers who derive their beliefs through emotionalism will be influenced by the charisma of the source, and their perceptions of how dynamic the source is will subsequently influence their liking of the source (Bentar, 1997; Dillard, 1995; Hamilton, 1997; Lemieuz, Hale, & Mongeau, 1996; Nabi, 1997a, 1997b).

Most persuasion studies attempt to change peripheral beliefs by making one, or occasionally two, of the three justification processes salient to receivers—examples include Petty and Cacioppo's (1981, 1986) elaboration likelihood model (ELM) and Chaiken's (1980) heuristic-systematic model (HSM). Outside of the laboratory, receivers may use two or even three justification processes for their peripheral beliefs. The extent to which receivers employ given justification processes is supposed to depend on the organization of their central beliefs. If belief systems theory is correct, then the impact that source credibility variables, argument quality variables, and affective response variables have on peripheral belief change will be moderated by variables found in the central region. Due to their interconnectedness within the belief system, central beliefs are particularly resistant to change.

Figure 2.1. Organization of the Belief System

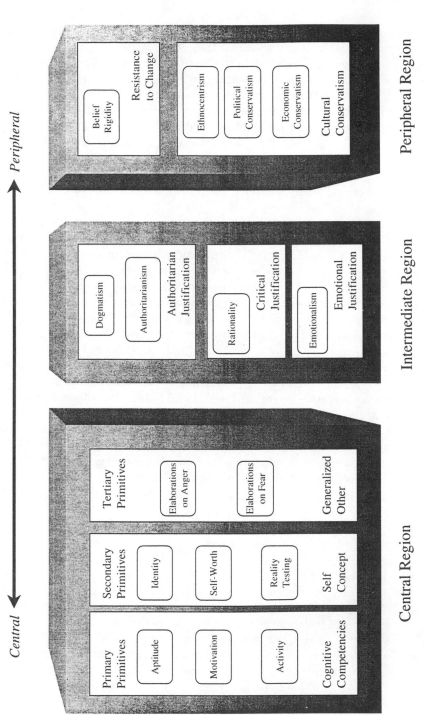

Message Effects Research

Researchers in the Information Systems Division have frequently employed meta-analyses to determine which results replicate across studies (Hunter & Hamilton, 1998). Meta-analyses have helped to resolve many long-standing conflicts within the message effects area.

Conclusions for Attitude Change

Meta-analyses, many done by information systems scholars, have provided a much clearer picture of the persuasion process than the one available to early persuasion theorists. Consider the propositions regarding "message discrepancy" found in the persuasion literature. Message discrepancy is the difference between the position advocated by the source and the premessage position of the receiver. Attitude change has been shown to be an increasing monotonic function of discrepancy with negative acceleration (Hamilton, 1997; McGuire, 1969). That is, the more belief change sources advocate, the more change they generally obtain—but with diminishing returns as the difference between source position and receiver position becomes large. This negative acceleration (the diminishing returns) is due to counterarguing. As message discrepancy increases, so does counterarguing. These propositions are as close to lawlike generalizations as can be found in the field of communication. These effects are as powerful as they are reliable.

People's use of information they possess in memory to counterargue persuasive messages is a subject often studied by information systems researchers. For many years, researchers disagreed as to whether distraction enhanced attitude change by decreasing counterarguing or inhibited attitude change by decreasing comprehension (see Buller, 1986; Buller & Hall, 1998). In fact, meta-analysis has shown that *both* counterarguing and comprehension mediate the effect of distraction on attitude change (Hamilton & Hunter, 1998b). On average, the indirect effect of distraction on attitude change mediated by counterarguing is positive but small, whereas the indirect effect of distraction mediated by comprehension is negative but even smaller. Thus the combined overall effect of distraction on attitude change is slightly positive.

Meta-analyses conducted by members of the Information Systems Division have also resolved key disputes in the message effects literature. Meta-analyses of the fear-appeal literature have shown support for the drive model (Boster & Mongeau, 1984; Mongeau, 1998). The meta-analytic results indicate that greater fear in a message has a moderately large effect on perceived fear in receivers, with perceived fear having a large positive effect on attitude change and attitude change having a very large positive effect on behavior change.

In another message effects meta-analysis, Allen (1998) found two-sided messages with refutation to be more persuasive than one-sided messages and one-sided messages to be more persuasive than two-sided messages without refutation. Hamilton and Hunter (1998a) found that language intensity influenced attitude change only if the message was discrepant and the source had high credibility. For the credible source delivering a discrepant message, intensity had a moderately small positive effect on attitude change for receivers who were uninvolved with the topic, but a moderately small negative effect on attitude change for receivers involved with the topic. If the source had low credibility or the message was congruent with receivers' position on the issue, then intensity had no effect on receiver attitudes.

Conclusions for Source Evaluation

Across studies, there is a mounting body of evidence that stronger messages improve ratings of source dynamism but lead receivers to evaluate the messages as more extreme. Dynamism and source position produce antagonistic effects on ratings of source competence. On the positive side, dynamism increases message clarity, with clarity improving ratings of competence, in part by improving evaluations of argument quality. On the negative side, a more extreme counterattitudinal message reduces competence ratings. Competence, in turn, increases trustworthiness, and trustworthiness increases liking of the source and attitude change. This model helps to explain the results of Cruz's (1998) meta-analysis on conclusion drawing. Cruz found that explicitly drawing conclusions had a very large positive effect on message comprehension, with comprehension having an extremely large positive effect on perceived extremity of source position. Source position, however, had only a slight positive effect on attitude change. The results of Burrell and Koper's (1998) meta-analysis are also consistent with the proposed model. They indicate that powerful language had a moderately positive effect on perceived source credibility, and perceived source credibility had a massive positive effect on attitude change. Additionally, in his meta-analysis of equivocal language effects, Hamilton (1998) found that opinionated language that evaluates receivers for the positions they hold has a large negative effect on competence, as does extremity of source position.

Implications for Future Persuasion Research

As researchers have gained a better understanding of how belief systems are organized and how people process persuasive messages, they have become better able to track the effects of messages on the message reception and yielding processes. These trends suggest that the most progressive research will possess two features. First, it will examine the belief targeted by a persuasive message not in isolation but within the belief hierarchy in which that belief is embedded. Suppose, for example, that a source's objective is to change people's attitudes toward bovine growth hormone. It would be useful for the source to know how people view food additives in general and to know what their attitudes are toward milk, as well as toward other dairy products. Second, progressive research will explore the complex relationships among the key dependent variables in the study. For instance, how does distraction disrupt attention, and what impact does this disruption have on comprehension of message content and the counterarguing of that content? Studies can thus be used to track the effects of message variables on receivers' exposure to the message; their attention, comprehension, and evaluation of its content (leading to bolstering thoughts or counterarguments); and the potential integration of the new information contained in the message into receiver belief systems.

SYSTEMS APPROACHES TO THE STUDY OF COMMUNICATION

History of Systems Approaches

The interests of the Information Systems Division described in the preceding three sections reflect an abiding commitment to the identification of underlying theoretical *mechanisms* in *systems* that explain how, and with what results, individuals process information.[1] The first section has described, at the intrapersonal level, the human as an information-processing system, reacting to structural and other characteristics of the message. The second section has described the mechanisms of co-constructing meaning and interpretation in a system that includes the media and the individual. The third section has examined the mechanisms of persuasion and attitude change by considering both the system of beliefs, articulated as knowledge structures, and the dynamics of interaction between sender and receiver articulated in terms of such concepts as refutation, distraction, and counterarguments.

This shared commitment to a focus on underlying mechanisms in systems at different levels undergirds a fourth area of interest for members of the Information Systems Division: a metatheoretical, sometimes philosophical, and increasingly empirical interest in the study of systems at and, more intriguingly, between different levels of analyses. Starting in the late 1970s, the tenets of systems theory have influenced scholarship in the field of communication (Monge, 1977; for a historical review, see Barnett, 1997). In his overview of the Information Systems Division in the first volume of the *Communication Yearbook,* Krippendorf (1977) outlined three critical aspects of general systems theory: structure, process, and function. *Structural functionalists* sought to identify the structures and processes that keep a system functioning in a stable state. A move away from equilibrium was seen as a symptom of a dysfunctional system. *Open-systems* theory recognized that the system's undesirable departure from an equilibrium state was often predicated by activities in the environment. *Cybernetic* systems underscored the importance of communication as a feedback mechanism to restore the system to its stable state. With their emphasis on stability and feedback, traditional systems theories were not well suited to model the dynamic emergence, mutual causality, historicity, time irreversibility, and discontinuity that imbued the intellectual discourse surrounding late-20th-century social systems (Barnett, 1997; Contractor, 1994; Poole, 1997).

Contemporary Systems Approaches

The diversity of responses to the shortcomings of traditional systems perspectives is well reflected in the research interests of members of the Information Systems Division. The division has witnessed at least three interrelated strands of theorizing and research from contemporary systems perspectives. First, starting in the late 1970s, communication researchers have studied the emergent and evolving structures of systems from a networks perspective. Second, starting in the late 1980s, the interest in underlying nonlinear generative mechanisms has been fueled by a renewed interest in the concepts introduced in contemporary systems theories, such as chaos theory, self-organizing systems theory, and autopoietic systems. Third, starting in the mid-1990s, the proliferation of computational tools has spawned a renewed interest in extending the study of systems from a metaphoric approach to a computational modeling approach.

Network Approach to Systems

Grounded in the mathematical subdiscipline called graph theory, sociometry (Moreno, 1934, 1953, 1978) was introduced as a mathematical representation of the structure of social systems. Today, the field commonly known as network analysis (Stohl, 1995; Wasserman & Faust, 1994) offers communication researchers a framework to describe the emergence of social systems based on the individual attributes of actors (e.g., individuals, families, and organizations) as well as communication relationships (at the dyadic, triadic, and global levels) among these actors. For instance, the stability of a system of interpersonal relationships is shown to be a function of the attributes (e.g., personality characteristics, age, gender) not only of the individuals, but also of the triads, groups, and larger networks in which the individuals are embedded. As such, it provides scholars an opportunity to articulate and test theories that often cross different levels of analyses. For instance, Valente (1995) has used network characteristics to model the diffusion of innovations by specifically incorporating individual and collective characteristics of the system. New network-analytic techniques, such as p* (Wasserman & Pattison, 1996), offer great promise for moving network analysis from a primarily descriptive endeavor to one that provides an omnibus test for cross-level inferences.

In recent years there has been substantial interest within the Information Systems Division in applying network analysis to the study of meaning and interpretation systems. Traditional network analysis had been criticized for its focus on the structure of systems without due recognition of the content of the relationships.

Catalyzed by Monge and Eisenberg's (1987) coinage of the concept of "semantic networks," communication researchers have examined social systems as networks of shared interpretations among key concepts and symbols (Danowski, 1988; Jang & Barnett, 1994; Rice, 1994; Stohl, 1993). Richards and Seary (1997) have used network analysis to articulate convergence theory—the ways in which individuals' configurations of concepts converge—from a systems perspective. These researchers have examined the correspondence (or lack thereof) between the communication and semantic structures within social systems. In a related line of research, building on an influential essay by Richards (1985), Corman and his colleagues (Corman & Scott, 1994; McPhee & Corman, 1995) have argued for the importance of conceptually distinguishing, and theoretically privileging, an actor's perceptions (or interpretations) of the communication network from what may be the "actual" self-reported communication network.

As we enter the 21st century, network theories and methods are poised to study the creation, maintenance, and dissolution of flexible, interconnected social systems (Contractor, Zink, & Chan, 1998; Monge & Contractor, 2001) precipitated by the inexorable forces of globalization (Kincaid, 1987; Monge, 1998; Stohl, 2000).

Nonlinear Complex Systems

Some scholars within the Information Systems Division have responded to their disillusionment with traditional systems approaches by introducing to the field of communication systems some of the more recent developments in the study of complex systems. *Complex systems* is an umbrella term used to describe a large family of contemporary systems theories and models that have as their goal the explanation of nonlinear phenomena. Members of this family of interest to members of the Information Systems Division have included autopoietic systems, second-order cybernetics, the second cybernetics, morphogenetic systems, chaos theory, self-organizing systems theory, dissipative structures, neural networks, and fractals.

Recent work on second cybernetics, self-referential systems, and autopoiesis has challenged the received view that communication systems are more profitably conceptualized as open, rather than closed, systems (Hawes, 1998; Krippendorf, 1998; McFarland, 1997). Maturana (1991) argues that "it is the organization of a system that characterizes its unity, not its relations with an environment" (p. 377). Luhmann (1992) proposes that a communication system is a "completely closed system that creates the components out of which it arises through communication itself" (p. 254). This view of a system as being closed may appear to signal a counterintuitive challenge to earlier attempts by systems theorists to "open" the system to informational and energy exchange from the environment. In fact, the use of the term *closed* in the contemporary context refers explicitly to logical and organizational closure of a system, where the boundary of a system is defined more expansively to include what earlier scholars had considered the environment. According to Krippendorf (1987): "Organizational processes of communication are explainable only from within a social form and are in the true sense self-referential. Living systems, indigenous culture, self-government, or organizationally autonomous social systems exemplify the empirical domain of this paradigm" (p. 208). Further, Krippendorf states that it is the "processes of communication that make a society see itself as distinct and that make it retain its indigenous form of organization, culture, or mind" (p. 208). From this perspective—sometimes termed *second-order cybernetics*—the organizational and logical closure of a system precludes not only the influence of but observation by elements outside the system. As such, it offers a radical constructivist challenge to the study of systems by problematizing the role of researchers "observing" a system without being a part of that system (Krippendorf, 1984; Steier & Smith, 1985). Specifically, it eschews the traditional social scientific researcher's role of dispassionate, unobtrusive "outside" observer of the system.

Conceptually distinct from the development of second-order cybernetics, but equally influential among scholars in the Information Systems Division, is Maruyama's (1963) introduction of the "second cybernetics." Unlike the focus of traditional cybernetics on regulating a system by using negative feedback to reduce deviation, Maruyama argues that many systems exhibit positive deviation-amplifying feedback. Salem (1997) has used the arguments of the second cybernetics to articulate a four-stage model (emergence, divergence, transformation, and convergence) to study morphogenesis in social systems. Unlike traditional cybernetics, which examines how systems regulate themselves, the focus here is on examining how large deviations from a system "morph" it into a system with new structures. As such, the second cybernetics offers a powerful framework for identifying, from a systems perspective, the mechanisms that explain fundamental changes in social systems resulting from interventions, such as new technological innovations.

Perhaps the two most popular of the nonlinear complex systems theories of the past two decades have been chaos theory (Gleick, 1987) and self-organizing systems theory (Prigogine & Stengers, 1984). These two theories are premised on closely related sets of nonlinear mechanisms that underscore the system's sensitivity to initial conditions and the system's ability to exhibit discontinuous behavior. Despite their similarities, however, the two theories manifest very different patterns of emergent dynamic behavior (Briggs & Peat, 1989). Chaos theory is concerned with the processes and conditions that lead deceptively simple systems to exhibit seemingly random or chaotic dynamic behavior. Tutzauer (1997) discusses how chaos theory could be used, for instance, to model the longitudinal data collected by Rice (1993) about the dynamically changing self-reported appropriateness of seven types of media (face-to-face, telephone, meetings, videoconferencing, voice mail, text, and electronic mail) used in organizational settings. Self-organizing systems theory, on the other hand, seeks "to explain the emergence of patterned behavior in systems that are initially in a state of disorganization" (Contractor, 1994, p. 51). Thus, whereas chaos theory seeks to explain the creation of chaos from order, self-organizing systems theory seeks to explain the emergence of order from chaos.

Computational Models

Closely related to the developments in chaos theory and self-organizing systems theory is the investment of effort by scholars in the Information Systems Division in the exploration of various modeling environments (such as cellular automata, neural networks, and object-oriented programming) for nonlinear systems. These environments characterize the system in terms of the attributes and relations among a set of actors. The actors are called *cells* in cellular automata models, *neurons* in neural network models, and *objects* in object-oriented environments. The system uses simple rules (the underlying theoretical mechanisms) to explain the changes in the attributes of, and relationships among, the actors in the system on the basis of the attributes and relations among other actors in the system. Thus these models can help uncover complex, emergent, and, in many cases, unanticipated collective "global" behavior resulting from individual actors' enactment of simple rules based on their "local" conditions. Corman (1996) argues that computer simulations using cellular automata (CA) modeling techniques offer "a new method of challenging explanations of communication that assume a collective intent. . . . If CA models can account for observed structure in collective communication, it becomes questionable why more complex postulates of collective-level intent are necessary" (p. 201). Woelfel (1993) offers neural networks as a viable modeling environment for policy research. Neural network models attempt to capture the emergent collective behavior of a system resulting from, for instance, a change in policies that are applied to individuals within the system. Likewise, Hyatt, Contractor, and Jones (1997) have used social information-processing theory and structural theory of action to develop an "object-oriented" model of the adoption and diffusion of a new information technology in an organization.

Future Directions

Despite their differences, systems theorists working from network, complex systems, and computational modeling perspectives share a fundamental intellectual commitment to the examination of the underlying generative mechanisms that explain changes in the system (Houston, 1998). However, these perspectives offer only a metatheoretical language; future research needs to build, extend, and test more specific communication-based theoretical mechanisms from a systems perspective.

Members of the Information Systems Division are also increasingly aware of the limitations of computational models and simulations that are not validated by empirical studies. They are increasingly committed to statistical validation of their computational models through the use of empirical data. With these efforts, their contributions will further attract the attention and engagement of communication scholars in other divisions of the ICA who share a commitment to the intellectual domain of communication, but not necessarily to a systems perspective.

SOME FINAL COMMENTS

As the field of communication moves from questions of the effects of communication to explaining the how and why of communication, the work of the Information Systems Division becomes more and more central to communication scholarship. Information systems scholars are not just a collection of nerds focused on abstract methodological issues (although we are proud to say that does describe some of us). Information Systems Division members are aggressively explaining the processes at the heart of mass, interpersonal, and organizational communication. We believe our focus on the psychological, social, and cultural systems of communication is the key to a mature understanding of communication that will emerge in the future.

NOTE

1. National Science Foundation Grant ECS-94-27730 supported preparation of this part of the chapter. Material in this section is excerpted from a paper by Noshir S. Contractor that was presented at a session on self-organizing systems jointly sponsored by the Information Systems Division and the Organizational Communication Division at the 1998 annual meeting of the International Communication Association. A summary of the session appears as a dialogue in *Management Communication Quarterly,* 1999, vol. 13, no. 1.

REFERENCES

Adoni, H., Cohen, A. A., & Mane, S. (1984). Social reality and television news: Perceptual dimensions of social conflicts in selected life areas. *Journal of Broadcasting, 28,* 33-49.

Adoni, H., & Mane, S. (1984). Media and the social construction of reality: Toward an integration of theory and research. *Communication Research, 11,* 323-340.

Allen, M. (1998). Comparing the persuasive effectiveness of one- and two-sided messages. In M. Allen & R. W. Preiss (Eds.), *Persuasion: Advances through meta-analysis.* Cresskill, NJ: Hampton.

Allen, M., & Preiss, R. W. (1996, May). *Comparing the persuasiveness of narrative and statistical evidence using meta-analysis.* Paper presented at the annual meeting of the International Communication Association, Chicago.

Anderson, D. R., & Levin, S. R. (1976). Young children's attention to "Sesame Street." *Child Development, 47,* 806-811.

Anderson, D. R., Levin, S. R., & Lorch, E. P. (1977). The effects of TV program pacing on the behavior of preschool children. *AV Communication Review, 25,* 159-166.

Anderson, D. R., & Lorch, E. P. (1983). Looking at television: Action or reaction? In J. Bryant & D. R. Anderson (Eds.), *Children's understanding of television* (pp. 1-34). Hillsdale, NJ: Lawrence Erlbaum.

Armstrong, G. B. (1997, May). *Context and effects of background television on reading: A test of TV effect on encoding, recall, and recognition.* Paper presented to the Information Systems Division at the annual meeting of the International Communication Association, Montreal.

Austin, E. W., Roberts, D. F., & Nass, C. I. (1990). Influences of family communication on children's television-interpretation. *Communication Research, 17,* 545-564.

Ball-Rokeach, S. J., & DeFleur, M. L. (1976). A dependency model of mass media effects. *Communication Research, 3,* 3-21.

Barnett, G. A. (1997). Organizational communication systems: The traditional perspective. In G. A. Barnett & L. Thayer (Eds.), *Organizational communication: Emerging perspectives V. The renaissance in systems thinking* (pp. 1-46). Greenwich, CT: Ablex.

Basil, M. D. (1994a). Multiple resource theory I: Application to television viewing. *Communication Research, 21,* 177-207.

Basil, M. D. (1994b). Secondary reaction-time measures. In A. Lang (Ed.), *Measuring psychological responses to media messages* (pp. 85-98). Hillsdale, NJ, Lawrence Erlbaum.

Basil, M. D. (1995, May). *Identification effects in persuasion.* Paper presented at the annual meeting of the International Communication Association, Albuquerque, NM.

Basil, M. D. (1996, May). *Real time and on line indices of message elaboration.* Paper presented at the annual meeting of the International Communication Association, Chicago.

Bentar, J. E. (1997, May). *Message-irrelevant affect in persuasion: A meta-analysis.* Paper presented at the annual meeting of the International Communication Association, Montreal.

Berkowitz, L. (1984). Some effects of thoughts on anti- and prosocial influence of media events: A cognitive-neoassociation analysis. *Psychological Bulletin, 95,* 410-427.

Berkowitz, L., & Donnerstein, E. (1982). External validity is more than skin deep: Some answers to criticisms of laboratory experiments. *American Psychologist, 37,* 245-257.

Berkowitz, L., & Rogers, K. H. (1986). A priming effect analysis of media influences. In J. Bryant & D. Zillmann (Eds.), *Perspectives on media effects* (pp. 57-81). Hillsdale, NJ: Lawrence Erlbaum.

Biocca, F. (1991). Viewers' mental models of political messages: Toward a theory of the semantic processing of television. In F. Biocca (Ed.), *Television and political advertising: Vol. 1. Psychological processes* (pp. 27-89). Hillsdale, NJ: Lawrence Erlbaum.

Bolls, P. D., Lang, A., Potter, R. F., & Snyder, J. F. (1999, May). *How can I tell if you love me? The effects of message valence on emotional and cognitive responses to radio.* Paper presented to the Information Systems Division at the annual meeting of the International Communication Association, San Francisco.

Bolls, P. D., Yoon, K., Dent, D. R., Potter, R. F., & Lang, A. (1997, May). *The hard cell: The effects of pacing and content arousal of television commercials on viewers' attention, arousal, and storage of commercial information.* Paper presented to the Information Systems Division at the annual meeting of the International Communication Association, Montreal.

Boster, F. J., & Levine, K. J. (1997, May). *The impact of the channel variable on persuasive messages: A beta-analytic review.* Paper presented at the annual meeting of the International Communication Association, Montreal.

Boster, F. J., & Mongeau, P. A. (1984). Fear-arousing persuasive messages. In R. N. Bostrom (Ed.), *Communication yearbook 8* (pp. 330-375). Beverly Hills, CA: Sage.

Briggs, J., & Peat, F. D. (1989). *Turbulent mirror: An illustrated guide to chaos theory and the science of wholeness.* New York: Harper & Row.

Bryant, J. (1997, May). *The interplay of emotional, cognitive, and experiential factors in responding to the emotion-eliciting messages.* Paper presented to the Information Systems Division at the annual meeting of the International Communication Association, Montreal.

Bryant, J., Carveth, R. A., & Brown, D. (1981). Television viewing and anxiety: An experimental examination. *Journal of Communication, 31*(1), 106-119.

Buller, D. B. (1986). Distraction during persuasive communication: A meta-analytic review. *Communication Monographs, 53,* 91-114.

Buller, D. B., & Hall, J. R. (1998). The effects of distraction during persuasion. In M. Allen & R. W. Preiss (Eds.), *Persuasion: Advances through meta-analysis.* Cresskill, NJ: Hampton.

Burrell, N. A., & Koper, R. J. (1998). The efficacy of powerful/powerless language on attitudes and source credibility. In M. Allen & R. W. Preiss (Eds.), *Persuasion: Advances through meta-analysis.* Cresskill, NJ: Hampton.

Chaffee, S. H., & Schleuder, J. (1986). Measurement and effects of attention to media news. *Human Communication Research, 13,* 76-107.

Chaiken, S. (1980). Heuristic versus systematic information processing and the use of source versus message cues in persuasion. *Journal of Personality and Social Psychology, 39,* 752-766.

Chaiken, S., Liberman, A., & Eagly, A. H. (1989). Heuristic and systematic information processing within and beyond the persuasion context. In J. S. Uleman & J. A. Bargh (Eds.), *Unintended thought* (pp. 212-252). New York: Guilford.

Cohen, A. A., Adoni, H., & Drori, G. (1983). Adolescents' perceptions of social conflicts in television news and social reality. *Human Communication Research, 10,* 203-225.

Contractor, N. S. (1994). Self-organizing systems perspective in the study of organizational communication. In B. Kovacic (Ed.), *New approaches to organizational communication* (pp. 39-65). Albany: State University of New York Press.

Contractor, N. S., Zink, D., & Chan, M. (1998). IKNOW: A tool to assist and study the creation, maintenance, and dissolution of knowledge networks. In T. Ishida (Ed.), *Community computing and support systems: Lecture notes in Computer Science 1519* (pp. 201-217). Berlin: Springer-Verlag.

Cooper, E., & Jahoda, M. (1947). The evasion of propaganda: How prejudiced people respond to anti-prejudice propaganda. *Journal of Psychology, 23,* 15-25.

Corman, S. R. (1996). Cellular automata as models of unintended consequences of organizational communication. In J. H. Watt & C. A. Van Lear (Eds.), *Dynamic patterns in communication processes* (pp. 191-212). Thousand Oaks, CA: Sage.

Corman, S. R., & Scott, C. R. (1994). Perceived networks, activity, foci, and observable communication in social collectives. *Communication Theory, 4,* 171-190.

Crano, W. D., & Chen, X. (1997, May). *Message strength, involvement, and persistence of majority and minority influence.* Paper presented at the annual meeting of the International Communication Association, Montreal.

Cruz, M. G. (1998). Explicit and implicit conclusions in persuasive messages In M. Allen & R. W. Preiss (Eds.), *Persuasion: Advances through meta-analysis* (pp. 217-230). Cresskill, NJ: Hampton.

Danowski, J. (1988). Organizational infographics and automated auditing: Using computers to unobtrusively gather and analyze communication. In G. M. Goldhaber & G. A. Barnett (Eds.), *Handbook of organizational communication* (pp. 335-384). Norwood, NJ: Ablex.

David, P., & King, J. (1996, May). *When a picture is worth a hundred words and when it is not.* Paper presented to the Information Systems Division at the annual meeting of the International Communication Association, Chicago.

David, P., & Peay, D. (1998, May). *News concreteness, audio-video reinforcement and news recall.* Paper presented to the Information Systems Division at the annual meeting of the International Communication Association, Jerusalem.

Deitz, R. B., & Lang, A. (1999, August). *Effective agents: Effects of agent affect on arousal, attention, liking and learning.* Paper presented at the Cognitive Technology Conference, San Francisco.

Dervin, B. (1981). Mass communicating: Changing conceptions of the audience. In R. E. Rice & W. J. Paisley (Eds.), *Public communication campaigns* (pp. 71-87). Beverly Hills, CA: Sage.

Dervin, B. (1989). Audience as listener and learner, teacher and confidante: The sense-making approach. In R. E. Rice & C. K. Atkin (Eds.), *Public communication campaigns* (2nd ed., pp. 67-86). Newbury Park, CA: Sage.

Detenber, B. (1996, May). *Pleasure, arousal, and memory for pictures.* Paper presented to the Information Systems Division at the annual meeting of the International Communication Association, Chicago.

Detenber, B., Simon, R. F., & Bennett, G. B. (1997, May). *The effect of picture motion on affective judgment and psychophysiological responses.* Paper presented to the Information Systems Division at the annual meeting of the International Communication Association, Montreal.

Dillard, J. P. (1995, May). *Message forms and affective response.* Paper presented at the annual meeting of the International Communication Association, Albuquerque, NM.

Ditton, T. B., Lombard, M., Kaynak, M. S., Linder, J., & Pemrick, J. (1998, May). *Presence and structural features of television: The illusion of nonmediation in television programming.* Paper presented to the Information Systems Division at the annual meeting of the International Communication Association, Jerusalem.

Doob, A. N., & MacDonald, G. E. (1979). Television viewing and fear of victimization: Is the relationship causal? *Journal of Personality and Social Psychology, 37,* 170-179.

Elliott, W. R., & Slater, D. (1980). Exposure, experience and perceived TV reality for adolescents. *Journalism Quarterly, 57,* 409-414, 431.

Fazio, R. H. (1986). How do attitudes guide behavior? In R. M. Sorrentino & E. T. Higgins (Eds.), *Handbook of motivation and cognition foundations of social behavior.* New York: Guilford.

Fazio, R. H. (1990). Multiple processes by which attitudes guide behavior: The mode model as an integrative framework. In M. P. Zanna (Ed.), *Advances in experimental social psychology* (Vol. 23, pp. 75-109). San Diego: Academic Press.

Flora, J. A., & Maibach, E. W. (1990). Cognitive responses to AIDS information: The effects of issue involvement and message appeal. *Communication Research, 17,* 759-774.

Fox, J. R. (1996, May). *Audio/video redundancy: Typical television news radio.* Paper presented to the Information Systems Division at the annual meeting of the International Communication Association, Chicago.

Geiger, S., & Newhagen, J. (1993). Revealing the black box: Information processing and media effects. *Journal of Communication, 43*(4), 42-50.

Geiger, S., & Reeves, B. (1993). The effects of scene changes and semantic relatedness on attention to television. *Communication Research, 20,* 155-175.

Gerbner, G., Gross, L., Morgan, M., & Signorielli, N. (1980). The mainstreaming of America: Violence Profile No. 11. *Journal of Communication, 30*(3), 10-29.

Gerbner, G., Gross, L., Morgan, M., & Signorielli, N. (1986). *Living with television: The dynamics of the cultivation process.* Hillsdale, NJ: Lawrence Erlbaum.

Gleick, J. (1987). *Chaos: Making a new science.* New York: Penguin.

Grabe, M., Lang, A., Zhou, S., & Bolls, P. D. (1999, May). *The impact of education on information processing: An experimental investigation of the knowledge gap.* Paper presented to the Information Systems Division at the annual meeting of the International Communication Association, San Francisco.

Greenwald, A. G. (1968). Cognitive learning, cognitive response to persuasion, and attitude change. In A. G. Greenwald, T. C. Brock, & T. M. Ostrom (Eds.), *Psychological foundations of attitudes* (pp. 147-170). New York: Academic Press.

Grimes, T. (1991). Mild auditory-visual dissonance in television news may exceed viewer attentional capacity. *Human Communication Research, 18,* 268-298.

Hamilton, M. A. (1997). The phase interfaced omnistructure underlying the processing of persuasive messages. In F. J. Boster & G. A. Barnett (Eds.), *Progress in communication sciences* (Vol. 13). Norwood, NJ: Ablex.

Hamilton, M. A. (1998). Message variables that mediate and moderate the effect of equivocal language on source credibility. *Journal of Language and Social Psychology, 17,* 109-143.

Hamilton, M. A., & Hunter, J. E. (1998a). The effect of language intensity on receiver evaluations of message, source, and topic. In M. Allen & R. W. Preiss (Eds.), *Persuasion: Advances through meta-analysis* (pp. 99-138). Cresskill, NJ: Hampton.

Hamilton, M. A., & Hunter, J. E. (1998b). A framework for understanding: Meta-analyses of the persuasion literature. In M. Allen & R. W. Preiss (Eds.), *Persuasion: Advances through meta-analysis* (pp. 1-28). Cresskill, NJ: Hampton.

Hamilton, M. A., & Mineo, P. J. (1996). Personality and persuasibility: Developing a multidimensional model of belief systems. *World Communication, 24,* 1-16.

Hamilton, M. A., & Mineo, P. J. (1999). Self-esteem and the authoritarian justification of ethnocentrism and rigidity. *Politics, Groups, and the Individual 8,* 85-110.

Hansen, C. H. (1989). Priming sex-role stereotypic event schemas with rock music videos: Effects on impression favorability, trait inferences, and recall of a subsequent male-female interaction. *Basic and Applied Social Psychology, 10,* 371-391.

Hansen, C. H., & Hansen, R. D. (1988). How rock music videos can change what is seen when boy meets girl: Priming stereotypic appraisal of social interactions. *Sex Roles, 19,* 287-313.

Hastie, R., & Park, B. (1986). The relationship between memory and judgment depends on whether the judgment task is memory-based or on-line. *Psychological Review, 93,* 258-268.

Hawes, L. (1998, May). *Dialogics, cybernetics, and post-human communication theory.* Paper presented to the special panel "Interdisciplinary Approach to Using Self-Organizing Systems to Theorize Human Organization and Experience" at the annual meeting of the International Communication Association, Jerusalem.

Hewes, D. E., & Planalp, S. (1987). The individual's place in communication science. In C. R. Berger & S. H. Chaffee (Eds.), *Handbook of communication science* (pp. 146-183). Newbury Park, CA: Sage.

Hibbs, H., Bolls, P. D., & Lang, A. (1995, May). *The medium is the memory: Using structural features to predict memory for random television messages.* Paper presented to the Information Systems Division at the annual meeting of the International Communication Association, Albuquerque, NM.

Higgins, E. T. (1989). Knowledge accessibility and activation: Subjectivity and suffering from unconscious sources. In J. S. Uleman & J. A. Bargh (Eds.), *Unintended thought* (pp. 75-123). New York: Guilford.

Higgins, E. T., & King, G. (1981). Social constructs: Information-processing consequences of individual and contextual variability. In N. Cantor & J. F. Kihlstrom (Eds.), *Personality, cognition and social interaction* (pp. 69-121). Hillsdale, NJ: Lawrence Erlbaum.

Hirsch, P. M. (1980). The "scary world" of the nonviewer and other anomalies: A reanalysis of Gerbner et al.'s findings on cultivation analysis, part 1. *Communication Research, 7,* 403-456.

Hitchon, J., Thorson, E., & Duckler, P. (1994). Effects of ambiguity and complexity on consumer response to music video commercials. *Journal of Broadcasting & Electronic Media, 38,* 289-306.

Hoijer, B. (1992). Socio-cognitive structures and television reception. *Media, Culture & Society, 14,* 583-603.

Houston, R. (1998, May). *Fragmented oneness.* Paper presented to the special panel "Interdisciplinary Approach to Using Self-Organizing Systems to Theorize Human Organization and Experience" at the annual meeting of the International Communication Association, Jerusalem.

Hunter, J. E., & Hamilton, M. A. (1998). Meta-analysis of controlled message designs. In M. Allen & R. W. Preiss (Eds.), *Persuasion: Advances through meta-analysis* (pp. 29-52). Cresskill, NJ: Hampton.

Hyatt, A., Contractor, N. S., & Jones, P. M. (1997). Computational organizational network modeling: Strategies and an example. *Computational and Mathematical Organizational Theory, 4,* 285-300.

Iyengar, S. (1990). *Shortcuts to political knowledge: The role of selective attention and accessibility.* Chicago: University of Illinois Press.

Jang, H., & Barnett, G. A. (1994). Cultural differences in organizational communication: A semantic network analysis. *Bulletin de Methodologie Sociologique, 44,* 31-59.

Kawahara, K., Bolls, P. D., Hansell, R., & Lang, A. (1996, May). *The effects of production pacing and content arousal on viewers' allocation of capacity to encoding and storage of television messages.* Paper presented to the Information Systems Division at the annual meeting of the International Communication Association, Chicago.

Kim, T., & Biocca, F. (1997, May). *Seeing is believing: Effects of telepresence on memory and persuasion.* Paper presented to the Information Systems Division at the annual meeting of the International Communication Association, Montreal.

Kincaid, D. L. (Ed.). (1987). *Communication theory: Eastern and Western perspectives.* New York: Academic Press.

King, P. E., & Behnke, R. R. (1998, May). *Effects of communication load on affect and listening performance.* Paper presented to the Information Systems Division at the annual meeting of the International Communication Association, Jerusalem.

Krippendorf, K. (1977). Information systems: An overview. In B. D. Ruben (Ed.), *Communication yearbook 1* (pp. 149-171). New Brunswick, NJ: Transaction.

Krippendorf, K. (1984). Paradox and information. In B. Dervin & M. Voigt (Eds.), *Progress in communication sciences* (Vol. 5, pp. 45-72). Norwood, NJ: Ablex.

Krippendorf, K. (1987). Paradigms for communication and development with emphasis on autopoiesis. In D. L. Kincaid (Ed.), *Communication theory: Eastern and Western perspectives* (pp. 189-208). New York: Academic Press.

Krippendorf, K. (1998, May). *Beyond coherence.* Paper presented to the special panel "Interdisciplinary Approach to Using Self-Organizing Systems to Theorize Human Organization and Experience" at the annual meeting of the International Communication Association, Jerusalem.

Lang, A. (1990). Involuntary attention and physiological arousal evoked by structural features and mild emotion in TV commercials. *Communication Research, 17,* 275-299.

Lang, A. (Ed.). (1994). *Measuring psychological responses to media messages.* Hillsdale, NJ: Lawrence Erlbaum.

Lang, A. (1995). Defining audio/video redundancy from a limited capacity information processing perspective. *Communication Research, 22,* 86-115.

Lang, A. (1997, May). *Physiological processes related to attention and motivation.* Paper presented to the Information Systems Division at the annual meeting of the International Communication Association, Montreal.

Lang, A., & Basil, M. D. (1996, May). *What do secondary task reaction times measure anyway?* Paper presented to the Information Systems Division at the annual meeting of the International Communication Association, Chicago.

Lang, A., & Basil, M. D. (1998). Attention, resource allocation, and communication research: What do secondary task reaction times measure, anyway? In M. E. Roloff (Ed.), *Communication yearbook 21* (pp. 443-474). Thousand Oaks, CA: Sage.

Lang, A., & Bolls, P. D. (1995, May). *Memory for emotional television messages: Arousal, valence, and capacity.* Paper presented to the Information Systems Division at the annual meeting of the International Communication Association, Albuquerque, NM.

Lang, A., Bolls, P. D., Potter, R. F., & Kawahara, K. (in press). The effects of production pacing and arousing content on the information processing of television messages. *Journal of Broadcasting & Electronic Media.*

Lang, A., Dhillon, P., & Dong, Q. (1995). Arousal, emotion, and memory for television messages. *Journal of Broadcasting & Electronic Media, 38,* 1-15.

Lang, A., Newhagen, J., & Reeves, B. (1996). Negative video as structure: Emotion, attention, capacity, and memory. *Journal of Broadcasting & Electronic Media, 40,* 460-477.

Lang, A., Potter, R. F., & Bolls, P. D. (1999). Something for nothing: Is visual encoding automatic? *Media Psychology, 1,* 145-164.

Lang, A., Schneider, E., & Deitz, R. B. (1999, August). *Emotional experience and physiological arousal during violent video game playing: Gender, experience, and presence matter.* Paper presented to the Theory and Methodology Division at the annual meeting of the Association for Education in Journalism and Mass Communication, New Orleans.

Lang, A., Schwartz, N., & Snyder, J. (1999, August). *Slow down, you're movin' too fast: Pacing, arousing content, and middle-age.* Paper presented to the Theory and Methodology Division at the annual meeting of the Association for Education in Journalism and Mass Communication, New Orleans.

Lemieuz, R., Hale, J. L., & Mongeau, P. A. (1996, May). *The effects of sadness on the cognitive processing of fear-arousing messages.* Paper presented at the annual meeting of the International Communication Association, Chicago.

Liebes, T., & Katz, E. (1986). Patterns of involvement in television fiction: A comparative analysis. *European Journal of Communication, 1,* 151-171.

Livingstone, S. M. (1992). The resourceful reader: Interpreting television characters and narratives. In S. A. Deetz (Ed.), *Communication yearbook 15* (pp. 58-90). Newbury Park, CA: Sage.

Lombard, M., Campanella, C. M., Linder, J., Snyder, J., Ditton, T. B., Kaynak, S., Pemrick, J., & Steward, G. (1996, May). *This state the media: A content analysis of television form.* Paper presented to the Information Systems Division at the annual meeting of the International Communication Association, Chicago.

Lombard, M., & Ditton, T. B. (1997, May). *At the heart of it all: The concert presence.* Paper presented at the annual meeting of the International Communication Association, Montreal.

Luhmann, N. (1992). Autopoiesis: What is communication? *Communication Theory, 2,* 251-259.

Mares, M. L. (1996). The role of source confusions in television's cultivation of social reality judgments. *Human Communication Research, 23,* 278-297.

Maruyama, M. (1963). The second cybernetics: Deviation amplifying mutual causal processes. *American Scientist, 51,* 164-179, postscript 250A-256A.

Maturana, H. R. (1991). Response to Jim Birch. *Journal of Family Therapy, 13,* 375-393.

McFarland, D. S. (1997). Ontogeny, structural drift, and self-organizing: An autopoietic perspective. In G. A. Barnett & L. Thayer (Eds.), *Organizational communication: Emerging perspectives V. The renaissance in systems thinking* (pp. 191-211). Greenwich, CT: Ablex.

McGuire, W. (1969). The nature of attitudes and attitude change. In G. Lindzey & E. Aronson (Eds.), *Handbook of social psychology* (2nd ed., Vol. 3, pp. 136-314). Reading, MA: Addison-Wesley.

McPhee, R. D., & Corman, S. R. (1995). An activity-based theory of communication networks in organizations, applied to the case of a local church. *Communication Monographs, 62,* 1-20.

Meadowcroft, J. M., & Zillmann, D. (1987). Women's comedy preferences during the menstrual cycle. *Communication Research, 14,* 204-218.

Mendelson, A., & Ognianova, E. (1998, May). *Children of lower socioeconomic status and the arousal effects of advertising.* Paper presented to the Information Systems Division at the annual meeting of the International Communication Association, Jerusalem.

Meyer, J. (1996, May). *Addressing secondary goals in messages: Effects of goal accessibility on a concurrent memory load.* Paper presented at the annual meeting of the International Communication Association, Chicago.

Mineo, P. J. (1995, May). *The role of rationality in message processing.* Paper presented at the annual meeting of the International Communication Association, Albuquerque, NM.

Mineo, P. J. (1996, May). *Assessment of critical thinking while message processing.* Paper presented at the annual meeting of the International Communication Association, Chicago.

Monge, P. R. (1977). The systems perspective as a theoretical basis for the study of human communication. *Communication Quarterly, 25,* 19-29.

Monge, P. R. (1998). Communication theory for a globalizing world. In J. S. Trent (Ed.), *Communication: Views from the helm for the 21st century* (pp. 3-7). Boston: Allyn & Bacon.

Monge, P. R., & Contractor, N. S. (2001). Emergence of communication networks. In F. M. Jablin & L. L. Putnam (Eds.), *The new handbook of organizational communication: Advances in theory, research, and methods* (pp. 440-502).Thousand Oaks, CA: Sage.

Monge, P. R., & Eisenberg, E. M. (1987). Emergent communication networks. In F. M. Jablin, L. L. Putnam, K. H. Roberts, & L. W. Porter (Eds.), *Handbook of organizational communication* (pp. 304-342). Newbury Park, CA: Sage.

Mongeau, P. A. (1996, May). *Argument quality and the elaboration likelihood model of persuasion.* Paper presented at the annual meeting of the International Communication Association, Chicago.

Mongeau, P. A. (1998). Another look at fear-arousing persuasive appeals. In M. Allen & R. W. Preiss (Eds.), *Persuasion: Advances through meta-analysis.* Cresskill, NJ: Hampton.

Moreno, J. L. (1934). *Who shall survive? Foundations of sociometry, group therapy, and sociodrama.* Washington, DC: Nervous and Mental Disease Publishing.

Moreno, J. L. (1953). *Who shall survive? Foundations of sociometry, group therapy, and sociodrama* (2nd ed.). Beacon, NY: Beacon House.

Moreno, J. L. (1978). *Who shall survive? Foundations of sociometry, group therapy, and sociodrama* (3rd ed.). Beacon, NY: Beacon House.

Nabi, R. L. (1995, May). *"Feeling" resistance: The role of visuals in the induction of inoculation.* Paper presented at the annual meeting of the International Communication Association, Albuquerque, NM.

Nabi, R. L. (1997a, May). *A cognitive-functional model for the effects of discrete negative emotions on information processing, attitude change, and recall.* Paper presented at the annual meeting of the International Communication Association, Montreal.

Nabi, R. L. (1997b, May). *The persuasive effect of disgust: A first look.* Paper presented at the annual meeting of the International Communication Association, Montreal.

Nabi, R. L. (1998, May). *Anger, fear, uncertainty, and attitudes: A test of the cognitive functional model.* Paper presented to the Information Systems Division at the annual meeting of the International Communication Association, Jerusalem.

Nabi, R. L. (1999). A cognitive-functional model for the effects of discrete negative emotions on information processing, attitude change, and recall. *Communication Theory, 3,* 292-320.

Nass, C., & Steuer, J. (1993). Voices, boxes, and sources of messages. *Communication Research, 19,* 504-527.

Newhagen, J., & Reeves, B. (1992). This evening's bad news: Effects of compelling negative television news images on memory. *Journal of Communication, 42*(2), 25-41.

O'Keefe, G. J. (1984). Public views on crime: Television exposure and media credibility. In R. N. Bostrom (Ed.), *Communication yearbook 8* (pp. 514-535). Beverly Hills, CA: Sage.

Orton, P., Reeves, B., Leshner, G., & Nass, C. (1994, May). *Effects of subjective camera angle (POV) and negatively-valenced footage.* Paper presented at the annual meeting of the International Communication Association, Sydney.

Perry, D. K. (1987). The image gap, how international news affects perceptions of nations. *Journalism Quarterly, 64,* 416-421, 433.

Petty, R. E., & Cacioppo, J. T. (1981). *Attitudes and persuasion: Classic and contemporary approaches.* Dubuque, IA: William C. Brown.

Petty, R. E., & Cacioppo, J. T. (1986). *Communication and persuasion.* New York: Springer-Verlag.

Pfau, M., Tusing, K. J., Koerner, A. F., Penaloza, L. J., Godbold, L. C., Lee W.-P., Yang, V. S., & Hong, Y. (1996, May). *Enriching the inoculation construct: The role of critical components in the process of resistance.* Paper presented at the annual meeting of the International Communication Association, Chicago.

Poole, M. S. (1997). A turn of the wheel: The case for a renewal of systems inquiry in organizational communication research. In G. A. Barnett & L. Thayer (Eds.), *Organizational communication: Emerging perspectives V. The renaissance in systems thinking* (pp. 47-63). Greenwich, CT: Ablex.

Potter, W. J. (1986). Perceived reality and the cultivation hypothesis. *Journal of Broadcasting & Electronic Media, 30,* 159-174.

Potter, W. J. (1988). Perceived reality in television effects research. *Journal of Broadcasting & Electronic Media, 32,* 23-41.

Potter, W. J. (1991). The linearity assumption in cultivation research. *Human Communication Research, 17,* 562-583.

Potter, W. J., & Chang, I. C. (1990). Television exposure measures and the cultivation hypothesis. *Journal of Broadcasting & Electronic Media, 34,* 313-333.

Preston, J. M. (1996, May). *Cognitive processing of visual and verbal stimuli.* Paper presented to the Information Systems Division at the annual meeting of the International Communication Association, Chicago.

Preston, J. M. (1997, May). *Cognitive processing: Modality and memory.* Paper presented to the Information Systems Division at the annual meeting of the International Communication Association, Montreal.

Prigogine, I., & Stengers, I. (1984). *Order out of chaos.* New York: Bantam.

Reep, D. C., & Dambrot, F. H. (1989). Effects of frequent television viewing on stereotypes: "Drip, drip" or "drench"? *Journalism Quarterly, 66,* 542-550.

Reeves, B., Lang, A., Kim, E., & Tatar, D. (1997, May). *The effect of screen size and message content on attention and arousal.* Paper presented to the Information Systems Division at the annual meeting of the International Communication Association, Montreal.

Reeves, B., Lang, A., Kim, E., & Tatar, D. (1999). The effects of screen size and message content on attention and arousal. *Media Psychology, 1,* 49-68.

Reeves, B., & Nass, C. (1996). *The media equation: How people treat computers, television, and new media like real people and places.* Stanford, CA: Stanford University, Center for the Study of Language and Information.

Reeves, B., Thorson, E., Rothschild, M., McDonald, D., Hirsch, J., & Goldstein, R. (1985). Attention to television: Intrastimulus effects of movement and scene changes on alpha variation over time. *International Journal of Neuroscience, 25,* 241-255.

Reynolds, R. (1996, May). *A validation test of a message elaboration measure.* Paper presented at the annual meeting of the International Communication Association, Chicago.

Rice, R. E. (1993). Media appropriateness: Using social presence theory to compare traditional and new organizational media. *Human Communication Research, 19,* 451-484.

Rice, R. E. (1994). Network analysis and computer-mediated communication systems. In S. Wasserman & J. Galaskiewicz (Eds.), *Advances in social network analysis: Research in the social and behavioral sciences* (pp. 167-206). Thousand Oaks, CA: Sage.

Richards, W. D. (1985). Data, models, and assumptions in network analysis. In R. D. McPhee & P. K. Tompkins (Eds.), *Organizational communication: Themes and new directions* (pp. 109-147). Beverly Hills, CA: Sage.

Richards, W. D., & Seary, A. J. (1997). Convergence analysis of communication networks. In G. A. Barnett & L. Thayer (Eds.), *Organizational communication: Emerging perspectives V. The renaissance in systems thinking* (pp. 141-189). Greenwich, CT: Ablex.

Ritchie, L. D. (1995, May). *Knowledge schemas among college students.* Paper presented at the annual meeting of the International Communication Association, Albuquerque, NM.

Ritchie, L. D. (1997, May). *Knowledge and relevance: An information processing model.* Paper presented at the annual meeting of the International Communication Association, Montreal.

Ritchie, L. D., & Good, L. T. (1996, May). *The concept of knowledge in communication contexts 2: Inter-group differences.* Paper presented at the annual meeting of the International Communication Association, Chicago.

Rokeach, M. (1960). *The open and closed mind.* New York: Basic Books.

Rokeach, M. (1969). *Beliefs, attitudes and values: A theory of organization and change.* San Francisco: Jossey-Bass.

Roskos-Ewoldsen, D. R. (1996, May). *Attitude measurement, attitude ambivalence and the effects of persuasive messages.* Paper presented at the annual meeting of the International Communication Association, Chicago.

Salem, P. (1997). Information and change: Social morphogenesis. In G. A. Barnett & L. Thayer (Eds.), *Organizational communication: Emerging perspectives V. The renaissance in systems thinking* (pp. 105-119). Greenwich, CT: Ablex.

Sanders, R. E., Gonzalez, E. G., Murphy, M. D., Liddle, C. L., & Vitina, J. R. (1987). Frequency of occurrence and the criteria for automatic processing. *Journal of Experimental Psychology: Learning, Memory, and Cognition, 13,* 241-250.

Schlesinger, P., Dobash, R. E., Dobash, R. P., & Weaver, C. K. (1992). *Women viewing violence.* London: British Film Institute.

Schneider, W., Dumais, S. T., & Shiffrin, R. M. (1984). *Automatic and control processing and attention.* Orlando, FL: Academic Press.

Shapiro, M. A. (1994). Think-aloud and thought-list procedures in investigating mental processes. In A. Lang (Ed.), *Measuring psychological responses to media messages* (pp. 1-14). Hillsdale, NJ: Lawrence Erlbaum.

Shapiro, M. A. (1995, May). *An interpretation/motivation theory of mental processing of television content.* Paper presented at the annual meeting of the International Communication Association, Albuquerque, NM.

Shapiro, M. A., & Chock, T. M. (1998). *Psychological processes in perceiving reality.* Paper presented at the annual meeting of the Association for Education in Journalism and Mass Communication, Baltimore.

Shapiro, M. A., & Fox, J. (1995, May). *The effect of media dependency and perceived reality on memory for stories.* Paper presented at the annual meeting of the International Communication Association, Albuquerque, NM.

Shapiro, M. A., & Fox, J. (1996, May). *Schema intrusions in memory for mass media stories.* Paper presented at the annual meeting of the International Communication Association, Chicago.

Shapiro, M. A., & Han, M. (1994). *Thinking-aloud about impersonal impact.* Paper presented at the annual meeting of the Association for Education in Journalism and Mass Communication, Atlanta, GA.

Shapiro, M. A., & Han, M. (1996, May). *Thinking-aloud about the personal and social risk of cigarette smoking.* Paper presented at the annual meeting of the International Communication Association, Chicago.

Shapiro, M. A., & Lang, A. (1991). Making television reality: Unconscious processes in the construction of social reality. *Communication Research, 18,* 685-705.

Shapiro, M. A., & McDonald, D. G. (1992). I'm not a real doctor, but I play one in virtual reality: Implications of virtual reality for judgments about reality. *Journal of Communication, 42*(4), 94-114.

Shiffrin, R. M., & Schneider, W. (1977). Controlled and automatic human information processing: II. Perceptual learning, automatic attending and a general theory. *Psychological Review, 84,* 127-189.

Shrum, L. J. (1997). The role of source confusion in cultivation effects may depend on processing strategy: A comment on Mares (1996). *Human Communication Research, 24,* 349-358.

Shrum, L. J. (1999). The relationship of television viewing with attitude strength and extremity: Implications for the cultivation effect. *Media Psychology, 1,* 3-25.

Shrum, L. J., & O'Guinn, T. C. (1993). Processes and effects in the construction of social reality: Construct accessibility as an explanatory variable. *Communication Research, 20,* 436-471.

Shrum, L. J., Wyer, R. S. J., & O'Guinn, T. C. (1998). The effects of television consumption on social perceptions: The use of priming procedures to investigate psychological processes. *Journal of Consumer Research, 24,* 447-458.

Singer, J. L. (1980). The power and limitations of television: A cognitive-affective analysis. In P. Tannenbaum (Ed.), *The entertainment functions of television.* Hillsdale, NJ: Lawrence Erlbaum.

Slater, M. D., & Rouner, D. (1995, May). *The influence of types of evidence on message processing, beliefs, and confidence in beliefs.* Paper presented at the annual meeting of the International Communication Association, Albuquerque, NM.

Snyder, L., & Rouse, R. A. (1992, May). *The media do not have only an impersonal impact: The case of AIDS risk perceptions and behavior.* Paper presented at the annual meeting of the International Communication Association, Miami, FL.

Sopory, P., & Dillard, J. P. (1996, May). *The effects of metaphor on persuasion: A meta-analysis.* Paper presented at the annual meeting of the International Communication Association, Chicago.

Steier, F., & Smith, K. K. (1985). Organizations and second order cybernetics. *Journal of Strategic and Systemic Therapies, 4*(4), 53-65.

Stiff, J. (1995, May). *Motivated receivers with limited knowledge.* Paper presented at the annual meeting of the International Communication Association, Albuquerque, NM.

Stohl, C. (1993). European managers' interpretations of participation: A semantic network analysis. *Human Communication Research, 20,* 97-117.

Stohl, C. (1995). *Organizational communication: Connectedness in action.* Thousand Oaks, CA: Sage.

Stohl, C. (2000). Globalizing organizational communication: Convergences and divergences. In F. M. Jablin & L. L. Putnam (Eds.), *Handbook of organizational communication: Advances in theory, research, and methods.* Thousand Oaks, CA: Sage.

Tamborini, R., Zillmann, D., & Bryant, J. (1984). Fear and victimization: Exposure to television and perceptions of crime and fear. In R. N. Bostrom (Ed.), *Communication yearbook 8* (pp. 492-513). Beverly Hills, CA: Sage.

Thorson, E., & Lang, A. (1992). Effects of television videographics and lecture familiarity on adult cardiac orienting responses and memory. *Communication Research, 19,* 346-369.

Thorson, E., Reeves, B., & Schleuder, J. (1985). Message complexity and attention to television. *Communication Research, 12,* 427-454.

Thorson, E., Reeves, B., & Schleuder, J. (1987). Attention to local and global complexity in television messages. In M. L. McLaughlin (Ed.), *Communication yearbook 10* (pp. 366-383). Newbury Park, CA: Sage.

Tremain Koch, P. L., & Crano, W. D. (1996, May). *Elaborating the ELM: Examining initial attitude and susceptibility to persuasion.* Paper presented at the annual meeting of the International Communication Association, Chicago.

Turner, C., & Berkowitz, L. (1972). Identification with film aggressor (covert role taking) and reactions to film violence. *Journal of Personality and Social Psychology, 21,* 256-264.

Tutzauer, F. (1997). Chaos and organization. In G. A. Barnett & L. Thayer (Eds.), *Organizational communication: Emerging perspectives V. The renaissance in systems thinking* (pp. 213-227). Greenwich, CT: Ablex.

Tyler, T. R. (1980). Impact of directly and indirectly experienced events: The origin of crime-related judgments and behaviors. *Journal of Personality and Social Psychology, 39,* 13-28.

Tyson, C. B., & Hamilton, M. A. (1996, May). *The effects of individual versus community messages on conservation behavior.* Paper presented at the annual meeting of the International Communication Association, Chicago.

Valente, T. W. (1995). *Network models of the diffusion of innovations.* Cresskill, NJ: Hampton.

Vaughn, M. W. (1996, May). *Testing the importance of user-friendly designed to computer interfaces.* Paper presented at the annual meeting of the International Communication Association, Chicago.

Vidmar, N., & Rokeach, M. (1974). Archie Bunker's bigotry: A study in selective perception and exposure. *Journal of Communication, 24*(1), 36-47.

Viser, V. J., & Gordon, T. F. (1996, May). *Mental imagery and emotional responses to opposing types of music.* Paper presented to the Information Systems Division at the annual meeting of the International Communication Association, Chicago.

Wasserman, S., & Faust, K. (1994). *Social network analysis: Methods and applications.* New York: Cambridge University Press.

Wasserman, S., & Pattison, P. (1996). Logit models and logistic regressions for social networks: I. An introduction to Markov graphs and p*. *Psychometrika, 61,* 401-425.

Weaver, J. B. (1997, May). *Personality and individual differences in response to emotionally laden stimuli.* Paper presented to the Information Systems Division at the annual meeting of the International Communication Association, Montreal.

Weaver, J. B., & Wakshlag, J. (1986). Perceived vulnerability to crime, criminal victimization experience, and television viewing. *Journal of Broadcasting & Electronic Media, 30,* 141-158.

West, D. M. (1993). *Air wars: Television advertising in election campaigns, 1952-1992.* Washington, DC: Congressional Quarterly Press.

Whaley, B. B., & Weber, D. C. (1996, May). *Persuasion and likeability: Rebuttal analogy as heuristic cue.* Paper presented at the annual meeting of the International Communication Association, Chicago.

Woelfel, J. (1993). Artificial neural networks in policy research: A current assessment. *Journal of Communication, 43*(1), 63-80.

Zillmann, D. (1982). Television and arousal. In D. Pearl, L. Bouthilet, & J. Lazar (Eds.), *Television and behavior: Ten years of scientific progress and implications for the eighties.* Washington, DC: U.S. Department of Health and Human Services.

Zillmann, D. (1991). The logic of suspense and mystery. In J. Bryant & D. Zillmann (Eds.), *Responding to the screen: Reception and reaction processes* (pp. 281-303). Hillsdale, NJ: Lawrence Erlbaum.

CHAPTER CONTENTS

3 Interpersonal Communication Research: An Overview

MICHAEL E. ROLOFF
LEFKI ANASTASIOU
Northwestern University

This chapter examines theory and research associated with three perspectives of interpersonal communication: psychological/relational, symbolic interactionist, and interactional. The authors describe the origins and key assumptions of each perspective and
discuss major theories, current research, and critiques associated with each. The chapter
concludes with a discussion of some possible directions for future research.

IN his groundbreaking review of interpersonal communication research, Berger (1977) identified a significant shift in scholarly interest. At that time, fewer studies were being published that focused on small group communication and on attitude change as researchers were beginning to explore the dynamics of interaction processes within interpersonal relationships. Although research on small group dynamics and persuasion has since enjoyed resurgent interest in other research contexts (e.g., health communication), the volume of scholarship focused on interaction processes has increased tremendously in the past two decades and continues to dominate the attention of interpersonal communication scholars. The richness of this area of inquiry is evident in articles published in major communication journals (e.g., *Communication Monographs, Communication Research,* and *Human Communication Research*) and in interdisciplinary journals focused on nonverbal communication (*Journal of Nonverbal Behavior*), language (e.g., *Journal Language and Social Psychology*), and interpersonal relationships (e.g., *Journal of Social and Personal Relationships* and *Personal Relationships*). To help make sense of this burgeoning area, several edited volumes have been dedicated to summarizing, critiquing, and pointing to new scholarly directions within

Correspondence: Michael E. Roloff, Department of Communication Studies, Northwestern
University, 1881 Sheridan Road, Evanston, IL 60208-2236; e-mail m-roloff@northwestern.edu

Communication Yearbook 24, pp. 51-71

the major domains of interpersonal communication research. For example, two volumes in the series Sage Annuals of Communication Research have highlighted new directions in interpersonal communication scholarship (Miller, 1976; Roloff & Miller, 1987), and the *Handbook of Interpersonal Communication* has gone through two editions, each of substantial length and coverage (Knapp & Miller, 1985, 1994). Moreover, a number of volumes were published in the 1990s that focus on specialized topics in interpersonal communication, including conflict (Cahn, 1992), relational maintenance (Canary & Stafford, 1994), self-disclosure (Derlega, Metts, Petronio, & Margulis, 1993), family violence (Cahn & Lloyd, 1996), and family communication (Fitzpatrick & Vangelisti, 1995). Finally, the mass of literature focused on particular research questions within given topics has grown sufficiently that meta-analytic studies are becoming more common (e.g., Preiss, Gayle, Burrell, & Allen, in press).

Although the aforementioned body of literature provides testimony to the wide variety of topics under investigation, it makes evident the difficulty of reviewing the large volume of research in interpersonal communication. Because of the limitations imposed on a single chapter, we offer here a review that is admittedly selective and cast at a high level of abstraction. Our intent is to provide an overview of current conceptions of interpersonal communication and some examples of current theories associated with each conception. However, we provide key citations for the reader who wishes to pursue a more detailed and thorough analysis of a particular research topic.

Our overview is divided into two major sections. First, we examine three major perspectives used to define interpersonal communication. Within each perspective, we highlight its origins, assumptions, theories that guide research, and critiques. Finally, we speculate about the future directions of interpersonal communication research.

THE NATURE OF INTERPERSONAL COMMUNICATION

In the most recent edition of the *Handbook of Interpersonal Communication,* Knapp, Miller, and Fudge (1994) observe that the notion of what constitutes interpersonal communication is constantly changing. Hence attempts to define the characteristics of interpersonal communication and, consequently, to set the central focus and boundaries of interpersonal communication research have rarely achieved long-standing consensus among scholars who self-identify as interpersonal communication researchers. Although Knapp et al.'s observations are well-taken, one can identify three conceptions of interpersonal communication that seem consistent with current research: the psychological/relational, the symbolic interactionist, and the interactional. Each conception emphasizes a different central focus for the defining characteristic of interpersonal communication and thereby provides a means of differentiating it from other types of communication.

Psychological/Relational Perspective

Scholars have noted a variety of trends (Knapp et al., 1994) and assumptions (Baxter, 1998) reflected in interpersonal communication research. Although differing in some respects, observers note that most research reflects a psychological and relational orientation. Indeed, one could argue that interpersonal communication research has increasingly focused on the cognitive antecedents and consequences of individuals' communicative attempts to exert influence within their close relationships. The roots of this perspective can be traced to Miller and Steinberg's (1975) characterization of interpersonal communication. These authors assert that people communicate to control their environment so as to receive certain physical, economic, or social rewards from it. To facilitate goal attainment, individuals make predictions about how the receivers of their messages will react. If these predictions are based on cultural or sociological data about the receivers, the communicators are engaged in noninterpersonal communication. On the other hand, if their communicative predictions are based on psychological data, they are engaged in interpersonal communication. Finally, the predominant form of communication defines the nature of the relationship such that if most of the communication is interpersonal in nature, the individuals can be thought to have an interpersonal relationship.

Miller and Steinberg's (1975) observations imply three fundamental characteristics of interpersonal communication. First, interpersonal communication is distinguishable from other forms of communication based upon the psychological processes of the interactants. This move is critical because it draws researchers' attention toward ascertaining and understanding an individual's perception of a target and only secondarily toward the behavior that the individual enacts as a result of those perceptions. Second, Miller and Steinberg's perspective posits an inherent link between communication interchanges and relationships and makes the study of intimate relationships the central context for studying interpersonal communication. Although Miller and Steinberg note that noninterpersonal relationships can be more frequent than interpersonal associations, can play an important role in a person's life, and can escalate into interpersonal relationships, the label *noninterpersonal* serves to reduce their centrality to the research enterprise. Finally, Miller and Steinberg's perspective privileges person perception as a key feature of interpersonal communication and relationships. As such, it is unclear what, if any, role other factors such as emotion might play within interpersonal interchanges.

Although the aforementioned set the scope of conditions for interpersonal communication research, Miller and Steinberg's definition also posits that the central function of all communication for the individual is control of the environment, so that the individual can gain needed resources. In the case of interpersonal communication, that function is served by the communicator's (a) gathering information about other individuals so as to predict their responses to communication more accurately, (b) constructing and enacting communication strategies that will maximize positive responses, and (c) tailoring responses so as to address the communicator's needs. The aforementioned processes are evident in three theoretical perspectives that guide current interpersonal communication research: uncertainty reduction theory, the goal-planning-action model, and the functional/hierarchical approach to comforting.

Uncertainty Reduction Theory

If, as Miller and Steinberg (1975) assert, a key feature of interpersonal communication involves individuals' predicting the actions of their targets, then individuals should engage in behaviors intended to reduce their uncertainty about their targets so as to increase the accuracy of their predictions. This process is the central focus of uncertainty reduction theory (URT), and this perspective has had lasting influence (see Berger, 1987; Berger & Calabrese, 1975; Berger & Gudykunst, 1991). Initially, URT and a great deal of the research associated with it focused on uncertainty reduction in initial encounters. Within Miller and Steinberg's perspective, this focus is reasonable given that relative strangers should have to rely upon their impressions of cultural or group tendencies to predict each other's reactions, which may prove to be a faulty base from which to predict individuals' reactions. When individuals anticipate continued interaction with each other, they should be motivated to reduce their uncertainty. Individuals could gather information about each other through passive observation, active manipulation of the environment, or conversational information exchange. Of course, they could also thwart others' attempts to learn about them and thereby keep their partners uncertain or perhaps create an "illusion of certainty." As individuals acquire more information about one another, their uncertainty should decrease and their relationship should escalate to a more intimate level. However, a relationship's becoming more intimate does not necessarily mean that the partners become impervious to uncertainty about each other. Moreover, individuals often experience uncertainty about events unrelated to intimate partners (e.g., health problems) and seek support from their intimates as a means of better understanding their environment (Albrecht & Adelman, 1987). Because of the aforementioned implications for close relationships, URT is often categorized as a theory of relational communication (e.g., Littlejohn, 1999). However, it has also been profitably employed in cross-cultural contexts (e.g., Gudykunst & Kim, 1984).

Although URT enjoys a favored position among some interpersonal communication researchers, shortcomings of the theory have been identified. Indeed, Berger (1987) acknowledges that some of URT's initial notions have proved to be of dubious validity. Some scholars have argued that uncertainty reduction is not aimed primarily at understanding another person but instead is driven by a desire to understand the nature of the consequences of interacting with the person (Sunnafrank, 1990). Moreover, some studies have found that uncertainty does not always prompt information seeking (e.g., Kellermann & Reynolds, 1990), and research in health contexts suggests that some forms of uncertainty may actually be desirable (e.g., Ford, Babrow, & Stohl, 1996). Although some of the tenets of

URT have proved to be inaccurate, it remains a central theory of interpersonal communication.

Goal-Plan-Action Model

Miller and Steinberg (1975) argue that in order to gain needed resources, individuals turn to others, and especially intimates, for support. At minimum, individuals must signal their desire to their targets, and, in some cases, they must convince reluctant targets to comply with their desires. Over the past two decades, research on interpersonal influence and compliance gaining has increased dramatically (see Seibold, Cantrill, & Meyers, 1994). Although several theoretical perspectives have been used to guide this research, goal-based models have become popular (e.g., Cody, Canary, & Smith, 1994), and among these, the goal-plan-action (GPA) model has been especially influential (Dillard, 1990, 1997). Essentially, the GPA model posits that social influence can be conceived of as a sequential process involving feedback loops. Initially, an individual senses that some discrepancy exists between the current state of affairs and some ideal. If the deviation is of sufficient magnitude and importance, the person will develop an influence goal that motivates action by stimulating planning and persistent attempts to achieve the goal, and the content of the influence goal characterizes the influence attempt (e.g., to gain assistance). Although exerting influence is the primary objective, secondary goals emerge that influence the precise nature of the planned influence attempt by limiting strategic options. Hence a compliance seeker who is concerned about maintaining a positive relationship with the target may refrain from appearing too demanding. Once a plan is generated and selected, a particular tactic is enacted. The target's response then feeds back to affect the influence goals and planned action. Research conducted within this framework has identified types of primary and secondary goals, examined the interrelationship between primary and secondary goals, and demonstrated their relationship to various parts of the compliance-gaining sequence.

Goal-directed models and the GPA model have not been without their critics. For example, Shepherd (1998) argues that the GPA model arises from a "mechanistic, psychologistic, and egoistic legacy" that limits its ability to describe communication processes accurately, shifts attention to psychological processes rather than communication, and privileges the communicator's interpretation of the meaning of an interaction over the interpretations of others (for a response to Shepherd, see Dillard & Schrader, 1998). As an alternative, the critics of goal-directed approaches argue for perspectives that focus on the emergent and social qualities of human interaction.

The Functional/Hierarchical Approach to Comforting

Miller and Steinberg (1975) observe that skillful communicators are empathic, assessing the individual characteristics and special needs of others and then creating messages that adapt to those characteristics and needs. Although this implies that skillful communicators are better able to gain support from others, it also implies that they may be better able to provide support. The latter is evident in research focused on the creation of comforting messages. When emotionally distressed, individuals sometimes turn to friends and family members for support, and in some cases, unsolicited support may be offered. Unfortunately, not all messages intended to alleviate distress prove to be comforting. The functional/hierarchical approach (FHA) posits that messages that acknowledge, elaborate, legitimate, and contextualize the viewpoint of a distressed person are more sophisticated and more likely to reduce distress than are those that are less person-centered (Burleson, 1994). Moreover, person-centered messages are generally seen as more appropriate than are less person-centered ones, although the perceived appropriateness of less person-centered messages is affected by the degree to which the distressed other is to blame for his or her fate (Jones & Burleson, 1997). Generally, individuals who are prone to create person-centered comforting messages are better liked by their partners than are those who are less likely to create such messages, although there is suggestive evidence that partner similarity in the level of comforting skills may be a more important determinant of interpersonal attraction (Burleson & Samter, 1994).

Although FHA has provided useful insights into comforting messages, Burleson and Goldsmith (1997) argue that it does not provide an adequate explanation for why comforting messages work. They posit that comforting results from conversational processes in which an individual helps a distressed individual create a reappraisal of the stressful situation. Such a reappraisal may reflect a new understanding of the causes of the distress, the precise nature of the individual's feelings, and a means of coping with the problem. Although appealing, this perspective is rather new, and limited research has been conducted to test its veracity.

Critique

Although their fundamental distinctions among types of data used to predict reactions quickly fell by the wayside, the observations embodied in Miller and Steinberg's (1975) perspective stimulated a great deal of research. However, some scholars have suggested that the widespread and uncritical acceptance of these assumptions has had negative by-products. Lannamann (1991) argues that much interpersonal communication research reflects an ideological commitment to "(1) individualism and cognitivism, (2) subjectivism, (3) subjective intentionally and (4) ahistoricism" (p. 179), which runs the risk that scholarship may only serve the interests of the current order. Baxter (1998) argues that interpersonal communication is dominated by the following three assumptions:

> First, the assumption that interpersonal communication is centered in intersubjective understanding; second, interpersonal communication is centered exclusively in our relational havens of intimacy, far removed from the arena of societal discourse; and

third, the assumption that interpersonal life will be experienced as consensual orderly, and stripped of its "bumps and warts" if communication is effective. (p. 60)

Although she does not advocate the abandonment of the psychological/relational research frame, Baxter asserts the need for a debate about the veracity of these assumptions and the development of alternative perspectives. In a particularly critical assessment, Cronen (1998) argues that the adoption of a psychological frame for the study of communication has led to intellectual, social, and personal "wreckage." He then lays out a set of guidelines for an alternative approach that might undo the carnage.

Clearly, there is not complete agreement about the value of the psychological/relational perspective and the quantitative methods typically used to study it. However, as of this writing, even critics acknowledge that the psychological/relational perspective is the dominant paradigm, although they assert that its time has passed. Of course, the veracity of that assertion is itself contestable.

Symbolic Interactionist Perspective

Just as the psychological/relational focus has caused some researchers to have an affinity for social psychological perspectives, the symbolic interactionist tradition has directed scholarly attention toward sociology (e.g., Goffman, 1967; Mead, 1934). Essentially, scholars working within this framework view interpersonal communication as a symbolic process involving the presentation and validation of the self. Cushman and Craig introduced this perspective to interpersonal communication researchers in their chapter in Miller's 1976 edited volume *Explorations in Interpersonal Communication.* They argue that the fundamental function of all forms of communication is to regulate consensus, in effect to coordinate the actions of diverse individuals. Within this frame, interpersonal communication systems

> regulate consensus with respect to individual's self-conception. The typical network form of an interpersonal system is the dyad (two people) within a friendship or family network. An interpersonal system tends to evolve a private code based on personal styles and experiences of the individuals. The typical processes of interpersonal communication systems are those involving the development, presentation, and validation of self-conceptions. (p. 44)

Although Cushman and Craig posit that interpersonal communication systems differ from other forms of communication in terms of their networks, codes, and processes, the primary difference is thought to be their function. Organizational systems regulate consensus about production, cultural systems regulate consensus about institutions (Cushman & Craig, 1976), and cross-cultural systems regulate consensus about cultural identity and interest (Cushman & Cahn, 1985). Cushman and Craig note that the function served by each communication system is mutually exclusive, but they also note that each communication system is interdependent. Thus the ability of two individuals to present and validate each other's self-concept can be influenced by the production needs of an organization in which they are employed and by the institutional definitions imposed by their culture. Also, the ability of an organization to regulate consensus about production or of a culture to regulate consensus about institutions can be influenced by the ability of individuals to achieve stable and rewarding self-conceptions. Although this perspective has many implications for the study of interpersonal communication research, its influence is most apparent in three current areas of research: politeness, account sequences, and face sensitivity.

Politeness

Brown and Levinson (1987) argue that a norm of politeness exists across cultures. Essentially, this norm dictates that a speaker use language that is sensitive to the feelings of the hearer (Brown & Gillman, 1989). Such sensitivity is reflected in the speaker's concern for two face needs. Positive face needs constitute the desires of individuals to receive approval and acceptance from others. Negative face needs reflect the desire of the individual to maintain a level of autonomy or not to be imposed upon. Unfortunately, some situations are inherently face threatening. For example, requesting something from another inherently constitutes a threat to that person's autonomy. In such cases, politeness norms dictate that the requester find some means of mitigating the threat to the hearer's face. In some cases, the speaker may simply choose to forgo making the request. In other cases, the speaker might act in an indirect fashion to mask his or her intent (e.g., drop a hint). Alternatively, the speaker might make the request but include linguistic mitigators such as apologies (negative politeness attempts) or compliments (positive politeness attempts). Finally, the speaker may simply choose to make the request baldly, with no mitigation at all. The degree to which speakers engage in facework is thought to vary with the social distance between the interactants, the relative power of the interactants, and the degree of imposition as defined by the culture.

Politeness theory has generated a great deal of research, and some of it suggests that the perspective needs revision. For example, Lim and Bowers (1991) found three rather than two different types of face wants (fellowship, competence, and face), each of which is associated with its own set of linguistic mitigating devices. Wilson, Aleman, and Leatham (1998) discovered evidence that although, to some degree, requests are intrinsically face threatening, speakers also rely upon their tacit knowledge about other facets of the situation to identify and mitigate potential threats to their own and the targets' face. Moreover, after having a request rebuffed, individuals become increasingly less concerned with maintaining the target's face and become more willing to force compliance (Hample & Dallinger, 1998). Dillard, Wilson, Tusing, and Kinney (1997) studied the underlying features of the politeness strategies identified by Brown and Levinson (1987) and found only partial support for the theory. Finally, some researchers have demonstrated that the exclusive focus on verbal politeness strategies should be expanded to include nonverbal cues (Trees & Manusov, 1998).

In addition to these noted areas of weakness, it is also important to acknowledge that research has verified some of politeness theory's central tenets (e.g., Leichty & Applegate, 1991), and the theory has provided insights into comforting messages (Goldsmith, 1994) and into aspects of organizational (Fairhurst, Green, & Snavely, 1984) and cross-cultural communication (Kim & Wilson, 1994).

Account Episodes

Occasionally, an individual is confronted by someone who claims that the individual has committed some offense. In such cases, the person confronted sometimes feels that he or she must account for the actions in question, and an account episode ensues. An account episode involves a three-part sequence, beginning with a reproach, which is followed by an account for the failure, which is then evaluated (Cody & Braaten, 1992). Although having a personal performance failure brought to one's attention may be inherently stigmatizing, research suggests that the form of the reproach can exacerbate the situation. When a reproach is rude, the target loses face, which has a variety of negative consequences. As Cody and Braaten (1992) note: "Severely reproaching another has a significant effect on the accounting process. Several forms of reproach that involve a personal attack, which derogates the self concept, elicit defensive reactions, result in negative evaluations, and cause negative interpersonal and emotional consequences" (p. 242). Moreover, to deflect responsibility for performance failures, individuals often express accounts in which they portray themselves in a positive light and keep private reasons that make them appear insensitive (e.g., Folkes, 1982). Individuals who notice performance failures are aware of this tendency (Dickson, Manusov, Cody, & McLaughlin, 1996).

Although the aforementioned research is interesting, Cody and Braaten (1992) note that it is at a preliminary stage of development and is limited by the lack of a clear theoretical perspective. It is possible that the social confrontation model might provide such a perspective (Newell & Stutman, 1991). This model focuses on how individuals deal with perceived rule violations and features of confrontational episodes such as goals, complaints, responses, and outcomes.

Face Sensitivity

Current research has focused on the degree to which individuals vary in their sensitivity to face issues. For example, there is a large body of research focused on verbal aggressiveness (Infante & Rancer, 1996). Verbally aggressive individuals are those who attack "the self-concepts of others in order to inflict psychological pain, such as humiliation, embarrassment, depression, and other negative feelings about self" (Infante & Rancer, 1996, p. 323). Verbally aggressive individuals are sufficiently face sensitive so as to understand how to attack another's image but at the same time are desensitized to the harm resulting from their actions. In part, verbal aggressiveness may result from a deficit in argumentative skills. Also, some individuals are prone to take conflict personally, which could make them overly sensitive to any disagreements or criticisms (Hample, 1999). As a result, individuals who tend to take conflict personally wish to avoid arguments and hence are both less argumentative and less verbally aggressive.

Critique

Although criticism has been leveled at particular theories, the symbolic interactionist perspective has been generally well received. However, one concern may arise from an underlying ideology reflected in this perspective. Much of the face-related research suggests that face sensitivity is a desirable trait/skill and that face attacks are to be avoided. Some might question whether this perspective simply reflects "a feel-good" ideology aimed at making individuals happy (see Burgoon, 1995). Hence researchers within this perspective may give insufficient attention and credence to contexts in which disconfirming another's self-concept and face might be justified and desirable.

Interactional Perspective

The perspectives discussed in the preceding pages posit that the defining characteristic of interpersonal communication is found in the psychological processes associated with it, the relational context, or the function the communication serves. However, others have argued that interpersonal communication should be conceived of as human interaction. Pearce (1976) notes that interpersonal communication involves "the sequencing of messages in conversations and the sequencing of conversations into relationships" (p. 17). Cappella (1987) has taken this position a step further by arguing, "If interpersonal communication has any essential features, it is that persons influence one another's behavior over and above that attributed to normal baselines of action" (p. 228). Hence the sequencing of conversational messages noted by Pearce reflects contingent responses or an interaction. Cappella describes his definition as minimalist in that it does not take a stand as to whether interpersonal communication (a) is intentional; (b) is influenced by psychological, affective, or social factors; or (c) occurs only within certain relational contexts. This rather broad conception of interpersonal communication expands the boundaries of the area. Specifically, Cappella argues that interpersonal communication researchers explore four fundamental classes of questions, which he calls zero-order questions, first-order questions, second-order questions, and third-order questions.

Zero-Order Questions

Zero-order questions focus on identifying the behaviors to be observed during an interaction and the time unit during which they are to be observed. In a sense, these questions have methodological implications for the ways we perform our research. For example, Kellermann and Cole (1994) have uncovered substantial problems in the ways in which influence messages have been operationalized. To avoid such problems, they argue, researchers should first identify the underlying dimensions that differentiate interaction behaviors and then devise and test theories that explain those dimensions. Such an approach seems consistent with research conducted on the appraisal of influence messages (Dillard, Kinney, & Cruz, 1996), the interpretation of relational communication (Dillard, Solomon, & Palmer, 1999), and the social meaning of nonverbal communication (e.g., Burgoon & Le Poire, 1999).

Issues related to the duration of an interaction are also important. Although interpersonal communication researchers have assumed that interactions can be seen as episodes (e.g., Pearce, 1976), the notion of where they begin and end is still unclear. Often researchers arbitrarily select time units within a given interchange or arbitrarily set limits on how long an interaction takes place. However, a few researchers have gone into the field to study the length of episodes. For example, Vuchinich (1990) studied family quarrels at the supper table and Benoit and Benoit (1987) used diaries and questionnaires to assess the length of arguments among college students. Both sets of studies suggest that everyday arguments are relatively short. Moreover, there is evidence that many arguments end unresolved and therefore recur (Benoit & Benoit, 1987). This raises the possibility that interpersonal communication researchers should expand their focus from single episodes to linked episodes (see Johnson & Roloff, 1998).

First-Order Questions

First-order questions focus on situational, cognitive, or psychological factors related to the encoding or decoding of interaction behaviors. A great deal of this research has studied message production, and two of the more popular theories are action assembly theory and planning theory. Greene's (1984, 1997; Greene & Geddes, 1993) action assembly theory posits that communicators use their knowledge of actions to assemble output representations that reflect their plans for accomplishing their goals. These representations are hierarchically structured and consist of goals, ideas to be communicated, appropriate language, and neural commands required to produce the language. The assembly process can be complicated and requires cognitive effort. When an individual strives to accomplish multiple goals, he or she must expend greater effort. Current research within this perspective is focused on how individuals acquire message production skills (e.g., Caplan & Greene, 1999). In a similar vein, Berger's planning theory (1997) posits that interactants sometime form plans or "hierarchical cognitive representations of goal-directed action sequences" (p. 25). Plans are hierarchically organized such that they contain abstract elements (such as strategies) and concrete actions (such as specific statements that the person intends to make). When enacting these plans, individuals sometimes fail. Assuming that they are sufficiently committed to achieving their goals that they persist, they could alter their plans by changing a more abstract element, such as the basic strategy, or a concrete element, such as repeating the same point in a different way. To avoid the excessive cognitive work that would arise from changing an abstract element, individuals tend to make minor changes in their plans by changing the concrete elements. This is referred to as the *hierarchy principle.* Current research suggests that it is valid (Berger, Knowlton, & Abrahams, 1996). However, in some cases, lower-level changes are insufficient, and individuals are forced to alter more abstract elements. In such cases, the cognitive load resulting from such changes depends upon the number of alternative ways the individuals created to achieve their goals. Individuals who had planned one way or many ways have been found to experience greater cognitive load when changing abstract elements than do those who had developed a moderate number of ways (Knowlton & Berger, 1997).

Interpersonal detection theory (Buller & Burgoon, 1996) is one of the few perspectives to examine the interplay between the perceptions of interactants. The theory posits that when an interactant sees signs of deceit, he or she becomes suspicious and enacts deception-detection strategies but also exhibits nonstrategic signs of impaired communication performance (e.g., low involvement, anxiety). His or her partner perceives the suspicious attempt to mask any decision but also exhibits signs of impaired communication. Thus the behavior of one person affects the perceptions of the partner, which in turn sets the tone for subsequent behavior. Research generally has verified this perspective (e.g., Burgoon, Buller, Ebesu, White, & Rockwell, 1996).

Second-Order Questions

Second-order questions focus directly on the patterns of behavior of which the interaction is composed. A variety of terms have been used to characterize the interrelationships among interaction behaviors (see Burgoon, Dillman, & Stern, 1993; Burgoon et al., 1998), and a variety of theories have attempted to explain and predict their occurrence, including discrepancy arousal theory (Cappella & Greene, 1982), expectancy violations theory (Burgoon & Hale, 1988), sequential functional theory (Patterson, 1982), communication accommodation theory (Giles, Coupland, & Coupland, 1991), and cognitive valence theory (Andersen, 1998). Interpersonal adaptation theory (IAT) is an attempt to tie together the various components of the aforementioned theories and patterns (Burgoon, 1998; Burgoon, Stern, & Dillman, 1995; Burgoon et al., 1998). In brief, IAT assumes that for biological and social reasons, interactants are prone to reciprocate (match) their interaction behaviors; hence reciprocity is the default pattern for most interactions. However, under certain conditions, individuals may intentionally or unintentionally engage in complementary patterns of behavior (engage in dissimilar actions). Individuals are thought to enter an interaction with requirements, expectations, and desires for interaction behaviors that combine to form an interaction position reflecting the anticipated, preferred, and needed pattern of behavior. During a conversation, individuals compare their interaction positions with the actual behaviors emitted by their partners. When the partner's behavior matches or nearly matches the interaction position, the individual will reciprocate the partner's behavior. When the partner's behavior is grossly at variance with the interaction position, the individual examines its valence. When the behavior is more positive than the interaction position, the individual should reciprocate (match) the behavior, but when the behavior is more negative, the individual will compensate (enact dissimilar behavior) or maintain his or her current behavior. Within this model, compensation could result from increased arousal or from a strategic reaction designed to preempt frustration by altering another's behavior (Burgoon, 1998). Initial research is supportive of many of IAT's predictions (see Floyd & Burgoon, 1999; Le Poire & Yoshimura, 1999).

Third-Order Questions

Third-order questions examine the relationship between interaction patterns and relational states. As noted earlier, the study of relational communication has grown to include the examination of issues related to relational maintenance (Canary & Zelley, 2000), dialectics (Baxter & Montgomery, 1996), relational abuse (Roloff, 1996), and marital and family communication (Fitzpatrick, 1988). One approach that is directly tied to interaction patterns has focused on demand/withdrawal sequences. During arguments, one individual (in heterosexual couples, the female) may issue a forceful, demanding statement toward the partner (in heterosexual couples, the male) to which the partner responds by withdrawing from the conversation (e.g., Klinetob & Smith, 1996). Self-reports of this complementary pattern have been linked to difficulty in resolving conflict (e.g., Johnson & Roloff, 1998) and to reduced relational quality (e.g., Heavey, Christensen, & Malamuth, 1995). Researchers have used a social structure perspective to explain this pattern (e.g., Christensen & Heavey, 1990). Essentially, this perspective argues that in a heterosexual couple the female is relatively less powerful than the male. This decreases the female's relational satisfaction, and she is prone to confront her male partner in a demanding fashion. The male, being more powerful and satisfied, sees little reason to change and simply withdraws from the conversation as a means of maintaining the status quo. Continued confrontations cause the pattern to be repeated, and eventually both parties become dissatisfied. Interestingly, when a male becomes dissatisfied with his female partner, he becomes demanding and she responds by withdrawing. Although there is some support for this reasoning, a recent study suggests that it is not entirely valid (Caughlin & Vangelisti, 1999).

Critique

The interactional approach to defining interpersonal communication has a great deal of appeal. It clearly makes communication the central focus and does not privilege any psychological or social process. Hence it provides an excellent umbrella to cover the numerous and diverse perspectives on interpersonal communication. At the same time, it serves only as an organizational pattern. The psychological/relational and symbolic perspectives advance theoretical perspectives that have heuristic value. Moreover, it is unclear as to whether most interpersonal communication researchers would define interaction in the same way. Certainly, Capella (1987) provides a very distinctive definition and includes within it a means of operationalizing interaction that some might find too restrictive. Finally, it is unclear how the various questions that flow from this perspective fit with one another. Indeed, few theorists and researchers have attempted to create a perspective that answers each question. The view of the field that is provided by this perspective is one of different perspectives being used to study a given question, but none that addresses all of them. Hence this approach uncovers a degree of incoherence and disjointedness to interpersonal communication research that may indeed be an accurate characterization.

FUTURE DIRECTIONS

Predicting the future of interpersonal communication research is risky. If one examines Berger's (1977) initial review, it is apparent that some research issues and perspectives have come and gone. However, at the risk of being proved wrongheaded, we posit the following directions.

First, we see a continuing trend focused on the study of everyday communication processes. Several scholars have noted a growing body of research that attempts to understand how ordinary individuals communicate so as to make sense of their everyday existence (Duck, 1998; Roloff, 1998). This observation implies that interpersonal communication researchers will need to access everyday practices so as to determine the degree to which our theories and methods map onto those experienced by ordinary individuals (Benoit & Benoit, 1987; Duck, Rutt, Hurst, & Strejc, 1991; Vuchinich, 1990). In doing so, we believe, interpersonal communication researchers will make contributions that will benefit individuals, but at the same time they may run the risk of appearing trivial. After all, the ordinary is sometimes thought to be obvious and of little value. Moreover, if our notion of everyday processes continues to be defined primarily by undergraduates in dating relationships, our perspective on everyday communication will likely be quite limited.

Second, we suspect that researchers will expand the contextual boundaries of our focus of study. This review clearly indicates that the study of interpersonal communication has increasingly become defined as the study of communication in close relationships. Although one could argue that this focus has generally served us well, it has narrowed our focus. We see two ways in which our focus might be expanded. First, one could argue that in everyday life, the boundaries between our close relationships and those that are less intimate are becoming more permeable. Hence it becomes important to study the interfaces between different parts of individuals' lives (Petronio, Ellemers, Giles, & Gallois, 1998). For example, a rather large literature examines the interface between the family and the workplace (e.g., Frone, Yardley, & Markel, 1997), but only a few communication researchers have made contributions to this body of knowledge (e.g., Kirby, 1999). This implies that interpersonal communication researchers will collaborate more with scholars from other communication specializations. Second, we could develop perspectives that specify how the nature of the relationship between communicators influences interaction processes (e.g., Roloff, 1987) and conduct research that compares given communication processes within different relational contexts (e.g., Buzzanell & Burrell, 1997).

Third, with the technological revolution arising from the Internet, the notion of what constitutes interaction will need to be broadened from our predominant focus on face-to-face interaction. Perspectives such as Walther's (1996) hyperpersonal communication represent valuable attempts to demonstrate how interactants deal with a new communication medium.

Fourth, we anticipate that interpersonal communication researchers will increasingly tie their scholarship to the significant issues facing society. In a sense, the study of interpersonal communication has enjoyed a certain sense of insularity. By and large, we have been able to set our own research agendas and to evaluate their value. If current trends in universities continue, others will be evaluating the worthiness of our agenda. This will make it essential for us to demonstrate that the fundamental process that defines interpersonal communication is related to issues that are of central concerns to larger society. Fortunately, it is possible to demonstrate that interpersonal communication plays a critical role in such social problems as violent crime, societal alienation, incivility, inadequate health care, and divorce (see Roloff, in press). Unfortunately, much of this research is being conducted by individuals who are not in communication departments and in all likelihood would not spontaneously identify themselves as interpersonal communication researchers. This last comment implies that interpersonal communication research will continue to have a multidisciplinary flavor. We will continue to draw from scholarship in fields and disciplines such as psychology and sociology, but some of us may also turn to less familiar fields, such as neurobiology (e.g., Beatty, McCroskey, & Heisel, 1998). However useful and inevitable, multidisciplinarity makes it imperative that we have something unique and of value to add. Although we are doubtful that there will ever be consensus about a definition of the field or a central theory, if there is not something of value among the multitude of approaches adopted by interpersonal communication researchers, then our demise is assured and deserved.

At the outset, we noted the formidability of the task of summarizing such a large and diverse literature in a single chapter. We suspect that some readers will believe that we have overlooked key perspectives, and some will find our analysis of those we have covered to be superficial. We may have offended friends and foes alike, and for that we apologize. However, we believe we have provided a picture of the diversity and richness of the field of interpersonal communication research.

REFERENCES

Albrecht, T. L., & Adelman, M. B. (Eds.). (1987). *Communicating social support.* Newbury Park, CA: Sage.

Andersen, P. A. (1998). The cognitive valence theory of intimate communication. In M. T. Palmer & G. A. Barnett (Eds.), *Progress in communication sciences: Vol. 14. Mutual influence in interpersonal communication: Theory and research in cognition, affect, and behavior* (pp. 39-72). Stamford, CT: Ablex.

Baxter, L. A. (1998). Locating the social in interpersonal communication. In J. S. Trent (Ed.), *Communication: Views from the helm for the 21st century* (pp. 60-64). Boston: Allyn & Bacon.

Baxter, L. A., & Montgomery, B. M. (1996). *Relating: Dialogues and dialectics.* New York: Guilford.

Beatty, M. J., McCroskey, J. C., & Heisel, A. D. (1998). Communication apprehension as temperamental expression: A communibiological paradigm. *Communication Monographs, 65,* 197-219.

Benoit, W. J., & Benoit, P. J. (1987). Everyday argument practices of naive social actors. In J. W. Wentzel (Ed.), *Argument and critical practices* (pp. 465-473). Annandale, VA: Speech Communication Association.

Berger, C. R. (1977). Interpersonal communication theory and research: An overview. In B. D. Ruben (Ed.), *Communication yearbook 1* (pp. 217-228). New Brunswick, NJ: Transaction.

Berger, C. R. (1987). Communicating under uncertainty. In M. E. Roloff & G. R. Miller (Eds.), *Interpersonal processes: New directions in communication research* (pp. 39-62). Newbury Park, CA: Sage.

Berger, C. R. (1997). *Planning strategic interaction: Attaining goals through communicative action.* Mahwah, NJ: Lawrence Erlbaum.

Berger, C. R., & Calabrese, R. J. (1975). Some explorations in initial interactions and beyond: Toward a developmental theory of interpersonal communication. *Human Communication Research, 1,* 99-112.

Berger, C. R., & Gudykunst, W. (1991). Uncertainty and communication. In B. Dervin & M. Voigt (Eds.), *Progress in communication sciences* (Vol. 10, pp. 21-66). Norwood, NJ: Ablex.

Berger, C. R., Knowlton, S. W., & Abrahams, M. F. (1996). The hierarchy principle in strategic communication. *Communication Theory, 6,* 111-142.

Brown, P., & Levinson, S. (1987). *Politeness: Some universals in language use.* Cambridge: Cambridge University Press.

Brown, R., & Gillman, A. (1989). Politeness theory and Shakespeare's four major tragedies. *Language and Society, 18,* 159-212.

Buller, D. B., & Burgoon, J. K. (1996). Interpersonal deception theory. *Communication Theory, 6,* 203-242.

Burgoon, J. K. (1998). It takes two to tango: Interpersonal adaptation and implications for relational communication. In J. S. Trent (Ed.), *Communication: Views from the helm for the 21st century* (pp. 53-59). Boston: Allyn & Bacon.

Burgoon, J. K., Buller, D. A., Ebesu, A. S., White, C. S., & Rockwell, P. A. (1996). Testing interpersonal detection theory: Effects of suspicion on communication behaviors and perceptions. *Communication Theory, 6,* 243-267.

Burgoon, J. K., Dillman, L., & Stern, L. A. (1993). Adaptation in dyadic interaction: Defining and operationalizing patterns of reciprocity and compensation. *Communication Theory, 3,* 295-316.

Burgoon, J. K., Ebesu, A. S., White, C. H., Koch, P., Alvaro, E. M., & Kikuchi, T. (1998). The multiple faces of interaction adaptation. In M. T. Palmer & G. A. Barnett (Eds.), *Progress in communication sciences: Vol. 14. Mutual influence in interpersonal communication: Theory and research in cognition, affect, and behavior* (pp. 191-220). Stamford, CT: Ablex.

Burgoon, J. K., & Hale, J. L. (1988). Nonverbal expectancy violations: Model elaboration and application. *Communication Monographs, 55,* 58-79.

Burgoon, J. K., & Le Poire, B. A. (1999). Nonverbal cues and interpersonal judgments: Participants and observer perceptions of intimacy, dominance, composure and formality. *Communication Monographs, 66,* 105-124.

Burgoon, J. K., Stern, L. A., & Dillman, L. (1995). *Interpersonal adaptation: Dyadic interaction patterns.* New York: Cambridge University Press.

Burgoon, M. (1995). A kinder, gentler discipline: Feeling good about being mediocre. In B. R. Burleson (Ed.), *Communication yearbook 18* (pp. 464-479). Thousand Oaks, CA: Sage.

Burleson, B. R. (1994). Comforting messages: Significance, approaches, and effects. In B. R. Burleson, T. L. Albrecht, & I. G. Sarason (Eds.), *Communication of social support: Messages, interactions, relationships, and community* (pp. 3-28). Thousand Oaks, CA: Sage.

Burleson, B. R., & Goldsmith, D. J. (1997). How the comforting process works: Alleviating emotional distress through conversationally induced reappraisals. In P. Andersen & L. K. Guerrero (Eds.), *Handbook of communication and emotion: Theory, applications and contexts* (pp. 245-280). San Diego, CA: Academic Press.

Burleson, B. R., & Samter, W. (1994). A social skills approach to relationship maintenance: How individual differences in communication skills affect the achievement of relationships functions. In D. J. Canary & L. Stafford (Eds.), *Communication and relational maintenance* (pp. 61-90). San Diego, CA: Academic Press.

Buzzanell, P. M., & Burrell, N. A. (1997). Family and workplace conflict: Examining metaphorical conflict schemas and expressions across context and sex. *Human Communication Research, 24,* 109-146.

Cahn, D. D. (1992). *Conflict in intimate relationships.* New York: Guilford.

Cahn, D. D., & Lloyd, S. A. (Eds.). (1996). *Family violence from a communication perspective.* Thousand Oaks, CA: Sage.

Canary, D. J., & Stafford, L. (Eds.). (1994). *Communication and relational maintenance.* San Diego, CA: Academic Press.

Canary, D. J., & Zelley, E. D. (2000). Current research programs on relational maintenance behaviors. In M. E. Roloff (Ed.), *Communication yearbook 23* (pp. 305-339). Thousand Oaks, CA: Sage.

Caplan, S. E., & Greene, J. O. (1999). Acquisition of message production skill by younger and older adults: Effects of age, task complexity, and practice. *Communication Monographs, 66,* 31-48.

Cappella, J. N. (1987). Interpersonal communication: Definitions and fundamental questions. In C. R. Berger & S. H. Chaffee (Eds.), *Handbook of communication science* (pp. 184-238). Newbury Park, CA: Sage.

Cappella, J. N., & Greene, J. O. (1982). A discrepancy-arousal explanation of mutual influence in expressive behavior for adult-adult and infant-adult interaction. *Communication Monographs, 49,* 89-114.

Caughlin, J. P., & Vangelisti, A. L. (1999). Desire for change in one's partner as a predictor of the demand/withdraw pattern of marital communication. *Communication Monographs, 66,* 66-89.

Christensen, A., & Heavey, C. L. (1990). Gender and social structure in the demand/withdraw pattern of martial conflict. *Journal of Personality and Social Psychology, 59,* 73-81.

Cody, M. J., & Braaten, D. O. (1992). The social-interactive aspects of account-giving. In M. L. McLaughlin, M. J. Cody, & S. J. Read (Eds), *Explaining oneself to others: Reason-giving in a social context* (pp. 225-243). Mahwah, NJ: Lawrence Erlbaum.

Cody, M. J., Canary, D. J., & Smith, S. W. (1994). Compliance-gaining goals: An inductive analysis of actors' goal types, strategies, and successes. In J. A. Daly & J. M. Wiemann (Eds.), *Strategic interpersonal communication* (pp. 33-90). Hillsdale, NJ: Lawrence Erlbaum.

Cronen, V. E. (1998). Communication theory for the twenty-first century: Cleaning up the wreckage of the psychology project. In J. S. Trent (Ed.), *Communication: Views from the helm for the 21st century* (pp. 18-38). Boston: Allyn & Bacon.

Cushman, D. P., & Cahn, D. D. (1985). *Communication in interpersonal relationships.* Albany: State University of New York Press.

Cushman, D. P., & Craig, R. T. (1976). Communication systems: Interpersonal implications. In G. R. Miller (Ed.), *Explorations in interpersonal communication* (pp. 37-58). Beverly Hills, CA: Sage.

Derlega, V. J., Metts, S., Petronio, S., & Margulis, S. T. (1993). *Self-disclosure.* Newbury Park, CA: Sage.

Dickson, R. E., Manusov, V., Cody, M. J., & McLaughlin, M. L. (1996). When hearing's not believing; Perceived differences between public and private explanations for two compliance failures. *Journal of Language and Social Psychology, 15,* 27-40.

Dillard, J. P. (1990). A goal-driven model of interpersonal influence. In J. P. Dillard (Ed.), *Seeking compliance: The production of interpersonal influence messages* (pp. 41-56). Scottsdale, AZ: Gorsuch Scarisbrick.

Dillard, J. P. (1997). Explicating the goal construct: Tools for theorists. In J. O. Greene (Ed.), *Message production: Advances in communication theory* (pp. 47-70). Mahwah, NJ: Lawrence Erlbaum.

Dillard, J. P., Kinney, T. A., & Cruz, M. G. (1996). Influence, appraisals, and emotions in close relationships. *Communication Monographs, 63,* 105-130.

Dillard, J. P., & Schrader, D. C. (1998). Reply: On the utility of the goals-plan-action sequence. *Communication Studies, 49,* 300-304.

Dillard, J. P., Solomon, D. H., & Palmer, M. T. (1999). Structuring the concept of relational communication. *Communication Monographs, 66,* 49-65.

Dillard, J. P., Wilson, S. R., Tusing, K. J., & Kinney, T. A. (1997). Politeness judgments in personal relationships. *Journal of Language and Social Psychology, 16,* 297-325.

Duck, S. (1998). Helms and bridges: Relational communication as conceptual and personal linkage. In J. S. Trent (Ed.), *Communication: Views from the helm for the 21st century* (pp. 47-52). Boston: Allyn & Bacon.

Duck, S., Rutt, D. J., Hurst, M. H., & Strejc, H. (1991). Some evident truths about conversations in everyday relationships: All communications are not created equal. *Human Communication Research, 18,* 228-267.

Fairhurst, G. T., Green, S. G., & Snavely, B. K. (1984). Face support in controlling poor performance. *Human Communication Research, 11,* 272-295.

Fitzpatrick, M. A. (1988). *Between husbands and wives: Communication in marriage.* Newbury Park, CA: Sage.

Fitzpatrick, M. A., & Vangelisti, A. L. (Eds.). (1995). *Explaining family interactions.* Thousand Oaks, CA: Sage.

Floyd, K., & Burgoon, J. K. (1999). Reacting to nonverbal expressions of liking: A test of interaction adaptation theory. *Communication Monographs, 66,* 217-239.

Folkes, V. S. (1982). Communicating reasons for social rejection. *Journal of Experimental Social Psychology, 18,* 235-252.

Ford, L. A., Babrow, A. S., & Stohl, C. (1996). Social support messages and the management of uncertainty in the experiences of breast cancer: An application of problematic integration theory. *Communication Monographs, 63,* 189-207.

Frone, M. R., Yardley, J. K., & Markel, K. S. (1997). Developing and testing an integrative model of the work-family interface. *Journal of Vocational Behavior, 50,* 145-167.

Giles, H., Coupland, N., & Coupland, J. (1991). Accommodation theory: Communication, context, and consequence. In H. Giles, N. Coupland, & J. Coupland (Eds.), *Contexts of accommodation: Developments in applied sociolinguistics* (pp. 1-68). Cambridge: Cambridge University Press.

Goffman, E. (1967). *Interaction ritual: Essays on face-to-face behavior.* Garden City, NY: Anchor.

Goldsmith, D. J. (1994). The role of facework in supportive communication. In B. R. Burleson, T. L. Albrecht, & I. G. Sarason (Eds.), *Communication of social support: Messages, interactions, relationships, and community* (pp. 29-49). Thousand Oaks, CA: Sage.

Greene, J. O. (1984). A cognitive approach to human communication: An action assembly theory. *Communication Monographs, 51,* 289-306.

Greene, J. O. (1997). A second generation action assembly theory. In J. O. Greene (Ed.), *Message production: Advances in communication theory* (pp. 151-170). Mahwah, NJ: Lawrence Erlbaum.

Greene, J. O., & Geddes, D. (1993). An action assembly perspective on social skill. *Communication Theory, 3,* 26-49.

Gudykunst, W. B., & Kim, Y. Y. (1984). *Communicating with strangers.* Reading, MA: Addison-Wesley.

Hample, D. (1999). The life space of personalized conflicts. In M. E. Roloff (Ed.). *Communication yearbook 22* (pp. 171-207). Thousand Oaks, CA: Sage.

Hample, D., & Dallinger, J. M. (1998). On the etiology of the rebuff phenomenon: Why are persuasive messages less polite after rebuff? *Communication Studies, 49,* 305-321.

Heavey, C. L., Christensen, A., & Malamuth, N. M. (1995). The longitudinal impact of demand and withdrawal during marital conflict. *Journal of Consulting and Clinical Psychology, 63,* 683-687.

Infante, D. A., & Rancer, A. S. (1996). Argumentativeness and verbal aggressiveness: A review of recent theory and research. In B. R. Burleson (Ed.), *Communication yearbook 19* (pp. 319-351). Thousand Oaks, CA: Sage.

Johnson, K. L., & Roloff, M. E. (1998). Serial arguing and relational quality: Determinants and consequences of perceived resolvability. *Communication Research, 25,* 327-343.

Jones, S. M., & Burleson, B. R. (1997). The impact of situational variables on helpers' perceptions of comforting messages: An attributional analysis. *Communication Research, 24,* 530-555.

Kellermann, K., & Cole T. (1994). Classifying compliance-gaining messages: Taxonomic disorder and strategic confusion. *Communication Theory, 4,* 3-60.

Kellermann, K., & Reynolds, R. (1990). When ignorance is bliss: The role of motivation to reduce uncertainty in uncertainty reduction theory. *Human Communication Research, 17,* 3-75.

Kim, M. S., & Wilson, S. R. (1994). A cross-cultural comparison of implicit theories of requesting. *Communication Monographs, 61,* 210-235.

Kirby, E. L. (1999, November). *Understudied communication: Balancing work and family in organizations.* Paper presented at the annual meeting of the National Communication Association, Chicago.

Klinetob, N. A., & Smith, D. S. (1996). Demand-withdraw communication in marital interaction: Tests of interspousal contingency and gender role hypothesis. *Journal of Marriage and the Family, 58,* 866-883.

Knapp, M. L., & Miller, G. R. (Eds.). (1985). *Handbook of interpersonal communication.* Beverly Hills, CA: Sage.

Knapp, M. L., & Miller, G. R. (Eds.). (1994). *Handbook of interpersonal communication* (2nd ed.). Thousand Oaks, CA: Sage.

Knapp, M. L., Miller, G. R., & Fudge, K. (1994). Background and current trends in the study of interpersonal communication. In M. L. Knapp & G. R. Miller (Eds.), *Handbook of interpersonal communication* (2nd ed., pp. 3-20). Thousand Oaks, CA: Sage.

Knowlton, S. W., & Berger, C. R. (1997). Message planning, communication failure, and cognitive load: Further explorations of the hierarchy principle. *Human Communication Research, 24,* 4-30.

Lannamann, J. W. (1991). Interpersonal communication research as ideological practice. *Communication Theory, 1,* 179-203.

Leichty, G., & Applegate, J. L. (1991). Social-cognitive and situational influences on the use of face-saving persuasive strategies. *Human Communication Research, 17,* 451-484.

Le Poire, B. A., & Yoshimura, S. M. (1999). The effects of expectancies and actual communication on nonverbal adaptation and communication outcomes: A test of interaction adaptation theory. *Communication Monographs, 66,* 1-30.

Lim, T. S., & Bowers, J. W. (1991). Facework: Solidarity, approbation, and tact. *Human Communication Research, 17,* 415-450.

Littlejohn, S. W. (1999). *Theories of human communication* (6th ed.). Belmont, CA: Wadsworth.

Mead, G. H. (1934). *Mind, self, and society: From the standpoint of a social behaviorist* (C. W. Morris, Ed.). Chicago: University of Chicago Press.

Miller, G. R. (Ed.). (1976). *Explorations in interpersonal communication.* Beverly Hills, CA: Sage.

Miller, G. R., & Steinberg, M. (1975). *Between people: A new analysis of interpersonal communication.* Chicago: Science Research Associates.

Newell, S. E., & Stutman, R. K. (1991). The episodic nature of social confrontation. In J. A. Anderson (Ed.), *Communication yearbook 14* (pp. 359-392). Newbury Park, CA: Sage.

Patterson, M. L. (1982). A sequential functional model of nonverbal exchange. *Psychological Review, 89,* 231-249.

Pearce, W. B. (1976). The coordinated management of meaning: A rules-based theory of interpersonal communication. In G. R. Miller (Ed.), *Explorations in interpersonal communication* (pp. 17-36). Beverly Hills, CA: Sage.

Petronio, S., Ellemers, N., Giles, H., & Gallois, C. (1998). (Mis)communicating across boundaries: Interpersonal and intergroup considerations. *Communication Research, 25,* 618-640.

Preiss, R. W., Gayle, B., Burrell, N. A., & Allen, M. (Eds.). (in press). *Interpersonal communication: Advances through meta-analysis.* Mahwah, NJ: Lawrence Erlbaum.

Roloff, M. E. (1987). Communication and reciprocity within intimate relationships. In M. E. Roloff & G. R. Miller (Eds.), *Interpersonal processes: New directions in communication research* (pp. 11-38). Newbury Park, CA: Sage.

Roloff, M. E. (1996). The catalyst hypothesis: Conditions under which coercive communication leads to physical aggression. In D. D. Cahn & S. A. Lloyd (Eds.), *Family violence from a communication perspective* (pp. 20-36). Thousand Oaks, CA: Sage.

Roloff, M. E. (1998). How people make sense of everyday, interpersonal events: Examining the perceived connection among conflict episodes. In J. S. Trent (Ed.), *Communication: Views from the helm for the 21st century* (pp. 67-72). Boston: Allyn & Bacon.

Roloff, M. E. (in press). The state of the art of interpersonal communication research: Are we addressing socially significant issues? In R. W. Preiss, B. Gayle, N. A. Burrell, & M. Allen (Eds.), *Interpersonal communication: Advances through meta-analysis.* Mahwah, NJ: Lawrence Erlbaum.

Roloff, M. E., & Miller, G. R. (Eds.). (1987). *Interpersonal processes: New directions in communication research.* Newbury Park, CA: Sage.

Seibold, D. R., Cantrill, J. G., & Meyers, R. A. (1994). Communication and interpersonal influence. In M. L. Knapp & G. R. Miller (Eds.), *Handbook of interpersonal communication* (2nd ed., pp. 542-588). Thousand Oaks, CA: Sage.

Shepherd, G. J. (1998). Response: The trouble with goals. *Communication Studies, 49,* 294-299.

Sunnafrank, M. (1990). Predicted outcome value and uncertainty reduction theories: A test of competing perspectives. *Human Communication Research, 17,* 76-103.

Trees, A. R., & Manusov, V. (1998). Managing face concerns in criticism: Integrating nonverbal behaviors as a dimension of politeness in female friendship dyads. *Human Communication Research, 24,* 564-583.

Vuchinich, S. (1990). The sequential organization of closing in verbal family conflict. In A. D. Grimshaw (Ed.), *Conflict talk: Sociolinguistic investigations of arguments in conversations* (pp. 118-138). Cambridge: Cambridge University Press.

Walther, J. B. (1996). Computer mediated-communication: Impersonal, interpersonal, and hyperpersonal interactions. *Communication Research, 23,* 3-43.

Wilson, S. R., Aleman, C. G., & Leatham, G. B. (1998). Identity implications of influence goals: A revised analysis of face-threatening acts and application to seeking compliance with same-sex friends. *Human Communication Research, 25,* 64-98.

CHAPTER CONTENTS

4 Mass Communication Research at the Dawn of the 21st Century

ALAN M. RUBIN
PAUL M. HARIDAKIS
Kent State University

This chapter reviews the current state of research according to dominant mass communication theories and lines of research. Theoretical perspectives addressed include agenda setting, framing, diffusion of innovations, gap hypotheses, third-person effects, cultivation, priming, social cognition, uses and gratifications, and critical/cultural studies. Prominent lines of research falling within or between these perspectives include media portrayals, media constructions, health issues, newer technologies, cultural maintenance and change, children and media, and political communication. The perspectives reflect different beliefs as to the roles of the audience, media, and society. Some emphasize purposeful individual selection and use, whereas others stress the power of media to influence societal directions and audience beliefs. Investigations reflect both differences and commonalities in assumptions and approaches. Regardless of discipline, concentration, or perspective, however, the expansive research in these areas suggests that mass communication researchers are on a productive path toward understanding how media affect and fit within the lives of people and societies.

T RADITIONALLY, mass communication research has been defined as inquiry into one-to-many information dissemination involving a physical or electronic interpose. Especially in light of newer interactive technologies, however, mass communication research also can be viewed as inquiry about mediated interaction that bridges communication contexts. For example, newer media have mass, interpersonal, organizational, political, economic, and cultural dimensions and have altered how people communicate in a variety of settings. In addition, theories developed in other communication contexts have been applied more frequently to the study of mediated communication.

Correspondence: Alan M. Rubin, School of Communication Studies, P.O. Box 5190, Kent State University, Kent, OH 44242-0001; e-mail arubin@kent.edu

Communication Yearbook 24, pp.73-97

Despite the blurring of boundaries across communication contexts, many theories developed about mass media are viable for the study of new and lingering questions. Accordingly, growth and expansion characterize the state of mass communication theory and research. The diversity of mass communication research foreshadows continued interest in the uses and effects of newer and older media as producers and users seek to attain goals and to meet needs.

We focus our discussion on dominant mass communication theories and lines of research as reflected in current literature, mostly in scholarly journals. The theoretical perspectives we address include agenda setting, framing, diffusion of innovations, gap hypotheses, third-person effects, cultivation, priming, social cognition, uses and gratifications, and critical/cultural studies. These theories were developed about or have been applied to mass communication and continue to generate a sizable body of research. We also focus on prominent lines of research, some of which span or fall between the theoretical cracks, including media portrayals, media constructions, health, new technologies, cultural maintenance and change, children and media, and politics. We seek to review the state of mass communication research as we embark on the new century.

THEORETICAL PERSPECTIVES

Agenda Setting

The agenda-setting hypothesis has generated a great deal of research since the early 1970s, and it continues to attract research attention (McCombs, 1994; McCombs & Shaw, 1993). Traditional agenda-setting research has focused on how the media set the public's agenda (Brosius & Kepplinger, 1990; Fan, Brosius, & Kepplinger, 1994). The general argument is that we can predict the public agenda from media coverage. Scholars have extended the theory to assess how the media's agenda is set (Rogers & Dearing, 1988) and the relationships among public policy, the media agenda, and the public agenda (Ader, 1995).

Historical evidence of agenda setting also has been a popular topic. For example, Wilke (1995) has reported how the American Revolution became a main topic in the German press in the 1770s. Curtin (1995) has assessed press coverage of a Japanese American combat team during World War II, and how the military tried to influence public opinion about this regiment.

Some have analyzed how news sources try to build the media's agenda. Research suggests that powerful sources influence media agendas. Salwen (1995) explained that high-level sources can influence the media's focus on issues. This is evidenced in Cassara's (1998) study of how President Carter's human rights policy affected the media's lax attitude toward human rights and media coverage of Latin America. Johnson, Wanta, Byrd, and Lee (1995) have found, however, that powerful sources have not always been so effective. They noted that, rather than influencing coverage, Franklin Roosevelt often reacted to issues he read in the newspaper in his State of the Union addresses. Wanta and Foote (1994) concluded that presidential influence on news and public agendas reflects the inability of the president to control media or to prioritize issues.

Salwen's (1995) research shows that ordinary citizens also can influence the media's agenda (e.g., providing human interest stories). Walters, Walters, and Gray (1996) studied the limited agenda-building effectiveness of press releases by presidential candidates, and suggested that we need to consider several players in agenda setting. Further, McCombs and Zhu (1995) argued that the complexity of the process is magnified by agenda diversity and issue volatility, which result in the instability of public opinion. Ader (1995) suggested that agenda-setting studies should not ignore relationships among world conditions, the media agenda, and the public agenda.

Framing

Framing is an important aspect of agenda setting. How the media package events and issues affects how readers and viewers understand and respond to the events (Pan & Kosicki, 1995; Shah, Domke, & Wackman, 1996). Research continues to be stimulated by how media select and use sources, visuals, and commentary to direct attention toward certain aspects of reality and away from others (Liebler & Bendix, 1996; Shah et al., 1996; Zoch & Turk, 1998).

International conflicts have led to studies of how news media framed these conflicts. For example, German (1995) looked at how the Bush administration justified intervention in the Gulf War and overcame the negative public meaning of Vietnam by using language aimed at recalling images of World War II. Reese and Buckalew (1995) focused on how television news stories developed frames supporting Gulf War policy. Local news media framed antiwar protesters as opposing patriotism. Park and Kosicki (1995) examined news frames during the Iran-Contra affair.

Framing social movements and social issues also has stimulated inquiries. Subjects have included racial issues (Goshorn & Gandy, 1995), civil rights movements (Ross, 1998), and peace movements (Meyer, 1995). Competing frames on such issues offered by media and by activists or elites have been juxtaposed. In a study of how television news framed the environmental controversy about the preservation of old-growth forests and spotted owls, Liebler and Bendix (1996) found that the pro-cut side was likely to be shown because it was "amenable to encapsulation" (p. 62).

Researchers also have considered how media frames influence thought and meaning. News frames may not affect the number of cognitive responses (Price, Tewksbury, & Powers, 1997), because people tend to be cognitive misers (Park & Kosicki, 1995). However, news frames influence the focus on and evaluation of topics. Rhee (1997) looked at how frames in news stories affect voters' campaign interpretations. Audience interpretations influenced by media frames, in turn, affect decision-making behavior (Price et al., 1997; Shah et al., 1996).

Diffusion of Innovations

New innovations have provided research topics about the diffusion of innovations. Not surprisingly, newer communication technologies have received attention. Contemporary subjects have included the adoption of computers (Atkin, Jeffres, & Neuendorf, 1998; Lin, 1998), the Internet (Atkin et al., 1998), and interactive television news (Elberese, 1998). Researchers have sought to identify predictors of new media adoption (Jeffres & Atkin, 1996), such as demographics (Perse & Dunn, 1998). Some have suggested that features such as perceived complexity (Trevino & Webster, 1992) may have been early impediments to computer adoption.

Research demonstrates the continued viability of innovation attributes identified by Rogers (1995) for explaining the rate of adoption. For example, a need for innovativeness (Jeffres & Atkin, 1996) and perceived utility (Perse & Dunn, 1998) predict new technology adoption. Some have suggested that the introduction of new media requires us to rethink our uses and views of newer and older media (James, Wotring, & Forrest, 1995). Newer media, however, do not necessarily displace older media easily (Perse & Courtright, 1993).

Health interventions also have generated attention. Communication, especially interpersonal communication, is integral to diffusion and adoption processes of intervention campaigns aimed at changing health behaviors (Basil & Brown, 1994). Rogers (1995) noted that interpersonal and mass channels work in tandem, and researchers continue to assess the effectiveness of different channels. For example, Valente and Saba (1998) looked at the role of mass media and personal networks in contraceptive adoption in Bolivia. McDivitt, Simicki, and Hornik (1997) conducted similar research on a vaccination campaign in the Philippines. Interpersonal channels are effective for people with personal networks that include innovators. Where personal networks are not present or when knowledge about the innovation is minimal, media can be effective in enhancing knowledge and encouraging adoption (McDivitt et al., 1997; Valente & Saba, 1998).

Gap Hypotheses

The underlying premise of the knowledge-gap hypothesis is that, as media information flows into a social system, groups of higher socioeconomic status (SES) acquire the information at a faster rate than do lower-SES groups. Although all groups may gain knowledge, those of higher SES gain more, so the relative knowledge gap between groups increases (Viswanath & Finnegan, 1996). Research on gaps also has extended to areas such as technology literacy and the digital divide, or gaps in computer knowledge.

Researchers also have applied gap hypotheses when assessing the effectiveness of communication campaigns. These efforts have included analyses of knowledge of health issues (Engelberg, Flora, & Nass, 1995; McDivitt et al., 1997; Wanta & Elliott, 1995) and whether less-advantaged groups benefit from computer-disseminated health information (Pingree et al., 1996). Such studies suggest the need for assessment of the individual and structural mediators that lead to differential knowledge acquisition by groups.

Researchers have sought to identify such contributors to knowledge-gap effects. Individual-level mediators include motivation and interest (Chew & Palmer, 1994; Viswanath & Finnegan, 1996), prior knowledge of a topic (Price & Zaller, 1993), and education (Chew & Palmer, 1994; Price & Zaller, 1993; Wanta & Elliott, 1995). Structural mediators include the social environment (Viswanath & Finnegan, 1996), relied-upon communication channels (Engelberg et al., 1995; McLeod & Perse, 1994), and the use of celebrities to enhance knowledge (Wanta & Elliott, 1995).

Third-Person Effects

The third-person effects hypothesis has grown in popularity. Researchers have tried to explain why people feel the media have a greater impact on others than on themselves, as well as the behavioral consequences of such perceptions (Perloff, 1993; Schoenbach & Becker, 1995).

Third-person effects have perceptual and behavioral components (Salwen, 1998). The perceptual component includes the extent to which people overestimate media impact on others and underestimate the effect on themselves (McLeod, Eveland, & Nathanson, 1997; Price, Tewksbury, & Huang, 1998). The behavioral component focuses on what people do with that information. For example, third-person perceptions may lead to support for censorship of pornography or rap lyrics (Gunther, 1995; McLeod et al., 1997), restriction of election campaign messages (Salwen, 1998), and the placement of constraints on editorials (Price et al., 1997).

Several factors influence third-person effects. More knowledgeable people may overestimate media effects on others (Price et al., 1997), although findings about the role of knowledge have been inconsistent (McLeod et al., 1997; Price et al., 1997; Shah, Faber, & Youn, 1999). Mason (1995) found that participants in a jury sample exaggerated third-person perceptions when the media disseminated the message in comparison to when the message came directly from the source. Gunther (1998) argued that it is a logical extension of the third-person effects model "to expect that when people perceive substantial media influences on others, they should perceive consonant influences on aggregated public opinion" (p. 488).

Some researchers have offered cognitive explanations for third-person perceptions. Salwen (1998) suggested that these perceptions may be attributable to self-serving biases or to how "people employ media schemas that assume the media are powerful, persuasive, and manipulative" (p. 261). Shah et al. (1999) found that estimates of susceptibility to media effects (cognitive effects) and appraisal of perceived severity of effects (affective effects) underlie third-person perceptions.

Recent studies, however, raise questions about the predictive strength of the hypothesis and about links between perceptions and outcomes. Some suggest that feelings of personal vulnerability, lower education, older age, and gender (female) are salient predictors of third-person effects such as support for media content restrictions (David & Johnson, 1998; Salwen, 1998; Shah et al., 1999). Price et al. (1998) found that those who exhibited greater third-person effects were more likely to oppose publication of a Holocaust ad in a student newspaper, but the opposition was motivated more by respondents' perceptions of effects on themselves than by their perceptions of effects on others. Perceptual bias is a complex predictor, and other explanations for third-person effects must be considered.

Cultivation

Cultivation has been an enduring perspective over the past 30 years. Researchers have assessed cultivation theory's (a) assumptions that television content is uniform and viewing is nonselective and (b) premise that television shapes and distorts perceptions of reality (Gerbner, Gross, Morgan, & Signorielli, 1994; Morgan & Shanahan, 1997). Because some have suggested that the assumptions of cultivation theory are flawed, scholars have sought to understand the psychological processes affecting cultivation judgments (Perse, 1990; Potter, 1997; Shrum, 1995, 1996; Shrum & O'Guinn, 1993). Researchers have addressed the role of psychological variables (e.g., locus of control), perceived realism, and viewer motivation and involvement (Perse, 1990; Potter, 1993; Rubin, Perse, & Taylor, 1988) in cultivation effects.

Whereas early cultivation research focused on identifying distorted views attributable to television viewing, recent studies have sought to explain how cultivation might occur. A recent focus has been the role of memory in cultivation. Shrum (1996) found television information to be more accessible in heavy viewers' memories. This "accessibility bias" mediated viewing frequency estimates. Shrum argued that factors such as recency of information, frequency with which it is accessed, vividness of portrayals, and distinctiveness of presentation affect memory accessibility. Tapper (1995) asserted that episodic memories reflect personal experience, and that people who experience events may interpret them differently. Mares (1996) has also found evidence that errors in memory such as source confusion may explain how people acquire television-biased beliefs. In Mares's study, cultivation effects were strongest for those who remembered fictional programming as news.

Cultivation is applicable to a range of perceptions attributable to television viewing. Signorielli and Staples (1997) found a link between viewing and perceptions about unhealthy nutrition. Shanahan, Morgan, and Stenbjerre (1997) found a relationship between viewing and environmentalism: Those who viewed more tended to be less concerned about the environment than those who viewed less. Pfau et al. (1999) applied cultivation to the socializing effects of political talk radio. They found that talk radio presents political institutions negatively and that listeners have less confidence in these institutions.

Priming

By activating some ideas, feelings, or values, media can encourage certain thoughts and lead us to arrive at certain conclusions. Priming is a cognitive process by which the activation of thoughts radiates from particular nodes (neural networks) along associated pathways to other nodes. Related thoughts come to mind and create a priming effect (Jo & Berkowitz, 1994).

Research suggests how media content may prime thoughts. Pan and Kosicki (1997) analyzed how media coverage affected President Bush's approval rating. They found that when news was dominated by an issue the president was felt to be handling well (i.e., the Gulf War), presidential approval ratings were high. When news was dominated by an issue he was seen as handling poorly (i.e., the recession), his approval ratings sank. Similarly, Willnat and Zhu (1996) found that newspaper coverage of a reform plan in Hong Kong inflated the felt importance of the proposal in readers' evaluations of its sponsor. By controlling for other factors, such as political events and the economy, Willnat and Zhu determined that this evaluation was a priming effect. In addition, Power, Murphy, and Coover (1996) found that media portrayals cue people's interpretations to prime positive or negative stereotypes of women and minorities.

Bushman (1998) tested the accessibility of aggressive constructs and found that exposure to violent media depictions primed aggressive constructs in memory. He argued that people who are already aggressive may have more aggressive associations to be activated. This idea of "chronic" accessibility of cognitive tendencies suggests that priming effects may not be transient (Hansen & Hansen, 1991; Power et al., 1996). After controlling for self-esteem and personal vulnerability, David and Johnson (1998) found that media priming can enhance first- and third-person effects.

Social Cognition

Like priming, social learning is a cognitive theory that has been applied to the effects of violent media portrayals (Bandura, 1994; Hogben, 1998). The basic premise of social cognitive theory, as applied to the media, is that media representations can enhance learning. Despite the theory's ties to violence, it continues to be used as a theoretical framework to study how media use contributes to learning. For example, Shrum (1995) applied a social cognitive perspective to identify psychological processes underlying cultivation judgments. And in a study of emotional presentations in family-oriented situation comedies, Weiss and Wilson (1996) found that social cognitive theory explains television's socializing role in children's learning.

Social cognitive modeling effects have been suggested to explain eating disorders owing to media portrayals of body image. Harrison and Cantor (1997), for example, examined how dieting behaviors can be socially learned from the media; they suggested that "once incentives (i.e., rewards associated with thinness) are recognized and assigned positive value, the drive to achieve these incentives engages and the behaviors necessary to achieve them (i.e., dieting or exercise or both) will be performed" (p. 61). Harrison (1997) found that interpersonal attraction to thin media performers predicted symptoms of eating disorders.

Uses and Gratifications

Uses and gratifications is a social psychological, audience-centered perspective that draws upon models of indirect effects. It is premised on the belief that people are variably active in their selection and use of media and other communication vehicles to satisfy their social and psychological needs and wants. Individual differences mediate effects of exposure (Rubin, 1994).

Much of the recent uses and gratifications research has built upon earlier research, looking at such concepts as personality traits and media use (Conway & Rubin, 1991; Finn, 1997), audience needs and goals (Tewksbury, 1999; Vincent & Basil, 1997), motivation and gratifications sought (Kim & Rubin, 1997; Marghalani, Palmgreen, & Boyd, 1998; Perse & Dunn, 1998; Vincent & Basil, 1997), and audience activity (Kim & Rubin, 1997).

Some researchers have applied uses and gratifications to newer media. Perse and Dunn (1998), for example, found that the most common use of computers among members of their sample was a ritualistic orientation to fill time. They speculated that the lack of perceived utility by potential users may explain the home computer's slow diffusion. Marghalani et al. (1998) found that a complex "mix of technological, political, economic, cultural, and religious forces" gave rise to several motives "to embrace the myriad benefits perceived to be offered by direct satellite broadcasting" in Saudi Arabia (p. 311). Such benefits included the ability to transcend communication limitations (e.g., receiving a variety of programs, enhancing surveillance of the environment). These studies suggest that new technologies may help people satisfy some needs better than do older media.

Research has supported past observations that life situations in which people find themselves affect the salience of needs and gratifications sought. Vincent and Basil (1997), for example, found that salient surveillance needs among college students increased their use of various media. Harwood (1999) looked at the role of social identity gratifications in television viewing and found that age identity predicted the viewing of "shows featuring casts of similar age to respondents and themes close to respondents' experience" (p. 130).

Other research has focused on identifying individual factors that affect media use. These include relationships among personality traits and preferences for mediated and nonmediated (e.g., interpersonal) communication (Finn, 1997), and effects of consumption goals on how people process information from television

(Tewksbury, 1999). Kim and Rubin (1997) examined the variability of audience activity and its mediating impact on cultivation and parasocial interaction. They found that different types of activity deter or facilitate media effects.

Parasocial interaction (PSI) has been examined as affective involvement that influences media behaviors and outcomes. Skumanich and Kintsfather (1998) found that viewer relationships with television shopping program hosts and callers predicted purchase behavior. Their study reinforces connections between inter-personal and mass communication and between perspectives such as dependency and uses and gratifications. Two other studies suggest gender differences in parasocial relationships. Hoffner (1996) found that intelligence and attractiveness predicted PSI with children's favorite male characters on television, but only attractiveness predicted PSI with favorite female characters. And Cohen (1997) found that males who were less secure about their dating partners tended to have stronger parasocial relationships than did females.

In addition, Tsao (1996) discovered, in a finding that supports earlier research, that whereas a deficiency paradigm (e.g., less empathy, less extroversion) pre-dicted more television viewing, it did not lead to PSI. Rather than social compen-sation, cognitive and affective empathy predicted PSI with favorite characters. Tsao's study points to the continued need to focus on media consumers' personal-ity characteristics and personal involvement in audience-media relationships.

Critical and Cultural Studies

Critical/cultural research encompasses disparate theoretical and philosophical positions advanced by several theorists, including Habermas, Gramsci, Foucault, Hall, Marx, and Adorno. Unlike other perspectives discussed in this section, criti-cal/cultural theories generally have not been derived from mass communication, but are more broadly aimed at addressing how societies and social experiences are developed and shaped. When applied to mass communication, critical theories often focus on evaluating the media's role in social change associated with the growth of mass culture and mass society (Davis & Puckett, 1992; Real, 1992).

Critical and cultural writers have not always agreed on several issues. Although some have argued that cultural theories have enough in common to be incorpo-rated within a single culture-centered media paradigm (Davis & Puckett, 1992), discussion has revolved around fundamental differences. Different interpretations of constructs have triggered debates about, for example, Habermas's conception of the "public sphere" (Goodnight, 1997) and postmodernity (Harms & Dickens, 1996). Others have argued for the explanatory value of hegemony theory instead of Marxism in the study of how the media engage in cultural production (Park, 1998).

Critical/cultural theorists see communication as a social process in which audi-ences construct views of reality by interpreting the cultural products often pro-vided by the media. The media are seen as powerful and as serving those who hold political and economic power. They play a central role in creating and maintaining mass society. They do this by presenting images that subordinate deviant societal elements and control social change.

Studies in the critical/cultural tradition have focused on how the media affect the way we perceive reality and the world around us. Much of the research has focused on media practices, including: how media marginalize social groups such as women and minorities (Edge, 1999; Lule, 1995; Wilkins, 1999); how power affects news production (Berkowitz & Terkeurst, 1999; Kieran, 1997); what role the media have in postmodern socialization (Buckingham, 1997); how the media construct individual identities (Dickerson, 1996), national identity (Brookes, 1999; Chang, Wang, & Chen, 1998), and collective memory (Barnhurst & Wartella, 1998); and how media forms such as rap music (Bennett, 1999), talk radio (Dauncey & Hare, 1999), and Disney heroines (Henke, Umble, & Smith, 1996) have evolved. There also has been a growing interest in political economy studies (Mosco, 1998) and in critical interpretations of media content, such as reception studies that focus on media content, frames, and discourse as texts or narratives (Durham, 1998).

Feminist studies often take a critical approach, premised on the recognition that institutional processes reflect patriarchal gender systems (Wilkins, 1999). Recent studies have addressed how women are marginalized in the political arena. Parry-Giles and Parry-Giles (1996) argued that despite the presence of a "feminine" style of political communication that may benefit female candidates, the dominant political image remains rooted in "a hegemonic masculinity" that supports a patriarchal system. Vavrus (1998) asserted that in the 1992 campaign (dubbed the "year of the woman"), mass-mediated discourse framed female candidates as being outside the mainstream or as challengers to the status quo. In studying women in local Israeli politics, Herzog (1998) found that the media's reporting on female politicians was shaped by "exclusionary" social interpretive frames.

Critical theorists have noted that there are times when the media present alternative positions that are at odds with dominant political and economic groups' interests. In a study of news reporting, Berkowitz and Terkeurst (1999) found evidence suggesting that in homogeneous communities journalists may provide interpretations of events more in accord with the community's power structure, but this may not be the case in diverse, pluralistic communities. Kieran (1997) contended that the media are not, as other cultural theorists have argued, inherently ideological. Rather, different news media provide different accounts of what they cover. Thus some studies suggest that the media may not always serve the dominant social order.

Relationships among media, audiences, and societal institutions are complex. Accordingly, critical/cultural researchers share common concerns with researchers working in other theoretical perspectives. For example, Lewis (1997) noted that cultivation has demonstrated that television has a "hegemonic role in contemporary culture" (p. 89). Cultivation's assumption that television shapes perceptions of reality is in accord with critical/cultural notions. Berkowitz and Terkeurst's (1999) observations about social construction of interpretations by journalists and sources is similar to agenda setting's interest in relationships between the media's agenda and sources' agendas. Vavrus's (1998) study of political campaigns in the "Year of the Woman" parallels framing research. And researchers working in most mass communication perspectives have been interested in the media's role in socialization, cultural transmission, and interpretation of the environment. Future research should illuminate consistencies rather than emphasize dissimilarities.

LINES OF RESEARCH

Media Portrayals

Several lines of research emerge within and across the various theoretical perspectives. For example, researchers continue to examine media portrayals, often assuming that such presentations adversely affect consumers' attitudes and behaviors. One would be hard-pressed to find an area that has generated more recent research attention than media portrayals. A sampling suggests that many portrayals studied have focused on women and on ethnic and minority groups.

Authors of several of these studies have provided descriptive portraits of the groups examined (Elasmar, Hasegawa, & Brain, 1999; Greenberg & Collette, 1997), whereas others have addressed possible consequences of the portrayals. For example, Herzog (1998) argued that media strengthen and entrench the social order by presenting women in Israeli local politics in "cultural frames that are part of the hegemonic view of the structure of society, women's roles in it, and the notions of masculinity and femininity" (pp. 44-45). Van Zoonen (1998) reached similar conclusions in her study comparing coverage of Dutch female and male politicians.

Some have suggested that such portrayals have been unproductive for women and minorities. Liebler and Smith (1997) found that gender-biased reporting occurred whether male or female news correspondents were used. Romer, Jamieson, and DeCoteau (1998) found that the news presented ethnocentric bias: Persons of color were overrepresented as perpetrators of crime, and Caucasians were overrepresented as victims. Goshorn and Gandy (1995) found that lead stories about mortgage loans emphasized black failure rather than white success in obtaining loans. Griffin and Sen (1995) applied attribution theory and found that media presentations affect public perceptions about judgments of group responsibility and blame for problems people face.

Other researchers have examined portrayals of interaction. For example, Honeycutt, Wellman, and Larson (1997) found that television's depiction of family interaction is egocentric, focusing on monologues rather than responsiveness and empathic listening. Brinson and Winn (1997) studied how interpersonal conflict is presented on television talk shows. They found that men and women behaved similarly in the programs analyzed, but women tended to dominate arguments. In analyzing male-female courtship in television comedy, Scodari (1995) observed that series' texts tended to perpetuate culturally assumed masculine conventions.

Another dimension of this research has been political portrayals. Topics have included portrayals of nations, leaders, national identity, and political groups. For example, researchers have examined how media portrayals of U.S. policy toward another nation (i.e., Iran) can affect public opinion (Brown & Vincent, 1995), how news photos can marginalize events such as murders in the Northern Ireland conflict (Edge, 1999), and how political cartoons in U.S. newspapers can dehumanize political enemies such as Saddam Hussein (Conners, 1998).

Media Constructions

These latter studies highlight a focus on how the media construct reality in their presentations of nations, groups, events, and subjects. This is an issue that is fundamental to cultivation, framing, and critical/cultural studies, in particular. Media constructions are important in shaping perceptions of national and international identity. Barnhurst and Wartella (1998) argued that television news creates "collective memory," a sort of "communal experience" that "helps form national identity" (p. 303).

Some writers have examined the construction of media and communication technology. They have found that media and newer technology are used to help local cultures adapt to globalization (e.g., Wheeler's [1998] study of Internet use in Kuwait), to maintain local or national identities for the geographically displaced (e.g., Boczkowski's [1999] study of the development of an Argentine mailing list to create a "national virtual community"), to connect and reconstruct a sense of community (e.g., Sampedro's [1998] observation of international students living in a different culture), and to maintain old identities and construct new ones (e.g., Glasser's [1997] study of Chinese magazine fiction and Sakamoto's [1999] study of Japanese women's magazines).

Health Issues

A great deal of attention has been given to the role of the media in health-related issues. Some of this research has been conducted within a diffusion of innovations framework (McDivitt et al., 1997; Valente & Saba, 1998), as investigators have considered communication in health campaign effectiveness. Researchers have addressed knowledge gaps, mass and interpersonal channels, audience characteristics, message appeals, and persuasive strategies (Murry, Stam, & Lastovicka, 1996; Rimal, Flora, & Schooler, 1999).

Exposure to health-related information via mediated sources can lead to behavioral change (McDivitt et al., 1997) and encourage information seeking and interpersonal communication, which, in turn, can affect health behaviors (Pingree et al., 1996). The research points to a link between awareness and behavioral change

(Wanta & Elliott, 1995) and to the need for a focus on the effectiveness of communication to achieve desired results (Myrick, 1996). It also points to a need for careful assessment of the audience, so that campaigns can be tailored to target marginalized and diverse populations (Myrick, 1996).

Aside from health campaigns, researchers have addressed the possible influence of media portrayals on health, such as potential negative effects related to body image. Research suggests that media can adversely affect healthy behaviors. David and Johnson (1998) argued that the media perpetuate a thin ideal that is almost impossible to achieve, leading to body image dissatisfaction and eating disorders. Signorielli and Staples (1997) found that children who spend considerable time watching television tend to have unhealthy perceptions of nutrition.

Newer Technologies

Much of the research surrounding newer communication technologies has revolved around concerns about why people choose certain media or other channels to achieve goals or to satisfy needs. Toward that end, investigators have examined channels based on their social presence or media richness (Perse & Courtright, 1993; Rice, 1993). Although some scholars have noted why the Internet should be studied as a mass medium (Morris & Ogan, 1996), it is difficult to categorize research on newer technologies as falling just within the mass communication context. Computer-mediated communication, for example, has been examined in interpersonal (Parks & Floyd, 1996) and political (Margolis, Resnick, & Tu, 1997) settings.

Recent discourse research suggests that how a medium like the Internet is characterized affects evaluations of its utility. Berdayes and Berdayes (1998) argued that the "information superhighway" has been constructed in magazines in such a way that potential users may view themselves as powerless. Gunkel and Gunkel (1997) also stressed the importance of discourse in their focus on how the image of "cyberspace" has been presented via metaphors such as "new world" and "frontier." They argued that the future of cyberspace will be determined "through the names we employ to describe it" (p. 133). In addition, Warnick (1999) asserted that "persuasive appeals to women to come on line have marginalized and excluded some women" (p. 4).

Some scholars have examined newly introduced media systems in different countries. This work is exemplified by research on the introduction of television and cable television in Israel (Katz, Haas, & Gurevitch, 1997; Weimann, 1996), the diffusion of satellites in Saudi Arabia (Marghalani et al., 1998), and interactive television use in the Netherlands (Elberese, 1998). These studies suggest the popularity of research on the variety and convergence of communication technologies.

Evolving technologies impact people's lives around the world. Investigators have sought to address how newer technologies have influenced people's media use (Johnson-Smaragdi, d'Haenens, Krotz, & Hasebrink, 1998; van der Voort et al., 1998) and family lifestyles (Pasquier, Buzzi, d'Haenens, & Sjöberg, 1998), as well as how they have affected how domestic space is used and organized (Gumpert & Drucker, 1998). Changes in technologies and means of communication will garner even greater research attention as we seek to uncover the uses and effects associated with an increasingly diverse media environment.

Cultural Maintenance and Change

An examination of media constructions of communities demonstrates important links between culture and the media (Kellner, 1995). Spurred by interconnected economies, conflicts around the world, and increasing immigration, many nations are becoming more diverse. Investigators have examined the media's role in cultural change given such characteristics as increased diversity. They have considered whether an open political and media environment has led to more balance in election coverage (Lo, Neilan, & King, 1998) and to greater democratization (Mollison, 1998).

Some scholars have referenced concerns with media and cultural imperialism (Roach, 1997; Schiller, 1992; Wasko, 1995). Other scholars have focused on specific media uses to serve cultural needs and to further localism. For example, Rios and Gaines (1999) explored how Latinos use English- and Spanish-language media for cultural maintenance. Hindman (1998) considered how a community newspaper that focused on neighborhood culture presented a view of the world from a community perspective and maintained community culture.

Children and Media

Children have often been a major focus of inquiry in mass communication research. The media's function of transmitting social heritage has been of long-standing interest to media scholars. Much socialization research has focused on children and adolescents. For example, Tan, Nelson, Dong, and Tan (1997) examined television's socialization effects on adolescents from different ethnic groups. They found that socialization was predicted based on whether individuals see socialization outcomes as being functional. When examining political socialization, Eveland, McLeod, and Horowitz (1999) found that age and cognitive capacity moderated socialization effects. Specifically, media information influenced younger children more than it did older children.

Research supports the idea that children are active and purposive in selecting what they like (Cantor & Nathanson, 1997). Several investigators have examined children's television selection and understanding, especially in relation to coviewing and family mediation. Valkenburg, Krcmar, and de Roos (1998) found that children acquired more knowledge about content when a coviewing adult provided information. Nathanson (1999) suggested that parental coviewing with children can mediate effects such as television-induced aggression. Valkenburg, Krcmar, Peeters, and Marseille (1999) identified instructive, restrictive, and social mediation strategies that parents use when coviewing and found that they used social mediation most frequently. And Krcmar and Cantor (1997) found that television advisories affected parent-child interaction about viewing choices.

Most researchers have studied children's television use outside of coviewing situations. They have looked at what children like or appreciate in television programs and how they evaluate or make judgments about the programs. Valkenburg and Janssen (1999) found that both Dutch and U.S. children value comprehensibility and action in television programs. Lemish (1997), however, suggested that how children comprehend and understand television may depend on cultural differences. She found that U.S. kindergartners tended to be more television literate than Israeli children, but Israeli children knew more about the news and its societal role.

Researchers also have focused on children's attraction or reactions to specific content, such as frightening portrayals and violence (Cantor & Nathanson, 1997; Hoffner, 1997; Krcmar, 1998) and portrayals of the family (Weiss & Wilson, 1996). Hoffner (1997) suggested that children engage in coping mechanisms when watching frightening films. Symptoms of fear, however, can persist (Cantor & Nathanson, 1997). This has been highlighted by Potter and Warren (1996), who argued that televised aggressive portrayals showing weapons increase children's fear.

Violence continues to be a subject of intense inquiry. Recent high school shootings have added fuel to the debate about the media's role in such incidents. Children are attracted to some violent content, particularly cartoons (Cantor & Nathanson, 1997), which often contain significant amounts of violence (*National Television Violence Study,* 1998). Concerns about the effects of televised violence on children have led to studies of ratings and advisories (Cantor & Nathanson, 1997) and to legislative and industry proposals such as family viewing hours, ratings, advisories, and blocking devices such as the V-chip to protect children from media violence (Edwards & Berman, 1995; Potter & Warren, 1996). Research has tended to support the position that violent media content has possible harmful effects on children, but the precise roles of many contributory factors are still not understood (*National Television Violence Study,* 1998; Paik & Comstock, 1994; Potter, 1997).

Media literacy also has been an important subject. Media literacy efforts have focused on teaching children how to interpret and make sense out of media messages. Several scholars have advocated media literacy training as a means of enabling children to evaluate media messages, ameliorate potentially harmful effects, and achieve prosocial outcomes (Kubey, 1997; Silverblatt, 1995). Complex issues remain about how to conceptualize media literacy, how to implement literacy programs, who to involve in the process, and how to finance the programs (Hobbs, 1998).

Political Communication

The relationships among the media and between the media and the political systems within which they operate, as well as the policy questions generated by these relationships, are integral parts of media history, development, and operation. Virtually every mass communication perspective has been applied at one time or another to the study of specific political questions. This includes cultivation, third-person effects, agenda setting, framing, priming, and uses and gratifications. Because separate chapters in this volume are devoted to political communication and to policy, we only touch upon these areas here.

Mass communication scholars remain interested in a variety of political issues. Recent examples include talk radio's political influence (Pfau et al., 1999), use of the Internet for campaign information dissemination (Margolis et al., 1997), political advertising's role in constructing candidate images (Kern & Just, 1995), political advertising as a source of political information (Zhao & Chaffee, 1995), gender bias in political advertising (Hitchon, Chang, & Harris, 1997), political campaign strategies (Fredin, Kosicki, & Becker, 1996), the packaging of political campaigns (Rawnsley, 1997), coverage of political campaigns in different countries (Semetko, 1996), election polls and political knowledge (Meyer & Potter, 1998), election polls and issue learning (Zhao & Bleske, 1998), and media impact on voting (Chang & Hitchon, 1997; Pinkleton, Austin, & Fortman, 1998).

In short, no aspect of media use for political purposes or the effects of media coverage on political processes and structures has escaped the attention of communication scholars. These scholars have sought to link media with relevant political processes such as voting and socialization from a variety of theoretical perspectives.

CONCLUSIONS AND DIRECTIONS

Mass communication researchers continue to pursue interesting and significant questions within several theoretical perspectives and lines of research. The perspectives reflect beliefs as to differential roles of the audience and media. Some emphasize cognitive and affective activity of audience members in selecting and using media and their messages. Others emphasize the strength of the media in influencing the society's direction and evolution and the audience's attitudes and behaviors. Given differing assumptions and methodologies, it is likely that mass communication research will continue to reflect these variations, although vehicles like the Internet make it clear that people will need to select carefully the information to which they attend. People will continue to choose from among the available personal and mediated communication channels they find most satisfactory to interact, to seek information, to make sense of their worlds, to be socialized, to conduct business, to be entertained, to escape, and so on.

Past and present research, regardless of discipline, area of concentration, or theoretical perspective applied, suggests that we are on a productive path toward understanding how media affect and fit within the lives of people and societies. Differences in assumptions and approaches can be productive, given the nuances in questions asked and answered. This, of course, depends on whether the questions pursued are worthwhile and the methods used are valid and reliable. Access and attention to research literatures across disciplines, areas of concentration, and theoretical perspectives are crucial to any assessment of the value of the findings of too-often isolated inquiries.

It also is clear that communication no longer is able to separate its traditional divisions based on features such as numbers, identities, and interaction of sources and receivers, and the implementation of physical or electronic media. Future research should be influenced by commonalities among these entities of the field and academic disciplines. Our questions in all areas of communication will continue to involve psychology, sociology, politics, economics, history, and the like. Our questions in mass communication will continue to involve interpersonal, group, organizational, and political communication, among other areas. These questions will be influenced by and must recognize the instantaneous accessibility of enormous databases in an electronically connected global environment. Questions of literacy, utility, access, control, and impact will be even more important in this environment.

REFERENCES

Ader, C. R. (1995). A longitudinal study of agenda setting for the issue of environmental pollution. *Journalism & Mass Communication Quarterly, 72,* 300-311.

Atkin, D. J., Jeffres, L. W., & Neuendorf, K. A. (1998). Understanding Internet adoption as telecommunications behavior. *Journal of Broadcasting & Electronic Media, 42,* 475-490.

Bandura, A. (1994). Social cognitive theory of mass communication. In J. Bryant & D. Zillmann (Eds.), *Media effects: Advances in theory and research* (pp. 61-90). Hillsdale, NJ: Lawrence Erlbaum.

Barnhurst, K. G., & Wartella, E. (1998). Young citizens, American TV newscasts and the collective memory. *Critical Studies in Mass Communication, 15,* 279-305.

Basil, M. D., & Brown, W. J. (1994). Interpersonal communication in news diffusion: A study of "Magic" Johnson's announcement. *Journalism Quarterly, 71,* 305-320.

Bennett, A. (1999). Hip hop am Main: The localization of rap music and hip hop culture. *Media, Culture & Society, 21,* 77-91.

Berdayes, L. C., & Berdayes, V. (1998). The information highway in contemporary magazine narrative. *Journal of Communication, 48*(2), 109-124.

Berkowitz, D., & Terkeurst, J. V. (1999). Community as interpretive community: Rethinking the journalist-source relationship. *Journal of Communication, 49*(3), 125-136.

Boczkowski, P. J. (1999). Mutual shaping of users and technologies in a national virtual community. *Journal of Communication, 49*(2), 86-108.

Brinson, S. L., & Winn, J. E. (1997). Talk shows' representations of interpersonal conflicts. *Journal of Broadcasting & Electronic Media, 41,* 25-39.

Brookes, R. (1999). Newspapers and national identity: The BSE/CJD crisis and the British press. *Media, Culture & Society, 21,* 247-263.

Brosius, H-B., & Kepplinger, H. M. (1990). The agenda-setting function of television news: Static and dynamic views. *Communication Research, 17,* 183-211.

Brown, W. J., & Vincent, R. C. (1995). Trading arms for hostages? How the government and print media "spin" portrayals of the United States' policy toward Iran. *Political Communication, 12,* 65-79.

Buckingham, D. (1997). News media, political socialization and popular citizenship: Towards a new agenda. *Critical Studies in Mass Communication, 14,* 344-366.

Bushman, B. J. (1998). Priming effects of media violence on the accessibility of aggressive constructs in memory. *Personality and Social Psychology Bulletin, 24,* 537-545.

Cantor, J., & Nathanson, A. I. (1997). Predictors of children's interest in violent television programs. *Journal of Broadcasting & Electronic Media, 41,* 155-167.

Cassara, C. (1998). U.S. newspaper coverage of human rights in Latin America, 1975-1982: Exploring President Carter's agenda-building influence. *Journalism & Mass Communication Quarterly, 75,* 478-486.

Chang, C., & Hitchon, J. (1997). Mass media impact on voter response to women candidates: Theoretical development. *Communication Theory, 7,* 29-52.

Chang, T-K., Wang, J., & Chen, C-H. (1998). The social construction of international imagery in the post-Cold War era: A comparative analysis of U.S. and Chinese national TV news. *Journal of Broadcasting & Electronic Media, 42,* 277-296.

Chew, F., & Palmer, S. (1994). Interest, the knowledge gap, and televised programming. *Journal of Broadcasting & Electronic Media, 38,* 271-287.

Cohen, J. (1997). Parasocial relations and romantic attraction: Gender and dating status differences. *Journal of Broadcasting & Electronic Media, 41,* 516-529.

Conners, J. L. (1998). Hussein as enemy: The Persian Gulf War in political cartoons. *Harvard International Journal of Press/Politics, 3*(3), 96-114.

Conway, J. C., & Rubin, A. M. (1991). Psychological predictors of television viewing motivation. *Communication Research, 18,* 443-464.

Curtin, P. A. (1995). Press coverage of the 442nd Regimental Combat Team (separate—Nisei): A case study in agenda building. *American Journalism, 12,* 225-241.

Dauncey, H., & Hare, G. (1999). French youth talk radio: The free market and free speech. *Media, Culture & Society, 21,* 93-108.

David, P., & Johnson, M. A. (1998). The role of self in third-person effects about body image. *Journal of Communication, 48*(4), 37-58.

Davis, D. K., & Puckett, T. F. N. (1992). Mass entertainment and community: Toward a culture-centered paradigm for mass communication research. In S. A. Deetz (Ed.), *Communication yearbook 15* (pp. 3-34). Newbury Park, CA: Sage.

Dickerson, P. (1996). Let me tell us who I am: The discursive construction of viewer identity. *European Journal of Communication, 11,* 57-82.

Durham, F. D. (1998). News frames as social narrative: TWA flight 800. *Journal of Communication, 48*(4), 100-117.

Edge, S. (1999). Why did they kill Barney? Media, Northern Ireland and the riddle of loyalist terror. *European Journal of Communication, 14,* 91-116.

Edwards, H. T., & Berman, M. N. (1995). Regulating violence on television. *Northwestern University Law Review, 89,* 1487-1566.

Elasmar, M., Hasegawa, K., & Brain, M. (1999). The portrayal of women in U.S. prime time television. *Journal of Broadcasting & Electronic Media, 44,* 20-34.

Elberese, A. J. T. (1998). Consumer acceptance of interactive news in the Netherlands. *Harvard International Journal of Press/Politics, 3*(4), 62-83.

Engelberg, M., Flora, J. A., & Nass, C. I. (1995). AIDS knowledge: Effects of channel involvement and interpersonal communication. *Health Communication, 7,* 73-91.

Eveland, W. P., Jr., McLeod, J. M., & Horowitz, E. M. (1999). Communication and age in childhood political socialization: An interactive model of political development. *Journalism & Mass Communication Quarterly, 75,* 699-718.

Fan, D. P., Brosius, H.-B., & Kepplinger, H. M. (1994). Predictions of the public agenda from television coverage. *Journal of Broadcasting & Electronic Media, 38,* 163-177.

Finn, S. (1997). Origins of media exposure: Linking personality traits to TV, radio, print, and film use. *Communication Research, 24,* 507-529.

Fredin, E. S., Kosicki, G. M., & Becker, L. B. (1996). Cognitive strategies for media use during a presidential campaign. *Political Communication, 13,* 23-42.

Gerbner, G., Gross, L., Morgan, M., & Signorielli, N. (1994). Growing up with television: The cultivation perspective. In J. Bryant & D. Zillmann (Eds.). *Media effects: Advances in theory and research* (pp. 17-41). Hillsdale, NJ: Lawrence Erlbaum.

German, K. M. (1995). Invoking the glorious war: Framing the Persian Gulf conflict through directive language. *Southern Communication Journal, 60,* 292-302.

Glasser, C. K. (1997). Patriarchy, mediated desire, and Chinese magazine fiction. *Journal of Communication, 47*(1), 85-108.

Goodnight, C. T. (1997). Opening up "the spaces of public dissension." *Communication Monographs, 64,* 270-275.

Goshorn, K., & Gandy, O. H., Jr. (1995). Race, risk and responsibility: Editorial constraint in the framing of inequality. *Journal of Communication, 45*(2), 133-151.

Greenberg, B. S., & Collette, L. (1997). The changing faces on TV: A demographic analysis of network television's new seasons, 1966-1992. *Journal of Broadcasting & Electronic Media, 41,* 1-13.

Griffin, R. J., & Sen, S. (1995). Causal communication: Movie portrayals and audience attributions for Vietnam veterans' problems. *Journalism & Mass Communication Quarterly, 72,* 511-524.

Gumpert, G., & Drucker, S. J. (1998). The mediated home in the global village. *Communication Research, 25,* 422-438.

Gunkel, D. J., & Gunkel, A. H. (1997). Virtual geographies: The new worlds of cyberspace. *Critical Studies in Mass Communication, 14,* 123-137.

Gunther, A. C. (1995). Overrating the X-rating: The third-person perception and support for censorship of pornography. *Journal of Communication, 45*(1), 27-38.

Gunther, A. C. (1998). The persuasive press inference: Effects of mass media on perceived public opinion. *Communication Research, 25,* 486-504.

Hansen, C. H., & Hansen, R. D. (1991). Constructing personality and social reality through music: Individual differences among fans of punk and heavy metal music. *Journal of Broadcasting & Electronic Media, 35,* 335-350.

Harms, J. B., & Dickens, D. R. (1996). Postmodern media studies: Analysis or symptom? *Critical Studies in Mass Communication, 13,* 210-227.

Harrison, K. (1997). Does interpersonal attraction to thin media personalities promote eating disorders? *Journal of Broadcasting & Electronic Media, 41,* 478-500.

Harrison, K., & Cantor, J. (1997). The relationship between media consumption and eating disorders. *Journal of Communication, 47*(1), 40-67.

Harwood, J. (1999). Age identification, social identity gratifications, and television viewing. *Journal of Broadcasting & Electronic Media, 43,* 123-136.

Henke, J. B., Umble, D. Z., & Smith, N. J. (1996). Construction of the female self: Feminist readings of the Disney heroine. *Women's Studies in Communication, 19,* 229-249.

Herzog, H. (1998). More than a looking glass: Women in Israeli local politics and the media. *Harvard International Journal of Press/Politics, 3*(1), 26-47.

Hindman, E. B. (1998). Community, democracy, and neighborhood news. *Journal of Communication, 48*(2), 27-39.

Hitchon, J. C., Chang, C., & Harris, R. (1997). Should women emote? Perceptual bias and opinion change in response to political ads for candidates of different genders. *Political Communication, 14,* 49-69.

Hobbs, R. (1998). The seven great debates in the media literacy movement. *Journal of Communication, 48*(1), 16-32.

Hoffner, C. (1996). Children's wishful identification and parasocial interaction with favorite television characters. *Journal of Broadcasting & Electronic Media, 40,* 389-402.

Hoffner, C. (1997). Children's emotional reactions to a scary film: The role of prior outcome information and coping style. *Human Communication Research, 23,* 323-341.

Hogben, M. (1998). Factors moderating the effect of televised aggression on viewer behavior. *Communication Research, 25,* 220-247.

Honeycutt, J. M., Wellman, L. B., & Larson, M. S. (1997). Beneath family role portrayals: An additional measure of communication influence using time series analyses of turn at talk on a popular television program. *Journal of Broadcasting & Electronic Media, 41,* 40-57.

James, M. L., Wotring, C. E., & Forrest, E. J. (1995). An exploratory study of the perceived benefits of electronic bulletin board use and their impact on other communication activities. *Journal of Broadcasting & Electronic Media, 39,* 30-50.

Jeffres, L., & Atkin, D. (1996). Predicting use of technologies for consumer and communication needs. *Journal of Broadcasting & Electronic Media, 40,* 318-330.

Jo, E., & Berkowitz, L. (1994). A priming effect analysis of media influences: An update. In J. Bryant & D. Zillmann (Eds.). *Media effects: Advances in theory and research* (pp. 43-60). Hillsdale, NJ: Lawrence Erlbaum.

Johnson, T. J., Wanta, W., Byrd, J. T., & Lee, C. (1995). Exploring FDR's relationship with the press: A historical agenda-setting study. *Political Communication, 12,* 157-172.

Johnson-Smaragdi, U., d'Haenens, L., Krotz, F., & Hasebrink, U. (1998). Patterns of old and new media use among young people in Flanders, Germany and Sweden. *European Journal of Communication, 13,* 479-501.

Katz, E., Haas, H., & Gurevitch, M. (1997). Twenty years of television in Israel: Are there long-run effects on values, social connectedness, and cultural practices? *Journal of Communication, 47*(2), 3-20.

Kellner, D. (1995). Media communications vs. cultural studies: Overcoming the divide. *Communication Theory, 5,* 162-177.

Kern, M., & Just, M. (1995). The focus group method, political advertising, campaign news, and the construction of candidate images. *Political Communication, 12,* 127-145.

Kieran, M. (1997). News reporting and the ideological presumption. *Journal of Communication, 47*(2), 79-96.

Kim, J., & Rubin, A. M. (1997). The variable influence of audience activity on media effects. *Communication Research, 24,* 107-135.

Krcmar, M. (1998). The contribution of family communication patterns to children's interpretations of television violence. *Journal of Broadcasting & Electronic Media, 42,* 250-264.

Krcmar, M., & Cantor, J. (1997). The role of television advisories and ratings in parent-child discussion of television viewing choices. *Journal of Broadcasting & Electronic Media, 41,* 393-411.

Kubey, R. (Ed.). (1997). *Media literacy in the information age: Current perspectives.* New Brunswick, NJ: Transaction.

Lemish, D. (1997). Kindergartners' understandings of television: A cross-cultural comparison. *Communication Studies, 48,* 109-126.

Lewis, J. (1997). What counts in cultural studies. *Media, Culture & Society, 19,* 83-97.

Liebler, C. M., & Bendix, J. (1996). Old-growth forests on network news: News sources and the framing of an environmental controversy. *Journalism & Mass Communication Quarterly, 73,* 53-65.

Liebler, C. M., & Smith, S. J. (1997). Tracking gender differences: A comparative analysis of network correspondents and their sources. *Journal of Broadcasting & Electronic Media, 41,* 58-68.

Lin, C. A. (1998). Exploring personal computer adoption. *Journal of Broadcasting & Electronic Media, 42,* 95-112.

Lo, V-H., Neilan, E., & King, P-T. (1998). Television coverage of the 1995 legislative election in Taiwan: Rise of cable television as a force for balance in media coverage. *Journal of Broadcasting & Electronic Media, 42,* 340-355.

Lule, J. (1995). The rape of Mike Tyson: Race, the press and symbolic types. *Critical Studies in Mass Communication, 12,* 176-195.

Mares, M-L. (1996). The role of source confusions in television's cultivation of social reality judgments. *Human Communication Research, 23,* 278-297.

Marghalani, K., Palmgreen, P., & Boyd, D. A. (1998). The utilization of direct satellite broadcasting (DBS) in Saudi Arabia. *Journal of Broadcasting & Electronic Media, 42,* 297-314.

Margolis, M., Resnick, D., & Tu, C-C. (1997). Campaigning on the Internet: Parties and candidates on the World Wide Web in the 1996 primary season. *Harvard International Journal of Press/Politics, 2*(1), 59-78.

Mason, L. (1995). Newspaper as repeater: An experiment on defamation and third-person effect. *Journalism & Mass Communication Quarterly, 72,* 610-620.

McCombs, M. (1994). News influence on our pictures of the world. In J. Bryant & D. Zillmann (Eds.). *Media effects: Advances in theory and research* (pp. 1-16). Hillsdale, NJ: Lawrence Erlbaum.

McCombs, M. E., & Shaw, D. L. (1993). The evolution of agenda-setting research: Twenty-five years in the marketplace of ideas. *Journal of Communication, 43*(2), 58-67.

McCombs, M. E., & Zhu, J-H. (1995). Capacity, diversity, and volatility of the public agenda: Trends from 1954 to 1994. *Public Opinion Quarterly, 59,* 495-525.

McDivitt, J. A., Simicki, S., & Hornik, R. C. (1997). Explaining the impact of a communication campaign to change vaccination knowledge and coverage in the Philippines. *Health Communication, 9,* 95-118.

McLeod, D. M., Eveland, W. P., Jr., & Nathanson, A. I. (1997). Support for censorship of violent and misogynist rap lyrics: An analysis of the third-person effect. *Communication Research, 24,* 153-174.

McLeod, D. M., & Perse, E. M. (1994). Direct and indirect effects of socioeconomic status on public affairs knowledge. *Journalism Quarterly, 71,* 433-442.

Meyer, D. S. (1995). Framing national security: Elite public discourse on nuclear weapons during the Cold War. *Political Communication, 12,* 173-192.

Meyer, P., & Potter, D. (1998). Preelection polls and issue knowledge in the 1996 U.S. presidential election. *Harvard International Journal of Press/Politics, 3*(4), 35-43.

Mollison, T. A. (1998). Television broadcasting leads Romania's march toward an open, democratic society. *Journal of Broadcasting & Electronic Media, 42,* 128-141.

Morgan, M., & Shanahan, J. (1997). Two decades of cultivation research: An appraisal and meta-analysis. In B. R. Burleson (Ed.), *Communication yearbook 20* (pp. 1-45). Thousand Oaks, CA: Sage.

Morris, M., & Ogan, C. (1996). The Internet as mass medium. *Journal of Communication, 46*(4), 39-50.

Mosco, V. (1998). Political economy, communication, and labor. In G. Sussman & J. A. Lent (Eds.), *Global productions: Labor in the making of the "information society"* (pp. 13-38). Cresskill, NJ: Hampton.

Murry, J. P., Jr., Stam, A., & Lastovicka, J. L. (1996). Paid- versus donated-media strategies for public service announcement campaigns. *Public Opinion Quarterly, 60,* 1-29.

Myrick, R. (1996). Speaking from the margins: Communication strategies used in African American HIV prevention campaigns in Alabama. *Howard Journal of Communications, 7,* 241-255.

Nathanson, A. I. (1999). Identifying and explaining the relationship between parental mediation and children's aggression. *Communication Research, 26,* 124-143.

National Television Violence Study (Vol. 3). (1998). Thousand Oaks, CA: Sage.

Paik, H., & Comstock, G. (1994). The effects of television violence on antisocial behavior: A meta-analysis. *Communication Research, 21,* 516-546.

Pan, Z., & Kosicki, G. M. (1995). Framing analysis: An approach to news discourse. *Political Communication, 10,* 55-75.

Pan, Z., & Kosicki, G. M. (1997). Priming and media impact on the evaluations of the president's performance. *Communication Research, 24,* 3-30.

Park, E., & Kosicki, G. M. (1995). Presidential support during the Iran-Contra affair: People's reasoning process and media influence. *Communication Research, 22,* 207-236.

Park, H-W. (1998). A Gramscian approach to interpreting international communication. *Journal of Communication, 48*(4), 79-99.

Parks, M. R., & Floyd, K. (1996). Making friends in cyberspace. *Journal of Communication, 46*(1), 80-97.

Parry-Giles, S. J., & Parry-Giles, T. (1996). Gendered politics and presidential image construction: A reassessment of the "feminine style." *Communication Monographs, 63,* 337-353.

Pasquier, D., Buzzi, C., d'Haenens, L., & Sjöberg, U. (1998). Family lifestyles and media use patterns: An analysis of domestic media among Flemish, French, Italian and Swedish children and teenagers. *European Journal of Communication, 13,* 503-519.

Perloff, R. M. (1993). Third-person effect research 1983-1992: A review and synthesis. *International Journal of Public Opinion Research, 5,* 167-184.

Perse, E. M. (1990). Cultivation and involvement with local television news. In N. Signorielli & M. Morgan (Eds.), *Cultivation analysis: New directions in media effects research* (pp. 51-69). Newbury Park, CA: Sage.

Perse, E. M., & Courtright, J. A. (1993). Normative images of communication media: Mass and interpersonal channels on the new media environment. *Human Communication Research, 19,* 485-503.

Perse, E. M., & Dunn, D. G. (1998). The utility of home computers and media use: Implications of multimedia and connectivity. *Journal of Broadcasting & Electronic Media, 42,* 435-456.

Pfau, M., Moy, P., Holbert, R. L., Szabo, E. A., Lin W-K., & Zhang, W. (1999). The influence of political talk radio on confidence in democratic institutions. *Journalism & Mass Communication Quarterly, 75,* 730-745.

Pingree, S., Hawkins, R. P., Gustafson, D. H., Boberg, E., Bricker, E., Wise, M., Berhe, H., & Hsu, E. (1996). Will the disadvantaged ride the information highway? Hopeful answers from a computer-based health crisis system. *Journal of Broadcasting & Electronic Media, 40,* 331-353.

Pinkleton, B. E., Austin, E. W., & Fortman, K. K. J. (1998). Relationships of media use and political disaffection to political efficacy and voting behavior. *Journal of Broadcasting & Electronic Media, 42,* 34-49.

Potter, W. J. (1993). Cultivation theory and research: A conceptual critique. *Human Communication Research, 19,* 564-601.

Potter, W. J. (1997). The problem of indexing risk of viewing television aggression. *Critical Studies in Mass Communication, 14,* 228-248.

Potter, W. J., & Warren, R. (1996). Considering policies to protect children from TV violence. *Journal of Communication 46*(4), 116-137.

Power, J. G., Murphy, S. T., & Coover, G. (1996). Priming prejudice: How stereotypes and counter-stereotypes influence attribution of responsibility and credibility among ingroups and outgroups. *Human Communication Research, 23,* 36-58.

Price, V., Tewksbury, D., & Huang, L.-N. (1998). Third-person effects on publication of a holocaust-denial advertisement. *Journal of Communication, 48*(2), 3-26.

Price, V., Tewksbury, D., & Powers, E. (1997). Switching trains of thought: The impact of news frames on readers' cognitive responses. *Communication Research, 24,* 481-506.

Price, V., & Zaller, J. (1993). Who gets the news? Alternative measures of news reception and their implications for research. *Public Opinion Quarterly, 57,* 133-164.

Rawnsley, G. D. (1997). The 1996 presidential campaign in Taiwan: Packaging politics in a democratizing state. *Harvard International Journal of Press/Politics, 2*(2), 47-61.

Real, M. (1992). The challenge of a culture-centered paradigm: Metatheory and reconciliation in media research. In S. A. Deetz (Ed.), *Communication yearbook 15* (pp. 35-46). Newbury Park, CA: Sage.

Reese, S. D., & Buckalew, B. (1995). The militarism of local television: The routine framing of the Persian Gulf War. *Critical Studies in Mass Communication, 12,* 40-59.

Rhee, J. W. (1997). Strategy and issue frames in election campaign coverage: A social cognitive account of framing effects. *Journal of Communication, 47*(3), 26-48.

Rice, R. E. (1993). Media appropriateness: Using social presence theory to compare traditional and new organizational media. *Human Communication Research, 19,* 451-484.

Rimal, R. N., Flora, J. A., & Schooler, C. (1999). Achieving improvements in overall health orientation: Effects of campaign exposure, information seeking, and health media use. *Communication Research, 26,* 322-348.

Rios, D. I., & Gaines, S. O., Jr. (1999). Latino media use for cultural maintenance. *Journalism & Mass Communication Quarterly, 75,* 746-761.

Roach, C. (1997). Cultural imperialism and resistance in media theory and literary theory. *Media, Culture & Society, 19,* 47-66.

Rogers, E. M. (1995). *Diffusion of innovations* (4th ed.). New York: Free Press.

Rogers, E. M., & Dearing, J. W. (1988). Agenda-setting research: Where has it been, where is it going? In J. A. Anderson (Ed.), *Communication yearbook 11* (pp. 555-594). Newbury Park, CA: Sage.

Romer, D., Jamieson, K. H., & DeCoteau, N. J. (1998). The treatment of persons of color in local television news: Ethnic blame discourse or realistic group conflict? *Communication Research, 25,* 286-305.

Ross, S. D. (1998). "Their rising voices": A study of civil rights, social movements, and advertising in the *New York Times. Journalism & Mass Communication Quarterly, 75,* 518-534.

Rubin, A. M. (1994). Media uses and effects: A uses-and-gratifications perspective. In J. Bryant & D. Zillmann (Eds.), *Media effects: Advances in theory and research* (pp. 417-436). Hillsdale, NJ: Lawrence Erlbaum.

Rubin, A. M., Perse, E. M., & Taylor, D. (1988). A methodological examination of cultivation. *Communication Research, 15,* 107-134.

Sakamoto, K. (1999). Reading Japanese women's magazines: The construction of new identities in the 1970s and 1980s. *Media, Culture & Society, 21,* 173-193.

Salwen, M. B. (1995). News of Hurricane Andrew: The agenda of sources and the sources' agendas. *Journalism & Mass Communication Quarterly, 72,* 826-840.

Salwen, M. B. (1998). Perceptions of media influence and support for censorship: The third-person effect in the 1996 presidential election. *Communication Research, 25,* 259-285.

Sampedro, V. (1998). Grounding the displaced: Local media reception in a transnational context. *Journal of Communication, 48*(2), 125-143.

Schiller, H. I. (1992). *Mass communication and American empire* (2nd ed.). Boulder, CO: Westview.

Schoenbach, K., & Becker, L. B. (1995). Origins and consequences of mediated public opinion. In T. L. Glasser & T. Salmon (Eds.), *Pubic opinion and the communication of consent* (pp. 323-347). New York: Guilford.

Scodari, C. (1995). Possession, attraction, and the thrill of the chase: Gendered myth-making in film and television comedy of the sexes. *Critical Studies in Mass Communication, 12,* 23-39.

Semetko, H. A. (1996). Political balance on television: Campaigns in the United States, Britain, and Germany. *Harvard International Journal of Press/Politics, 1*(1), 51-71.

Shah, D., Domke, D., & Wackman, D. B. (1996). "To thine own self be true": Values, framing, and voter decision-making strategies. *Communication Research, 23,* 509-560.

Shah, D. V., Faber, R. J., & Youn, S. (1999). Susceptibility and severity: Perceptual dimensions underlying the third-person effect. *Communication Research, 26,* 240-267.

Shanahan, J., Morgan, M., & Stenbjerre, M. (1997). Green or brown? Television and the cultivation of environmental concern. *Journal of Broadcasting & Electronic Media, 41,* 305-323.

Shrum, L. J. (1995). Assessing the social influence of television: A social cognition perspective on cultivation effects. *Communication Research, 22,* 402-429.

Shrum, L. J. (1996). Psychological processes underlying cultivation effects: Further tests of construct accessibility. *Human Communication Research, 22,* 482-509.

Shrum, L. J., & O'Guinn, T. C. (1993). Processes and effects in the construction of social reality. *Communication Research, 20,* 436-471.

Signorielli, N., & Staples, J. (1997). Television and children's conceptions of nutrition. *Health Communication, 9,* 289-301.

Silverblatt, A. (1995). *Media literacy: Keys to interpreting media messages.* Westport, CT: Praeger.

Skumanich, S. A., & Kintsfather, D. P. (1998). Individual media dependency relations within television shopping programming: A causal model reviewed and revised. *Communication Research, 25,* 200-219.

Tan, A., Nelson, L., Dong, Q., & Tan, G. (1997). Value acceptance in adolescent socialization: A test of a cognitive-functional theory of television effects. *Communication Monographs, 64,* 82-97.

Tapper, J. (1995). The ecology of cultivation: A conceptual model for cultivation research. *Communication Theory, 5,* 36-57.

Tewksbury, D. (1999). Differences in how we watch the news: The impact of processing goals and expertise on evaluations of political actors. *Communication Research, 26,* 4-29.

Trevino, L., & Webster, J. (1992). Flow in computer-mediated communication: Electronic mail and voice mail evaluation and impacts. *Communication Research, 19,* 539-573.

Tsao, J. (1996). Compensatory media use: An exploration of two paradigms. *Communication Studies, 47,* 89-109.

Valente, T. W., & Saba, W. P. (1998). Mass media and interpersonal influence in a reproductive health communication campaign in Bolivia. *Communication Research, 25,* 96-124.

Valkenburg, P. M., & Janssen, S. C. (1999). What do children value in entertainment programs? A cross-cultural investigation. *Journal of Communication, 49*(2), 3-21.

Valkenburg, P. M., Krcmar, M., & de Roos, S. (1998). The impact of a cultural children's program and adult mediation on children's knowledge of and attitudes towards opera. *Journal of Broadcasting & Electronic Media, 42,* 315-326.

Valkenburg, P. M., Krcmar, M., Peeters, A. L., & Marseille, N. M. (1999). Developing a scale to assess three styles of television mediation: "Instructive mediation," "restrictive mediation," and "social coviewing." *Journal of Broadcasting & Electronic Media, 43,* 52-66.

van der Voort, T. H. A., Beentjes, J. W. J., Bovill, M., Gaskell, G., Koolstra, C. M., Livingstone, S., & Marseille, N. M. (1998). Young people's ownership and uses of new and old forms of media in Britain and the Netherlands. *European Journal of Communication, 13,* 457-477.

Van Zoonen, L. (1998). "Finally, I have my mother back": Politicians and their families in popular culture. *Harvard International Journal of Press/Politics, 3*(1), 48-64.

Vavrus, M. (1998). Working the Senate from the outside in: The mediated construction of a feminist political campaign. *Critical Studies in Mass Communication, 15,* 213-235.

Vincent, R. C., & Basil, M. D. (1997). College students' news gratifications, media use, and current events knowledge. *Journal of Broadcasting & Electronic Media, 41,* 380-392.

Viswanath, K., & Finnegan, J. R., Jr. (1996). The knowledge gap hypothesis: Twenty-five years later. In B. R. Burleson (Ed.), *Communication yearbook 19* (pp. 187-227). Thousand Oaks, CA: Sage.

Walters, T., Walters, L. M., & Gray, R. (1996). Agenda building in the 1992 presidential campaign. *Public Relations Review, 22,* 9-24.

Wanta, W., & Elliott, W. R. (1995). Did the "magic" work? Knowledge of HIV/AIDS and the knowledge gap hypothesis. *Journalism & Mass Communication Quarterly, 72,* 312-321.

Wanta, W., & Foote, J. (1994). The president-news media relationship: A time series analysis of agenda-setting. *Journal of Broadcasting & Electronic Media, 38,* 437-448.

Warnick, B. (1999). Masculinizing the feminine: Inviting women on line ca. 1997. *Critical Studies in Mass Communication, 16,* 1-19.

Wasko, J. (1995). *Hollywood in the information age: Beyond the silver screen.* Austin: University of Texas Press.

Weimann, G. (1996). Cable comes to the holy land: The impact of cable TV on Israeli viewers. *Journal of Broadcasting & Electronic Media, 40,* 243-257.

Weiss, A. J., & Wilson, B. J. (1996). Emotional portrayals in family television series that are popular among children. *Journal of Broadcasting & Electronic Media, 40,* 1-29.

Wheeler, D. L. (1998). Global culture or culture clash: New information technologies in the Islamic world. A view from Kuwait. *Communication Research, 25,* 359-376.

Wilke, J. (1995). Agenda-setting in an historical perspective: The coverage of the American Revolution in the German press (1773-83). *European Journal of Communication, 10,* 63-86.

Wilkins, K. (1999). Development discourse on gender and communication in strategies for social change. *Journal of Communication, 49*(1), 46-68.

Willnat, L., & Zhu, J-H. (1996). Newspaper coverage and public opinion in Hong Kong: A time-series analysis of media priming. *Political Communication, 13,* 231-246.

Zhao, X., & Bleske, G. L. (1998). Horse-race polls and audience issue learning. *Harvard International Journal of Press/Politics, 3*(4), 13-34.

Zhao, X., & Chaffee, S. H. (1995). Campaign advertisements versus television news as sources of political issue information. *Public Opinion Quarterly, 59,* 41-65.

Zoch, L. M., & Turk, J. V. (1998). Women making news: Gender as a variable in source selection and use. *Journalism & Mass Communication Quarterly, 75,* 762-775.

CHAPTER CONTENTS

5 Organizational Communication Research: Key Moments, Central Concerns, and Future Challenges

JAMES R. TAYLOR
University of Montreal

ANDREW J. FLANAGIN
University of California, Santa Barbara

GEORGE CHENEY
University of Montana–Missoula

DAVID R. SEIBOLD
University of California, Santa Barbara

This chapter summarizes the state of theory and research in organizational communication. The authors highlight the central concerns and major challenges addressed by organizational communication researchers. They begin by isolating the central intellectual and practical currents, and then they identify defining and constituting concepts in organizational communication. The chapter concludes with the authors' proposals of fruitful areas for future research.

ORE than a generation ago, Katz and Kahn (1966) argued that organizations are best conceptualized as open systems in which the behavior of members takes on a structure that is properly viewed at a collective, organizational level. In contrast to earlier perspectives that concentrated almost exclusively on the individual psychology and interpersonal relations among organizational members, the open-systems view emphasized that organizations are

Correspondence: James R. Taylor, Department of Communication, University of Montreal, CP 6128, Succ Centre-Ville, Montreal, Quebec, H3C 3J7 Canada; e-mail taylor@com.umontreal. ca

Communication Yearbook 24, pp. 99-137

psychological, social, and symbolic constructions in and through which individuals respond to their environments. Control mechanisms such as norms and rules serve to curtail strictly individual needs in favor of wider organizational ones. In this manner, organizations function by balancing the changing demands of the environment with control mechanisms that guard against potentially overwhelming uncertainty.

Katz and Kahn thus framed individual action within a *network* of relationships, in effect foregrounding communication in the construction and enactment of organizations. This dynamic perspective on organizations—central to the open-systems view—simultaneously stressed the role of interconnectedness and the inherent importance of the external environment. Absent from the perspective, however, was an explicit focus on social interaction per se, an oversight soon redressed in Weick's (1979) claim that through processes of enactment, selection, and retention, organizational members construct their organizations through communicative processes.

In Weick's view, organizational members create their environments through enactment, or ongoing interaction, that emphasizes the phenomena to which they pay attention. They then select from among many possible interpretations of the enacted environment, thus attaining a degree of collective sensemaking through communication. Finally, members retain the interpretations that seem to work for them, setting up a locus of choice for future patterns of interaction and attention (enactment). It is through communication, Weick suggested, that we continually construct the reality of which we are a part and engage in "retrospective sensemaking" in order to rationalize the meanings of our actions. Communication is the core process in organizations, or, in Weick's terms, the core process of *organizing*.

Communication is thus viewed *as organization*—constituting organizations and not just occurring within them. Weick both precipitated and navigated the shift from the metaphor of the organization as "container" of communication to a view of communication as fundamental to the study of organizations. This shift has been crucial to the development of organizational communication as a distinct area of study, away from the strictly container view predominant from the 1940s to the 1960s and toward perspectives that explicitly consider communication phenomena as central processes of organizing (Cheney & Christensen, 2000; Farace, Monge, & Russell, 1977; Monge, 1973; Smith, 1993; Taylor, 1993). At the same time, however, this devaluing has come at some cost to the discipline.

In examining the state of contemporary organizational communication research, we stand to learn from the open-systems perspective and its dual emphasis on the environment as a source of organizational input and on the importance of diverse communication phenomena in organizations. In view of current social, political, technological, and economic developments, the centrality of the environment and the diversity of communication processes are critical to the study of organizational communication, with a far greater magnitude than a generation ago. Pressures toward globalization, new types of social movements and organizations, tensions between integration and segregation, team-based restructuring, the imperative of customer service, and the rise of network and virtual organizations, to name only a few developments, suggest ways in which contemporary organizational communication theories and concerns parallel, and of course expand, open-systems perspectives initiated a generation ago.

At the same time, we have recently come to appreciate organizational "closedness," in its dialectical relationship with openness, as organizational boundaries become problematic (see Luhmann, 1990). That is to say, with greater fluidity of organizational boundaries there is a concomitant desire to reassert organizational identity and to maintain coherence and cohesion. In this regard, we invoke the systems perspective (Poole, 1997) and, later in this essay, interpretivism (the other predominant perspective on organizational communication during the past two decades) as heuristics for clarifying current themes in the study of organizational communication.

In this essay we highlight the central concerns and major challenges addressed by organizational communication researchers who study the communication-related aspects of diverse organizational phenomena in the world today. We proceed by first examining key moments in the study of organizational communication in order to sketch central intellectual and practical currents. We explicate both "explicit" and "implicit" histories of the field, treat reviews of the metatheoretical perspectives and methodological orientations in organizational communication, and then describe the interpretive and critical "turn" in the field during the 1980s. Throughout this discussion, we identify defining and constituting concepts of organizational communication. In the final section we review continuing preoccupations in organizational communication research, and we propose areas for further work and exploration. Cutting across theoretical, methodological, and practical concerns, we hope to challenge researchers to confront directly the complexities of contemporary organizational environments and communication processes.

KEY MOMENTS IN THE HISTORY AND DEVELOPMENT OF ORGANIZATIONAL COMMUNICATION

In order to examine where the field of organizational communication has been, and thus where it is going, we propose to delineate its historical development, outline its theoretical perspectives and methodological orientations, and examine prevalent research topics to date. In doing so, we focus on organizational communication's "explicit" history, or its documented and recounted pedigree, as well as on its "implicit" history, or factors that are typically overlooked in such "recipe" treatments. In turn and in the subsequent section, we detail the evolution of the field's interpretive/critical turn in an effort to provide a richer understanding of roots, key moments, and directions.

Explicit History

Although the study of organizational communication phenomena in a sense dates back to antiquity (Allen, Tompkins, & Busemeyer, 1996), extant histories generally locate the genesis of organizational communication as an identifiable academic field in the 1940s and 1950s (Putnam & Cheney, 1983, 1985; Redding, 1985; Redding & Tompkins, 1988). Three sources account for the discipline's conceptual roots: traditional rhetorical theory, human relations prototheories, and parallel models of early management/organization theories (Redding & Tompkins, 1988). Organizational communication currently enjoys a rich interplay with the allied academic disciplines of administrative science, anthropology, business communication, corporate communication, industrial organizational psychology, management communication, organizational behavior, political science, social psychology, sociolinguistics, sociology, rhetoric, and even literary criticism (Poole, Putnam, & Seibold, 1997).

In tracing the emergence of organizational communication as an academic field, Redding and Tompkins (1988) have sketched three major periods of development. During the foundational "era of preparation" (1900-1940), the emphasis was primarily on communication skills training. The "era of identification and consolidation" (1940-1970) saw the emergence of what was termed "business and industrial communication." According to Redding (1985), it was during the decades of the 1940s and 1950s that the seeds of organizational communication (as a unique and identifiable discipline) were sown, largely through a series of seminal academic publications, several social science programs, and the birth of graduate programs in organizational communication. In the "era of maturity and innovation" (after 1970), empirical research under the rubric of "organizational communication" proliferated, and efforts were made to develop the theoretical premises and philosophical bases of organizational communication.

Implicit History

Clair (in press) questions the utility of defining and articulating the explicit history of organizational communication at all, due to issues of self-definition, legitimacy, and the "diversified heritage" that doing so implicitly ignores. In her view—essentially a Foucauldian perspective (e.g., Foucault, 1984)—any historical account or self-definition of organizational communication is framed in a dominant and constraining organizational discourse. If organizational communication exists only when we establish the discipline as "officially" recognized—or legitimated—by a university, this fails to recognize or acknowledge the larger philosophical conversations that preceded our "academic birth" and from which organizational communication has in part sprung. Accordingly, in most historical accounts of the genesis of organizational communication, figures such as Aristotle, Marx, and Mead are given lip service at best, and our "diversified heritage" is partially lost. In addition, of course, certain interests become privileged over others. And along with the prevalence of the container metaphor has flourished an administrative or managerial bias, in which the organization itself is seen as a social actor with ever-expanding rights and power (see, e.g., the sociohistorical critique in Coleman, 1974).

Although we can take issue with aspects of Clair's (in press) critique (see McPhee & Seibold, in press), we should perhaps worry less about self-definition while continuing to explore diverse theoretical and methodological options. Accordingly, we have the opportunity to take advantage of our "loose coupling" as a discipline, rather than rush toward constraining attempts at *capturing* organizational communication. Similar to Beniger (1993), who calls for communication researchers to realign and embrace the *subject* of communication and not the *field* (which he views as blind to many important communication phenomena), Clair urges us to focus less on disciplinary boundaries and more on communication and organization as the basis of and impetus for our work.

Metatheoretical Perspectives and Methodological Orientations

Historical/Evolutionary Orientations

Redding and Tompkins (1988) have outlined three somewhat overlapping historical phases of the development of organizational communication theory and research from 1900 to 1970. During the "formulary-prescriptive" phase (1900-1950), organizational communication focused primarily on skills-based training and prescriptive advice aimed at achieving "effective" communication. For example, early studies of organizational communication prescribed media choice, timing, and message structure for managers. During the "empirical-prescriptive" phase (1950-1970), largely descriptive, empirical studies began to emerge. Although methodological sophistication and the depth of information in studies began to increase, the overall emphasis remained on prescriptive advice for managers, rather than on the articulation and testing of theoretical perspectives. During a parallel "applied-scientific" phase (late 1940s-1970s), researchers sought to position themselves as neutral and objective observers of communication phenomena, working toward a science of organizational communication. Emphasis was placed on measurement, variable analysis, and hypothetico-deductive designs intended to test competing perspectives.

In reviewing the contents of 15 communication journals from 1979 to 1989, Wert-Gray, Center, Brashers, and Meyers (1991) found that the most heavily researched topics were information flow and channels; climate and culture; superior-subordinate communication; power, conflict, and politics; and public organizational communication. In an ambitious review of 889 articles from 61 journals between 1980 and 1991, Allen, Gotcher, and Seibert (1993) identified 19 areas of organizational communication research. In descending order of the areas most frequently researched, they list interpersonal relations (including superior-subordinate, interviewing, stress, conflict, and gender and race); communication skills and strategies; culture and symbolism; information flow and channels; power and influence; positive outcomes of communication; decision making and problem solving; communication networks; cognitive, communication, and management styles; organization-environment communication interface; technology; language and message content; structure; uncertainty and information adequacy; groups and organizational effectiveness; ethics; cross-cultural research; climate; and theoretical advances. We can thus see an expansion of organization communication's scope, especially since 1980, to include a broader range of topics and research perspectives.

Perhaps the most wide-ranging review of the development of organizational communication research is that provided by Putnam, Phillips, and Chapman (1996; see also Putnam, 1998). These reviewers identify seven "metaphor clusters" that, implicitly or explicitly, have framed lines of research in organizational communication and their attendant views of communication: conduit, in which organizations are treated as containers or channels for information flow and communication is seen as transmission of messages; lens, in which organizations are conceived as perceptual systems or eyes for environmental scanning, gatekeeping, and the like, and communication is filtered; linkage, in which organizations are represented as networks or systems of nodes linked by communication that functions to connect them; performance, in which organizations emerge as coordinated actions—the performative result of communicative social interactions; symbol, in which members' interpretive communication activities produce organizations as novels; voice, in which "communication is expression and organization becomes a chorus of stilled or singing voices" (p. 379); and discourse, in which organizations appear as texts consisting of genres and dialogues, manifestations of communication as conversation. Most interesting about this review is Putnam et al.'s recognition of the variety of understandings of communication itself as embedded in different studies of organizational communication.

Allied Perspectives

Beyond historical perspectives on the evolution of scholarly emphases, organizational communication research also has been located in metatheoretical stances that are roughly consistent with Burrell and Morgan's (1979) classic two-dimensional typology of schools of sociological thought and inquiry. The dimensions address assumptions about (a) the nature of social science (objectivist/subjectivist) and (b) the nature of society (maintenance or regulation/enlightenment or radical change). When the two dimensions are crossed, four main paradigms emerge. Briefly, *functionalists* view reality as significantly external to the individual's experience of it and behavior as concrete and tangible. Research within this paradigm aims to arrive at empirical knowledge by means of scientifically rigorous methods, as traditionally understood. *Radical humanists* take reality to be socially and intersubjectively constructed, yet ultimately dominated by the ideological factors that individuals both create and maintain. *Radical structuralists* view society as objective, like functionalists, but by contrast view many aspects of the social order as oppressive and dominating. Their goal is to attempt to uncover the sources of this oppression. *Interpretivists* view reality as socially constructed by the interplay of individuals' subjective experiences, and research is aimed at uncovering the nature and role of symbolic forms that maintain social order. Unfortunately, these terms have sometimes been employed in simplistic ways (especially so with *functionalism*) that ignore both metatheoretical assumptions and blurred genres (Cheney, in press; Geertz, 1973).

Scholars have applied Burrell and Morgan's model to organizational communication (e.g., Daniels & Spiker, 1994; Putnam, 1983), despite the fact that its importation from sociology necessarily neglects research traditions actually reflected in organizational communication (Clair, in press; Mumby & Stohl, 1996). For example, Putnam (1982) used Burrell and Morgan's typology to examine the basic assumptions underlying research on prevalent concerns of communication channels, networks, communication climates, supervisor-subordinate communication, and symbol systems in organizations. She noted the contribution that each paradigm can make to the study of organizational communication phenomena and outlined problematic applications as well. Later, Rosengren (1993) observed that, due to political and intellectual changes, the relative importance of the Burrell-Morgan typology's two major dimensions (objective/subjective versus regulation/change) has shifted toward the objective/subjective side. He called for cross-fertilization across this divide to invigorate the study of communication. Although the typology provides a structure by which to organize theoretical perspectives, the boundaries between these perspectives should be seen as somewhat fluid. More recently, Deetz (1996) and Mumby (1997a) have both reconfigured the typology for special application to organizational communication, recognizing subtle distinctions between and among different postures toward interpretation and critique.

Alternatively, Euske and Roberts (1987) have noted traditional organizational metatheories (classical-structural, human relations, behavioral decisions, and systems theory) and have offered recent organizational theory perspectives that assume a distinct organization-environment view. They demonstrate how resource-dependence, population ecology/organizational life-cycle, and institutionalization theories all address complex and important relations between organizations and their environments, and they encourage increased attention to this relationship among organizational communication researchers. Especially, Euske and Roberts call attention to some of the physical and biological structures and constraints of organizing.

Communication-Centered Approaches

Krone, Jablin, and Putnam (1987) developed a more communication-oriented perspective for classifying theoretical paradigms by pointing out that researchers' views on human communication guide the study of organizational phenomena. Krone et al. mapped four conceptual frameworks (mechanistic, psychological, interpretive-symbolic, and systems-interaction), each reflecting basic assumptions about human communication. The mechanistic view approaches communication as a transmission process in which truthfulness is a goal of communicators. Adopting an essentially psychological view takes into account how individual characteristics influence communication by casting communicators as active participants in the communication process. An interpretive-symbolic approach emphasizes the action of communicating by taking into account the collective and cultural contexts of communication. In this way, the communication is seen as it creates and sustains the organization. Finally, the systems-interaction perspective assumes that the overall communication system shapes organizational behavior and treats communication as an evolving system. From this perspective, the sequences of communication behaviors are considered the locus of communication.

Other theorists' reviews of the field have been grounded in the view that organizational communication is composed of complementary but distinct theoretical and methodological perspectives. Redding and Tompkins (1988) note modernist, naturalist, and critical orientations to communication inquiry, characterized, respectively, by emphases on prediction and control, understanding and anticipation, and consciousness-raising and emancipation. Putnam and Cheney (1983) employed Habermas's (1971) three modes of scientific inquiry to analyze and critique dominant research traditions in organizational communication: the empirical-analytic (exemplified by the positivist tradition), historical-hermeneutic (which focuses on interaction and language in order to understand shared norms and experiences), and critical (which emphasizes liberation from unnecessary means of domination) approaches to the study of organizational communication phenomena. Putnam and Cheney sought to promote a "healthy pluralism" that might serve to revitalize traditional areas of organizational communication research. They later outlined several emerging approaches to the study of organizational communication, such as information-processing, rhetorical, cultural, and political perspectives (Putnam & Cheney, 1985; they would now add technological approaches to this list). These terms refer to "families" of perspectives in which core concepts and concerns are shared; they do not correspond to specific epistemological and theoretical perspectives.

In surveying the development of key constructs in organizational communication between 1985 and 1999, Conrad (1999; Conrad & Haynes, 2000) has identified five "clusters of scholarship"—all unified by an underlying theoretical concern with the relationship between symbolic action and social/organizational structure, but differing in how scholars in each deal with the dualism between action and structure. Conrad (1999) characterizes organizational communication scholarship as reflecting research that privileges structure over action (e.g., functionalist research on information exchange, superior-subordinate relationships, and interpersonal interaction) or action over structure (e.g., interpretivist studies of culture, meanings/messages, symbolism, and ambiguity); three subclusters that strive to integrate action and structure (i.e., structuration, research on unobtrusive [concertive] control/identification, and critical theory); challenging perspectives to the constructs that developed in the 1980s and 1990s (e.g., resistance/transformation, postmodernism); and studies that cross organizational boundaries (e.g., member-client relationships, organizational rhetoric). Conrad's framework is interesting especially because it attempts to position various organizational communication research approaches in terms of one of the most basic issues in all of social inquiry: individual action or agency versus social structure or constraint.

Taylor and Trujillo (2000) and Miller (2000) provide detailed treatments of qualitative and quantitative methods, respectively, in organizational communication research. In addition to charting a variety of criteria for evaluating qualitative research (on a continuum from quasi-positivist to interpretivist to critical-postmodern), Taylor and Trujillo discuss how critical theories, feminism, and postmodernism challenge investigators to confront and critique power issues in the research process. Miller surveys a variety of quantitative research practices (experimental research, survey and interview research, and coding of communication behavior and archives) and addresses criteria and challenges relevant to each.

Also prominent among recent metatheoretical attempts to analyze the contours of organizational communication research is the work of Deetz (1996, 2000), who offers an update to Burrell and Morgan's (1979) typology in proposing schools of thought that he terms "discourses." He replaces the categories of functionalist, interpretivist, radical humanist, and radical structuralist with those of normative, interpretive, critical, and dialogic—directing attention explicitly to communication processes. Deetz argues that clarifying each perspective's claims and procedures will help to foster greater understanding across perspectives and more rigor within them. Although this reframing incorporates postmodern organizational communication perspectives, Clair (in press) notes that it fails to account sufficiently for feminist and multicultural views. Notwithstanding these limitations, Deetz's approach highlights key developments emanating from the interpretive turn in organizational communication scholarship during the 1980s, which we address in the following section.

Before we examine the interpretive turn in organizational communication (and related developments in postmodernism and critical theory), it is worth noting that the area of organizational communication is vibrant and flourishing. New journals and book series in the area, increases in Ph.D. degrees, the proportion of Organizational Communication Division members in the International Communication Association (forming the second-largest division), awards to scholars in this area, major federal grants, interdisciplinary collaboration, and a host of other indicators reflect the vitality of scholarship focusing on the description, analysis, understanding, and critique of communication practices in contemporary organizational life.

In no small part, this has been associated with the advances and continued importance of scholarship loosely coupled within the broad "systems" perspective we have noted thus far (see Farace et al., 1977). Indeed, many of the new theoretical understandings of communication and organization that we identify later in this essay are those of researchers working within the systems tradition: self-organizing systems theory (Contractor, 1994), reticulation theory (Corman & Scott, 1994), public goods perspectives (Fulk, Flanagin, Kalman, Monge, & Ryan, 1996; Monge et al., 1998), assimilation perspectives (Jablin, 1987; Kramer, 1993), and adaptive structuration theory (Poole & DeSanctis, 1990). Similarly, investigations arising out of the community of scholars with a systems orientation are central to the emerging research foci we identify later: technology (Corman, 1997), groups and organizations (DeSanctis & Poole, 1997; Lammers & Krikorian, 1997; Poole, Seibold, & McPhee, 1996), networks (Heald, Contractor, Koehly, & Wasserman, 1998; Monge & Contractor, 2000; Rice, 1993; Stohl, 1993a), change (Lewis & Seibold, 1996; Miller, Johnson, & Grau, 1994), and globalization (Monge & Fulk, 1999; Stohl, 2000). As but one example of current activity in these areas, the 1997 Alta conference was devoted to the theme of "self-organizing processes," especially to generative mechanisms of various social systems that help systems both "know themselves" and create the conditions necessary for social reproduction and adaptation. Further, this same subject was the topic of a jointly sponsored theme session between the Organizational Communication and Information Systems Divisions at the 1998 ICA conference, and papers from these sessions appeared subsequently in a "Dialogue" section of *Management Communication Quarterly* (Contractor, 1999; Hawes, 1999; Houston, 1999; Krippendorff, 1999). Finally, important conceptual, technological, and methodological advances have emanated from researchers in this area: computational modeling (Hyatt, Contractor, & Jones, 1997), collaborative technologies (Contractor, Zink, & Chan, 1998; Flanagin, in press), and methods for coding and data-analytic techniques (Holmes & Poole, 1991; Poole & DeSanctis, 1992).

THE INTERPRETIVE MOVEMENT
IN ORGANIZATIONAL COMMUNICATION

The year 1981 was a critical time for organizational communication studies, for during that summer a group of communication scholars met at a mountain retreat just south of Salt Lake City, Utah, to consider where the field had been and where it should be going. The outcome of this summer conference was a volume edited by Putnam and Pacanowsky (1983) that has become a landmark in the evolution of the field and in the field's narrative about itself. The contributors to that volume pointed the way to more adventurous approaches to the conduct of research than were previously recognized as valid. In a real sense, the conference and the book signaled a commitment to the establishment of a genuine discipline of organizational communication, in the full academic meaning of that term. It brought to the center of our attention two concepts of research that are referred to as *interpretivism* and *critical perspectives* (Putnam, 1983).

In retrospect, there seem to have been two principal motives behind the rethinking of the bases of the field of study that led to the Alta conference and Putnam and Pacanowsky's book. The first was a determination to distance organizational communication research somewhat from the preoccupations of management. As we have noted in our discussion above of the reviews by Redding (1985) and Redding and Tompkins (1988), the field of organizational communication began as a practical concern with teaching communication skills to people in organizations. Practitioners tended to take on the attitudes of their managerial partners: a kind of top-down view of organizational process and structure, not unlike that prevalent in management science. The people at Alta were determined to stake out an independent role for organizational communication research, one that was clearly distinct from that taught in business schools. That motive still seems to be operative (Mumby & Stohl, 1996).

The second motivation can be traced to a growing dissatisfaction with the then-prevailing mode of research and its restrictive view of what constitutes both data and theory. The social sciences in North America had for some time subscribed to a version of research that emphasizes the centrality of attributions of cause and effect, the necessity for a precise operational definition of variables, the meticulous collection and categorization of data, investigator objectivity, and quantitative (preferably statistical) analysis. This amalgam of commitments has been variously termed *positivism, functionalism,* and *operationalism,* although none of these terms would be accepted today as fully representative because each stands for no more than one of the component elements of *strict empiricism,* typically associated with some particular school or author. By the end of the 1970s, empiricism, to use the term that is most neutral in its associations, was drawing fire because it so limited research possibilities that some believed it had become an intellectual straitjacket. The Alta conference thus had some of the qualities of a manifesto in that it announced an opening up to new kinds of research.

Intellectual Roots of the Interpretive Tradition

In outlining alternatives, the innovators could draw on a rich 20th-century intellectual tradition. Two principal influences can be seen in the transformation of perspective from empiricism to interpretivism: phenomenology and structuralism, or, more specifically, semiotics. The two great innovators of 20th-century phenomenology were German professors: Husserl (1964, 1976) and Heidegger (1962). Husserl's particular contribution was to turn attention to the cognitive processes involved in arriving at knowledge. He reminded us that knowledge is not simply a recording of experience but an active construction of it, in which the categories we begin with delimit what we can subsequently know. Heidegger, the more radical of the two thinkers, challenged the entire tradition of Western philosophy, and its preoccupation with prejudice-free knowledge, by reiterating the situatedness of all experience and the circumstantial limits such situatedness imposes on knowledge. Together, Husserl and Heidegger problematized the pretensions of any empirical inquiry that aims to produce value-free findings.

Phenomenology, in its pristine expression in Husserl and Heidegger, is dauntingly abstruse and almost inaccessible to any but professional philosophers. It evolved to become an important influence on social research initially through the interpretations of one of Husserl's students, Schutz (1962, 1964), and subsequently through others whom Schutz in turn influenced—Garfinkel (1967), Cicourel (1964, 1973), and Sacks (1989), who transformed phenomenology into ethnomethodology and then into conversation analysis. In this revised form phenomenology emphasized two ideas, both of which have had profound effects on how we conceive of organizational communication: (a) the *indexicality* of all language (i.e., its inevitable situatedness in some identifiable sphere or domain of life) and (b) the *reflexivity* of language (i.e., that property of language-in-use that has as its consequences not merely that the meaning of an expression is tied to an occasion of use but that the occasion itself is a construction of language that is being used by people to do practical things).

Structuralism (or, more specifically, semiotics) is the other great interpretive innovation of the 20th century. Its first proponent was the Swiss philologist Ferdinand de Saussure (1915/1966), who is credited with being the founder of modern linguistics. His conceptualization greatly transcends linguistics, however, because what he was aiming for was a general science of *signs*. What Saussure accomplished is still a matter of debate (Harris, 1987; Thibault, 1997), but on one point there is no disagreement: It was Saussure who obliged us to take seriously the idea that language, like other symbolic modes of communication, is a system, with its own internal dynamic and logic. Language is not merely a passive instrument, or neutral medium, by which we represent the world; instead, it is a kind of active agent that imposes on us an ideological filtering of experience (Burke, 1966). Language becomes an object of study in its own right.

Structuralism and semiotics flourished in the 1960s, but their impact on interpretivism was mediated by two influential figures, neither of whom can be counted as a structuralist, although the thinking of both exhibits a structuralist influence: Foucault (1969/1972) and Derrida (1976, 1988). Foucault most cogently exemplifies Saussure's counsel to look at, rather than through, language and to understand how its "discursive formations" (as Foucault calls broad patterns of thought and talk) establish the patterns of social life even as they mediate its processes. In Habermas's (1970, 1984, 1987) and Deetz's (1992) colorful phrase, language is capable of "colonizing" an organization, and as it does so it instantiates relations of power that inevitably privilege some voices while silencing others. Derrida's central concern is to counter what he feels to be the ingrained prejudice of seeing language as no more than a secondary accessory to experience—like the "decorative" view of rhetoric prevalent from the 16th through the early 20th centuries. Our experience of the world, Derrida has consistently argued, is not made immediately "present" to us; it has to be first "written" so that we can recognize (re-cognize) it. Text is not just an incidental by-product of living and interacting but its essential basis.

Trends in Interpretive Research

All of these ideas can be found, singly or in combination, in the organizational communication literature that was inspired by the interpretivist turn, even though scholars have only occasionally referred to the origins of their perspectives. What is truly remarkable is the diversity and fecundity of this research. It is not our intention to review in detail the intellectual expansion that followed the Alta conference; this has already been done. Instead, to illustrate our theme, we recall in brief summary some of the principal directions of research that have emerged during the past two decades.

Ethnographically Oriented Research

The interpretive movement in communication studies coincided with another development in an allied field, the increasing preoccupation of ethnographers with their own society (Van Maanen, 1988). The result has been the emergence of a new kind of communication study, one that features what Geertz (1973) has called "thick description." The researcher employs the methodology of the anthropologist to conduct highly detailed observation of people in organizational contexts, over a protracted period of time and through prolonged interaction, in order to produce an interpretation of their culture. To the extent possible, the observer tries to see the world as his or her informants see it through their own eyes.

One interesting consequence of the ethnographic turn in organizational studies was the highlighting of the centrality of organizational culture as a construct. There was in the 1980s a fad in management studies centered on the idea that culture is something that can be molded and managed, and as such culture is the key to enhanced productivity. But here the frontier between management and organizational communication thinking reemerged. As Smircich (1983) reminded us, thinking of culture as something that an organization *has* is not the same as seeing culture as what an organization *is*. If culture is something an organization "has," then it can be shaped; if it is what the organization "is," then even the attempt to "shape" it becomes one additional index of what it is. To the interpretivist the practice of "managing" culture is merely an instance of managerial culture.

Rhetoric and Narrativity

Interpretivism has provided a renewed stimulus to rhetoric, one of the traditional branches of communication studies. The modern organization faces a constant challenge in its internal and external relations to sustain a positive image of itself (Cheney & McMillan, 1990). Organizations often speak for populations and constituencies whose views, considered at the individual level, may be far from unanimous. The rhetorical perspective on organization reveals a complication of Aristotle's rhetorical situation (with its elements of speaker, message, and audience) today, messages often exist in public discourse without clearly identifiable sources, the discrete message may not be as important as a broader pattern of discourse, and audiences internal and external to the organization are likely to be both heterogeneous and overlapping (Cheney & Frenette, 1993; Heath, 1994). Organizational rhetoric then becomes a delicate balancing act of taking positions that are representative, but not alienating, a challenge well illustrated by Cheney's (1991) study of the public positions of the Roman Catholic Church on controversial issues. The value of rhetorical analysis similarly becomes evident in contexts where constructing an effective public argument is the difference between survival and serious loss, as in the case of a recent dispute in which a major hydroelectric developer was pitted against a Native population that risked seeing its territory and means of sustenance invaded by dams (Cooren & Taylor, in press). In the rhetorical context, Eisenberg's (1984) concept of strategic ambiguity in communication and Markham's (1996) study of the ethics of ambiguity in managerial directives take on particular relevance.

The interpretive approach has similarly revitalized the study of *narrative* in organizational contexts, in recording both how members create meaning out of ambiguous circumstances (Boje, 1991) and how the organization itself can be thought of as a tissue of narrativity (Cooren, in press; Czarniawska, 1997). As an organizing principle narrative also implicates the study of organizational identity in that every organization will struggle to tell and retell its own story, with some concern for coherence and while addressing multiple audiences. Some researchers believe that narrative is not just about storytelling; it is the basis on which events are structured in the first place—a view that is reminiscent of Burke's "dramaturgical" view (see, e.g., Robichaud, 1999; Taylor & Van Every, in press).

Critical Theory and Feminist Approaches

What is known as *critical theory* (in its strict sense referring to the Frankfurt school and in its broader sense referencing approaches that feature power, ideology, and undecidability in their analytic schemes) resembles structuration theory in its preoccupation with the bases of power, but it differs significantly from the latter in the emphasis it lays on the power of discourse to inform organizational worlds of experience. A principal source of inspiration for critical theory is the work of French philosopher and sociologist Michel Foucault (1984), who encourages us to take seriously the substantiality of language (hence his term *discursive formations,* which echoes the idea of geological formations). The constructions of language are not neutral; they have a history of emergence in social practices, and they engender a world of sense in which structures of domination and power are sanitized and naturalized. Take, for example, modern Western conceptions of the individual that stress autonomy, uniqueness, and agency. We should be looking for power not in the persons of a few leaders, or in the monopolization of resources by a privileged few, Foucault argues, but in the ideology that made such distortions of power possible in the first place. Power is thus seen to be diffuse, inherent in the very language we speak. Deetz (1992) elaborates on the relevance of critical theories to the study of organizational communication.

Critical theory addresses themes that crosscut other preoccupations, including fields such as social semiotics (Hodge & Kress, 1988, 1993; Kress & Hodge, 1979) and feminism (Buzzanell, 1994; Clair, 1993; Mumby, 1987, 1988). Feminist scholars have made a great contribution to organizational communication research by demonstrating in their analyses of the unfolding of discourse in interactive situations how privilege and power are exercised and amplified to instantiate gender relations.

Not all the critical work on interaction, however, would normally be classified under this heading. Barker, Tompkins, and Cheney (Barker, 1993; Barker & Cheney, 1994; Tompkins & Cheney, 1985) have shown how concertive control is exercised to discipline individual behavior even in so-called self-organizing groups. A preoccupation with interactive processes, and how they can produce bias, is shared by a large community of scholars who study phenomena such as conflict and negotiation (Putnam, 1989) and how discourse is framed (Clair, 1993; Fairhurst & Sarr, 1996). Dialogue has become in fact an important focus of research in communication, just as it has become a popular term for organizational practitioners (Senge, 1990). The latest in the series of Alta conferences has been devoted to this topic.

This critical work has a larger significance in that it has brought to our attention the issue of how to achieve a democratic form of organization. Much of the traditional literature on organization assumed a basis in a kind of machine rationality, but, as Habermas (1984, 1987) points out, there is another rationality that a student of communicative action should bear in mind: the rationality of open and honest exchange and dialogue. It is this preoccupation that has led a number of researchers to explore the organizational dynamics of comparatively nonhierarchical models of organizing, such as cooperatives and collectives (Cheney, 1999; Glaser, 1994; Harrison, 1994). This work similarly brings to the fore international comparisons and has immensely enriched our understanding of what an organization actually is.

RESEARCH EMPHASES IN ORGANIZATIONAL COMMUNICATION: CURRENT CONCERNS AND FUTURE CHALLENGES

Problematics and Prospects

Mumby and Stohl (1996) identify four central "problematics" or key issues for the contemporary study of organizational communication that scholars in the discipline must address. First is the issue of *voice,* or the notion that organizational communication researchers, rather than sharing managerial concerns and goals such as profit, are more typically concerned with organizations as "social collectivities that pose particularly complex communication issues" (p. 56). Voices exist partially outside of our unit of study and stand to inform important aspects of modern organizational life, as when we consider that certain stakeholding groups are being represented in administrative or managerial deliberations and decisions.

Another problematic is that of *rationality,* or the notion that modern organizations are bound to instrumentally (purposive) and technically (predictable) rational goals such as efficiency. However, a tension exists due to coexistent, but often neglected, socially constructed individual goals that might not appear to be plainly instrumentally/technically rational. In this manner, communication phenomena in organizations such as negotiation or interpretation can be understood as incorporating fundamentally important (and rational) information about participants' definitions of the situation that might transcend narrowly rational views of organizational efficiency. For instance, Feldman and March (1981) made problematic the very notion of information in organizations by showing how the acts of collecting and presenting information themselves serve as important organizational messages.

Third is the problematic of *organization.* Beyond linear transmission of messages occurring primarily within the container of the organization, organizational communication scholars problematize the very notion of organization and organizing by emphasizing that communication behaviors serve to establish and affirm organizations continually via participants' interactions. In this view, organizations are constituted in their enactment and exist as individuals strive to make sense of them (Weick, 1979). In this respect, studies of organizational identities and the organizational properties of language (Taylor, Cooren, Giroux, & Robichaud, 1996) come into view.

Finally, the *organization-environment relationship* is a problematic because boundaries between organizations and society are increasingly indistinct and permeable. For instance, pressures toward globalization highlight flexible and emergent communication networks (Monge & Contractor, 2000; Monge & Fulk, 1999), and in various ways organizations are increasingly viewed as sites for democratic forms of participation and decision making (Cheney et al., 1998; Stohl, 1995). In each instance, pressures from the external environment are indistinct from those within organizations—as can be seen, for instance, with the application of the concept of the "internal market" to all of an organization's activities (e.g., Halal, 1996).

These four problematics serve as useful frames for critiquing traditional organizational communication concerns and encourage the development of additional frames for critique. For example, although the socialization (Van Maanen & Schein, 1979) or assimilation (Jablin, 1987) perspective has resulted in a considerable body of scholarship, and Jablin and Krone (1994) and Bullis (1993) have urged a life-span perspective, most research has focused on newcomers' organizational experiences (for a notable exception, see Kramer, 1993). Importantly, the work socialization/assimilation stage model has been challenged as privileging organizations' over individuals' interests (Cheney, 1987; Smith & Turner, 1995), valuing organizational "real jobs" and devaluing other forms of work (Clair, 1997), and limiting socialization foci to organization-centered dynamics and as a predetermined process (Giddens, 1979; McPhee, 1986). In many respects, the research on organizational socialization spans all four of Mumby and Stohl's (1996) problematics. Furthermore, although this corpus certainly deals with rationality, organization, environment, and (recently) voice, we would additionally frame socialization research as implicitly focused on *relationship*—another prospective problematic for organizational communication researchers. A further noteworthy feature of this research is that it has involved empirical, interpretive, and critical perspectives (Cheney, in press). Ultimately, we might reflect on how postmodern organizational socialization research would look.

Some New Theoretical Understandings of Communication and Organization

Even from our far-from-encyclopedic survey of some key moments and constructs in organizational communication (i.e., systems theory and interpretivism), it is clear that the field is characterized by exceptionally open boundaries. Although one can lament the resulting lack of a clear disciplinary identity (Mumby & Stohl, 1996), this permeability and the ready receptiveness to ideas, whatever their origin, may well be the mark of a new kind of discipline and a source of genuine vitality rather than simple eclecticism. In a world whose contours are increasingly global, what we have described will almost certainly become the pattern of all 21st-century disciplines concerned with social practice. What are some of the new influences just now being felt by organizational communication researchers? Again it is impossible to enumerate them all, but the following can be identified. We begin with a focus on theory and then turn to some topical areas.

Pursuing Elaboration and Refinement of Structurational Analyses

The concept of structuration is the brainchild of a British sociologist, Anthony Giddens (1976, 1979, 1984). Many of its roots are shared by the interpretivism that we have described above, so it is hardly surprising that it would find a ready reception in communication circles (Browning & Beyer, 1998; Poole & McPhee, 1983; Poole et al., 1996; Riley, 1983; Scott, Corman, & Cheney, 1998). Giddens's central idea is that both the structures of society and the day-to-day systems of people at work emerge out of the processes of interpretation of those caught up in activity. As they make sense of their own daily experiences by interpreting the flow of events retrospectively, people attribute meanings to what is happening that unconsciously reiterate the patterns of larger institutional forms. Society is continually being reinstantiated and, as it is, structures of power are elaborated and confirmed, worlds of meaning are legitimated, and society's sanctions are enforced.

One of the central concerns of structurational research in organizational communication has been the implementation of technology into organization. Here again the boundaries between communication and other closely related fields have proven to be fluid. One feature of both communication and noncommunication studies has been the conviction that the properties of technology are not fixed in the developer's laboratory. Technology is a malleable object whose definition is ultimately determined in the context of its use, where it is given meaning in the same way as other facets of experience, through retrospective interpretation. Some of the work studying the implementation of technology employs basically qualitative methods in a naturalistic field situation (Orlikowski, 1992; Orlikowski & Robey, 1991); some follows a more traditional approach of experimentalism, featuring operationalization of variables and a controlled laboratory situation (Poole & DeSanctis, 1992); some exhibits a mixed strategy (Barley, 1986).

Exploring the Potentials for Activity Theory and Translation Theory

Two bodies of theory closely associated with organizational communication but originating in other disciplines are now beginning to make their influence felt in the field; these are activity theory and translation theory. Activity theory is inspired by a Russian school of learning theory elaborated by Vygotsky, Luria, and Leontiev, but it is its reinterpretation by the Finnish scholar (and professor of communication at the University of California at San Diego) Engeström (1987, 1990; Engeström & Middleton, 1996) that has demonstrated its relevance to communication research. Activity theory emphasizes very strongly the material grounding of communication in a context of purposive work, within a physical situation, and mediated by technology. One of Engeström's notable contributions has been to show in his careful analysis of professional dialogue how the worldview of a certain community of discourse is made present in the voices of people belonging to that community as they carry out their tasks. Activity theory aims at uncovering the underlying tensions of overlapping discursive formations that presage and motivate organizational change.

Translation theory emerged out of the sociology of scientific knowledge as a way of explaining how certain views of reality come to dominate and eventually to be taken for granted ("black-boxed," to use the colorful term applied by Latour, 1992). It aims to show how otherwise diverse interests come to be associated with each other to produce networks that take on the single voice of an actor. This work, known in organizational communication studies through the interpretations of Cooren (in press; Cooren & Taylor, 1997, 1999) and Robichaud (1999), thus touches on the essence of organization: its ability to "translate" collectively fragmented human endeavors into a single entity of action. It thus aims to reveal the bases of power as well as to reexamine the ontology of organization.

Understanding Artificial Intelligence and Its Possibilities

Recent developments in the field of artificial intelligence (AI) are now making their influence felt in organizational communication studies. The new concept of computing is called variously *connectionism, subsymbolicism,* and *parallel distributed processing.* It makes the claim that knowledge is not restricted to forms that can be encoded into a symbolic medium such as language to become the basis of cognition (human or artificial). Instead, one of AI's aims is to demonstrate that there is another form of knowledge—subsymbolic knowledge—that is a property of the network of interaction rather than something possessed by any particular node within the network, human or otherwise. This somewhat abstract construction of an alternative form of knowledge has been given a much more recognizable face by Weick and Roberts (1993) and Hutchins (1995), whose careful analysis of teamwork on naval vessels points to the ability of collaborating members to respond successfully to complex environments employing a form of knowledge that they collectively generate, in interaction with technology, that no single one of them can be said to possess, or even to be fully aware of. Weick and Roberts refer to the "collective mind"; Hutchins prefers to call the phenomenon "distributed cognition." Taylor and Van Every (in press) show that the assumption of distributed cognition is consistent with the work of some conversation analysts. The implications of this shift of perspective for organizational research remain to be explored, but it is clear that it entails a radical change in how we view organizational rationality and the role of management strategy.

Seeking the Further Examination of Discursive Fields
In and Around Organizations

Consistent with moves to get beyond the container metaphor for organizational communication, a number of scholars have stretched analyses to include broad patterns in discourse that not only manifest themselves within organizations but also extend beyond the sites of organizations. Research by Deetz (1992) and Mumby (1997b) features the patterns of power that are represented within organizational contexts, such as meetings and narratives, but also are parallel to and influenced by broader patterns in the exercise of social power. Clair's (1997) essay on the colloquialism "Get a real job" is an excellent example of how organizational patterns of power are shaped to some extent by discourses that have a broader cultural life (in the "common sense" of the society). Holmer-Nadesan (1996) shows linkages between certain discourses of human resources management, such as personality testing, and wider cultural knowledge. May (1999) has recently examined the implicit cultural and political assumptions of employee-assistance and wellness programs of many contemporary organizations. Cheney (1998, 1999), McMillan and Cheney (1996), and Cheney and Zorn (1999) have considered how metaphors of the market and the customer/consumer are pervading organizational life today, thus drawing a connection between discourses of marketing and the internal affairs of organizations. Such studies remind us to pay greater attention to the diffusion of knowledge within and between organizations, considering especially how it is that certain ideas come to have the status of trends to which clusters of organizations, whole industries, or entire sectors appeal.

The discursive turn that has marked communication studies over the past decade is almost certainly due to expand as rhetorical, sociolinguistic, semiotic, critical discourse-analytic, and other language-centered perspectives become more a part of organizational communication's mainstream research agendas (see the review by Fairhurst & Putnam, 1999). In part, the trend is the result of innovative research by scholars already identified with the field (Mumby & Clair, 1997), but there have also emerged styles of analysis that reflect other disciplinary imperatives. One case in point is the work of Boden (1994), whose analysis is grounded in the tradition of conversation analysis but who has adapted it to the exigencies of organizational inquiry by introducing the notion of a "lamination" of conversations. This allows her to explore features of the flow of information in an organizational context that would otherwise remain unremarked. Another instance of innovation that began outside the field but is very much in the spirit of organizational communication work is the work of Star and Ruhleder (1996), who explore "boundary objects," or discourse themes among groups where each group holds an object in different significance even though all groups are co-oriented to it. Finally, Czarniawska's (1997) work on the role of narrative in and around organizations is highly sensitive to the dynamics of both internal and external organizational communication.

Coming to Grips With the Material
as Well as the Symbolic Dimensions of Organizational Life

All theoretical perspectives, like all metaphors, have their blind spots or areas that they leave far in the background, largely outside of view (Lakoff & Johnson, 1980). If interpretivism and the discursive turn have a major limitation, at least as they have been influential in organizational communication, it is found in their neglect of the biological and physical dimensions of organizational life. Recently, there has been a reaction against these "interpretive excesses" by some scholars, although thus far this movement can be seen largely outside the community of scholars who ally themselves under the rubric of *organizational communication.* For example, Cloud's (1994) work in rhetorical criticism is helpful in articulating the material constraints on discourse production, as when she considers the resource limits for persuasive campaigns conducted by today's labor unions in the face of still-strong antiunion corporate postures. And Aune's (1997) rhetorical-critical investigations have drawn greater attention to both the material and the symbolic aspects of economic forces. Finally, Ballard and Seibold (1999) have explored both objective and subjective dimensions of time as they relate to our understandings of organizational communication, and sociologist Russell (1996) has enjoined organizational communication scholars to pay closer attention to the *nature of work activities themselves*—the actual types of work being done—as they examine messages, interactions, networks, and discourses.

Returning to the Sociological Roots of Organizational Analysis While
Transforming Its Central Concepts With Insights From Communication Studies

Through most of its history, organizational communication research has offered
relatively little insight into broader institutional concerns: issues that transcend the
domains of distinct organizations and speak to broad social processes and problems (see Euske & Roberts, 1987). As a number of trends mentioned above reveal,
that is beginning to change. Although institution-level concerns have figured more
prominently in sociology (Meyer & Rowan, 1977), what can organizational communication researchers say about organizational mimicry (trend setting and trend
following) or cross-fertilization (across sectors—as when religious organizations
begin to look like businesses and businesses take on characteristics and functions
formerly ascribed to religious institutions), or the diffusion of what counts as practical "managerial knowledge"? In this way, organizational communication scholars can return to the societywide concerns that motivated Marx, Weber,
Durkheim, Simmel, and other founders of organizational theory. Furthermore, a
distinctly communicative approach to these traditionally sociological preoccupations could help explain the ironies, twists, and turns in the transformation of symbols and organizations that have been missing in accounts of organizations that
have often taken social structures for granted.

Seeing Groups as Crucial "Mediating Structures"
in Organizational Communication

Organizational groups invite greater attention from communication researchers
for theoretical, empirical, and practical reasons (Poole, 1998; Seibold, 1998;
Weick, 1979). Theoretically, groups are at the nexus of organizational interaction
and structure. Members' groups have pervasive effects that channel individual
agency yet mediate larger organizational structures in processes that constrain and
condition individuals. Empirically, and owing to dynamics endemic to task
demands and jurisdiction, resource distribution and competition, temporal constraints on performance, multiple levels of operation across groups and organizations (Lammers & Krikorian, 1997), multiparty/multimotive interactions, relational intricacies and power structures, and coordinating/collaborative needs
challenge researchers to untangle the empirical complexities of organizational
groups. Not only do organizational groups abound (e.g., work groups, cross-func-
tional teams, short-term project groups, ad hoc task forces, perennial agenda committees, support and adjudicating groups, executive/administrative teams, quality
and oversight groups—not to mention groups as emergent organizations), but
group-based organizational structures and activities are becoming increasingly
prevalent for philosophical, competitive, and political reasons (Seibold & Shea,
2000). Notwithstanding efforts to apply strong theoretical frameworks to organizational groups (Barker & Cheney, 1994; Poole et al., 1996; Putnam & Stohl,
1996), groups remain much understudied by organizational communication

researchers. Allen et al. (1993) identified only 41 (4.6%) group-related studies among the 889 organizational communication pieces appearing between 1980 and 1991. Cragan and Wright (1990) found that only 9 (11%) of 72 empirical investigations (among a total of 96 articles on group communication published in communication journals during the 1980s) studied groups in organizational settings. After surveying what we estimate to be more than 3,000 articles published in 88 social science journals between 1993 and 1995, Greenbaum and Query (1999) found 311 articles relevant to the subject of organizational work group behavior. Only 27% were natural work group studies, and only 55 were studies of communication in natural work groups. Much more work needs to be done.

Taking Seriously the Adoption of Diverse Perspectives

Organizational communication is on the brink of taking diversity seriously, not only within its traditional domain of North America but around the world. Reaching out to examine the full potential for feminist, multicultural, and multinational perspectives is a worthy pursuit for ethical reasons alone. But this intellectual and practical expansion of the discipline also stands to challenge many of our accustomed ways of thinking about communication and organization as well as to introduce some wholly new ideas. A genuine commitment to this kind of theoretical diversity means not so much reinterpreting newly encountered theoretical discourses—such as feminist analyses of bureaucracy (Ferguson, 1984) or Chinese understandings of socialization at work (Krone, Chen, Sloan, & Gallant, 1997)—in terms of the usual ways of thinking, but seeing what it really means to adopt another point of view on some of our most cherished constructs. Munshi (1999), for example, is developing a thorough critique of the literature on "diversity management" (inside and outside of organizational communication circles), revealing its strong instrumental and neocolonialist biases. Even in supposedly humanistic and sensitive accounts of diversity management and multiculturalism in organizations, most writers are insisting on conformity by the so-called diverse groups rather than taking diverse influences seriously. In the coming years, we should expect studies emanating from a variety of sources that challenge some of our most fundamental notions of rationality, organizational structure, decision making, and relationships.

Emerging and New Topics in Organizational Communication Research

Having considered a number of recent and emerging theoretical developments in organizational communication, we now turn to a brief listing of topics to be explored. Where the topics are familiar, we suggest new avenues of exploration. Where they are new, we simply try to introduce them to organizational communication scholars.

What Count as Organizations: New and Nonmainstream Organizational Forms

Several organizational forms stand in contrast to traditional, vertically integrated organizations. Global, network, and virtual organizations, formed on the basis of partnerships, joint ventures, alliances, flexible manufacturing, and the outsourcing of services, rely heavily on advanced communication and information technologies that enable organizational members to coordinate their actions across space and time (Heckscher, 1994; Monge & Fulk, 1999; Nohria & Berkley, 1994; Powell, 1990; Stohl, 2000). Because these organizational forms emphasize multiparty cooperative work, nonproximate work teams, and strong links between activities and individuals across organizational boundaries, communication processes assume a critical role in our attempts to understand them. Further, such interorganizational and quasi-organizational developments make problematic customary notions of collaboration and competition (Golden, 1993).

Communication researchers will also be challenged to expand the variety of places we "find" organizing and organization. Although we have begun to focus beyond traditional sites (North American corporations and governmental organizations) and on nonprofits, cooperatives, and collectives, the scope of organizational scholarship can undoubtedly widen. Stohl (1993b) outlines three types of international organizations (international governmental organizations such as the United Nations, international nongovernmental organizations such as Amnesty International, and multinational corporations), all of which invite study in the face of globalization. Trujillo (1999) raises the important point that nonmainstream organizations and groups have received little attention from organizational communication scholars. Notwithstanding many analyses in Frey's (1994) edited volume on group communication, we have not seen many studies of labor unions and nonprofit agencies, let alone neighborhood associations, community movements, and street gangs.

Technology, Organizations, and Society

The role of technology is crucial in many issues confronted by contemporary organizational communication scholars, and, because it is interwoven so thoroughly into organizational practice, it cannot be meaningfully separated from the organizational contexts in which it is used. Perspectives such as structurational accounts of technology acknowledge this mutual causality of structure and action, and technology's role in the relation (Jackson, 1996; Markus & Robey, 1988; Orlikowski, 1992; Poole & DeSanctis, 1990). As Barley (1986) has convincingly demonstrated, technologies in effect offer "occasions for structuring" that serve to highlight their "second-level" effects over more narrow and intended ones (see Sproull & Kiesler, 1991, pp. 1-17). The implication for organizational communication researchers is that technology should be considered a fundamental part of organizational communication phenomena, and studies of technology should explicitly consider the role of organizational context (rather than viewing technology as a separate area of study). In this regard, compelling work is being produced at the group (McGrath & Hollingshead, 1994, pp. 7-31), organizational (Fulk, 1993), and interorganizational (Monge et al., 1998) levels. Related research treats technology as a patterned discourse that is seen to shape interaction; indeed, from this broad perspective, frameworks for gathering organizational knowledge, like marketing, are heuristically seen as technologies (Christensen, 1999).

As a consequence, although technological innovation has occasionally been the topic of organizational communication studies, there is now an urgent need to focus on the implications of the transformations that accompany the implementation of new technologies. To this end, we can learn from some of the excellent field studies of organizational work that have been conducted over the past decade (e.g., Trujillo, 1992). This work has once again reiterated the remarkable complexity of situated activities and the complex interaction of human and technological agents, but it has also pointed to the strikingly different images of how to organize that characterize, on the one hand, conventional management thinking and, on the other, the perspective of situated action (Suchman, 1987, 1996). Although such conflicts of imagery are at least as old as the famous Hawthorne studies of 1927-1932, they take on a singular relevance in the present era. The result is the emergence in recent organizational communication studies of cutting-edge research into dispersed organizations (Monge et al., 1998), fluid forms of organization that are not so much networks as "knotworks" (Engeström, Engeström, & Vähäaho, 1999; Krikorian, Taylor, & Harms, 1998), and self-organizing forms of association that are in large part enabled through new communication technologies (Contractor, 1994; Corman, 1997). This is work we can expect to see expand very rapidly as the implications of the Internet's spectacular success are felt (Flanagin, Farinola, & Metzger, in press; Flanagin & Metzger, in press).

Groups and/in Organizations

In light of technological, global, and economic forces shaping organizations today, a focus on group-based structures and processes seems imperative (Poole, 1998). Consider global, virtual, or networked organizations characterized by multiparty cooperative work, nonproximate work teams, and strong links between activities and individuals across organizational boundaries (Davidow & Malone, 1992; Miles & Snow, 1986; Nohria & Berkley, 1994; Powell, 1990). Based on interactions in network (versus more traditional, vertically integrated) organizations, DeSanctis and Poole (1997), identify potential changes in team-based structures, processes, and social identities. They propose that teamwork may undergo such changes as increasingly heterogeneous team membership, shifts in team-based social identification, and less reliance on formal procedures and more on information-sharing technologies. These changes suggest that core organizational communication issues such as organizational identification, team commitment, communication satisfaction, and communicative competence may become problematic, demanding reinterpretation. In turn, this suggests specific communication phenomena that researchers might examine in order to understand more fully changes such as those that might occur in (inter)organizational teamwork. For instance, the study of discourse at the team and organizational levels can help us to make sense of diverse, multicultural teams and organizations; researchers can examine symbols in order to assess degrees of commonality or meaningful differences among members of different cultures; and we can explore cross-team interaction networks as a means of examining factors that enhance or inhibit information sharing.

Leadership: Old and New

As suggested by the prevalence of team-based organization and organizational restructuring noted above, new conceptions of leadership are gaining additional significance. Leadership research is now moving beyond even the popular transformational model (Burns, 1978) to consider what it means when leadership is emergent, negotiated, shared, and facilitative in nature. In management studies, Manz and Sims (1984) have written extensively about the dilemmas of the "unleader." And within communication studies, scholars such as Barker (1993), Fairhurst (2000), Seibold (1995), and Zorn and Thompson (in press) have explored the micro-level communicative aspects of leadership within the team context. From a critical standpoint, of course, it is important to consider the extent to which the reframing of leadership in managerial movements is actually as liberating as it sounds.

Organizing for and Talking About Change

Organizational change and change-oriented persuasion represent important new topics for organizational communication scholars. Lewis and Seibold (1998) delineate the phases of organizational change in explicitly communication-oriented terms: They identify the two broad categories of interaction surrounding implementation (including information sharing, vision and motivation, social support, and evaluation/feedback) and communication-related structures (reward, participation, and role). To some degree, traditional studies of innovation and innovation diffusion (see especially Rogers, 1995, pp. 252-280; but see also Albrecht & Hall, 1981; Bach, 1989) have been supplanted by a focus on change, not because such traditional studies fail to provide continued insight but because of the broad rhetoric of change sweeping organizations today (Zorn, Christensen, & Cheney, 1999). A social critic outside our discipline, Sennett (1998), has called attention to the limitations of our obsession with change in organizations and urges a revaluing of continuity, stability, and loyalty. As with a number of other topics we discuss here, change can thus be conceptualized on several different levels for message analysis—from the distinct change program or organizational innovation to a discourse cohering more or less around a central term or symbol.

We also propose resistance to change as an important area of investigation. Here we refer to both organized (e.g., through labor unions and professional associations) and unorganized attempts to oppose, undermine, or modify managerially driven programs of organizational change. However, so far the topic of resistance has been little explored by organizational communication scholars (for exceptions, see Markham, 1996; Mumby, 1997b; in sociology, see Graham, 1995; in management, see Jermier, Knights, & Nord, 1994). Paradoxically, new forms of resistance to organizational programs may develop as employees are reconfigured as internal "customers" and "suppliers": They may make new demands for participation at work (Cheney, 1999).

New Forms of Network Research

Stemming from a diverse set of concerns with social structure (Bateson, 1972; Giddens, 1976; Homans, 1958; Weber, 1947), network perspectives have flourished under equally diverse positional, relational, and cultural traditions (for an in-depth discussion, see Monge & Eisenberg, 1987). Positional views emphasize the patterns of relations among formally defined positions (in the group, organization, or society). In this view, exchange patterns are largely dictated by the responsibilities that are incumbent on the individual occupying a specific position or role. Relational network perspectives, by contrast, focus on the emergent nature of association among entities (individuals, groups, or organizations) and the resultant networks of relations that are formed. Research in the cultural tradition extends this concern by exploring the establishment, transmission, and reproduction of meaning as facilitated by networks among individuals. Importantly, recent work (Monge & Contractor, 2000) has responded to a call for greater theoretical specificity and rigor (Salancik, 1995), beyond these metatheoretical traditions.

Network perspectives currently enjoy tremendous vitality and growth in organizational communication research. Stohl (1995) demonstrates that multiple, overlapping, and interconnected relationships create and sustain contemporary organizational life. Network theory and analysis have been invoked to examine common meaning in semantic networks (Fiol, 1989; Monge & Eisenberg, 1987; Rice & Danowski, 1993; Stohl, 1993a), cognitive conceptualizations of organizational structures (Heald et al., 1998; Krackhardt, 1987), social influence among individuals (Marsden & Friedkin, 1994; Rice, 1993), the diffusion of innovations (Rice, Grant, Schmitz, & Torobin, 1990; Valente, 1995, 1996), and organizational commitment and turnover (Eisenberg, Monge, & Miller, 1984; Feeley & Barnett, 1996). Network perspectives in organizational communication include interpersonal (Liedka, 1991), intraorganizational (Krackhardt & Brass, 1994), interorganizational (Grandori & Soda, 1995; Mizruchi & Galaskiewicz, 1994; Powell, Koput, & Smith-Doerr, 1996), and multilevel (Seabright, Levinthal, & Fichman, 1992) analyses.

Finally, there is developing work on community-based networks. In recent years, several studies of practical aspects of networking in different cities have appeared. What is especially interesting about these cases is that they rely on both computer-mediated communication and face-to-face interaction. Rogers and his colleagues (e.g., Schmitz, Rogers, Phillips, & Paschal, 1993) have analyzed the highly successful Santa Monica, California, Public Electronic Network (PEN), which was established to promote both knowledge sharing and intergroup interaction. Contractor and his colleagues (1998) have developed a similar system in Champaign-Urbana, Illinois, based on an elaboration of network methodology that links people not only through their own shared information but also through mediating individuals and groups.

Work and Nonwork Domains

Just as changes in society have made organizational boundaries more fluid, so they make for reconfigurations of relationships at work and in the home. The area of study concerned with work and nonwork domains has enjoyed a great revival in recent years in sociology, owing in large part to the well-known work of Hochschild (1983, 1989). Again, working largely within the container metaphor, organizational communication scholars have until recently generally ignored the ways relationships at work relate to those outside of work. But trends such as telecommuting, open-ended work hours for many professions, threats to the idea of a lifelong career, and the growth of wellness programs at work challenge us to examine patterns of organizing activities at home and in public settings outside of places of employment. This is a case where longitudinal and multimethod studies of interaction would allow organizational communication scholars to make important practical as well theoretical contributions.

Ethics

As Redding (1996) noted several years ago, ethics suffers from neglect in organizational communication research and consulting. This is not to say that most organizational communication scholars are without ethical concerns; rather, they have not generally pushed those ideals to the forefront of their analyses and writing. This is certainly evident in most organizational communication textbooks, which tend to give only passing attention to ethical issues.

Here we would argue for the examination of ethics in organizational communication on two broad levels: first, the ethical dimensions of communication-related functions, such as the dimensions of dissent in organizations (Kassing & Avtgis, 1999; Mattson & Buzzanell, 1999); second, the construction of presumably ethical and *a*-ethical or nonethically relevant "spaces" through the invocation of concepts such as "just business" (Cheney, 1998, 1999). In other words, we urge organizational communication scholars to analyze both the ethical dimensions of a problem and the very ways that discourses about ethics and ethical practices in organizations are delineated.

The Local and the Global

Social, economic, technological, and political developments are producing organizational alternatives beyond just the traditional sectors of public, private, and so-called independent while also cutting across industries and nations (Poole, 1997). Consequently, organizational communication should continue a trend toward the study of more and different types of organizations that span nationalities, functional domains, and organizational types (Stohl, 1993b). Furthermore, exigencies from outside the organization demand a rethinking of organizational practices with a simultaneous concern for the local and the global. For instance, Stohl (2000) notes how members of global organizations must manage environmental, technological, and social pressures to become more similar to organizational members from cultures other than their own while also maintaining their own distinct cultural identities. Missteps in this complex identity management can result in disastrous organizational outcomes (Seelye & Seelye-James, 1995).

Increasingly, organizational communication scholarship is turning to case studies that implicate a range of processes related to globalization (which is admittedly and importantly a polysemic term). There are studies on international business negotiations, in which the insights of intercultural communication are crucial to the examination of both the microinteractional and macrocontextual features of interorganizational relations. There are studies of multicultural influences within both "home-based" and transplanted multinational corporations, emphasizing multiple levels of understanding of "organizational culture" (Smircich & Calás, 1987). Studies of differences among national and cultural interpretations of key concepts such as "employee participation" have been conducted within the European Union (e.g., Stohl, 1993a). Studies comparing employee relations and organizational rationality in North America and Latin America have appeared, and there have been case studies of global market and related political pressures on long-standing organizational traditions in the public sector of Sweden (Czarniawska-Joerges, 1994), of private worker-owned cooperatives in the Basque Provinces of Spain (Cheney, 1999), and of indigenous empowerment movements in Canada (Cooren & Taylor, 2000), Bangladesh (Auwal, 1999; Papa, Auwal, & Singhal, 1995), and India (Kandath, Papa, & Singhal, 1999; Papa, Singhal, & Papa, 1999). The studies in India and Bangladesh bring organizational communication scholarship into direct contact with issues of international development while relating to specific questions of local empowerment, feminism, and values-based organizations.

Societal changes of various types pose great challenges for the study of contemporary organizations, but we think communication researchers are well positioned to address issues such as those mentioned here (see also Mumby & Stohl, 1996; Putnam, 1998). We are hopeful that in the coming years the field of organizational communication will offer some of the most intriguing explanations, interpretations, and critiques found in any area of social inquiry.

REFERENCES

Albrecht, T. L., & Hall, B. (1981). Relational and content differences between elites and outsiders in innovation networks. *Human Communication Research, 7,* 535-561.

Allen, B. J., Tompkins, P. K., & Busemeyer, S. (1996). Organizational communication. In M. B. Salwen & D. W. Stacks (Eds.), *An integrated approach to communication theory and research* (pp. 383-395). Mahwah, NJ: Lawrence Erlbaum.

Allen, M. W., Gotcher, J. M., & Seibert, J. H. (1993). A decade of organizational communication research: Journal articles 1980-1991. In S. A. Deetz (Ed.), *Communication yearbook 16* (pp. 252-330). Newbury Park, CA: Sage.

Aune, J. A. (1997, November). *Discourses of inevitability in contemporary economics.* Paper presented at the annual meeting of the National Communication Association, San Diego, CA.

Auwal, M. (1999). *Communication, poverty, and development.* Manuscript in preparation, California State University, Los Angeles.

Bach, B. W. (1989). The effect of multiplex relationships upon innovation adoption: A reconsideration of Rogers' model. *Communication Monographs, 56,* 133-150.

Ballard, D. I., & Seibold, D. R. (1999, November). *A test of the dimensionality of time: Implications for group communication research.* Paper presented at the annual meeting of the National Communication Association, Chicago.

Barker, J. R. (1993). Tightening the iron cage: Concertive control in self-managing teams. *Administrative Science Quarterly, 38,* 408-437.

Barker, J. R., & Cheney, G. (1994). The concept and practices of discipline in contemporary organizational life. *Communication Monographs, 61,* 19-43.

Barley, S. (1986). Technology as an occasion for structuring: Evidence from observations of CT scanners and the social order of radiology departments. *Administrative Science Quarterly, 31,* 78-108.

Bateson, G. (1972). *Steps to an ecology of mind.* New York: Ballantine.

Beniger, J. R. (1993). Communication: Embrace the subject, not the field. *Journal of Communication, 43*(3), 18-25.

Boden, D. (1994). *The business of talk; Organizations in action.* Cambridge: Polity.

Boje, D. (1991). The storytelling organization: A study of storytelling performance in an office supply firm. *Administrative Science Quarterly, 36,* 106-126.

Browning, L. D., & Beyer, J. M. (1998). The structuring of shared voluntary standards in the U.S. semiconductor industry. *Communication Monographs, 65,* 220-243.

Bullis, C. (1993). Organizational communication research: Enabling, constraining, and shifting perspectives. *Communication Monographs, 60,* 10-17.

Burke, K. (1966). *Language as symbolic action: Essays on life, literature and method.* Berkeley: University of California Press.

Burns, J. M. (1978). *Leadership.* New York: Harper & Row.

Burrell, G., & Morgan, G. (1979). *Sociological paradigms and organizational analysis.* London: Heinemann.

Buzzanell, P. (1994). Gaining a voice: Feminist organizational communication theorizing. *Management Communication Quarterly, 7,* 339-383.

Cheney, G. (1987, November). *A rhetorical-critical look at the process of socialization: Or what does it mean to be an "individual" in an organizational society?* Paper presented at the annual meeting of the Speech Communication Association, Boston.

Cheney, G. (1991). *Rhetoric in an organizational society: Managing multiple identities.* Columbia: University of South Carolina Press.

Cheney, G. (1998). "It's the economy, stupid!" A rhetorical-communicative perspective on today's market. *Australian Journal of Communication, 25*(1), 25-44.

Cheney, G. (1999). *Values at work: Employee participation meets market pressure at Mondragón.* Ithaca, NY: Cornell University Press.

Cheney, G. (in press). *Interpreting interpretive research: Toward perspectivism without relativism.* In S. R. Corman & M. S. Poole (Eds.), *Paradigm dialogues in organizational communication.* New York: Guilford.

Cheney, G., & Christensen, L. T. (2000). Identity at issue: Linkages between "internal" and "external" organizational communication. In F. M. Jablin & L. L. Putnam (Eds.), *Handbook of organizational communication: Advances in theory, research, and methods.* Thousand Oaks, CA: Sage.

Cheney, G., & Frenette, G. (1993). Persuasion and organization: Values, logics, and accounts in contemporary corporate public discourse. In C. Conrad (Ed.), *Ethical nexus: Communication, values, and organizational decisions* (pp. 49-74). Norwood, NJ: Ablex.

Cheney, G., & McMillan, J. (1990). Organizational rhetoric and the practice of criticism. *Journal of Applied Communication Research, 18,* 95-114.

Cheney, G., Straub, J., Speirs-Glebe, L., Stohl, C., DeGooyer, D., Jr., Whalen, S., Garvin-Doxas, K., & Carlone, D. (1998). Democracy, participation, and communication at work: A multidisciplinary review. In M. E. Roloff (Ed.), *Communication yearbook 21* (pp. 35-91). Thousand Oaks, CA: Sage.

Cheney, G., & Zorn, T. (1999, January-February). Is serving the customer a noble mission or mistaken ideology? *At Work,* pp. 12-14.

Christensen, L. T. (1999). *Discourses of technology* (Working paper). Odense, Denmark: Odense Universitet.

Cicourel, A. V. (1964). *Method and measurement in sociology.* New York: Free Press.

Cicourel, A. V. (1973). *Cognitive psychology: Language and meaning in social interaction.* Harmondsworth, Middlesex: Penguin.

Clair, R. P. (1993). The use of framing devices to sequester organizational narratives: Hegemony and harassment. *Communication Monographs, 60,* 113-136.

Clair, R. P. (1997). The political nature of the colloquialism, "Get a real job": Implications for organizational socialization. *Communication Monographs, 63,* 249-267.

Clair, R. P. (1999). Standing still in an ancient field: A contemporary look at the organizational communication discipline. *Management Communication Quarterly, 13*(2), 283-293.

Cloud, D. (1994). The materiality of discourse as oxymoron: A challenge to critical rhetoric. *Western Journal of Communication, 58,* 141-163.

Coleman, J. S. (1974). *Power and the structure of society.* New York: W. W. Norton.

Conrad, C. (1999, May). *Bibliographic addendum, 1996-1999 [to Conrad & Haynes].* Paper presented at the annual meeting of the International Communication Association, San Francisco.

Conrad, C., & Haynes, J. (2000). The development of key constructs. In F. M. Jablin & L. L. Putnam (Eds.), *Handbook of organizational communication: Advances in theory, research, and methods.* Thousand Oaks, CA: Sage.

Contractor, N. S. (1994). Self-organizing systems perspective in the study of organizational communication. In B. Kovacic (Ed.), *New approaches to organizational communication* (pp. 39-66). Albany: State University of New York Press.

Contractor, N. S. (1999). Self-organizing systems research in the social sciences: Reconciling the metaphors and models. *Management Communication Quarterly, 13,* 154-166.

Contractor N. S., Zink, D., & Chan, M. (1998). IKNOW: A tool to assist and study the creation, maintenance, and dissolution of knowledge networks. In T. Ishida (Ed.), *Community computing and support systems, lecture notes in Computer Science 1519* (pp. 201-217). Berlin: Springer-Verlag.

Cooren, F. (2000). *The organizing property of communication.* Philadelphia: John Benjamins.

Cooren, F., & Taylor, J. R. (1997). Organization as an effect of mediation: Redefining the link between organization and communication. *Communication Theory, 7,* 219-259.

Cooren, F., & Taylor, J. R. (1999). The procedural and rhetorical modes of the organizing dimension of communication: Discursive analysis of a parliamentary commission. *Communication Review, 3*(1-2), 65-101.

Cooren, F., & Taylor, J. R. (2000). Association and dissociation in an ecological controversy: The Great Whale case. In N. W. Coppola & W. Karis (Eds.), *Connections and directions: Technical communication, deliberative rhetoric, and environmental discourse* (pp. 171-190). Norwood, NJ: Ablex.

Corman, S. R. (1997). The reticulation of quasi-agents in systems of organizational communication. In G. A. Barnett & L. Thayer (Eds.), *Organizational communication: Emerging perspectives V. The renaissance in systems thinking* (pp. 65-81). Greenwich, CT: Ablex.

Corman, S. R., & Scott, C. R. (1994). Perceived networks, activity foci, and observable communication in social collectives. *Communication Theory, 4,* 171-190.

Cragan, J. F., & Wright, D. W. (1990). Small group communication research of the 1980s: A synthesis and critique. *Communication Studies, 41,* 212-236.

Czarniawska, B. (1997). *Narrating the organization: Dramas of institutional identity.* Chicago: University of Chicago Press.

Czarniawska-Joerges, B. (1994). Narratives of individual and organizational identities. In S. A. Deetz (Ed.), *Communication yearbook 17* (pp. 193-221). Thousand Oaks, CA: Sage.

Daniels, T., & Spiker, B. (1994). *Perspectives in organizational communication* (3rd ed.). Dubuque, IA: William C. Brown.

Davidow, W. H., & Malone, M. S. (1992). *The virtual corporation.* New York: HarperCollins.

Deetz, S. A. (1992). *Democracy in an age of corporate colonization: Developments in communication and the politics of everyday life.* Albany: State University of New York Press.

Deetz, S. A. (1996). Describing differences in approaches to organization science: Rethinking Burrell and Morgan and their legacy. *Organization Science, 7,* 191-207.

Deetz, S. A. (2000). Conceptual foundations for organizational communication studies. In F. M. Jablin & L. L. Putnam (Eds.), *Handbook of organizational communication: Advances in theory, research, and methods.* Thousand Oaks, CA: Sage.

Derrida, J. (1976). *Of grammatology* (G. C. Spivak, Trans.). Baltimore: Johns Hopkins University Press.

Derrida, J. (1988). *Limited Inc.* Evanston, IL: Northwestern University Press.

DeSanctis, G., & Poole, M. S. (1997). Transitions in teamwork in new organizational forms. *Advances in Group Processes, 14,* 157-176.

Eisenberg, E. M. (1984). Ambiguity as strategy in organizational communication. *Communication Monographs, 51,* 227-242.

Eisenberg, E. M., Monge, P. R., & Miller, K. I. (1984). Involvement in communication networks as a predictor of organizational commitment. *Human Communication Research, 10,* 179-201.

Engeström, Y. (1987). *Learning by expanding: An activity-theoretical approach to developmental research.* Helsinki, Finland: Orienta-Konsultit Oy.

Engeström, Y. (1990). *Learning, working and imagining.* Helsinki, Finland: Orienta-Konsultit Oy.

Engeström, Y., Engeström, R., & Vähäaho, T. (1999, May). *When the center doesn't hold: The importance of knotworking.* Paper presented at the annual meeting of the International Communication Association, San Francisco.

Engeström, Y., & Middleton, D. (Eds.). (1996). *Cognition and communication at work.* Cambridge: Cambridge University Press.

Euske, N. A., & Roberts, K. H. (1987). Evolving perspectives in organization theory: Communication implications. In F. M. Jablin, L. L. Putnam, K. H. Roberts, & L. W. Porter (Eds.), *Handbook of organizational communication: An interdisciplinary approach* (pp. 41-69). Newbury Park, CA: Sage.

Fairhurst, G. T. (2000). Dualisms in leadership communication research. In F. M. Jablin & L. L. Putnam (Eds.), *Handbook of organizational communication: Advances in theory, research, and methods.* Thousand Oaks, CA: Sage.

Fairhurst, G. T., & Putnam, L. L. (1999). Reflections on the organization-communication equivalency question: The contributions of James Taylor and his colleagues. *Communication Review, 3*(1-2), 1-19.

Fairhurst, G. T., & Sarr, R. A. (1996). *The art of framing*. San Francisco: Jossey-Bass.

Farace, R. V., Monge, P. R., & Russell, H. M. (1977). *Communicating and organizing*. Reading, MA: Addison-Wesley.

Feeley, T. H., & Barnett, G. A. (1996). Predicting employee turnover from communication networks. *Human Communication Research, 23,* 370-387.

Feldman, M. S., & March, J. G. (1981). Information in organizations as sign and symbol. *Administrative Science Quarterly, 26,* 171-186.

Ferguson, K. E. (1984). *The feminist case against bureaucracy*. Philadelphia: Temple University Press.

Fiol, C. M. (1989). A semantic analysis of corporate language: Organizational boundaries and joint venturing. *Administrative Science Quarterly, 34,* 277-303.

Flanagin, A. J. (1999). Theoretical and pedagogical issues in computer-mediated interaction and instruction. *Electronic Journal of Communication/La revue électronique de communication*. [Available online: http://www.cios.org/]

Flanagin, A. J., Farinola, W. J., & Metzger, M. J. (in press). The technical code of the Internet/World Wide Web. *Critical Studies in Mass Communication.*

Flanagin, A. J., & Metzger, M. J. (in press). Internet use in the contemporary media environment. *Human Communication Research.*

Foucault, M. (1972). *The archeology of knowledge* (G. Nakhnian, Trans.). New York: Pantheon. (Original work published 1969)

Foucault, M. (1984). *The Foucault reader* (P. Rabinow, Ed.). New York: Pantheon.

Frey, L. R. (Ed.). (1994). *Group communication in context: Studies of natural groups*. Hillsdale, NJ: Lawrence Erlbaum.

Fulk, J. (1993). Social construction of communication technology. *Academy of Management Journal, 36,* 921-950.

Fulk, J., Flanagin, A. J., Kalman, M., Monge, P. R., & Ryan, T. (1996). Connective and communal public goods in interactive communication systems. *Communication Theory, 6,* 60-87.

Garfinkel, H. (1967). *Studies in ethnomethodology*. Englewood Cliffs, NJ: Prentice Hall.

Geertz, C. (1973). *The interpretation of cultures: Selected essays*. New York: Basic Books.

Giddens, A. (1976). *New rules of sociological method: A positive critique of interpretative sociologies*. New York: Basic Books.

Giddens, A. (1979). *Central problems in social theory: Action, structure, and contradiction in social analysis*. Berkeley: University of California Press.

Giddens, A. (1984). *The constitution of society: Outline of the theory of structuration*. Berkeley: University of California Press.

Glaser, H. (1994). *Structure and struggle in egalitarian groups: Reframing the problems of time, emotion, and inequity as defining characteristics*. Unpublished doctoral dissertation, University of Illinois, Urbana-Champaign.

Golden, J. R. (1993, Summer). Economics and national strategy: Convergence, global networks, and cooperative competition. *Washington Quarterly,* pp. 91-113.

Graham, L. (1995). *On the line at Subaru-Isuzu: The Japanese model and the American worker*. Ithaca, NY: ILR.

Grandori, A., & Soda, G. (1995). Inter-firm networks: Antecedents, mechanisms, and forms. *Organization Studies, 16,* 183-214.

Greenbaum, H. H., & Query, J. L. (1999). Communication in organizational work groups: A review and synthesis of natural work group studies. In L. R. Frey, D. S. Gouran, & M. S. Poole (Eds.), *The handbook of group communication theory and research* (pp. 539-564). Thousand Oaks, CA: Sage.

Habermas, J. (1970). Toward a theory of communicative competence. In H. P. Dreitzel (Ed.), *Recent sociology* (Vol. 2, pp. 114-148). London: Collier-Macmillan.

Habermas, J. (1971). *Knowledge and human interests* (J. J. Shapiro, Trans.). Boston: Beacon.

Habermas, J. (1984). *Theory of communicative action: Vol. 1. Reason and the rationalization of society* (T. McCarthy, Trans.). Boston: Beacon.

Habermas, J. (1987). *Theory of communicative action: Vol. 2. Lifeworld and system: A critique of functionalist reason* (T. McCarthy, Trans.). Boston: Beacon.

Halal, W. E. (1996). *The new management.* San Francisco: Berrett-Koehler.

Harris, R. (1987). *Reading Saussure: A critical commentary on the* Cours de linguistic générale. La Salle, IL: Open Court.

Harrison, T. M. (1994). Communication and interdependence in democratic organizations. In S. A. Deetz (Ed.), *Communication yearbook 17* (pp. 247-274). Thousand Oaks, CA: Sage.

Hawes, L. C. (1999). Dialogics, posthumanist theory, and self-organizing systems. *Management Communication Quarterly, 13,* 146-153.

Heald, M. R., Contractor, N. S., Koehly, L. M., & Wasserman, S. (1998). Formal and emergent predictors of coworkers' perceptual congruence on an organization's social structure. *Human Communication Research, 24,* 536-563.

Heath, R. L. (1994). *Management of corporate communication: From interpersonal contacts to external affairs.* Hillsdale, NJ: Lawrence Erlbaum.

Heckscher, C. (1994). Defining the post-bureaucratic type. In C. Heckscher & A. Donnellon (Eds.), *The post-bureaucratic organization: New perspectives on organizational change* (pp. 14-62). Thousand Oaks, CA: Sage.

Heidegger, M. (1962). *Being and time.* New York: Harper & Row.

Hochschild, A. R. (1983). *The managed heart: Commercialization of human feeling.* Berkeley: University of California Press.

Hochschild, A. R., with MacHung, A. (1989). *The second shift: Working parents and the revolution at home.* New York: Viking.

Hodge, R., & Kress, G. (1988). *Social semiotics.* Ithaca, NY: Cornell University Press.

Hodge, R., & Kress, G. (1993). *Language as ideology* (2nd ed.). London: Routledge.

Holmer-Nadesan, M. (1996). Organizational identity and space of action. *Organization Studies, 17,* 49-81.

Holmes, M., & Poole, M. S. (1991). The longitudinal analysis of interaction. In B. Montgomery & S. Duck (Eds.), *Studying interpersonal interaction* (pp. 286-302). New York: Guilford.

Homans, G. C. (1958). Social behavior as exchange. *American Journal of Sociology, 19,* 22-24.

Houston, R. (1999). Self-organizing systems theory: Historical challenges to new sciences. *Management Communication Quarterly, 13,* 119-134.

Husserl, E. (1964). *The idea of phenomenology* (W. Alston & G. Nakhnian, Trans.). The Hague: Martinus Nijhoff.

Husserl, E. (1976). *Logical investigations* (Vols. 1-2) (J. N. Findlay, Trans.). London: Routledge.

Hutchins, E. (1995). *Cognition in the wild.* Cambridge: MIT Press.

Hyatt, A., Contractor, N. S., & Jones, P. (1997, May). *Computational organizational network modeling: Strategies and an exemplar.* Paper presented at the annual meeting of the International Communication Association, Montreal.

Jablin, F. M. (1987). Organizational entry, assimilation, and exit. In F. M. Jablin, L. L. Putnam, K. H. Roberts, & L. W. Porter (Eds.), *Handbook of organizational communication: An interdisciplinary approach* (pp. 679-740). Newbury Park, CA: Sage.

Jablin, F. M., & Krone, K. J. (1994). Task/work relationships: A life-span perspective. In M. L. Knapp & G. R. Miller (Eds.), *Handbook of interpersonal communication* (2nd ed., pp. 621-675). Thousand Oaks, CA: Sage.

Jackson, M. H. (1996). The meaning of "communication technology": The technology-context scheme. In B. R. Burleson (Ed.), *Communication yearbook 19* (pp. 229-267). Thousand Oaks, CA: Sage.

Jermier, J. M., Knights, D., & Nord, W. R. (Eds.). (1994). *Resistance and power in organizations.* New York: Routledge.

Kandath, K. P., Papa, M. J., & Singhal, A. (1999, May). *Paradoxes and contradictions in organizing for social change.* Paper presented at the annual meeting of the International Communication Association, San Francisco.

Kassing, J. W., & Avtgis, T. A. (1999). Examining the relationship between organizational dissent and aggressive communication. *Management Communication Quarterly, 13,* 100-115.

Katz, D., & Kahn, R. L. (1966). *The social psychology of organizations.* New York: John Wiley.

Krackhardt, D. (1987). Cognitive social structures. *Social Networks, 9,* 109-134.

Krackhardt, D., & Brass, D. J. (1994). Intraorganizational networks: The micro side. In S. Wasserman & J. Galaskiewicz (Eds.), *Advances in social network analysis: Research in the social and behavioral sciences* (pp. 207-229). Thousand Oaks, CA: Sage.

Kramer, M. W. (1993). Communication and uncertainty reduction during job transfers: Leaving and joining processes. *Communication Monographs, 60,* 178-198.

Kress, G., & Hodge, R. (1979). *Language as ideology.* London: Routledge & Kegan Paul.

Krikorian, D. H., Taylor, J. R., & Harms, C. (1998, November). *Knotting by netting: Thread emergence in electronic newsgroups.* Paper presented at the annual meeting of the National Communication Association, New York.

Krippendorff, K. (1999). Beyond coherence. *Management Communication Quarterly, 13,* 135-145.

Krone, K. J., Chen, L., Sloan, D. K., & Gallant, L. M. (1997). Managerial emotionality in Chinese factories. *Management Communication Quarterly, 11,* 6-50.

Krone, K. J., Jablin, F. M., & Putnam, L. L. (1987). Communication theory and organizational communication: Multiple perspectives. In F. M. Jablin, L. L. Putnam, K. H. Roberts, & L. W. Porter (Eds.), *Handbook of organizational communication: An interdisciplinary approach* (pp. 18-40). Newbury Park, CA: Sage.

Lakoff, G., & Johnson, M. (1980). *Metaphors we live by.* Chicago: University of Chicago Press.

Lammers, J. C., & Krikorian, D. H. (1997). Theoretical extension and operationalization of the bona fide group construct with an application to surgical teams. *Journal of Applied Communication Research, 25,* 18-41.

Latour, B. (1992). *We have never been modern.* Cambridge, MA: Harvard University Press.

Lewis, L. K., & Seibold, D. R. (1996). Communication during intraorganizational innovation adoption: Predicting users' behavioral coping responses to innovations. *Communication Monographs, 63,* 131-157.

Lewis, L. K., & Seibold, D. R. (1998). Reconceptualizing organizational change implementation as a communication problem: A review of literature and research agenda. In M. E. Roloff (Ed.), *Communication yearbook 21* (pp. 93-151). Thousand Oaks, CA: Sage.

Liedka, R. V. (1991). Who do you know in the group? Location of organizations in interpersonal networks. *Social Forces, 70,* 455-474.

Luhmann, N. (1990). *Essays on self-reference.* New York: Columbia University Press.

Manz, C. C., & Sims, H. P. (1984). Searching for the "unleader": Organizational member views on leading self-managed groups. *Human Relations, 37,* 409-424.

Markham, A. (1996). Designing discourse: A critical analysis of strategic ambiguity and workplace control. *Management Communication Quarterly, 9,* 389-421.

Markus, M. L., & Robey, D. (1988). Information technology and organizational change: Causal structure in theory and research. *Management Science, 34,* 583-598.

Marsden, P. V., & Friedkin, N. E. (1994). Network studies of social influence. In S. Wasserman & J. Galaskiewicz (Eds.), *Advances in social network analysis: Research in the social and behavioral sciences* (pp. 3-25). Thousand Oaks, CA: Sage.

Mattson, M., & Buzzanell, P. M. (1999). Traditional feminist organizational communication analyses of messages and issues surrounding an actual job loss case. *Journal of Applied Communication Research, 27,* 49-72.

May, S. K. (1999, May-June). Therapy at work. *At Work,* pp. 12-14.

McGrath, J. E., & Hollingshead, A. B. (1994). *Groups interacting with technology: Ideas, evidence, issues, and an agenda.* Thousand Oaks, CA: Sage.

McMillan, J. J., & Cheney, G. (1996). The student as consumer: The implications and limitations of a metaphor. *Communication Education, 45,* 1-15.

McPhee, R. D. (1986, May). *Political and critical perspectives on socialization.* Paper presented at the annual meeting of the International Communication Association, Chicago.

McPhee, R. D., & Seibold, D. R. (1999). Response to the finalist essays. *Management Communication Quarterly, 13* (2), 327-336.

Meyer, J., & Rowan, B. (1977). Institutionalized organizations: Formal structure as myth and ceremony. *American Journal of Sociology, 83,* 340-363.

Miles, R. E., & Snow, C. C. (1986). Organizations: New concepts for new forms. *California Management Review, 28*(3), 62-73.

Miller, K. (2000). Quantitative research in organizational communication: Practices and challenges. In F. M. Jablin & L. L. Putnam (Eds.), *Handbook of organizational communication: Advances in theory, research, and methods.* Thousand Oaks, CA: Sage.

Miller, V. D., Johnson, J. R., & Grau, J. (1994). Antecedents to willingness to participate in a planned organizational change. *Journal of Applied Communication Research, 22,* 59-80.

Mizruchi, M. S., & Galaskiewicz, J. (1994). Networks of interorganizational relations. In S. Wasserman & J. Galaskiewicz (Eds.), *Advances in social network analysis: Research in the social and behavioral sciences* (pp. 230-253). Thousand Oaks, CA: Sage.

Monge, P. R. (1973). Theory construction in the study of communication: The system paradigm. *Journal of Communication, 23*(1), 5-16.

Monge, P. R., & Contractor, N. S. (2000). Emergence of communication networks. In F. M. Jablin & L. L. Putnam (Eds.), *Handbook of organizational communication: Advances in theory, research, and methods.* Thousand Oaks, CA: Sage.

Monge, P. R., & Eisenberg, E. M. (1987). Emergent communication networks. In F. M. Jablin, L. L. Putnam, K. H. Roberts, & L. W. Porter (Eds.), *Handbook of organizational communication: An interdisciplinary approach* (pp. 304-342). Newbury Park, CA: Sage.

Monge, P. R., & Fulk, J. (1999). Communication technology for global network organizations. In G. DeSanctis & J. Fulk (Eds.), *Shaping organization form: Communication, connection, and community.* Thousand Oaks, CA: Sage.

Monge, P. R., Fulk, J., Kalman, M., Flanagin, A. J., Parnassa, C., & Rumsey, S. (1998). Production of collective action in alliance-based interorganizational communication and information systems. *Organization Science, 9,* 411-433.

Mumby, D. K. (1987). The political function of narrative in organizations. *Communication Monographs, 54,* 113-127.

Mumby, D. K. (1988). *Communication and power in organizations: Discourse, ideology and domination.* Norwood, NJ: Ablex.

Mumby, D. K. (1997a). Modernism, postmodernism, and communication studies: A rereading of an ongoing debate. *Communication Theory, 7,* 1-28.

Mumby, D. K. (1997b). The problem of hegemony: Rereading Gramsci for organizational communication studies. *Western Journal of Communication, 61,* 343-375.

Mumby, D. K., & Clair, R. (1997). Organizational discourse. In T. A. van Dijk (Ed.), *Discourse studies: A multidisciplinary introduction: Vol. 2. Discourse as social interaction* (pp. 181-205). Thousand Oaks, CA: Sage.

Mumby, D. K., & Stohl, C. (1996). Disciplining organizational communication studies. *Management Communication Quarterly, 10,* 50-72.

Munshi, D. (1999). *Neo-colonialism in organizational communication discourses.* Doctoral dissertation in preparation, University of Waikato, Hamilton, New Zealand.

Nohria, N., & Berkley, J. D. (1994). The virtual organization: Bureaucracy, technology, and the implosion of control. In C. Heckscher & A. Donnellon (Eds.), *The post-bureaucratic organization: New perspectives on organizational change* (pp. 108-128). Thousand Oaks, CA: Sage.

Orlikowski, W. J. (1992). The duality of technology: Rethinking the concept of technology in organizations. *Organization Science, 3,* 398-426.

Orlikowski, W. J., & Robey, D. (1991). Information technology and the structuring of organizations. *Information Systems Research, 2*(3), 143-169.

Papa, M. J., Auwal, M. A., & Singhal, A. (1995, May). *Dialectic of control and emancipation in organizing for social change: Concertive control systems within the Grameen Bank.* Paper presented at the annual meeting of the International Communication Association, Albuquerque.

Papa, M. J., Singhal, A., & Papa, W. (1999, May). *Organizing for social change through feminist action: The paradoxes and contradictions of communicative empowerment.* Paper presented at the annual meeting of the International Communication Association, San Francisco.

Poole, M. S. (1997). A turn of the wheel: The case for the renewal of systems inquiry in organizational communication research. In G. A. Barnett & L. Thayer (Eds.), *Organizational communication: Emerging perspectives V. The renaissance in systems thinking* (pp. 47-63). Greenwich, CT: Ablex.

Poole, M. S. (1998). The small group should be the fundamental unit of communication research. In J. S. Trent (Ed.), *Communication: Views from the helm for the 21st century* (pp. 94-97). Boston: Allyn & Bacon.

Poole, M. S., & DeSanctis, G. (1990). Understanding the use of group decision support systems: The theory of adaptive structuration. In J. Fulk & C. W. Steinfield (Eds.), *Organizations and communication technology* (pp. 173-193). Newbury Park, CA: Sage.

Poole, M. S., & DeSanctis, G. (1992). Microlevel structuration in computer-supported group decision making. *Human Communication Research, 19,* 5-49.

Poole, M. S., & McPhee, R. D. (1983). A structurational theory of organizational climate. In L. L. Putnam & M. E. Pacanowsky (Eds.), *Communication and organizations: An interpretive approach* (pp. 195-219). Beverly Hills, CA: Sage.

Poole, M. S., Putnam, L. L., & Seibold, D. R. (1997). Organizational communication in the 21st century. *Management Communication Quarterly, 11,* 127-138.

Poole, M. S., Seibold, D. R., & McPhee, R. D. (1996). The structuration of group decisions. In R. Y. Hirokawa & M. S. Poole (Eds.), *Communication and group decision making* (2nd ed., pp. 114-146). Thousand Oaks, CA: Sage.

Powell, W. W. (1990). Neither market nor hierarchy: Network forms of organization. *Research in Organizational Behavior, 12,* 295-336.

Powell, W. W., Koput, K. W., & Smith-Doerr, L. (1996). Interorganizational collaboration and the locus of innovation: Networks of learning in biotechnology. *Administrative Science Quarterly, 41,* 116-145.

Putnam, L. L. (1982). Paradigms for organizational communication research: An overview and synthesis. *Western Journal of Speech Communication, 46,* 192-206.

Putnam, L. L. (1983). The interpretive perspective: An alternative to functionalism. In L. L. Putnam & M. E. Pacanowsky (Eds.), *Communication and organizations: An interpretive approach* (pp. 31-54). Beverly Hills, CA: Sage.

Putnam, L. L. (1989). Negotiation and organizing: Two levels of analysis within the Weickian world. *Communication Studies, 40,* 249-257.

Putnam, L. L. (1998). Metaphors of communication and organization. In J. S. Trent (Ed.), *Communication: Views from the helm for the 21st century* (pp. 145-152). Boston: Allyn & Bacon.

Putnam, L. L., & Cheney, G. (1983). A critical review of research traditions in organizational communication. In M. S. Mander (Ed.), *Communication in transition* (pp. 206-224). New York: Praeger.

Putnam, L. L., & Cheney, G. (1985). Organizational communication: Historical developments and future directions. In T. W. Benson (Ed.), *Speech communication in the 20th century* (pp. 130-159). Carbondale: Southern Illinois University Press.

Putnam, L. L., & Pacanowsky, M. E. (Eds.). (1983). *Communication and organizations: An interpretive approach.* Beverly Hills, CA: Sage.

Putnam, L. L., Phillips, N., & Chapman, P. (1996). Metaphors of communication and organization. In S. R. Clegg, C. Hardy, & W. R. Nord (Eds.), *Handbook of organization studies* (pp. 375-408). Thousand Oaks, CA: Sage.

Putnam, L. L., & Stohl, C. (1996). Bona fide groups: An alternative perspective for communication and small group decision making. In R. Y. Hirokawa & M. S. Poole (Eds.), *Communication and group decision making* (2nd ed., pp. 147-178). Thousand Oaks, CA: Sage.

Redding, W. C. (1985). Stumbling toward identity: The emergence of organizational communication as a field of study. In R. D. McPhee & P. K. Tompkins (Eds.), *Organizational communication: Traditional themes and new directions* (pp. 15-54). Beverly Hills, CA: Sage.

Redding, W. C. (1996). Ethics and the study of organizational communication: When will we wake up? In J. A. Saska & M. S. Pritchard (Eds.), *Responsible communication: Ethical issues in business, industry, and the professions* (pp. 16-40). Cresskill, NJ: Hampton.

Redding, W. C., & Tompkins, P. K. (1988). Organizational communication: Past and present tenses. In G. M. Goldhaber & G. A. Barnett (Eds.), *Handbook of organizational communication* (pp. 5-33). Norwood, NJ: Ablex.

Rice, R. E. (1993). Using network concepts to clarify sources and mechanisms of social influence. In G. A. Barnett & W. Richards, Jr. (Eds.), *Advances in communication network analysis* (pp. 1-21). Norwood, NJ: Ablex.

Rice, R. E., & Danowski, J. (1993). Is it really just like a fancy answering machine? Comparing semantic networks of different types of voice mail users. *Journal of Business Communication, 30,* 369-397.

Rice, R. E., Grant, A., Schmitz, J., & Torobin, J. (1990). Individual and network influences on the adoption of perceived outcomes of electronic messaging. *Social Networks, 12,* 27-55.

Riley, P. (1983). A structurationist account of political culture. *Administrative Science Quarterly, 28,* 414-437.

Robichaud, D. (1999). Looking at organization in communication: Two processes of organizing in discourse: Textualisation and actualization. *Communication Review, 3*(1-2).

Rogers, E. M. (1995). *Diffusion of innovations* (4th ed.). New York: Free Press.

Rosengren, K. E. (1993). From field to frog ponds. *Journal of Communication, 43*(1), 6-17.

Russell, R. (1996, November). *Communication in organizations.* Paper presented at the annual meeting of the Speech Communication Association, San Diego, CA.

Sacks, H. (1989). Harvey Sacks: Lectures 1964-1965 (G. Jefferson, Ed.). *Human Studies, 12*(3-4).

Salancik, G. R. (1995). Wanted: A good network theory of organization. *Administrative Science Quarterly, 40,* 345-349.

Saussure, F. de. (1966). *Course in general linguistics* (C. Bally & A. Sechehaye, Eds.; W. Baskin, Trans.). New York: McGraw-Hill. (Original work published 1915)

Schmitz, J., Rogers, E., Phillips, K., & Paschal, D. (1993, May). *The Public Electronic Network (PEN) and the homeless in Santa Monica.* Paper presented at the annual meeting of the International Communication Association, Washington, DC.

Schutz, A. (1962). *Collected papers* (Vol. 1). The Hague: Martinus Nijhoff.

Schutz, A. (1964). *Collected papers* (Vol. 2). The Hague: Martinus Nijhoff.

Scott, C. R., Corman, S. R., & Cheney, G. (1998). Development of a structurational model of identification in the organization. *Communication Theory, 8,* 298-336.

Seabright, M. A., Levinthal, D. A., & Fichman, M. (1992). Role of individual attachments in the dissolution of interorganizational relationships. *Academy of Management Journal, 35,* 122-160.

Seelye, H., & Seelye-James, A. (1995). *Culture clash: Managing in a multicultural world.* Lincolnwood, IL: NTC Business Books.

Seibold, D. R. (1995). Developing the "team" in a team-managed organization: Group facilitation in a new design plant. In L. R. Frey (Ed.), *Innovations in group facilitation techniques: Case studies of applications in naturalistic settings* (pp. 282-298). Cresskill, NJ: Hampton.

Seibold, D. R. (1998). Groups and organizations: Premises and perspectives. In J. S. Trent (Ed.), *Communication: Views from the helm for the 21st century* (pp. 162-168). Boston: Allyn & Bacon.

Seibold, D. R., & Shea, C. (2001). Participation and decision making. In F. M. Jablin & L. L. Putnam (Eds.), *The new handbook of organizational communication: Advances in theory, research, and methods* (664-703). Thousand Oaks, CA: Sage.

Senge, P. M. (1990). *The fifth discipline: The art and practice of the learning organization.* New York: Doubleday/Currency.

Sennett, R. (1998). *The corrosion of character.* New York: W. W. Norton.

Smircich, L. (1983). Concepts of culture and organizational analysis. *Administrative Science Quarterly, 28,* 339-358.

Smircich, L., & Calás, M. B. (1987). Organizational culture: A critical assessment. In F. M. Jablin, L. L. Putnam, K. H. Roberts, & L. W. Porter (Eds.), *Handbook of organizational communication: An interdisciplinary approach* (pp. 228-263). Newbury Park, CA: Sage.

Smith, R. C. (1993, May). *Images of organizational communication: Root-metaphors of the organization-communication relation.* Paper presented at the annual meeting of the International Communication Association, Washington DC.

Smith, R. C., & Turner, P. K. (1995). A social constructionist reconfiguration of metaphor analysis: An application of "SMCA" to organizational socialization theorizing. *Communication Monographs, 62,* 152-181.

Sproull, L., & Kiesler, S. (1991). *Connections: New ways of working in the networked organization.* Cambridge: MIT Press.

Star, S. L., & Ruhleder, K. (1996). Steps toward an ecology of infrastructure: Design and access for large information spaces. *Information Systems Research, 7*(1), 111-134.

Stohl, C. (1993a). European managers' interpretations of participation: A semantic network analysis. *Human Communication Research, 20,* 97-117.

Stohl, C. (1993b). International organizing and organizational communication. *Journal of Applied Communication Research, 21,* 377-384.

Stohl, C. (1995). *Organizational communication: Connectedness in action.* Thousand Oaks, CA: Sage.

Stohl, C. (2000). Globalizing organizational communication: Convergences and divergences. In F. M. Jablin & L. L. Putnam (Eds.), *Handbook of organizational communication: Advances in theory, research, and methods.* Thousand Oaks, CA: Sage.

Suchman, L. (1987). *Plans and situated action: The problem of human-machine communication.* New York: Cambridge University Press.

Suchman, L. (1996). Constituting shared workspaces. In Y. Engeström & D. Middleton (Eds.), *Cognition and communication at work* (pp. 35-60). Cambridge: Cambridge University Press.

Taylor, B., & Trujillo, N. (2000). Qualitative research in organizational communication. In F. M. Jablin & L. L. Putnam (Eds.), *Handbook of organizational communication: Advances in theory, research, and methods.* Thousand Oaks, CA: Sage.

Taylor, J. R. (1993). *Rethinking the theory of organizational communication: How to read an organization.* Norwood, NJ: Ablex.

Taylor, J. R., Cooren, F., Giroux, F., & Robichaud, D. (1996). The communicational basis of organization: Between the conversation and text. *Communication Theory, 6,* 1-39.

Taylor, J. R., & Van Every, E. J. (2000). *The emergent organization: Communication as its site and surface.* Mahwah, NJ: Lawrence Erlbaum.

Thibault, P. J. (1997). *Re-reading Saussure: The dynamics of signs in social life.* London: Routledge.

Tompkins, P. K., & Cheney, G. (1985). Communication and unobtrusive control in contemporary organizations. In R. D. McPhee & P. K. Tompkins (Eds.), *Organizational communication: Traditional themes and new directions* (pp. 179-210). Beverly Hills, CA: Sage.

Trujillo, N. (1992). Interpreting the work and talk of baseball: Perspectives on ballpark culture. *Western Journal of Communication, 56,* 350-371.

Trujillo, N. (1999). [Review of the book *Case studies in organizational communication 2*]. *Management Communication Quarterly, 12,* 474-476.

Valente, T. W. (1995). *Network models of the diffusion of innovations.* Cresskill, NJ: Hampton.

Valente, T. W. (1996). Social network thresholds in the diffusion of innovations. *Social Networks, 18,* 69-89.

Van Maanen, J. (1988). *Tales of the field: On writing ethnography.* Chicago: University of Chicago Press.

Van Maanen, J., & Schein, E. H. (1979). Toward a theory of organizational socialization. *Research in Organizational Behavior, 1,* 209-264.

Weber, M. (1947). *The theory of social and economic organization* (A. H. Henderson & T. Parsons, Eds. & Trans.). Glencoe, IL: Free Press.

Weick, K. E. (1979). *The social psychology of organizing* (2nd ed.). Reading, MA: Addison-Wesley.

Weick, K. E., & Roberts, K. H. (1993). Collective mind in organizations: Heedful interrelating on flight decks. *Administrative Science Quarterly, 38,* 357-381.

Wert-Gray, S., Center, C., Brashers, D. E., & Meyers, R. A. (1991). Research topics and methodological orientations in organizational communication: A decade in review. *Communication Studies, 42,* 141-154.

Zorn, T. E., Christensen, L. T., & Cheney, G. (1999). *Constant change and extreme flexibility: Do we really want this?* (Beyond the Bottom Line pamphlet series, Vol. 3). San Francisco: Berrett-Koehler.

Zorn, T. E., & Thompson, G. H. (in press). Communication in top management teams. In L. P. Frey (Ed.), *New directions in group communication.* Thousand Oaks, CA: Sage.

CHAPTER CONTENTS

6 Mapping the Domain of Intercultural Communication: An Overview

YOUNG YUN KIM
University of Oklahoma

This essay takes a close look at the domain of intercultural communication and its subdomains, cultural and cross-cultural communication, and distinguishes intercultural communication from related areas such as international communication and cultural studies. Recent theoretical and research developments in the area are examined in terms of neopositivist, systems, interpretive, and critical methodological underpinnings. Five main themes of studies in intercultural communication are identified: intrapersonal processes in intercultural communication, intercultural communication competence, adaptation to a new culture, cultural identity in intercultural contexts, and power inequality in intercultural relations. In addition, studies of cultural and cross-cultural communication are examined in two categories: emic studies of cultural communication and etic studies of cross-cultural communication. The essay ends with a summary of key recent theoretical and research advancements in the area and a discussion of some of the challenges that lie ahead.

THE DOMAIN

Since the 1960s, when this relatively young area took shape, intercultural communication has enjoyed rapid growth and an increasing presence within and outside the field of communication. Within the field, we have witnessed a gradual mainstreaming of intercultural communication. Conference programs of the International Communication Association and other communication associations feature many sessions and individual papers that address issues of culture and intercultural interface in various contexts. In addition, intercultural communication theories and research findings have been increasingly incorporated into communication textbooks (e.g., Beebe & Masterson, 1997; Gudykunst, Ting-Toomey, Sudweeks, & Stewart, 1995; Infante, Rancer, & Womack, 1996). Facilitating this growth have been publications dedicated to theoretical and research development

Correspondence: Young Yun Kim, Department of Communication, University of Oklahoma, 610 Elm Avenue, Norman, OK 73019; e-mail youngkim@ou.edu

Communication Yearbook 24, pp. 139-157

in intercultural communication, including handbooks of international and/or intercultural communication (Asante & Gudykunst, 1989; Asante, Newmark, & Blake, 1979; Gudykunst & Mody, in press) and the International and Intercultural Communication Annual book series (e.g., Tanno & Gonzalez, 1998; Wiseman, 1995; Wiseman & Shuter, 1994). As is the case in most other areas of communication, the intellectual roots of intercultural communication cut across the traditions of various older social science disciplines. In particular, intercultural communication owes its development significantly to the works of anthropologists (e.g., Hall, 1976), psychologists (e.g., Berry, 1980; Hofstede, 1980; Triandis, 1988), sociologists (e.g., Simmel, 1908/1950), and linguists (e.g., Whorf, 1952), among others.

Definition and Boundaries

Scholars in the area generally agree that one element distinguishing intercultural communication from the rest of the communication field is the relatively high degree of difference in the cultural experiential backgrounds of the communicators. Intercultural communication, thus, is commonly defined as the communication process in which individual participants of *differing cultural backgrounds* come into direct contact and interaction with one another. The term *culture* is employed as a label for the collective life experiences of commonly recognizable large groups, such as national and ethnic/racial groups. It is also applied to other smaller, subcultural social groups with discernible life patterns (e.g., groups based on gender, sexual orientation, geographic area, or physical dis/ability). This inclusive conception of culture allows for the viewing of all communication encounters as potentially "intercultural," with varying degrees of "interculturalness" or heterogeneity in the experiential backgrounds of interactants (see Dodd, 1998; Ellingsworth, 1977; Martin & Nakayama, 1997; Samovar, Porter, & Stefani, 1998; Sarbaugh, 1988). Gudykunst and Kim (1997), for example, have employed the concept of "stranger" (Simmel, 1908/1950; see also Rogers, 1999) to integrate various types of intercultural situations (including intergroup and interethnic) into a continuum of interculturalness, with differing degrees of cultural difference, unfamiliarity, and psychological distance involved in specific communication encounters.

Integral to the domain of intercultural communication are the subdomains of cultural communication (which focuses on understanding communication in particular cultural or subcultural communities) and cross-cultural communication (which compares communication in two or more cultural or subcultural communities). Cultural and cross-cultural communication studies have been a vital part of the theorizing and research activities in the area. On the other hand, it is generally agreed that the domain excludes studies of mass-mediated and other technological forms of communication within and across different cultural and subcultural systems. These mediated communication activities are the objects of inquiry primarily in areas such as international communication, comparative mass communication, and media cultural studies. Also excluded are studies of development communication, which address various issues associated with modernization and sociocultural change in traditional societies.

Methodological Approaches

Guiding the current theorizing and research activities in intercultural communication (as well as cultural and cross-cultural communication) are four methodological perspectives: the neopositivist, systems, interpretive, and critical approaches. The prevailing neopositivist methodology emphasizes the "normal science" practices of objectivism, reductionism, nomothesis, and quantitative data (e.g., Gudykunst, 1995; Ting-Toomey, 1988). Neopositivist investigators conceptualize intercultural (as well as cultural and cross-cultural) communication phenomena in terms of predictive, generalizable propositions, often consisting of "independent" and "dependent" variables. Closely aligned with neopositivismis systems methodology (e.g., Kim, 1988, 1995a; Ruben, 1983). Systems methodologists share with neopositivists the scientific goal of arriving at lawlike principles and patterns in human behavior. At the same time, systems theorists emphasize the emergent and dynamic properties of a communication system as a whole, the "structure-function" of its interacting parts, and the system's interaction with its "environment."

The main alternative to the neopositivist and systems approaches is what is broadly called interpretive methodology, which is rooted in the phenomenological tradition. Commonly employed in this tradition are "qualitative" research methods, including ethnographic field studies of different cultural groups (e.g., Broome, 1990; Carbaugh, 1993) or specific intercultural encounters (e.g., Collier & Bornman, 1999), rhetorical analysis of texts and speeches (e.g., McPhail, 1998), discourse analysis (e.g., van Dijk, 1989), and conversation analysis (e.g., Chen, 1998). Branching out from this tradition is critical methodology. Like feminist communication scholars, critical (or "postcolonial") analysts of intercultural communication (e.g., Orbe, 1997; Tsuda, 1986) question the legitimacy of traditional methodologies and engage in ideological critiques aimed at the emancipatory political goals of "privileging" the voices of historically underprivileged groups.

STUDIES OF INTERCULTURAL COMMUNICATION

The above-described four methodological systems underpin the current studies of intercultural communication that focus on situations of direct, face-to-face encounters between individuals of dissimilar cultural or subcultural backgrounds. These studies address one or more of five interrelated and often overlapping themes: (a) intrapersonal processes in intercultural communication, (b) intercultural communication competence, (c) adaptation to a new culture, (d) cultural identity in intercultural contexts, and (e) power inequality in intercultural relations. Together, these themes help to organize the following review of theories and related research activities that have played prominent roles in the recent development of intercultural communication scholarship.

Intrapersonal Processes in Intercultural Communication

A significant number of investigators have focused on intrapersonal (psychological) processes in describing and/or explaining the inherently problematic nature of intercultural communication, notably, stereotype, ethnocentrism, prejudice, and related factors such as racism and intolerance. Extensively investigated in the branch of social psychology called *intergroup psychology,* these intrapersonal factors continue to draw the attention of intercultural communication researchers (e.g., Baldwin & Hecht, 1995; Hecht, 1998). Among the most prominent works in this category are van Dijk's discourse analyses of "prejudicial talk" (e.g., Smitherman-Donaldson & van Dijk, 1988; van Dijk, 1989). Based on analyses of interview data and mass-media messages, van Dijk offers a theoretical account that links micro-level prejudicial talk patterns to the macro-level societal condition of unequal intergroup power relations.

Problematic psychological tendencies and language behaviors such as these serve as examples of communicative "divergence" in the multilayered neopositivist communication accommodation theory developed by Gallois, Giles, Jones, Cargile, and Ota (1995) and its original rendition, speech accommodation theory (Giles, Mulac, Bradac, & Johnson, 1987). Grounded in social identity theory (Tajfel, 1982), communication accommodation theory explains different types of intergroup communication behavior (convergent, divergent, and maintenance) based on the intrapersonal explanatory factor of "accommodative orientation" of interactants. Also included in this theory are factors of "immediate situation" (e.g., goals and addressee focus) and of broader sociohistorical context (e.g., history of rivalry or conflict between groups) influencing the interactants' evaluation of the encounter and future intentions. The theory has generated a substantial amount of empirical research, including a recent study by Petronio, Ellemers, Giles, and Gallois (1998) that focused on the "sociostructural relations between groups" and the individual communicators' "identity choices" contributing to the level of "miscommunication."

In recent years, initial efforts have been made to apply Burgoon's (1995) expectancy violation theory and interaction adaptation theory (Burgoon, Stern, & Dillman, 1995) to intercultural contexts. Focusing on nonverbal behaviors from a neopositivist perspective, Burgoon, Allspach, and Miczo (1997) have reported that, despite cultural differences, communicators tend to enter intercultural encounters with similar relational expectations. In another study, partners in intercultural dyads were found to exhibit more awkwardness and asynchrony initially, but they quickly became as coordinated as their intracultural counterparts

(Burgoon et al., 1998). Similar observations have been made by other researchers from different theoretical perspectives. Chen (1997) has documented, for example, that micro-level "verbal adaptation strategies" are naturally employed by communicators in intercultural dyads in the form of "alignment talk" (Stokes & Hewitt, 1976) and other convergent adaptive behaviors (Ellingsworth, 1988) such as "meaning negotiation" with the use of conversational "repair" and "understanding checks" (Chen, 1998). Relatedly, Varonis and Gass (1985) have reported that "negotiation of nonunderstanding" occurs most often between nonnative speakers, followed by between native and nonnative speakers and between native speakers. Varonis and Gass employ the concept of "face" to explain this finding—that is, nonnative speakers recognize their shared incompetence, which encourages them to negotiate nonunderstandings without losing face.

The theoretical concepts described above that depict intrapersonal processes in relation to intercultural communication behaviors have been incorporated into my own integrative model of interethnic communication (Kim, 1994). In this model, variations in intercultural communication behavior are conceptualized as falling on a continuum between "associative" and "dissociative" behaviors (verbal and nonverbal, encoding and decoding). Behaviors closer to the associative end of the continuum are described as increasing the likelihood of mutual understanding, cooperation, and the "coming together" of the involved persons into a constructive relationship. Conversely, behaviors at the dissociative end are described as contributing to misunderstanding, competition, and the "coming apart" of the relationship. Grounded in a systems perspective, this theory presents a multilayered model consisting of psychological, situational, and macroenvironmental contextual factors that simultaneously interact with one another to influence a given individual's communication behavior in a specific interethnic encounter.

Intercultural Communication Competence

Adding to researchers' efforts to explain intercultural communication behaviors by focusing on intrapersonal processes is an extensive amount of work devoted to the investigation of the notion of intercultural communication competence (ICC). By and large, ICC (and various similar or related concepts, such as intercultural effectiveness, intercultural communication effectiveness, perceived communication competence, linguistic competence, and relational competence) has been viewed as a culture-general phenomenon consisting of a set of factors that facilitate successful outcomes of intercultural communication (e.g., satisfaction and other positive assessments of the interaction and the interaction partner).

Given this general consensus, investigators have offered varying descriptions of ICC that emphasize different constituent elements. For example, Gudykunst's (1995) anxiety/uncertainty management (AUM) theory explains "communication effectiveness" of individual communicators based on three core psychological variables: uncertainty, anxiety, and mindfulness. The theory further incorporates various other psychological factors (e.g., motivation and social categorization) and situational factors (e.g., informality and institutional support) that indirectly affect intercultural communication effectiveness by influencing the three core variables. A substantial amount of research evidence in social psychology and intercultural communication has been incorporated in the development of this theory, as well as in the testing of the proposed relationships among the three core variables (e.g., Gudykunst & Nishida, in press; Kimberly, Gudykunst, & Guerrero, 1999).

Other investigators from both interpretive and neopositivist perspectives have proposed ICC models that emphasize the centrality of cultural identity. Collier and Thomas (1988) offer an interpretive perspective on ICC as an individual's ability to negotiate his or her identities. Likewise, cultural identity is at the heart of neopositivists' conceptions of ICC, including that of Cupach and Imahori (1993), who highlight the ability of individuals to "manage" one another's cultural identities as essential to ICC. A broader theoretical account of ICC from the "identity negotiation" perspective is provided in Ting-Toomey's (1993) multidimensional model of communicative resourcefulness, also referred to as "facework competence" (Ting-Toomey & Kurogi, 1998). Building on her earlier theoretical work on cross-cultural differences in "facework" and "conflict styles" (Ting-Toomey, 1988), as well as on the ideas of several psychological theories, Ting-Toomey (1993) predicts "effective identity negotiation" based on cognitive, affective, and behavioral resourcefulness of communicators in intercultural encounters.

Still other researchers have offered more broadly based models that conceive ICC in terms of a range of communication abilities along cognitive (e.g., cognitive complexity, cognitive flexibility, and mindfulness), affective (e.g., positive attitude, motivation, and sensitivity), and/or operational lines (e.g., verbal and non-verbal skills, listening skills, and interaction management skills) (see, e.g., Chen & Starosta, 1996; Hammer, 1989; Kim, 1991; Koester & Olebe, 1988; Ruben & Kealey, 1979). For example, the systems model of ICC (Kim, 1991) defines ICC as a system of interrelated cognitive, affective, and operational abilities that increase the likelihood of successful communication regardless of the particular cultural makeup of an intercultural encounter. I have argued that ICC is a necessary, but not sufficient, condition of communication outcomes such as "perceived competence" and "perceived effectiveness" (Kim, 1991).

Adaptation to a New Culture

The crossing of cultural boundaries and adaptation to a new and unfamiliar environment has been a salient phenomenon of interest to researchers across social science disciplines for the past several decades. The term *adaptation* and related terms such as *acculturation, assimilation, adjustment,* and *integration* have been employed in investigations of the process through which individual immigrants and sojourners increase their functional and psychological "fitness" in new cultural environments.

Since 1977, when I proposed a "path model" based on a study of Korean immigrants' acculturation in the United States (Kim, 1977), the phenomenon of adaptation has been one of the most extensively investigated research issues in intercultural communication. Building on this initial model, and based on a synthesis of various theoretical concepts and an extensive compilation of empirical data available across the social sciences, I have subsequently developed an integrative theory of communication and cross-cultural adaptation (Kim, 1988, 1995a, in press). This expanded and revised theory is grounded in a systems perspective, which conceives of adaptation as a dialectic process that unfolds over time. In this theory, I propose a process model depicting the "stress-adaptation-growth" dynamic that leads to a gradual intercultural transformation of the individual. The theory further offers a multidimensional structural model designed to predict the rate at which the individual in a particular environment undergoes adaptive transformation. Defining adaptation not as an independent or dependent variable but as the entirety of the phenomenon itself, this structural model identifies key factors that facilitate (or impede) the adaptation process, including factors of (intra)personal, interpersonal, and mass communication, as well as of the new environment and the individual's own background.

In addition to this integrative theory, theoretical models developed in other disciplines, such as Berry's (1980, 1990) psychological adaptation model, have often been employed by intercultural communication researchers (e.g., Kim, Lujan, & Dixon, 1998). Based on the identity orientations of immigrants and ethnic minorities toward their own ethnic group and toward the larger society, Berry's model highlights differential subjective adaptation orientations by identifying four categories: integration, assimilation, separation, and marginalization. An additional psychologically based explanation is offered by Gudykunst's (1998) anxiety/uncertainty management theory, mentioned above. Gudykunst applies the same three core variables of this theory—anxiety, uncertainty, and mindfulness—to explain and predict the adaptation levels of sojourners who cross individualist and collectivist cultural boundaries.

Cultural Identity in Intercultural Contexts

Cultural identity (as well as such related concepts as national, ethnic, ethnolinguistic, racial, and group identity) has received increasing attention in recent years from intercultural communication researchers, coinciding with the rising interest in critical analysis of intercultural communication phenomena. By and large, investigators have conceived cultural identity to be integral to an individual's identity, offering a sense of historical connection and embeddedness and of a "larger" existence in the collectivity of a group. As such, cultural identity has been conceptualized as an essentially uniform and stable social category or a communal entity, with little attention to individual variations within a group and the dynamic, evolutionary nature of cultural identity as it is enacted in an individual's everyday life. Most researchers, from neopositivists (e.g., Ting-Toomey, 1993;

Ting-Toomey & Kurogi, 1998) and interpretive investigators (e.g., Carbaugh, 1993; Wieder & Pratt, 1990) to critical analysts (e.g., Tsuda, 1986; Young, 1996), have treated an individual's cultural identity as if it were an ascription-based, monolithic entity or communally shared symbolic system exclusive to a particular group of people.

Given this prevailing conception, however, recent efforts have been directed toward stressing the complex nature of cultural identity. Collier, for example, has emphasized "identity negotiation" in theorizing about intercultural communication competence (see Collier & Bornman, 1999; Collier & Thomas, 1988). Ting-Toomey (1988, 1993, 1999; Ting-Toomey & Kurogi, 1998) makes a similar point; as noted previously, she places face negotiation at the core of intercultural communication activities. Moving beyond identity flexibility and complexity, I have explained the dynamic and evolving nature of identity from a systems perspective (Kim, 1988, 1995a, 1995b; Kim & Ruben, 1988). As an aspect of my adaptation theory, I have explained that an individual's identity is not a fixed entity, but can be transformed by extensive and cumulative intercultural communication experiences. Accordingly, I have addressed the phenomenon of "achieved identity" (compared with ascribed identity) and have explained the evolution of an individual's identity into an intercultural identity as more than one set of cultural elements are incorporated. In this developmental process, two interrelated changes tend to occur in an individual's self-other orientation: "individualization" (i.e., particularization of group categories) and "universalization" (i.e., transcendence of group boundaries). This systems conception is consistent with Casmir's (1999) model of "third-culture building" as a desirable goal for intercultural communicators. Empirical findings from a number of studies of immigrant and ethnic groups in the United States have provided data that suggest identity transformation, including the study of Asian Indian immigrants in the United States (Boekestijn, 1988; Dasgupta, 1983) and in England (Hutnik & Bhola, 1994), as well as of Cuban Americans (Szapocznik & Kurines, 1980).

Power Inequality in Intercultural Relations

Issues of power and intercultural interaction have gained prominence, spurred by recent works employing critical analysis to challenge some of the existing theories developed from the more traditional methodological perspectives of neopositivist, systems, and, to a lesser extent, interpretive approaches. Critical analysts have tended to question the legitimacy of some traditional theoretical accounts for their inherent "flaw" of reflecting and serving to reproduce the status quo of the dominant cultural ideology within and across cultures, ethnic/racial groups, and genders. In introducing an anthology of essays presented largely from a critical perspective, for example, Gonzalez, Houston, and Chen (1994) state their goal of presenting the perspectives of the authors' own cultural experiences "instead of writing to accommodate the voice that is culturally desirable by the mainstream Anglo standards" (p. xiv; see also Gonzalez & Tanno, 1997; Moon, 1998).

Critical analysts thus place a spotlight on the politics of identity and the subjective experiences of identity conflict and perpetual struggle on the part of nondominant group members as "victims." Collier and Bornman (1999), for instance, focus on the "dialectic tensions in group and individual identity orientations" in studying several historically dominant and nondominant ethnic groups in South Africa. Likewise, based on interviews with a small group of Asian Indian immigrant women in the United States, Hedge (1998) characterizes immigrant adaptation experiences mainly in terms of "displacement," "struggle," and "contradictions" in the "world in which hegemonic structures systematically marginalize certain types of difference" (p. 36). This depiction of adaptation stands in sharp contrast to the "stress-adaptation-growth" dynamic articulated in my own adaptation theory, described earlier. Other critical studies of intercultural communication similarly cast "traditionally muted groups" (Orbe, 1997) in the position of "victims" of power asymmetry rooted in the "oppressive" and "imperialistic" cultural practices of Western civilizations (e.g., Tsuda, 1986; Young, 1996).

STUDIES OF CULTURAL AND CROSS-CULTURAL COMMUNICATION

Complementing the above-described intercultural communication foci are studies of cultural communication (that focus on understanding a particular culture or subculture) and of cross-cultural communication (that compare similarities and differences in two or more cultures or subcultures). Cultural and cross-cultural communication studies have been a vital subdomain within intercultural communication. By and large, cultural communication studies are rooted in the interpretive "emic" (insider or culture-specific) methodological perspective rooted in varying degrees of the philosophical grounding in "cultural relativism." In contrast, the neopositivist "etic" (outsider or culture-general) studies of cross-cultural communication reflect the philosophy of "cultural universalism."

Emic Studies of Cultural Communication Systems

Many investigators have attempted to describe salient features of communication operating within cultural or subcultural groups from the insiders' perspectives. Emic studies are predicated on the conception of culture as a relatively stable "intersubjective" meaning system and are largely atheoretical and descriptive. Whereas neopositivist and systems methodological interests lie in theorizing about universal phenomena into generalizable knowledge claims (propositions), emic studies of cultural communication are often aimed at illuminating the essential features of culture-specific communication practices unique to the particular cultural or subcultural community being studied.

Commonly employed in these studies are interpretive research methods such as ethnographic field study, discourse analysis, conversation analysis, and rhetorical analysis. Among the notable studies in this group are Broome's (1990) study of the core features in Greek interpersonal communication, Carbaugh's (1993) study of Russian "cultural pragmatics" in the context of Russian-American encounters, Chang's (1998) description of "indeterminacy" in Chinese conversation, and Fitch's (1998) analysis of interpersonal communication and relationship patterns in Colombia. Emic studies have also generated descriptions of defining communication features in various subcultural communities within the United States, including an urban neighborhood subculture that Philipsen (1990) calls "Teamsterville," African Americans (e.g., Daniel & Smitherman-Donaldson, 1990; Hecht, Collier, & Ribeau, 1993; Kochman, 1990), Native Americans (e.g., Wieder & Pratt, 1990), and white Americans (e.g., Martin, Krizek, Nakayama, & Bradford, 1996). (For additional emic studies of cultural and subcultural communities, see Carbaugh, 1990.)

Emic analysis has been extended beyond studies of cultural or subcultural communities to the investigation of particular individuals' communication messages in the context of intercultural relations or of particular intercultural communication events. For example, Hall (1994) employed a rhetorical analysis to understand the persuasive message strategies used by the Native American community and the surrounding largely white community in Wisconsin. McPhail (1998) used a rhetorical analysis to examine Louis Farrakhan's messages and to identify patterns of his reasoning on race.

Etic Studies of Cross-Cultural Communication

In contrast to the insider perspective taken in the emic studies described above, researchers undertaking etic studies have adopted the perspectives of objective outsiders in comparing two or more cultural groups and have sought to design their studies based on culture-general theoretical concepts. The objective of such research is to identify cross-cultural variations in communication-related phenomena along certain universal dimensions. Clearly topping the list of such etic-theoretical issues is *individualism/collectivism,* a dimension of cross-cultural variations extensively theorized and researched across disciplines (e.g., Hofstede, 1980; Kluckhohn & Strodtbeck, 1961; Triandis, 1988). The individualism/collectivism dimension is widely employed to reflect differences across societies in cultural values concerning social relations, such as self-direction and self-achievement salient in individualist cultures and in-group loyalty and conformity prominent in collectivist cultures. (For an argument that this conventional theoretical scheme has mistakenly attributed the characteristics of "communalism" to collectivism, see Moemeka, 1998.)

The group-level individualism/collectivism dimension has been extended to a personality equivalent, *idiocentrism/allocentrism* (or "independent-interdependent self-construal"), by Triandis, Leung, Villareal, and Clark (1985). This individual-level dimension, along with the group-level individualism/collectivism dimension, has allowed many cross-cultural communication researchers to account for variations in individual communication behaviors both within and across cultural groups (see Gudykunst & Bond, 1997; Singelis & Brown, 1995). Among the various individual communication behaviors investigated in this theoretical approach are competitive and cooperative behaviors (Oetzel, 1998), conversational constraints (Kim, 1993; Kim & Sharkey, 1995), speaking behavior (Gao, 1998), handling of disagreement (Smith, Dugan, Peterson, & Leung, 1998), silence (Hasegawa & Gudykunst, 1998), embarrassability (Singelis & Sharkey, 1995), facework and conflict style (Gao, 1998; Gao & Ting-Toomey, 1998), in-group and out-group communication patterns (Gudykunst et al., 1992), and anxiety, uncertainty, and perceived communication effectiveness (Gudykunst & Nishida, in press).

Closely linked to the individualism/collectivism dimension of cross-cultural variation is Hall's (1976) theory that differentiates cultures along a continuum from *low-context* (explicit, verbal, direct) to *high-context* (implicit nonverbal, indirect) communication systems. Even though this theory grew out of Hall's own ethnographic field studies, its characterizations of high- and low-context communication systems are closely associated with the characteristics of individualism and collectivism (Gudykunst & Ting-Toomey, 1988). Accordingly, both individualism/collectivism and high- and low-context communication are employed in Ting-Toomey's (1988) face-negotiation theory, which identifies facework patterns in conflict situations in individualist, low-context cultures ("self-face concerns" and "negative face need") and in collectivist, high-context cultures ("other-face concerns" and "positive face need"). The theory then links these differing cultural facework patterns to "direct" and "indirect" modes of conflict style.

ADVANCEMENTS AND CHALLENGES

Although far from exhaustive or complete, the preceding overview has been an attempt to draw a map of the area of intercultural communication as broadly as possible within the allotted space and, at the same time, to place spotlights on those major works that currently constitute the intellectual core of the area of intercultural communication.

Theoretical and Research Advancements

Emerging from these works is a significant trend toward development of a number of broad-based theories that integrate multiple layers of explanatory factors. Theoretical integration is evident in many of the major theories reviewed in this essay, including van Dijk's (1989) theory of prejudicial talk; Giles et al.'s (1987) speech accommodation and its subsequent version, communication accommodation theory (Gallois et al., 1995); Gudykunst's (1995, 1998) AUM theory;

Ting-Toomey's (1988) theory of identity (or face) negotiation and communicative resourcefulness; my own theory of cross-cultural adaptation including identity development (Kim, 1988); and my theory of interethnic communication (Kim, 1994). (For additional integrative theoretical models that have been proposed recently, see Baldwin & Hecht, 1995; Lindsley, 1999.) In varying degrees, each of these theories is interdisciplinary in nature, with its concepts and empirical evidence drawn from other relevant theories across disciplines. Rather than repeating or merely "translating" the works of anthropologists, sociologists, psychologists, and linguists, these theories incorporate relevant existing ideas into a broad framework with a focus on a specific communication phenomenon involving individuals or groups from culturally or subculturally dissimilar backgrounds.

The above review has also shown a substantial advancement in neopositivistetic studies of cross-cultural communication, mainly in providing a great deal of insight into the way the cultural-level phenomenon of individualism/collectivism is manifested in various features of communication behaviors. There has also been a notable increase in the number of interpretive-emic studies of various cultural and subcultural communities and specific intercultural communication events. Employing qualitative research methods, investigators have contributed significantly to a deepening of our understanding of the communication practices unique to given cultural or subcultural communities. Recently, critical analysts have strengthened their presence in the area of intercultural communication. They have raised the salience of the issue of power and power inequality as a fundamental dilemma confronting many intercultural communicators.

Methodological Plurality and Refinements

Justifiably or not, the increasing methodological diversity in intercultural communication studies appears to be fostering a growing sense of division and fragmentation, as well as a need to find better ways to understand, debate, reconcile, and cross-pollinate seemingly divergent knowledge claims made by investigators working from differing methodological perspectives. Martin and Nakayama (1999), for example, have advocated "a dialectical approach to scholarship that facilitates interparadigmatic dialogue and offers new ways to conceptualize and study intercultural communication" (p. 1). Some initial efforts have been made in this regard, including attempts to integrate emic and etic perspectives in the conduct of studies (e.g., Hubbert, Gudykunst, & Guerrero, 1999; Kim et al., 1998) and to nest the traditional interpretive methodology in a critical-postcolonialist perspective (Collier, 1998). Efforts like these should continue as investigators working from differing methodological perspectives strive for greater clarity and refinement in articulating their respective systems of inquiry. It is through such methodological clarity and refinement that the seemingly divergent perspectives may be accurately contrasted and consensus may be reached on at least some basic prerequisite criteria that can serve as a common basis for the appreciation and critique of knowledge claims made across the methodological systems.

To this end, normative scientists (neopositivists and systems investigators) should benefit from continuing to improve on their current research practices. In particular, improvements are needed in the obtainment of samples from outside college classrooms for more accurate representation of given cultural or subcultural groups and in the employment of bicultural or multicultural research teams, which would allow an integration of emic and etic perspectives. More efforts need to be directed to the design and implementation of longitudinal studies of many important intercultural issues, such as the process of adaptation to a new culture, development of intercultural communication competence, evolution of cultural identity, and formation and change in intercultural relationships. The same improvements may also benefit interpretive and critical investigators by making their knowledge claims more rigorously substantiated by generalizable and balanced empirical data beyond historically situated and localized cases.

As cultures and subcultures of the world continue to interface in coming years, and given the recent advances in intercultural communication studies, we may look to the future of this research area with a degree of optimism and confidence. Such an outlook, however, requires a collective resolve to continue to make methodological refinements in search of knowledge claims that can withstand the test of time.

REFERENCES

Asante, M. K., & Gudykunst, W. B. (Eds.). (1989). *Handbook of international and intercultural communication.* Newbury Park, CA: Sage.

Asante, M. K., Newmark, E., & Blake, C. (1979). *Handbook of intercultural communication.* Beverly Hills, CA: Sage.

Baldwin, J., & Hecht, M. L. (1995). The layered perspective of cultural (in)tolerance(s): The roots of a multidisciplinary approach. In R. L. Wiseman (Ed.), *Intercultural communication theory* (pp. 59-91). Thousand Oaks, CA: Sage.

Beebe, S., & Masterson, J. (1997). *Communication in small groups: Principles and practices* (5th ed.). New York: Longman.

Berry, J. W. (1980). Acculturation as varieties of adaptation. In A. Padilla (Ed.), *Acculturation: Theory, models and some new findings* (pp. 9-25). Boulder, CO: Westview.

Berry, J. W. (1990). Psychology of acculturation: Understanding individuals moving between cultures. In R. W. Brislin (Ed.), *Applied cross-cultural psychology* (pp. 232-253). Newbury Park, CA: Sage.

Boekestijn, C. (1988). Intercultural migration and the development of personal identity: The dilemma between identity maintenance and cultural adaptation. *International Journal of Intercultural Relations, 12,* 387-404.

Broome, B. (1990). "Palevome": Foundations of struggle and conflict in Greek interpersonal communication. *Southern Journal of Communication, 55,* 260-275.

Burgoon, J. K. (1995). Cross-cultural and intercultural applications of expectancy violations theory. In R. L. Wiseman (Ed.), *Intercultural communication theory* (pp. 194-214). Thousand Oaks, CA: Sage.

Burgoon, J. K., Allspach, L., & Miczo, N. (1997, February). *Needs, expectancies, goals and initial interaction: A view from interaction adaptation theory.* Paper presented at the annual meeting of the Western States Communication Association, Monterey, CA.

Burgoon, J. K., Ebesu, A. S., White, C. H., Koch, P., Alvaro, E. M., & Kikuchi, T. (1998). The multiple faces of interaction adaptation. In M. T. Palmer & G. A. Barnett (Eds.), *Progress in communication sciences: Vol. 14. Mutual influence in interpersonal communication: Theory and research in cognition, affect, and behavior* (pp. 191-220). Stamford, CT: Ablex.

Burgoon, J. K., Stern, L. A., & Dillman, L. (1995). *Interpersonal adaptation: Dyadic interaction patterns*. New York: Cambridge University Press.

Carbaugh, D. (Ed.). (1990). *Cultural communication and intercultural contact*. Hillsdale, NJ: Lawrence Erlbaum.

Carbaugh, D. (1993). Competence as cultural pragmatics: Reflections on some Soviet and American encounters. In R. L. Wiseman & J. Koester (Eds.), *Intercultural communication competence* (pp. 168-183). Newbury Park, CA: Sage.

Casmir, F. (1999). Foundations for the study of intercultural communication based on a third-culture building model. *International Journal of Intercultural Relations, 23*, 91-116.

Chang, H. (1998). The "well-defined" is "ambiguous": Indeterminacy in Chinese conversation. *Journal of Pragmatics, 31*, 535-556.

Chen, G.-M., & Starosta, W. J. (1996). Intercultural communication competence: A synthesis. In B. R. Burleson (Ed.), *Communication yearbook 19* (pp. 353-383). Thousand Oaks, CA: Sage.

Chen, L. (1997, December). Verbal adaptive strategies in U.S. American dyadic interactions with U.S. American or East-Asian partners. *Communication Monographs, 64*, 302-323.

Chen, L. (1998, December). Repair in the initial encounter: A comparison of native-native speakers' and native-nonnative speakers' conversations. *RASK* [International Journal of Language and Communicaton], pp. 79-107.

Collier, M. (1998). Researching cultural identity: Reconciling interpretive and postcolonial perspectives. In D. V. Tanno & A. Gonzalez (Eds.), *Communication and identity across cultures* (pp. 122-147). Thousand Oaks, CA: Sage.

Collier, M., & Bornman, E. (1999). Core symbols in South African intercultural friendships. *International Journal of Intercultural Relations, 23*, 133-156.

Collier, M., & Thomas, M. (1988). Cultural identity: An interpretive perspective. In Y. Y. Kim & W. B. Gudykunst (Eds.), *Theories in intercultural communication* (pp. 99-120). Newbury Park, CA: Sage.

Cupach, W., & Imahori, T. (1993). Identity management theory: Communication competence in intercultural episodes and relationships. In R. L. Wiseman & J. Koester (Eds.), *Intercultural communication competence* (pp. 112-131). Newbury Park, CA: Sage.

Daniel, J., & Smitherman-Donaldson, G. (1990). How I got over: Communication dynamics in the black community. In D. Carbaugh (Ed.), *Cultural communication and intercultural contact* (pp. 27-40). Hillsdale, NJ: Lawrence Erlbaum.

Dasgupta, S. (1983). Indian immigrants: The evolution of an ethnic group (Doctoral dissertation, University of Delaware, 1983). *Dissertation Abstracts International, 44*, 1938A.

Dodd, C. H. (1998). *Dynamics of intercultural communication* (5th ed.). New York: McGraw-Hill.

Ellingsworth, H. (1977). Conceptualizing intercultural communication. In B. D. Ruben (Ed.), *Communication yearbook 1* (pp. 345-350). New Brunswick, NJ: Transaction.

Ellingsworth, H. (1988). A theory of adaptation in intercultural dyads. In Y. Y. Kim & W. B. Gudykunst (Eds.), *Theories in intercultural communication* (pp. 259-279). Newbury Park, CA: Sage.

Fitch, K. (1998). *Speaking relationally: Culture, communication, and interpersonal connection*. New York: Guilford.

Gallois, C., Giles, H., Jones, E., Cargile, A., & Ota, H. (1995). Accommodating intercultural encounters: Elaborations and extensions. In R. L. Wiseman (Ed.), *Intercultural communication theory* (pp. 115-147). Thousand Oaks, CA: Sage.

Gao, G. (1998). "Don't take my word for it": Understanding Chinese speaking practices. *International Journal of Intercultural Relations, 22*, 163-186.

Gao, G., & Ting-Toomey, S. (1998). *Communicating effectively with the Chinese.* Thousand Oaks, CA: Sage.

Giles, H., Mulac, A., Bradac, J. J., & Johnson, P. (1987). Speech accommodation theory: The first decade and beyond. In M. L. McLaughlin (Ed.), *Communication yearbook 10* (pp. 13-48). Newbury Park, CA: Sage.

Gonzalez, A., Houston, M., & Chen, V. (1994). *Our voices: Essays in culture, ethnicity, and communication: An intercultural anthology.* Los Angeles: Roxbury.

Gonzalez, A., & Tanno, D. V. (Eds.). (1997). *Politics, communication, and culture.* Thousand Oaks, CA: Sage.

Gudykunst, W. B. (1995). Anxiety/uncertainty management (AUM) theory: Current status. In R. L. Wiseman (Ed.), *Intercultural communication theory* (pp. 8-58). Thousand Oaks, CA: Sage.

Gudykunst, W. B. (1998). Applying anxiety/uncertainty management (AUM) theory to intercultural adjustment training. *International Journal of Intercultural Relations, 22,* 227-250.

Gudykunst, W. B., & Bond, M. (1997). Intergroup relations across cultures. In J. W. Berry, M. Segall, & C. Kagitcibasi (Eds.), *Handbook of cross-cultural psychology* (2nd ed., pp. 118-161). Boston: Allyn & Bacon.

Gudykunst, W. B., Gao, G., Schmidt, K., Nishida, T., Bond, M., Leung, K., Wang, G., & Barraclough, R. (1992). The influence of individualism-collectivism on communication in ingroup and outgroup relationships. *Journal of Cross-Cultural Psychology, 23,* 196-213.

Gudykunst, W. B., & Kim, Y. Y. (1997). *Communicating with strangers: An approach to intercultural communication* (3rd ed.). New York: McGraw-Hill.

Gudykunst, W. B., & Mody, B. (Eds.). (in press). *Handbook of international and intercultural communication* (3rd ed.). Thousand Oaks, CA: Sage.

Gudykunst, W. B., & Nishida, T. (in press). Anxiety, uncertainty, and perceived effectiveness of communication across relationships and cultures. *International Journal of Intercultural Relations.*

Gudykunst, W. B., & Ting-Toomey, S. (1988). *Culture and interpersonal communication.* Newbury Park, CA: Sage.

Gudykunst, W. B., Ting-Toomey, S., Sudweeks, S., & Stewart, L. (1995). *Building bridges: Interpersonal skills for a changing world.* Boston: Houghton Mifflin.

Hall, B. (1994). Understanding intercultural conflict through an analysis of kernel images and rhetorical visions. *International Journal of Conflict Management, 5*(1), 62-86.

Hall, E. T. (1976). *Beyond culture.* Garden City, NY: Anchor.

Hammer, M. R. (1989). Intercultural communication competence. In M. K. Asante & W. B. Gudykunst (Eds.), *Handbook of international and intercultural communication* (pp. 247-260). Newbury Park, CA: Sage.

Hasegawa, T., & Gudykunst, W. B. (1998). Silence in Japan and the United States. *Journal of Cross-Cultural Psychology, 29,* 668-684.

Hecht, M. L. (Ed.). (1998). *Communicating prejudice.* Thousand Oaks, CA: Sage.

Hecht, M. L., Collier, M. J., & Ribeau, S. A. (1993). *African American communication: Ethnic identity and cultural interpretation.* Newbury Park, CA: Sage.

Hedge, R. (1998). Swinging the trapeze: The negotiation of identity among Asian Indian immigrant women in the United States. In D. V. Tanno & A. Gonzalez (Eds.), *Communication and identity across cultures* (pp. 34-55). Thousand Oaks, CA: Sage.

Hofstede, G. (1980). *Culture's consequences: International differences in work-related values.* Beverly Hills, CA: Sage.

Hubbert, K., Gudykunst, W. B., & Guerrero, S. (1999). Intergroup communication over time. *International Journal of Intercultural Relations, 23,* 13-46.

Hutnik, N., & Bhola, P. (1994, July). *Self-categorization and response to threat.* Paper presented at the 5th International Conference on Language and Social Psychology, Brisbane, Queens, Australia.

Infante, D. A., Rancer, A. S., & Womack, D. F. (1996). *Building communication theory* (3rd ed.). Prospect Heights, IL: Waveland.

Kim, M. (1993). Culture-based interactive constraints in explaining intercultural strategic competence. In R. L. Wiseman & J. Koester (Eds.), *Intercultural communication competence* (pp. 132-150). Newbury Park, CA: Sage.

Kim, M., & Sharkey, W. (1995). Independent and interdependent construals of the self: Explaining cultural patterns of interpersonal communication in multi-cultural settings. *Communication Quarterly, 43,* 20-38.

Kim, Y. Y. (1977). Communication patterns of foreign immigrants in the process of acculturation. *Human Communication Research, 4,* 66-77.

Kim, Y. Y. (1988). *Communication and cross-cultural adaptation: An integrative theory.* Clevedon, England: Multilingual Matters.

Kim, Y. Y. (1991). Intercultural communication competence: A systems view. In S. Ting-Toomey & F. Korzenny (Eds.), *Cross-cultural interpersonal communication* (pp. 259-275). Newbury Park, CA: Sage.

Kim, Y. Y. (1994). Interethnic communication: The context and the behavior. In S. A. Deetz (Ed.), *Communication yearbook 17* (pp. 511-538). Thousand Oaks, CA: Sage.

Kim, Y. Y. (1995a). Cross-cultural adaptation: An integrative theory. In R. L. Wiseman (Ed.), *Intercultural communication theory* (pp. 170-193). Newbury Park, CA: Sage.

Kim, Y. Y. (1995b). Identity development: From cultural to intercultural. In H. Mokros (Ed.), *Interaction and identity* (pp. 347-369). New Brunswick, NJ: Transaction.

Kim, Y. Y. (in press). *Becoming intercultural: An integrative theory of communication and cross-cultural adaptation.* Thousand Oaks, CA: Sage.

Kim, Y. Y., Lujan, P., & Dixon, L. (1998). "I can walk both ways": Identity integration of American Indians in Oklahoma. *Human Communication Research, 25,* 252-274.

Kim, Y. Y., & Ruben, B. (1988). Intercultural transformation: A systems theory. In Y. Y. Kim & W. B. Gudykunst (Eds.), *Theories in intercultural communication* (pp. 299-321). Newbury Park, CA: Sage.

Kimberly, N., Gudykunst, W. B., & Guerrero, S. (1999). Intergroup communication over time. *International Journal of Intercultural Relations, 22*(4), 1-34.

Kluckhohn, F. R., & Strodtbeck, F. L. (1961). *Variations in value orientations.* Evanston, IL: Row, Peterson.

Kochman, T. (1990). Forcefields in black and white communication. In D. Carbaugh (Ed.), *Cultural communication and intercultural contact* (pp. 193-217). Hillsdale, NJ: Lawrence Erlbaum.

Koester, J., & Olebe, M. (1988). The behavioral assessment scale for intercultural communication effectiveness. *International Journal of Intercultural Relations, 12,* 233-246.

Lindsley, S. (1999). A layered model of problematic intercultural communication in U.S.-owned maquiladoras in Mexico. *Communication Monographs, 66,* 145-167.

Martin, J. N., Krizek, R., Nakayama, T. K., & Bradford, L. (1996). Exploring whiteness: A study of self labels for White Americans. *Communication Quarterly, 44,* 125-144.

Martin, J. N., & Nakayama, T. K. (1997). *Intercultural communication in contexts.* Mountain View, CA: Mayfield.

Martin, J. N., & Nakayama, T. K. (1999). Thinking dialectically about culture and communication. *Communication Theory, 1,* 1-25.

McPhail, M. (1998). Passionate intensity: Louis Farrakhan and the fallacies of racial reasoning. *Quarterly Journal of Speech, 84,* 416-429.

Moemeka, A. (1998). Communalism as a fundamental dimension of culture. *Journal of Communication, 48*(4), 118-141.

Moon, D. G. (1998). Performed identities: "Passing" as an inter/cultural discourse. In J. N. Martin, T. K. Nakayama, & L. A. Flores (Eds.), *Readings in cultural contexts* (pp. 322-330). Mountain View, CA: Mayfield.

Oetzel, J. (1998). Culturally homogeneous and heterogeneous groups: Explaining communication processes through individualism-collectivism and self-construal. *International Journal of Intercultural Relations, 22*(2), 135-161.

Orbe, M. P. (1997). *Constructing co-cultural theory: An explication of culture, power, and communication.* Thousand Oaks, CA: Sage.

Petronio, S., Ellemers, N., Giles, H., & Gallois, C. (1998). (Mis)communicating across boundaries: Interpersonal and intergroup considerations. *Communication Research, 25,* 571-595.

Philipsen, G. (1990). Speaking "like a man" in Teamsterville: Culture patterns and role enactment in an urban neighborhood. In D. Carbaugh (Ed.), *Cultural communication and intercultural contact* (pp. 11-20). Hillsdale, NJ: Lawrence Erlbaum.

Rogers, E. (1999). Georg Simmel's concept of the stranger and intercultural communication research. *Communication Theory, 1,* 58-74.

Ruben, B. (1983). A system-theoretic view. In W. B. Gudykunst (Ed.), *Intercultural communication theory: Current perspectives* (pp. 131-145). Beverly Hills, CA: Sage.

Ruben, B., & Kealey, D. (1979). Behavioral assessment of communication competency and the prediction of cross-cultural adaptation. *International Journal of Intercultural Relations, 3,* 15-48.

Samovar, L., Porter, R., & Stefani, L. (1998). *Communication between cultures* (3rd ed.). Belmont, CA: Wadsworth.

Sarbaugh, L. (1988). *Intercultural communication.* New Brunswick, NJ: Transaction.

Simmel, G. (1950). The stranger. In G. Simmel, *The sociology of Georg Simmel* (K. H. Wolff, Ed. & Trans.). New York: Free Press. (Original work published 1908)

Singelis, T., & Brown, W. (1995). Culture, self, and collectivist communication: Linking culture to individual behavior. *Human Communication Research, 21,* 354-389.

Singelis, T., & Sharkey, W. (1995). Culture, self-construal, and embarrassability. *Journal of Cross-Cultural Psychology, 26,* 622-644.

Smith, P., Dugan, S., Peterson, M., & Leung, K. (1998). Individualism: Collectivism and the handling of disagreement. A 23 country study [*sic*]. *International Journal of Intercultural Relations, 22,* 351-367.

Smitherman-Donaldson, G., & van Dijk, T. A. (1988). *Discourse and discrimination.* Detroit, MI: Wayne State University Press.

Stokes, R., & Hewitt, J. (1976). Aligning actions. *American Sociological Review, 41,* 838-849.

Szapocznik, J., & Kurines, W. (1980). Acculturation, biculturalism and adjustment among Cuban Americans. In A. Padilla (Ed.), *Acculturation: Theory, models and some new findings* (pp. 139-159). Boulder, CO: Westview.

Tajfel, H. (1982). *Human groups and social categories.* Cambridge: Cambridge University Press.

Tanno, D. V., & Gonzalez, A. (Eds.). (1998). *Communication and identity across cultures.* Thousand Oaks, CA: Sage.

Ting-Toomey, S. (1988). Intercultural conflict styles: A face-negotiation theory. In Y. Y. Kim & W. B. Gudykunst (Eds.), *Theories in intercultural communication* (pp. 213-235). Newbury Park, CA: Sage.

Ting-Toomey, S. (1993). Communicative resourcefulness: An identity negotiation perspective. In R. L. Wiseman & J. Koester (Eds.), *Intercultural communication competence* (pp. 72-111). Newbury Park, CA: Sage.

Ting-Toomey, S. (1999). *Communicating across cultures.* New York: Guilford.

Ting-Toomey, S., & Kurogi, A. (1998). Facework competence in intercultural conflict: An updated face-negotiation theory. *International Journal of Intercultural Relations, 22,* 187-225.

Triandis, H. C. (1988). Collectivism vs. individualism: A reconceptualization of a basic concept in cross-cultural psychology. In C. Bagley & G. K. Verma (Eds.), *Cross-cultural studies of personality, attitudes, and cognition* (pp. 60-95). London: Macmillan.

Triandis, H. C., Leung, K., Villareal, M., & Clark, F. (1985). Allocentric versus idiocentric tendencies. *Journal of Research in Personality, 19,* 395-415.

Tsuda, Y. (1986). *Language inequality and distortion in intercultural communication: A critical theory approach.* Amsterdam: John Benjamins.

van Dijk, T. A. (1989). Structures of discourse and structures of power. In J. A. Anderson (Ed.), *Communication yearbook 12* (pp. 18-59). Newbury Park, CA: Sage.

Varonis, E., & Gass, S. (1985). Native/non-native conversations: A model for negotiation of meaning. *Applied Linguistics, 6,* 71-90.

Whorf, B. L. (1952). *Language, culture and reality: Selected writings of Benjamin Lee Whorf* (J. Carroll, Ed.). Cambridge: MIT Press.

Wieder, L., & Pratt, S. (1990). On being a recognizable Indian among Indians. In D. Carbaugh (Ed.), *Cultural communication and intercultural contact* (pp. 45-64). Hillsdale, NJ: Lawrence Erlbaum.

Wiseman, R. L. (Ed.). (1995). *Intercultural communication theory.* Thousand Oaks, CA: Sage.

Wiseman, R. L., & Shuter, R. M. (Eds.). (1994). *Communicating in multinational organizations.* Thousand Oaks, CA: Sage.

Young, R. (1996). *Intercultural communication: Pragmatics, genealogy, deconstruction.* Philadelphia: Multilingual Matters.

CHAPTER CONTENTS

7   "We Are All Natives Now": An Overview of International and Development Communication Research

SANDRA BRAMAN
University of Alabama

HEMANT SHAH
JO ELLEN FAIR
University of Wisconsin—Madison

This chapter reviews the historical and conceptual parameters of the international communication research area, followed by a focus on communication and development. Both parts of the chapter define the scope of the areas discussed, summarize the main theoretical approaches, and present major trends in research. The chapter concludes with suggestions for future research.

D ECADES ago, the question for those studying international communication was how communications turns "others" into "ourselves" (propaganda). Now the question is who we are, ourselves, and where the "other" has gone. As a subject, international communication has moved from "low" to "high" policy; corporations and communities struggle to adapt to conditions created by a qualitatively new information infrastructure, and every social science

AUTHORS' NOTE: This chapter was prepared in two major parts separately by two sets of authors: Braman on international communication and Shah and Fair on communication and national development. Authorship is listed in order of appearance of their contributions. Division 5 of the International Communication Association expresses appreciation to the editor for allowing all three areas of the division's mandate to be represented for the first time. Due to space limitations, the two discussions originally prepared by the authors were shortened and merged into one chapter by Bella Mody, chair of the Intercultural and Development Division of the ICA.

Correspondence: Sandra Braman, Department of Telecommunication and Film, P.O. Box 870152, University of Alabama, Tuscaloosa, AL 35487-0152; e-mail sandra.braman@mail. ua.edu

Communication Yearbook 24, pp. 159-187

attends to "who says what to whom with what effects." The continued importance of Lasswell's formula (Korzenny & Schiff, 1992) is evidence that its development as a research agenda for international communication (Gary, 1996) succeeded. Indeed, this agenda long served the field of communication as a whole. Yet across the history of international communication study, "individual and social" identity has dissolved into a site of conflict, transaction, and accommodation. In this subfield there has thus been a shift from a first-order to a second-order investigation.

When Clifford Geertz (1983) said, "We are all natives now" (p. 151), he meant that the conversations across communal borders of the past now effectively take place across communicative borders within individual identities, and he meant that we all, irrespective of the types of societies from which we come, include within ourselves the mixture of the premodern, modern, and postmodern that has come to characterize the anthropological "native" on the frontiers of a qualitatively changed communication, and therefore social, environment. The second major section of this chapter explores the special contexts of the 5 billion majority of the world's 6 billion population whose communication challenges are studied in the specialization called communication and development.

INTERNATIONAL COMMUNICATION

Definition

After a 19th-century "prehistory" during which journalists thought about news and war, and users accumulated anecdotal evidence about then-new technologies (Headrick, 1990), communication formed its identity after World War I through efforts to understand and manage propaganda (Lasswell, 1927/1971). After World War II, foreign policy goals supported a second surge of interest; the next major section of this chapter explores the development communication literature this phase spawned. Digitization and globalization launched today's third phase, during which international questions have again become coextant with the field of communication as a whole.

Distinguishing international communication as a subfield has always been difficult. Often *international* simply means "not American" (Stevenson, 1994). Such self-absorption is no longer either acceptable or possible. Historically there has been a cost, as when U.S. and British scholars have ignored work on public opinion well-known in Germany by the 1920s (Keane, 1991). Also, research around the world has exploded, in journals such as the *Asian Journal of Communication, Nordicom Review, Journal of International Communication, Australian Journal of Communication, Canadian Journal of Communication, European Journal of Communication,* and *Gazette* and surveys of communication scholarship in different countries appearing in other journals. National and regional associations are getting stronger, international participation in and coproduction of conferences is on the rise, and large-scale comparative research projects are under way.

It can be hard to know where international communication begins (Albarran & Chan-Olmsted, 1998). Important borders are often not those of the nation-state, but intrastate, suprastate, or organizational. Mediated communication in both developed and developing societies (International Telecommunication Union, 1996) is dominated by corporations based elsewhere. The constitutional locus is itself moving to the international level; largely in response to the need to deal with global information flows (Petersmann, 1991), private decision-making entities and contract law are setting precedents for the development of international law (Dezalay & Garth, 1996).

A pragmatic approach defines international communication as communication that flows between nation-states. This distinguishes it from comparative, intercultural, and development communication. Every element, however, has become problematized. Issues include the following:

- *What is the message?* Attention is moving toward the economic and cultural fields in which flows occur and away from the flows themselves.
- *Who is the sender?* Although mainstream media organizations and governments remain important, a wide variety of other types of content providers are also of interest.
- *Who is the audience?* Is the receiver a member of civil society, citizen, consumer, audience, community member, participant in a diffusion process, avatar, intelligent agent, or machine?

Theory

Because the subfield of international communication deals with every phase of communication processes, theories of all kinds (micro, meso, and macro) and at every level of analysis (from the individual to the global) apply. A study of the impacts of messages on decision makers, for example, may draw from cognitive information-processing theory (Suedfeld & Tetlock, 1977), analysis of audience reactions to popular culture may start from cultural studies and reception theory (Lull, 1987), and a look at international constraints on national telecommunications policy making may rely on political economy (Comor, 1994).

Because theories are themselves shaped by and in response to specific contexts, many believe that communication theory developed in one society cannot be applied, at least without adaptation or further articulation, in another. Different types of theories may arise out of disparate intellectual traditions (Kincaid, 1987), as Mowlana and Wilson (1990) show in their discussion of communication theory based in Islamic religious thought. They may also arise out of differing experiences, as exemplified by Ito's (1990) conceptualization of a type of communication that does not exist in Western culture, *kuuki,* the Japanese process of consensus building, and Michaels's (1994) analysis of Australian Aboriginal communications. Even such concepts as Bourdieu's cultural capital need adaptation for use in transforming societies (Palumbo-Liu & Gumbrecht, 1993). The situation is complex, for, as Ito (1990) notes, some Western theories may not apply at all in a country such as Japan, whereas others may apply there but not elsewhere. One concern is that theory developed in relatively stable societies may not be useful in those undergoing change (Downing, 1996; Pye, 1967). For Rosenau (1997), however, the "cascading interdependence" of the early 1980s has become general geopolitical turbulence, and theorists such as Guattari (1995) start their analyses of global communications from this point.

Today's flows are so complex that they are no longer confinable within simple or singular versions of either media imperialism or the free market. There has been a threefold response:

1. The range of flows of interest has expanded. Having begun with studies of mass-media content, research now looks at flows of knowledge structures, organizational form, narrative form, and the hardware and software of the infrastructure itself.
2. Conceptualization of the forces shaping flows has become more complex, including flows within flows (Tracey, 1985), contraflows and disparities between and within different areas of media activity (Boyd-Barrett, 1998), unevenness in the global economic context (Amin, 1993), asymmetries (Straubhaar, 1991), and "swirls" such as the influence of a Japanese serial about a peasant woman in places like Iran and Poland (Mowlana & Rad, 1990). Flows are influenced by such classic processes as gatekeeping (Chang & Lee, 1993), agenda setting (Hu & Wanta, 1993), and framing (Entman, 1991).
3. Communication flows are now understood to occur within structured fields that are replacing flows themselves at the center of attention.

Increasingly, however, there are no flows, as in cases of what is variously called syncretism, hybridity, and *mestizaje* (Martin-Barbero, 1993), in which negotiations occur among multiple cultural, ethnic, and social forces within individual identities. There are also no flows when messages are, effectively, distributed globally instantaneously, making chronopolitics (power over time) of more interest than geopolitics (power over space) (Virilio, 1995). Similarly, today's merger of medium and message—including the economy—eclipses flows. Product innovations today involve concurrent design of both content and the infrastructure needed for distribution and use (Owen & Wildman, 1992).

"Information" entered discussions of international communication when information systems models became popular in the 1950s. Quantitative flow analysis undertaken by political scientists (Cioffi-Revilla, Merritt, & Zinnes, 1987; Pool, Inose, Taksaki, & Hurwitz, 1984) took the "A bit is a bit is a bit" approach to an interest in numbers of messages rather than their content. From the beginning, the "new world information order" debate included explicit concerns about data flows as well as news (Richstad & Anderson, 1981). Today the merger of archival and distribution functions in the global information infrastructure—and of library and information science schools with those of communication—further deepens interest in all kinds of international information flows.

From the perspective of culture, a bit is *not* a bit; content is all. The concept of culture appeared early, as a filter for diffusion processes and as a set of contextual dimensions. Said's seminal *Orientalism* (1978) offered a Foucaultian vision of the production and reproduction of culture, and Wallerstein's (1990) pronouncement that culture is the "battleground of the world-system" marked a turning point. Contemporary analysts, inspired by Bourdieu on cultural capital and habitus, Stuart Hall on identity and power, and Derrida on difference, see culture as critical to global capital.

The state is not only a "sender" but an informational entity itself, reaching modernity concurrent with the building of the global information infrastructure. Public administration as a discipline was launched by a Woodrow Wilson piece of 1887 in which he emphasized the role of information in governance, an insight he acted upon in his position as U.S. president with his vision of ending war with "open covenants openly arrived at" (Blanchard, 1986). Richards's (1993) study of the archival activities of the British Empire suggests that informational control over colonies penetrated more deeply and more successfully than did military control. Telecommunications policy is a key site for states trying to exercise informational forms of power today because the informational profile of a state proscribes its effective boundaries (Braman, 1996). James N. Rosenau (1992) describes the current problematic of state identity as a "puzzle" in which there is a "perplexing globalization of patterns wherein the loci of authority [are] relocated and restructured" (p. 253). In citizenship, individual identity issues merge with those of the state.

Studies of normative media-state relations—how things ought to be rather than how they are—explain some aspects of state behaviors as intervening variables for effects. Thus the four theories of the press (Peterson, Schramm, & Siebert, 1956) and Hachten's (1992) five theories have been important and continue to be so despite their obsolescence.

International relations theory has also turned to "symbolic technologies" (Laffey & Weldes, 1997), beginning with the role of the media in the construction of international realities (Tehranian, 1997). Constructivism, including notions of epistemic communities and consensual knowledge, is increasingly used to study political processes (Checkel, 1998). Theories of organizations as information technologies are applied to international players (Haas, 1990). Recent work has directly addressed the impact of the use of new information technologies on international relations (Deibert, 1997).

Of the many conceptualizations of globalization (Featherstone, 1990), Wallerstein's world-system theory has had the most influence. In Wallerstein's view, the inherently globalizing tendencies of capital create a system out of which nation-states become articulated in response to economic forces. All theories of globalization break from the international perspective by abandoning the latter's state-centrism; nonstate entities are thus also important, including multinational and transnational corporations, nongovernmental organizations (NGOs), and international organizations.

The global is produced and reproduced in the local, where a variety of dimensions can be distinguished for analysis: The local can be understood as geographic (*local*), the site of human agency (*locus*), a cultural and historical environment (*locale*), or surface physical features (*location*), and primary, secondary, and tertiary processes of localization can be distinguished (Braman, 1996). Appadurai (1993) separates *history,* which leads outward toward global universes of interaction, from *genealogy,* which leads inward toward the particularities of the local, suggesting multiple chronopolitical processes in any specific cultural act or identity. Others prefer the term *immediate,* which has the attraction that it can be used for both chronopolitical and geopolitical analysis. *Propinquity* was first used to describe the local in electronic space in the 1970s (Korzenny, 1978). Traditional local knowledge is meanwhile now extremely valuable to corporations anxious to mine genetic information in plants, animals, and organisms with biotechnologies, also informational metatechnologies. Other types of corporations are interested in the local because it is there that blockages of capital and information flows occur and the "cultural discount" is determined (Hoskins & Mirus, 1988).

Theories of cultural or media imperialism are much used. Based on the implications of world-system theory for those in developing societies (dependency theory; Mattelart, 1978), media imperialism theory claims that international communication flows reproduce colonial relationships (Lee, 1980; Salwen, 1991; Schiller, 1971). Debate turns on whether and how media imperialism exists, to whom it applies, whether its existence matters, and how it can be resisted. There are critiques—beginning with the methodological—that there is little work actually being done on the ground, researchers keep returning to a set of aberrant statistics, and specific cases are overgeneralized (Boyd-Barrett, 1998; Chaffee, 1992; Cioffi-Revilla & Merritt, 1981). Hamelink (1983) prefers the notion of cultural synchronization because it acknowledges two-way transfer interactions. Wasser's (1995) study of "Hollywood" films—no longer American except in name—elegantly makes the point that theory can lag behind empirical reality. The discourse of imperialism is described as itself mythic, overly simple, and obsolete in a post-Marxian and poststructural era (Sreberny-Mohammadi, 1995). Lull (1995) suggests that constructivism is more useful today. Meanwhile, the classic view remains: Herman and McChesney (1997) assert that media corporations run the world, Gonzalez-Manet (1988) sees a return of colonialism in new information technologies, and Schiller (1991) and his supporters continue to tell us that his version of media imperialism still applies.

There are multiple ways of thinking of the receiver, each associated with different theories and research practices: member of civil society, citizen, audience, consumer, reader, participant in diffusion processes, contested site of identity, and, now, avatar (identity representation in virtual reality) and intelligent agent (software extensions of individual identity and agency). The audience is now content provider. For the increasingly large proportions of international information flows that are not final products such as books but, rather, secondary inputs into other manufacturing, distribution, and consumption processes (60-80% of all international information flows today are intracorporate), the concepts of sender and receiver do not apply. Rather, analysts must look at all activity that takes place in and through the net, what the French call the *filiere electronique.*

Research

Here only a few dominant, useful, or particularly interesting streams of international communication research can be introduced. There is no one-to-one correspondence between theories and research: Theoretical approaches are at times combined, and each is associated with more than one research method. Too much work has been descriptive and atheoretical; in turn, critique of theory often focuses on its failure to reach research operationalization.

State-Oriented Research

International political communication is communication that tries to influence geopolitical relations—affairs between states qua states—or through which such relations are conducted. The types of political communication used are affected by venue, culture, and the degree to which affairs are conflictual. Communication among nation-states that is ongoing (diplomacy) is different from communication that takes place during conflict that is low intensity (public diplomacy, propaganda, intelligence), medium intensity, (terrorism, revolution), or high intensity (arms and arms control) (Frederick, 1993).

Formalized rules for diplomatic communication were established as part of the reification of the modern nation-state, early in the 19th century (Tran, 1987); under these rules, only "official" speakers can speak. Thus some contemporary work looks at uses of the media by diplomats and efforts on the part of the media to fulfill diplomatic roles (Davison, 1997). The low-intensity conflict of the Cold War introduced the concept of public diplomacy as communication with entire peoples in efforts to affect their governments; the United States is also the target of such efforts (Manheim, 1994).

Public diplomacy is one point on a scale of political persuasion at the end of which is propaganda, intentional efforts to shape public opinion as distinct from the structural effects of the influence of media imperialism (Jowett & O'Donnell, 1992). The two perspectives come together in their interest in the images of states. This staple of the field is of long-standing interest (Buchanan & Cantril, 1953; Messaris, 1993) and is sometimes today known as *cognitive-strategic research* (Herrmann & Fischerkeller, 1995). Several streams of literature look at factors affecting the internal identity of the state, including interactions between ethnicity and geopolitical relations (Cunningham & Jacka, 1996) and new forms of community in the net environment (Elkins, 1997).

Certainly national security concerns have been an influence throughout (Simpson, 1994). Today the illusions, interpretation, and verification exercises associated with the use of mandated information flows for peacekeeping purposes—called confidence- and security-building measures (CSBMs) in arms-control parlance—are a central site for the struggle for transparency in international information flows. The Gulf War is understood as narrative as much as it has been studied as a military operation (Dufour-Gompers, 1992). Weapons and the practice of war have also been transformed by the use of new information technologies (DeLanda, 1991; Dudley, 1991).

"Unofficial" content providers include terrorists (Paletz & Schmid, 1992), revolutionary movements (Sussman, 1993), indigenous groups (Michaels, 1994), the women's movement (Viezzer, 1986), and others (Boyd, 1991). In the Internet environment, everyone who has a Web page, sends messages to a list, shows up in virtual reality, or participates in chat is a player in the media world; thus the range of content of importance, too, has expanded beyond those products and services traditionally conceived of as commodities.

Flow Studies

Flow studies examine the directions, quantities, and content of communications between states. The complexities of analyses of contemporary flows have been described above. Key early work explored biases in news flows (Galtung & Ruge, 1965; Hester, 1971) and factors shaping those biases (Hester, 1973; Peterson, 1979). Entertainment flows were soon studied as well (Pool, 1977; Varis, 1992). By the mid-1980s, so many flow studies had been conducted that meta-analyses began to appear (Elasmar & Hunter, 1997; Hur, 1984; McQuail, 1986; Wu, 1998). The digital mixture of data types now generally referred to as *the net* was first known as transborder data flow; methodologies are still being developed for analysis of flow in the environment of the Internet. Global and regional flow dynamics interact (Kim & Barnett, 1996), requiring multistep analyses (Sepstrup, 1989). Other recent trends include a historical turn and an absorption in flows about and directed at Americans.

Narrative forms flow. Each type of content is received differently within as well as across societies (Roeh & Cohen, 1992). Even within a genre there can be significant structural variants as well as surface particularities (Cooper-Chen, 1994). Narrative styles change in response to media exposure and political conditions (Chan & Lee, 1991). Genre is equated with niche, whether in the marketplace (Liebes & Livingstone, 1998), in the political environment (Blommaert, 1990), or in relationships between the two (Snyder, Willenborg, & Watt, 1991). Genre is evolving rapidly on the World Wide Web (Aune, 1997), and Elmer (1997) notes that in that environment, links from one Web page to another, a form of citation, serve as both genre and medium. Narrative form is important because it structures cognition. Other ways of transmitting knowledge structures are also global flows of interest in today's environment, such as publishing (Kobrak & Luey, 1992) and research and development (Pearce & Singh, 1992).

Because organizations can be seen as information technologies, the diffusion of organizational form and development of transnational and multinational corporations are also flows of interest (Strang & Soule, 1998). There has been a lot of work conducted concerning the diverse ways in which media firms have become internationalized as well as the impacts of new information technologies on firms of all kinds (Hoskins, McFadyen, & Finn, 1996). Although some studies of multinational and transnational organizations ignore cultural difference altogether, the more useful look at cultural difference both within firms and within the cultures in which they operate (De Bernardy, Boisgontier, & Goyet, 1993). Studies of networked interpersonal, intrapersonal, and small group communications within organizations—the literatures of computer-mediated communication, computer-supported cooperative work, group decision support systems, and the like—are also pertinent to the understanding of international communication today (Walther, 1997).

Audiences, too, flow. Thus there is a nascent literature on migration as communication (Castles, 1998) and a burgeoning one on tourism (Pearce & Butler, 1992). And, finally, trade in information goods and services now drives economic arrangements and conflicts. The General Agreement on Trade in Services, the World Trade Organization, and international intellectual property rights law cover both the hardware and the software of the infrastructure and the international information flows of both final products and production inputs that are its content (Braman, 1990; Drake & Nicolaides, 1992).

Globally Oriented Research

Myriad studies have looked at the impact of globalization on specific cultures or settings. One stream of work debates the possibility and/or reality of global civil society: Waterman (1990) says yes, Sparks (1998) says no, and Hallin and Mancini (1991) say yes, but only for short moments. Another looks at the all-important international and global regulatory structures for what is now clearly a single global information infrastructure (Branscomb, 1986). In this environment, meta-analyses of comparative studies have gained in value for policy makers who must now reach consensual and effective agreement with players from many states in order even to operate domestically (Mansell, 1994; Mody, Straubhaar, & Bauer, 1995). Cyberspace is seen by political economists and those in cultural studies as a frontier for new types of community identity as well as a venue for contestation over identity among communities that are geopolitically or ethnically based (Mitra, 1997).

Many content flow studies are intended to find support for or to disprove the media imperialism thesis, although it is impossible to reach conclusions about effects by looking at either content or quantities. Other research on media imperialism has included attention to such diverse matters as analysis of the impact of American television on Latin Americans (Beltran, 1978), radio wars between Cuba and the United States (Frederick, 1986), and the semiology of popular culture (Dorfman & Mattelart, 1975), what Eco (1990) refers to as "semiological guerrilla warfare."

Methodology

Many methodological issues raised by international communication research are endemic, such as the difficulties raised by efforts to achieve equivalence across cultures (Halloran, 1995). There are inconsistencies; as Chaffee (1992) notes, for example, whereas effects in other societies are explained by media imperialism theories, those in the United States are generally addressed with cognitive information-processing theories. Little has been done to develop research methods from theories based in non-Western cultures, although Blake (1997) offers Afrocentric rhetorical analysis. The engagement of feminist theory with international communication (Hegde, 1998) may bring innovations in research methods.

Some descriptive work is necessary—inductive analysis of unknown ground is an important stage in the life of a research question, and the phenomena and processes being studied are endlessly varied and constantly changing. Such work is not, however, sufficient: Lerner's *The Passing of Traditional Society* (1958) was based on data collected 8 years before the conceptual framework emerged (Golding, 1974). As others have noted, mere accumulations of such work are essentially pointless.

Concern about the quality of quantitative data focuses on their inability to deal with issues of equity, non-state-oriented globalization processes (Beck, 1992), or the "thick" dimensions of the local. There are access issues: Data don't exist, aren't comparable, or are inaccessible by law, culture, or institutional intention or failure. There is a need for more longitudinal analyses and midrange work. Funding has an impact; Sreberny-Mohammadi (1995) notes that large-scale projects have declined since UNESCO funding dropped, and a BBC researcher admits that even that organization's surveys are too random and ad hoc (Mytton, 1993).

Theoretical developments demand methodological adaptation and invention. Effects research has assumed a stable and passive audience receiving changing messages, but international communication researchers are often looking at active and changing audiences who may be receiving stable message flows (Chaffee, 1992). The global/local assemblage encourages the use of qualitative research methods, with the "local" sited variously in the body (Ang, 1990), the home (Gumpert & Drucker, 1998), and the city (Jussawalla, Toh, & Low, 1992).

Among the many things to be learned from Michaels (1994) is that the first and most difficult task may be to figure out not which questions to ask, but which questions are even possible. Moral issues arise from the Hawthorne effect, the impact on a society of questions asked, although one NGO (Canada-based IDRC) has foregrounded use of this effect in research design as a selling point with policy makers. Too many research products sit in libraries in the developed world, inaccessible to planners in the societies studied (O'Brien, 1983).

Summary

The ideal for international communication has changed several times since the middle of the 19th century; the late 19th century saw efforts on the part of media organizations to distinguish themselves institutionally as autonomous, or "free." Since the close of World War I, the United States has promoted the international goal of the "free flow of information." Developing society experience shifted attention from the late 1960s on to the "free and balanced flow of information" as an orienting goal. In the 1990s, the target became "transparency."

With transparency come problems of identity. Because there is no mirror, we cannot see ourselves. It is possible to gaze through the transparency, but what we see may be fractured, or refracted, or the dimensions may be confused. More information is not necessarily better information, and its granularity can be manipulated according to political, economic, and technological constraints and desires.

Rather than doing research on how entities with agency construct images with their messages for intended effect, whether political or social or commercial, the problem for international communication research has shifted to that of identifying the locus of agency itself. This locus, "identity," may be multiple, shifting, permeable, and self-contradictory (Hall, 1996). In Lalvani's (1995) terms, both international communication and its study are now processes of "consuming the exotic other—and the 'other' remains ourselves."

COMMUNICATION IN DEVELOPING COUNTRIES

On January 20, 1949, U.S. President Harry S Truman announced the formation of policy intended to make the benefits and advances of Western science, technology, and progress available to the "underdeveloped areas" of the world. So began the era of development.[1]

In practical terms, making Western benefits and advances available to "underdeveloped areas" to relieve these regions of the burden of being "underdeveloped,"—the ideology of modernization—involved a wholesale transfer and infusion of U.S. and European cultural assumptions, political premises, and economic values. But modernization has been and is more than political and economic endeavor. Modernization is a perception, a way of imagining the world and so managing social order. At a discursive level, Truman's declaration that certain areas of the world—and by extension their cultures and peoples—were "underdeveloped" reinforced an old, often-used hierarchy of pitting "us" against "them" to justify Western intervention on behalf of development in much the same way that

Christian, then Western, imperialism and colonization had been rationalized (Amin, 1989; Memmi, 1965; Mudimbe, 1988; Said, 1978).

During this post-World War II era, policy makers began to view mass communication as a powerful modernizing force. Guided by concerns over communist intrusion into Africa, Asia, the Middle East, and Latin America, U.S. government offices and international organizations were keen to fund research investigating links between communication and socioeconomic change (Samarajiwa, 1987). Thus the field of mass communication and national development emerged. In the following pages, we provide an overview of mass communication and development research, highlighting its conceptual and historical parameters, major theoretical approaches, and current research trends.

Defining National Development

Development refers to the operational implementation of modernization ideology in the nation-state. For decades now, social scientists have constructed elaborate theories to dissect and measure various aspects of development. Politicians likewise have pursued development strategies and projects. While social scientists and politicians have tinkered with the specifics of development, its measurement and application, the need for development—whether top-down, participatory, socialist, basic-needs oriented—has remained largely unquestioned. Thus, in the social imaginary, development has become powerful in its ability to organize cultural practices and representations as well as political and economic spheres (Escobar, 1995, pp. 3-20; Tomlinson, 1991, pp. 154-169).

Despite the West's emphasis on the development of the developing world, many critics suggest that the search for mass prosperity has failed.[2] Indeed, regional inequalities, both macro and micro, have widened. For example, in 1960, the world's top 20% possessed wealth 30 times that of the bottom 20%, whereas in 1989, the upper 20% had nearly 60% more (U.N. Development Program, 1992, p. 34). The 1980s, popularly labeled by journalists the "lost decade,"[3] was for the Third World a period of crushing foreign debt, budget deficits, capital flight, falling commodity prices, declines in foreign assistance, and structural adjustment (Bradshaw & Wahl, 1991; Brown & Tiffen, 1992; Glasberg & Ward, 1993; Watson & McCluskie, 1994). Still, the idea and policies of development persist, although it is continually transformed to account for changing global economic and political trends (Mehmet, 1995; Waters, 1995).

Indeed, the policy and practice of development, which originate in the ideology of modernization, are often traced back to U.S. plans to revitalize Europe after much of the continent was destroyed during World War II. But a case can be made for tracing the lineage of modernization ideology much further back in history than 1945. In fact, Luke (1990) suggests that the notion of "modernization" represents only "the latest sophistication" in a long chain of "imperialistic language to suit new political relations with the developing countries" (p. 222). The first of these sophistications was the idea of Christianization of newly "discovered" populations in Africa, Asia, and Latin America. As early as the 16th century—and earlier, if we include the Crusades to what we now call the Middle East—European nations embarked on religious missions to the "new worlds," their mission to bring the light of the Christian God to these regions and to save souls. The dawn of the Enlightenment created a need for a secular version of Christianization that could be used to argue for "objective" and "rational" reasons for continued Western dominance of Third World countries.

This new sophistication was called Westernization. Through what was understood in the West to be the rationale of objective indicators, the West was "defined as the cultural center of the world, from which all other regions borrowed or learned in order to evolve or progress" (Luke, 1990, p. 222). Despite the seemingly innocuous language of Westernization, the process often involved violent imposition of values and practices that aroused anger, anguish, and resistance to Westernization. Criticism of the spatial biases and assumptions of cultural superiority embedded in the notion of Westernization (during the era of European colonialism and up through the end of World War II) brought about the need for a despatialized term to describe the relationship between the West and the Third World.

Thus the next sophistication was *modernization*. The term denoted neither a spatial bias toward the West nor a zeal for saving souls. The notion promised only a vision of a modern society and offered a process that could bring "primitive," "backward" peoples and societies into the modern present. It is interesting to note that the spatial bias of Westernization had been replaced by the temporal bias (toward the modern present) of modernization. It is also important to note that despite the discursive movement toward a secular and spatially neutral terminology, modernization (and its operational existence as developmentalism) still bears the imprint of the Western church. Pieterse (1991) has observed that "developmentalism [and modernization] conforms to a Christian format and logic in viewing history as a salvific process" (p. 15). In modernization, "providence is recast as Progress. Predestination reformulated as determinism. The basic scenario of the scripture, Paradise-Fall-Redemption, comes replicated in evolutionary schemes [such as] primeval simplicity and innocence (the good savage), followed by the fall from grace (corruption), which in turn is followed by redeeming change (modernity)" (p. 16).

There is yet another sophistication in terminology that describes the relations between nations. As modernization has come under fire for, among other issues, its temporal bias (the claim that the future of the Third World is located in the present of urban centers in the West), a universalized version of modernization has made its way into discussion of relations between the West and the Third World. This newest sophistication is *globalization*. Waters (1995) forcefully reveals the connection between globalization and its antecedents:

> Globalization is an obvious object for ideological suspicion because, like modernization, a predecessor and related concept, it appears to justify the spread of Western cul-

ture and of capitalist society by suggesting that there are forces operating beyond human control that are transforming the world. Globalization is the direct consequence of the expansion of European culture. (p. 3)

Because modernization has had clear historical and ideological connections with processes of Western imperialism and colonialism, it has been criticized from various intellectual perspectives.

Major Theoretical Approaches to Development

In the context of the Cold War, the U.S. State Department, the U.S. military, institutions of higher education, and private foundations (Ford, Rockefeller, and the like) formed a cooperative relationship through which academics were encouraged to study the new nations of the Third World as a way of promoting economic development and political stability so as to avoid the "loss" of the new states to the Soviets (So, 1990). A generation of political scientists, sociologists, anthropologists, and communication scholars cut their academic teeth on research into various aspects of the new Third World nations (Gendzier, 1985; Samarajiwa, 1987; So, 1990). By the 1950s, "an interdisciplinary modernization school was in the making" (So, 1990, p. 18).

So (1990, pp. 18-23) has summarized the main theoretical assumptions of the modernization school. They are rooted in ideas about evolution and functionalism. From these roots, the following critiques, among others, were proposed: Development is assumed to be unidirectional; development requires the elimination of "traditional" values; development is understood as an internal process to the extent that foreign domination by states and transnational corporations is ignored; and there is an ideology underlying the development idea that justifies U.S. intervention in the Third World. These critiques have led to the rise of other ways of looking at the process and idea of development. These are the neomodernization, dependency, world-system, and postmodern approaches. We briefly summarize the first three of these approaches here because they are fairly well-known. We discuss the postmodern view of development a bit more thoroughly because it is relatively new to development studies.

The neomodernization school retains some key ideas and concepts about the development process from the modernization school, such as a focus on nations and the view that modernization is generally beneficial but recognizes and revises certain faulty assumptions (So, 1990, pp. 60-87). Dependency is a neo-Marxist critique of modernization that came out of Latin America in the 1960s and is a response to the shortcomings of the liberal economic program proposed by the U.N. Economic Commission on Latin America. Dependency theory finds little hope for optimism in Third World countries' retaining ties to the imperialist core countries and proposes socialist revolution to bring about change in the unequal relations between the West and the Third World (Portes, 1976; So, 1990, pp. 91-109). A related model (because it also is rooted in neo-Marxist orientation) is the world-system approach to analysis of development, associated most closely with Immanuel Wallerstein. Wallerstein claims that dependency cannot adequately explain continued economic growth in East Asian countries, the economic stagnation of several socialist countries, and the declining hegemony of U.S. capitalism. Wallerstein's world-system approach divides the world into core, semiperiphery, and periphery states; all nation-states can move among these three modes over time. Thus, from the world-system perspective, the focus on development studies is a longitudinal view of the global political economy rather than a view of the economy of a single nation-state (as it is in the dependency and modernization approaches; see So, 1990, pp. 110-134).

The postmodern critique of modernization is rooted in what might be called a crisis of modernity. The recognition of the ecological limits to growth (see Chatterjee & Finger, 1994), new social movements that challenge the notion of linear social change (see Melucci, 1989), and the realization that the very process of modernity is, in theory and practice, more exclusionary than inclusive (see Kothari, 1988; Pieterse, 1991; Said, 1978) are among the factors that set the stage for a postmodern critique of modernization. There are two broad strands in this critique.[4] One is optimistic and embraces the possibilities for local and particularistic types of and strategies for development (e.g., Burkey, 1993). The second is skeptical about development and examines how the "discourse of development" works to perpetuate the paradigm despite the fact that development efforts are rarely successful (e.g., Crush, 1995; Escobar, 1995). The tasks that postmodern development skeptics have identified for themselves are to identify and deconstruct the institutional, political, and cultural interests and processes involved in postwar theorizing that "recycles key development ideas which appear, disappear, and reappear under changed political-economic and ideological circumstances" (Peet & Watt, 1994, p. 232).

Communication Research for National Development

Throughout the modernization era, communication was seen as a key element in the West's project of developing the Third World. In the decade and a half after Lerner's influential 1958 study of communication and development in the Middle East, communication researchers assumed that the introduction of media and certain types of educational, political, and economic information into a social system could transform individuals and societies from traditional to modern. Conceived as having fairly direct and powerful effects on Third World audiences, the media were seen as magic multipliers, able to accelerate and magnify the benefits of development.

In 1976, Rogers suggested that the dominant paradigm, as the direct and powerful effects model of communication and development came to be known, had passed. Guided by the works of critical mass communication scholars in Latin America, Rogers recognized that the effects of communication are mediated by social structures, interpersonal networks, the accessibility of communication hardware and software, and the quality of messages. In this revision, Rogers suggested that the effects of communication not only may be limited but also may not necessarily be direct or large.

Fair's (1989) examination of 224 studies of communication and development published in the first three decades of this specialization (1958-1986) reveals that much of the research was informed by models predicting either powerful effects or limited effects. About 40 years after Lerner, 20 years after Rogers, and nearly 10 years since Fair's metaresearch, Fair and Shah (1997) examined the research literature between 1987 and 1996 about media effects on Third World audiences to discover how the field had evolved in that decade.

Theoretical Frameworks

In the first four decades of the life of this problem-solving research area, the majority of studies had no theoretical base. In the fourth decade studied (1987-1996), the situation showed some improvement. The increase in theoretical research perhaps marks some movement toward more conceptual precision and clarity in thinking about how to describe, explain, or predict the effects of media in the Third World. What is interesting across time periods is the nature of the theories used in research. In the earlier period, Lerner's model specifying the relationships of urbanization, literacy, and media use on political and economic participation accounted for approximately one-third of the studies using some kind of theoretical framework. The use of Lerner's ideas largely occurred early in the history of communication and development literature, prior to the beginning of criticism of the dominant paradigm in 1976.

In the 1987-1996 period, Lerner's modernization model completely disappeared. Instead, the most frequently used theoretical framework was participatory development, a postmodern optimist orientation, which is almost the polar opposite of Lerner, who viewed mass communication as playing a top-down role in social change. Also vanishing from research in this latter period was the two-step flow model. Research in both periods did make use of such theories or approaches as knowledge gap, indirect influence, and uses and gratifications.

Research appearing from 1987 through 1996 can be characterized as much more theoretically diverse than that published between 1958 and 1986. In the more recent period, along with participatory development notions, researchers used a number of frameworks—information environment, cultural integration, community structure, interactivity, imagined community, public sphere, dialogic, feminist—that attempt to address media effects more critically in a broader social, economic, and political context.

Another indicator of the state of the field is to be found within the Intercultural and Development Communication Division of the International Communication Association. We examined the convention programs of the 1997 and 1998 ICA conferences to learn what kinds of research approaches—modernization or neomodernization, dependency or world-system, postmodern optimist or postmodern skeptic—were in use. We made our judgments based on paper titles and abstracts. To be sure, this is a rough guide at best, but we tried to systematize our classification process by first compiling a set of keywords that likely would be associated with each of the approaches and using this scheme to categorize the conference papers. In 1997 and 1998, a total of 20 papers on communication and development were presented. Among these papers, 7 took a modernization approach, 3 took a neomodernization approach, 9 took a postmodern optimist approach, and 1 took a postmodern skeptic approach. In other words, 10 studies were in a modernization school and 10 were in a postmodern school. None of the studies was judged to be taking a neo-Marxist approach.

Conceptual and Operational Definitions

Over the two metaresearch periods, how scholars conceived of media effects varied in terms of whether effects were seen as direct (going from the media straight to individuals or society) or complementary (acting indirectly or with other individual or societal variables). The most pronounced change in the conceptualization of media between the 1958-1986 and 1987-1996 periods was a shift from a view of the media as having direct effects to a view of the media's effects as complementary.

The research conducted in the more recent period tried to account for the complexity of national development by downplaying the media's direct role in both individual modernization and social change. It looked to the media's relationship to macro-level or structural variables consistent with the dependency and world-system critiques of modernization. An increased complexity in approach is reflected by the wider range of disciplines, including some from the humanities, cited in the literature reviews. In the earlier period, literature reviews cited three primary fields: mass communication, sociology, and political science. In the later period, mass communication, sociology, and political science represented the most frequently cited fields, but fields such as education, philosophy, cultural anthropology, religion, feminist studies, and literature were also represented.

The conceptual and operational definitions of national development were also examined. In the earlier metaresearch, more than half the studies conceptualized national development as having to do with modern attitudes or behaviors (Fair, 1988, p. 152). From 1987 to 1996, national development seems still largely to have been defined within parameters of modernization theories, despite ongoing debates and revisions in fields outside of communication. However, in a change from the previous period, about a third of studies did incorporate a conceptualization of development that stems from rethinking modernization: Those studies defined development in terms of the abilities of societies to meet basic needs or to have self-reliance, ideas that have been incorporated by the optimist postmodern critique.

National development is a complex issue to think about and difficult to measure. In both periods, the majority of studies contained no operationalization of development. Although the absence of conceptual and/or operational definitions of media effects and national development highlights the difficulty of defining such terms, it also may reflect a lack of clarity or rigor in organizing the framework of study. The neglect of definitions can serve only as a hindrance to substantive theory building and exploration of media effects in the Third World.

Media as Variables in the Development Process

Researchers found several variables to be important in influencing or mediating media effects. In the first metaresearch, the primary factors mitigating media impacts generally were individual or personal characteristics: interpersonal and family relations, literacy, education level, socioeconomic status, and gender.[5] In the second metaresearch, studies cited a greater diversity of mediating factors. With the exception of interpersonal and family relations, which remained the mediating factor most often provided, variables were less often personal and more often structural, reflecting the attention to structural factors proposed by critiques of modernization—especially the dependency and world-system schools of thought. Government policies, the state of the polity or economy, cultural pressures, credibility of the message or message sender, poor infrastructure or lack of media availability, and world capitalism represent the new prominent mediating influences.

Methods, Data, and Levels of Analysis

Of the studies conducted in the earlier three decades, about 50% were quantitative survey projects. In the most recent decade studied (1987-1996), a vast majority of the researchers used some form of qualitative methods (such as description, historical methods, and field observation). Quantitative methods were used in less than 20% of the studies examined. Specific approaches included surveys, content analysis, and econometrics. In both periods, however, the focus of empirical studies was mainly on rural audiences of mass-media development messages. Also, most empirical studies in both periods were cross-sectional as opposed to longitudinal.

In the 1958-1986 period, Asian countries were the most frequent focus of studies, followed by Latin American, African, and Middle Eastern nations, in that order. In the 1987-1996 period, Asian countries continued to be the most frequent focus of studies, but these were followed by African, Latin American, Middle Eastern, and Eastern European countries. The fact that there was more focus on Africa than on Latin America in this period may be reflective of Western determination to "democratize" Africa in the 1980s. The appearance of Eastern Europe in communication and development studies indicates the Third World-like status of many Eastern and Central European countries as they emerged (after 1989) from an era of neocolonial relations with the Soviet Union.

Although macro-level analysis increased in the 1987-1996 studies, micro-level analysis remained the most used. When it came to actual measurement of development and media use, researchers tended to rely on measures of individual characteristics and change.

From the earlier period to the later, the biggest change in the pattern of funding was that non-U.S. governments and intergovernmental organizations were getting involved. University funding had become scarcer, and funding from the U.S. government had declined.

Conclusions

In the first three decades of the field of development communication research, the most commonly mentioned conclusions of research studies were that mass media had positive impacts on individual modernity. Less frequently mentioned were conclusions calling for expanded thinking about development communication and the need to examine other forms of communication. In the 1987-1996 study reviewed above, the most commonly stated conclusion was that mass media have positive impacts on social structure; this was followed by a call for expanded thinking about development communication. These most frequently stated conclusions reveal, once again, that macro-level concerns were of primary importance to researchers in the 1987-1996 era. Concerns about negative and positive impacts on individuals were mentioned relatively infrequently. The conclusions suggest a number of other areas of concern for researchers that are worth highlighting. Researchers indicated that they were interested in thinking more expansively about mass communication and development, that other forms of media should be examined, and that participation in participatory communication projects should be more inclusive.

Directions for Future Research

In the 1958-1986 study, the directions for future research most commonly suggested by the authors included closer examination of the relevance of message content, the need for more comparative research, and the need for more policy research. In the 1987-1996 period, the most frequent suggestion concerned the need for more policy research, including institutional analysis of development-agency coordination. This was followed by the need for research on and development of indigenous models of communication and development through participatory research, and two other suggestions that researchers examine the relevance of development communication messages and establish new normative models for development communication. The results suggest that since the earlier study, policy research has come to be perceived as an even more pressing need, as has the need to create models of communication and development that reflect indigenous priorities and needs. The latter is clearly in line with the optimist postmodern view.

A Look at the Past and a Look Toward the Future

Clearly, there are significant continuities and discontinuities in the way the field of development communication research has evolved since the first metaresearch discussed above was completed. The 1987-1996 metaresearch reveals that research on communication and development has become more complex in several respects, but also that some features of the field remain relatively unchanged.

For some researchers, development is no longer only a Third World concern. Eastern European nations and marginalized groups in the West are receiving attention from communication and development researchers. Technological advances in communication have forced researchers to incorporate new media such as video and fax into their understanding of the role of communication in development. At the same time, researchers have recognized that the mass media act as contributory factors in socioeconomic development. Thus explanations of mass-media impacts on development have included a greater number of intervening variables. In particular, structural factors, such as infrastructure and political economy, are becoming more central to analyses of communication and development. Individual-level concerns have not disappeared, but individual blame for lack of development is no longer common because researchers acknowledge the structural constraints under which people live. In an effort to understand this complex relationship between the micro and macro levels more clearly, scholars have begun to rely upon a number of critical perspectives—such as feminist, dialogic, participatory, and public sphere perspectives—that are relatively new for this field.

Despite the trend toward complexity and change, studies of communication and development are still characterized by some of the shortcomings found in the first metaresearch. For example, in both research periods, few studies provided operational definitions of either development or how mass media might influence it, which was ostensibly the purpose of the research in the first place. When development or mass-media impact was operationalized in the 1987-1996 period, the definitions were almost identical to those in the earlier period. Moreover, in both periods there was little face-to-face interaction between researchers and the people they studied. Women, children, and other marginalized groups remained largely outside of researchers' concern.

Our review indicates increasing epistemological and methodological tolerance as a greater number of studies with diverse frameworks appeared in the 1987-1996 period. However, it seems clear that conceptualizing communication and development based on critical theories has raced ahead of empirical research (whether quantitative or qualitative). Indeed, this metaresearch of the field found many conceptual think pieces and reflexive essays, with few applications of these ideas in the field. What we are unable to ascertain is the extent to which funding agencies view the projects they support and the data they generate as proprietary and, therefore, unavailable for publication.

Finally, the thinking about communication and development has to some extent reflected the critiques of modernization. One aspect of the modernization critiques largely absent in the communication and development literature to date, however, is the skeptical postmodernist orientation. For future research, this kind of approach would involve a discursive turn in which communication and development studies would be examined not just for what and how they might describe the media's impact in the Third World and other "developing" areas, but also for the ways in which they reinforce existing power relations and structures of inequalities. For example, such an approach would explore why particular groups—women, children, the dispossessed—continue to be ignored despite the fact that the rhetoric of development suggests these groups are of central concern. In other words, the skeptical postmodern approach provides analytic tools that can aid researchers in discovering the relationships among discourse, structure, and agency. The importance of analyzing the discourse of development from a skeptical postmodern perspective is that it helps us to reveal who actually benefits from communication and development activities, including research. After nearly five decades of development efforts led by the Western development industry, the Third World has seen little tangible gain. At this historical moment in relations between the West and the Third World, knowing who benefits and who loses from "development" is key to reorganizing the development industry, in which communication and development researchers are central actors.

NOTES

1. For further discussion of the Truman Doctrine, see Esteva (1995), Gendzier (1985), and Luke (1990, pp. 211-240).

2. For overviews on this point, see Mehmet (1995), Momsen (1993), and Webster (1990).

3. Although the decade might have been lost to Western business interests in the Third World and perhaps to Third World elites, disastrous effects of declining economies and living standards were certainly not "lost" to Third World peoples.

4. Writing in very broad terms, Pauline M. Rosenau (1992) describes two general orientations to postmodernism. On the one hand there are the skeptical postmodernists, who offer a negative and sometimes gloomy assessment. They claim that the postmodern age is characterized by "fragmentation, disintegration, malaise, meaninglessness, a vagueness, if not an absence of moral parameters and societal chaos" (p. 15), and there is little hope for political action or social change. According to Rosenau, this orientation is inspired by European philosophers such as Heidegger and Nietzsche. On the other hand are the affirmative postmodernists, who agree with the skeptics' critique of the postmodern age but have a more hopeful outlook on the possibilities for political struggle and resistance. These postmodernists celebrate "personal nondogmatic projects . . . and lifestyles" (p. 16).

5. These figures are based on percentages of responses obtained from multiple responses in which coders recorded up to three variables having mediating impact on the media. The total number of studies coded for mediating factors was 224 in the first metaresearch and 129 in the second.

REFERENCES

Albarran, A. B., & Chan-Olmsted, S. (1998). *Global media economics: Commercialization, concentration and integration of world media markets.* Ames: Iowa State University Press.

Amin, A. (1993). The globalization of the economy: An erosion of regional networks? In G. Grabher (Ed.), *The embedded firm: On the socioeconomics of industrial networks* (pp. 278-295). New York: Verso.

Amin, S. (1989). *Eurocentrism* (R. Moore, Trans.). New York: Monthly Review Press.

Ang, I. (1990). Culture and communication: Towards an ethnographic critique of media consumption in the transnational media system. *European Journal of Communication, 5,* 239-260.

Appadurai, A. (1993). Consumption, duration, and history. In D. Palumbo-Liu & H. U. Gumbrecht (Eds.), *Streams of cultural capital: Transnational cultural studies* (pp. 23-46). Stanford, CA: Stanford University Press.

Aune, J. A. (1997). The work of rhetoric in the age of digital dissemination. *Quarterly Journal of Speech, 83,* 230-268.

Beck, U. (1992). *Risk society: Towards a new modernity* (M. Ritter, Trans.). London: Sage.

Beltran, L. R. (1978). TV etchings in the minds of Latin Americans: Conservatism, materialism, and conformism. *Gazette, 24,* 61-85.

Blake, C. (1997). Afrocentric tokens: Afrocentric methodology in rhetorical analysis. *Howard Journal of Communications, 8*(1), 1-14.

Blanchard, M. A. (1986). *Exporting the First Amendment: The press-government crusade of 1945-1952.* New York: Longman.

Blommaert, J. (1990). Modern African political style: Strategies and genre in Swahili political discourse. *Discourse and Society, 1,* 115-131.

Boyd, D. A. (1991). Lebanese broadcasting: Unofficial electronic media during a prolonged civil war. *Journal of Broadcasting & Electronic Media, 35,* 269-287.

Boyd-Barrett, O. (1998). Media imperialism reformulated. In D. K. Thussu (Ed.), *Electronic empires: Global media and local resistance* (pp. 157-176). London: Arnold.

Bradshaw, Y. W., & Wahl, A.-M. (1991). Foreign debt expansion, the International Monetary Fund, and regional variation in Third World poverty. *International Studies Quarterly, 35,* 251-272.

Braman, S. (1990). Trade and information policy. *Media, Culture & Society, 12,* 361-385.

Braman, S. (1996). Interpenetrated globalization: Scaling, power, and the public sphere. In S. Braman & A. Sreberny-Mohammadi (Eds.), *Globalization, communication, and transnational civil society* (pp. 21-36). Cresskill, NJ: Hampton.

Branscomb, A. W. (Ed.). (1986). *Toward a law of global communication networks.* New York: Longman.

Brown, M. B., & Tiffen, P. (1992). *Short-changed: Africa and world trade.* London: Pluto.

Buchanan, W., & Cantril, H. (1953). *How nations see each other.* Urbana: University of Illinois Press.

Burkey, S. (1993). *People first: A guide to self-reliant, participatory rural development.* London: Zed.

Castles, S. (1998). New migrations in the Asia-Pacific region: A force for social and political change. *International Social Science Journal, 50,* 215-228.

Chaffee, S. H. (1992). Search for change: Survey studies of international media effects. In F. Korzenny & S. Ting-Toomey (Eds.), *Mass media effects across cultures* (pp. 35-54). Newbury Park, CA: Sage.

Chan, J. M., & Lee, C.-C. (1991). *Mass media and political transition: The Hong Kong press in China's orbit.* New York: Guilford.

Chang, T.-K., & Lee, J. (1993). U.S. gatekeepers and the new world information order: Journalistic qualities and editorial positions. *Political Communication, 10,* 303-316.

Chatterjee, P., & Finger, M. (1994). *The Earth brokers: Power, politics, and world development.* London: Routledge.

Checkel, J. T. (1998). The constructivist turn in international relations theory. *World Politics, 50,* 324-349.

Cioffi-Revilla, C., & Merritt, R. L. (1981). Communication research and the new world information order. *Journal of International Affairs, 35,* 233-234.

Cioffi-Revilla, C., Merritt, R. L., & Zinnes, D. A. (Eds.). (1987). *Communication and interaction in global politics.* Newbury Park, CA: Sage.

Comor, E. (Ed.). (1994). *The global political economy of communication: Hegemony, telecommunication and the information economy.* London: Macmillan.

Cooper-Chen, A. (1994). *Games in the global village: A 50-nation study of entertainment television.* Bowling Green, OH: Bowling Green State University Popular Press.

Crush, J. S. (1995). Introduction: Imagining development. In J. S. Crush (Ed.), *Power of development* (pp. 1-23). London: Routledge.

Cunningham, S., & Jacka, E. (1996). The role of television in Australia's paradigm shift to Asia. *Media, Culture & Society, 18,* 619-637.

Davison, P. M. (1997). *Global communications, international affairs and the media since 1945.* London: Routledge.

De Bernardy, M., Boisgontier, P., & Goyet, G. (1993). The ecology of innovation: The cultural substratum and sustainable development. *International Social Science Journal, 45,* 55-67.

Deibert, R. J. (1997). *Parchment, printing, and hypermedia: Communication in world order transformation.* New York: Columbia University Press.

DeLanda, M. (1991). *War in the age of intelligent machines.* New York: Zone.

Dezalay, Y., & Garth, B. G. (1996). *Dealing in virtue: International commercial arbitration and the construction of a transnational legal order.* Chicago: University of Chicago Press.

Dorfman, A., & Mattelart, A. (1975). *How to read Donald Duck: Imperialist ideology in the Disney comic.* London: Internationale General.

Downing, J. D. H. (1996). *Internationalizing media theory: Transitions, power, culture—Reflections on media in Russia, Poland and Hungary 1980-95.* London: Sage.

Drake, W. J., & Nicolaides, K. (1992). Ideas, interests, and institutionalization: Trade in services and the Uruguay Round. *International Organization, 46*(1), 37-100.

Dudley, L. M. (1991). *The word and the sword: How techniques of information and violence have shaped our world.* Cambridge, MA: Blackwell.

Dufour-Gompers, R. Y. (1992). Watching the violence of warfare in the "theatre" of operations. *International Social Science Journal, 44,* 247-268.

Eco, U. (1990). Towards a semiological guerrilla warfare. In U. Eco, *Travels in hyperreality* (W. Weaver, Trans.) (pp. 135-144). San Diego, CA: Harcourt Brace Jovanovich.

Elasmar, M. G., & Hunter, J. E. (1997). The impact of foreign TV on a domestic audience: A meta-analysis. In B. R. Burleson (Ed.), *Communication yearbook 20* (pp. 47-69). Thousand Oaks, CA: Sage.

Elkins, D. J. (1997). Globalization, telecommunication, and virtual ethnic communities. *International Political Science Review, 18,* 139-152.

Elmer, G. (1997). Spaces of surveillance: Indexicality and solicitation on the Internet. *Critical Studies in Mass Communication, 14,* 182-191.

Entman, R. M. (1991). Framing U.S. coverage of international news: Contrasts in narratives of the KAL and Iran air incidents. *Journal of Communication, 41*(4), 6-27.

Escobar, A. (1995). *Encountering development: The making and unmaking of the Third World.* Princeton, NJ: Princeton University Press.

Esteva, G. (1995). Development. In W. Sachs (Ed.), *The development dictionary: A guide to knowledge as power* (pp. 6-25). London: Zed.

Fair, J. E. (1988). *A meta-research of mass media effects on audiences in developing countries from 1958 through 1986.* Unpublished doctoral dissertation, Indiana University.

Fair, J. E. (1989). 29 years of theory and research on media and development: The dominant paradigm impact. *Gazette, 44,* 129-150.

Fair, J. E., & Shah, H. (1997). Continuities and discontinuities in communication and development since 1958. *Journal of International Communication, 4*(2), 3-23.

Featherstone, M. (Ed.). (1990). *Global culture: Nationalism, globalization and modernity.* London: Sage.

Frederick, H. H. (1986). *Cuban-American radio wars: Ideology in international telecommunication.* Norwood, NJ: Ablex.

Frederick, H. H. (1993). *Global communication and international relations.* Belmont, CA: Wadsworth.

Galtung, J., & Ruge, M. H. (1965). The structure of foreign: The presentation of the Congo, Cuba, and Cyprus crises in four foreign newspapers. *Journal of International Peace Research, 1,* 64-90.

Gary, B. (1996). Communication research, the Rockefeller Foundation, and mobilization for the war on words, 1938-1944. *Journal of Communication, 46*(3), 124-148.

Geertz, C. (1983). *Local knowledge: Further essays in interpretive anthropology.* New York: Basic Books.

Gendzier, I. L. (1985). *Managing political change: Social scientists and the Third World.* Boulder, CO: Westview.

Glasberg, D. S., & Ward, K. B. (1993). Foreign debt and economic growth in the world system. *Social Science Quarterly, 74,* 703-720.

Golding, P. (1974). Media role in national development: A critique of a theoretical orthodoxy. *Journal of Communication, 24*(3), 39-53.

Gonzalez-Manet, E. (1988). *The hidden war of information* (L. Alexandre, Trans.). Norwood, NJ: Ablex.

Guattari, F. (1995). *Chaosmosis: An ethico-aesthetic paradigm* (J. Petaris & P. Bains, Trans.). Bloomington: Indiana University Press.

Gumpert, G., & Drucker, S. J. (1998). The mediated home in the global village. *Communication Research, 25,* 422-438.

Haas, E. B. (1990). *When knowledge is power: Three models of change in international organizations.* Berkeley: University of California Press.

Hachten, W. A. (1992). *The world news prism* (3rd ed.). Ames: Iowa State University Press.

Hall, S. (1996). Introduction: Who needs "identity"? In S. Hall & P. du Gay (Eds.), *Questions of cultural identity* (pp. 1-17). London: Sage.

Hallin, D. C., & Mancini, P. (1991). Summits and the constitution of an international public sphere: The Reagan-Gorbachev meetings as televised media events. *Communication, 12*(4), 249-266.

Halloran, James D. (1995). Some problems in international comparative research. *Electronic Journal of Communication, 5*(2-3).

Hamelink, C. (1983). *Cultural autonomy in global communications.* New York: Longman.

Headrick, D. R. (1990). *The invisible weapon: Telecommunications and international relations, 1851-1945.* New York: Oxford University Press.

Hegde, R. S. (1998). A view from elsewhere: Locating difference and the politics of representation from a transnational feminist perspective. *Communication Theory, 8,* 271-297.

Herman, E. S., & McChesney, R. W. (1997). *The global media: The new missionaries of corporate capitalism.* London: Cassell.

Herrmann, R. K., & Fischerkeller, M. P. (1995). Beyond the enemy image and spiral model: Cognitive-strategic research after the Cold War. *International Organization, 49,* 415-450.

Hester, A. (1971). An analysis of news flow from developed and developing nations. *Gazette, 17,* 29-43.

Hester, A. (1973). Theoretical considerations in predicting volume and direction of international information flow. *Gazette, 19,* 239-247.

Hoskins, C., McFadyen, S., & Finn, A. (1996). A comparison of domestic and international joint ventures in television program and feature film production. *Canadian Journal of Communication, 21*(1), 77-94.

Hoskins, C., & Mirus, R. (1988). Reasons for the US dominance of the international trade in television programmes. *Media, Culture & Society, 10,* 499-515.

Hu, Y. W., & Wanta, W. (1993). The agenda setting effect of international news coverage: An examination of differing news frames. *International Journal of Public Opinion Research, 5,* 250-265.

Hur, K. K. (1984). A critical analysis of international news flow research. *Critical Studies in Mass Communication, 1,* 365-378.

International Telecommunication Union. (1996). *World telecommunication development report 1996.* Geneva: Author.

Ito, Y. (1990). Mass communication theories from a Japanese perspective. *Media, Culture & Society, 12,* 423-464.

Jowett, G. S., & O'Donnell, V. (1992). *Propaganda and persuasion* (2nd ed.). Newbury Park, CA: Sage.

Jussawalla, M., Toh, M. H., & Low, L. (1992). Singapore: An intelligent city-state. *Asian Journal of Communication, 2*(3), 31-54.

Keane, J. (1991). Democracy and the media. *International Social Science Journal, 43,* 523-541.

Kim, K., & Barnett, G. A. (1996). The determinants of international news flow: A network analysis. *Communication Research, 23,* 323-353.

Kincaid, D. L. (Ed.). (1987). *Communication theory: Eastern and Western perspectives.* San Diego, CA: Academic Press.

Kobrak, F., & Luey, B. (Eds.). (1992). *The structure of international publishing in the 1990s.* New Brunswick, NJ: Transaction.

Korzenny, F. (1978). A theory of electronic propinquity: Mediated communication in organizations. *Communication Research, 5,* 3-24.

Korzenny, F., & Schiff, E. (1992). Media effects across cultures: Challenges and opportunities. In F. Korzenny & S. Ting-Toomey (Eds.), *Mass media effects across cultures* (pp. 1-10). Newbury Park, CA: Sage.

Kothari, R. (1988). *Rethinking development: In search of humane alternatives.* New Delhi: Ajanta.

Laffey, M., & Weldes, J. (1997). Beyond belief: Ideas and symbolic technologies in the study of international relations. *European Journal of International Relations, 3,* 193-238.

Lalvani, S. (1995). Consuming the exotic other. *Critical Studies in Mass Communication, 12,* 263-286.

Lasswell, H. D. (1971). *Propaganda technique in World War I.* Cambridge: MIT Press. (Original work published 1927)

Lee, C.-C. (1980). *Media imperialism reconsidered.* Beverly Hills, CA: Sage.

Lerner, D. (1958). *The passing of traditional society.* Glencoe, IL: Free Press.

Liebes, T., & Livingstone, S. (1998). European soap operas: The diversification of a genre. *European Journal of Communication, 13,* 147-180.

Luke, T. W. (1990). *Social theory and modernity: Critique, dissent, and revolution.* Newbury Park, CA: Sage.

Lull, J. (Ed.). (1987). *Popular music and communication.* Newbury Park, CA: Sage.

Lull, J. (1995). *Media, communication, and culture: A global approach.* New York: Columbia University Press.

Manheim, J. B. (1994). *Strategic public diplomacy and American foreign policy.* New York: Oxford University Press.

Mansell, R. E. (1994). *The new telecommunications: A political economy of network evolution.* Thousand Oaks, CA: Sage.

Martin-Barbero, J. (1993). *Communication, culture, and hegemony: From the media to mediations.* Newbury Park, CA: Sage.

Mattelart, A. (1978). The nature of communication practice in a dependent society. *Latin American Perspectives, 5*(1), 13-34.

McQuail, D. (1986). International information flows: Evidence of content analysis. In U. Kivikuru & T. Varis (Eds.), *Approaches to international communication* (pp. 131-152). Helsinki: Finnish National Commission for UNESCO.

Mehmet, O. (1995). *Westernizing the Third World: The Eurocentricity of economic development theories.* London: Routledge.

Melucci, A. (1989). *Nomads of the present.* Philadelphia: Temple University Press.

Memmi, A. (1965). *The colonizer and the colonized.* Boston: Beacon.

Messaris, P. (1993). *Visual "literacy": Image, mind, and reality.* Boulder, CO: Westview.

Michaels, E. (1994). *Bad Aboriginal art.* Minneapolis: University of Minnesota Press.

Mitra, A. (1997). Diasporic Web sites: Ingroup and outgroup discourse. *Critical Studies in Mass Communication, 14,* 158-181.

Mody, B., Straubhaar, J. D., & Bauer, J. M. (Eds.). (1995). *Telecommunications politics: Ownership and control of the information highway in developing countries.* Mahwah, NJ: Lawrence Erlbaum.

Momsen, J. H. (1993). *Women and development in the Third World.* London: Routledge.

Mowlana, H., & Rad, M. M. (1990, June). *Japanese programs on Iranian television: A study in international flow of information.* Paper presented at the annual meeting of the International Association for Mass Communication Research, Bled, Yugoslavia.

Mowlana, H., & Wilson, L. J. (1990). *The passing of modernity: Communication and the transformation of society.* New York: Longman.

Mudimbe, V. Y. (1988). *The invention of Africa: Gnosis, philosophy, and the order of knowledge.* Bloomington: Indiana University Press.

Mytton, G. (Ed.). (1993). *Global audiences: Research for worldwide broadcasting, 1993.* London: John Libbey.

O'Brien, R. C. (Ed.). (1983). *Information, economics, and power: The North-South dimension.* London: Hodder & Staughton.

Owen, B. M., & Wildman, S. S. (1992). *Video economics.* Cambridge, MA: Harvard University Press.

Paletz, D. L., & Schmid, A. P. (Eds.). (1992). *Terrorism and the media.* Newbury Park, CA: Sage.

Palumbo-Liu, D., & Gumbrecht, H. U. (Eds.). (1993). *Streams of cultural capital: Transnational cultural studies.* Stanford, CA: Stanford University Press.

Pearce, D., & Butler, R. (Eds.). (1992). *Tourism research: Critiques and challenges.* New York: Routledge.

Pearce, D., & Singh, S. (1992). *Globalizing research and development.* New York: St. Martin's.

Peet, R., & Watts, M. (1994). Introduction: Development theory and environment in an age of market triumphalism. *Economic Geography, 69,* 227-253.

Petersmann, E.-U. (1991). *Constitutional functions and constitutional problems of international economic law.* Fribourg, Switzerland: University Press.

Peterson, S. (1979). Foreign news coverage and criteria of newsworthiness. *Journalism Quarterly, 56,* 116-125.

Peterson, T., Schramm, W., & Siebert, F. S. (1956). *Four theories on the press.* Chicago: University of Chicago Press.

Pieterse, J. N. (1991). Dilemmas of development discourse: The crisis of developmentalism and the comparative method. *Development and Change, 22,* 5-29.

Pool, I. de S. (1977). The changing flow of television. *Journal of Communication, 27*(2), 139-149.

Pool, I. de S., Inose, H., Taksaki, N., & Hurwitz, R. (1984). *Communication flows: A census in the United States and Japan.* Tokyo: University of Tokyo Press.

Portes, A. (1976). On the sociology of national development: Theories and issues. *American Journal of Sociology, 82,* 55-85.

Pye, L. W. (1967). Communication, institution building, and the reach of authority. In D. Lerner & W. Schramm (Eds.), *Communication and change in the developing countries* (pp. 35-55). Honolulu: East-West Center Press.

Richards, T. (1993). *The imperial archive: Knowledge and the fantasy of empire.* New York: Verso.

Richstad, J., & Anderson, M. H. (Eds.). (1981). *Crisis in international news.* New York: Columbia University Press.

Roeh, I., & Cohen, A. A. (1992). One of the bloodiest days: A comparative analysis of open and closed television news. *Journal of Communication, 42*(2), 42-55.

Rogers, E. (1976). Communication and development: The passing of the dominant paradigm. In E. Rogers (Ed.), *Communication and development: Critical perspectives* (pp. 121-149). Beverly Hills, CA: Sage.

Rosenau, J. N. (1992). The relocation of authority in a shrinking world. *Comparative Politics, 24,* 253-272.

Rosenau, J. N. (1997, March). *Imposing global order: A synthesized ontology for a turbulent era.* Paper presented at the annual meeting of the International Studies Association, Toronto.

Rosenau, P. M. (1992). *Post-modernism and the social sciences: Insights, inroads, and intrusions.* Princeton, NJ: Princeton University Press.

Said, E. W. (1978). *Orientalism.* New York: Pantheon.

Salwen, M. (1991). Cultural imperialism: A media effects approach. *Critical Studies in Mass Communication, 8,* 29-38.

Samarajiwa, R. (1987). The murky beginnings of the communication and development field: Voice of America and "the passing of traditional society." In N. Jayaweera & S. Amunugama (Eds.), *Rethinking development communication* (pp. 3-19). Singapore: AMIC.

Schiller, H. I. (1971). *Mass communication and American empire.* Boston: Beacon.

Schiller, H. I. (1991). Not yet the post-imperialist era. *Critical Studies in Mass Communication, 8,* 13-28.

Sepstrup, P. (1989). Research into international television flows: A methodological contribution. *European Journal of Communication, 4,* 393-407.

Simpson, C. (1994). *The science of coercion: Communication research and psychological warfare 1945-1960.* New York: Oxford University Press.

Snyder, L. B., Willenborg, B., & Watt, J. (1991). Advertising and cross-cultural convergence in Europe, 1953-89. *European Journal of Communication, 6,* 441-468.

So, A. Y. (1990). *Social change and development: Modernization, dependency, and world-system theories.* Newbury Park, CA: Sage.

Sparks, C. (1998). Is there a global public sphere? In D. K. Thussu (Ed.), *Electronic empires: Global media and local resistance* (pp. 108-124). London: Arnold.

Sreberny-Mohammadi, A. (1995). International news flow in the post-Cold War world: Mapping the news and the news producers. *Electronic Journal of Communication, 5*(2-3).

Stevenson, R. L. (1994). *Global communication in the twenty-first century.* New York: Longman.

Strang, D., & Soule, S. A. (1998). Diffusion in organizations and social movements: From hybrid corn to poison pills. *Annual Review of Sociology, 24,* 265-290.

Straubhaar, J. D. (1991). Beyond media imperialism: Asymmetrical interdependence and cultural proximity. *Critical Studies in Mass Communication, 8,* 39-59.

Suedfeld, P., & Tetlock, P. E. (1977). Integrative complexity of communications in international crises. *Journal of Conflict Resolution, 21,* 169-184.

Sussman, G. (1993). Revolutionary communications in Cuba. *Critical Studies in Mass Communication, 10,* 199-218.

Tehranian, M. (1997). Global communication and international relations: Changing paradigms and policies. *International Journal of Peace Studies, 2*(1), 39-64.

Tomlinson, J. (1991). *Cultural imperialism.* Baltimore: Johns Hopkins University Press.

Tracey, M. (1985). The poisoned chalice? International television and the idea of dominance. *Daedalus, 114*(4), 17-55.

Tran, V. D. (1987). *Communication and diplomacy in a changing world.* Norwood, NJ: Ablex.

U.N. Development Program. (1992). *Human development report.* New York: Oxford University Press.

Varis, T. (Ed.). (1992). *The new media: Cultural identity and integration in the new media world.* Helsinki, Finland: University of Industrial Arts, Center for Advanced Studies.

Viezzer, M. (1986). Communication for women's movements in Latin America. In M. Traber (Ed.), *The myth of the information revolution: Social and ethical implications of communication technology* (pp. 117-125). London: Sage.

Virilio, P. (1995). *The art of the motor* (J. Rose, Trans.). Minneapolis: University of Minnesota Press.

Wallerstein, I. (1990). Culture as the ideological battleground of the modern world-system. In M. Featherstone (Ed.), *Global culture: Nationalism, globalization and modernity* (pp. 31-55). London: Sage.

Walther, J. B. (1997). Group and interpersonal effects in international computer-mediated collaboration. *Human Communication Research, 23,* 342-369.

Wasser, F. (1995). Is Hollywood America? The transnationalization of the American film industry. *Critical Studies in Mass Communication, 12,* 423-437.

Waterman, P. (1990). Reconceptualizing the democratization of international communication. *International Social Science Journal, 42,* 77-92.

Waters, M. (1995). *Globalization.* London: Routledge.

Watson, R. P., & McCluskie, S. (1994). U.S. aid to the Third World: Testing aid theories and programs of the 1980s. *Journal of Third World Studies, 11,* 202-239.

Webster, A. (1990). *Introduction to the sociology of development* (2nd ed.). Atlantic Highlands, NJ: Humanities Press International.

Wu, H. D. (1998). Investigating the determinants of international news flow: A meta-analysis. *Gazette, 60,* 493-512.

CHAPTER CONTENTS

8 Political Communication Research and the Mutations of Democracy

DAVID L. SWANSON
University of Illinois

In recent years many political communication researchers have attempted to relate the attributes of political messages to the circumstances of the generative institutions of political communication, political institutions and media institutions. This mode of analysis helps reveal why the political messages produced by actors within these institutions have the attributes that define them and lead to their civic consequences. As its generative institutions undergo fundamental changes in response to altered circumstances, raising the possibility of corresponding but not yet known changes in democratic processes and practices, the study of political communication has taken on particular urgency. This essay describes some of the current research that endeavors to appreciate the wider context of political communication and illustrates some of the main themes of political communication study.

THE closing decades of the 20th century witnessed an unprecedented expansion of democracy. The proportion of democracies increased from 25% of the world's independent nations in 1974 to 66% in 1996 (Schwartzman, 1998). Noting that "virtually the only countries that are explicitly non-democratic are the last remaining semi-feudal states," Giddens (1999) has described democracy as "perhaps the most powerful energising idea of the 20th century." But at the same time, in the old, established democracies of Europe and the United States—and in some of new democracies as well—there was widespread and growing disillusionment with democratic politics and institutions (Dogan, 1997; Norris, 1999). Thus the 21st century dawned on the irony of growing concern about the future of democracy in the full bloom of democracy's most victorious era.

Various writers have identified communication as a contributory, sometimes even causal, agent in both of these contradictory developments. Television news, for example, has been hailed as leading the march toward democratization (e.g.,

Correspondence: David L. Swanson, Department of Speech Communication, University of Illinois, 702 S. Wright Street, Room 244, Urbana, IL 61801; e-mail dswanson@uiuc.edu

Communication Yearbook 24, pp. 189-205

Mollison, 1998) and also as fostering cynicism and discontent in the older democracies (e.g., Cappella & Jamieson, 1997).

Concerns about the world's rapidly changing political landscape and the future possibilities for democracy, together with wide acceptance of the belief that representative institutions and governments depend on communication to a large extent for their support and success, give particular importance and relevance to the many questions pursued by political communication researchers in the region where communication processes and political processes intersect.

Political communication has been defined in many ways during the quarter century or so since the field coalesced as a more or less distinct domain of study (for a brief history, see Nimmo & Swanson, 1990). One of the most serviceable definitions was also one of the earliest: "a focus upon communication in generating and regulating social conflict—and in achieving social order (or disorder)" (Nimmo, 1977, p. 441). As this definition suggests, the field's research portfolio is broad, ranging from studies of political journalism and election propaganda to studies of citizens' everyday conversations about political subjects. In order to understand the flow and consequences of information and influence in political processes, the field is multidisciplinary, drawing especially on the viewpoints associated with communication studies, political science, and sociology, and on the range of levels of analysis and methodological practices typical of those fields as well. What perhaps mark the field as distinctive are (a) commitment to research questions, concepts, and explanations that span, rather than merely apply, these multiple disciplinary perspectives, and (b) a focus on communication as central to and generative of, rather than merely reflective of, political processes.

Despite its diverse analytic concepts, research questions, and methods, the study of political communication is typified by some central tendencies that can be noted. Most research concerns the role of communication in political processes and institutions associated with electoral campaigning and governing. Most research focuses on the influence of media messages—both messages created by political advocates, such as campaign advertising, and messages created by journalists in the form of political news—on political processes and citizens' responses. Underlying most research is an ethical commitment to the discovery and promotion of means by which communication can best contribute to effective democratic institutions. Although these central tendencies give some definition to the diverse field, it is important to note that a great array of other research topics and interests is pursued around and beyond these central tendencies.

A number of reviews of political communication research—some quite comprehensive, others more focused in their scope—have been written over the years. Recent reviews include those undertaken by Bucy and D'Angelo (1999), Graber (1993), Kaid (1996), and Stuckey and Antczak (1998). Major research anthologies have been assembled by Nimmo and Sanders (1981) and Swanson and Nimmo (1990). Important reviews in earlier volumes in the *Communication Yearbook* series have been contributed by Nimmo (1977), Sanders and Kaid (1978), Larson and Wiegele (1979), Jackson-Beeck and Kraus (1980), and Mansfield and Weaver

(1982). Taken together, these reviews chart many of the research interests and accomplishments of the field of political communication, as well as its evolution over time.

Review papers in the 1970s and 1980s were organized by topical schemes that emphasized the field's scope. The most commonly used scheme was that offered by Nimmo (1977), who described research in terms of the Lasswellian rubrics of political communicators (who); use of languages, symbols, and techniques (says what); media of political communication (through what channel); audiences of political actors (to whom); and effects of communication in politics (with what effect). Such schemes reflected the character of the research, which charted the then-new terrain in mostly topical studies. As the field matured, topical theories and research began to be complemented in the 1990s, especially, by the emergence of broader viewpoints and approaches that integrated topical concerns within more general conceptions of political communication.

Current political communication theory and research spread across a much larger terrain than can be reviewed in a short essay. In this chapter my more modest goal is to describe some, but by no means all, of the more important trends that have emerged to dominate much current interest and work in the field. This essay focuses on trends that illustrate the more macro-level, integrative conceptions that now characterize much political communication research. It is my hope that a description of these trends will convey some of the recent accomplishments and future aspirations that today characterize scholarship in political communication.

WIDENING THE CONTEXT: RECOGNIZING LIMITATIONS ON THE AUTONOMY OF POLITICAL COMMUNICATION

In a synoptic essay published in 1999, Blumler and Kavanagh proposed that political communication in the 1990s was entering a new, third "age." Writing with specific reference to experience in the United States and the United Kingdom, they proposed that the first age—roughly the two decades following World War II—was defined by political parties and leaders enjoying ready access to the media, offering comparatively substantive messages concerning their views on issues of the day, but with little effect on citizens, who voted largely on the basis on long-standing party loyalties. The second age, beginning in the 1960s, was characterized by a greater willingness of more open-minded voters to consider alternative views and parties but less substantive political messages produced by politicians and operatives who were more interested in using sophisticated communication techniques to create appealing "images" to manipulate voters. The still-emerging third age, Blumler and Kavanagh suggest, is "more complex than its predecessors, molded more by conflicting cross currents than by a dominant tendency" (p. 213). This age is marked by the proliferation of traditional and new communication media, an abundance of news outlets and forms, 24-hour news services and news cycles, intensified professionalization of political communication, increased competitive pressures on the media, popularization of political journalism and discourse, diversification and fragmentation of media, and the enhanced ability of citizens to include messages about politics in their "media diets" in the forms, at the times, and to the extent they prefer.

Blumler and Kavanagh's important analysis offers purchase on how present trends in political communication may be understood and illuminated by their historical predecessors. An especially interesting feature of the analysis is the way in which the authors attempt to understand the essential features of political communication in each period by attending to the actors, influences, and practices that shape the subject's broad context: parties and political institutions, relations between parties and citizens, the character of media institutions in the competitive marketplace, citizens' relations to media, and the way each of these shapes the main messages of political communication—political journalism and the political discourse of parties and leaders.

Blumler and Kavanagh's approach represents an important emerging trend: the attempt on the part of researchers to understand particular political communication practices, such as habits of television news reporting about politics, in part by identifying connections between the practices and the wider context of institutions and influences that shape them. In contrast to earlier, more fragmented conceptions of the field, Blumler and Kavanagh's appreciation of the full context of political communication, and especially of the generative institutions of political communication in parties and media, leads us to recognize limitations on the autonomy of political communication. Recognizing how the choices of political communicators are shaped by the institutions in which they act and the contexts they inhabit helps us to appreciate why political messages have the features we notice.

In one sense, the analytic habit of seeking connections within political communication's institutional and social context reflects the European tradition of social theory and research (Gurevitch, 1999). Equally, however, attention to the importance of institutions characterizes the traditional approach to political communication in American political science (e.g., Key, 1958). However its provenance is conceived, this analytic trend enlivens and integrates many themes of current political communication research, as shown in the following sections of this essay.

THE POLITICAL CONTEXT: ACTORS AND INSTITUTIONS

Political actors and institutions produce many of the forms of messages that political communication researchers study: campaign speeches, political advertising in some countries and party political programs in others, the public discourse of government officials, press releases, political actors' media-centered events (such as photo opportunities, interviews, and press conferences), and so on. During the second and third ages of political communication as described by Blumler and

Kavanagh (1999), political communication researchers have identified changes in the character of such messages and sought to discover the consequences of these changes. In the United States, for example, political campaigns have been criticized for becoming increasingly negative in tone, consisting more of attacks on the opposition and less of proposals for addressing pressing issues. In Europe, political campaigns have been criticized for becoming less programmatic—diagnosing national programs and prescribing remedies from the viewpoint of contrasting ideologies—and more calculated, employing tactics and themes suggested by public relations professionals to win votes. Increasingly and almost everywhere, the practice of electoral politics seems to be intertwined with sophisticated marketing strategies. In order to understand and assess these trends, researchers are turning to their contexts, the circumstances of political actors and institutions.

Party Dilemmas

A host of studies have documented the decline in traditional forms of support for political parties in the established democracies across the past two decades or so. In the United States, this decline has been linked to voters' declining willingness to define their identities in terms of the collectivities of class or region that are the traditional bases of political party affiliation, the hollow ring of the parties' continued appeals to social and economic cleavages that no longer describe fault lines of the changing economy, the consequent erosion of voters' feelings of loyalty and connection to the parties, the parties' inability to offer persuasive responses to new issues (such as the environment and lifestyle concerns) that do not easily relate to traditional party doctrines, and, in short, the parties' loss of relevance to voters' experiences and concerns (see Åsard & Bennett, 1997; Bennett, 1996a; Sigelman & Whicker, 1988; Wattenberg, 1990). Parties in other established democracies have experienced similar, although typically less dramatic, erosion of their connections to traditional constituencies (see Dogan, 1997; Giddens, 1999; Mayobre, 1996; Mazzoleni, 1996; Mazzoleni & Schulz, 1999; Waisbord, 1996).

Political parties are no longer able to command the loyalties of their traditional partisans in the traditional ways by following the timeworn paths of political discourse. Instead, they face the need to find new bases for appealing to voters in an increasingly volatile electoral environment.

Party Propaganda

To maintain their viability in elections, parties in many countries have turned to similar strategies involving the use of experts in public relations and marketing, intensive use of the mass media to appeal to voters, sophisticated opinion polling, and emphasis on appealing personalities of candidates and leaders. The strategies of professionalization and personalization of campaigning are, of course, efforts to use political communication to win the support of voters with new kinds of techniques and appeals. These strategies, and the messages they produce, have been the subject of a large body of research.

The use of professional campaign consultants and sophisticated marketing communications techniques is familiar in the United States. An important body of research has examined characteristically personalized U.S. campaigns and the influence of professional communications and polling experts on the conduct of campaigns and the resultant qualities of campaign discourse (e.g., Bennett, 1996a; Herbst, 1993; Mauser, 1983; Mayhew, 1997; Medvic & Lenart, 1997; Newman, 1994; Sabato, 1981). In general, researchers have been critical of the effects of marketing strategies on political discourse. Such strategies encourage a superficial "adlike," sloganeering treatment of political issues; fabrication of pretested, prepackaged "images" for candidates; and only limited spontaneity and substance in political discourse. One of the discourse domains most often controlled by political professionals—political advertising—is a particular focus of research, and the civic consequences of negative advertising have come under intense scrutiny (e.g., Ansolabehere & Iyengar, 1995; Diamond & Bates, 1992; Garramone, Atkin, Pinkleton, & Cole, 1990; Jamieson, 1992; Johnson-Cartree & Copeland, 1991; Kaid & Johnston, 1991; Mayer, 1996; Pfau & Kenski, 1990; Pinkleton, 1997; West, 1997). In both experimental studies and detailed case studies, researchers have shown that, all other things being equal, negative advertising tends to polarize attitudes and may diminish turnout at the polls on election day. At the same time, however, negative advertising is memorable and informative.

Emerging from the extensive studies of U.S. political campaigns is the general conclusion that in each succeeding election cycle, campaigns employ more sophisticated marketing techniques, devoted to style more than substance, practicing manipulation strategies that are increasingly transparent to voters, in part because they are revealed by political journalists. The targets of these campaigns, the voters, become steadily more skeptical and cynical, research suggests.

Outside the United States, researchers have investigated the growing use of communications and public relations professionals, advertising and sophisticated communications strategies, polling, and marketing approaches in the political communication in a number of countries (e.g., Blumler, Kavanagh, & Nossiter, 1996; Franklin, 1994; Harrop, 1990; Kavanagh, 1995; Maarek, 1995, 1997; Negrine, 1996; Rawnsley, 1997; Scammell, 1995). Some particularly interesting work along these lines has been comparative in nature (e.g., Butler & Ranney, 1992; Farrell, 1996; Holtz-Bacha, 1999; Kaid & Holtz-Bacha, 1995; Mancini, 1999; Mazzoleni & Schulz, 1999; Swanson & Mancini, 1996; Tak, Kaid, & Lee, 1997). Studies such as these have documented the rising importance of media and professionals in many countries, shaping political communication in ways similar to that noted in the United States. A particular theme of this work concerns the relative power in producing political communication of traditional party organizations and operatives versus media and marketing professionals. In general, campaign strategies and discourse have been shown to remain more under the control of politicians than has been observed in some U.S. campaigns. Although the influence of communications and marketing strategies on campaign discourse is marked, it is thought to be less dominant in countries other than in the United States because of the greater subordination of professional consultants to political actors and party organizations in those countries. In part, this reflects the greater power of political party organizations in parliamentary systems and in electoral systems where voters cast ballots for party lists rather than for individual candidates. The weaker position of parties in the United States, where campaigns are run by individual candidates and their professional advisers, creates a context in which political marketing experts may exert considerable power in decision making.

When researchers examine the public discourse of political actors by setting the discourse in the broader context facing political institutions, it becomes possible to understand the forces shaping the discourse and to appreciate how those forces have changed over time, changes noticeable in particular qualities of political discourse. The negativity and superficiality of U.S. campaigns, for example, are seen to reflect the weakened institutional position of parties and candidates who, finding that their traditional rhetoric no longer works, are seeking a way of capturing the attention and at least momentary support of voters who doubt their sincerity and relevance. No one doubts that these styles of campaigning are corrosive to the health of democracy, but those who seek to propose effective reforms must begin by appreciating the causes of current practices. Revealing those causes is a particular strength of the more integrative, institution-oriented approach seen in some of the best political communication research.

THE MEDIA CONTEXT: PRESSURES ON POLITICAL JOURNALISM

In virtually every country, the news media are key to the functioning of politics and government. News media are the major source of the public's information about politics and government. As such, their influence on the public's perceptions of political institutions and support for political leaders is considerable. During the second and third ages of political communication as described by Blumler and Kavanagh (1999), the news media have experienced institutional pressures and changes fully as profound as those faced by political parties. Important political communication research has revealed how those changes have been reflected in news coverage of politics and government, and also has considered the civic consequences of today's political journalism.

Throughout the first age and much of the second age of political communication, the news media were a relatively stable set of institutions: in the United States, network television newscasts, the major newspapers with national or regional distribution, and a handful of influential newsmagazines; in Europe and most other countries, public service broadcasters that produced television news in each country, the major national newspapers (sometimes aligned with, sometimes organs of, particular political viewpoints), and major journals of opinion. During the past few years, this stable world has been turned on its head by both internal and external forces. Internally, commercialization has come to broadcasting, leading to proliferation of media outlets and intensified competition for audiences. Externally, political actors and their professional advisers have pursued sophisticated strategies for manipulating news media, leading journalists in many countries to feel the need to resist and assert their independent voices in the political dialogue. Both pressures have had important consequences for political communication.

Intensified Competition and Political Manipulation

Electronic media, especially, are proliferating in virtually every region of the world. International satellite broadcasters such as Sky News and CNN complement national broadcasters; commercial broadcasting has developed in many countries where formerly only public service broadcasting existed; public service broadcasting has been privatized in a number of countries; cable television is spreading in most countries. The effects of these developments are that viewers have more choices than ever before, audiences are more fragmented across different news sources than before, and broadcasters face keener competition for audiences.

Because political journalism is a key source of information about politics and government for the public, political communication researchers have been concerned with discovering whether the changing media environment is affecting the quality of political news. An analytic focus of much research is news values, the principles that guide editors' and journalists' choices of what political actors, events, and subjects to cover, how to cover them, and how much coverage to provide. These choices are reflected in the content of the news, so content analysis has become the dominant method for assessing whether and how the changing media environment influences political journalism.

The United States is the world's most intensely competitive media marketplace. U.S. households receive a dozen different broadcast television stations, on average, and the majority of households subscribe to cable services through which they receive more than three dozen different channels (Swanson, Crigler, Gurevitch, & Neuman, 1998). As competitive pressures on "mainstream" news outlets have increased, researchers have produced findings suggesting that political journalism has not prospered (e.g., Baum & Kernell, 1999). "Sound bite" coverage of politicians and campaigns has increased, with political actors being granted steadily diminishing opportunities to express themselves in their own words (Hallin, 1992; Kurtz, 1996; Lowry & Shidler, 1995). The total amount of news coverage given to campaigns is declining as well. In the last 2 months of the 1996 U.S. presidential campaign, broadcast media gave the campaign 55% less coverage than they gave the 1992 campaign over the same period; coverage in major newspapers declined by more than 40% (Jamieson, Waldman, & Devitt, 1998). Desire to make political coverage appealing to news audiences has been implicated in the U.S. media's continuing devotion to covering policy conflicts and political campaigns as "horse races"—dramatic, suspenseful, conflict-filled contests—as much as or more than as substantive policy disagreements (Cappella & Jamieson, 1996, 1997; Patterson, 1993). The thread that unifies these various changes appears to be a desire to make political journalism more lively, entertaining, and brief, presumably palatable fare for a public that is not much interested in politics. In the U.S. media market, attracting large audiences to news programs is an essential requirement of commercial media institutions.

Similar developments have been observed to affect, although generally to lesser degrees, the mainstream media and their political coverage in other countries as well (Blumler, 1992; Franklin, 1997; Hvitfelt, 1994; Mazzoleni, 1995; Okigbo, 1992; Pfetsch, 1996; Statham, 1996; Thussu, 1999). Among the issues raised by these developments is the possible blurring of genres between news and entertainment, endeavoring to attract wider audiences by injecting entertainment values into news stories (Brants, 1998; Brants & Neijens, 1998; Pfetsch, 1996). This development has been described as reflecting adoption of a more commercial approach to news in countries where media institutions find themselves in more spirited competition for audiences.

A particular focus of research has been the competition between journalists and politicians to shape the news and control the public agenda. As political actors have become more sophisticated and effective at manipulating news coverage (for example, by creating events tailored to providing journalists' desired news values), in some countries journalists have been motivated to resist the manipulation and assert their independence more forcefully. This growing adversarialism, within a broader framework of cooperation where each side is quite dependent on the other, and its consequences for news coverage of politics have been investigated in a number of recent studies (e.g., Bennett, 1996b; Blumler, 1990; Blumler & Gurevitch, 1995; Fallows, 1997; Semetko, Blumler, Gurevitch, & Weaver, 1991; Swanson, 1992, 1997). Among its consequences in the United States, researchers suggest, is an increasingly negative view of politics and politicians offered by journalists who are featured more prominently in their own more heavily interpretive stories (e.g., Barnhurst & Steele, 1997; Patterson, 1993, 1996; Sabato, 1991; Steele & Barnhurst, 1996). Cappella and Jamieson (1997), among others, have attempted to show that this enhanced negativity in political news fosters cynicism about politics and politicians among the electorate, further weakening the institutional position of political parties.

A currently popular methodological approach to discovering these and other qualities of news is the study of news frames, or the way in which news stories frame the events and subjects they cover. Based chiefly on Goffman's (1974) work, frame analysis was developed specifically as a method for examining the content of news by Gamson (1988, 1989; Gamson & Modigliani, 1989). Essentially, frame analysis attempts to identify key features of the narrative framework of a news story that create the overall meaning and coherence of the story. Thus a frame integrates the individual elements of a story (disparate facts, personalities, events) into a meaningful whole. Frame analysis has been employed by political communication researchers in two different ways. First, researchers have used the method to reveal the interpretive frames that journalists construct in order to make news stories coherent and meaningful (e.g., Cohen & Wolfsfeld, 1993; Valkenburg & Semetko, 1998; Wolfsfeld, 1997). Frames most often used to cover politics focus on conflict and competition (elections and policy disputes as horse races or boxing matches, where it is who wins, not ideas and policies, that is most important). Second, researchers have attempted to chart the effectiveness of advocates in leading journalists to adopt the advocates' frames in reporting about issues (e.g., Coy & Woehrle, 1996; Entman & Rojecki, 1993). Despite the popularity of the concept of frames, however, researchers have not always used the concept in precise and consistent ways, as Entman (1993) points out in his call for clarification of this important approach to content analysis.

Cybermedia and Political Communication

Political communication scholars have been greatly interested in the advent and rapid diffusion of the Internet, the Usenet, the World Wide Web, and e-mail, as well as the growing use of these tools by news media, political parties and campaigns, and governments. Researchers have endeavored particularly to discover what new possibilities for political communication these media offer and what their long-term effects will be on the role of communication in political processes.

A number of studies have charted the use of cybermedia in political campaigns and government in the United States and elsewhere (e.g., Bimber, 1998, in press; Coleman, 1998; Gibson & Ward, 1998; Hill & Hughes, 1997, 1998; Klotz, 1997, 1998; Margolis, Resnick, & Tu, 1997; Wu & Weaver, 1997). Perhaps the greatest interest focuses on whether the Internet, with its possibilities for interactive communication and participatory democracy, will alter the nature of citizens' relations to government in the future. Also of great interest is the effect of the Internet on political journalism, as it provides journalists access to new sources of information and provides citizens access to new sources of political news. We have not yet enough experience with these media to foresee what their ultimate contributions will be, and scholars thus far disagree about the prognosis (e.g., Davis, 1999; Friedland, 1996; Graber, 1996; Groper, 1996; Hacker, 1996). Some, such as Graber (1996), foresee greatly enlarged opportunities for citizens to become engaged with government and participate in politics. Others, such as Davis (1999), contend that the Internet will come to be dominated by the same institutions and organizations that control traditional media; thus they see little reason to expect revolutionary changes.

THE CONTEXT OF RECEPTION: CITIZENS AND AUDIENCES

Political communication researchers have long been concerned with determining how and to what extent messages from politicians and news media influence citizens' political knowledge, attitudes, and participation in political processes, as previous reviews of this field amply demonstrate. These major themes of research continue in current work, which investigates such topics as citizens' learning of political information from the mainstream media (e.g., Chaffee & Frank, 1996; Chaffee & Kanihan, 1997), learning from nontraditional media such as talk shows (e.g., Hollander, 1995), cognitive and attitudinal effects of voters' exposure to campaign debates (e.g., Drew & Weaver, 1998; Yawn, Ellsworth, Beatty, & Kahn, 1998), "bandwagon" and other effects of reporting findings of candidate preference polls (e.g., Mehrabian, 1998), effects of newspapers' editorial content on candidate preferences (e.g., Dalton, Beck, & Huckfeldt, 1998), and the effects of "ad watch" news stories that critique political advertisements (e.g., Jamieson & Cappella, 1997). This work emphasizes the importance of individual differences in how voters come to understand the meanings of messages from journalists and politicians. Such work underscores the need for researchers to connect content analysis, which is the most common form of political communication studies of news and politicians' discourse, to audience studies in order to understand the ultimate effects of messages on audiences.

In addition to continuing to explore traditional questions about communication effects, political communication researchers in recent years have shed additional light on the complex processes by which individual voters come to understand the meanings and significance of political messages, integrate the messages with information they already have, and draw on all their beliefs and information to make action decisions in particular contexts. The processing of political information has been studied from a psychological viewpoint for a considerable period, and studies of the roles of political schemata in information processing are particularly well-known, from the groundbreaking studies of Fiske, Kinder, and their colleagues (Fiske, 1986; Fiske & Kinder, 1981; Fiske, Kinder, & Larter, 1983) and Doris Graber (1984) in the 1980s to the recent work of Rhee and Cappella (1997) and Rahn and Cramer (1996).

Recently, the psychological point of view on information processing has been complemented by the attention researchers have given to social and interactional processes in what has come to be called the constructionist approach, which emphasizes an active, dynamic interchange between political communication and its audiences in which learning occurs iteratively and interactively (see Just et al., 1996; Neuman, Just, & Crigler, 1992). This approach is attracting interest because it enables us to understand how political learning and opinions form and evolve within the context of the life experience of citizens, and thus to see political communication from the viewpoint of its audiences.

LOOKING AHEAD: MUTATIONS OF DEMOCRACY?

The study of political communication arose from interest in how communication can contribute to the health and effectiveness of representative government.

In the current scene, the generative institutions of political communication—institutions of politics and journalism—are undergoing rapid change in response to fundamental changes in their contexts and circumstances. Already, these changes are leading to new forms and opportunities for the institutions and altered roles for communication. A theme that unifies the research topics examined above is interest in how the fundamental changes described are leading to corresponding changes in democratic processes and practices: new forms of parties, new relations between citizens and government, new sources of information, new roles for political communication in the lives of citizens. The prospects of "political activity without politics" as citizens come together to address common concerns outside of the structure of political parties and of the rise of a supranational politics appropriate to globalized media and economics raise the possibility of futures that are quite unlike the past.

Political communication research is vitally interested in these mutations —alterations in forms or qualities—of democratic processes and practices. Thus political communication researchers have attempted to prescribe and gauge the effectiveness of a number of reforms, from the civic journalism movement to involve citizens in the democratic dialogue (e.g., Eksterowicz, Roberts, & Clark, 1998; McGregor, Comrie, & Fountaine, 1999; Rosen, 1992) to suggestions for making television news more successful in communicating political information (e.g., Graber, 1994) to speculations about new, more participatory forms of democracy to be achieved through the Internet (e.g., Friedland, 1996). The special contribution of the new analytic attention to connections between political communication and its generative institutions is to help devise reforms that are realistic, given the circumstances of the relevant institutions, and that do not overestimate the independence of political communication from its institutional context. As all forms of representation come to depend increasingly on communication processes, political communication research endeavors to understand and critique how well communication performs its civic functions at the center of social and political life, and also to point the way toward shaping communication to better serve democratic processes.

REFERENCES

Ansolabehere, S., & Iyengar, S. (1995). *Going negative: How political advertisements shrink and polarize the electorate.* New York: Free Press.
Åsard, E., & Bennett, W. L. (1997). *Democracy and the marketplace of ideas.* Cambridge: Cambridge University Press.
Barnhurst, K. G., & Steele, C. A. (1997). Image-bite news: The visual coverage of elections on U.S. television, 1968-1992. *Harvard International Journal of Press/Politics, 2*(1), 40-58.
Baum, M. A., & Kernell, S. (1999). Has cable ended the golden age of presidential television? *American Political Science Review, 93,* 99-114.
Bennett, W. L. (1996a). *The governing crisis: Media, money, and marketing in American elections* (2nd ed.). New York: St. Martin's.
Bennett, W. L. (1996b). *News: The politics of illusion.* White Plains, NY: Longman.

Bimber, B. (1998). The Internet and political mobilization: Research note on the 1996 election season. *Social Science Computer Review, 16,* 391-401.

Bimber, B. (in press). The Internet and citizen communication with government: Does the medium matter? *Political Communication.*

Blumler, J. G. (1990). Elections, the media and the modern publicity process. In M. Ferguson (Ed.), *Public communication: The new imperatives* (pp. 101-113). London: Sage.

Blumler, J. G. (Ed.). (1992). *Television and the public interest: Vulnerable values in West European broadcasting.* London: Sage.

Blumler, J. G., & Gurevitch, M. (1995). *The crisis of public communication.* London: Routledge.

Blumler, J. G., & Kavanagh, D. (1999). The third age of political communication: Influences and features. *Political Communication, 16,* 209-230.

Blumler, J. G., Kavanagh, D., & Nossiter, T. J. (1996). Modern communications versus traditional politics in Britain: Unstable marriage of convenience. In D. L. Swanson & P. Mancini (Eds.), *Politics, media, and modern democracy* (pp. 49-72). Westport, CT: Praeger.

Brants, K. (1998). Who's afraid of infotainment? *European Journal of Communication, 13,* 315-335.

Brants, K., & Neijens, P. (1998). The infotainment of politics. *Political Communication, 15,* 149-164.

Bucy, E. P., & D'Angelo, P. (1999). The crisis of political communication: Normative critiques of news and democratic processes. In M. E. Roloff (Ed.), *Communication yearbook 22* (pp. 301-339). Thousand Oaks, CA: Sage.

Butler, D., & Ranney, A. (Eds.). (1992). *Electioneering: A comparative study of continuity and change.* Oxford: Clarendon.

Cappella, J. N., & Jamieson, K. H. (1996). News frames, political cynicism, and media cynicism. *Annals of the American Academic of Political and Social Science, 546,* 71-84.

Cappella, J. N., & Jamieson, K. H. (1997). *Spiral of cynicism: The press and the public good.* New York: Oxford University Press.

Chaffee, S. H., & Frank, S. (1996). How Americans get political information: Print versus broadcast news. *Annals of the American Academy of Political and Social Science, 546,* 48-58.

Chaffee, S. H., & Kanihan, S. F. (1997). Learning about politics from the mass media. *Political Communication, 14,* 421-430.

Cohen, A. A., & Wolfsfeld, G. (Eds.). (1993). *Framing the intifada: People and media.* Norwood, NJ: Ablex.

Coleman, S. (1998). Interactive media and the 1997 UK general election. *Media, Culture & Society, 20,* 687-694.

Coy, P. G., & Woehrle, L. M. (1996). Constructing identity and oppositional knowledge: The framing practices of peace movement organizations during the Persian Gulf War. *Sociological Spectrum, 16,* 287-327.

Dalton, R. J., Beck, P. A., & Huckfeldt, R. (1998). Partisan cues and the media: Information flows in the 1992 presidential election. *American Political Science Review, 92,* 111-126.

Davis, R. (1999). *The web of politics: The Internet's impact on the American political system.* New York: Oxford University Press.

Diamond, E., & Bates, S. (1992). *The spot: The rise of political advertising on television* (3rd ed.). Cambridge: MIT Press.

Dogan, M. (1997). Erosion of confidence in advanced democracies. *Studies in Comparative International Development, 32*(3), 3-29.

Drew, D., & Weaver, D. (1998). Voter learning in the 1996 presidential election: Did the media matter? *Journalism & Mass Communication Quarterly, 75,* 292-301.

Eksterowicz, A. J., Roberts, R., & Clark, A. (1998). Public journalism and public knowledge. *Harvard International Journal of Press/Politics, 3*(2), 74-95.

Entman, R. M. (1993). Framing: Toward clarification of a fractured paradigm. *Journal of Communication, 43*(4), 51-58.

Entman, R. M., & Rojecki, A. (1993). Freezing out the public: Elite and media framing of the U.S. anti-nuclear movement. *Political Communication, 10,* 155-173.

Fallows, J. (1997). *Breaking the news: How the media undermine American democracy.* New York: Vintage.

Farrell, D. M. (1996). Campaign strategies and tactics. In L. LeDuc, R. G. Niemi, & P. Norris (Eds.), *Comparing democracies: Elections and voting in global perspective* (pp. 161-183). Thousand Oaks, CA: Sage.

Fiske, S. T. (1986). Schema-based versus piecemeal politics: A patchwork quilt, but not a blanket, of evidence. In R. R. Lau & D. O. Sears (Eds.), *Political cognition* (pp. 41-53). Hillsdale, NJ: Lawrence Erlbaum.

Fiske, S. T., & Kinder, D. R. (1981). Involvement, expertise, and schema use: Evidence from political cognition. In N. Cantor & J. F. Kihlstrom (Eds.), *Personality, cognition and social interaction* (pp. 171-190). Hillsdale, NJ: Lawrence Erlbaum.

Fiske, S. T., Kinder, D. R., & Larter, W. M. (1983). The novice and the expert: Knowledge-based strategies in political cognition. *Journal of Experimental Social Psychology, 19,* 381-400.

Franklin, B. (1994). *Packaging politics: Political communications in Britain's media democracy.* London: Edward Arnold.

Franklin, B. (1997). *Newszak and news media.* London: Arnold.

Friedland, L. A. (1996). Electronic democracy and the new citizenship. *Media, Culture & Society, 18,* 185-212.

Gamson, W. A. (1988). The 1987 distinguished lecture: A constructionist approach to mass media and public opinion. *Symbolic Interaction, 11,* 161-174.

Gamson, W. A. (1989). News as framing. *American Behavioral Scientist, 33,* 157-161.

Gamson, W. A., & Modigliani, A. (1989). Media discourse and public opinion on nuclear power: A constructionist approach. *American Journal of Sociology, 95,* 1-37.

Garramone, G. M., Atkin, C. K., Pinkleton, B. E., & Cole, R. T. (1990). Effects of negative political advertising on the political process. *Journal of Broadcasting & Electronic Media, 34,* 299-311.

Gibson, R. K., & Ward, S. J. (1998). U.K. political parties and the Internet: "Politics as usual" in the new media? *Harvard International Journal of Press/Politics, 3*(3), 14-38.

Giddens, A. (1999, May 5). *Democracy* (Reith Lectures). London: BBC.

Goffman, E. (1974), *Frame analysis: An essay on the organization of experience.* New York: Harper & Row.

Graber, D. A. (1984). *Processing the news: How people tame the information tide.* New York: Longman.

Graber, D. A. (1993). Political communication: Scope, progress, promise. In A. W. Finifter (Ed.), *Political science: The state of the discipline II* (pp. 305-332). Washington, DC: American Political Science Association.

Graber, D. A. (1994). Why voters fail information tests: Can the hurdles be overcome? *Political Communication, 11,* 331-346.

Graber, D. A. (1996). The "new" media and politics: What does the future hold? *PS: Political Science & Politics, 24,* 33-36.

Groper, R. (1996). Electronic mail and the reinvigoration of American democracy. *Social Science Computer Review, 14,* 157-168.

Gurevitch, M. (1999). Whither the future? Some afterthoughts. *Political Communication, 16,* 281-284.

Hacker, K. L. (1996). Missing links in the evolution of electronic democratization. *Media, Culture & Society, 18,* 213-232.

Hallin, D. C. (1992). Sound bite news: Television coverage of elections, 1968-1988. *Journal of Communication, 42*(2), 5-24.

Harrop, M. (1990). Political marketing. *Parliamentary Affairs, 43,* 277-291.

Herbst, S. (1993). *Numbered voices: How opinion polling has shaped American politics.* Chicago: University of Chicago Press.

Hill, K. A., & Hughes, J. E. (1997). Computer-mediated political communication: The USENET and political communities. *Political Communication, 14,* 3-27.

Hill, K. A., & Hughes, J. E. (1998). *Cyberpolitics: Citizen activism in the age of the Internet.* Lanham, MD: Rowman & Littlefield.

Hollander, B. A. (1995). The new news and the 1992 presidential campaign: Perceived versus actual political knowledge. *Journalism & Mass Communication Quarterly, 72,* 786-798.

Holtz-Bacha, C. (1999). The American presidential election in international perspective: Europeanization of the U.S. electoral advertising through free-time segments. In L. L. Kaid & D. G. Bystrom (Eds.), *The electronic election: Perspectives on the 1996 campaign communication* (pp. 349-361). Mahwah, NJ: Lawrence Erlbaum.

Hvitfelt, H. (1994). The commercialization of the evening news: Changes in narrative technique in Swedish TV news. *Nordicom Review, 2,* 33-41.

Jackson-Beeck, M., & Kraus, S. (1980). Political communication theory and research: An overview. In D. Nimmo (Ed.), *Communication yearbook 4* (pp. 449-465). New Brunswick, NJ: Transaction.

Jamieson, K. H. (1992). *Dirty politics: Deception, distraction, and democracy.* New York: Oxford University Press.

Jamieson, K. H., & Cappella, J. N. (1997). Setting the record straight: Do ad watches help or hurt? *Harvard International Journal of Press/Politics, 2*(1), 13-22.

Jamieson, K. H., Waldman, P., & Devitt, J. (1998). Mapping the discourse of the 1996 U.S. Presidential campaign. *Media, Culture & Society, 20,* 323-328.

Johnson-Cartree, K. S., & Copeland, G. A. (1991). *Negative political advertising: Coming of age.* Hillsdale, NJ: Lawrence Erlbaum.

Just, M. R., Crigler, A. N., Alger, D. E., Cook, T. E., Kern, M., & West, D. M. (1996). *Crosstalk: Citizens, candidates, and the media in a presidential campaign.* Chicago: University of Chicago Press.

Kaid, L. L. (1996). Political communication. In M. B. Salwen & D. W. Stacks (Eds.), *An integrated approach to communication theory and research* (pp. 443-457). Mahwah, NJ: Lawrence Erlbaum.

Kaid, L. L., & Holtz-Bacha, C. (Eds.). (1995). *Political advertising in Western democracies.* Thousand Oaks, CA: Sage.

Kaid, L. L., & Johnston, A. (1991). Negative versus positive television advertising in presidential campaigns, 1960-1988. *Journal of Communication, 41*(3), 53-64.

Kavanagh, D. (1995). *Election campaigning: The new marketing of politics.* Oxford: Blackwell.

Key, V. O. (1958). *Politics, parties, and pressure groups* (4th ed.). New York: Thomas Y. Crowell.

Klotz, R. (1997). Positive spin: Senate campaigning on the Web. *PS: Political Science & Politics, 30,* 482-486.

Klotz, R. (1998). Virtual criticism: Negative advertising on the Internet in the 1996 Senate races. *Political Communication, 15,* 347-365.

Kurtz, H. (1996, October 12). Does the evening news still matter? *TV Guide,* pp. 20-23.

Larson, C. U., & Wiegele, T. C. (1979). Political communication theory and research: An overview. In D. Nimmo (Ed.), *Communication yearbook 3* (pp. 457-473). New Brunswick, NJ: Transaction.

Lowry, D. T., & Shidler, J. A. (1995). The sound bites, the biters, and the bitten: An analysis of network TV news bias in campaign 92. *Journalism & Mass Communication Quarterly, 72,* 33-44.

Maarek, P. J. (1995). *Communication and political marketing.* London: John Libbey.

Maarek, P. J. (1997). New trends in French political communication: The 1995 presidential elections. *Media, Culture & Society, 19,* 357-368.

Mancini, P. (1999). New frontiers in political professionalism. *Political Communication, 16,* 231-245.

Mansfield, M. W., & Weaver, R. A. (1982). Political communication theory and research: An overview. In M. Burgoon (Ed.), *Communication yearbook 5* (pp. 605-625). New Brunswick, NJ: Transaction.

Margolis, M., Resnick, D., & Tu, C. (1997). Campaigning on the Internet: Parties and candidates on the World Wide Web in the 1996 primary season. *Harvard International Journal of Press/Politics, 2*(1), 59-78.

Mauser, G. (1983). *Political marketing: A new approach to campaign strategy.* New York: Praeger.

Mayer, W. G. (1996). In defense of negative campaigning. *Political Science Quarterly, 111,* 437-455.

Mayhew, L. H. (1997). *The new public: Professional communication and the means of social influence.* Cambridge: Cambridge University Press.

Mayobre, J. A. (1996). Politics, media, and modern democracy: The case of Venezuela. In D. L. Swanson & P. Mancini (Eds.), *Politics, media, and modern democracy* (pp. 227-245). Westport, CT: Praeger.

Mazzoleni, G. (1995). Towards a "videocracy"? Italian political communication at a turning point. *European Journal of Communication, 10,* 291-319.

Mazzoleni, G. (1996). Patterns and effects of recent changes in electoral campaigning in Italy. In D. L. Swanson & P. Mancini (Eds.), *Politics, media, and modern democracy* (pp. 192-206). Westport, CT: Praeger.

Mazzoleni, G., & Schulz, W. (1999). "Mediatization" of politics: A challenge for democracy? *Political Communication, 16,* 247-261.

McGregor, J., Comrie, M., & Fountaine, S. (1999). Beyond the feel-good factor: Measuring public journalism in the 1996 New Zealand election campaign. *Harvard International Journal of Press/Politics, 4*(1), 66-77.

Medvic, S. K., & Lenart, S. (1997). The influence of political consultants in the 1992 congressional elections. *Legislative Studies Quarterly, 22,* 61-77.

Mehrabian, A. (1998). Effects of poll reports on voter preferences. *Journal of Applied Social Psychology, 28,* 2119-2130.

Mollison, T. A. (1998). Television broadcasting leads Romania's march toward an open, democratic society. *Journal of Broadcasting & Electronic Media, 42,* 128-141.

Negrine, R. (1996). *The communication of politics.* London: Sage.

Neuman, W. R., Just, M. R., & Crigler, A. N. (1992). *Common knowledge: News and the construction of political meaning.* Chicago: University of Chicago Press.

Newman, B. I. (1994). *The marketing of the president: Political marketing as campaign strategy.* Thousand Oaks, CA: Sage.

Nimmo, D. (1977). Political communication theory and research: An overview. In B. D. Ruben (Ed.), *Communication yearbook 1* (pp. 441-452). New Brunswick, NJ: Transaction.

Nimmo, D., & Sanders, K. R. (1981). *Handbook of political communication.* Beverly Hills, CA: Sage.

Nimmo, D., & Swanson, D. L. (1990). The field of political communication: Beyond the voter persuasion paradigm. In D. L. Swanson & D. Nimmo (Eds), *New directions in political communication* (pp. 7-47). Newbury Park, CA: Sage.

Norris, P. (1999). *Critical citizens.* Oxford: Oxford University Press.

Okigbo, C. (1992). Horserace and issues in Nigerian elections. *Journal of Black Studies, 22,* 349-365.

Patterson, T. E. (1993). *Out of order.* New York: Alfred A. Knopf.

Patterson, T. E. (1996). Bad news, bad governance. *Annals of the American Academy of Political and Social Science, 546,* 97-108.

Pfau, M., & Kenski, H. C. (1990). *Attack politics: Strategy and defense.* New York: Praeger.

Pfetsch, B. (1996). Convergence through privatization? Changing media environments and televised politics in Germany. *European Journal of Communication, 11,* 427-451.

Pinkleton, B. E. (1997). The effects of negative comparative political advertising on candidate evaluations and advertising evaluations: An exploration. *Journal of Advertising, 26,* 19-29.

Rahn, W. M., & Cramer, K. J. (1996). Activation and the application of political party stereotypes: The role of television. *Political Communication, 13,* 195-212.

Rawnsley, G. D. (1997). The 1996 presidential campaign in Taiwan: Packaging politics in a democratizing state. *Harvard International Journal of Press/Politics, 2*(2), 47-61.

Rhee, J. W., & Cappella, J. N. (1997). The role of political sophistication in learning from news: Measuring schema development. *Communication Research, 24,* 197-233.

Rosen, J. (1992). Politics, vision, and the press: Toward a public agenda for journalism. In J. Rosen & P. Taylor (Eds.), *The new news v. the old news: The press and politics in the 1990s* (pp. 3-33). New York: Twentieth Century Fund.

Sabato, L. J. (1981). *The rise of political consultants: New ways of winning elections.* New York: Basic Books.

Sabato, L. J. (1991). *Feeding frenzy: How attack journalism has transformed American politics.* New York: Free Press.

Sanders, K. R., & Kaid, L. L. (1978). Political communication theory and research: An overview. In B. D. Ruben (Ed.), *Communication yearbook 2* (pp. 375-389). New Brunswick, NJ: Transaction.

Scammell, M. (1995). *Designer politics: How elections are won.* Basingstoke, England: Macmillan.

Schwartzman, K. C. (1998). Globalization and democracy. *Annual Review of Sociology, 24,* 159-181

Semetko, H. A., Blumler, J. G., Gurevitch, M., & Weaver, D. H. (with Barkin, S., & Wilhoit, G. C.). (1991). *The formation of campaign agendas: A comparative analysis of party and media roles in recent American and British elections.* Hillsdale, NJ: Lawrence Erlbaum.

Sigelman, L., & Whicker, M. L. (1988). The growth of government, the ineffectiveness of voting, and the pervasive political malaise. *Electoral Studies, 7,* 95-108.

Statham, P. (1996). Television news and the public sphere in Italy: Conflicts at the media/politics interface. *European Journal of Communication, 11,* 511-556.

Steele, C. A., & Barnhurst, K. G. (1996). The journalism of opinion: Network news coverage of U.S. presidential campaigns, 1968-1988. *Critical Studies in Mass Communication, 13,* 187-209.

Stuckey, M. E., & Antczak, F. J. (1998). The rhetorical presidency: Deepening vision, widening exchange. In M. E. Roloff (Ed.), *Communication yearbook 21* (pp. 405-441). Thousand Oaks, CA: Sage.

Swanson, D. L. (1992). The political-media complex. *Communication Monographs, 59,* 397-400.

Swanson, D. L. (1997). The political-media complex at 50: Putting the 1996 presidential campaign in context. *American Behavioral Scientist, 40,* 1264-1282.

Swanson, D. L., Crigler, A. N., Gurevitch, M., & Neuman, W. R. (1998). The United States. In K. B. Jensen (Ed.), *News of the world: World cultures look at television news* (p. 144-163). London: Routledge.

Swanson, D. L., & Mancini, P. (Eds.). (1996). *Politics, media, and modern democracy.* Westport, CT: Praeger.

Swanson, D. L., & Nimmo, D. (Eds.). (1990). *New directions in political communication.* Newbury Park, CA: Sage.

Tak, J., Kaid, L. L., & Lee, S. (1997). A cross-cultural study of political advertising in the United States and Korea. *Communication Research, 24,* 413-430.

Thussu, D. K. (1999). Privatizing the airwaves: The impact of globalization on broadcasting in India. *Media, Culture & Society, 21,* 125-131.

Valkenburg, P. M., & Semetko, H. A. (1998, September). *On the way to framing effects: A content analysis of frames in the news.* Paper presented at the annual meeting of the American Political Science Association, Boston.

Waisbord, S. R. (1996). Secular politics: The modernization of Argentine electioneering. In D. L. Swanson & P. Mancini (Eds.), *Politics, media, and modern democracy* (pp. 207-225). Westport, CT: Praeger.

Wattenberg, M. P. (1990). *The decline of American political parties.* Cambridge, MA: Harvard University Press.

West, D. M. (1997). *Air wars: Television advertising in election campaigns, 1952-1996* (2nd ed.). Washington, DC: Congressional Quarterly Press.

Wolfsfeld, G. (1997). *Media and political conflict: News from the Middle East.* Cambridge: Cambridge University Press.

Wu, W., & Weaver, D. (1997). On-line democracy or on-line demagoguery? Public opinion "polls" on the Internet. *Harvard International Journal of Press/Politics, 2*(4), 71-86.

Yawn, M., Ellsworth, K., Beatty, B., & Kahn, K. F. (1998). How a presidential primary debate changed attitudes of audience members. *Political Behavior, 20,* 155-181.

CHAPTER CONTENTS

9 Instructional and Developmental Communication Theory and Research in the 1990s: Extending the Agenda for the 21st Century

JENNIFER H. WALDECK
University of Kansas, Lawrence

PATRICIA KEARNEY
TIMOTHY G. PLAX
California State University, Long Beach

In examining the state of the art in instructional and developmental communication, the authors define the scope of the Instructional and Developmental Communication Division of the International Communication Association. They then present an overview of the primary theories that have directed research in instructional communication since 1990 and identify the major areas of research, discussing representative studies within each area. Finally, they address major theoretical, conceptual, and methodological issues of importance to instructional and developmental communication researchers and, based on in-depth review of the literature in this area, recommend more research attention to (a) teacher-student interactions, as opposed to studies that examine just teacher or student communication alone; (b) student-student interactions, including collaborative learning; and (c) the impact of technology on student outcomes. Moreover, the authors note that to facilitate systematic advancement of this area, researchers should work to (a) acknowledge the distinction between instructional communication and communication education, (b) initiate and sustain *programs* of research, and (c) precisely define constructs to avoid confusion resulting from conceptual and operational overlap.

A S the 21st century begins, we are confronted with the fact that the instructional process continues to fail far too many students. In a recent report card for the nation, for example, the National Assessment of Educational Progress revealed that only 40% of high school seniors are proficient in reading (Donahue, Voelkl, Campbell, & Mazzeo, 1999) and only 30% are proficient in

---

Correspondence: Jennifer H. Waldeck, 5000 Clinton Parkway #207, Lawrence, KS 66047; e-mail jhwinca@aol.com

Communication Yearbook 24, pp. 207-229

math (Reese, Miller, Mazzeo, & Dossey, 1997). These and similar statistics have served as the basis for a nationwide call for testing, higher standards, and more teacher training in an effort to increase teacher competencies in both subject matter and pedagogy. Central to advancing teachers' pedagogical expertise is the research and thinking of instructional communication scholars. Researchers in this area have consistently recognized that teacher content competence is a necessary but insufficient condition for teaching effectiveness (e.g., Hall, Morreale, & Gaudino, 1999; Hurt, Scott, & McCroskey, 1978; Johnson & Roellke, 1999).

The public outcry for increased teacher competency is not a new idea. In fact, more than 20 years ago instructional communication researchers began to address that very concern (Scott & Wheeless, 1977; Lashbrook & Wheeless, 1978; Wheeless & Hurt, 1979). Over the years, communication researchers have demonstrated the central role of communication in effective instruction. We owe a lot to these early efforts—key terms and variables have been defined, processes and effects have been substantiated, and innovative studies have yielded important prescriptive implications for the classroom. But, as in any new area of study, these early research efforts were characterized by more energy than focus—evidenced by the number of studies versus themes of programmatic research. For instance, very few examples of theoretically grounded or programmatic research appear in the literature. If we are to legitimate and develop instructional communication further as an area of research and theory, we need to take time now to pause and reflect on what we have learned and what we still need to do.

In this chapter we examine the state of the art in instructional communication. Toward this end, we begin by defining the scope of the Instructional and Developmental Communication Division of the International Communication Association. We then provide an overview of the primary theories that have directed research in instructional communication. We next describe the criteria employed in our selection of the studies reviewed in this chapter, identify the major lines of research, and review representative studies. Finally, we address the major conceptual, theoretical, and methodological issues of importance that instructional communication researchers must consider as they move into the new century.

THE SCOPE OF THE INSTRUCTIONAL AND DEVELOPMENTAL COMMUNICATION DIVISION

Sorensen and Christophel (1992) have traced the origins of instructional communication in the International Communication Association. The area was not recognized widely by the field until the 1972 ICA convention, and the following year the Instructional Communication Division was founded (9 years later, the division was expanded to include developmental communication). In a series of three *Communication Yearbook* overviews, the parameters of instructional communication were defined to (a) introduce this area of scholarship to the field and (b) distinguish between "teaching speech" (communication education) and the role of communication in generalized instruction across disciplines (instructional communication). In reference to these objectives, Sorensen and Christophel indicate that "instructional communication is concerned with the implementation of communication systems that facilitate learning without regard for any specific academic discipline. At the other end, however, communication education focuses on instructional strategies specifically designed to teach the content of the speech communication discipline" (p. 36). Predicting that work conducted in the 1990s would lead to a greater understanding of this distinction, Sorensen and Christophel encouraged communication scholars to "use the titles that their colleagues prefer" (p. 39). Instructional communication research encompasses much wider concerns than teaching speech communication; thus the Instructional and Developmental Communication Division addresses issues relevant to educators within and outside of our discipline.

Important to our understanding of the distinction between instructional communication and communication education is the theory (or lack of theory) from which research has been generated. With few notable exceptions (see Daly, Vangelisti, & Weber, 1995), communication education scholars are essentially atheoretical in their concern for content-specific pedagogy. Conversely, instructional communication scholars, interested in a broader understanding of the role of communication in learning, operate deductively from a particular theoretical perspective or work inductively to build theory. In the next section, we briefly review the major theories that have dominated the area of instructional communication.

MAJOR THEORIES ASSOCIATED WITH INSTRUCTIONAL AND DEVELOPMENTAL COMMUNICATION RESEARCH

In reviewing the instructional and developmental communication research, we found that the following theories are representative of those employed by instructional and developmental communication researchers: arousal theory, Keller's model of instructional design, French and Raven's bases of power, attribution theory, expectancy or learned helplessness, arousal valence model, approach-avoidance, information-processing theory, social cognitive/learning theory, cultivation theory, and general theories of child development. We review each of these theories briefly below and provide representative examples of how they are used in particular lines of instructional/developmental communication research. These examples illustrate initial uses of each theory in the literature as well recent applications.

Arousal theory. Researchers rely on arousal theory to explain the role of teacher nonverbal immediacy in the learning process (Christophel & Gorham, 1995; Kelley & Gorham, 1988). In one representative study, Christophel and Gorham (1995) found that immediacy aroused students sufficiently to direct their attention toward learning the content. In this way, students' motivation to engage in task-related activities was enhanced and student learning was achieved.

Keller's ARCS model of instructional design. Keller's (1983, 1987) ARCS model indicates that teachers who make material relevant to students' lives or goals increase students' motivation to learn. More specifically, Keller contends that four conditions must be met for learning to occur: First, the instructor must gain students' attention (*A*); second, the content must be relevant (*R*) to students' needs; third, students must have confidence (*C*) in their ability to accomplish the task; and fourth, students must be satisfied (*S*) with the results of their efforts. In one instructional communication study, Frymier and Shulman (1995) found support for Keller's paradigm; their findings indicated that the more effectively teachers were able to communicate relevance in their instruction, the more motivated students were to learn.

French and Raven's bases of power. French and Raven (1959) conceptualized five power resources: coercive, referent, legitimate, reward, and expert. This perspective initiated a long line of research focusing on teacher use of behavior alteration techniques (BATs) and behavior alteration messages (BAMs) to gain student compliance. These studies focus on the implementation of teacher power—how teachers communicate their power resources, student and teacher perceptions of teacher power, and the relationship between teachers' selective power use and student learning. Research from this theoretical perspective has employed diverse samples of teachers, including elementary and secondary teachers, preteachers, graduate teaching assistants, and college/university professors. In their contribution to a volume examining power in the classroom, Kearney and Plax (1992) provide a comprehensive review of the literature on teacher power and student resistance.

Attribution theory. Attribution theory focuses on the processes by which we construct, interpret, and identify causes of our own behavior and that of others. Kearney, Plax, and Burroughs (1991) used attribution theory to explain students' decisions about resisting their teachers' control attempts. Kearney et al. found that students selected different strategies for resisting teachers based on their attributions regarding problem ownership (i.e., whether students attributed classroom problems to teachers or to themselves). Elsewhere, this theory has been used in investigations of teacher attire and credibility (Gorham, Cohen, & Morris, 1997; Morris, Gorham, Cohen, & Huffman, 1996).

Expectancy learning/learned helplessness. This theoretical perspective posits that individuals learn to predict or expect positive or negative outcomes of their own behavior over time. Learned helplessness results when behavioral consequences are random and therefore impossible to predict. McCroskey and Richmond (1987) first used this theoretical framework for predicting and explaining communication apprehension, setting the stage for a long line of theoretically informed research on communication anxiety (e.g., Chesebro et al., 1992; Rosenfeld, Grant, & McCroskey, 1995). Specifically, McCroskey and

Richmond found that when individuals' expectations regarding communication were unpredictable, they experienced a decrease in confidence and an increase in anxiety. When those expectations entailed negative outcomes that the individual believed would be difficult or impossible to avoid, fear resulted (see also Daly, McCroskey, Ayres, Hopf, & Ayres, 1997).

Arousal valence theory. Closely aligned with expectancy theory, arousal valence theory has been used to explain students' responses to teachers (Andersen, 1985; Neuliep, 1995; Sanders & Wiseman, 1990). Specifically, arousal valence theory indicates that individuals hold expectations for their environments. Such expectations are influenced by a variety of factors, including cultural background, past experiences, individual differences, and contextual characteristics. Exposure to stimuli that are inconsistent with an individual's expectations results in arousal—a heightened state of emotional and cognitive attention. Once arousal occurs, the individual assigns either a positive or a negative valence to the experience. The direction of the valence, then, influences the person's reactions to the experience. For instance, Collier and Powell (1990) and Sanders and Wiseman (1990) reasoned that students' cultures influence the valences of their reactions to specific teacher behaviors. Similarly, Neuliep (1995) found that both students' and teachers' cultural backgrounds influenced their expectations and subsequent reactions to one another in the classroom.

Approach/avoidance. A number of studies in instructional communication have relied on approach/avoidance tendencies to explain teacher-student interactions. Logically, individuals approach or move toward encounters that they like, evaluate highly, and prefer, and they avoid, or move away from, encounters that they dislike, evaluate negatively, and do not prefer (Mehrabian, 1971). This axiom has been employed in examinations of a number of instructional concerns, including immediacy, communication apprehension, extraclass communication, student motivation, receiver apprehension, willingness to communicate in the classroom, and use of communication technologies for instructional purposes. For example, positive student learning outcomes are associated with teacher immediacy (a set of approach-oriented behaviors), and negative learning outcomes are associated with teacher nonimmediacy (Frymier, 1994). Elsewhere, Neer (1990) found that students apprehensive about classroom communication were more likely to avoid classroom discussions than were students who had low anxiety about classroom communication.

Information-processing theory. Information-processing theory concerns how people decode messages from their environments based on their cognitive abilities to do so and the relative complexity of the messages (see Delia, O'Keefe, & O'Keefe, 1982; Wheeless, Preiss, & Gayle, 1997). Within the literature on instructional communication, this theory has been used to explain students' receiver apprehension. For instance, Ayres, Wilcox, and Ayres (1995) found that message complexity (e.g., difficulty of lecture material), motivation to process the message (e.g., desire to get a good grade), and antici- pation of the need to reproduce the message for evaluation (e.g., on a test) in- creased student receiver apprehension.

Social learning/cognitive theory. Also referred to as observational learning, social cognitive theory (Bandura, 1994) was originally developed by Bandura (1977) (and referred to as social learning theory) as an extension of earlier, more general reinforcement theories. As the name suggests, social learning theory explains how individuals learn not by performing actions themselves, but by observing how other people cope with problems that confront them. Ac- cording to this theory, looking to the behavior of others is the main way in which individuals discover what others expect of them. People watch how oth- ers behave and react to stimuli, and under some circumstances (e.g., when the role models are respected or emulated) they repeat those responses. Bandura (1994) posits that television viewers learn about the world from exposure to media. In a recent application of this theory, Cantor and Omdahl (1999) found that children who saw televised dramas of accidents with negative conse- quences (as opposed to benign consequences) comprehended the importance of adhering to safety guidelines in order to avoid accidents.

Cultivation theory. Gerbner, Gross, Morgan, and Signorielli (1994) explain the process by which heavy television viewing influences persons' percep- tions of reality. According to their perspective, the "reality" that is depicted on television becomes, over time, more believable to viewers than their actual ex- periences. Although cultivation theory has received minimal support (Morgan & Shanahan, 1997), Cantor and Omdahl (1991) found that children exposed to frightening scenes of natural disasters (ones with negative, life-threatening consequences) reported greater fear and worry that such incidents would occur in reality than did children exposed to benign stimuli (scenes with no apparent negative consequences).

Developmental theories. Developmental theorists argue that as children age, they are able to differentiate among stimuli in increasingly sophisticated ways (Flavell, 1985; Piaget, 1977). Developmental theories have been used to explain children's communication competence (Kline & Clinton, 1998) and reactions to media exposure. For instance, Wilson and Weiss (1991; Weiss & Wilson, 1998) examined children's emotional and cognitive responses to fright- and anger-inducing television scenes and found that older children per- ceived, interpreted, and responded to such portrayals differently than did younger ones.

MAJOR LINES OF RESEARCH AND OUTLETS FOR PUBLICATION IN INSTRUCTIONAL AND DEVELOPMENTAL COMMUNICATION

Given the limited space and parameters for this review, we needed to establish firm criteria on which to base our selection of the studies to be included. Specifically, we have directed our attention to studies that have been reported in the literature published since 1990, to contribute to the "state-of-the-art" nature of this chapter, and that have been reported in journals indexed by the National Communication Association's publication *Index to Journals in Communication Studies Through 1995* (Matlon & Ortiz, 1997). We have also limited our selection to studies that were empirical and data based and that addressed issues that fit within the parameters of the Instructional and Developmental Communication Division.

Analysis of the instructional/developmental literature from 1990 to winter 1999 that fit these criteria allowed for classification by publication outlet. Overwhelmingly, the majority of instructional and developmental communication studies appeared in *Communication Education* (n = 88 out of a total of 186 studies). The bulk of the remaining studies appeared in *Communication Research Reports* (n = 31) and *Communication Quarterly* (n = 22). Other represented outlets included the *Journal of Broadcasting & Electronic Media, Journal of Applied Communication Research, Human Communication Research, Southern Communication Journal,* and *Communication Monographs.* (See Table 9.1 for a complete report on the number of instructional communication studies in each journal.)

After reviewing and analyzing the studies, we found that we could classify the instructional and developmental communication research into six major categories: classroom management, teacher-student interaction, pedagogical methods and technology use, student communication variables, teacher communication variables, and the impact of mass media on children. Across these six major categories we found 186 studies published in the communication literature. Because a number of these studies were not mutually exclusive in terms of major variables examined, they were referenced in more than one category. (See Table 9.2 for complete lists of topics covered within each of the six categories.)

In the following review of representative research within each of the six categories, we include studies that (a) represent the relevant category, (b) demonstrate sound research design and assessment practices, (c) have heuristic value, and (d) were conducted by scholars who are known for their research within the particular category.

Student Communication Variables

The largest category of research focused on student communication variables (N = 113). Studies within this category examined student characteristics and communication behaviors that influence the instructional process and learning out-

TABLE 9.1
Instructional and Developmental Communication
Research by Journal, 1990-April 1999

Journal	Number	Percentage
Communication Education	88	47
Communication Research Reports	31	7
Communication Quarterly	22	12
Journal of Broadcasting & Electronic Media	8	4
Journal of Applied Communication Research	6	3
Human Communication Research	6	3
Southern Communication Journal	6	3
Communication Monographs	4	2
Communication Reports	3	2
Journal of Communication	3	2
Journalism Quarterly	3	2
Communication Research	2	—
Western Journal of Communication	1	—
Women's Studies in Communication	1	—
Journal of the Association for Communication Administration	1	—
Communication Studies	0	—
Communication Theory	0	—
Critical Studies in Mass Communication	0	—
Howard Journal of Communications	0	—
Journal of Communication and Religion	0	—
Philosophy and Rhetoric	0	—
Quarterly Journal of Speech	0	—
Text and Performance Quarterly	0	—
TOTAL	186	100

comes. For instance, this category was dominated by studies that focused on students' communication apprehension or public speaking anxiety ($n = 53$). Second in ranking was student culture/gender ($n = 26$), followed by studies that examined student motivation ($n = 14$).

Communication apprehension research. Although a number of scholars speculated that the state anxiety experienced by a speaker during a presentation is influenced by a number of situational factors, particularly novelty, conspicuousness, and subordinate status, no research to this point has actually tested that assumption. Suspecting that more traitlike characteristics affect state anxiety, Beatty and Friedland (1990) examined both trait and state versions of novelty, conspicuousness, and subordinate state, along with the traitlike public speaking component of the PRCA-24. Undergraduate students presented a short informative speech. They completed all trait measures at the beginning of the term and the situational measures immediately following their performance. Analyses confirmed Beatty and Friedland's prediction: Trait measures better predicted students' public speaking state anxiety than did situational measures, with public speaking apprehension (trait) the single best predictor.

Although substantial attention has been given to the role of communication apprehension (CA) in public speaking, little has been directed toward the effect of CA on the speech preparation process. Assuming that individuals high in CA are averse to communication and consequently avoid real or imagined interaction when they can, Ayres (1996) predicted that, compared with persons low in CA, those high in CA would report less time discussing the assignment with instructors, conducting interviews, rehearsing, and analyzing their audience but more time doing library research, preparing notes, and preparing visual aids. Ayres also predicted that those high in CA would spend less time preparing and would receive lower grades on their speeches. Following the first prepared speech of the semester, undergraduate students completed a questionnaire that included the PRCA-24, a state measure of CA, and an instrument designed to assess a variety of speech preparation-type activities. As predicted, those with high CA scores reported spending more of their preparation time on non-communication-oriented activities than did those with low CA scores. In contrast, those with low CA spent proportionately more of their preparation time on communication-oriented activities. And even though those with high communication apprehension reported spending more time overall preparing their speeches, they received lower grades than did those whose CA was low.

Motivation to learn research. Recognizing that motivated students learn more than unmotivated students, Gorham and Christophel (Millette) (1992) asked college students to identify both motivating and demotivating class-specific factors that influenced them to "try hard and do their best" in class. Responses to open-ended questions revealed that students identified a number of student- and class-related factors to their own levels of motivation, but attributed primarily negative teacher behaviors to their levels of demotivation. Those findings led the researchers to speculate as to whether or not teachers' perceptions of what motivates and demotivates students were similarly aligned with students' reports. In a follow-up study, Gorham and Millette (1997) compared college teachers' responses to open-ended questions with those reported by students from their previous study. These analyses revealed substantial agreement between teachers and students on the range of factors affecting student motivation. However, the data supported a sharp difference between the two populations in assignment of credit or blame for motivating or

TABLE 9.2
Instructional and Developmental Communication Research by Category,
1990-Winter 1999

Area of Study	Number	Percentage
Student communication	113	42
Peer sexual harassment	1	
Learner empowerment	1	
Student culture/gender	26	
Student affinity seeking	1	
Communication competence	7	
Communication apprehension/ public speaking anxiety	53	
Motivation/demotivation	14	
Willingness to communicate in the classroom	3	
Social support	4	
Receiver apprehension/student uncertainty	3	
Teacher communication	85	31
Misbehaviors	7	
Ratings of teaching effectiveness	9	
Receptivity	1	
Powerful speech	1	
Immediacy-related behaviors	28	
Credibility	12	
Style	2	
Graduate student assistant training	4	
Burnout	2	
Content relevance	2	
Teacher affinity seeking	5	
Teacher communication apprehension	1	
Teacher sociocommunicative style	3	
Teacher communication concerns	1	
Clarity	3	
Attire	3	
Humor	2	

TABLE 9.2 *continued*

Area of Study	Number	Percentage
Mass-media effects on children	27	10
TV effects	14	
Film effects	7	
Print media	1	
Advertising	3	
Policy regulation	2	
Pedagogical methods/technology use	26	10
Televised classroom/distance learning	6	
Technology as a pedagogical aid	12	
Student/teacher technology apprehension	1	
Pedagogical methods	7	
Classroom management	10	3.7
Teacher power	5	
Student resistance	2	
Student challenges	1	
Graduate teaching assistant power	2	
Teacher-student interaction	10	3.7
Student clarifying tactics	1	
Student questions	4	
Mentoring	2	
Mediated interaction	1	
Interpersonal communication	1	
Extraclass communication	1	
TOTAL	271[a]	100

[a] Some studies are referenced in multiple categories; thus the actual total number of studies is <271 for this period (acutal $N = 186$)

demotivating students, respectively. Whereas teachers credited sources of motivation to what teachers do (e.g., how they organize and structure the class, assignments, and course requirements), students attributed sources of motivation more to what students do (e.g., interest in the subject matter, desire to get good grades and please their parents). Similarly, teachers attributed sources of demotivation more to student factors (e.g., students' low grades, lack of prerequisite skills, and heavy workload), whereas students attributed their demotivation more to teacher factors (e.g., poor presentational skills, lack of teacher enthusiasm). Apparently, teacher behaviors affect the motivational climate of the classroom—but not in the ways teachers have traditionally assumed.

Teacher Communication Variables

The second-largest category included studies examining teacher communication variables ($N = 85$). Investigations in this category focused on teacher characteristics and communication behaviors that influence the instructional process and student learning. Not surprisingly, teacher immediacy ($n = 28$) and credibility ($n = 12$) were the most frequently studied teacher variables. Others included graduate student assistant training, teacher style, teacher misbehaviors, and ratings of teaching effectiveness.

Teacher immediacy and credibility research. In a recent study that examined three of these teacher communication variables, Thweatt and McCroskey (1998) predicted that college teachers high in immediacy would be perceived as more credible (more competent, trustworthy, and caring) than teachers who are less immediate. They also hypothesized that teachers who engage in misbehaviors would be perceived as less credible than teachers who do not. Students in Thweatt and McCroskey's sample read one of four scenarios that manipulated descriptions of a teacher who was either high or low in nonverbal immediacy and who engaged in either three inappropriate behaviors (misbehaviors) or three appropriate behaviors. Even though results indicated significant main effects, interaction effects were also obtained. To interpret, students rated highest in credibility the nonmisbehaving, immediate teacher. Most interesting is the finding that ratings of credibility continued to be higher for the misbehaving, immediate teacher than for the nonmisbehaving, nonimmediate teacher. Apparently, engaging in nonverbal immediacy behaviors is one important way for teachers to increase perceptions of credibility and, at the same time, neutralize some of the negative impacts of certain kinds of teacher misbehaviors.

Teacher immediacy and culture research. In an effort to determine the relative importance of specific nonverbal immediacy behaviors on students' evaluations of their teachers, McCroskey, Richmond, Sallinen, Fayer, and Barraclough (1995) reasoned that immediacy behaviors might also be those same behaviors more traditionally defined as "good delivery" skills. Because they were also interested in the degree to which teacher immediacy behaviors and instructor evaluation are generalizable across divergent cultures, they sampled more than 1,000 students from the United States, Australia, Puerto Rico, and Finland. Based on the students' behavioral assessments and overall evaluations of their teachers, teacher immediacy was found to be highly and positively related to students' evaluations across all cultures. Interestingly, Puerto Rican and U.S. students reported having the most immediate teachers, whereas Finnish students reported having the least immediate teachers and, not coincidentally, the most negative affect. Specific nonverbal immediacy behaviors that contributed most to higher teacher ratings included vocal variety, relaxed body position, eye contact, smiling, and, to a lesser extent, gestures and body movement. Behaviors that seemed to be of little consequence were touch (perceived as inappropriate for college instruction) and whether the teacher stood or sat in class.

Teacher immediacy and content relevance research. Even though teacher immediacy has been known to have consistent and positive influence on students' (state) motivation to study, Frymier and Shulman (1995) were interested in the additional predictive power of content relevance. Relying on Keller's (1983, 1987) ARCS model of instructional design, these researchers explained how immediacy may help to influence three of the four factors requisite for motivation by affecting students' attention (A), confidence (C), and satisfaction (S). But the fourth factor, relevance (R), may require additional teacher behaviors or messages that communicate how course content/tasks meet students' needs. Frymier and Shulman hypothesized that student reports of teacher immediacy and content relevance would together contribute to students' state motivation more than would either set of behaviors alone, and undergraduates' responses to questionnaires confirmed their prediction.

Mass-Media Effects on Children

The distant third most frequently studied area concerned mass-media effects on children ($N = 27$). Within this category, researchers are interested in the effects of various media genres on children, including television ($n = 14$) and film ($n = 7$). Researchers concerned with the effects of popular but problematic media presentations on children have produced a long line of research that has systematically examined ways to prevent or reduce media-induced fear. Representative of that research program is Hoffner's (1997) study on children's emotional reactions to a scary film. Hoffner wanted to know if detailed, prior knowledge of a happy, safe outcome to a film along with individual differences in coping style would reduce children's fear. To test that interaction, Hoffner exposed 10-year-olds to scary film segments depicting a tornado destroying a family farm and trapping a grandfather and grandson under a truck or under a mound of corn. Half the children were told that the segment would conclude with a happy ending; the other half were not. Half were categorized as "blunters" (those who prefer to avoid or reinterpret threat-related information) and half as "monitors" (those who prefer to attend to threat-related information). Results indicated that prior knowledge of a happy outcome did not meaningfully reduce children's fear—except for blunters (accounting for 6% of the variance).

In a second important media effects study, Weiss and Wilson (1998) examined children's developmental comprehension of and emotional responses to negative emotions in televised family situation comedies. They were interested in whether including a humorous subplot precluded younger children from (a) understanding the negative main plot or (b) realistically understanding the impact that a similar negative event might have in their own lives. Boys and girls at two developmental levels viewed an episode of *Full House* with a main plot that produced a negative emotion (fear or anger). Two groups viewed the negative main plot with a positive subplot included, and the remaining children viewed only the negative main plot. Overall, results indicated that inclusion of the subplot (a) reduced comprehension of the major plot for younger children (who are less cognitively sophisticated) and (b) distorted children's perceptions of the characters' negative emotions (children who viewed the subplot reported that the characters were less angry or scared than did those who viewed the episode without the subplot), but (c) had relatively little impact on children's own emotional responses to the program. Finally, this study indicated that viewing negative emotional events in a sitcom may influence children's perceptions of the severity of similar events in their own lives, particularly for children who perceive what is televised as highly realistic and for older children whose thinking is more sophisticated.

Pedagogical Methods and Technology Use

Closely tied in rank to media effects studies were investigations of pedagogical methods and technology use ($N = 26$). These studies focused on specific classroom activities and exercises (pedagogical methods) and issues such as computer-mediated instruction ($n = 12$) and distance learning ($n = 6$).

Distance learning research. Witt and Wheeless (1999) examined the relationship between students' expectations for teacher nonverbal immediacy and their enrollment in a distance learning course. Because the telecourse teacher is typically physically distant, Witt and Wheeless hypothesized that students have lower expectancies for teacher nonverbal immediacy in telecourses than in traditional courses. However, citing evidence that telecourses can be interactive and participative, and can actually allow for highly immediate teacher behaviors, they examined whether previous experience with distance learning may positively influence students' expectations for teacher nonverbal immediacy. They found that (a) students enrolled in distance learning courses had lower expectations for teacher nonverbal immediacy than did students enrolled in traditional courses, and (b) students with previous distance learning experiences had significantly higher expectations for teacher nonverbal immediacy than did students with no telecourse experience. Witt and Wheeless reasoned that positive expectancies will influence students to enroll in distance learning courses and may possibly influence students' specific course selections. Thus they imply that telecourse teachers should make efforts to create "immediate" experiences and that distance learning programs, in their student recruitment efforts, should build positive student expectancies for nonverbal immediacy.

Videotaped instruction research. Guerrero and Miller (1998) examined the relationship between teacher nonverbal behaviors and student evaluations of videotaped instructors and courses. They exposed 180 students to one of four stimulus videotapes of instructors displaying varying levels of nonverbal (a) immediacy, (b) expressiveness, (c) smooth interaction management, (d) altercentrism, and (e) composure. As predicted, high levels of these characteristics were positively associated with students' favorable impressions of both instructor and video course. The most interesting finding emerging from this study was that when instructors of videotaped courses were perceived as highly involved, articulate, and warm, their being *too* composed had a negative impact on student impressions of the course. Guerrero and Miller suggest that in the video instruction context (which is by nature highly scripted and rehearsed), instructors who are extremely composed (who do not show anxiety cues, use only purposeful movements, and exhibit excessively fluent speech) *and* display high levels of other nonverbal skills may contribute to student perceptions of teacher insincerity. Students may then regard course content as "mechanical and uninteresting" (p. 39).

Classroom Management

The fifth most frequently studied area was classroom management ($N = 10$). Classroom management researchers are interested in instructional strategies for encouraging student compliance and maintaining discipline. More specifically, these studies focused on teacher ($n = 5$) and graduate assistant ($n = 2$) power.

Teacher power research. A long line of research initiated by McCroskey and Richmond (1983) examined teacher "power in the classroom." Later studies considered the active role of the student as a potential resister to teacher compliance-gaining attempts (see Burroughs, Kearney, & Plax, 1989) by identifying potential resistance strategies that students might use. In an extension of that research, Kearney et al. (1991) attempted to validate their original resistance typology, meaningfully reduce the category scheme, and test attribution theory as an explanation of strategies students select in their resistance attempts. College students responded qualitatively to teacher scenarios that included variations of nonverbal immediacy (immediate or nonimmediate) and compliance-gaining strategies (prosocial or antisocial). Content analysis of these data indicated the stability of the original category scheme. A second group of students responded to the same teacher scenarios, indicating their resistance on a scaled variation of the category scheme. Analysis of these quantitative data demonstrated that the original categories could be reduced to two underlying dimensions: teacher-owned (teacher is at fault) and student-owned (student assumes responsibility) resistance techniques. Testing the centrality of teacher immediacy as the primary attribute for students' resistance decisions, the researchers further found that teacher immediacy, not strategy type, directed students' resistance decisions. Students reported a greater likelihood of using teacher-owned techniques with nonimmediate teachers and student-owned strategies with immediate teachers—regardless of strategy type employed.

Graduate teaching assistant power research. Based on research indicating that teacher power use at all instructional levels influences students' motivation and, ultimately, learning, Roach (1995) argued for his examination of the effects of graduate teaching assistant (GTA) trait argumentativeness on students' perceptions of GTA power use and students' affective learning. Both GTAs and their students self-reported their own levels of argumentativeness; students also reported their perceptions of GTA power use and affective learning. Findings indicated significant differences in student affective learning for classes taught by low, moderate, and high argumentative GTAs. Lower GTA argumentativeness was shown to be positively associated with higher levels of affective learning. Conversely, when GTA argumentativeness was moderate or high, student affective learning was lower. Interestingly, lower GTA argumentativeness was associated with perceptions of increasingly *more* power use, but these GTAs relied less on coercive bases of power than did their more highly argumentative counterparts. Student levels of argumentativeness contributed only minimally to their overall perceptions of teacher power or learning.

Teacher-Student Interaction

Finally, tied with classroom management studies, teacher-student interaction research ($N = 10$) has focused on how students and teachers communicate with one another interdependently, as opposed to their individual communication behaviors that contribute to the learning process. Examples of issues within this category are student question asking in the classroom ($n = 4$) and mentoring ($n = 2$).

Mentoring research. Waldeck, Orrego, Plax, and Kearney (1997) (a) delineated a profile of graduate student-faculty mentorships, (b) inductively derived a typology of graduate student messages used to initiate mentoring relationships with faculty, and (c) assessed graduate student satisfaction with their attempts to obtain faculty mentors and the subsequent relationships they developed. Mentored graduate student participants represented multiple disciplines from 12 U.S. universities. Waldeck et al. reported 10 protégé initiation strategies and corresponding tactics: ensuring contact with the target professor, making a direct request to be mentored, excelling in class or work to make a favorable impression, communicating respect for the target, searching for similar interests, seeking counsel from the target, providing work assistance to the target, assuming the mentorship will "just happen," disclosing personal information, and participation in institutionalized mentoring programs. They found that protégés typically use multiple strategies and tactics, and that they perceive their initiation attempts to be difficult.

Moreover, graduate student protégés perceive more psychosocial (self-concept enhancing) than career (skill-enhancing) support from their mentors. Waldeck et al. found that this social support is more predictive of students' satisfaction with their mentored relationships than is career support. Finally, graduate student protégés reported being highly satisfied with their mentored relationships overall.

Student question-asking research. West and Pearson (1994) were interested in what types of questions students ask and what teachers say to elicit and respond to student questions across diverse classes and academic disciplines. Based on coders' observations of classroom dialogue and audiotape transcriptions, West and Pearson inductively derived six categories of student question types. The following three most frequently asked question types accounted for 70% of all questions: (a) procedural (pertaining to the operation of the classroom), (b) general inquiry regarding content (information seeking relevant to course content), and (c) clarification (eliciting further explanation of a point already broached by the teacher). Overall, across 30 1-hour classes, students asked 108 questions—an average of 3.6 questions per hour. Content analysis of interaction sequences also revealed a number of teacher antecedent, student question, and teacher consequent categories. Overall, based on their results, West and Pearson recommend that teachers (a) receive training on how to elicit student questions (especially higher-order questions that transcend the procedural types asked most frequently by their sample) and (b) employ positive responses to student questions in order to encourage further question asking.

The studies we have reviewed in this section represent the breadth of the research in instructional communication over the past decade. In the pages that follow, we offer an analysis of how far we have come and what we still need to do.

THE FUTURE OF INSTRUCTIONAL
AND DEVELOPMENTAL COMMUNICATION RESEARCH

During the 1990s, research in instructional communication flourished. An examination of the past 10 years of this literature has revealed more than 186 journal articles devoted to the area. So what do we know as a result? The bulk of this research has focused on one student-related construct, communication apprehension, and one teacher-related construct, immediacy. From this, we now know how communication apprehension is developed, how to alleviate it, and how it affects communication performance. Moreover, we know that teachers who engage in immediacy behaviors are better able to facilitate student learning and motivation, alter students' perceptions of occasional teacher "misbehaviors," and gain student compliance. And how do we know this? Over an extended period of time, instructional communication researchers have examined these two constructs systematically, both inductively and deductively. In this way, scholars have cultivated and sustained active, focused research programs that have eventuated into important knowledge claims.

What don't we know? For one, although we know about "teacher" behaviors and "student" behaviors independent of one another, we know very little about how teacher-student *interactions* influence learning. Thus we need more investigations of relational constructs such as extraclass communication, mentoring at the undergraduate and graduate levels, and teacher clarity/student clarifying tactics in order to uncover the dynamic interplay between teachers and students. Second, although peer groups have an influence on student socialization, very little communication research has examined student-to-student interaction or collaborative learning. Third, in light of the increasing ubiquity of technology, more substantive research is needed to help us understand the impact of computer- and video-aided instruction and distance learning on student outcomes. Finally, we know very little about the theoretical bases or implications of instructional communication research. Although the theoretical implications of some studies may be evident to sophisticated readers, researchers have made very little effort to contextualize their projects in explicit theoretical frameworks.

Thus we are concerned that although instructional and developmental communication researchers have been prolific, few large-scale knowledge claims have been advanced, and our more important findings have received little attention from educators outside the communication discipline. A number of complex factors account for this lack of systematic development and exposure. These include (a) the communication field's general inattention to the critical distinction between communication education and instructional communication and the associated bias against those who engage in instructional communication research, (b) variable-analytic (rather than programmatic) attention to the instructional process as a whole and the resulting inability to build theories of instructional communication or to interpret findings within any theoretical context, and (c) confusion resulting from conceptual and operational overlap among related constructs.

Distinction Between Communication Education and Instructional Research

We argue that the communication field has, in general, failed to acknowledge the critical distinction between communication education and instructional communication. Instructional communication should be recognized as foundational to and pervasive across our discipline because it focuses on the broader concern of the role of communication in learning—as opposed to the narrower focus of communication education scholars on how to teach speech in particular. An examination of publication outlets in the 1990s reveals that most instructional and developmental research has been showcased in one primary journal, *Communication Education.* This appears to be evidence of a prevailing tendency among scholars to categorize all education-related research as communication or speech education. An unfortunate consequence of this bias is the inaccurate assumption by individuals outside the Instructional and Developmental Communication Division that all instructional communication scholars are atheoretical or concerned only with the teaching of speech. Thus, as Sorensen and Christophel (1992) did almost 10 years ago, we urge members of the discipline to recognize the breadth and depth of what instructional communication scholars do.

To address this concern, we believe that *Communication Education* may be a misleading name for a journal that addresses much more than the pedagogy of communication. This publication could be better titled *Instructional Communication.* We also recommend that all published research reports include sections on theoretical implications, wherein the authors contextualize their findings within one or more relevant theoretical perspectives and indicate how their scholarship advances theory.

Lack of Programmatic Research

The preoccupation with variable-analytic (rather than programmatic) research further perpetuates the notion that instructional communication research is atheoretical. Although variable-analytic research has raised and answered valuable questions for instructional communication scholars, for the most part systematic efforts to build ongoing programs of research around specific issues important to instructional communication have been absent in the past 10 years. Instructional communication research efforts must serve the heuristic function of stimulating consideration of additional, related, and worthy issues for further examination. Only when scholars initiate and sustain research programs will they be able to draw sound, generalizable conclusions about communication and learning.

Conceptual and Operational Overlap of Constructs

Finally, related to our concern about the lack of programmatic research in instructional communication is the tendency of researchers to create and then justify their own constructs as separate and distinct from extant variables. When the conceptual antecedents for both constructs are similar, researchers are obligated to differentiate clearly between the two. For instance, how are the related constructs of student's state motivation to learn and student's affect similar and different? How are student challenges similar to and different from student resistance techniques? How is teacher's sociocommunicative style similar to and different from teacher's communication style? Such conceptual and operational overlaps preclude theoretical advances and minimize heuristic potential. Instructional communication researchers need to make more effort to extend their work from or link it to existing research and theoretical constructs.

All of the factors noted above, taken together, are likely to inhibit the growth and development of instructional communication theory and research essential for confronting the educational challenges of the 21st century. Alternatively, attention to programmatic research, application of rigorous methodology, precise explication of constructs, and concern for theory are likely to yield important knowledge about the role of communication in teaching and learning. Thoughtful consideration of these recommendations will position the Instructional and Developmental Communication Division more centrally within our discipline. Moreover, instructional communication researchers' work will become influential *outside* of the discipline. In this way, our work may help educators across the academy cope with 21st-century instructional challenges.

REFERENCES

Andersen, P. A. (1985). Nonverbal immediacy and interpersonal communication. In A. W. Siegman & S. Feldstein (Eds.), *Multichannel integrations of nonverbal behavior* (pp. 1-36). Hillsdale, NJ: Lawrence Erlbaum.

Ayres, J. (1996). Speech preparation processes and speech apprehension. *Communication Education, 45,* 228-235.

Ayres, J., Wilcox, A. K., & Ayres, D. M. (1995). Receiver apprehension: An explanatory model and accompanying research. *Communication Education, 44,* 223-235.

Bandura, A. (1977). *Social learning theory.* Englewood Cliffs, NJ; Prentice Hall.

Bandura, A. (1994). Social cognitive theory of mass communication. In J. Bryant & D. Zillmann (Eds.), *Media effects: Advances in theory and research* (pp. 61-90). Hillsdale, NJ: Lawrence Erlbaum.

Beatty, M. J., & Friedland, M. H. (1990). Public speaking state anxiety as a function of selected situational and predispositional variables. *Communication Education, 39,* 142-147.

Burroughs, N. F., Kearney, P., & Plax, T. G. (1989). Compliance-resistance in the college classroom. *Communication Education, 38,* 214-229.

Cantor, J., & Omdahl, B. L. (1991). Effects of fictional media depictions of realistic threats on children's emotional responses, expectations, worries, and liking for related activities. *Communication Monographs, 58,* 384-401.

Cantor, J., & Omdahl, B. L. (1999). Children's acceptance of safety guidelines after exposure to televised dramas depicting accidents. *Western Journal of Communication, 63,* 57-71.

Chesebro, J. W., McCroskey, J. C., Atwater, D. F., Bahrenfuss, R. M., Cawelti, G., Gaudino, J. L., & Hodges, H. (1992). Communication apprehension and self-perceived communication competence of at-risk students. *Communication Education, 41,* 345-360.

Christophel, D. M., & Gorham, J. (1995). A test-retest analysis of student motivation, teacher immediacy, and perceived sources of motivation and demotivation in college classes. *Communication Education, 44,* 292-306.

Collier, M. J., & Powell, R. (1990). Ethnicity, instructional communication and classroom systems. *Communication Quarterly, 38,* 334-349.

Daly, J. A., McCroskey, J. C., Ayres, J., Hopf, T., & Ayres, D. M. (Eds.). (1997). *Avoiding communication: Shyness, reticence, and communication apprehension* (2nd ed.). Cresskill, NJ: Hampton.

Daly, J. A., Vangelisti, A. L., & Weber, D. J. (1995). Speech anxiety affects how people prepare speeches: A protocol analysis of the preparation processes of speakers. *Communication Monographs, 62,* 383-397.

Delia, J. G., O'Keefe, B. J., & O'Keefe, D. J. (1982). The constructivist approach to communication. In F. E. X. Dance (Ed.), *Human communication theory* (pp. 147-191). New York: Harper & Row.

Donahue, P. L., Voelkl, K. E., Campbell, J. R., & Mazzeo, J. (1999, March). *NAEP 1998 reading report card for the nation and the states* [On-line]. Available Internet: http://nces.ed.gov/nationsreportcard/pubs/main1998/1999500.shtml

Flavell, J. H. (1985). *Cognitive development* (2nd ed.). Englewood Cliffs, NJ: Prentice Hall.

French, J. R. P., Jr., & Raven, B. H. (1959). The bases of social power. In D. Cartwright (Ed.), *Studies in social power* (pp. 150-167). Ann Arbor: University of Michigan Press.

Frymier, A. B. (1994). A model of immediacy in the classroom. *Communication Quarterly, 42,* 133-144.

Frymier, A. B., & Shulman, G. M. (1995). "What's in it for me?" Increasing content relevance to enhance students' motivation. *Communication Education, 44,* 40-50.

Gerbner, G., Gross, L., Morgan, M., & Signorielli, N. (1994). Growing up with television: The cultivation perspective. In J. Bryant & D. Zillmann (Eds.), *Media effects: Advances in theory and research* (pp. 17-41). Hillsdale, NJ: Lawrence Erlbaum.

Gorham, J., & Christophel, D. M. (1992). Students' perceptions of teacher behaviors as motivating and demotivating factors in college classes. *Communication Quarterly, 40,* 239-252.

Gorham, J., Cohen, S. H., & Morris, T. L. (1997). Fashion in the classroom II: Instructor immediacy and attire. *Communication Research Reports, 14,* 11-23.

Gorham, J., & Millette, D. M. (1997). A comparative analysis of teacher and student perceptions of sources of motivation and demotivation in college classes. *Communication Education, 46,* 245-261.

Guerrero, L. K., & Miller, T. A. (1998). Associations between nonverbal behaviors and initial impressions of instructor competence and course content in videotaped distance education courses. *Communication Education, 47,* 30-42.

Hall, B. I., Morreale, S. P., & Gaudino, J. L. (1999). A survey of the status of oral communication in the K-12 public educational system in the United States. *Communication Education, 48,* 139-148.

Hoffner, C. (1997). Children's emotional reactions to a scary film: The role of prior outcome information and coping style. *Human Communication Research, 23,* 323-341.

Hurt, H. T., Scott, M. D., & McCroskey, J. C. (1978). *Communication in the classroom.* Menlo Park, CA: Addison-Wesley.

Johnson, S. D., & Roellke, C. F. (1999). Secondary teachers' and undergraduate education faculty members' perceptions of teaching-effectiveness criteria: A national survey. *Communication Education, 48,* 127-138.

Kearney, P., & Plax, T. G. (1992). Student resistance to control. In V. P. Richmond & J. C. McCroskey (Eds.), *Power in the classroom: Communication, control, and concern* (pp. 85-99). Hillsdale, NJ: Lawrence Erlbaum.

Kearney, P., Plax, T. G., & Burroughs, N. F. (1991). An attributional analysis of college students' resistance decisions. *Communication Education, 40,* 325-342.

Keller, J. M. (1983). Motivational design of instruction. In C. M. Reigeluth (Ed.), *Instructional design theories: An overview of their current status* (pp. 383-434). Hillsdale, NJ: Lawrence Erlbaum.

Keller, J. M. (1987). Development and use of the ARCS model of instructional design. *Journal of Instructional Development, 10,* 2-10.

Kelley, D. H., & Gorham, J. (1988). Effects of immediacy on recall of information. *Communication Education, 37,* 198-207.

Kline, S. L., & Clinton, B. L. (1998). Developments in children's persuasive practices. *Communication Education, 47,* 120-136.

Lashbrook, V. J., & Wheeless, L. R. (1978). Instructional communication theory and research: An overview of the relationship between learning theory and instructional communication. In B. D. Ruben (Ed.), *Communication yearbook 2* (pp. 439-456). New Brunswick, NJ: Transaction.

Matlon, R. J., & Ortiz, S. P. (Eds.). (1997). *Index to journals in communication studies through 1995.* Annandale, VA: National Communication Association.

McCroskey, J. C., & Richmond, V. P. (1983). Power in the classroom I: Teacher and student perceptions. *Communication Education, 32,* 175-184.

McCroskey, J. C., & Richmond, V. P. (1987). Willingness to communicate. In J. C. McCroskey & J. A. Daly (Eds.), *Personality and interpersonal communication* (pp. 129-156). Newbury Park, CA: Sage.

McCroskey, J. C., Richmond, V. P., Sallinen, A., Fayer, J. M., & Barraclough, R. A. (1995). A cross-cultural and multi-behavioral analysis of the relationship between nonverbal immediacy and teacher evaluation. *Communication Education, 44,* 281-291.

Mehrabian, A. (1971). *Silent messages.* Belmont, CA: Wadsworth.

Morgan, M., & Shanahan, J. (1997). Two decades of cultivation research: An appraisal and meta-analysis. In B. R. Burleson (Ed.), *Communication yearbook 20* (pp. 1-45). Thousand Oaks, CA: Sage.

Morris, T. L., Gorham, J., Cohen, S. H., & Huffman, D. (1996). Fashion in the classroom: Effects of attire on student perceptions of instructors in college classes. *Communication Education, 45,* 135-148.

Neer, M. R. (1990). Reducing situational anxiety and avoidance behavior associated with classroom apprehension. *Southern Communication Journal, 56,* 49-61.

Neuliep, J. W. (1995). A comparison of teacher immediacy in African-American and Euro-American college classrooms. *Communication Education, 44,* 267-277.

Piaget, J. (1977). *The development of thought: Equilibration of cognitive structures.* New York: Viking.

Reese, C. M., Miller, K. E., Mazzeo, J., & Dossey, J. A. (1997, February). *NAEP 1996 mathematics report card for the nation and the states* [On-line]. Available Internet: http://nces.ed.gov/nationsreportcard/96report/97488.shtml

Roach, K. D. (1995). Teaching assistant argumentativeness: Effects on affective learning and student perceptions of power use. *Communication Education, 44,* 15-29.

Rosenfeld, L. B., Grant, C. H., III, & McCroskey, J. C. (1995). Communication apprehension and self-perceived communication competence of academically gifted students. *Communication Education, 44,* 79-86.

Sanders, J. A., & Wiseman, R. L. (1990). The effects of verbal and nonverbal teacher immediacy on perceived cognitive, affective, and behavioral learning in the multicultural classroom. *Communication Education, 39,* 341-353.

Scott, M. D., & Wheeless, L. R. (1977). Instructional communication theory and research: An overview. In B. D. Ruben (Ed.), *Communication yearbook 1* (pp. 495-511). New Brunswick, NJ: Transaction.

Sorensen, G. A., & Christophel, D. M. (1992). The communication perspective. In V. P. Richmond & J. C. McCroskey (Eds.), *Power in the classroom: Communication, control, and concern* (pp. 35-46). Hillsdale, NJ: Lawrence Erlbaum.

Thweatt, K. S., & McCroskey, J. C. (1998). The impact of teacher immediacy and misbehaviors on teacher credibility. *Communication Education, 47,* 348-358.

Waldeck, J. H., Orrego, V. O., Plax, T. G., & Kearney, P. (1997). Who gets mentored, how it happens, and to what end. *Communication Quarterly, 45,* 93-109.

Weiss, A. J., & Wilson, B. J. (1998). Children's cognitive and emotional responses to the portrayal of negative emotions in family-formatted situation comedies. *Human Communication Research, 24,* 584-609.

West, R., & Pearson, J. C. (1994). Antecedent and consequent conditions of student questioning: An analysis of classroom discourse across the university. *Communication Education, 43,* 299-311.

Wheeless, L. R., & Hurt, H. T. (1979). Instructional communication theory and research: An overview of instructional strategies as instructional communication systems. In D. Nimmo (Ed.), *Communication yearbook 3* (pp. 525-541). New Brunswick, NJ: Transaction.

Wheeless, L. R., Preiss, R. W., & Gayle, B. M. (1997). Receiver apprehension, informational receptivity, and cognitive processing. In J. A. Daly, J. C. McCroskey, J. Ayres, T. Hopf, & D. M. Ayres (Eds.), *Avoiding communication: Shyness, reticence, and communication apprehension* (2nd ed., pp. 151-187). Cresskill, NJ: Hampton.

Wilson, B. J., & Weiss, A. J. (1991). The effects of two reality explanations on children's reactions to a frightening movie scene. *Communication Monographs, 58,* 307-326.

Witt, P. L., & Wheeless, L. R. (1999). Nonverbal communication expectancies about teachers and enrollment behavior in distance learning. *Communication Education, 48,* 149-154.

CHAPTER CONTENTS

10 The Evolution and Advancement of Health Communication Inquiry

GARY L. KREPS
National Cancer Institute

This chapter examines the current state of health communication research, reviews the development of this area of inquiry, and suggests fruitful directions for advancing health communication inquiry in light of the communication revolution developing within the modern health care system. Particular attention is paid to the important role of information in health care and health promotion, power inequities within the health care system, and biases in health communication research. Rich opportunities for conducting health communication research that can increase public health literacy, enhance health information quality, improve health message design and delivery, and generally promote public health are suggested.

T HERE has never been a more exciting nor more propitious time than now to study the role of communication in health and health care. We are in the midst of a communication revolution in modern health care that is closely tied to the widespread availability of health information to both consumers and providers via a broad range of new and more traditional communication channels. The widespread availability of relevant and accurate health information offers the great promise of helping to demystify health care and the health care system for consumers, shedding light on health care processes that were once only the domain of health care professionals. Access to relevant health information can help consumers participate fully in health care decision making and encourage greater cooperation between health care providers and consumers than ever before. This information revolution can also help health care professionals access state-of-the-art prevention, diagnostic, and treatment information and, through easy contact with other providers, encourage multidisciplinary consultation in the coordination of health care services. However, on the negative side of the coin, this

Correspondence: Gary L. Kreps, Health Communication and Informatics Research Branch, Behavioral Research Program, Division of Cancer Control and Population Sciences, National Cancer Institute, Executive Plaza North, Room 4080, 6130 Executive Boulevard, MSC 7365, Bethesda, MD 20892-7365; e-mail gary.kreps@nih.gov

Communication Yearbook 24, pp. 231-253

information revolution has also led to a general overload of available health information of limited quality, which inevitably serves to confuse and misdirect health care consumers and providers, decreasing the quality of health care choices they make. Health communication scholars have a wonderful opportunity at this propitious point in time to help promote public health by focusing on the role of information in the modern health care system. Health communication research can help to sort out the ways communication can most profitably inform consumers and providers about relevant health issues, identify the best ways to develop and present high-quality health information to key audiences, and encourage effective collaborative decision making in modern health care efforts.

THE EVOLUTION OF HEALTH COMMUNICATION INQUIRY

Health communication inquiry has come a long way. Although it is a relatively young area of communication inquiry, research on this topic has grown tremendously in the past two decades, generating increasing numbers of important health communication publications (including several dedicated health communication scholarly journals and numerous professional and academic books). Health communication is a rich, exciting, and relevant research area that investigates and elucidates the many ways that human and mediated communication dramatically influence the outcomes of health care and health promotion efforts. In recognition of the growing stature of this area of inquiry, health communication issues are increasingly primary topics of large-scale funded research programs sponsored by numerous major government agencies, foundations, and health care corporations. Similarly, health communication divisions/interest groups have been established in almost all of the communication discipline's professional associations, as well as in many public health and health education professional societies. Well-attended scholarly conferences presenting cutting-edge health communication research and applications are held on a regular basis, both nationally and internationally. Indeed, increasing numbers of graduate theses and dissertations are being written concerning health communication inquiry, and health communication courses have become standard fare in many undergraduate and graduate communication educational programs across the United States and around the world. There is no doubt that health communication research has achieved a level of disciplinary maturation, generating strong scholarly interest, support, and productivity (for reviews of the growth and development of health communication inquiry, see, e.g., Kreps, Bonaguro, & Query, 1998; Rogers, 1994; Sharf, 1999).

A major reason for the tremendous growth and development of health communication inquiry is the importance of this research area for addressing the complex and challenging health care demands of society and guiding the promotion of public health. Over the past few decades, a large and growing body of scholarly health communication literature has been established that powerfully illustrates the centrality of communication processes in the achievement of important health care goals and the promotion of public health (for extensive reviews of much of this literature, see Kreps, 1988a; Kreps & O'Hair, 1995; Zook, 1994). There is growing recognition within the academy and throughout the health care delivery system, as well as in major centers for public health policy (such as the U.S. Centers for Disease Control and Prevention and the National Institutes of Health), that health communication is a most important and relevant area of inquiry for addressing salient health care and health promotion issues (Rogers, 1994; Zook, 1994).

Despite the major advances in health communication inquiry, health communication scholars who want to maximize their opportunities to enhance health care delivery and promote public health still have a very long way to go (Sharf, 1993, 1999). The quality of health communication research and intervention efforts can and must be improved (Arntson, 1985; Gabbard-Alley, 1995, Kreps et al., 1998; Lupton, 1994; Rootman & Hershfield, 1994; Zook, 1994). Knowledge gleaned from the very best health communication inquiry must be applied to refining health care delivery practices, directing health promotion efforts, and informing public health policy at the highest possible levels (Sharf, 1999; Zook, 1994). Ineffective communication practices and policies still consistently limit the effectiveness of health care/promotion efforts, causing unnecessary pain, suffering, and even deaths throughout the modern world (Kreps, 1996a, 1996c, 1998). As health communication inquiry truly comes of age, health communication scholars must increasingly focus their attention on working collaboratively with an interdisciplinary group of scholars, health care practitioners, and public officials to improve modern health care delivery and health promotion efforts (Kreps, 1989). In this chapter, I will assess the current state of health communication inquiry, examine key issues concerning the quality of health communication scholarship, and suggest that health communication scholars adopt a consumer orientation toward meaningfully addressing critical health care/promotion issues and effectively framing enlightened public health policy.

CURRENT PARAMETERS OF HEALTH COMMUNICATION INQUIRY

Levels of Health Communication Analysis

Health communication inquiry is an extremely broad research area, examining the important roles performed by human and mediated communication in health care and health promotion in a wide range of social contexts. Health communication is examined at many different levels of interaction, utilizing a wide array of communication media and communication channels. A frequently used framework for describing several primary levels of health communication analysis describes intrapersonal, interpersonal, group, organizational, and societal levels of health communication inquiry (Kreps, 1988a; Kreps & Thornton, 1992; Thornton & Kreps, 1993). The ability of health communication scholars to examine the influences of communication on health outcomes at multiple levels of interaction occurring within a broad range of social settings clearly illustrates the power and pertinence of health communication inquiry, yet it also illustrates the complexity of this area of inquiry. This complexity suggests that researchers need to adopt multiple analytic perspectives and perhaps even to develop interdisciplinary teams in order to address complex programs of health communication inquiry.

Intrapersonal health communication inquiry examines the internal mental and psychological processes that influence health care, such as the health beliefs, attitudes, and values that predispose individuals to particular health care behaviors and decisions (see, e.g., Babrow, Kasch, & Ford, 1998; Booth-Butterfield, Chory, & Beynon, 1997; Burgoon, 1996; Burgoon & Hall, 1994; Guttman, 1996; Hyde, 1990; Kelly, St. Lawrence, Smith, Hood, & Cook, 1987; Treichler, 1987). Scholars focusing on these intrapersonal issues in health communication often benefit from adopting a psychological frame of reference for their inquiry. There has been excellent progress in recent years in the integration of health communication and health psychology scholarship, and there should be great opportunities for collaboration between these interrelated areas of inquiry. (See, for example, my introductory guest editorial in a special issue of the *Journal of Health Psychology* examining this interdisciplinary interface between health communication and health psychology inquiry; Kreps, 1996b.)

Interpersonal health communication inquiry examines relational influences on health outcomes, focusing on provider-consumer relationships, dyadic provision of health education, therapeutic interaction, and the exchange of relevant information in health care interviews (e.g., Kim, Odallo, Thuo, & Kols, 1999; Kreps, 1988b; Makoul, 1998; Marshall, 1993; Miller & Zook, 1997; Phillips & Jones, 1991: Query & Kreps, 1996; Smith & Hoppe, 1991). The interpersonal perspective has been a dominant area of health communication inquiry over the years, focusing directly on important health care delivery issues. Researchers undertaking interpersonal health communication inquiry must take care to address fairly the important cultural, political, and power issues that underlie interpersonal relations in the delivery of health care (Cline & McKenzie, 1998).

Group health communication inquiry examines the role communication performs in the interdependent coordination of members of collectives, such as health care teams, support groups, ethics committees, and families, as these group members share relevant health information in making important health care decisions (see, e.g., Fabregas & Kreps, 1999; Ferguson, 1996; Gifford, 1983; Metts, Manns, & Kruzic, 1996; Query & James, 1989). As specialization of health care services and technologies continues to increase, there is growing dependence on health care teams in the delivery of modern health care. Similarly, the growing complexities of health care delivery demand greater input from groups of individuals when difficult and challenging health care decisions must be made (Fabregas & Kreps, 1999). Interdependent health care providers, administrators, and consumers must learn how to share relevant information and coordinate efforts in group settings.

Communication scholars are particularly well situated to study the communication demands inherent in these groups and to help facilitate effective coordination and cooperation in health care teams and important decision-making groups.

Organizational health communication inquiry examines the use of communication to coordinate interdependent groups, mobilize different specialists, and share relevant health information within complex health care delivery systems to enable effective multidisciplinary provision of health care and prevention of relevant health risks (see, e.g., Frey, Adelman, & Query, 1996; Geist & Hardesty, 1992: Klingle, Burgoon, Afifi, & Callister, 1995; Kreps, 1998; Lammers & Geist, 1997). With the rise of managed care, the delivery of health care services has become increasingly controlled by financial and bureaucratic concerns (Geist & Hardesty, 1992). There is growing frustration among many consumers about the quality of care they receive and their ability to participate actively in making important health care decisions (Jones, Kreps, & Phillips, 1995). There are many opportunities for health communication scholars to examine ways to promote greater receptivity, flexibility, and sensitivity toward consumers within the increasingly complex and highly regulated modern health care system (Kreps, 1998; Lammers & Geist, 1997; Sharf, 1999).

Societal health communication examines cultural influences on health care and the generation, dissemination, and utilization of health information communicated via diverse media to the broad range of professional and lay audiences in society that influence health education, promotion, and health care practices (see, e.g., Eng & Gustafson, 1999; Guttman, 1997; Kreps, Hubbard, & DeVita, 1988; Kreps & Kunimoto, 1994; Kreps, Ruben, Baker, & Rosenthal, 1987; Myrick, 1998; Pavlik et al., 1993; Quesada & Heller, 1977). Social marketing has been widely adopted by communication scholars as an important strategic framework for the design of sophisticated health promotion campaigns (see, e.g., the special forum section of the *Journal of Health Communication: International Perspectives,* 1997, vol. 2, no. 4, which describes an influential consensus conference on the future of social marketing in health promotion; see also Albrecht & Bryant, 1996; Dearing et al., 1996; Kotler & Roberto, 1989; Lefebvre & Flora, 1988; Maibach, Shenker, & Singer, 1997; Ratzan, 1999; Ressler & Toledo, 1997).

In the past, research focusing on the societal perspective on health communication inquiry was conducted primarily by media studies communication scholars, who examined the ways that various media can deliver health promotion and risk prevention messages to targeted audiences. However, as health promotion efforts have become more and more sophisticated, utilizing multiple message strategies and delivery systems, there are increasing opportunities for greater participation by communication scholars (and others) with expertise in intrapersonal, interpersonal, group, and organizational levels of health communication analysis (Engleberg, Flora, & Nass, 1995; Hafstad & Aaro, 1997; Korhonen, Uutela, Korhonen, & Puska, 1998; Maibach, Kreps, & Bonaguro, 1993; O'Keefe, Hartwig Boyd, & Brown, 1998; Reardon & Rogers, 1988; Valente, Poppe, & Merritt, 1996).

Health Communication Channels

Health communication inquiry also involves examination of many communication channels. Face-to-face communication between providers and consumers, among members of health care teams, and among support group members have been the focus of many health communication studies (e.g., Jones et al., 1995; Kim et al., 1999; Maibach & Kreps, 1986; Makoul, 1998; Phillips & Jones, 1991). A broad range of personal (telephone, mail, fax, e-mail) and mass (radio, television, film, billboards) communication media have also been the focus of health communication inquiry (e.g., Freimuth, Stein, & Kean, 1989; Gantz & Greenberg, 1990; Hammond, Freimuth, & Morrison, 1990; Hofstetter, Schultze, & Mulvihill, 1992; Larson, 1991; Signorielli & Lears, 1992; Stoddard, Johnson, Sussman, Dent, & Boley-Cruz, 1998). More and more, researchers are examining the importance of new communication technologies as health communication media (e.g., Cassell, Jackson, & Cheuvront, 1998; Chamberlain, 1996; Clark, 1992; Eng & Gustafson, 1999; Ferguson, 1996; Harris, 1995; Lieberman, 1992; Slack, 1997; Smaglik et al., 1998; Street, 1996; Street, Gold, & Manning, 1997). These new media, especially the use of interactive computer technologies and the Internet, have become increasingly important sources for relevant health information and support for many health care consumers and providers; they will clearly be a most promising topic for future health communication inquiry (Agency for Health Care Policy and Research, 1997; Eng & Gustafson, 1999; Sonnenberg, 1997).

The settings for health communication inquiry are also quite diverse. They include the wide range of settings where health information is generated and exchanged, such as homes, offices, schools, clinics, and hospitals. Health communication scholars must be aware of the ubiquitous nature of health communication so that they can design and conduct studies in many diverse field settings (Rootman & Hershfield, 1994). Health communication research has examined such diverse issues as the role of interpersonal communication in the development of cooperative health care provider-consumer relationships (Makoul, 1998; Smith & Pettegrew, 1986), the role of comforting communication in the provision of social support to those who are troubled (Metts et al., 1996; Query & James, 1989), the effects of various media and presentation strategies on the dissemination of health information to those who need such information (Baker, Friede, Moulton, & Ross, 1995; McGuiness, Deering, & Patrick, 1995; Sechrest, Backer, Rogers, Campbell, & Grady, 1994; Wallack, Dorfman, Jernigan, & Themba, 1993; Winnett & Wallack, 1996; Yom, 1996), the use of communication to coordinate the activities of interdependent health care providers (Freidson, 1970; Johnson, 1997; Kreps et al., 1988; Kreps & Kunimoto, 1994), and the use of communication in the administration of complex health care delivery systems (Geist & Hardesty, 1992; Lammers & Geist, 1997; Ray & Miller, 1990). Because health communication inquiry encompasses such a broad range of communication media, channels, levels, and settings, it is a convergent research area that benefits from the work of scholars representing multiple perspectives, research traditions, disciplines, and methodological and theoretical perspectives (Kreps et al., 1998; Lupton, 1994). Indeed, health communication is a *transdisciplinary* area of inquiry, attracting researchers representing multiple related social scientific, humanistic, and technical disciplines who conduct research that focuses on a diverse set of health issues in a broad range of health care settings.

The Central Role of Information in Health Communication Inquiry

Health information is a central focus of health communication inquiry. Relevant and timely health information is a critical resource in health care and health promotion because it is essential for practitioners who must guide strategic health behaviors, treatments, and decisions (Agency for Health Care Policy and Research, 1997; Freimuth et al., 1989; Johnson, 1997; Kreps, 1988a; McGuiness et al., 1995). Health information includes the knowledge gleaned from patient interviews and laboratory tests used to diagnose health problems, the precedents developed through clinical research and practice used to determine the best available treatment strategies for specific health threats, the data gathered in checkups used to assess the efficacy of health care treatments, the input practitioners and consumers need to evaluate bioethical issues and weigh consequences in making complex health care decisions, the recognition of warning signs needed to detect imminent health risks, and the direct health behaviors that have been determined to help individuals avoid these risks (Kreps et al., 1998). Health care providers and consumers depend on communication to generate, access, and exchange relevant health information for making important treatment decisions, for adjusting to changing health conditions, and for coordinating health-preserving activities. The process of communication also enables health promotion specialists to develop persuasive messages for dissemination over salient channels to provide target audiences with relevant health information to influence their health knowledge, attitudes, and behaviors. Health communication scholars are well poised to promote public health by examining and helping to enhance social mechanisms for disseminating relevant health information to consumers and providers of health care.

CRITIQUES OF HEALTH COMMUNICATION INQUIRY

Several complex issues and controversies have arisen concerning the directions and potential influences of health communication scholarship. These include questions about the theoretical foundations and contributions of health communication inquiry, unintended negative effects of health communication inquiry on health care practice, coordination of interpersonal and mediated perspectives on health communication inquiry, and provider biases in health communication research. Below, I examine these lingering research critiques and make some recommendations for addressing and ameliorating them.

Health Communication Inquiry and Theoretical Development

Critics have expressed concern about a lack of strong theoretical underpinnings and an atheoretical focus in too many health communication studies (Berger, 1991; Burgoon, 1992), although it must be noted that these same criticisms have also been leveled at other applied communication research areas. Although these concerns may be overstated, especially given what I see as many strong interdisciplinary theoretical rationales for and theory-building contributions made by numerous health communication studies, the concerns do reflect an important and widely accepted scholarly dictate that a primary goal of "good" communication scholarship is the intimate connection of research and theory. This dictate mandates that data-gathering efforts are best guided by theory and should also be used to help in testing and refining theory (Frey, Botan, & Kreps, 2000). Setting aside for the moment the case of grounded research, which is designed to generate theory without being biased by guiding theoretical presuppositions, the dictate recommending this circular relationship between research and theory is generally a very good standard for guiding health communication (and other forms of applied communication) research. Kreps, Frey, and O'Hair (1991) suggest that a major criterion for conducting meaningful applied communication research is to use "relevant theory to articulate research questions and hypotheses, as well as to explain research findings" (p. 79). Strong health communication inquiry should fully utilize theory in the conceptualization and design of research, as well as use data-gathering efforts to contribute to the development and refinement of theories to increase our understanding of complex communication phenomena. Kreps et al. also explain that field research—and the vast majority of all health communication research is conducted in field settings—is particularly conducive to field testing of the validity and applicability of theories. Health communication scholars should take advantage of the opportunities they have for testing and refining theory in their research efforts.

Iatrogenic Effects of Health Communication Inquiry

Concern has been expressed about the potential for unintentionally negative effects of health care research on health care delivery, the health care system, and public health as researchers conduct their research and intervention efforts (Burgoon, 1992; Witte, 1994). These potentially negative effects can be caused by researchers getting in the way of health care delivery efforts, infringing on the privacy of health care consumers, and naively recommending courses of action to health care providers and consumers that are not medically warranted. These are serious concerns that health care scholars must heed.

Burgoon (1992) suggests a "do no harm" guideline for directing health communication inquiry to safeguard against iatrogenic effects of research efforts. He recommends that communication scholars pay strict attention to the planned and unplanned influences of their studies, particularly to influences on important health outcomes. Arntson (1985) and Burgoon (1992) both suggest that the true impacts of health communication inquiry are often masked by a preoccupation with patient satisfaction measures, which may obfuscate real health outcomes. They recommend a greater focus on health psychological, behavioral, and physiological outcome variables in the design and conduct of communication research. This emphasis on the importance of relating health communication research to health outcomes has been echoed by several other scholars (see Kreps & O'Hair, 1995; Kreps, O'Hair, & Clowers, 1994).

Similarly, Witte (1994) and Guttman (1997) raise serious ethical concerns about health promotion research and intervention efforts. Witte (1994) warns of the potentially manipulative nature of health promotion, suggesting that health communication scholars must establish ethical guidelines to inform their research and intervention efforts. She recommends that health promotion efforts should construct messages to fit specific health promotion goals and should develop campaigns that are guided by "the common good," utilizing community standards for establishing the common good (Witte, 1994, p. 290). Guttman (1997) suggests that health promotion efforts should be guided by clear values that reflect the important underlying values of the audience members targeted by health communication campaigns. The larger issue here is that health communication inquiry can have powerful influences on health care and health promotion. Health communication scholars must take care to recognize the potentially positive and negative influences of their work and must strive to minimize negative influences and maximize positive ones.

Competing Perspectives in Health Communication Inquiry

There has been a long history of competition between two major interdependent branches of health communication inquiry: health care delivery and health promotion (Kreps et al., 1998). The health care delivery area of inquiry examines how communication influences the provision of health care, such as in provider-consumer relations, health care interviews, emergency room treatment, and other settings for health care delivery. The health promotion area of inquiry examines the persuasive use of communication messages and media to promote public health, such as in health education programs, health promotion campaigns, and health risk prevention efforts.

These two branches of the health communication subfield parallel a long-standing division within the larger discipline of communication studies between academic interest in human communication (interpersonal, group, and organizational) and academic interest in mediated communication (print, electronic, and new media) (Reardon & Rogers, 1988; Rogers, 1994; Rubin & Rubin, 1985). The health care delivery branch of the field has attracted communication scholars who have primary interests in the ways interpersonal and group communication influence health care delivery, focusing on issues concerning the provider-consumer relationship, therapeutic communication, health care teams, health care decision making, and the provision of social support. The health promotion branch has attracted many mass communication scholars who are concerned with the development, implementation, and evaluation of persuasive health communication campaigns to prevent major health risks and promote public health. For example, health communication scholars have developed communication campaign strategies aimed at preventing public risks for contracting diseases such as HIV/AIDS (Bandura, 1989; Dearing et al., 1996; Maibach et al., 1993; Myrick, 1998), heart disease (Flora, Maccoby, & Farquhar, 1989; Pavlik et al., 1993), and cancer (Hafstad & Aaro, 1997; Korhonen et al., 1998; Kreps et al., 1988). Many health promotion scholars are also concerned with evaluating the use of mediated channels of communication to disseminate relevant health information, as well as in examining the ways that health and health care are portrayed by popular media.

Unfortunately, many of the scholars representing the two branches of the field of health communication (health care delivery and health promotion) have perceived themselves as being in direct competition with each other for institutional resources, numbers of conference programs, journal space, and research grants. However, this competition has begun to diminish as more health communication scholars have started working across these areas, as health care delivery systems have begun utilizing an increasingly broader range of human and mediated channels of communication (in areas such as telemedicine, health care marketing, and health education), and as health promotion specialists have enlisted more interpersonal (support groups, personal appeals, family involvement programs) and macrosocial (neighborhood, workplace, and government interventions) health promotion strategies in recent years. Over time, these two branches of the health communication field should continue to grow closer together and eventually merge. The merging of these two areas will be most advantageous, because health care delivery and health promotion are closely related activities. Health promotion must be recognized as a primary professional activity of health care practice, with doctors, nurses, and other providers devoting increasing energy toward health education, and health promotion efforts must be coordinated with the many related activities and programs of the health care delivery system (Kreps, 1990, 1996a).

Biases in Health Communication Inquiry

Concerns have arisen about potential biases in health communication inquiry toward the perspectives and interests of health care providers over the interests of consumers of health care (see, e.g., the special issue of *Health Communication* titled "The Patient as a Central Construct in Health Communication Research," edited by Sharf & Street, 1997; see also Arntson, 1989; Freidson, 1970; Haug & Lavin, 1983; Kreps, 1996c). Similarly, there are concerns about the often unwitting patterns of bias in health communication inquiry toward privileging the perspectives of culturally powerful participants of the health care system over those of members of marginalized groups (e.g., advantaging the perspectives of participants who are wealthy, well-educated, male, middle-aged, and members of dominant cultural groups and professions over the perspectives of individuals who are poor, female, have minimal formal education, are elderly or are children, or are members of other stigmatized cultural groups) (Beck, Ragan, & Dupre, 1997; Corea, 1997; Fee, 1993; Gabbard-Alley, 1995; Kosa & Zola, 1975; Kreps, 1996a; Kreps & Kunimoto, 1994; Mahowald, 1993; Thornton, Marinelli, & Larson, 1993). The existence of a provider/mainstream bias in health communication research is a serious, insidious, and detrimental problem that must be addressed as this area of inquiry matures.

Communication scholars can promote greater equity in health care by examining practices that limit consumer access to relevant health information and enforce hegemony within the modern health care system (Eng et al., 1998; Ferguson, 1997). Communication is a primary social process that can help equalize power between providers and consumers of health care by promoting wide dissemination of relevant health information. Relevant health information can help both consumers and providers interpret symptoms of illness to discover the causes of ailments, facilitating diagnosis and helping consumers select from among available treatment options. Armed with relevant health information, consumers can better understand the actions and messages of health care practitioners, and they can use this information in establishing cooperative working relationships with their health care providers (Kreps, 1988b). Similarly, relevant information about the health care delivery system can help consumers manage the many complex rules, regulations, and procedures that so often get in the way of effective health care delivery.

Health communication scholars can help consumers become active participants in the health care process. Consumers (and their advocates) must communicate strategically and assertively to gain and share relevant health information, and they must use communication to participate fully in their health care (Jones et al., 1995; Kreps, 1993b). This active participation in the health care delivery process is similar to what Paul Arntson (1989) refers to as health care "citizenship," becoming a participating citizen of the modern health care system. Health care citizenship depends upon individuals' abilities to use communication as a tool for identifying and avoiding potential health care system perils, making informed health care decisions, and enlisting cooperation from providers in accomplishing health care goals. The work of health communication scholars can help promote active participation of consumers within the modern health care system.

DIRECTIONS FOR ADVANCING HEALTH COMMUNICATION INQUIRY

Health communication inquiry has come a long way and is continuing to mature, with research that is addressing significant social issues and employing sophisticated research designs and methodologies. The maturation of this body of research has resulted in growing interdisciplinary and institutional credibility for health communication scholars. Yet there is still a long way to go. It is important for scholars to pose research questions that address an array of critical emerging pragmatic communication issues relating to the promotion of public health. Health communication research has the great potential to minimize significantly the threat of many health risks, to decrease the incidence and duration of health problems, to reduce resulting morbidity and mortality, and generally to increase quality of life. There are several areas of research opportunity where health communication scholars can help promote public health issues concerning power, literacy, information quality, and social influence.

Power in Health Communication Inquiry

Similar to the critique of bias in health communication research, there has been a troubling imbalance of power in the health care system that serves to disenfranchise and marginalize many health care consumers; this issue should be investigated in health communication inquiry. Health communication scholars can focus research attention specifically on the ways in which communication can be used to fulfill the physical and psychological needs of health care consumers, equalize influence and control between providers and consumers, and empower consumers to make informed decisions about their health care to help promote social justice within the modern health care system. Such health communication research can identify mechanisms for increasing consumer participation in health care and promoting partnerships between providers and consumers.

A consumer orientation to health communication inquiry suggests a focus on the strategic use of communication by both health care consumers and providers to promote cooperation and sharing of relevant information. It suggests examination of how health care providers can best elicit information from their clients to diagnose health care problems and to develop and monitor appropriate treatment strategies. Such research also investigates the ways consumers gather relevant information from their providers and from other sources to make sense of their health care problems and to evaluate different courses of treatment. Health communication inquiry that adopts a consumer orientation examines how strategic communication is used to develop cooperation and coordination among interdependent members of health care teams. Health communication inquiry should help clarify the communication strategies that consumers and providers can use to work together cooperatively to accomplish their individual and shared health care goals.

Power issues also arise in the area of access to health care by members of different segments of society who may be marginalized within the health care system. Research data suggest that several groups of consumers (owing to their age, socioeconomic status, sex, race, ethnicity, and/or sexual orientation) often confront cultural barriers to receiving health care information and services (Beck et al., 1997; Cline & McKenzie, 1998; Corea, 1977; Fee, 1993; Kelly et al., 1987; Kosa & Zola,

1975; Kreps, 1986; Mahowald, 1993; Mondragon, Kirkmann-Liff, & Schneller, 1991; Quesada & Heller, 1977; Treichler, 1987; Yom, 1996). Health communication scholars can conduct research that will help document the differences in treatment and access to health information available to different groups of consumers, as well as help to develop strategies for promoting greater access and equity for all consumers within the modern health care system.

Information and Health Literacy

Health communication scholars can perform a major role in support of public health education by helping to promote increased public health literacy. It is very difficult for consumers to participate effectively in health care if they are medically illiterate (Jones et al., 1995; Phillips & Jones, 1991). To use health care advice effectively, consumers must know at least the basics of human physiology, have a working medical vocabulary, be able to explain their symptoms accurately and clearly, and understand their conditions well enough to interpret what their health care providers tell them and ask their providers useful questions. Skilled health care consumers go beyond these minimums to seek relevant health information actively and to stay up-to-date on key health care innovations, especially those innovations that are most relevant to their specific health conditions (Freimuth et al., 1989; Johnson, 1997). Health communication scholars can promote public health by helping to develop, test, and implement innovative health education media and message strategies for promoting enhanced public health literacy. For example, scholars can evaluate the effectiveness of different sources of health information, help tailor message strategies to meet the information needs of targeted audiences of health consumers and health care providers, and help develop new communication programs and technologies for health education.

Unfortunately, there are many popular (television, radio, print, and Internet-based) sources of inaccurate health information that act as potential barriers to health literacy (Eng & Gustafson, 1999; Jones et al., 1995). Popular books, magazine articles, and commercial advertising routinely recommend unusual diets, compulsive exercise, megavitamins, herbal supplements, and major life modifications as panaceas for human miseries. Although some popular health promotion strategies may have some merit, uninformed health care recommendations can cause serious harm. Similarly, family members, friends, and coworkers routinely recommend remedies to one another, often erroneously. Paradoxically, well-informed health care professionals armed with state-of-the-art prevention and treatment strategies often have great difficulty in providing their clients with relevant health information (Edwards, Matthews, Pill, & Bloor, 1998; Jones et al., 1995; Kreps, 1990; White & Malik, 1999). There is a dire need for research to evaluate the accuracy and appropriateness of popular sources of health information (Eng & Gustafson, 1999). Communication scholars can play a major role in this critically important evaluation process.

Sources of accurate and relevant scientifically based health information are not always as compellingly packaged for consumers as are the many commercial health information channels that may not be as "healthy" for public consumption. Physicians and other health care providers are also not always well prepared to provide their clients with accurate health information (Edwards et al., 1998; Jones et al., 1995; White & Malik, 1999). A national survey of a representative cross section of the American public identified primary care physicians as the most preferred source of health information, with 84% of the 1,250 consumers surveyed identifying a discussion with their personal physician as potentially their most useful source of health information (Kreps et al., 1987). A related survey conducted with primary care physicians found that although these providers were genuinely concerned with health education (providing their clients with relevant health information), a variety of communication barriers, such as lack of training in health education and counseling skills, were inhibiting their information dissemination efforts (Maibach & Kreps, 1986). In fact, there is abundant evidence that all too often current health care provider communication practices fail to supply consumers with satisfactory levels of health information (Hess, Liepman, & Ruane, 1983; Kreps, 1990; Newell & Webber, 1983; Orleans, George, Houpt, & Brodie, 1985; Relman, 1982; Wechsler, Levine, Idelson, Rohman, & Taylor, 1983). Health communication scholars can help identify and develop effective communication strategies, resources, and media that health care providers can use in supplying their clients with relevant information, as well as introduce and test training programs to help providers develop communication skills and strategies for effectively counseling their clients (White & Malik, 1999).

Quality of Health Information

Consumers of health care depend upon the quality of health information they can access to make important health care choices. There are many different sources of health information available today. In addition to gathering health information directly from their health care providers, consumers can consult resources at their public libraries or, if available, local university or medical libraries, which have access to health reference books, journals, and computerized sources such as the National Library of Medicine's MEDLINE database. A large and growing number of health information services are available to consumers via the Internet, which has rapidly become an extremely powerful source of health information for both health care consumers and providers (Cassell et al., 1998; Chamberlain, 1996; Ferguson, 1996; Street, 1996; Street et al., 1997). Yet the sheer number of information sources and the incredible volume of health information available today can sometimes overload and confuse consumers (Eng & Gustafson, 1999).

Consumers can get information from advocacy and research organizations about specific health care issues. Local and federal government agencies also provide excellent information on most serious diseases. For example, the National Cancer Institute operates a toll-free telephone information system, the Cancer Information Service (CIS, at 1-800-4-CANCER), that can be accessed from anywhere in the United States (Freimuth et al., 1989; Johnson, 1997). CIS telephone operators will try to answer any questions about cancer and provide referral and treatment information to callers (see the recent supplemental issue of the *Journal of Health Communication: International Perspectives* that describes the health information dissemination functions of the CIS; Ratzan, 1998). CIS operators can also have PDQ database searches conducted for callers to access the latest information about cancer treatment and clinical research being conducted (Kreps, 1993a; Kreps et al., 1988). Health communication scholars are in great demand to help such organizations and government agencies evaluate the effectiveness of their current health information delivery programs, tailor their message strategies for specific targeted audiences, and develop new and improved health information dissemination strategies and technologies. Such evaluation research can also help consumers decide which of the many available sources of health information are most credible, accurate, and up-to-date (Eng & Gustafson, 1999; Morra, 1998).

Social Influence and Health Promotion

Health communication scholars can help promote public health by examining the complex role of social influence in health promotion efforts. Too often, health promotion efforts do not use social influence theory and research to match planned message strategies to the unique social influence features of targeted audiences (Albrecht & Bryant, 1996; Dearing et al., 1996; Lefebvre & Flora, 1988). Kim Witte's provocative line of research on the use of fear appeals in risk communication illustrates the ways in which communication research and social influence theories can inform health promotion efforts (for a review of this research program, see Witte, 1995). Witte has found that fear appeals raise consumers' awareness of health risks, but, at a certain point, if health promotion messages do not help consumers also recognize good opportunities for confronting those risks, the consumers become defensive and tend to focus more on ways to relieve their fear than on responding to the health risk. If health care providers do not provide messages to their clients that not only help them to recognize health risks but also direct them to respond to those risks, their health promotion efforts will have limited success. Through the careful design of health promotion messages to match social influence processes, the effectiveness of these efforts can be greatly enhanced.

To be effective, health promotion efforts should always rise out of clear recognition of consumers' health needs, problems, beliefs, and behaviors, so that campaigns are developed to reflect target audiences' specific concerns and cultural perspectives (Kotler & Roberto, 1989; Lefebvre & Flora, 1988; Maibach et al., 1993). As Maibach et al. (1993) note, "Effective campaigns appeal to the interests and orientations of target audience members to gain their attention, increase the likelihood they will comprehend and be moved by campaign messages, encourage their participation in campaign activities, and ultimately to enable them to adopt the campaigns strategies and recommendations" (p. 20). Health communication scholars can provide much-needed data from audience analyses to direct sophisticated health promotion efforts that are tailored to carefully segmented audiences of consumers (Albrecht & Bryant, 1996).

Health communication scholars can help conduct formative and summative evaluations of health promotion campaigns, focusing specifically on the message strategies, communications media, and channels employed by campaign planners. Such research is essential for increasing the sophistication and reach of public health campaigns. Evaluation research data can provide relevant feedback to help campaign planners in tailoring their campaigns to meet the specific needs, expectations, and orientations of target audiences of consumers and in developing strategic and well-tailored health education messages. Such data can also aid planners in the selection and employment of appropriate communication channels and media to achieve their campaign goals.

Conclusions Concerning the Future of Health Communication Inquiry

I am heartened to see a growing emphasis on public advocacy, consumerism, and empowerment in health communication inquiry. This trend can help influence the revolution in modern health care in very positive ways. It can help equalize power between providers and consumers as well as relieve a great deal of strain on the modern health care system by encouraging disease prevention, self-care, and increased consumer participation in the health care enterprise (see Arntson, 1989; Kreps, 1993b, 1996a, 1996c; Sharf, 1999). Health communication research can also promote public health by helping to identify the information needs of consumers and suggesting sophisticated strategies for encouraging consumers to take control of their health and health care. Health communication research can also help identify and evaluate sources of relevant health information that are available to health care consumers and providers, gather data from consumers about the kinds of challenges and constraints they face within the modern health care system, and develop and field test educational and media programs for enhancing consumers' medical literacy (see Johnson, 1997). Such research will help consumers to negotiate their way through health care bureaucracies and develop communication skills for interacting effectively with health care providers.

Current and future health communication research should expand its focus on the effective dissemination of relevant health information to promote public health. Sophisticated health promotion efforts will recognize the multidimensional nature of health communication, identify communication strategies that incorporate multiple levels and channels of human communication, and implement a wide range of prevention messages and campaign strategies based on theories of social influence that target relevant and specific (well-segmented) audiences (Albrecht & Bryant, 1996; Maibach et al., 1993). Modern campaigns should also become more dependent upon integrating interpersonal, group, organizational, and mediated communication to disseminate relevant health information effectively to specific at-risk populations, recognizing the complexities of health promotion and the transdisciplinary nature of health communication.

Health communication inquiry should address growing concerns about the role of culture on health and health care. Health communication scholars can help to promote greater equity in the treatment of members of particular cultural groups who are too often marginalized within the modern health care system, such as people with AIDS, the poor, minorities, women, and the elderly. Future research should examine the health communication needs of such marginalized cultural groups and identify strategies for enhancing health communication with members of these groups.

Ideally, the field of health communication is moving toward a sophisticated transdisciplinary agenda for applied health communication research that will examine the role of communication in health care at multiple communication levels and in a broad range of communication contexts. The best health communication research will evaluate the use of established and emerging communication channels and assess the influences of communication on important psychological, behavioral, and physiological health outcomes. Future health communication inquiry and education can provide relevant information about the development of cooperative relationships between interdependent participants in the modern health care system, encourage the use of sensitive and appropriate interpersonal communication in health care, empower consumers to take charge of their own health care, enhance the dissemination of relevant health information, and promote the use of strategic communication message strategies in public health campaigns.

REFERENCES

Agency for Health Care Policy and Research. (1997). *Consumer health informatics and patient decision making: Final report* (Publication No. AHCPR 98-N001). Rockville, MD: U.S. Department of Health and Human Services.

Albrecht, T., & Bryant, C. (1996). Advances in segmentation modeling for health communication and social marketing campaigns. *Journal of Health Communication: International Perspectives, 1,* 65-80.

Arntson, P. (1985). Future research in health communication. *Journal of Applied Communication Research, 13,* 118-130.

Arntson, P. (1989). Improving citizens' health competencies. *Health Communication, 1,* 29-34.

Babrow, A. S., Kasch, C. R., & Ford, L. A. (1998). The many meanings of uncertainty in illness: Toward a systematic accounting. *Health Communication, 10,* 1-23.

Baker, E. L., Friede, A., Moulton, A. D., & Ross, D. A. (1995). A framework for integrated public health information and practice. *Public Health Management Practice, 1,* 43-47.

Bandura, A. (1989). Perceived self-efficacy in the exercise of control over AIDS infection. In V. M. Mays, G. W. Albee, & S. S. Schneider (Eds.), *Primary prevention of AIDS: Psychological approaches* (pp. 128-141). Newbury Park, CA: Sage.

Beck, C. S., Ragan, S. L., & Dupre, A. (1997). *Partnership for health: Building relationships between women and health caregivers.* Mahwah, NJ: Lawrence Erlbaum.

Berger, C. R. (1991). Curiouser and curiouser curios. *Communication Monographs, 59,* 101-107.

Booth-Butterfield, S., Chory, R., & Beynon, W. (1997). Communication apprehension and health communication and behaviors. *Communication Quarterly, 45,* 235-250.

Burgoon, M. (1992). Strangers in a strange land: The Ph.D. in the land of the medical doctor. *Journal of Language and Social Psychology, 11,* 101-106.

Burgoon, M. (1996). (Non)compliance with disease prevention and control messages: Communication correlates and psychological predictors. *Journal of Health Psychology, 1,* 279-296.

Burgoon, M., & Hall, J. R. (1994). Myths as health belief systems: The language of salves, sorcery, and science. *Health Communication, 6,* 97-115.

Cassell, M. M., Jackson, C., & Cheuvront, B. (1998). Health communication on the Internet: A effective channel for health behavior change? *Journal of Health Communication: International Perspectives, 3,* 71-79.

Chamberlain, M. (1996). Health communication: Making the most of new media technologies. *Journal of Health Communication: International Perspectives, 1,* 43-50.

Clark, F. (1992). The need for a national information infrastructure. *Journal of Biomedical Communication, 19,* 8-9.

Cline, R. J., & McKenzie, N. J. (1998). The many cultures of health care: Difference, dominance, and distance in physician-patient communication. In L. D. Jackson & B. K. Duffy (Eds.), *Health communication research: A guide to developments and direction* (pp. 57-74). Westport, CT: Greenwood.

Corea, G. (1977). *The hidden malpractice: How American medicine treats women as patients and professionals.* New York: William Morrow.

Dearing, J. W., Rogers, E. M., Meyer, G., Casey, M. K., Rao, N., Campo, S., & Henderson, G. M. (1996). Social marketing and diffusion-based strategies for communicating with unique populations: HIV prevention in San Francisco. *Journal of Health Communication: International Perspectives, 1,* 342-364.

Edwards, A., Matthews, E., Pill, R., & Bloor, M. (1998). Communication about risk: The responses of primary care professionals to standardizing the "language of risk" and communication tools. *Family Practice, 15,* 301-307.

Eng, T. R., & Gustafson, D. H. (Eds.). (1999). *Wired for health and well-being: The emergence of interactive health communication.* Washington, DC: U.S. Department of Health and Human Services, Office of Disease Prevention and Health Promotion.

Eng, T. R., Maxfield, A., Patrick, K., Deering, M. J., Ratzan, S. C., & Gustafson, D. H. (1998). Access to health information and support: A public highway or a private road? *Journal of the American Medical Association, 280,* 1371-1375.

Engleberg, M., Flora, J., & Nass, C. (1995). AIDS knowledge: Effects of channel involvement and interpersonal communication. *Health Communication, 7,* 73-92.

Fabregas, S. M., & Kreps, G. L. (1999). Bioethics committees: A health communication approach. *Puerto Rico Health Sciences Journal, 18*(1), 31-37.

Fee, E. (Ed.). (1993). *Women and health: The politics of sex in medicine.* Farmingdale, NY: Baywood.

Ferguson, T. (1996). *Health online: How to find health information support groups and self-help communities in cyberspace.* Reading, MA: Addison-Wesley.

Ferguson, T. (1997). Health care in cyberspace: Patients lead a revolution. *Futurist, 31,* 29-33.

Flora, J. A., Maccoby, N., & Farquhar, J. W. (1989). Communication campaigns to prevent cardiovascular disease: The Stanford community studies. In R. E. Rice & C. K. Atkin (Eds.), *Public communication campaigns* (2nd ed., pp. 233-252). Newbury Park, CA: Sage.

Freidson, E. (1970). *Professional dominance: The social structure of medical care.* Chicago: Aldine.

Freimuth, V. S., Stein, J. A., & Kean, T. J. (1989). *Searching for health information: The Cancer Information Service model.* Philadelphia: University of Pennsylvania Press.

Frey, L. R., Adelman, M. B., & Query, J. L. (1996). Communication practices in the social construction of health in an AIDS residence. *Journal of Health Psychology, 1,* 383-398.

Frey, L. R., Botan, C. H., & Kreps, G. L. (2000). *Investigating communication: An introduction to research methods* (2nd ed.). Boston: Allyn & Bacon.

Gabbard-Alley, A. S. (1995). Health communication and gender: A review and critique. *Health Communication, 7,* 35-54.

Gantz, W., & Greenberg, B. (1990). The role of informative television programs in the battle against AIDS. *Health Communication, 2,* 199-216.

Geist, P., & Hardesty, M. (1992). *Negotiating the crisis: DRGs and the transformation of hospitals.* Hillside, NJ: Lawrence Erlbaum.

Gifford, C. J. (1983). *Health team literature: A review and application with implications for communication research.* Paper presented at the annual meeting of the Eastern Communication Association, Ocean City, MD.

Guttman, N. (1996). Values and justifications in health communication interventions: An analytic framework. *Journal of Health Communication: International Perspectives, 1,* 365-396.

Guttman, N. (1997). Ethical dilemmas in health campaigns. *Health Communication, 9,* 155-190.

Hafstad, A., & Aaro, L. E. (1997). Activating interpersonal influence through provocative appeals: Evaluation of a mass media-based anti-smoking campaign targeting adolescents. *Health Communication, 9,* 253-272.

Hammond, S. L., Freimuth, V. S., & Morrison, W. (1990). Radio and teens: Convincing gatekeepers to air health messages. *Health Communication, 2,* 59-68.

Harris, L. M. (Ed.). (1995). *Health and the new media: Technologies transforming personal and public health.* Mahwah, NJ: Lawrence Erlbaum.

Haug, M., & Lavin, B. (1983). *Consumerism in medicine: Challenging physician authority.* Beverly Hills, CA: Sage.

Hess, J. W., Liepman, M. R., & Ruane, T. J. (1983). *Family practice and preventive medicine: Health promotion in primary care.* New York: Human Sciences.

Hofstetter, C. R., Schultze, W. A., & Mulvihill, M. M. (1992). Communications media, public health, and public affairs: Exposure in a multimedia community. *Health Communication, 4,* 259-272.

Hyde, M. J. (1990). Experts, rhetoric, and the dilemmas of medical technology: Investigating a problem of progressive ideology. In M. J. Medhurst, A. Gonzalez, & T. R. Peterson (Eds.), *Communication and the culture of technology* (pp. 115-136). Pullman: Washington State University Press.

Johnson, J. D. (1997). *Cancer related information seeking.* Cresskill, NJ: Hampton.

Jones, J. A., Kreps, G. L., & Phillips, G. M. (1995). *Communicating with your doctor: Getting the most out of health care.* Cresskill, NJ: Hampton.

Kelly, J. A., St. Lawrence, J. S., Smith, S., Hood, H. V., & Cook, D. J. (1987). Stigmatization of AIDS patients by physicians. *American Journal of Public Health, 77,* 789-791.

Kim, Y. M., Odallo, D., Thuo, M., & Kols, A. (1999). Client participation and provider communication in family planning counseling: Transcript analysis in Kenya. *Health Communication, 11,* 1-19.

Klingle, R. S., Burgoon, M., Afifi, W., & Callister, M. (1995). Rethinking how to measure organizational culture in the hospital setting: The Hospital Culture Scale. *Evaluation and the Health Professions, 18,* 166-186.

Korhonen, T., Uutela, A., Korhonen, H. J., & Puska, P. (1998). Impact of mass media and interpersonal health communication on smoking cessation attempts: A study in North Karelia, 1989-1996. *Journal of Health Communication: International Perspectives, 3,* 105-118.

Kosa, J., & Zola, I. (Eds.). (1975). *Poverty and health: A sociological analysis.* Cambridge, MA: Harvard University Press.

Kotler, P., & Roberto, E. (1989). *Social marketing: Strategies for changing public behavior.* New York: Free Press.

Kreps, G. L. (1986). Health communication and the elderly. *World Communication, 15,* 55-70.

Kreps, G. L. (1988a). The pervasive role of information in health and health care: Implications for health communication policy. In J. A. Anderson (Ed.), *Communication yearbook 11* (pp. 238-276). Newbury Park, CA: Sage.

Kreps, G. L. (1988b). Relational communication in health care. *Southern Speech Communication Journal, 53,* 344-359.

Kreps, G. L. (1989). Setting the agenda for health communication research and development: Scholarship that can make a difference. *Health Communication, 1,* 11-15.

Kreps, G. L. (1990). Communication and health education. In E. B. Ray & L. Donohew (Eds.), *Communication and health: Systems and applications* (pp. 187-203). Hillsdale, NJ: Lawrence Erlbaum.

Kreps, G. L. (1993a). Disseminating cancer treatment information to physicians: The case of the Physician Data Query (PDQ) system. In B. C. Thornton & G. L. Kreps (Eds.), *Perspectives on health communication* (pp. 146-152). Prospect Heights, IL: Waveland.

Kreps, G. L. (1993b). Refusing to be a victim: Rhetorical strategies for confronting cancer. In B. C. Thornton & G. L. Kreps (Eds.), *Perspectives on health communication* (pp. 42-47). Prospect Heights, IL: Waveland.

Kreps, G. L. (1996a). Communicating to promote justice in the modern health care system. *Journal of Health Communication: International Perspectives, 1,* 99-109.

Kreps, G. L. (1996b). The interface between health communication and health psychology [Guest editorial]. *Journal of Health Psychology, 1,* 259-260.

Kreps, G. L. (1996c). Promoting a consumer orientation to health care and health promotion. *Journal of Health Psychology, 1,* 41-48.

Kreps, G. L. (1998). Social responsibility and the modern health care system: Promoting a consumer orientation to health care. In P. Salem (Ed.), *Organizational communication and change* (pp. 293-304). Cresskill, NJ: Hampton.

Kreps, G. L., Bonaguro, E. W., & Query, J. L. (1998). The history and development of the field of health communication. In L. D. Jackson & B. K. Duffy (Eds.), *Health communication research: A guide to developments and direction* (pp. 1-15). Westport, CT: Greenwood.

Kreps, G. L., Frey, L. R., & O'Hair, D. (1991). Applied communication research: Scholarship that can make a difference. *Journal of Applied Communication Research, 19,* 71-87.

Kreps, G. L., Hubbard, S. M., & DeVita, V. T. (1988). The role of the Physician Data Query on-line cancer system in health information dissemination. In B. D. Ruben (Ed.), *Information and behavior* (Vol. 2, pp. 362-374). New Brunswick, NJ: Transaction.

Kreps, G. L., & Kunimoto, E. (1994). *Effective communication in multicultural health care settings.* Newbury Park, CA: Sage.

Kreps, G. L., & O'Hair, D. (Eds.). (1995). *Communication and health outcomes.* Cresskill, NJ: Hampton.

Kreps, G. L., O'Hair, D., & Clowers Hart, M. (1994). The influence of human communication on health care outcomes. *American Behavioral Scientist, 38,* 248-256.

Kreps, G. L., Ruben, B. D., Baker, M. W., & Rosenthal, S. R. (1987). Survey of public knowledge about digestive health and diseases: Implications for health education. *Public Health Reports, 102,* 270-277.

Kreps, G. L., & Thornton, B. C. (1992). *Health communication: Theory and practice* (2nd ed.). Prospect Heights, IL: Waveland.

Lammers, J. C., & Geist, P. (1997). The transformation of caring in the light and shadow of "managed care." *Health Communication, 9,* 45-60.

Larson, M. (1991). Health related messages embedded in prime-time television entertainment. *Health Communication, 3,* 175-184.

Lefebvre, C., & Flora, J. (1988). Social marketing and public health intervention. *Health Education Quarterly, 15,* 299-315.

Lieberman, D. (1992). The computer's potential role in health education. *Health Communication, 4,* 211-226.

Lupton, D. (1994). Toward the development of critical health communication praxis. *Health Communication, 6,* 55-67.

Mahowald, M. B. (1993). *Women and children in health care: An unequal majority.* New York: Oxford University Press.

Maibach, E. W., & Kreps, G. L. (1986, September). *Communicating with clients: Primary care physicians perspectives on cancer prevention, screening, and education.* Paper presented at the International Conference on Doctor-Patient Communication, University of Western Ontario.

Maibach, E. W., Kreps, G. L., & Bonaguro, E. W. (1993). Developing strategic communication campaigns for HIV/AIDS prevention. In S. Ratzan (Ed.), *AIDS: Effective health communication for the 90s* (pp. 15-35). Washington, DC: Taylor & Francis.

Maibach, E. W., Shenker, A., & Singer, S. (1997). Consensus conference on the future of social marketing. *Journal of Health Communication: International Perspectives, 2,* 301-303.

Makoul, G. (1998). Perpetuating passivity: Reliance and reciprocal determinism in physician-patient interaction. *Journal of Health Communication, 3,* 233-259.

Marshall, A. (1993). Whose agenda is it anyway: Training medical residents in patient-centered interviewing techniques. In E. B. Ray (Ed.), *Case studies in health communication* (pp. 15-29). Hillsdale, NJ, Lawrence Erlbaum.

McGuiness, J. M., Deering, M. J., & Patrick, K. (1995). Public health information and the new media: A view from the public health service. In L. M. Harris (Ed.), *Health and the new media: Technologies transforming personal and public health* (pp. 127-141). Mahwah, NJ: Lawrence Erlbaum.

Metts, S., Manns, H., & Kruzic, L. (1996). Social support structures and predictors of depression in persons who are seropositive. *Journal of Health Psychology, 1,* 367-382.

Miller, K., & Zook, E. G. (1997). Care partners for persons with AIDS: Implications for health communication. *Journal of Applied Communication Research, 25,* 57-74.

Mondragon, D., Kirkmann-Liff, B., & Schneller, E. (1991). Hostility to people with AIDS-risk perception and demographic factors. *Social Science and Medicine, 32,* 1137-1142.

Morra, M. E. (1998). Editorial. *Journal of Health Communication: International Perspectives, 3*(Suppl.), v-vii.

Myrick, R. (1998). In search of cultural sensitivity and inclusiveness: Communication strategies used in rural HIV prevention campaigns. *Health Communication, 10,* 65-86.

Newell, G. R., & Webber, C. F. (1983). The primary care physician in cancer prevention. *Family and Community Health, 5,* 77-84.

O'Keefe, G. J., Hartwig Boyd, H., & Brown, M. R. (1998). Who learns preventive health care information from where: Cross-channel and repertoire comparisons. *Health Communication, 10,* 25-26.

Orleans, C. T., George, L. K., Houpt, J. L., & Brodie, K. H. (1985). Health promotion in primary care: A survey of U.S. family practitioners. *Preventive Medicine, 14,* 636-647.

Pavlik, J. V., Finnegan, J. R., Strickland, D., Salman, C. T., Viswanath, K., & Wackman, D. B. (1993). Increasing public understanding of heart disease: An analysis of the Minnesota Heart Health Program. *Health Communication, 5,* 1-20.

Phillips, G. M., & Jones, J. A. (1991). Medical compliance: Patient or physician responsibility. *American Behavioral Scientist, 34,* 756-767.

Query, J. L., & James, A. C. (1989). The relationship between interpersonal communication competence and social support among elderly support groups in retirement communities. *Health Communication, 1,* 165-184.

Query, J. L., & Kreps, G. L. (1996). Testing a relational model of health communication competence among caregivers for individuals with Alzheimer's disease. *Journal of Health Psychology, 1,* 335-352.

Quesada, G., & Heller, R. (1977). Sociocultural barriers to medical care among Mexican Americans in Texas. *Medical Care, 15,* 93-101.

Ratzan, S. C. (Ed.). (1998). The impact and value of the Cancer Information Service: A model for health communication [Special issue]. *Journal of Health Communication: International Perspectives, 3*(Suppl.), 1-120.

Ratzan, S. C. (1999). Strategic health communication and social marketing of risk issues [Editorial]. *Journal of Health Communication: International Perspectives, 4,* 1-6.

Ray, E. B., & Miller, K. I. (1990). Communication in health care organizations. In E. B. Ray & L. Donohew (Eds.), *Communication and health: Systems and applications* (pp. 92-107). Hillsdale, NJ: Lawrence Erlbaum.

Reardon, K. K., & Rogers, E. M. (1988). Interpersonal versus mass media communication: A false dichotomy. *Human Communication Research, 15,* 284-303.

Relman, A. A. (1982). Encouraging the practice of preventive medicine and health promotion. *Public Health Reports, 97,* 216-219.

Ressler, W., & Toledo, E. (1997). A functional perspective on social marketing: Insights from Israel's bicycle helmet campaign. *Journal of Health Communication: International Perspectives, 2,* 145-156.

Rogers, E. M. (1994). The field of health communication today. *American Behavioral Scientist, 38,* 208-214.

Rootman, I., & Hershfield, L. (1994). Health communication research: Broadening the scope. *Health Communication, 6,* 69-72.

Rubin, A. M., & Rubin, R. C. (1985). Interface of personal and mediated communication: A research agenda. *Critical Studies in Mass Communication, 2,* 36-53.

Sechrest, L., Backer, T. E., Rogers, E. M., Campbell, T. F., & Grady, M. L. (Eds.). (1994). *Effective dissemination of health information.* Rockville, MD: Agency for Health Care Policy and Research.

Sharf, B. F. (1993). Reading the vital signs: Research in health care communication. *Communication Monographs, 60,* 35-41.

Sharf, B. F. (1999). The present and future of health communication scholarship: Overlooked opportunities. *Health Communication, 11,* 195-199.

Sharf, B. F., & Street, R. L., Jr. (Eds.). (1997). The patient as a central construct in health communication research [Special issue]. *Health Communication, 9*(1).

Signorielli, N., & Lears, M. (1992). Television and children's conceptions of nutrition: Unhealthy messages. *Health Communication, 4,* 245-258.

Slack, W. V. (1997). *Cybermedicine: How computers empower doctors and patients for better health care.* San Francisco: Jossey-Bass.

Smaglik, P., Hawkins, R. P., Pingree, S., Gustafson, D. H., Boberg, E., & Bricker, E. (1998). The quality of interactive computer use among HIV-infected individuals. *Journal of Health Communication: International Perspectives, 3,* 53-68.

Smith, D. H., & Pettegrew, L. S. (1986). Mutual persuasion as a model for doctor-patient communication. *Theoretical Medicine, 7,* 127-139.

Smith, R. C., & Hoppe, R. (1991). The patient's story: Integrating a patient-centered approach to interviewing. *Annals of Internal Medicine, 115,* 470-477.

Sonnenberg, F. A. (1997). Health information on the Internet: Opportunities and pitfalls. *Archives of Internal Medicine, 157,* 151-152.

Stoddard, J. L., Johnson, C. A., Sussman, S., Dent, C., & Boley-Cruz, T. (1998). Tailoring outdoor tobacco advertising to minorities in Los Angeles County. *Journal of Health Communication: International Perspectives, 3,* 137-146.

Street, R. L., Jr. (Ed.). (1996). *Health and multimedia.* Mahwah, NJ: Lawrence Erlbaum.

Street, R. L., Jr., Gold, W. R., & Manning, T. (Eds.). (1997). *Health promotion and interactive technology: Theoretical applications and future directions.* Mahwah, NJ: Lawrence Erlbaum.

Thornton, B. C., & Kreps, G. L. (Eds.). (1993). *Perspectives on health communication.* Prospect Heights, IL: Waveland.

Thornton, B. C., Marinelli, R. D., & Larson, T. (1993). Ethics and women's health care. In B. C. Thornton & G. L. Kreps (Eds.), *Perspectives on health communication* (pp. 186-195). Prospect Heights, IL: Waveland.

Treichler, P. (1987). AIDS, homophobia, and biomedical discourse: An epidemic of signification. *Cultural Studies, 1,* 263-305.

Valente, T. W., Poppe, P. R., & Merritt, A. P. (1996). Mass-media generated interpersonal communication as sources of information about family planning. *Journal of Health Communication: International Perspectives, 1,* 247-266.

Wallack, L., Dorfman, L., Jernigan, D., & Themba, M. (1993). *Media advocacy and public health.* Newbury Park, CA: Sage.

Wechsler, H., Levine, S., Idelson, R. K., Rohman, M., & Taylor, J. O. (1983). The physician's role in health promotion: A survey of primary care practitioners. *New England Journal of Medicine, 308*(2), 97-100.

White, M. K., & Malik, T. (1999). Teaching clinician-patient communication in the treatment of breast diseases. *Journal of Women's Health, 8*(1), 39-44.

Winnett, L. B., & Wallack, L. (1996). Advancing public health goals through the mass media. *Journal of Health Communication: International Perspectives, 1,* 173-196.

Witte, K. (1994). The manipulative nature of health communication research. *American Behavioral Scientist, 38,* 285-293.

Witte, K. (1995). Generating effective risk messages: How scary should your risk communication be? In B. R. Burleson (Ed.), *Communication yearbook 18* (pp. 229-254). Thousand Oaks, CA: Sage.

Yom, S. S. (1996). The Internet and the future of minority health. *Journal of the American Medical Association, 275,* 735.

Zook, E. G. (1994). Embodied health and constitutive communication: Toward an authentic conceptualization of health communication. In S. A. Deetz (Ed.), *Communication yearbook 17* (pp. 344-377). Thousand Oaks, CA: Sage.

CHAPTER CONTENTS

11 Ambivalence in the "New Positivism" for the Philosophy of Communication: The Problem of Communication and Communicating Subjects

ED McLUSKIE
Boise State University

The philosophy of communication in the United States grew out of a reaction to positivist approaches to communication research, which had managed to render processes of communication anonymous through the eradication of the epistemological subject. Although the pursuits varied among founding proponents of a "philosophy of communication" within the International Communication Association, the concepts nevertheless displayed partisanship for conceptualizations of communication that included communicating subjects. After the early responses to positivism, however, a "new positivism" emerged that challenged that vision. Linked to postmodernist developments in other fields, it joined the old positivist skepticism that subtracted epistemological subjects from knowledge by suggesting a path that would subtract "communicating subjects" and even "communication" from the work of the "philosophy of communication." Most recently, the new positivism has produced ambivalence over the prospects for communication with communicating subjects. In this essay the author concludes that this ambivalence signals a reconsideration of postmodern influences on the philosophy of communication, as well as the return of communication with communicating subjects.

> That we disavow reflection *is* positivism.
> —*Jürgen Habermas, Knowledge and Human Interests, 1971*

T HE philosophy of communication in the United States grew out of a reaction to positivist approaches to communication research, which had managed to render processes of communication anonymous through the eradication of the epistemological subject. Although the pursuits varied among founding proponents of a "philosophy of communication" within the International Communication Association, the concepts nevertheless displayed partisanship for

Correspondence: Ed McLuskie, Department of Communication, Boise State University, Boise, ID 83725; e-mail emclusk@boisestate.edu

Communication Yearbook 24, pp. 255-269

conceptualizations of communication that included communicating subjects. After the early responses to positivism, however, a "new positivism" emerged that challenged that vision. Linked to postmodernist developments in other fields, it joined the old positivist skepticism that subtracted epistemological subjects from knowledge by suggesting a path that would subtract "communicating subjects" and even "communication" from the work of the "philosophy of communication." Most recently, the new positivism has produced ambivalence over the prospects for communication with communicating subjects. In this essay, I will argue that this ambivalence signals a reconsideration of postmodern influences on the philosophy of communication, as well as the return of communication with communicating subjects.

The assumption that communication cannot be expected to spring out of the structures and infrastructures of daily life makes communication scholars automatically skeptical of contentions that "communication" is an empirical fact awaiting the academy's observations and analyses. Early work in the philosophy of communication was skeptical in that sense (Deetz, 1976; Grossberg, 1979; Hardt, 1972; McLuskie, 1976). Instead, philosophical investigations articulated perspectives of communication whose central concept—"communication"—was *counterfactual* in the field. This counterfactuality of communication extended to analyses of practices (Kersten, 1984; Lanigan & Deetz, 1979) that highlighted how struggles for actual participation in the life of society must be won case by case, suggesting that efforts to offer alternative perspectives on communication were suppressed as much by society as by the academy.

To pursuits of the counterfactual, positivism always turns a deaf ear. The culture of the United States supplies fertile ground for positivism. By midcentury, its staunchest supporter in the academy, logical empiricism, had successfully migrated into social research, provoking Mills (1959) to coin the term *abstracted empiricism* to designate both an obsessiveness with methodology *sans substance* and the persistently unfulfilled promise of theoretical explanation. This continuing apology of empiricism masked interests in knowledge, including 1940s "mass communication research" (Simpson, 1994), but it was sustainable for generations of Ph.D.s throughout the social sciences at least from the end of World War II through the first challenges emerging during the anti-Vietnam War period of the late 1960s and early 1970s (Gitlin, 1981). Alliances with inductive theory-building methodologies still dominate the social sciences today.

In a culture of realism, even of pluralist realisms, claims about states of affairs offered as "facts" make for the preferred debates; that which is not yet actual is "speculative," and thus, since the Vienna Circle of the 1920s, not worth even the philosopher's attention. The classic statement is Schlick's (1959) manifesto: "Investigations concerning the human 'capacity for knowledge' . . . are replaced by considerations regarding the nature of expression, of representation," including the subtraction of "the *cogito ergo sum* and related nonsense." The philosophy of communication in the United States was "born" in reaction to this positivist eradication of knowing subjects. "Minor" journals promoted the philosophy of communication as a corrective against the positivism of behaviorism and took aim at the antitheoretical indifference that anonymized human communication in theory and for practice (Delia & Grossberg, 1977; "Preface," 1974).

There seemed little substantive difference between philosophical arguments to annihilate epistemological subjects and behavioral research practices launching the same assault on communicating subjects. The role of the philosophy of communication as academic partisan for communication with communicating subjects was captured by the lead petitioner for a philosophy of communication division within the International Communication Association. Lanigan (1977b) detailed "the elements of lived-experience *which is strictly speaking a subjectivity born of intersubjectivity*" (p. 116; emphasis added), elements systematically lost in prevailing behavioral approaches. It is important to recognize that Lanigan's idea of subjectivity is not monadic, but refers instead to the experiences of an *intersubjective subject,* whose articulation spans at least two centuries of otherwise varied philosophies of the social, from von Humboldt (1973) to Mead (1934) to Habermas (1987). Such claims to the inevitability of intersubjectively generated subjectivity do not inevitably lead to a romantic harmonics of dialogue (teleologically or actually), nor do they require a thorough splitting off of subjectivity from its intersubjective roots. Yet these moves are necessary for contemporary offensives against intersubjective perspectives in the philosophy of communication. Nevertheless, Lanigan described the point of departure for the philosophy of communication, that is, an agreement that the philosophy of communication take up partisanship for *communication with communicating (that is, "intersubjective")* subjects.

Within the ICA, the movement to create the philosophical study of communication became visible during the 1977 Berlin conference, which signified the interests brewing in the United States to engage in a critique of positivism as a route toward more humanistic approaches to communication. There, papers began to appear about the role of positivism in promoting an atheoretical attitude in communication studies (Budd, 1977; McLuskie, 1977). Others used the European context as an occasion to rediscover humanistic and reform-minded communication research in the United States (Hardt, 1977), whereas others saw an opening for papers advocating alternative approaches drawn from European scholarship (Lanigan, 1977a). These efforts reflected a wider phenomenon in the United States, where the aim to abandon the pretense of "value neutrality" in favor of social research to extend freedom in social praxis was occurring in social philosophy—for example, in line with Apel's (1967) work in Germany. Dervin (1978) had given a name to the effort for communication scholars: "the human side of communication."

It seemed that the philosophy of communication would be responsible for and distinguished by explorations in the human side of communication. On the first count, the persistence of positivism is easily underestimated if one tracks merely the growth in the Philosophy of Communication Division of the ICA. Indeed, the original occasions for the philosophical study of communication seem tenacious.

Almost 20 years after MacLean (1976) questioned the assumptions of behavioral linearity and neglect of epistemological issues, Beniger (1993) argued that the field was still obsessed with the "narrow and long outmoded approaches" of "input and decoding," "encoding and decoding," and "computation or processing" (p. 19). This 1990s reminder of philosophy's failure to curb the excesses of positivism was met with another reiterated position: to create a paradigm shift to make "communication" the centerpiece of social science, which, although already proposed as early as 1968 (Thayer, 1968/1979), always had difficulty finding a hearing. This can be traced to an American preference for "liberal-pluralist ideas" at the level of "the politics of the academy," "the struggle for administrative power and recognition of [the] multidisciplinary" (Hardt, 1997, pp. 75, 77), displayed prominently in the field's version of *Methodenstreite* (Gerbner, 1983; Levy, 1993; Levy & Gurevitch, 1993). Perhaps the more visible debates have attracted the greatest interest in recent years, but the successes of positivism and its extensions beyond the academy generated the very occasions and many of the arguments for critical reactions in the philosophy of communication. These arguments have by now mutated, infiltrating the otherwise critical impulses and analyses in the field. New forms of positivism have defined research practices as necessary but confusing institutional efforts to win an intellectual sphere in the face of behaviorism and means-centered research methodologies. In the opening of substantive theoretical spaces emerged a new positivism, a mutation from within the philosophy of communication that encourages *communication without a communicating subject*. Coupled with the persistence of behavioral positivism, the idea of communication without a communicating subject has enjoyed something of a renaissance in the philosophy of communication. This consequence of a "new positivism" invites the philosophy of communication into an ambivalent reconsideration of its work—to explore, first, the move toward this new positivism and then the resulting new ambivalence as a harbinger of future directions.

FROM "OLD" TO "NEW POSITIVISM"

Today, the philosophy of communication is caught in a predicament the possibility of which was articulated 30 years ago, when Habermas (1971) demonstrated how positivism could and did emerge as an "inside job" of the *Geisteswissenschaften.* Then it was a surprising lesson. It was one thing to document positivism in obvious places, such as in varieties of behaviorism or inductively oriented data-gathering supplying vague promises of theoretical insight down the road (the empiricist's apologia). But it was quite another matter to document positivism in the very resources for its critique. Any thesis of an undifferentiated positivism—often read, for example, in the work of Horkheimer and Adorno (1972)—could, Habermas seemed to be warning, blind critical scholars to their own ways of manufacturing positivist programs. If Kant, Hegel, Fichte, Marx,

Peirce, Dilthey, Gadamer, Freud, Nietzsche, and Husserl could commit positivist maneuvers at key points in their works—that is, if positivism resides in pivotal moments of critical philosophy, Marxist social theory, pragmatist theories of meaning, historicist foundations for hermeneutics, the psychoanalytic bridge from society to emancipated egos, the nihilistic adherence to scientism as the occasion for its rejection, and ironically objectivist appeals to the phenomenologist's concept of actual, lived experience—then surely we must consider how positivism could once again become a problem for the philosophy of communication. One aspect of the "new positivism" is that, this time, the philosophy of communication must respond to its own "inside job."

Part of the explanation rests in the argumentative cues appropriated from other fields, through the discourse of modernity. In philosophy and social theory, postmodernists aim to free knowledge from the Enlightenment faith in reason and knowledge (Alexander, 1992). In this argument is a recurring stress on uncertainty everywhere, coupled with a totalizing discreteness of difference, that drives an assault on the epistemological subject not seen since the days of the Vienna Circle. Its debts lie with major figures in the postmodern movement, often traced to Lyotard's *The Postmodern Condition* (1984). Questions of how we know what we know, how we justify our research practices epistemologically, and systematic suspicions about empirical observation prompted discourse about the crumbling foundations of knowledge. The fracturing of knowledge has been variously described as computerization (Lyotard, 1984), as consumerism (Baudrillard, 1983), and even more generally as a rupture that is "political, economic, technical" (Derrida, 1966, p. 450). The state of knowledge in contemporary society is "altered as societies enter into what is known as the postindustrial age and cultures enter what is known as the postmodern age" (Lyotard, 1984, p. 3). To grasp these alterations, we focus on change in how we talk about structures (Derrida, 1966). The result is that we value an utter, totalizing state of change with which to criticize subject-centered reflectiveness. In this, Habermas's (1971, p. vii) definition of "positivism" as the disavowal of reflection meets the postmodern.

By the 1990s, postmodernism had become normalized within the philosophy of communication. But engagements with German idealism, specifically with the critical cultural studies of the Frankfurt school, were not generally addressed:

> Adorno built general social theory out of particular cultural readings illuminated by, and illuminating, total theory. . . . this symbiosis between general theory and particular cultural interpretations has largely given way to methodically-driven readings that are more technical than theoretical. (Agger, 1992, p. 77)

This was even more the case in the United States during its reception of postmodernism, a road that encourages competing versions of cultural studies.

U.S. versions of cultural studies, which freely borrow the skeptical conclusions about the possibility of social theory and knowledge in general, also borrow from

British cultural studies (Agger, 1992, p. 77). The decision is often not to worry about such questions at all: "Anglo-American cultural studies in general has tended to be rather a-theoretical," "unfocussed," and offering "ungrounded 'readings' that do not coalesce . . . nor lead to coherent political interventions"; the crisis in representation instead becomes a reason for interdisciplinarity (Agger, 1992, pp. 77, 79).

Instability and interdisciplinarity have been used as warrants for surfing the culture, making rare the concern for contributions to theorizing communication in the United States. Insisting on the instability of culture and society carries with it the decision to drop the question of whether or not continuity is possible in history, whether there are room and reason to consider continuity as well as fractures. Those influenced by Baudrillard (1983) see the role of the investigator as that of affirmer of instability and even undoer of existing forms. The goal here is to complicate knowledge. On the deathbed of the epistemological subject Baudrillard claimed the end of fixed or continuous positions from which to know. In such a world, only the seductions of alterations drive inquiry. Thus research inevitably becomes the study of seduction, and research is about wherever seduction takes us. Investigating the seductions of consumerism, the media, and the like helped to define an entire generation of cultural studies researchers in communication studies, including the philosophy of communication.

Having learned from Foucault, Lyotard, and Baudrillard that knowledge is uncertain and fractured, researchers face the demand to give up all illusions of order. Enter the postmodern avant-garde as the practice of cultural studies to disrupt knowledge, to reveal underlying contradictions, to emphasize conflicts, map and erase the contextual terrain, and articulate concealments. When we unravel knowledge and subvert it we are practicing the best of deconstruction. In a shifting mix of references to British cultural studies, we find the interplay of Foucault with Hall (Chang, 1986) and, according to Hall (1986) himself, Gramsci. Whereas British cultural studies depended on Gramscian versions of human needs often "blended with Althusser's theory of ideology" (Agger, 1992, p. 80), U.S.-based cultural studies became even more eclectic as it often essentialized fleeting moments of history into the multiple realms of the concrete.

Contemporary authors claim that postmodernism no longer needs to address the "nature of knowledge" question. All that is really left to do is work on the unprecedented happenings of the postmodern. A disconnected topography of unique conditions in contemporary society occupies several empirical postmodernists (Kellner, 1988, p. 258). Here conceptual work has created new terms to describe the allegedly developing postmodern world. The fascination with innovations associated with computerization and the Internet that are "autocatalytic" in their rates of change (Kellner, 1988, p. 267; Kumar, 1995, p. 186) takes the focus off communicating subjects and considers instead sped-up phenomena such as the progressive domination of media (Denzin, 1986, p. 194), the growth of advertising (Kellner, 1988, p. 239), commercialization of knowledge (Smart, 1993), and an increase in globalization (Smith, 1992, p. 503). Our new economic world "trans-territorializes production" (Smith, 1992, p. 503), spreading production throughout the planet to the sources of cheapest labor. Stories of the "jobless future" (Aronowitz, 1994) and of cultures "beyond employment" (Offe, 1985) encourage consumption cultures (Denzin, 1986; Kellner, 1988, p. 268; Smart, 1993, p. 74). The new forms of capitalism are "disorganized" (Lash & Urry, 1987; Offe, 1985), "post-Fordist" (Harvey, 1989), "late" (Habermas, 1975; Jameson, 1991), "techno" (Kellner, 1988, p. 267), and "fast" (Agger, 1989). Postmodern politics stresses the decline of national sovereignty and the cultural identity associated with the state (Beck, 1994, p. 38). Thus the postmodern political scene is marked in the rise of "new social movements" (Habermas, 1989). The public sphere retreats to "subpolitics" (Beck, 1994) and "life-politics" (Giddens, 1994), searching not for a renewal of national political life, but for the self whose identity has been ravaged by global production and consumer capitalism. At the same time, from now-inevitably particular locations, the inevitably marginalized seek impact where they can have none if the world is evolving over the heads of subpolitics.

Attention to such phenomena stresses the erosion of intersubjectivity as a "longing for a new version of relevance by social theorists" (Zukin, 1992, p. 464). Meanwhile, the case against the concepts to be replaced or forgone is more asserted than engaged. Exactly which old concepts and paradigms are now inadequate is a question that receives less agreement. Zukin (1992, p. 464) claims that traditional Marxism and the moral significance of feminism are dated, but leaves out the emerging marriage of class and gender in a reconstructed, critical appropriation of these "old" concepts (Hardt, 1998). This includes arguments against the human subject of intersubjectivity, in ethnomethodology and symbolic interactionism. Finally, *subculture* is a better term for understanding contemporary society than is *culture* in postmodern parlance (Wolfe, 1992, p. 764). The overarching paradox is that the increasing globalization of transnational cultures can be researched only in the ever-shrinking spaces where people reside but no longer count in the worst case and cannot be understood to be capable of action beyond the local in the best case. The predicament of the latter is the endemic manufacture of uncertainty where interpersonal relations have been replaced with indirect relations. Whether we trace this to a failure of "old Enlightenment concepts" or the mistake of those giving up on "the unfinished project of enlightenment" (Honneth, McCarthy, Offe, & Wellmer, 1989) is a debate we are in the midst of. It is not settled.

For the past 15 years, the philosophy of communication has pursued the path of communication without communicating subjects. Billig (1997) associates this development with the rise of cultural studies, which was launched through the philosophy of communication movement in the International Communication Association. Billig criticizes Grossberg, Nelson, and Treichler's (1992) well-known collection on cultural studies for ignoring the actual human subject. For all of the emphasis on language and the ways in which discourse embeds and is embedded by ideology, the compendium is, according to Billig, nowhere concerned with "analyzing utterances . . . in everyday conversations. Conversation analysis, pragmatics, ethnomethodology, rhetoric and discursive psychology find no place in the editors' list. Nor do they figure in the compendium's various contributions" (p. 207). Like an earlier generation's reduction of communication to content, both in behaviorism and in rhetorical studies, this version of cultural studies keeps alive the focus on, in Saussurian terms, *la langue,* whereas *"la parole,* or the use of language and practice, is absent. In this, the structuralist heritage of cultural studies is revealed" (Billig, 1997, p. 208). Even Stuart Hall (1988, p. 35) recognizing that tendency, has complained that cultural studies has become a "depopulated discipline" (Billig, 1994). "The pages of cultural studies have tended to be devoid of recognizable women and men," leaving "culture" to be analyzed only via "manufactured artifacts, such as magazines, films or academic books." With the exception of feminist theorists, "culture does not appear as something to be lived" (Billig, 1997, p. 205). One consequence of this blind spot is an unexamined reduction of consciousness to language, bypassing the question of language use: Bakhtin (1986) regards such a maneuver as blind to the *"real unit* of speech communication"—"the utterance," which always belongs "to a particular subject" (p. 71).

   Moreover, communication receded into the background as culture became the focus. "Intersubjectivity" is no more than "the measure of valorizing . . . aggregations" deployed in "particular structures of circulation or codes of relations" (Grossberg, 1982a, p. 202). The subjects themselves are, at best, remnants of subjectivity and intersubjectivity in this postmodern proposal that reads Foucault (1973, 1977, 1980) via Deleuze and Guattari (1981) into a geometric splash of lines through the lifeless metaphor of the crystal. There we imagine a time-lapsed hardening of residual, localized concepts of process, so that "processes" become discrete unto themselves, stressing change and difference in a "circuit of distribution." Intersubjectivity is now to be understood as a "residue of particular effects" of distribution. From there, an uncharacteristic modernist glance backward calls up an alliance with systems theory to "seek new understandings of what would constitute a scientific discourse on human existence" (Grossberg, 1982a, p. 203). Here, on the periphery of tentative suggestions, the old positivism meets the new if Lilienfeld (1978) was ever correct that the "basic thought forms of systems theory remain classical positivism and behaviorism" (p. 251). In any event, the call to forgo communication with communicating subjects is by now an established trait in the philosophy of communication.

EMERGING AMBIVALENCE WITH THE NEW POSITIVISM

   Outside the field, a retreat of sorts has been occurring. Signs of this can be read in the labeling supplied by Anthony Giddens (1991), and Beck, Giddens, and Lash (1994) note the appearance of such terms as *late modernism, reflexive modernism,* and *radicalized modernism.* Questions about the possibilities of social science at all (and of knowledge and proposals of alternative ways of gathering and analyzing data) are, they claim, receding into the background.

During the past decade, scholars in the philosophy of communication have explored the consequences of the debate over modernity as well (Angus & Langsdorf, 1993; Carey, 1993; Crowley & Mitchell, 1994; Hardt, 1997; Jensen, 1980; McChesney, 1993; McLuskie, 1993; McPhee, 1998; Peters, 1993; Phillips, 1996; Pollock & Cox, 1991). One author's work stands out, however, because it displays an ambivalence in the context of a sustained argument against the prospect of communication with communicating subjects. Chang (1996) accuses "communication theorists of encouraging and perpetuating a teleological interpretation of communicative events" and immediately associates this interpretation with "idealist philosophies of the subject and meaning to promote social harmony, collective identity, or romantic interpretive practice" (p. xvii)—theorists do not, however, "deliberately choose" these otherwise inevitable associations. Such ideas belong to one of two forms of nothingness: Either they eventually decline "into nothingness" for reasons "other than either our forgetfulness or the lack of clarity" or they conceal the triviality of encounters, mistaking Kierkegaardian chatter for genuine participation, thus vindicating the existentialist lesson of the regularity of inauthenticity at the heart of experience (wished for or actualized) (Chang, 1996, pp. 222-223). This explains why a recent work in the philosophy of communication does not utterly "denounce the vague charm of commonality, of dialogism, of the 'fusion of horizons,' of the 'ideal speech situation,' and the like" (p. xvii).

Interestingly, the model to which Chang (1996) appeals is the conversation situation, where the authentic communicative experience is one that makes the pragmatic demand of continued conversation when I "do not understand," where the philosophical principle "*communication implies noncomprehension*" (p. 225) creates memory and, therefore, a history that bespeaks finally the possibility of communication with communicating subjects whose experiences are memorable precisely because they break through the inauthenticity of day-to-day experience. When real communicating subjects experience breaks in their inauthentic lives, the existentialist notion of experience breaks into the postmodern scene of deconstruction in a way that produces a reconsideration of intersubjectivity on the plane of ambivalence.

What Chang calls subjectivity Habermas (1982) calls "diffracted intersubjectivity" (p. 218), which for Habermas but not Chang only gives the *appearance* of impossibility. Thus another way to read Chang's skepticism about the possibility of communication is to consider his thesis as a foregrounding of the practice of "pseudocommunication," the situation in which "the participants do not recognize" each other as persons, and, worse yet, fail to grasp "any communication disturbances" at all. But Chang does allow, ultimately, the recognition of one another as persons, to break through what Habermas (1970) refers to as the "system of reciprocal misunderstandings" that leads to "the pretense of pseudo-consensus" (p. 117). This prospect for authentic communication reproduces the interest in communication with communicating subjects not only as a remote possibility, but as an interest that guides the analysis. This ambivalence over the postmodern assault on intersubjectivity is introduced into the philosophy of communication.

There is hope in this ambivalence, because it persists in the tension between actualities and the counterfactual, between the hope of participation in communication and its systematic frustration. This is precisely where Hegel (1966) wanted dialectical philosophers to be. His version of a dialectical approach recommends the breaking down of polar opposites *without* eradicating them. From the point of view of dialectical philosophy since Hegel, the mistake of the new positivism has been its eradication of ambivalences, of oppositions, of connections between prevailing past and future practices. In terms of communication, the new positivism disembodies meanings—where communication occurs without communicating subjects—or reduces communication to an institutional crossroads for scholarship. Hegel's point, however, is to grasp the interconnection of opposites. This leads Hegel down an argument that establishes "contradiction" as a central problem for philosophy, and for theorizing as well. The response of a reductionist or dualist "either/or" has, in Chang's work, produced a welcome ambivalence.

For the communication scholar, defending a counterfactual concept like communication means facing the prospect of reductionist moments in one's own backyard. It is tempting to stress here the impossibility of communication, communicating subjects, and attendant concepts of intersubjectivity. To articulate something like an as-yet counterfactual "structure of nondistorted ordinary communication" (Habermas, 1970, p. 121) puts the philosophy of communication in the position of defending modernist positions in the midst of an ongoing debate over modernity that, in spite of its duration, is neither settled nor engaged in any sustained way in the field. Failure to engage the oppositions of actuality and counterfactuality is but one important consequence. It closes off consideration of counterfactual communicative practices as *projects* to be actualized, focusing instead on phenomena to be realistically or concretely grasped.

It is also tempting to romanticize or otherwise fetishize "communication" and "the field" that studies it, the substantive problem about which Grossberg (1982a, 1982b, 1993) has given ample and appropriate warnings. The mistake, however, is to take such warnings as warrants for giving up on the idea of communication with communicating subjects. Chang's (1996) sustained argument in this direction, in spite of its claims to the impossibility of communication, requires the reintroduction of communicating subjects struggling for what they, according to Chang, cannot have. And therein lies the decision point of the philosophy of communication today. This fundamental opposition sets the intersubjective subject up against *proposals for communication without communicating subjects.* It calls for submerging something like the hope for intersubjectivity to the reality of its eclipse. There is no doubt that as the lifeworld is colonized (Habermas, 1984), conditions for dialogue erode. But this is the dialectical opportunity in the philosophy of communication, where moves from concept to material history prevent utter assent to the new positivist eradication in practice. Related fundamental oppositions such as the lifeworld/system and communicative action/purposive-rational action ride an evolutionary trend that highlights the intersubjective subject at risk.

To confront the factual rather than the counterfactual is the dualist's, but not the dialectician's, choice. Signs of disaffection with the dualist's choice can be read in the ambivalence described above, and in the push for a dialectical encounter with the idea and the possibility of communication. To leave the counterfactuality of communicative practices as a farewell promotes *monadic* subjectivity. Why there should then be a *nomadic* search for the impossible is a mystery explainable only on the terrain of the intersubjective, whether that terrain is the community of deconstructionist investigators or the experiences of all communicating subjects who share the experience of the systematic frustration of meaning.

Putting intersubjectivity at risk is as old as alienation literature in sociology, as the atomistic implications of behaviorism for the *Geisteswissenschaften,* as an automatic Marxism for emancipatory theory and praxis. But this two-century issue has persisted since the industrial age spawned alienation (by any name) as an experience of the age. It was precisely because the grand social theories of Marx, Weber, Durkheim, and Tönnies were describing the ravages of modernity that subsequent work could even begin to conceive of critical research speaking for the subject whose shrinking lifeworld resources had to be explained, understood, and ultimately defended. Quarrel as we might with one or more of these and other theories of modern society, communication studies and cultural studies are linked to alienation-like understandings of developments since at least the Industrial Revolution. In fact, their concepts depend on them. At the center of those concepts is partisanship for communication, not as a field, but as something like an endangered species, an endangered experience of modernity that can be considered only when communicating subjects are seen as struggling for shared meaning.

The response of recent ambivalence reopens this critical project of reclaiming communication with communicating subjects. A fruitful place to begin is with the critical appropriation of ideas through a renewed interest to theorize in spite of, but not in reaction to, charges of committing "grand narratives." Already, scholars in other fields who work out of French, German, and British schools of cultural studies and postmodernism are backing away from strident arguments against theory and theorizing. Within our field, productive suggestions from Hardt (1992, 1998) to read, for example, the return to the concept of class in feminism offers a basis for concrete work in cultural studies while ensuring that the discourse of critical scholars remembers communicating subjects who exist and have histories in common, histories well described and well told by a variety of genealogies and other methods for conducting cultural studies. Excellent works outside the field take seriously the arguments and analyses born in the debates over modernity, marking out projects of retheorizing without obliterating the marginalized voices of many generations (Agger, 1992). Some works in the field explore these debates in detail, including more extensive accounts and clues about how communication studies lost its way when it did not have to through eradication of the intersubjective, by revisiting *Methodenstreite* (Anderson & Schoening, 1994; McPhee, 1998; Owen, 1984; Skupien, 1993).

Contending with positivism is difficult in this culture. For one thing, it seems a remote discourse. But it is a rather cunning phenomenon of daily life as well as of intellectual work. It essentializes, creates ontologies that, once created, go unquestioned. Just as its continuities are grasped as the disappearance of knowers in philosophy, positivism appears in the consequences of stressing discontinuities, a possibility German critical theory taught through Habermas's (1971) prehistory of modern positivism, the sensibilities of which guide the analyses of cultural studies by Agger (1992). In any event, failure to explore dialectically the positivist impulses within the philosophy of communication risks the continued eradication of the subject, intersubjectivity, and the ability to articulate a future history collectively. In many respects, the choice is the same today as it was a century ago: acquiesce to alleged realities of the age or pragmatically imagine realities worth having. The second choice puts knowing and communicating subjects at the center, however severely crippled their communicative practices may be. The new positivism encourages us to give up on, or severely retract our interest in, the second choice.

REFERENCES

Agger, B. (1989). *Fast capitalism: A critical theory of significance.* Chicago: University of Illinois Press.
Agger, B. (1992). *Cultural studies as critical theory.* London: Falmer.
Alexander, J. C. (1992). General theory in the postpositivist mode: The "epistemological dilemma" and the search for present reason. In S. Seidman & D. Wagner (Eds.), *Postmodernism and social theory.* Cambridge, MA: Blackwell.
Anderson, J. A., & Schoening, G. T. (1994, May). *Social action media studies: Foundational arguments and common premises.* Paper presented at the annual meeting of the International Communication Association, Sydney.
Angus, I. H., & Langsdorf, L. (1993). *The critical turn: Rhetoric and philosophy in postmodern discourse.* Carbondale: Southern Illinois University Press.
Apel, K.-O. (1967). *Analytic philosophy of language and the Geisteswissenschaften* (H. Holstelilie, Trans.). Dordrecht, Netherlands: Reidel.
Aronowitz, S. (1994). *The jobless future: Sci-tech and the dogma of work.* Minneapolis: University of Minnesota Press.
Bakhtin, M. M. (1986). *Speech genres and other late essays.* Austin: University of Texas Press.
Baudrillard, J. (1983). *In the shadow of the silent majorities, or the end of the social and other essays* (P. Foss, P. Patton, & J. Johnston, Trans.). New York: Semiotext(e).
Beck, U. (1994). The reinvention of politics: Towards a theory of reflexive modernization. In U. Beck, A. Giddens, & S. Lash (Eds.), *Reflexive modernization: Politics, tradition and aesthetics in the modern social order.* Cambridge: Polity.
Beck, U., Giddens, A., & Lash, S. (Eds.). (1994). *Reflexive modernization: Politics, tradition and aesthetics in the modern social order.* Cambridge: Polity.
Beniger, J. R. (1993). Communication: Embrace the subject, not the field. *Journal of Communication, 43*(3), 18-25.

Billig, M. (1994). Repopulating the depopulated pages of social psychology. *Theory and Psychology, 4,* 307-335.

Billig, M. (1997). From codes to utterances: Cultural studies, discourse and psychology. In M. Ferguson & P. Golding (Eds.), *Cultural studies in question* (pp. 205-226). London: Sage.

Budd, R. W. (1977, May). *Perspectives on a discipline.* Presidential address presented at the annual meeting of the International Communication Association, Berlin.

Carey, J. W. (1993). The mass media and democracy: Between the modern and the postmodern. *Journal of International Affairs, 47*(1).

Chang, B. G. (1996). *Deconstructing communication: Representation, subject, and economies of exchange.* Minneapolis: University of Minnesota Press.

Chang, C.-H. F. (1986). Post-Marxism or beyond: Hall and Foucault. *Journal of Communication Inquiry, 10*(4), 71-85.

Crowley, D., & Mitchell, D. (1994). Communication in a post-mass media world. In D. Crowley & D. Mitchell (Eds.), *Communication theory today* (pp. 1-24). Stanford, CA: Stanford University Press.

Deetz, S. A. (1976). Conceptualizing human understanding: Gadamer's hermeneutics and American communication studies. *Communication Quarterly, 26*(2), 12-23.

Deleuze, F., & Guattari, D. (1981). Rhizome. *I&C, 8,* 49-71.

Delia, J. G., & Grossberg, L. (1977). Interpretation and evidence. *Western Journal of Speech Communication, 41*(1).

Denzin, N. K. (1986). A postmodern social theory. *Sociological Theory, 4,* 194-204.

Derrida, J. (1966). Structure, sign, play in the discourse of the human sciences. In J. Derrida, *Writing and difference.* Chicago: University of Chicago Press.

Dervin, B. (1978, November). The human side of communication. *T&M Newsletter,* pp. 5-13.

Foucault, M. (1973). *The birth of the clinic: An archeology of medical perception* (A. M. Sheridan, Trans.). New York: Pantheon.

Foucault, M. (1977). *Discipline and punish: The birth of the prison* (A. M. Sheridan, Trans.). New York: Pantheon.

Foucault, M. (1980). *Power/knowledge: Selected interviews and other writings, 1972-1977* (C. Gordon, Ed.; L. Marshall, J. Mepham, & K. Soper, Trans.). New York: Pantheon.

Gerbner, G. (Ed.). (1983). Ferment in the field [Special issue]. *Journal of Communication, 33*(3).

Giddens, A. (1991). *Modernity and self-identity: Self and society in the late modern age.* Cambridge: Polity.

Giddens, A. (1994). Living in a post-traditional society. In U. Beck, A. Giddens, & S. Lash (Eds.), *Reflexive modernization: Politics, tradition and aesthetics in the modern social order.* Cambridge: Polity.

Gitlin, T. (1981). Media sociology: The dominant paradigm. In G. C. Wilhoit & H. Debock (Eds.), *Mass communication review yearbook 2* (pp. 73-121). Beverly Hills, CA: Sage.

Grossberg, L. (1979). Language and theorizing in the human sciences. In N. K. Denzin (Ed.), *Language in symbolic interaction* (Vol. 2). Greenwich, CT: JAI.

Grossberg, L. (1982a). Does communication theory need intersubjectivity? Toward an immanent philosophy of interpersonal relations. In M. Burgoon (Ed.), *Communication yearbook 6* (pp. 171-205). Beverly Hills, CA: Sage.

Grossberg, L. (1982b). The ideology of communication. *Man and World, 15,* 83-101.

Grossberg, L. (1993). Can cultural studies find true happiness in communication? *Journal of Communication, 43*(4), 89-97.

Grossberg, L., Nelson, C., & Treichler, P. A. (Eds.). (1992). *Cultural studies.* New York: Routledge.

Habermas, J. (1970). Toward a theory of communicative competence. In H. P. Dreitzel (Ed.), *Recent sociology no. 2: Patterns of communicative behavior.* New York: Macmillan.

Habermas, J. (1971). *Knowledge and human interests* (J. J. Shapiro, Trans.). Boston: Beacon.

Habermas, J. (1975). *Legitimation crisis* (T. McCarthy, Trans.). Boston: Beacon.

Habermas, J. (1982). A reply to my critics. In J. B. Thompson & D. Held (Eds.), *Habermas: Critical debates* (pp. 219-317). Cambridge: MIT Press.

COMMUNICATION YEARBOOK 24

Habermas, J. (1984). *Theory of communicative action: Vol. 1. Reason and the rationalization of society* (T. McCarthy, Trans.). Boston: Beacon.
Habermas, J. (1987). *Theory of communicative action: Vol. 2. Lifeworld and system: A critique of functionalist reason* (T. McCarthy, Trans.). Boston: Beacon.
Habermas, J. (1989). *The new conservatism: Cultural criticism and the historians' debate* (S. W. Nicholsen, Trans.). Cambridge: MIT Press.
Hall, S. (1986). Gramsci's relevance for the study of race and ethnicity. *Journal of Communication Inquiry, 10*(3), 5-27.
Hall, S. (1988). The toad in the garden: Thatcherism among the theorists. In C. Nelson & L. Grossberg (Eds.), *Marxism and the interpretation of culture* (pp. 35-57). London: Macmillan.
Hardt, H. (1972). Communication and philosophy: An approach to human communication. In R. W. Budd & B. D. Rubin (Eds.), *Approaches to human communication* (pp. 145-155). New York: Spartan.
Hardt, H. (1977, May). *Reformers of society: Small, Ross and Sumner on language, communication and the press.* Paper presented at the annual meeting of the International Communication Association, Berlin.
Hardt, H. (1992). *Critical communication studies: Communication, history and theory in America.* London: Routledge.
Hardt, H. (1997). Beyond cultural studies: Recovering the "political" in critical communication studies. *Journal of Communication Inquiry, 21*(2), 70-78.
Hardt, H. (1998). Looking for the working class: Class relations in communication studies. In H. Hardt, *Interactions: Critical studies in communication, media, and journalism* (pp. 41-62). Lanham, MD: Rowman & Littlefield.
Harvey, D. (1989). *The condition of postmodernity.* Cambridge, MA: Blackwell.
Hegel, G. W. F. (1966). *The phenomenology of mind* (J. B. Baillie, Trans.). London: Humanities.
Honneth, A., McCarthy, T., Offe, C., & Wellmer, A. (Eds.). (1989). *Philosophical interventions in the unfinished project of enlightenment.* Cambridge: MIT Press.
Horkheimer, M., & Adorno, T. W. (1972). *Dialectic of enlightenment* (J. Cumming, Trans.). New York: Herder.
Jameson, F. (1991). *Postmodernism; or, The cultural logic of late capitalism.* Durham, NC: Duke University Press.
Jensen, J. (1980). *Redeeming modernity: Contradictions in media criticism.* Beverly Hills, CA: Sage.
Kellner, D. (1988). Postmodernism as social theory: Some challenges and problems. *Theory, Culture & Society, 5,* 239-269.
Kersten, A. (1984, May). *Organizational control and the communication process.* Paper presented at the annual meeting of the International Communication Association, San Francisco.
Kumar, K. (1995). *From post-industrial to post-modern society: New theories of the contemporary world.* Cambridge, MA: Blackwell.
Lanigan, R. L. (1977a, May). *Critical theory as a philosophy of communication.* Paper presented at the annual meeting of the International Communication Association, Berlin.
Lanigan, R. L. (1977b). *Speech act phenomenology.* The Hague: Martinus Nijhoff.
Lanigan, R. L., & Deetz, S. A. (1979). *Unreflected ideology and the subversion of conventional critique.* Paper presented at the annual meeting of the Southern Speech Communication Association, Biloxi, MS.
Lash, S., & Urry, J. (1987). *The end of organized capitalism.* Cambridge: Polity.
Levy, M. R. (1993). The future of the field II [Special issue]. *Journal of Communication, 43*(4).
Levy, M. R., & Gurevitch, M. (Eds.). (1993). The future of the field I [Special issue]. *Journal of Communication, 43*(3).
Lilienfeld, R. (1978). *The rise of systems theory: An ideological analysis.* New York: John Wiley.
Lyotard, J.-F. (1984). *The postmodern condition: A report on knowledge* (G. Bennington & B. Massumi, Trans.). Minneapolis: University of Minnesota Press.

MacLean, M. S., Jr. (1976). Communication theory, research and the practical affairs of man. *Journal of Communication Inquiry, 2*(1), 1-6.

McChesney, R. W. (1993). Critical communication research at the crossroads. *Journal of Communication, 43*(4), 98-104.

McLuskie, E. (1976). Against a science of human communication: The role of hermeneutics in contributing arguments from the Frankfurt School. *Journal of Communication Inquiry, 2*(1), 7-19.

McLuskie, E. (1977, May). *Integration of critical theory with North American communication study: Barriers and prospects.* Paper presented at the annual meeting of the International Communication Association, Berlin.

McLuskie, E. (1993). Against transformations of communication into control: Continuities in the critical theory of Jürgen Habermas. *Journal of Communication, 43*(1), 154-165.

McPhee, R. D. (1998, May). *Traditional, interpretive, critical, and postmodern discourses in communication studies: Another telling of the paradigm debates story.* Paper presented at the annual meeting of the International Communication Association, Jerusalem.

Mead, G. H. (1934). *Mind, self, and society: From the standpoint of a social behaviorist* (C. W. Morris, Ed.). Chicago: University of Chicago Press.

Mills, C. W. (1959). *The sociological imagination.* London: Oxford University Press.

Offe, C. (1985). *Disorganized capitalism: Contemporary transformations of work and politics.* Cambridge: MIT Press.

Owen, J. L. (1984, May). *A critical analysis of behavioral paradigms and their implications for the study of communication context.* Paper presented at the annual meeting of the International Communication Association, San Francisco.

Peters, J. D. (1993). Genealogical notes on "the field." *Journal of Communication, 43*(4), 132-139.

Phillips, K. R. (1996). The spaces of public dissension: Reconsidering the public sphere. *Communication Monographs, 63,* 231-248.

Pollock, D., & Cox, J. R. (1991). Historicizing "reason": Critical theory, practice, and postmodernity. *Communication Monographs, 58,* 170-178.

Preface. (1974). *Journal of Communication Inquiry, 1*(1), i.

Schlick, M. (1959). The turning point in philosophy. In A. Ayer (Ed.), *Logical positivism.* New York: Free Press.

Simpson, C. (1994). *Science of coercion: Communication research and psychological warfare, 1945-1960.* New York: Oxford University Press.

Skupien, J. (1993, May). *Frege on anti-psychologism and the communicability of concepts.* Paper presented at the annual meeting of the International Communication Association, Washington, DC.

Smart, B. (1993). *Postmodernity.* New York: Routledge.

Smith, M. P. (1992). Postmodernism, urban ethnography, and the news social space of ethnic identity. *Theory and Society, 21,* 493-531.

Thayer, L. (1979). Communication: Sine qua non of the behavioral sciences. In R. W. Budd & B. D. Ruben (Eds.), *Interdisciplinary approaches to human communication.* Rochelle Park, NJ: Hayden. (Original work published 1968)

von Humboldt, W. (1973). *Schriften zur Sprache* (M. Böhler, Ed.). Stuttgart: Reclam.

Wolfe, A. (1992). Weak sociology/strong sociology: Consequences and contradictions of the field and turmoil. *Social Research, 59,* 759-779.

Zukin, S. (1992). Doing postmodernism: A forum. *Theory and Society, 21,* 463-465.

CHAPTER CONTENTS

12 Bridging the Subdisciplines: An Overview of Communication and Technology Research

LEAH A. LIEVROUW
University of California, Los Angeles

ERIK P. BUCY
Indiana University

T. ANDREW FINN
George Mason University

WOLFGANG FRINDTE
University of Jena

RICHARD A. GERSHON
Western Michigan University

CAROLINE
HAYTHORNTHWAITE
*University of Illinois,
Urbana-Champaign*

THOMAS KÖHLER
University of Jena

J MICHAEL METZ
University of Central Florida

S. SHYAM SUNDAR
Pennsylvania State University

Communication and technology (CAT) research is concerned with the development, uses, and consequences of information and communication technologies (ICTs) across all types of social, cultural, and institutional settings. Technology includes the artifacts or devices that enable and extend our abilities to communicate, the communication activities or practices in which we engage when developing and using those devices, and the social arrangements or organizations that form around those practices and devices. Together, these elements also constitute the central phenomenon of interest for CAT research, the mediation of communication processes by ICTs. ICTs are used across many social settings and applications, so CAT research does not fit easily into either the traditional "mass media" or "interpersonal" specializations within the communication discipline. The present essay is organized broadly around the contexts of ICT use and research in society and organizations and by individuals and groups. Three themes resonate throughout this literature: the pervasiveness of electronically mediated communication in contemporary society (ubiquity); the multiplex social formations and phenomena associated with ICTs, rather than effects on particular audiences or demographic groups (the network metaphor); and the changes entailed by the ongoing rearrangement and redefinition of ICTs to suit people's changing needs and circumstances (recombination).

COMMUNICATION and technology (CAT) research is concerned with the development, uses, and consequences of information and communication technologies (ICTs) across all types of social, cultural, and institutional settings. As Langdon Winner (1977) notes, technology is difficult to define; its meaning shifted during the 20th century "from something relatively precise, limited and unimportant to something vague, expansive and highly significant" (p. 8). However, a useful definition would include the *artifacts* or devices that enable and extend our abilities to communicate, the communication activities or *practices* in which we engage when developing and using those devices, and the *social arrangements* or organizations that form around those practices and devices. Together, these elements also constitute the central phenomenon of interest for CAT research, the mediation of communication processes by ICTs.

A line of studies dating back to Schramm (1977) has classified media technologies according to their technological attributes, features, or channel characteristics (e.g., Durlak, 1987; Pool, 1983; Steuer, 1995). Early communication technology studies, following this classificatory approach and the tradition of American media effects research, tended toward technological determinism (i.e., emphasizing the effects or "impacts" of ICTs on users, organizations, or society). This tradition is still influential; however, contemporary researchers consider both impacts and the ways in which individuals, groups, and institutions influence and reshape technologies in use.

Today, ICTs are used both for selective interpersonal or group communication and for the production, transmission, and reception of general-interest content. They incorporate computing, telephone, cable, broadcast, print, and satellite technologies, so research in this area is often framed in terms of point-to-point or networked interactions and information flows, in contrast to the more familiar media framework of institutional sources directing broad-based messages to mass audiences through established channels (e.g., publishing or broadcasting) (Rice & Holmes, 1996). ICTs are often said to be used in "demassified" ways (Rogers, 1986). Over the past two decades, the new media/mass media distinction has blurred as ICT systems have undergone increasing technological and institutional convergence (Baldwin, McVoy, & Steinfield, 1996).

ICTs are used in every kind of social setting and application, which makes it difficult to place CAT research easily into either the traditional "mass media" specialization or the "interpersonal" specialization within the communication discipline. CAT researchers often adapt and combine constructs, theories, and methods from diverse specialties within communication or from other disciplines according to the problem or question being investigated. They tend to view CAT research as a bridge between the subdisciplines of mass-media communication and interpersonal communication (Hawkins, Wiemann, & Pingree, 1988; Rogers, 1999).

Although it has lately acquired some trendy connotations in the multimedia, entertainment, and e-commerce industries, the term *new media* has been used by CAT researchers since the late 1970s in social, psychological, economic, political, and cultural studies of ICTs; often, they have applied the term to the field itself (see Rice & Associates, 1984; Rogers, 1986, 1994; for an overview of current thinking about the term new media, see the inaugural issue of the journal *New Media & Society*).[1]

CAT research is an international effort. In Canada, the specialty grew from the Innis-McLuhan tradition at the University of Toronto, Simon Fraser University, and McGill University. Quebec boasts a large concentration of CAT researchers, encouraged by Canadian government initiatives on computer communications and videotex. Theory-driven researchers such as Armand Mattelart and others connected to the Minitel/Teletel and related projects have led a significant stream of work in France. The engineering-based work of Colin Cherry, the supradisciplinary work of Raymond Williams, and investigations of the service economy laid the groundwork for research in the United Kingdom in the 1980s, especially the Program in Information and Communication Technology of the Economic and Social Research Council. Today, degree programs specializing in communication and technology are found in universities throughout Europe, the United Kingdom, and Asia, as well as in North and South America, and investigators engage in both basic research and applications for business and education.

Although most communication technology studies have taken a social science approach, concentrating on technological, economic, or behavioral issues, in the past decade new media have also become the subject of a vigorous and growing scholarly literature in critical and cultural studies, social theory, and social history. CAT research has a strong grounding in historical scholarship (e.g., Beniger, 1986; Carey, 1989; Fischer, 1992; Marvin, 1988). Technology policy studies in particular have benefited from historical perspectives on key issues such as universal service (Dordick, 1990; Mueller, 1993).

In this chapter our aim is to provide a broad overview of important concepts and an introduction to the essential literatures of the field. Because space is strictly limited, we cannot probe any single issue or researcher's work in great depth, and we may overlook some worthwhile contributions or studies. Nonetheless, we believe that what we present here is reasonably representative of the recent history and current state of research. In general, we cite the most recent, classic, or comprehensive works by particular authors; we encourage readers to seek out their other publications.

This essay is organized broadly around the contexts of ICT use and research in society and organizations and by individuals and groups. Three themes resonate throughout this research: the pervasiveness of electronically mediated communication in contemporary society; the network formations and phenomena associated with ICTs, rather than effects on particular audiences or demographic groups; and the changes entailed by the ongoing rearrangement and redefinition of ICTs to suit people's changing needs and circumstances.

ICTs AND SOCIETY

At the societywide level, communication technology research deals with broad-based social change and movements associated with ICTs as well as with the specific legal, ethical, social, and economic issues that accompany those changes.

The Information Society

Information society research grew out of the influential work of economists and sociologists who detected the movement within developed societies from industrial to postindustrial economies. This was by no means an exclusively American phenomenon; the *johoka shakai* approach in Japan (Ito, 1981) and the recognition of *informatique* by Simon Nora and Alain Minc (1980) in France defined the information society from the outset as an international development.

Fritz Machlup (1962) was among the first economists to recognize and document the increasing numbers of "knowledge workers" in the United States in the postwar period. Daniel Bell (1973) argued that under the influence of new ICTs and the growing dependence on information as an economic good, developed societies were moving to a postindustrial stage characterized by the growth of the service and professional sectors of the economy. Porat and Rubin (1977) refined Machlup's occupational framework and produced the first input-output table of the U.S. *information economy*. Subsequent work in this line focused on defining *information work* and identifying the information workforce (Schement & Lievrouw, 1984), *information industries,* and their relative contribution to national and regional productivity.

In the 1980s an important perspective emerged to challenge the widespread view of a new society driven inevitably by the imperatives of ICT development, the prospect of ever-growing productivity, and swelling ranks of white-collar knowledge workers. This critical view, best illustrated in the work of Herb Schiller, Dallas Smythe, Jennifer Daryl Slack, Colin Cherry, Frank Webster, Kevin Robins, and others, argued that the use of new media technologies tends to reinforce rather than break down existing relations of power and capital. Indeed, the critics said, new ICTs were being implemented in ways that extended the deskilling, alienating patterns of industrial work to industries and workers that had previously seemed immune to assembly-line-style rationalization (e.g., health care, education, and the professions; Slack & Fejes, 1987; Webster, 1995).

The ongoing disagreements between the so-called *discontinuity* and *continuity* viewpoints led Shields and Samarajiva (1993) to conclude that the information society literature could be organized into four major schools: postindustrialists, industrialists, long-wave theorists, and power theorists. Likewise, Webster (1995) has summarized the contributions of social theorists such as Anthony Giddens, Jürgen Habermas, and notably Mark Poster's (1990) *mode of information.* Recently, the information society rubric has taken on a new and more specific form in the European Community as policies of infrastructural expansion and member states' unity or cohesion (see, e.g., European Commission, 1997a).

Globalization

Certainly, Marshall McLuhan had a strong influence on early visions of the information society. In the 1960s he used the term *global village* to describe and critique the effects he observed of worldwide electronic communications (McLuhan, 1964). Today, the word *globalization* dominates discussions of international trade, information flows and infrastructures, national sovereignty and governance, and popular culture and consumption.

The globalization idea draws on the economics of information (e.g., studies by Kenneth Arrow and Donald Lamberton) and on theories of the nation-state and of new technologies and organizing (see the discussion below). It is also based in the communication and development research tradition that was first associated with the work of Daniel Lerner, moved through the "passing of the dominant paradigm" documented by Everett Rogers, and now recognizes the value of local knowledge and grassroots approaches (see, in this volume, Braman, Shah, & Fair, Chapter 7; Kim, Chapter 6).

Perhaps more than any other technology, communication satellites (and the ancillary technologies of cable networking and multichannel systems) have materially affected perceptions of globalization (see Anderson, 1985; Baldwin et al., 1996; Elasmar, 1995; Gershon & Kanayama, 1995; Marghalani, Palmgreen, & Boyd, 1993; Parsons & Frieden, 1998). Communication satellites have played an integral role in the development process, especially for remote education and access to information about agriculture, industry, health care, and social services. Some of the first communication technology studies in the 1960s and 1970s explored satellite communication and development (Rogers, 1986; see also Hudson, 1997; Mody, 1987).

Globalization is studied empirically in terms of international telecommunications markets, organizations, and treaties, as well as the worldwide extension of the technological networks themselves. Policy researchers have considered the emergence of a global information infrastructure (Drake, 1995) and the implications of international regimes such as the Global Agreement on Tariffs and Trade and the World Intellectual Property Organization for transborder data flows, intellectual property, law enforcement, language, culture, education, and national identity. The International Telecommunications Union has been an important player in the allocation of access to satellite "slots" in geosynchronous orbit, especially claims to slots by countries that lack either technical or financial means to place satellites in orbit themselves.

Observers have also noted the changing perceptions of space and place associated with ICTs (e.g., Curry, 1998; Meyrowitz, 1985). Manuel Castells (1996) describes the "space of flows." International, indeed global, information flows have considerable geopolitical and cultural consequences, raising the question of whether a government or other organization has the right to transmit data or programs to another country without the latter's permission (McBride Commission, 1980; Pelton & Howkins, 1988; Pelton & Snow, 1977; Ploman, 1984; Powell, 1985).

Some question whether the existence of international communication networks necessarily leads to globalization, or claim that the notion itself reflects mainly the perspectives of economic and national elites. Critics have begun to ask whether moves toward "deglobalization" are under way (see recent special issues of *Foreign Policy* and *New Perspectives Quarterly*). Many observers consider the world today to be a network of economic centers, information hubs, or technopoles that involve nation-states, transnational corporations and other organizations, urban centers, and high-tech regions (see Castells, 1989; Garnsey, 1998; Graham & Marvin, 1996; Saxenian, 1994).

Access and Equity

A major theme of research informing ICT policy and regulation is the equitable distribution of technologies and services. The concern with equity underlies much of the issue-based research that is undertaken in response to policy makers' needs for information on current problems, including the privacy implications of caller ID and similar services (for a fuller discussion of privacy, see Gandy, 1993); reconsiderations of universal service beyond the specific case of POTS (plain old telephone service); concentration of new media ownership and the rise of global oligopolies; the effects of computerization on employment, especially in the telecommunications industry; spectrum allocation and auction; and changes in intellectual property law and speech rights prompted by new technologies, especially related to copyright, fair use, and the public domain (Katsh, 1995; Pool, 1983).

Different approaches to the policy-making process cast access and equity differently. Melody and Mansell (1983) have suggested that *administrative* policy research tends to maintain or reinforce the roles and interests of existing organizations, government and legal authorities, and technologies, whereas *critical* policy research tends to focus on power issues, the political economy of information and technology, and the emancipatory potential of new technologies. Mansell (1993) has also proposed that two competing frameworks guide policy makers' views of how networked ICT systems should develop. The *idealist model* assumes that there are few technical, organizational, or political barriers to the development of open, ubiquitous, and "seamless" networks that cannot be overcome. The *strategic model*, on the other hand, assumes that networks are likely to be fragmented and to diffuse unevenly due to the divergent political, cultural, and monopolistic interests of the players involved.

Uneven access has led to a growing concern about the rise of a *digital divide* between information haves and have-nots based on race, income, family structure, and other demographic characteristics (Cooper & Kimmelman 1999; National Telecommunications and Information Administration, 1998). Such disparities raise a familiar idea in communication research, namely, that the introduction of a new communication medium can create an *information gap* between the best-positioned members of society and the less fortunate.

Although the number of computer users is growing rapidly in the United States and around the world, a majority of the public still does not have Internet access and may not for years to come. Recent surveys suggest that nearly as many people have discontinued using the Internet as remain current users (Katz & Aspden, 1998). Use of on-line services is particularly low among nonwhites, the poor, and single-parent, female-headed households (National Telecommunications and Information Administration, 1998). Only 60% of American households have cable service, and about 60% of American households do not have Internet access. The number of households with basic telephone service declined after the AT&T divestiture, due to marked increases in local telephone rates associated with the loss of subsidies from long-distance service (Schement, 1995). Overcoming the divide may depend on policy initiatives that promote fair access, such as the Clinton-Gore administration's *e-rate* policy.

Given the Internet's growing importance as a news source (Morris & Ogan, 1996) and the depth of information now available on-line, the potential for the rise of a political and economic "overclass" populated by information elites seems increasingly real. The issue takes on a certain urgency as more governmental functions and educational opportunities become available through the World Wide Web and political campaigns are waged on-line. The digital divide may also exclude a large segment of society from entrepreneurial and career opportunities.

The most affluent people are often assumed to have the most access, opportunity, and competence to communicate. However, different types of inequities may develop as people segregate themselves into ever-smaller communities of interest, using new media to select and interact only with others who are most like themselves (Lievrouw, 1998).

Moreover, even if universal technological access is achieved, substantial social investments in education and training must be made to allow people to benefit from the complex and constantly evolving new media environment (Anderson, Bikson, Law, & Mitchell, 1995). Kling (1999) refers to the mix of professional knowledge, economic resources, and technical skills required for effective use of ICTs as *social access*. Cronin and Davenport (1993) argue that *social intelligence* can affect information seeking and social participation.

Equity is a concern across societies as well as within them. It is often observed that most people in the world have never placed or received a phone call, much less used on-line information services or e-mail. Even in relatively affluent areas such as the European Community, subtle regional differences in the distribution of ICTs have been documented. It is doubtful that systems and services will develop or be distributed in underserved areas as evenly as they have been in affluent societies.

Social Networks and Community

In the past decade, researchers have begun to examine the ways in which certain technologies, especially computer-mediated communication (CMC), support *virtual communities* or societies (Jones, 1998; Kiesler, 1996; Kollock & Smith, 1998; Ludlow, 1996; Rheingold, 1993) and social networks (Wellman et al., 1996).

On-line communicators share language conventions, maintain distinctive social and professional roles, establish boundaries, enact rituals, show commitment to communal goals, follow standards of (n)etiquette, and engage in socioemotional exchanges in both work and leisure settings, much as traditional communities do (Haythornthwaite & Wellman, 1998; Rice & Love, 1987; Walther, 1992). CMC appears to sustain and extend complex interpersonal and community ties. It allows users to increase their range of contacts and form relationships with others who may share their interests but with whom they are unacquainted (Constant, Kiesler, & Sproull, 1996).

Diffusion of innovations theory describes and predicts the ways in which new ideas or practices spread in a community through networks of social relationships (for an overview of the theory and recent studies, see Rogers, 1995). This theory's emphasis on communication and social structure parallels the technological and institutional infrastructures and information flows associated with ICTs. As noted previously, it has been applied widely in studies of economic development, productivity, and technology transfer, as well as in attempts to understand community networks.

Several researchers have extended or elaborated the basic outlines of diffusion of innovations theory. Adopters may *reinvent* innovations, creating new uses for them that were unintended by the originators. *Critical mass theory* (Markus, 1990) suggests that some minimum number of participants must adopt an interactive system, such as telephone or e-mail, before it provides a relative advantage to users. Moreover, because the system provides additional benefit with every additional user, some early users actually contribute more than they benefit from the system as they initiate group use. Where effort and benefit are mismatched, systems may fail to reach critical mass (Grudin, 1989).

Other researchers have taken an explicitly cultural approach to the analysis of social relations and practices among ICT users (Levy, 1997). Reid (1991) argues that the notion of culture is an appropriate concept for the study of users of Internet relay chat (IRC). Curtis's (1996) study of XeroxPARC's LambdaMOO is a seminal work in MUD (multiuser domain) ethnography. Baym (1995) applied ethnographic techniques in her study of Usenet newsgroups; Metz (1995) systematically outlines the cultural attributes of real-time CMC communities as a foundation for examining synchronous and asynchronous CMC from a cultural perspective. One of the most frequently cited cases of the violation of cultural norms and rules in a computer-mediated community is reported by Dibbell (1996), who describes a virtual "rape" and its aftermath. Stone (1995) juxtaposes themes from critical and feminist theory and science fiction with case studies of high-tech firms, research labs, and everyday users of on-line technologies.

Nonetheless, the definition and significance of virtual communities, electronic cultures, and the like remain open questions. In future studies, ethnography may be used to explore further the notion of virtual "community standards" and how they might differ from ordinary (geographic) community standards, the competing value systems and possible culture clashes among Internet user groups or between

Internet users and other social groups, and the process of affiliation and group formation on-line.

Home and School

Although a few pioneering studies were conducted in the 1980s (e.g., Chen & Paisley, 1985; Dutton, Kovaric, & Steinfield, 1985), until recently relatively few empirical data have been available on the adoption and use of new media technologies in the home. Data have been gathered about household CMC in large suburban communities near Toronto (Hampton & Wellman, 1999). The HomeNet study was one of the first longitudinal studies of home Internet use (Kraut, Patterson, & Scherlis, 1998). And a new multiyear project under way at UCLA's Center for Communication Policy will track new media adoption and use in a large-scale longitudinal survey of U.S. households. Taking a different approach, studies of the *domestication* of ICTs—that is, their incorporation into home life and leisure (Silverstone & Hirsch, 1992)—draw on cultural and sociological studies of consumption and popular culture.

ICTs have long been used as instructional media in classrooms, laboratories, consultants' offices, and informal settings. Wilbur Schramm (1977) conducted studies of instructional media in the early days of communication research; the applications of satellite systems and slow-scan television in long-distance schooling and remote medical consultation were studied at Stanford University in the 1970s and 1980s (McAnany, 1983).

Today some believe that ICTs have "become a force for a new form of education" (Harasim, Hiltz, Teles, & Turoff, 1995, p. 271). We encourage interested readers to see the contribution to this volume by Waldeck, Kearney, and Plax (Chapter 4) for a more detailed discussion of instructional media. For our purposes in this essay, one issue in particular merits attention: *distance education.*

Distance learning using the World Wide Web and other new media modalities, especially in higher education, has become an area of intense research interest (Dede, 1996; Mood, 1995). Although critical observers such as David Noble (1998a, 1998b) have noted the economic, privacy, and intellectual property, as well as instructional, implications of the rapid adoption of new media by universities, others note the potential of Web-based technologies for real-time distance instruction, information seeking, and media use as a social process (Lyman, 1996). Some projects are explicitly designed to integrate learning technologies into companies, organizations, and workforces as a means of enhancing their performance; these projects promote the transfer of successful learning technology R&D to the marketplace and focus on the implementation, marketing, and evaluation of learning technologies (European Commission, 1997b; Frindte & Köhler, 1999).

With the growing emphasis in postsecondary education on the cultivation of students' critical thinking skills, researchers have explored uses of the World Wide Web for general education, where close student-teacher interaction is desirable. The integration of *learning companion* systems with sophisticated networking capabilities and user-friendly interfaces into social learning systems is also being explored, and trial systems have been demonstrated and discussed.

Interactive mechanisms for Web-based teaching situations are still relatively undeveloped, but might include forums similar to newsgroups or chat rooms. New Web-based learning software environments that are specifically designed to integrate the didactic and social needs of learning in a single system incorporate specialized content databases, safe personal environments, and multimedia or hypertextual information from the World Wide Web (Frindte, Köhler, Stauche, & Suckfüll, 1998; Hegarty, Phelan, & Kilbridge 1998). They allow teachers to supervise and help students individually and enable the capture of comprehensive evaluation data.

Social accounts of learning and human knowledge have led researchers and teachers to reorganize educational institutions as school-based and work-based *learning communities* (Koschmann, 1996). ICTs, and in particular the World Wide Web, are seen as playing important roles in the creation and operation of learning communities, provided such communities have sufficient access to specialized information about relevant data and analysis tools and personnel trained to handle the demands of the progressively more complex levels of interaction that are involved (O'Neill, Gomez, & Edelson, 1994).

Distance learning studies have provided detailed descriptions of multimedia system features (Hegarty et al., 1998; Lehrer, 1992) and have demonstrated and evaluated techniques for representing comprehensive knowledge in hypermedia structures. Some researchers have considered the World Wide Web as a means for disseminating information, generating and accessing resource materials, and enhancing communication among participants during learning; others have explored techniques and methodologies for integrating computers and telecommunications technology into existing curricula. Some observers believe that use of the Web encourages independent learning, and a number of studies have considered the Web as an information resource and communication channel among younger students in different schools and countries (e.g., Donath, 1994).

Despite these advances, however, system developers and users often seem to assume that multimedia systems will transform the whole process of learning into an open, personalized, interactive experience. They tend to emphasize large-scale distance education projects and the development of technologically mediated communities based on regular and consistent feedback (see, e.g., Barrett, 1992; Issing & Klimsa, 1996; Murray, 1995), rather than the problems of integrating media into local teaching settings. These scenarios have been criticized for underestimating the limitations of new media technologies, including the accessibility of the technology and its fit or suitability for particular pedagogical uses (Hart, 1998; Kawalek, 1996). Some researchers have noted the pedagogical problems associated with use of the Web for teaching elementary and secondary students (e.g., Hegarty et al., 1998; Noack, 1996). The need remains for specific guidelines and techniques for employing ICTs in elementary and secondary teaching and learning.

ICTs AND ORGANIZING

The uses of ICTs in organizational contexts constituted one of the first major re-search fronts in communication and technology studies. Although technologies and organizational communication are covered more fully elsewhere in this vol-ume, we briefly discuss below two important areas of investigation: ICTs and or-ganizational structure, and ICTs and organizational communication processes.

Organizational Structure and ICTs

New technologies (especially satellites and wireless systems) have had major effects on the organizational structures and processes of the firms that use them (Egan, 1997; Frieden, 1997; Pelton, 1995). The *intelligent network* permits the integration of internal and external organizational information and communica-tion; economies of scale can be realized because the costs of satellite and wireless transmission bear little relationship to the distance involved and/or the number of receivers (Elbert, 1997; Gordon & Morgan, 1993; Richharia, 1999).

Companies that provide satellite communication services have also been affected by international privatization trends and advancing technology. For example, Intelsat, founded in 1964 as a nonprofit international cooperative to deliver global satellite communications services, today finds its core mission being challenged by private satellite carriers and business consortia that offer suboceanic fiber alternatives (Fields, 1994; Gershon, 1990; Wright, 1998).

Over the past few decades, major public and private concerns have undergone an evolutionary process of organizational restructuring and realignment, delegat-ing more decision making and operations to local or peripheral units and forming new types of affiliations and alliances with suppliers, competitors, and clients. Telecommunications and distributed data processing have eliminated many of the time and distance barriers that once separated organizational centers from their affiliate sites and other organizations (Sproull & Kiesler, 1991). Today, widely dispersed organizations operate globally and communicate in real time as so-called *network firms* or *virtual enterprises*. The study of these new organiza-tional forms has been influenced by social network research (see previous section) and self-organizing systems theory (see the reviews by Braman, 1994; Roberts & Grabowski, 1996).

Communication Processes in Organizations

Many of the earliest studies of ICTs in the workplace evaluated their channel capacities or features and compared mediated versus face-to-face communication for particular types of work situations and decision-making tasks (Culnan & Markus, 1987; Daft & Lengel, 1986). These studies concentrated on the use of e-mail and computer conferencing and were frequently designed as laboratory studies (Rice, 1992). They suggested that computer messaging was similar to telegraphy and probably best for simple, unambiguous, task-related messages.

Investigators found that CMC can give users control over the flow of information. New technologies can reach more people at one time than other channels, provide information simultaneously to remote and local workers, and increase the involvement of both groups (Eveland & Bikson, 1988).

Media richness theory (Daft & Lengel, 1986; Daft, Lengel, & Trevino, 1987; Trevino & Webster, 1992) hypothesizes that certain systems are suitable for certain types of communication, depending on system bandwidth (the capacity to carry interpersonal and nonverbal cues and symbolic content that reduce message uncertainty, equivocality, or ambiguity). It predicts that effective communicators will match the communication channel they select with the degree of richness required for any particular communicative act. Thus simple task-related information exchange can be accomplished with ICTs that are "lean" (low in media richness), whereas bargaining and negotiation require "richer" systems. Rice (1993) refines this approach and proposes the concept of *media appropriateness.*

System- or channel-centered studies were later criticized because they failed to capture the complexity of real communication (Culnan & Markus, 1987; Rudy, 1996). Current analytic frameworks place more emphasis on social processes within groups and organizations, including group and organizational dynamics, norms, and constraints (Fulk & Steinfield, 1990; Lea, 1992; Markus, 1994). Fulk and her colleagues have formulated *social influence theory* to explain how other people and groups within an organization affect an individual's choice of media and the social construction of ICTs (see Fulk, 1993; Fulk, Schmitz, & Steinfield, 1990).

Poole and DeSanctis (1990) have proposed *adaptive structuration* to describe the uses of technologies in organizations (especially group decision support systems). Based on Anthony Giddens's theory of structuration and social studies of technology, adaptive structuration theory outlines the iterative and interdependent relationships among ICTs, people, and organizational structures, and ways that groups create their own local definitions and uses of technologies.

The social studies of technology literature, especially the sociology of computing and, more recently, *social informatics* (Kling, 1999), has been an important influence in studies of ICTs and organizing. Key concepts here include the web of computing (Kling, 1980; Kling & Scacchi, 1982), boundary objects and the social construction of infrastructure (Bowker, Star, Turner, & Gasser, 1997; Star & Ruhleder 1996), and technological trajectories (Hughes, 1989). This *sociotechnical* perspective has been especially influential in studies of collaborative work using new media technologies (Dourish, 1998; Galegher, Kraut, & Egido, 1990; Kraut, 1987; Orlikowski, 1993; Twidale & Nichols, 1999) and of the participatory design of information systems (Clement & Van den Besselaar, 1993).

ICTs AND INTERACTION

The study of communication technologies and interpersonal interaction takes several different directions. Some researchers consider technologies as a *source* of communication or information; this work has its roots in the media effects tradition, uses and gratifications theory, and extensive literatures in computer science and information science on human-computer interaction and interface design. A second group of researchers conceive of technologies as communication *channels* among human communicators; their work draws from the social psychology of telecommunications and computing. A third research perspective moves away from the "source/channel" transmission metaphor of communication and instead looks at ICTs as settings for *social interaction* and the social construction of identity and shared meaning. We review each of these streams of work briefly below.

Technology as Source

A central question for many CAT researchers is whether the technologies themselves generate psychological effects in, and elicit social and behavioral responses from, users. Much of the applied research in this stream is devoted to developing interfaces that conform to people's social and communicative expectations rather than to engineering specifications alone.[2] The emphasis has been on technological or structural features and attributes that may be unique to certain technologies; specific technological features may affect users' reception of different types of content, such as news or advertising (Sundar, Narayan, Obregon, & Uppal, 1998).

The *media equation* thesis suggests that people treat computers, television, and new media as if these technologies were real people and places. Asserting that encounters with communication technologies are "fundamentally social and natural," Reeves and Nass (1996) argue not only that people anthropomorphize communication appliances but also that people's cognitive processing of media content is affected by the formal features and design elements of the interface. Reeves and Nass's research demonstrates that individuals are polite to computers, attribute notions of "self" and "other" as well as personality types to machines, and even apply gender stereotypes to voice-based computers.

The uses and gratifications approach has been applied in CAT studies since the 1980s. Uses and gratifications theory assumes an active audience, that media use is goal oriented, and that media compete with other sources of need satisfaction. Perse and Dunn (1998) found that networked computers satisfied user needs for learning, entertainment, social interaction, escapism, and passing the time, and that they were used out of habit. Ritualistic (as opposed to instrumental) uses, such as passing time and habitual use, indicate that gratifications may not be tied to specific content but rather to the technology or medium itself. Perse and Dunn suggest that ritualistic uses of computer connectivity might influence personal well-being, possibly leading to addiction.

Studies of information retrieval (IR) systems, such as those that allow users to search distributed databases, library collections, and the World Wide Web (Twidale & Nichols, 1999), also contribute to the understanding of technologies as information sources. IR and information-seeking research tend to focus on the varying abilities and aptitudes of different social or professional groups, such as scientists and historians, to search on-line databases. Borgman (1989), for example, found that the differing technical aptitudes and personality characteristics of engineering, psychology, and English majors had consequences for their uses of information retrieval systems. Lieberman (1992) found that the effectiveness of individuals in retrieving information from a health care information systems depended on important individual-level predictors of learning, such as involvement, motivation, perceived self-efficacy, and sense of personal control.

A key theoretical concept in IR research is *relevance* (Saracevic, 1975), or the degree to which the materials a system retrieves actually match the searcher's request or satisfy his or her query or need. Relevance feedback, for example, is employed in World Wide Web search engines that show percentage figure estimates as indicators of how closely the retrieved items match the user's request. Relevance is a complex phenomenon, however, and some critics have rejected simple matching approaches in favor of *psychological relevance* (Harter, 1992) or other conceptualizations that capture the searcher's sense that the retrieved material is meaningful or appropriate for his or her purposes (Schamber, 1994).

Technology as Channel

Another group of studies has examined systematic changes in interpersonal and small group interactions that may be attributable to media technologies, especially computers, compared to face-to-face communication. Here, investigators have asked whether, and how well, new media channels facilitate interpersonal and small group interaction.

In the 1970s and 1980s, studies of the social psychology of telecommunications and of computing produced several fundamental constructs in this stream, including those of *social presence* (Short, Williams, & Christie, 1976) and *telepresence* (Johansen, Vallee, & Spangler, 1979). Researchers analyzed the use of computer bulletin boards ("bboards"), computer conferencing, the Arpanet, and other computer-based messaging systems by researchers and scientists in academic and military settings to see how well these technologies supported interaction among widely dispersed groups (Hiltz & Turoff, 1993).

Early studies explored the psychological states of individual participants as well as group dynamics in computer-mediated communication (e.g., Rice & Love, 1987, adapted Bales's Interaction Process Analysis). Anonymity, for example, was found to be an attractive feature of CMC for many communicators. New technologies were thought to influence these individual psychological states, and therefore individuals' behavior and group decision-making processes, differently than would face-to-face encounters. More recently, Kraut et al. (1998) found increased use of the Internet to be associated with depression and loneliness.

The absence of *social context cues* in CMC (status and nonverbal, visual cues) was noted in the early 1980s. Researchers argued that because it reduces or removes these cues, CMC compares poorly with the quality of face-to-face communication. The absence of cues may also contribute to *disinhibition*, a reduction in communicators' adherence to social norms and constraints (Kiesler, Siegel, & McGuire, 1984), and encourage a greater degree of aggressive communication such as *flaming* (Sproull & Kiesler, 1991).

Walther's (1992, 1996) *social information processing* theory rejects the idea that CMC is inherently more impersonal than face-to-face communication and assumes that communicators in any setting are motivated to develop social relationships, but that the limitations of text-based technology may slow the development of interpersonal ties. Over time, users will adapt to text as the sole channel for relational communication and develop warm and personal relationships. Walther (1996) argues that research should focus instead on the "critical factors that *interact* with CMC to foster impersonality" (p. 13).

The reduced nonverbal cues and increased disinhibition associated with CMC have also been characterized as a status-equalization function of the technology that empowers individual users. Some observers, however, claim that CMC can actually reinforce power relations (Lea & Spears, 1991). To the extent that interpersonal cues are reduced, the influence of the remaining social cues (status, role, and category membership markers that are explicit in CMC but often only implied in face-to-face contexts) may be magnified rather than diminished (Spears & Lea, 1994). Spears and Lea (1994) developed the SIDE (Social Identity-Deindividuation) model, which hypothesizes that the deindividuating isolation generated by CMC can (depending on whether group identity is important to the person) strengthen or weaken an individual's level of group identification, thereby promoting or undermining conformity to group norms in intergroup contexts.

Rafaeli (1988) was among the first to suggest the centrality of *interactivity* in the study of new media. Since the 1980s, scholars have attempted to define and explain interactivity, either as a quality of mediated dialogue or discourse (Williams, Rice, & Rogers, 1988) or as a function of interface or system features (Durlak, 1987). Whether defined as the degree of relatedness among messages (Rafaeli & Sudweeks, 1997), features that encourage greater user engagement with the system and a sense of telepresence (Reeves & Nass, 1996), or the modifiability of a mediated environment in real time (Steuer, 1995), interactivity has been considered roughly analogous to semantic feedback or reciprocity (see Sims, 1997).

Based on a content analysis of audience e-mail messages to *NBC Nightly News,* Newhagen, Cordes, and Levy (1995) defined *perceived interactivity* as the user's expectation of receiving a response. Bucy and Newhagen (1999) contend that perceived interactivity can be extended beyond mass media and CMC and applied to the study of other systems.

Social Interaction

From a different perspective, new media technologies are sites for social interaction, allowing users to express and work out personal issues and identities. Schegloff, Mandelbaum, and their colleagues have analyzed interaction in telephone conversations. In *The Second Self* (1984), Sherry Turkle argues that computers (and, by extension, computer-based communication systems) are "projective devices" or "evocative objects"—like Rorschach inkblots—that give inhibited or awkward communicators more control over their self-presentation and allow them to communicate more confidently and effectively than they can in face-to-face communication.

In contrast to claims that prolonged, intensive on-line activity can be harmful, the literature on gender and identity play regards chat rooms, MUDs, role-playing games, and other digitally based worlds as safe havens where individuals can explore different aspects of the self. They can adopt new personas and play in worlds that have no counterpart in "real life" (Sudweeks, McLaughlin, & Rafaeli, 1998). Turkle (1995) asserts that, rather than regarding Internet use as a type of addiction or compulsion, researchers should examine the inherent appeal of multiplicity and the contingent psychological possibilities of exploring a "flexible" self without punitive social repercussions. Although reliance on on-line relationships has been criticized for fostering real-world isolation, there are many prosocial aspects to "life on the screen," such as community building and the ability to work through personal concerns. Similarly, Gergen (1991) has advanced the idea that ICTs may produce the "saturated self," where identity extends across networks of social relationships and roles rather than inhering "in" the individual.

CONCLUSION

After this necessarily brief overview of a growing research front, it may be helpful to ask what has been learned and what themes might unify or organize such a disparate range of work. As we noted at the outset of this chapter, we find that CAT research assumes the *ubiquity* of electronically mediated communication. This sensibility accounts for the prominence of certain research issues in the CAT literature, such as access and equity, "flows" of information and communication content, and cultural influence.

On one hand, this view runs the risk of obscuring the crucial role that face-to-face interaction and nonelectronic media continue to play in everyday social life. On the other hand, many CAT studies also make the implicit assumption that face-to-face interaction is the ideal-typical form of communication, and that media channels should try to simulate face-to-face as closely as possible, despite ample evidence that people understand face-to-face and mediated modes as inseparable aspects of the whole experience of communicating and interacting (Lievrouw & Finn, 1990). CAT research may bridge the interpersonal and media specializations of communication study, but it reveals a persistent habit of bracketing face-to-face interaction as a separate and usually preferable form of engagement. In future studies this implicit assumption should be explicitly questioned and analyzed.

Second, we find that CAT researchers characteristically portray technological and cultural ubiquity by employing a *network* metaphor for communication across levels and contexts of analysis, in contrast to analytic categories such as "audience" and "demographic" that are associated with a "mass" metaphor. To some extent, the network metaphor is derived from the technologies themselves, as Carey (1989) and Hughes (1989) have shown, but it is also rooted firmly in the idea that social, communication, workplace, kinship, and community relations are complex "webs of affiliation" (to use Simmel's phrase) that change over time.

The confluence or mutual shaping of technological and social networks is a view of the reality of communication processes that is different from linear or exchange models of communication. By invoking a network metaphor, CAT researchers suggest that people, organizations, and institutions are not simply either "sources" or "receivers" of content; rather, network roles and positions may entail both aspects of communication simultaneously according to communicators' contexts, meanings, and purposes. This theme is well illustrated in the work of researchers who find that constructs such as family, culture, markets, community, hierarchical corporate organizational forms, and even the nation-state no longer adequately describe or explain contemporary social formations and processes.

Third, one of the most important implications of the network metaphor is that communication practices, technologies, and institutions are constantly changing and rearranging to suit people's needs and circumstances. Networks are mutable phenomena or experiences rather than fixed categories—sets of relations and meanings among, rather than "states" or attributes of, communicators. The metaphor raises the question: What is the nature of change in networked social and technical milieux?

We might also say that mediated communication today is *recombinant*. It is an ongoing process of hybridization arising from communicators' deliberate choices of messages, products, meanings, technologies, and relationships, as well as from a kind of sociotechnical natural selection that shapes languages, genres, contexts, cultures, markets, and communities over time. Existing ("old") and innovative ("new") technologies or their functions are recombined according to the particular communicative needs or applications at hand, the product of a richly interconnected, networked, and adaptive institutional environment.

The metaphor of recombination suggests that ICTs are products of human action and decisions; they are certainly influenced by the existing technological environment, and may have unforeseen consequences, but they are not determined by an inevitable evolutionary process. Recombination creates an unstable technological landscape and compels CAT researchers to treat artifacts, practices, and social arrangements—the components of technology outlined at the beginning of this chapter—as moving targets. It accounts for both the technological convergence of media systems and the persistent sense of "newness" that characterize this literature—and everyday life in societies and settings where ICTs are prevalent.

These three themes—ubiquity, the network metaphor, and recombination—only begin to suggest possible directions for future research. They are certainly not fully theorized; other concepts may be more useful or enduring. However, we offer them as a challenge for the generation of new questions and as a platform for research and scholarship that continues to bridge the interpersonal and mass-media sides of our disciplinary "house." We hope that this review and brief synthesis have contributed to a better understanding of mediated communication.

NOTES

1. The Communication and Technology Division of the International Communication Association was founded in the early 1980s as the Human Communication Technology Interest Group. The membership changed the name in the early 1990s to accommodate a rapidly growing and broadening range of issues and research problems. For an analysis of the growth of the specialty as reflected in ICA conference submissions, see Rice and Holmes (1996).

2. *Interface* may be defined as the "contact surface" between the user and the technology; the meaning of the term has become more complicated as technologies have grown more sophisticated (Laurel & Mountford, 1990).

REFERENCES

Anderson, J. W. (1985). The economic, legal and scientific implications of direct broadcast satellites. *Communications and the Law, 7*(1), 3-25.

Anderson, R., Bikson, T. K., Law, S. A., & Mitchell, B. M. (1995). *Universal access to e-mail: Feasibility and societal implications.* Santa Monica, CA: RAND Corporation.

Baldwin, T. F., McVoy, D. S., & Steinfield, C. (Eds.). (1996). *Convergence: Integrating media, information and communication.* Thousand Oaks, CA: Sage.

Barrett, E. (1992). *Sociomedia: Multimedia, hypermedia and the social construction of knowledge.* Cambridge: MIT Press.

Baym, N. K. (1995). The emergence of community in computer-mediated communication. In S. G. Jones (Ed.), *Cybersociety: Computer-mediated communication and community* (pp. 138-163). Thousand Oaks, CA: Sage.

Bell, D. (1973). *The coming of post-industrial society: A venture in social forecasting.* New York: Basic Books.

Beniger, J. R. (1986). *The control revolution: Technological and economic origins of the information society.* Cambridge, MA: Harvard University Press.

Borgman, C. L. (1989). All users of information retrieval systems are not created equal: An exploration into individual differences. *Information Processing and Management, 25,* 237-251.

Bowker, G. C., Star, L. S., Turner, W., & Gasser, L. (1997). *Social science, technical systems, and cooperative work.* Mahwah, NJ: Lawrence Erlbaum.

Braman, S. (1994). Entering chaos: Designing the state in the information age. In S. Splichal, A. Calabrese, & C. Sparks (Eds.), *Information society and civil society* (pp. 157-184). West Lafayette, IN: Purdue University Press.

Bucy, E. P., & Newhagen, J. E. (1999). The micro- and macrodrama of politics on television: Effects of media format on candidate evaluations. *Journal of Broadcasting & Electronic Media 43*(2), 193-210.

Carey, J. W. (1989). *Communication as culture: Essays on media and society.* Winchester, MA: Unwin Hyman.

Castells, M. (1989). *The informational city.* Oxford: Blackwell.

Castells, M. (1996). *The rise of the network society.* Oxford: Blackwell.

Chen, M., & Paisley, W. J. (Eds.). (1985). *Children and microcomputers: Research on the newest medium.* Beverly Hills, CA: Sage.

Clement, A., & Van den Besselaar, P. (1993). A retrospective look at PD projects. *Communications of the ACM, 36*(4), 29-37.

Constant, D., Kiesler, S. B., & Sproull, L. S. (1996). The kindness of strangers: The usefulness of electronic weak ties for technical advice. *Organization Science, 7,* 119-135.

Cooper, M., & Kimmelman, G. (1999). *The digital divide confronts the Telecommunications Act of 1996: Economic reality versus public policy.* Washington, DC: Consumer Federation of America/Consumers Union.

Cronin, B., & Davenport, E. (1993). Social intelligence. In M. E. Williams (Ed.), *Annual review of information science and technology* (Vol. 28, pp. 3-44). Medford, NJ: Learned Information.

Culnan, M. J., & Markus, M. L. (1987). Information technologies. In F. M. Jablin, L. L. Putnam, K. H. Roberts, & L. W. Porter (Eds.), *Handbook of organizational communication: An interdisciplinary perspective* (pp. 420-443). Newbury Park, CA: Sage.

Curry, M. R. (1998). *Digital places: Living with geographic information technologies.* New York: Routledge.

Curtis, P. (1996). MUDDING: Social phenomena in text-based virtual realities. In S. B. Kiesler (Ed.), *Cultures of the Internet* (pp. 121-142). Mahwah, NJ: Lawrence Erlbaum.

Daft, R. L., & Lengel, R. H. (1986). Organizational information requirements, media richness, and structural determinants. *Management Science, 32,* 554-571.

Daft, R. L., Lengel, R. H., & Trevino, L. K. (1987). Message equivocality, media selection, and manager performance: Implications for information systems. *MIS Quarterly, 11,* 355-366.

Dede, C. J. (1996). The evolution of distance education: Emerging technologies and distributed learning. *American Journal of Distance Education, 10*(2), 4-36.

Dibbell, J. (1996). A rape in cyberspace; or, How an evil clown, a Haitian trickster spirit, two wizards, and a cast of dozens turned a database into a society. In P. Ludlow (Ed.), *High noon on the electronic frontier: conceptual issues in cyberspace* (pp. 375-395). Cambridge: MIT Press.

Donath, R. (1994). Rauf auf die Daten-Autobahn! *Paed Extra, 22,* 10-14.

Dordick, H. S. (1990). The origins of universal service: History as a determinant of telecommunications policy. *Telecommunications Policy, 14,* 223-231.

Dourish, P. (Ed.). (1998). Interaction and collaboration in MUDs [Special issue]. *Computer-Supported Cooperative Work, 7*(1-2).

Drake, W. J. (Ed.). (1995). *The new information infrastructure: Strategies for U.S. policy.* New York: Twentieth Century Fund Press.

Durlak, J. T. (1987). A typology for interactive media. In M. L. McLaughlin (Ed.), *Communication yearbook 10* (pp. 743-756). Newbury Park, CA: Sage.

Dutton, W. H., Kovaric, P., & Steinfield, C. (1985). Computing in the home: A research paradigm. *Computers and the Social Sciences, 1*(1), 5-18.

Egan, B. (1997). The role of wireless communications in the global information infrastructure. *Telecommunications Policy, 21,* 357-386.

Elasmar, M. G. (1995). The direct broadcast satellite industry in the U.S.: Development and economic concerns. *Journal of Broadcasting & Electronic Media, 39,* 200-214.

Elbert, B. R. (1997). *The satellite communication applications handbook.* Norwood, MA: Artech House.

European Commission. (1997a). *Building the European information society for us all: Final policy report of the High Level Expert Group.* Brussels: Author.

European Commission. (1997b). *Telematics for flexible and distance learning.* Brussels: Author.

Eveland, J. D., & Bikson, T. K. (1988). Work group structures and computer support: A field experiment. *ACM Transactions on Office Information Systems, 6,* 354-379.

Fields, A. (1994). Intelsat at a crossroads. *Law and Policy in International Business, 25,* 1335-1355.

Fischer, C. (1992). *America calling: A social history of the telephone to 1940.* Berkeley: University of California Press.

Frieden, R. (1997). Widespread deployment of wireless telephony: Business, legal, regulatory and spectrum challenges. *Telecommunications Policy, 21,* 451-460.

Frindte, W., & Köhler, T. (1999). *Internet communication.* Frankfurt: Peter Lang.

Frindte, W., Köhler, T., Stauche, H., & Suckfüll, M. (1998). *State-of-the-art report: Internet based teaching and learning.* Brussels: European Commission.

Fulk, J. (1993). Social construction of communication technology. *Academy of Management Review, 36,* 921-950.

Fulk, J., Schmitz, J., & Steinfield, C. (1990). A social influence model of technology use. In J. Fulk & C. Steinfield (Eds.), *Organizations and communication technology* (pp. 117-140), Newbury Park, CA: Sage.

Fulk, J., & Steinfield, C. (Eds.). (1990). *Organizations and communication technology.* Newbury Park, CA: Sage.

Galegher, J., Kraut, R. E., & Egido, C. (Eds.). (1990). *Intellectual teamwork: Social and technological foundations of cooperative work.* Hillsdale, NJ: Lawrence Erlbaum.

Gandy, O. (1993). *The panoptic sort: A political economy of personal information.* Boulder, CO: Westview.

Garnsey, E. (1998). The genesis of the high technology milieu: A study in complexity. *International Journal of Urban and Regional Research, 22,* 361-377.

Gergen, K. J. (1991). *The saturated self: Dilemmas of identity in contemporary life.* New York: Basic Books.

Gershon, R. A. (1990). Intelsat: Global cooperation in an era of deregulation. *Telecommunications Policy, 14,* 249-259.

Gershon, R. A., & Kanayama, T. (1995). Direct broadcast satellites in Japan: A case study in government-business partnerships. *Telecommunications Policy, 19,* 217-231.

Gordon, G., & Morgan, W. L. (1993). *Principles of communication satellites.* New York: John Wiley.

Graham, S., & Marvin, S. (1996). *Telecommunications and the city: Electronic spaces, urban places.* London: Routledge.

Grudin, J. (1989). Why groupware applications fail: Problems in design and evaluation. *Office: Technology and People, 4,* 245-264.

Hampton, K. N., & Wellman, B. (1999). Netville online and offline: Observing and surveying a wired suburb. *American Behavioral Scientist 43*(3), 475-492.

Harasim, L., Hiltz, S. R., Teles, L., & Turoff, M. (1995). *Learning networks: A field guide to teaching and learning online.* Cambridge: MIT Press.

Hart, A. (1998). *Teaching the media.* Mahwah, NJ: Lawrence Erlbaum.

Harter, S. (1992). Psychological relevance and information science. *Journal of the American Society for Information Science, 43,* 602-615.

Hawkins, R., Wiemann, J. M., & Pingree, S. (Eds.). (1988). *Advancing communication science: Merging mass and interpersonal processes.* Newbury Park, CA: Sage.

Haythornthwaite, C., & Wellman, B. (1998). Work, friendship and media use for information exchange in a networked organization. *Journal of the American Society for Information Science, 46,* 1101-1114.

Hegarty, M., Phelan, A., & Kilbridge, L. (1998). *Classrooms for distance teaching and learning: A blueprint.* Leuven, Belgium: Leuven University Press.

Hiltz, S. R., & Turoff, M. (1993). *The network nation: Human communication via computer* (Rev. ed.). Cambridge: MIT Press.

Hudson, H. E. (1997). *Global connections: International telecommunications infrastructure and policy.* New York: Van Nostrand Reinhold.

Hughes, T. P. (1989). *American genesis: A century of invention and technological enthusiasm, 1870-1970.* New York: Penguin.

Issing, L. J., & Klimsa, P. (1995). *Information and learning with the help of multimedia.* Weinheim: Psychologie Verlags Union.

Ito, Y. (1981). The "Johoka Shakai" approach to the study of communication in Japan. *Keio Communication Review, 1,* 13-40.

Johansen, R., Vallee, J., & Spangler, K. (1979). *Electronic meetings: Technical alternatives and social choice.* Reading, MA: Addison-Wesley.

Jones, S. G. (Ed.). (1998). *Cybersociety 2.0: Revisiting computer-mediated communication and community.* Thousand Oaks, CA: Sage.

Katsh, M. E. (1995). *Law in a digital world.* New York: Oxford University Press.

Katz, J. E., & Aspden, P. (1998). Internet dropouts in the USA: The invisible group. *Telecommunications Policy, 22,* 327-339.

Kawalek, J. (1996). *Unterricht am Bildschirm.* Frankfurt: Peter Lang.

Kiesler, S. B. (Ed.). (1996). *Cultures of the Internet.* Mahwah, NJ: Lawrence Erlbaum.

Kiesler, S. B., Siegel, J., & McGuire, T. W. (1984). Social psychological aspects of computer-mediated communication. *American Psychologist, 39,* 1123-1134.

Kling, R. (1980). Social analyses of computing: Theoretical orientations in recent empirical research. *Computing Surveys, 12*(1), 61-110.

Kling, R. (1999). What is social informatics and why does it matter? *D-Lib Magazine* [On-line], *5*(1). Available Internet: http://www.dlib.org/dlib/january99/kling/01kling.html

Kling, R., & Scacchi, W. (1982). The web of computing: Computer technology as social organization. *Advances in Computing, 21,* 1-90.

Kollock, P., & Smith, M. (Eds.). (1998). *Communities in cyberspace.* London: Routledge.

Koschmann, T. (1996). *CSCL: Theory and practice of an emerging paradigm.* Mahwah, NJ: Lawrence Erlbaum.

Kraut, R. E. (Ed.). (1987). *Technology and the transformation of white-collar work.* Hillsdale, NJ: Lawrence Erlbaum.

Kraut, R. E., Patterson, M., & Scherlis, W. (1998). Internet paradox: A social technology that reduces social involvement and psychological well-being. *American Psychologist, 53,* 1017-1031.

Laurel, B., & Mountford, S. J. (1990). Introduction. In B. Laurel & S. J. Mountford (Eds.), *The art of human-computer interface design* (pp. xi-xvi). Reading, MA: Addison-Wesley.

Lea, M. (Ed.). (1992). *Contexts of computer-mediated communication.* New York: Harvester Wheatsheaf.

Lea, M., & Spears, R. (1991). Computer-mediated communication, de-individuation and group decision making. *International Journal of Man-Machine Studies, 34,* 283-301.

Lehrer, R. (Ed.). (1992). New directions in technology-mediated learning [Special issue]. *Educational Psychologist, 27*(3).

Levy, P. (1997). *Cyberculture.* Paris: Éditions Odile Jacob.

Lieberman, D. (1992). The computer's potential role in health education. *Health Communication, 4,* 211-225.

Lievrouw, L. A. (1998). Our own devices: Heterotopic communication, discourse and culture in the information society. *Information Society, 14,* 83-96.

Lievrouw, L. A., & Finn, T. A. (1990). Identifying the common dimensions of communication: The communication systems model. In B. D. Ruben & L. A. Lievrouw (Eds.), *Mediation, information, and communication: Information and behavior, vol. 3* (pp. 37-65). New Brunswick, NJ: Transaction.

Ludlow, P. (Ed.). (1996). *High noon on the electronic frontier: Conceptual issues in cyberspace.* Cambridge: MIT Press.

Lyman, P. (1996). Is using a computer like driving a car, reading a book, or solving a problem? The computer as machine, text and culture. In M. A. Shields (Ed.), *Work and technology in higher education: The social construction of academic computing* (pp. 19-36). Hillsdale, NJ: Lawrence Erlbaum.

Machlup, F. (1962). *The production and distribution of knowledge in the United States.* Princeton, NJ: Princeton University Press.

Mansell, R. (1993). *The new telecommunications: A political economy of network evolution.* London: Sage.

Marghalani, K., Palmgreen, P., & Boyd, D. A. (1993). The utilization of direct satellite broadcasting in Saudi Arabia. *Journal of Broadcasting & Electronic Media, 42,* 297-314.

Markus, M. L. (1990). Toward a "critical mass" theory of interactive media. In J. Fulk & C. Steinfield (Eds.), *Organizations and communication technology* (pp. 194-218). Newbury Park, CA: Sage.

Markus, M. L. (1994). Electronic mail as the medium of managerial choice. *Organization Science, 5,* 502-527.

Marvin, C. (1988). *When old technologies were new: Thinking about electric communication in the late nineteenth century.* New York: Oxford University Press.

McAnany, E. G. (Ed.). (1983). *Distance education: Evaluating new approaches in education for developing countries.* Oxford: Pergamon.

McBride Commission. (1980). *Many voices, one world* (Report for UNESCO). London: Kogan Page.

McLuhan, M. (1964). *Understanding media: The extensions of man.* New York: Mentor.

Melody, W. H., & Mansell, R. E. (1983). The debate over critical vs. administrative research: Circularity or challenge. *Journal of Communication, 33*(3), 103-116.

Metz, J. (1995). CMC and the question of culture. *New Jersey Journal of Communication, 3*(1), 1-25.

Meyrowitz, J. (1985). *No sense of place.* New York: Oxford University Press.

Mody, B. (1987). Contextual analysis of the adoption of a communications technology: The case of satellites in India. *Telematics & Informatics, 4*(2).

Mood, T. A. (1995). *Distance education: An annotated bibliography.* Englewood, CO: Libraries Unlimited.

Morris, M., & Ogan, C. (1996). The Internet as mass medium. *Journal of Communication, 46*(1), 39-50.

Mueller, M. (1993). Universal service in telephone history: A reconstruction. *Telecommunications Policy, 17,* 352-369.

Murray, J. H. (1995). The pedagogy of cyberfiction: Teaching a course on reading and writing interactive narrative. In E. Barrett & M. Redmond (Eds.), *Contextual media.* Cambridge: MIT Press.

National Telecommunications and Information Administration. (1998, July 28). *Falling through the net II: New data on the digital divide* [On-line]. Available Internet: http://www.ntia.doc.gov/ntiahome/net2/falling.html

Newhagen, J. E., Cordes, J. W., & Levy, M. R. (1995). Nightly@nbc.com: Audience scope and the perception of interactivity in viewer mail on the Internet. *Journal of Communication, 45*(3), 164-175.

Noack, M. (1996). Schule im Internet: Die Datenbahn im Unterricht. *Die Deutsche Schule, 88,* 494-508.

Noble, D. F. (1998a). Digital diploma mills, part 1: The automation of higher education. *October, 86,* 107-117.

Noble, D. F. (1998b). Digital diploma mills, part 2: The coming battle over online instruction. *October, 86,* 118-129.

Nora, S., & Minc, A. (1980). *The computerization of society: A report to the president of France.* Cambridge: MIT Press.

O'Neill, D. K., Gomez, L. M., & Edelson, D. C. (1994). Collaborative hypermedia for the classroom and beyond: A year's experiences with the collaboratory notebook. In J. M. Haake (Ed.), *Proceedings of the CSCW '94 Workshop on collaborative hypermedia systems.* Chapel Hill: University of North Carolina Press.

Orlikowski, W. (1993). Learning from notes: Organizational issues in groupware implementation. *Information Society, 9,* 237-250.

Parsons, P. R., & Frieden, R. M. (1998). *The cable and satellite television industries.* Boston: Allyn & Bacon.

Pelton, J. N. (1995). *Wireless and satellite telecommunications: The technology, the market, and the regulations.* Upper Saddle River, NJ: Prentice Hall.

Pelton, J. N., & Howkins, J. (Eds.). (1988). *Satellites international.* New York: Stockton.

Pelton, J. N., & Snow, M. (Eds.). (1977). *Economic and policy problems in satellite communications.* New York: Praeger.

Perse, E. M., & Dunn, D. G. (1998). The utility of home computers and media use: Implications of multimedia and connectivity. *Journal of Broadcasting & Electronic Media, 42,* 435-456.

Ploman, E. (1984). *Space, earth and communication.* Westport, CT: Quorum.

Pool, I. de S. (1983). *Technologies of freedom.* Cambridge, MA: Harvard University Press.

Poole, M. S., & DeSanctis, G. (1990). Understanding the use of group decision support systems: The theory of adaptive structuration. In J. Fulk & C. Steinfield (Eds.), *Organizations and communication technology* (pp. 173-193). Newbury Park, CA: Sage.

Porat, M. U., & Rubin, M. R. (1977). *The information economy* (OT Special Publication 77-12; 9 vols.). Washington, DC: U.S. Department of Commerce, Office of Telecommunications.

Poster, M. (1990). *The mode of information: Poststructuralism and social context.* Chicago: University of Chicago Press.

Powell, J. T. (1985). *International broadcasting by satellite.* Westport, CT: Quorum.

Rafaeli, S. (1988). Interactivity: From new media to communication. In R. Hawkins, J. M. Wiemann, & S. Pingree (Eds.), *Advancing communication science: Merging mass and interpersonal processes* (pp. 124-181). Newbury Park, CA: Sage.

Rafaeli, S., & Sudweeks, F. (1997). Networked interactivity. *Journal of Computer Mediated Communication* [On-line], *2*(4). Available Internet: http://jcmc.ascusc.org/vol2/issue4/rafaeli. Sudweeks. html

Reeves, B., & Nass, C. (1996). *The media equation: How people treat computers, television, and new media like real people and places.* Stanford, CA: Stanford University, Center for the Study of Language and Information.

Reid, E. M. (1991). Electropolis: Communication and community on Internet relay chat. *Intertek, 3*(3), 7-13.

Rheingold, H. (1993). *The virtual community: Homesteading on the electronic frontier.* Reading, MA: Addison-Wesley.

Rice, R. E. (1992). Contexts of research on organizational computer-mediated communication: a recursive review. In M. Lea (Ed.), *Contexts of computer-mediated communication* (pp. 113-144). New York: Harvester Wheatsheaf.

Rice, R. E. (1993). Media appropriateness: Using social presence theory to compare traditional and new organizational media. *Human Communication Research, 19,* 451-484.

Rice, R. E., & Associates. (1984). *The new media: Communication, research, and technology.* Beverly Hills, CA: Sage.

Rice, R. E., & Holmes, M. E. (1996, April). *Research themes of the Communication and Technology Division of the International Communication Association, derived from the conceptual structure of conference paper titles.* Unpublished manuscript, Rutgers University and University of Utah.

Rice, R. E., & Love, G. (1987). Electronic emotion: Socioemotional content in a computer-mediated communication network. *Communication Research, 14,* 85-108.

Richharia, M. (1999). *Satellite communication systems.* New York: McGraw-Hill.

Roberts, K. H., & Grabowski, M. (1996). Organization, technology and structuring. In S. R. Clegg, C. Hardy, & W. R. Nord (Eds.), *Handbook of organization studies* (pp. 409-423). Thousand Oaks, CA: Sage.

Rogers, E. M. (1986). *Communication technology: The new media in society.* New York: Free Press.

Rogers, E. M. (1994). *A history of communication study: A biographical approach.* New York: Free Press.

Rogers, E. M. (1995). *Diffusion of innovations* (4th ed.). New York: Free Press.

Rogers, E. M. (1999). Anatomy of the two subdisciplines of communication study. *Human Communication Research, 25,* 618-631.

Rudy, I. (1996). A critical review of research on electronic mail. *British Journal of Information Systems, 4,* 198-213.

Saracevic, T. (1975). Relevance: A review of a framework for thinking on the notion of information science. *Journal of the American Society for Information Science, 26,* 321-343.

Saxenian, A. (1994). *Regional advantage: Culture and competition in Silicon Valley and Route 128.* Cambridge, MA: Harvard University Press.

Schamber, L. (1994). Relevance and information behavior. In M. E. Williams (Ed.), *Annual review of information science and technology* (Vol. 29, pp. 3-48). Medford, NJ: Information Today.

Schement, J. R. (1995). Beyond universal service: Characteristics of Americans without telephones, 1980-1993. *Telecommunications Policy, 19,* 477-485.

Schement, J. R., & Lievrouw, L. A. (1984). A behavioural measure of information work. *Telecommunications Policy, 8,* 321-334.

Schramm, W. (1977). *Big media, little media: Tools and technologies for instruction.* Beverly Hills, CA: Sage.

Shields, P., & Samarajiva, R. (1993). Competing frameworks for research on information-communication technologies and society: Toward a synthesis. In S. A. Deetz (Ed.), *Communication yearbook 16* (pp. 349-380). Newbury Park, CA: Sage.

Short, J., Williams, E., & Christie, B. (1976). *The social psychology of telecommunications.* New York: John Wiley.

Silverstone, R., & Hirsch, E. (Eds.). (1992). *Consuming technologies: Media and information in domestic spaces.* London: Routledge.

Sims, R. (1997). Interactivity: A forgotten art? *Computers in Human Behavior, 13,* 157-180.

Slack, J. D., & Fejes, F. (Eds.). (1987). *The ideology of the information age.* Norwood, NJ: Ablex.

Spears, R., & Lea, M. (1994). Panacea or panopticon? The hidden power in computer-mediated communication. *Communication Research, 21,* 427-459.

Sproull, L. S., & Kiesler, S. B. (1991). *Connections: New ways of working in the networked organization.* Cambridge: MIT Press.

Star, S. L., & Ruhleder, K. (1996). Steps toward an ecology of infrastructure: Design and access for large information spaces. *Information Systems Research, 7*(1), 111-134.

Steuer, J. (1995). Defining virtual reality: Dimensions determining telepresence. In F. Biocca & M. R. Levy (Eds.), *Communication in the age of virtual reality* (pp. 33-56). Mahwah, NJ: Lawrence Erlbaum.

Stone, A. R. (1995). *The war of desire and technology at the close of the mechanical age.* Cambridge: MIT Press.

Sudweeks, F., McLaughlin, M. L., & Rafaeli, S. (Eds.). (1998). *Network and netplay.* Cambridge: MIT Press.

Sundar, S. S., Narayan, S., Obregon, R., & Uppal, C. (1998). Does Web advertising work? Memory for print vs. online media. *Journalism & Mass Communication Quarterly, 75,* 822-835.

Trevino, L. K., & Webster, J. (1992). Flow in computer-mediated communication: Electronic mail and voice mail evaluation and impacts. *Communication Research, 19,* 539-573.

Turkle, S. (1984). *The second self: Computers and the human spirit.* New York: Simon & Schuster.

Turkle, S. (1995). *Life on the screen: Identity in the age of the Internet.* New York: Simon & Schuster.

Twidale, M. B., & Nichols, D. M. (1999). Computer supported cooperative work in the information search and retrieval process. In M. E. Williams (Ed.), *Annual review of information science and technology* (Vol. 33, pp. 259-319). Medford, NJ: Information Today.

Walther, J. B. (1992). Interpersonal effects in computer-mediated interaction: A relational perspective. *Communication Research, 19,* 52-90.

Walther, J. B. (1996). Computer-mediated communication: Impersonal, interpersonal, and hyperpersonal interaction. *Communication Research, 23,* 3-43.

Webster, F. (1995). *Theories of the information society.* London: Routledge.

Wellman, B., Salaff, J., Dimitrova, D., Garton, L., Gulia, M., & Haythornthwaite, C. (1996). Computer networks as social networks: Collaborative work, telework, and virtual community. *Annual Review of Sociology, 22,* 213-238.

Williams, F., Rice, R. E., & Rogers, E. M. (1988). *Research methods and the new media.* New York: Free Press.

Winner, L. (1977). *Autonomous technology: Technics out-of-control as a theme in political thought.* Cambridge: MIT Press.

Wright, D. (1998). The European Commission and the satellite industry combine forces to open markets. *Telecommunications Policy, 22,* 267-272.

CHAPTER CONTENTS

13 Popular Communication in the Contemporary Age

BARBIE ZELIZER
Annenberg School for Communication
University of Pennsylvania

This essay explores the field of popular communication as an arena worthy of academic attention. Beginning with the assumption that the label *popular communication* is something of a misnomer, the author argues that the study of popular communication underlies much of what communication scholars do. She then discusses the different domains examined under the rubric of popular communication and posits that the study of popular communication can create alliances of unpredictable shapes between people in different disciplines, using different theoretical perspectives, and moving toward different practical aims. This makes the study of popular communication fertile ground for enhancing people's ties with others not like themselves.

T HE label *popular communication* is something of a misnomer, in that it implies that all other communication is unsavory, unwanted, and undesired. The truth, however, is that all communication has popular dimensions, and it is the challenge that this poses to our scholarly endeavors that I hope to address in this essay. Assuming that part of our task as educators is to demystify the features of everyday life, then popular communication—that is, communication in its everyday form—offers a venue in critical need of attention. The Popular Communication Division of the International Communication Association, currently the only division of any national or international communication association with an explicitly "popular" title, has taken as its mission the clarification, elaboration, and analysis of what popular communication and popular culture might mean in the contemporary age, exploring the ways in which they take shape and maintain resonance over time and space. In doing so, the division has hoped to raise the level of public awareness concerning the value of popular communication and popular culture not only among ICA members but also in the population at large.

Correspondence: Barbie Zelizer, Annenberg School for Communication, University of Pennsylvania, 3620 Walnut Street, Philadelphia, PA 19104; e-mail bzelizer@asc.upenn.edu

Communication Yearbook 24, pp. 297-316

DEFINING THE POPULAR

One of the primary problems that confronts scholars intent on studying popular culture and popular communication lies in the many inadequate attempts to define what *the popular* means. The popular is commonly understood to be that which is not elite or elitist, and the broad nature of that solitary premise has produced an array of competing and often contradictory definitions. Each of these makes a stab at defining *the popular,* but none sufficiently includes the dimensions suggested in other lexical endeavors. As Tony Bennett (1980) has argued, "As it stands, the concept of popular culture is virtually useless, a melting pot of confused and contradictory meanings capable of misdirecting inquiry on any number of theoretical blind alleys" (p. 18; cited in Storey, 1993, p. 1).

The numerous definitions of *popular communication* and *popular culture* do, however, have certain traits in common, even if they do not encompass all that might be classified as "popular." Dick Hebdige (1988) has defined popular culture simply as "a set of generally available artifacts: films, records, clothes, TV programs, modes of transport, etc." (p. 47). John Fiske (1989a) argues that the art of popular culture is "the art of making do" (p. 4). In *Key Concepts in Communication,* O'Sullivan, Hartley, Saunders, and Fiske (1983) define the popular and popular culture simply as "of people in general; for people in general, well liked by people in general—usually synonymous with 'good' " (p. 74). Although McGuigan (1992) has taken popular cultural studies to task for what he calls an overload of populism that celebrates popular culture more than it critically investigates it, the prevailing view has been that popular culture and popular communication are defined by some degree of engagement with the public, broadly defined.

The most comprehensive definition of popular culture has been provided by British literary and cultural critic Raymond Williams. Arguing that popular culture as we understand it today derives from a transitional shift in perspective between the 18th and 19th centuries that introduced the notion of "well-liked" or "widely favored," Williams (1976) contends that *the popular* was originally a legal and political term, derived from the Latin word *popularis*—"belonging to the people" (p. 236). He opines that the popular as it exists today retains four distinct dimensions, not all of which are complementary. First, the popular has long been seen as that which represents the perspective of "the people" rather than those who wield power over them. Popular culture, then, has become culture that is made by people for and largely by themselves. Additionally, however, Williams (1975) argues that the popular has also retained an aura of inferiority when compared with other cultural productions, artifacts, experiences, or processes that are amorphously situated "above" it. In this view, the popular press might be seen as qualitatively inferior to the elite press, or romance novels less valuable than classic literature. Williams (1976) further claims that the popular also includes culture that is "well-liked by many people" and work that "deliberately sets out to win favor with the people" (p. 237). The different meanings of the word *popular* therefore connect in different contexts in different ways. In fact, as Storey (1995) has argued, by tracking the ways in which they intersect, we can trace the historical trajectory through which "the popular" has come to embody meaning in the public imagination.

Much of the concern with the popular has focused upon popular culture—that is, those cultural artifacts, processes, effects, and meanings that are popular by definition, derivation, or general understanding. However, Williams (1976) himself has argued that *culture* is "one of the two or three most complicated words in the English language" (p. 87). He contends that culture itself has three broad dimensions: first, a "general process of intellectual, spiritual and aesthetic development," as seen in the classics, the works of great poets and philosophers; second, a "particular way of life, whether of a people, a period or a group," as seen in certain holidays, religious celebrations, and sports happenings; and third, "the works and practices of intellectual and especially artistic activity," as in the actual signifying practices of art, ballet, music, and the like.

However, due to the aforementioned aura of inferiority that has accompanied popular culture, "the popular" continues to be dealt an unfair blow in the public imagination. We need only think of how people tend to evaluate opera as opposed to rap music. Synonyms for *popular,* as noted by the *OED,* have tended to include adjectival death sentences such as "gross, base, vile, riff-raff, common, low, vulgar, plebian [and] cheap" (cited in O'Sullivan et al., 1983, p. 174). Moreover, the popular has come to be understood less in terms of what it "is" than in terms of what it "is not," a juxtaposition that has long placed "popular culture" in a comparison with "high culture" that leaves it coming up short. High culture—the opera, ballet, canonical literature—has been seen as the standard against which all else is examined. Whereas high culture has been taken as an honorific category that includes that which is thought to elevate, refine, teach, and better those with whom it makes contact, popular culture has been seen as that which fails to elevate or refine and does nothing but sedate, vulgarize, and entertain its audiences.

POPULAR CULTURE AND THE CULTURE WARS

To be sure, the "is/is not" split between high culture and popular culture has a historic trajectory. Although "that which is not high" has been differently nominalized by context—variously called *low culture, mass culture, popular culture,* and *folk culture*—the impulse to trivialize the low so as to valorize the high has echoed a familiar theme in diverse culture wars in different eras and different locations. This impulse produces numerous problems, not the least of which has to do with the transformative quality of popular culture over time. The works of Charles Dickens and William Shakespeare, originally panned as vulgar art, are poignant cases in point.

Several distinct strands to the debates over culture have emerged over time. During the mid-1800s, British cultural critic Matthew Arnold (1869/1932) launched one of the most well-known conservative wars on low culture; his criticism derived from the romantic critique of industrialism. His argument, informally called the culture and civilization tradition, was in keeping with Samuel Coleridge's distinction between "civilization" for everybody and "cultivation" for the select few. It tackled the threat posed by the idea of culture for the masses. In Arnold's view, culture needs to provide "sweetness and light"—the body of knowledge that represents the best in the world plus the ability to make reason and the will of God prevail. High culture is a way to refine, educate, enlighten, and, not incidentally, control the public. Popular culture, by contrast, encourages anarchy and disrupts the working classes' acceptance of their lot in life. Arnold's arguments, although articulated early on, have echoed repeatedly in the years that have since elapsed. They can be found at the heart of fears about the attraction of novels for 18th-century women, in discussions about mass-circulation newspapers and the 19th-century working class, in concern over the draw of nickelodeons for immigrants at the beginning of the 20th century, in the fears about the effects of cinema, in the anxiety over the appeal of comic books for youth during the 1940s and 1950s, in the fears related to the growth of television and the simultaneous rise of the 1960s counterculture, and in concerns about the appeal of rap music for African American urban youth. In other words, the same argument has been used time and again in critiques of different popular cultural forms.

One of the most often cited invocations of Arnold's premises about popular culture came during the 1930s, when the British literary critic Q. D. Leavis attacked Edgar Rice Burroughs and his novel *Tarzan*. Leavis's concern with the modern novel and with popular fiction in general produced a fertile attack on popular culture that became the mainstay premise of the arts journal *Scrutiny,* for which Leavis served as editor. Leavis argued that cultural work like *Tarzan* distracts people from the circumstances of their everyday lives. In her view, coupled with other ills, such as urbanization and industrialization, popular fiction generates a loss of primary experience as a foundation for knowing the world and addicts people to a fantasy world (see Leavis, 1978). Although Leavis's arguments were launched in the 1930s, they were later echoed in the writings of T. S. Eliot, Otto Spengler, and José Ortega y Gasset. They have also found more contemporary resonance in discussions of the effects of Hollywood films, radio, advertising, television, and even, today, the Internet.

In the years that immediately followed the Leavisite attacks on popular culture, the philosophers of the Frankfurt school introduced an argument in Germany that, although Marxist rather than conservative, expressed a surprisingly similar disdain for popular culture. The school's proponents—among them Max Horkheimer, Theodor Adorno, Erich Fromm, Herbert Marcuse, and Leo Lowenthal—declared war on mass culture from the left because they believed that it narcotizes the public and prevents individuals from thinking critically. In their view, mass culture is no better than a drug that blunts awareness and provides spurious satisfaction for needs that have been commercially stimulated (Horkheimer & Adorno, 1979). Horkheimer and Adorno (1979) have noted that they criticized mass culture not because it gives people too much or makes their lives too secure, but because it contributes to conditions whereby people get too little, and what they do get is bad. The targets of this lament—poverty, injustice, political passivity, elitism—went unnoticed, as mass culture, which came to be known as the culture industry, produced cultural homogeneity and intellectual passivity. Yet for all of the voracity of their mass culture critique, the proponents of the Frankfurt school failed to explore adequately the tenets by which mass culture could be used for positive impacts upon the public. In fact, this Marxist tour de force against the workings of mass culture neglected to offer many positive thoughts about the function of culture for the public. As Adorno (1992) has offered in his classic essay on popular music, popular music is simply no better than "a multiple-choice questionnaire." For many, concern came to center on the effects of "Americanization" on popular culture. Critics feared that the populist tendencies of American democracy would inevitably break down all traditional hierarchies of class and taste.

Interestingly, adherents of both the culture and civilization tradition and the mass culture critique saw popular culture as inherently powerful. Although they rejected it on radically opposing grounds, proponents of both schools of thought assumed that popular culture is capable of having forceful effects on the people at whom it is directed. That premise has also figured into later arguments about the nature of popular culture, and it provides much of the legitimation for the contemporary study of popular culture and popular communication.

At approximately the same time the Frankfurt school was drawing attention, American cultural critic Dwight MacDonald gave additional life to the general disdain for popular culture when, writing during the 1930s, he attempted to integrate the public into high culture. Ultimately, however, he came to see high culture and popular culture as two distinct entities that cannot be merged, and he resigned himself to accepting popular culture as inescapable. Despite his negativity about popular culture, however, MacDonald diversified the notion of "the mass" because he was particularly troubled by a type of experience he called "mid-cult." Wrestling with the distinctions between high and low, he coined this in-between term to address those kinds of cultural productions that are mass-produced yet paraded as high culture. MacDonald held that such productions—his examples included *Life* magazine, the paintings of Norman Rockwell, and the Book-of-the-Month Club—are particularly dangerous because they suggest to the public that they are receiving high culture when in fact they are not (see MacDonald, 1962). In this sense, MacDonald can be seen as representing both the height and the exhaustion of the negativity of the mass culture critique.

In the United States of the 1950s, other voices also began debating the nature of popular culture. In their edited volume *Mass Culture: Popular Art in America* (1957), Bernard Rosenberg and David Manning White cautioned against what they saw as the Russian influence on popular cultural forms. During this post-McCarthy period, which gave way to the Cold War ideology of containment, critics such as Rosenberg and White argued for two strands of self-protection: the need to maintain a healthy body politic from the outside (resulting from the dangers of communism) and the need to maintain a healthy body politic from the inside (resulting from the dangers of mass culture). Mass culture, in this view, was seen as decidedly Russian, mass-conformist, and uniform.

Yet there were more optimistic voices on the horizon. The American liberal pluralists of the 1950s offered yet another way to stratify culture that was derived primarily from their discomfort with the negativity of both the Frankfurt school position and the Cold War isolationists vis-à-vis popular culture. Derived from a general postwar consensus that was based on liberalism, pluralism, egalitarianism, and classlessness, the liberal pluralists—who included Herbert Gans, Edward Shils, and Gilbert Seldes—argued for a more positive embrace of popular culture and a more diversified notion of the mass that could recognize alternative cultural experiences. Key here was the notion that members of the public can be trusted to know what is best for them. Gans (1974), for instance, argued for "taste cultures," groups by which different groups come to experience culture differently, rather than a hierarchy of cultures from high to low. Shils (1978) studied the effect of the periphery and the center in shaping cultural experience and argued that three kinds of culture appeal to three levels of people. More recently, Schudson (1987) echoed many of the liberal pluralist assumptions about popular culture in offering a retrospective tracking of the study of popular culture in the academy.

From the 1960s onward, the optimism of the liberal pluralists met up with ongoing concerns about power and domination that emerged during the breakdown of consensus in the 1960s over what constitutes legitimate authority. This breaking apart of a recognizable monolithic culture, hastened by events such as the Kennedy assassination, the war in Vietnam, and Watergate, offered a new sensibility about what constitutes legitimate cultural formations and for whom (Carey, 1989; Zelizer, 1992). Concerns such as these proved a good breeding ground for the emerging Centre for Contemporary Cultural Studies at the University of Birmingham, which took as its mission the elaboration of popular cultural forms in conjunction with Marxist cultural studies (Hall, 1981; Hall & Jefferson, 1976; Hall & Whannel, 1964). The impulse among scholars at the Birmingham Centre was to renovate popular culture by seeing it as something that is potentially positive because it resonates with the will of the public (Angus & Jhally, 1989; Chambers, 1987; Collins, 1989; Fiske, 1989a; Hebdige, 1979, 1988; McRobbie, 1994).

Thus in many, but not all, studies of popular communication and popular culture, the background suppositions have been Marxist in nature. Following primarily upon the work of Stuart Hall, the authors of these studies have claimed that popular communication and popular culture address "an arena of consent and resistance . . . where hegemony arises, and where it is secured" (see Hall, 1981). At the very least, however, these lines presuppose a political nature to the workings of popular culture and communication. Popular culture and communication are seen as sites through which meaning about everyday life is shaped, contested, challenged, and reinstated. Moreover, the extent to which having a popular tilt is seen as either a "good" thing or a "bad" thing depends, ultimately, on one's larger pre-suppositions about "the people" and the public at large. Those presuppositions are linked in turn to one's assumptions about whether said culture is made of the experiences of the public or whether it is imposed by those who think they know better.

Such definitions of the popular have provided a background against which the Popular Communication Division came into place. Unlike its closest cohort, the Popular Culture Association, which operates from Bowling Green State University, the Popular Communication Division attempts to apply communication theories and perspectives to popular cultural phenomena. According to its charter divisional statement, the overall purpose of the division is

> to promote communication-related research that draws from a variety of theoretical approaches in furthering the understanding of popular communication and popular culture. The Division is committed to scholarship that explores a wide range of artifacts, processes, effects, and meanings associated with the shaping of popular communication and popular culture. It is also committed to promoting critical research that regards popular communication and popular culture as a locus from which to generate useful and provocative questions about everyday life. (Divisional By-Laws, p. 1)

This statement suggests three fundamental points about the nature of scholarship on popular communication:

1. It is interdisciplinary.
2. It is eclectic in its embrace of theoretical focus, methodological perspective, and focus of inquiry.
3. It strives to connect the academy and real life.

THE POPULAR IN ITS CONTEMPORARY CONTEXT

Given these premises, what does it mean to study popular communication and, by implication, popular culture? This question generates increasing degrees of relevance as popular communication—in forms as wide-ranging as news, political speeches, karaoke, public auctions, bathroom graffiti, and serial dramas—becomes more available, more accessible, and more ever present. Popular communication can be had in an increasing number of forums, which provide growing numbers of options for engaging in communication of a popular sort. Moreover, everyday life in modern societies appears to be increasingly affected by popular culture itself. From televised talk shows to teen magazines to self-help literature, our growing dependence on popular culture to draw for us the outlines of our lives suggests that popular culture and popular communication constitute an arena in need of closer perusal.

Thus, as contemporary circumstances have made popular communication and popular culture more available rather than less so, the territory that popular communication and culture inhabit has come to be looked at in numerous ways, from numerous disciplines, from numerous perspectives, and using numerous methods. It is time, then, to have a conversation about the study of popular culture and popular communication—to think together about what that study is, what it is not, and how it might figure most effectively within the International Communication Association.

Three main areas of argument have shaped inquiries into popular culture in the contemporary age. As articulated by Dominic Strinati (1995), these are as follows:

- *Questions of agency:* Who or what determines popular culture and popular communication? Where do popular culture and popular communication come from? Are they products of the people themselves or are they imposed by larger power structures?

- *Questions of commodification:* What is the impact of advertising and commercialization on popular culture and popular communication? How do issues such as profit and marketability affect integrity, quality, and artistry? Is there a universal market for popular culture and popular communication?

- *Questions of ideology:* What is the role of ideology in the production and consumption of popular culture and popular communication? Does ideology encourage submission to the status quo or independence? Are there ways to maintain both submission and independence?

These questions, and others, remain the core focus of the study of popular culture and popular communication, and the analyses of popular culture researchers now stretch across geographic domains and across disciplinary areas of inquiry.

Alongside enthusiasm for the study of popular culture and popular communication, however, remains what Cary Nelson has called an "ingrained contempt" for such study (cited in Morley & Chen, 1996, p. 396). In trying to figure out how to make the study of popular culture and popular communication a respected "thing to do" in the academy, we have not quite determined the boundaries of the spaces in which we conduct our work, despite scholarship that grows even as I write this. What, in the end, can and should be the appropriate study of popular culture and communication? I would like to offer, as a partial solution, some rules of communication relay—specifically, the rules of the journalistic lead—to help define the shape of this study.

It is fair to say that the study of popular culture and popular communication is itself interdisciplinary. The analysis of popular culture and communication is found all over the academy, and whenever it appears it borrows quite actively from an array of conceptual starting points—in literature, sociology, anthropology, history, literary criticism, and psychoanalysis, to name a few. Film studies has been one enclave that has traditionally examined popular cinema, but largely within the confines of separate film programs or English departments. The points at which these disciplinary interests intersect have produced a rather large and often unwieldy body of scholarly inquiry that goes far beyond the initial attempts to define popular culture and communication as that which is *not* something else. Yet at the same time, the fertile routes of cross-fertilization by which these different arenas of inquiry meet over the issue of popular culture and popular communication underscore how conceptually rich this field of study is.

As inquiry has grown, however, what has *not* grown at its side is the kind of reflexive impulse that keeps the study of popular culture and communication on track. Consequently, we still seem to know better what popular culture and communication *are not* than what they are, and we know even less about how newly arriving studies fit alongside those that came before. It is here that the journalistic lead—or what Robert Manoff and Michael Schudson (1986) more than a decade ago called the "commandment questions of journalism"—offers a formula to point us toward definitional clarity in the study of popular culture and popular communication. What if we were to ask the 5 Ws and an H of popular culture and popular communication—who, when, where, what, why, and how do we study it? Figuring out which of these six questions is most salient in our analyses can provide an index to where our studies fit against the larger body of preexisting scholarship. The journalistic lead thus gives us a platform from which we can see how we study what we study.

WHAT IS POPULAR CULTURE AND COMMUNICATION?

First, *what* is the study of popular culture and communication? There are a number of answers to this question, each of which is connected to the basic issue of what popular culture and popular communication are. We alternately invoke popular culture and popular communication as systems of beliefs and attitudes, skills and habits, preferences and values, uses of technology, just mind frames, or all of the above. Sometimes popular culture is conflated with "mass media." Prevalent here have been binary distinctions about what we figure are popular culture's most telling features; we argue that popular culture is internal versus external, implicit versus explicit, formal versus informal, general versus specialized. Invoking distinctions like these has helped us establish a certain anthropological validity to our study and has allowed us to locate popular culture and popular communication through many material prisms that have drawn in folklorists, scholars interested in poetics and aesthetics, and anthropologists in particular.

Yet even here questions remain about when a production or artifact is codified as popular versus elite. In 1991, Luciano Pavarotti performed for free before an audience of some 100,000 people in London's Hyde Park. Was this popular culture because it was outside, free of charge, and open to the masses, or was it high culture because of its operatic nature (Storey, 1993)? Within the Popular Communication Division, such concerns have produced many responses and a wide range of scholarship. Division members have sought to examine popular culture and communication as process, behavior, institution, artifact, and text. Division programs have provided forums for the debate of such issues as karaoke bars (Drew, 1997), lingerie ads (Valdivia, 1997), children and consumer culture (Mazzarella & Pecora, 1999), cinematic and televisual portrayals of marginalized groups (Hanke, 1998; Tucker, 1997), the production of documentary television (Dornfeld, 1998), comic books (Tankel & Murphy, 1998), and the values implicit in news leads (Corrigan, 1990).

The arenas of inquiry that constitute the study of popular culture within the Popular Communication Division have been widespread. A perusal of the division's conference programming over the past 10 years reveals that topics covered have included space and cultural geography (Fry, 1998); discourse on sex (Banks & Zimmerman, 1996); youth practices and subcultures (Valdivia, 1998); popular journalism (Bird, 1996); fandom, cults, and celebrity practices; comics and animation (Lamb, 1990; Uricchio & Pearson, 1991); popular culture across nation-states and across popular dimensions of advertising (Tucker, 1998); artifacts (Cooks & Aden, 1995); and popular culture pedagogy. By attending to each arena's popular dimensions, this scholarship extends public understanding beyond the taken-for-granted assumptions about how each arena works and what effects it has.

Popular Literature

A large proportion of scholarship on popular culture and popular communication has focused on texts, both formally defined and creatively extended beyond the more obvious textual realms. The general thrust of this work has been to complicate the common assumption that high literature enlightens and educates. Much of this work has tackled assumptions concerning what education or enlightenment might actually mean under different circumstances.

In its most recent incarnation, the study of popular literature has valorized those types of literature that have typically been deemed unworthy of critical study by the academy and the reigning intelligentsia (e.g., Moffitt, 1993). This, too, has had a historic trajectory, dating back to Q. D. Leavis's (1978) aforementioned view that Edgar Rice Burroughs's novel *Tarzan* dissociates the common folk from their agrarian roots. In arguing that popular literature offers a template for daily living to the common folk, who have few lessons for real experience, Leavis unwittingly offered a challenge to those who followed and wanted to prove that lessons, although different from those offered by high literature, could be gleaned from popular genres. An example is the study of comics as popular literature. With the renaissance of the comic book industry in the 1960s sparked by the popularity of Marvel Comics, a generation of scholars who grew up on comics came into their own from the early 1990s onward. The use of comic-book characters such as Batman and the Incredible Hulk as fodder for television shows and feature films generated a steady increase in academic attention (Lamb, 1990; Uricchio & Pearson, 1991).

Thus much of the study of popular literature in the present day is aimed at elevating popular literature by demonstrating either that it offers alternative views of the world or that it offers alternative functions for those who use it (Bennett, 1990; Crane, 1992). John Fiske (1987, 1989b), for instance, has shown how different texts are able to empower groups and collectives in ways that underscore their independence from the powers that be. At the same time, much of the current work takes its lead from Janice Radway's *Reading the Romance* (1984), in which Radway argues that reading romance novels offers serious advances for women seeking escape from the drudgery of housewifery. Following Radway's work, the investigation of popular literature has ranged from studies of *Star Trek* fanzines (Bacon-Smith, 1992) to studies of conspiracy literature (Fenster, 1999) and James Bond (Bennett & Woollacott, 1987).

Popular News

The capacity to define dimensions of the news and journalism as popular has created a crossroads in thinking about how "the popular" can infiltrate and permeate the more highly regarded elite discourses of information relay. Whereas news has typically been seen as the relay of information only, discussions of its popular dimensions have sought to go beyond the function of information relay. This scholarship has focused on issues such as narrative and storytelling practices, rhetorical forms, rites and rituals, folklore, and the establishment of collective authority.

Back in the 1970s, John Fiske and John Hartley (1978) were perhaps the first in this field to point to the notion of popular journalism. Fiske (1996) has continued this strand of interest in his more recent work, which has focused primarily on journalism, including a discussion of the ways in which tabloid news reading encouraged and legitimated a certain mode of thought processing among jury members in the O.J. Simpson murder trial. Following Fiske's lead, scholars such as Hartley (1982, 1996), Peter Dahlgren (1995), and Dave Morley (1980) have independently examined the popular dimensions of contemporary news.

But in truth, popular dimensions of news have been around for at least as long as news itself. Tabloid news, jazz journalism, sensationalism, feature writing—all offer different dimensions of news performance, production, and consumption that go beyond the notion of conveying important information. Relevant here has been the work of Elizabeth Bird (1992) and Matthew Ehrlich (1996) on tabloids as well as David Eason's (1986) and my own work on journalistic authority (Zelizer, 1992, 1993). James Carey (1989) has been particularly instrumental in helping us to see that the popular dimensions of news have always inhabited the journalistic world.

Popular Advertising

A growing body of scholarship has also pushed beyond the view that advertising is primarily the work of persuasion. Matthew McAllister (1996), Jib Fowles (1996), Robin Andersen (1995), and Robert Goldman and Stephen Papson (1996) have all begun to complicate the meaning of advertising in its popular dimensions. The issues examined have included the function of nostalgia in advertising, the blurring of televisual and commercial programming, the role of gender and race in advertising, and the targeting of constructed identities in audiences. All of these complicate our default understanding of advertising as simply something that persuades.

The impetus for examining advertising texts can be traced back to the work of Marshall McLuhan, whose *Mechanical Bride* (1951) helped establish the tone and technique for the close reading of advertising texts on which other scholars, such as semiotician Roland Barthes (1972), Erving Goffman (1979), and Judith Williamson (1978), later built. More recent scholarship has begun to unpack the ways in which different identity markers have been used in advertising. Goldman (1992), for instance, has tracked the ways in which the "mortise," or logo of an advertisement, is fitted to the image associated with the product, such as beauty or social acceptance. O'Barr (1994) discusses the advertising world's portrayals of race and ethnicity. Similarly, Kern-Foxworth (1994) has traced the ways in which African Americans have been portrayed in advertisements and commercials from the 17th century to the present, and Valdivia (1997) has examined the gender and class assumptions at work in lingerie catalogs.

Popular Television and Film

In something of an about-face, scholarship on popular television and film has had to work significantly *against* the assumption that television, and sometimes film, primarily entertains. There seems to be a lingering public attitude that implies the question, What are television and film, if they are not popular? Thus much academic work on the popular dimensions of television and film has had to complicate the notion of "the popular" within a larger bias against the medium of television in its broadest form (Allen 1992; MacCabe, 1986; Modleski, 1986; Williamson, 1986). For instance, in their book *Prime Time, Prime Movers,* David Marc and Robert J. Thompson (1992) apply an auteurist mode of criticism to the work of television producers. Ian Ang (1985, 1995) has uncovered underlying ideological premises at work in television programming. The production of *The Cosby Show* and audience reactions to that program have been examined both across national boundaries and against a template of racial identity (Fuller, 1992; Tucker, 1997). In film, even topics that have pushed the boundaries of what constitutes cinema, such as Hollywood cartoons, have had a certain appeal to scholars (Smoodin, 1993).

Gender identity has occupied a similar place in the imagination of scholars of popular communication and popular culture. Mary Ellen Brown (1999) demonstrates that television both creates and recycles predominant representations of reality. In *Television and Women's Culture,* Brown examines issues such as women's televisual genres in relation to television programming. Ang (1985, 1995) focuses on women in her analysis of *Dallas* and other television programming, whereas Scodari (1995) discusses the gendered messages of situation comedies. Similarly, both Craig (1992) and Hanke (1998) have explored the ways in which men's different identities have come to play in the media.

Programming at conferences on popular culture and communication has focused on notions of generations on prime-time television, gender and the landscape of public communication, explorations of television soap operas, the export of television programming across national boundaries, and the consumption of television drama by marginalized groups.

In large part, this scholarship has helped bridge the gap between the study of popular culture and communication and the kinds of film studies conducted in film programs and English programs with concentrations in film. Valdivia (1998), for instance, takes up the issue of single mothers in contemporary family films in a way that relates directly back to larger social configurations. By the same token, these works have taken up issues of representation that in an earlier academic configuration might have been overlooked. For instance, a focus on reality-based television programming has opened up new venues for thinking about televisual representation (Consalvo, 1998; Fishman, 1999).

Popular Music

The work of such scholars as James Lull (1987), Simon Frith (1983, 1988), Larry Grossberg (1992), and Steve Jones (1992) has been instrumental in elevating different kinds of musical performance and production to the level of public scholarly awareness. Jonathan Tankel's (1998) studies of radio have provided a more institutional vision of the practices of radio making.

From pop, easy listening, and Tin Pan Alley to disco, rock, and jazz, the elaborations of what popular music means have been vast (Frith, Goodwin, & Grossberg, 1991; Kaplan, 1987). The study of popular music has given rise to consideration of the ways in which authenticity takes on different styles according to communal or group identity. Researchers have undertaken examinations of productions as unusual as cassette culture in India (Manuel, 1993).

Included here are questions of race, ethnicity, age, and gender in relation to the use of popular music, the role of popular music in nostalgia, and practices of music production and music consumption. For instance, Steve Jones (1992) discusses the ways in which technology and music have blended to create what we call rock music. Similarly, the contributors to James Lull's edited collection *Popular Music and Communication* (1987) examine the proliferation of popular music across different communicative contexts.

WHO IS POPULAR CULTURE AND COMMUNICATION?

A range of similar issues surrounds a second question: Who is the *who* in the study of popular culture and communication? Here again, a number of identities, both individual and collective, are involved in shaping culture, and the issue of "who counts" varies according to who is doing the asking.

Sociological inquiry has been central here, prompting us to examine questions of identity in many activities surrounding the production of culture. Who produces popular culture? Who uses it? Who consumes it, challenges it, promotes it? It is possible that much of our concern with the "who" in the study of popular culture has been a bottoms-up interest that has set in place a frame that focuses attention more on popular culture's distinctiveness than on its similarities to the so-called nonpopular. Emphasis on the "who" has been further legitimated by scholarship a priori grounded in issues of identity, such as women's studies, gay and lesbian studies, and ethnic studies—each of which has rendered the "who" question a primary analytic tenet. What might be worth thinking about here is the point at which these different identities come together, for we may have lost sight of the larger population beyond the pockets we study. On this point it is perhaps Michael Schudson who has most pointedly directed us in thinking about the value of popular communication and popular culture (see, e.g., Mukerji & Schudson, 1991; Schudson, 1987). Certain work has also moved us in the direction of ethnography, which many researchers see as a tool for studying the audiences of popular communication (Drew, 1997).

It is relevant to note that some scholars have been situated not only in the Popular Communication Division of the ICA but elsewhere in the organization, the field, and the academy. Work by British and Australian cultural studies scholars such as Stuart Hall, John Fiske, Richard Johnson, and Graham Turner has done much to facilitate serious thinking about popular culture and popular communication.

Other work has been closer to the home front. Sharon Mazzarella and Angharad Valdivia have both worked on youth cultures. Larry Gross (1993), writing about the cultural practices of outing in the American gay and lesbian community over the past century, connects the issue of identity politics with prevalent media practices. Jonathan Tankel and Jane Banks (1996) have focused on gender identity and popular communication, looking at the processes by which gender is constructed in the media.

Also of relevance here are the ongoing discussions within the division about the representation of national groups in the mass media. Whether the subject has been the images of South Africans in American films, the representation of Yanks in

British cinema, or the experience of Vietnam in Australian film, the emphasis in much of this scholarship has been on the ways in which collectives are seen by other collectives.

WHEN IS POPULAR CULTURE AND COMMUNICATION?

The *when* in the study of popular communication and culture is another index worth contemplating. Here, we tend to think first of historians, although that affinity becomes more complicated the more closely we examine it. Even among historians, the "when" question has become increasingly intertwined with other indices of inquiry. We could, for instance, characterize the Annale school's recoding of the history of the West as a decision to look differently at the "what" in its analysis (i.e., looking at objects and habits of the masses rather than at the documents of the literate elite). Moreover, the "when" of popular culture has become a popular site of study for nonhistorians who consider "when we are" as a template for understanding contemporary life. Studies of collective memory are another example, where groups as wide-ranging as sociologists and literary scholars are examining dimensions of culture's "when" (Schudson, 1992; Zelizer, 1992, 1998).

Significantly, the emphasis on the popular has often altered the traditional focal points within recognizable realms of analysis. Particularly prevalent, for instance, has been an interest in celebrity. This has produced work as wide-ranging as scholarship on the Elvis legend (Rodman, 1996) and the trajectories of various national heroes (Drucker & Cathcart, 1994). Additionally, nearly every conference on popular communication has included in its program some focus on historical studies in popular communication, ranging from the use of popular music as history to Hollywood and the "Jewish question" to the cultural politics of the Communist Party during the 1930s.

WHERE IS POPULAR CULTURE AND COMMUNICATION?

Where is the study of popular culture and communication? There are many answers to this question, all connected to a fundamental ambivalence concerning the "where" of popular culture itself. For instance, is popular culture antecedent to human activity (as anthropologists might have it) or consequent to that activity (as sociologists would argue)? Is it in the domestic setting or in the broad-based institution? Is it in one place or many—as in the export and import of culture, or in the transformation of cultural artifacts from one setting to another? The fluid and transformative nature of popular culture extends to the "where" of its study too. Some issues worth mentioning include the following: Is the study of popular culture confined to or even promoted by certain disciplines? Certain institutions?

Certain geographic locations? The many settings in which popular culture deserves and receives analysis may be patterned enough that they, too, merit attention.

Although the study of popular communication and culture has been addressed by scholars in numerous disciplines (e.g., literary studies, sociology, anthropology, and historical studies) and in numerous associations (e.g., the American Studies Association, the American Sociological Association, and the Popular Culture Association), the focus on popular communication as a target of inquiry is relatively novel. Although concerned with popular culture, the study of popular communication moves beyond issues of cultural production to the communicative processes by which communication is "made popular." The recent establishment of the Popular Communication Division is a testament to the growing interest in the popular dimensions of communication.

Of relevance here are numerous studies dealing with spatial location and place identity. Fry (1995), for instance, has examined spatial practices as they relate to regional magazines. Mark Neumann (1999) and Joli Jensen (1990) have worked on the sites of tourism and the ways in which popular spaces create collective identities.

WHY AND HOW IS POPULAR CULTURE AND COMMUNICATION?

Finally, we have the twin issues of *why* and *how*. Because so much of the study of popular culture is devoted to distinguishing it from other kinds of culture, we find that the "why" and "how" underlie all of the other indices, but in varying configurations. Those in literary criticism or folklore might combine these issues with the "what" question, explaining the aesthetics of popular music, for instance, as a function of class placement. Sociologists, on the other hand, who regard popular culture and communication as a resource people draw upon to coordinate activity, direct us first to the question of "how," to the practices involved in maintenance, legitimation, and what is routinely called the politics of culture.

What does any of this tell us? To anyone sensitive to interdisciplinary inquiry, this kind of formula reinforces the varied linkages that the study of popular culture and popular communication can generate both across the academy and between the academy and the larger nonacademic world. Obviously, no index is always applicable, mutually exclusive, or self-containing. But when taken together, these indices offer a platform from which we can view inquiry about the study of popular culture.

Extending an idea proposed by Ann Swidler (1986), they suggest that the study of culture functions like culture itself—as a "tool kit" that people use differently try to resolve different kinds of problems. This means that the multiple sites of analysis from which popular culture can—and should—be studied are instrumental not only because they clarify definitional ambiguity and stake out a place for new study, but because they create alliances of unpredictable shapes between people in different disciplines, using different theoretical perspectives, and moving toward different practical aims. This makes the study of popular culture fertile ground for enhancing people's ties with others not like themselves.

Equally important, the long-touted "pleasures of the popular" reign as a default setting for the analysis of much of popular culture and popular communication. The reasons that cultural artifacts become popular, and what difference that makes, offer substantially different answers to issues that have long been seen as the industrialized imperatives of late capitalism and the hegemonic issues those imperatives raise. In other words, the relatively newfound focus on responses and effects such as empowerment and emancipation ring a different bell from that rung by the long-standing debate between hegemony theorists and enthusiasts for dominant ideology.

REFERENCES

Adorno, T. W. (1992). On popular music. In A. Easthope & K. McGowan (Eds.), *A critical and cultural theory reader.* Milton Keynes: Open University Press.

Allen, R. (Ed.). (1992). *Channels of discourse, reassembled.* New York: Routledge.

Andersen, R. (1995). *Consumer culture and TV programming.* Boulder, CO: Westview.

Ang, I. (1985). *Watching Dallas: Soap opera and the melodramatic imagination.* London: Methuen.

Ang, I. (1995). *Living room wars.* London: Routledge.

Angus, I., & Jhally, S. (1989). *Cultural politics in contemporary America.* New York: Routledge.

Arnold, M. (1932). *Culture and anarchy.* London: Cambridge University Press. (Original work published 1869)

Bacon-Smith, C. (1992). *Enterprising women: Television fandom and the creation of popular myth.* Philadelphia: University of Pennsylvania Press.

Banks, J., & Zimmerman, P. R. (1996). Dr. Ruth Westheimer: Talking sex as a technology of power. *Journal of Film and Video, 45*(2-3), 60-71.

Barthes, R. (1972). *Mythologies* (A. Lavers, Trans.). New York: Hill & Wang.

Bennett, T. (1980). Popular culture: A teaching object. *Screen Education, 34.*

Bennett, T. (Ed.). (1990). *Popular fiction.* London: Routledge.

Bennett, T., & Woollacott, J. (1987). *Bond and beyond: The political career of a popular hero.* London: Methuen.

Bird, S. E. (1992). *For enquiring minds.* Knoxville: University of Tennessee Press.

Bird, S. E. (1996). CJ's revenge: Media, folklore, and the cultural construction of AIDS. *Critical Studies in Mass Communication, 13,* 44-58.

Brown, M. E. (1990). *Television and women's culture: The politics of the popular.* Newbury Park, CA: Sage.

Carey, J. W. (1989). *Communication as culture: Essays on media and society.* Winchester, MA: Unwin Hyman.

Chambers, I. (1987). *Popular culture: The metropolitan experience.* New York: Methuen.

Collins, J. (1989). *Uncommon cultures: Popular culture and post-modernism.* London: Routledge.

Consalvo, M. (1998). Hegemony, domestic violence, and "Cops": A critique of concordance. *Journal of Popular Film and Television, 26*(2), 62-70.

Cooks, L. M., & Aden, R. C. (1995). "Northern Exposure" 's sense of place: Constructing and marginalizing the matriarchal community. *Women's Studies in Communication, 18,* 1-17.

Corrigan, D. (1990). Value coding consensus in front page news leads. *Journalism Quarterly, 67,* 653-662.

Craig, S. (Ed.). (1992). *Men, masculinity and the media.* Newbury Park, CA: Sage.

Crane, D. (1992). *The production of culture: Media and the urban arts.* Newbury Park, CA: Sage.

Dahlgren, P. (1995). *Television and the public sphere: Citizenship, democracy and the media.* London: Sage.

Dornfeld, B. (1998). *Producing public television, producing public culture.* Princeton, NJ: Princeton University Press.

Drew, R. S. (1997). Embracing the role of amateur: How karaoke bar patrons become regular performers. *Journal of Contemporary Ethnography, 25,* 449-468.

Drucker, S., & Cathcart, R. S. (Eds.). (1994). *American heroes in a media age.* Cresskill, NJ: Hampton.

Eason, D. (1986). On journalistic authority. *Critical Studies in Mass Communication, 3,* 429-447.

Ehrlich, M. (1996, February). The journalism of outrageousness: Tabloid television news vs. investigative news. *Journalism and Mass Communication Monographs, 155.*

Fenster, M. (1999). *Conspiracy theories.* Minneapolis: University of Minnesota Press.

Fishman, J. (1999). The populace and the police: Models of social control in reality-based crime television. *Critical Studies in Mass Communication, 16,* 268-288.

Fiske, J. (1987). *Television culture.* New York: Routledge.

Fiske, J. (1989a). *Reading the popular.* Winchester, MA: Unwin Hyman.

Fiske, J. (1989b). *Understanding popular culture.* Winchester, MA: Unwin Hyman.

Fiske, J. (1996). *Media matters: Everyday culture and political change.* Minneapolis: University of Minnesota Press.

Fiske, J., & Hartley, J. (1978). *Reading television.* London: Methuen.

Fowles, J. (1996). *Advertising and popular culture.* Thousand Oaks, CA: Sage.

Frith, S. (1983). *Sound effects: Youth, leisure and the politics of rock 'n' roll.* New York: Pantheon.

Frith, S. (1988). *Music for pleasure: Essays in the sociology of pop.* New York: Routledge.

Frith, S., Goodwin, A., & Grossberg, L. (Eds.). (1991). *Sound and vision: The music television reader.* Boston: Unwin Hyman.

Fry, K. (1995). Regional magazines and the ideal white reader: Constructing and retaining geography as text. In D. Abrahamson (Ed.), *The American magazine: Research perspectives and prospects.* Ames: Iowa State University Press.

Fry, K. (1998). A cultural geography of Lake Wobegon. *Howard Journal of Communications, 9,* 303-321.

Fuller, L. (1992). The Cosby Show: *Audiences, impact and implications.* Westport, CT: Greenwood.

Gans, H. (1974). *Popular culture and high culture: An analysis and evaluation of taste.* New York: Basic Books.

Goffman, E. (1979). *Gender advertisements.* Cambridge, MA: Harvard University Press.

Goldman, R. (1992). *Reading ads socially.* New York: Routledge.

Goldman, R., & Papson, S. (1996). *Sign wars: The cluttered landscape of advertising.* New York: Guilford.

Gross, L. (1993). *Contested closets: The ethics and politics of outing.* Minneapolis: University of Minnesota Press.

Grossberg, L. (1992). *We gotta get out of this place: Popular conservatism and postmodern culture.* New York: Routledge.

Hall, S. (1981). Cultural studies: Two paradigms. In T. Bennett (Ed.), *Culture, ideology, and social process.* Milton Keynes: Open University Press.

Hall, S., & Jefferson, T. (Eds.). (1976). *Resistance through rituals: Youth subculture in post-war Britain.* London: Hutchinson.

Hall, S., & Whannel, P. (1964). *The popular arts.* London: Pantheon.

Hanke, R. (1998). The "mock-macho" situation comedy: Hegemonic masculinity and its reiteration. *Western Journal of Communication, 62*(1), 74-93.

Hartley, J. (1982). *Understanding news*. London: Methuen.

Hartley, J. (1996). *Popular reality: Journalism, modernity, popular culture*. London: Arnold.

Hebdige, D. (1979). *Subculture: The meaning of style*. New York: Routledge.

Hebdige, D. (1988). *Hiding in the light: On images and things*. London: Routledge.

Horkheimer, M., & Adorno, T. W. (1979). *Dialectic of enlightenment*. London: Verso.

Jensen, J. (1990). *Redeeming modernity: Contradictions in media criticism*. Newbury Park, CA: Sage.

Jones, S. (1992). *Rock formation: Music, technology, and mass communication*. Newbury Park, CA: Sage.

Kaplan, E. A. (1987). *Rocking around the clock: Music television, postmodernism, and consumer culture*. New York: Methuen.

Kern-Foxworth, M. (1994). *Aunt Jemima, Uncle Ben, and Rastus: Blacks in advertising yesterday, today and tomorrow*. Westport, CT: Greenwood.

Lamb, C. (1990). Changing with the times: The world according to Doonesbury. *Journal of Popular Culture, 23*(4), 113-129.

Leavis, Q. D. (1978). *Fiction and the reading public*. London: Chatto & Windus.

Lull, J. (Ed.). (1987). *Popular music and communication*. Newbury Park, CA: Sage.

MacCabe, C. (Ed.). (1986). *High theory/low culture: Analyzing popular television and film*. New York: St. Martin's.

MacDonald, D. (1962). *Against the American grain: Essays on the effects of mass culture*. New York: Random House.

Manoff, R., & Schudson, M. (1986). *Reading the news*. New York: Pantheon.

Manuel, P. (1993). *Cassette culture: Popular music and technology in India*. Chicago: University of Chicago Press.

Marc, D., & Thompson, R. J. (1992). *Prime time, prime movers: From I Love Lucy to L.A. Law—America's greatest TV shows and the people who created them*. Boston: Little, Brown.

Mazzarella, S., & Pecora, N. (1999). *Growing up girls: Popular culture and the construction of identity*. New York: Peter Lang.

McAllister, M. (1996). *The commercialization of American culture: New advertising, control, and democracy*. Thousand Oaks, CA: Sage.

McGuigan, J. (1992). *Cultural populism*. New York: Routledge.

McLuhan, M. (1951). *The mechanical bride: Folklore of industrial man*. New York: Vanguard.

McRobbie, A. (1994). *Postmodernism and popular culture*. London: Routledge.

Modleski, T. (Ed.). (1986). *Studies in entertainment: Critical approaches to mass culture*. Bloomington: Indiana University Press.

Moffitt, M. A. (1993). Articulating meaning: Reconceptions of the meaning process, fantasy/reality, and identity in leisure activities. *Communication Theory, 3*, 231-251.

Morley, D. (1980). *The "Nationwide" audience*. London: British Film Institute.

Morley, D., & Chen, K.-H. (Eds.). (1996). *Stuart Hall: Critical dialogues in cultural studies*. London: Routledge.

Mukerji, C., & Schudson, M. (1991). *Rethinking popular culture: Contemporary perspectives in cultural studies*. Berkeley: University of California Press.

Neumann, M. (1999). *On the rim: Looking for the Grand Canyon*. Minneapolis: University of Minnesota Press.

O'Barr, W. (1994). *Culture and the ad: Exploring otherness in the world of advertising*. Boulder, CO: Westview.

O'Sullivan, T., Hartley, J., Saunders, D., & Fiske, J. (1983). *Key concepts in communication*. London: Methuen.

Radway, J. (1984). *Reading the romance: Women, patriarchy and popular literature*. Chapel Hill: University of North Carolina Press.

Rodman, G. (1996). *Elvis after Elvis: The posthumous career of a living legend*. New York: Routledge.

Rosenberg, B., & White, D. W. (Eds.). (1957). *Mass culture: The popular arts in America.* New York: Macmillan.

Schudson, M. (1987). The new validation of popular culture: Sense and sentimentality in Academia. *Critical Studies in Mass Communication, 4,* 51-68.

Schudson, M. (1992). *Watergate in American memory: How we remember, forget, and reconstruct the past.* New York: Basic Books.

Scodari, C. (1995). Profession, attraction, and the thrill of the chase: Gendered myth-making in film and television comedy of the sexes. *Critical Studies in Mass Communication, 12,* 23-39.

Shils, E. (1978). Mass society and its culture. In P. Davison, R. Meyersohn, & E. Shils (Eds.), *Culture and mass culture.* Cambridge: Cambridge University Press.

Smoodin, E. (1993). *Animating culture: Hollywood cartoons from the sound era.* New Brunswick, NJ: Rutgers University Press.

Storey, J. (1993). *An introductory guide to cultural theory and popular culture.* Athens: University of Georgia Press.

Storey, J. (Ed.). (1995). *Cultural theory and popular culture: A reader.* Athens: University of Georgia Press.

Strinati, D. (1995). *An introduction to theories of popular culture.* New York: Routledge.

Swidler, A. (1986). Culture in action: Symbols and strategies. *American Sociological Review, 51,* 273-286.

Tankel, J. D. (1998). Reconceptualizing call-in talk radio as listening. *Journal of Radio Studies, 5*(1), 36-48.

Tankel, J. D., & Banks, J. (1996). Lifetime Television and women: Narrowcasting as electronic space. In S. Drucker & G. Gumpert (Eds.), *Voices in the street: Explorations in gender, media and public space* (pp. 255-269). Cresskill, NJ: Hampton.

Tankel, J. D., & Murphy, B. K. (1998). Collecting comic books: A study of the fan and curatorial consumption. In C. Harris & A. Alexander (Eds.), *Theorizing fandom: Fans, subculture and identity* (pp. 53-66). Cresskill, NJ: Hampton.

Tucker, L. R. (1997). Was the revolution televised? Professional criticism about "The Cosby Show" and the essentialism of black cultural expression. *Journal of Broadcasting & Electronic Media, 41,* 90-108.

Tucker, L. R. (1998). The framing of Calvin Klein: A frame analysis of media discourse about the August 1995 Calvin Klein jeans advertising controversy. *Critical Studies in Mass Communication, 15,* 141-157.

Uricchio, W., & Pearson, R. (Eds.). (1991). *The many lives of the Batman: Critical approaches to a superhero and his media.* New York: Routledge.

Valdivia, A. N. (1997). The secret of my desire: Gender, class, and sexuality in lingerie catalogs. In K. Frith (Ed.), *Undressing the ad: Reading culture in advertising.* New York: Peter Lang.

Valdivia, A. N. (1998). Clueless in Hollywood: Single moms in contemporary family movies. *Journal of Communication Inquiry, 22,* 272-292.

Williams, R. (1975). *Television: Technology and cultural form.* New York: Schocken.

Williams, R. (1976). *Keywords.* London: Fontana.

Williamson, J. (1978). *Decoding advertisements: Ideology and meaning in advertising.* New York: Marion Boyars.

Williamson, J. (1986). *Consuming passions: The dynamics of popular culture.* London: Marion Boyars.

Zelizer, B. (1992). *Covering the body: The Kennedy assassination, the media, and the shaping of collective memory.* Chicago: University of Chicago Press.

Zelizer, B. (1993). Journalists as interpretive communities. *Critical Studies in Mass Communication, 10,* 219-237.

Zelizer, B. (1998). *Remembering to forget: Holocaust memory through the camera's eye.* Chicago: University of Chicago Press.

CHAPTER CONTENTS

14 Public Relations: An Emerging Social Science Enters the New Millennium

GABRIEL M. VASQUEZ
University of Houston

MAUREEN TAYLOR
Rutgers University

The field of public relations is one of the newest additions to the International Communication Association. Public relations is both a social science field of study and a professional practice. Public relations research is similar to other disciplines in that scholars
utilize social science models, research methods, and both quantitative and qualitative
techniques to describe, explain, and predict specific phenomena. In business, public relations is a professional practice with an organizational role and function, communication
processes, and a code of ethics that guides the responsible use of strategies and tactics.
This chapter provides an overview of public relations scholarship as it contributes to the
objectives of the ICA. The authors trace the development of public relations from a
one-way communication tool to a theoretically grounded communication function that
builds relationships between organizations and the public.

T HE field of public relations has grown from an early emphasis on the available means of public communication to a professional practice grounded in
social science. The roots of today's public relations can be found as forms
of public communication dating to the earliest of civilizations. The origins are
found in early treatises that detailed how public communication can and should be
used to create strategic messages. These messages were designed and tailored to
achieve specific objectives with key audiences in ways that would develop relationships. The building and maintenance of strategic ethical relationships are the
essence of public relations research and practice today.

Correspondence: Maureen Taylor, Department of Communication, Rutgers University,
4 Huntington Street, New Brunswick, NJ 08901-1071; e-mail maureent@scils.rutgers.edu

Communication Yearbook 24, pp. 319-342

Our purpose in this chapter is to provide a state-of-the-discipline analysis of public relations. Several questions underlie this examination: How did public relations develop as a social science field of study? What is the relationship of public relations to other communication disciplines? What are the major lines of research? What are the major issues for researchers and practitioners? What are the metatheoretical assumptions guiding public relations research into the new millennium? We address these questions in the sections that follow.

THE DEVELOPMENT OF PUBLIC RELATIONS
AS A SOCIAL SCIENCE FIELD OF STUDY

Public relations is both a social science field of study and a professional practice. In the academy, public relations research is similar to other disciplines in that scholars utilize social science models, research methods, and both quantitative and qualitative techniques to describe, explain, and predict specific phenomena. Simultaneously, in the business world, public relations is a professional practice with an organizational role and function, communication processes, and a code of ethics that guides the responsible use of strategies and tactics. Today's public relations scholarship is a convergence of academic and professional communication research. Some scholars conduct research that builds communication theory, whereas others conduct research for the purpose of enhancing professional practice. Professionals also conduct research to identify the best public relations practices. Public relations scholars and public relations professionals are united in that they seek to understand the most ethical, strategic, and effective uses of communication to build relationships with key publics. Public relations scholarship and the professional practice of public relations, thus, are opposite sides of the same coin.

An understanding of how public relations developed as a social science discipline requires some knowledge about how public relations came to be the professional practice that exists today. Sadly, many scholars from the communication discipline as well as other disciplines lack an appreciation of the rich history and function of public relations. As a result, misperceptions of public relations persist. Because the nature, ethics, and even appropriateness of public relations as an area of serious academic study have been called into question, one of our goals in this chapter is to enhance communication scholars' understanding of the place of public relations in the academic community. A second goal is to contextualize public relations as a social science and locate it within the interests and objectives of the International Communication Association.

THE DEVELOPMENT OF PUBLIC RELATIONS PRACTICE

How did public relations develop? Although most undergraduate public relations textbooks note that activities resembling some modern practices have their roots in ancient Babylonia, Greece, and Rome, the public relations function that is studied and practiced today is usually traced from roots in mid-18th-century America. From the mid-1700s to the new millennium, the development of public relations as a professional practice and social science field of study can be broken into five stages: foundations, expansion, institutionalization, maturation, and professionalization. These stages are not always distinct, nor are they mutually exclusive. Rather, each stage reflects a maturing of public relations that has contributed to an emphasis on the building of strategic, ethical communication relationships.

Foundations

Although there are now detailed histories of the American practice (Cutlip, 1994, 1995; Miller, 1998), few agree as to where, when, and how public relations began (Cutlip, Center, & Broom, 1999). Sriramesh, Kim, and Takasaki (1999) note that descriptions of public relations exist from prebiblical and biblical times, and Wilcox, Ault, and Agee (1998) trace public relations back to Germany in the late 1800s. Although there has been a long tradition all over the world of activities that can be described as resembling practices of public relations, most of the historical understanding of the field's development has been traced from an American timeline. We recognize that this historical contextualization may appear to be ethnocentric, but we argue that because public relations has rested, until recently, on a tradition of Western scholarship, it is important to know how it developed in the nation of scholarly concentration before we can examine it in other cultural settings.

The foundations stage accounts for the early use of public relations in the colonization of America and in gaining support for the American Revolution (Pimlott, 1951). The beginning of public relations in the United States coincides with the exploration, settlement, and eventual independence of the American colonies. Some scholars have identified the basic elements of a successful public relations effort within the American Revolution (Cutlip et al., 1999).

Many of the public relations strategies that contributed to the birth of United States are occurring today in the developing nations of Latin America and Asia and in emerging democracies in Eastern Europe. Public relations in these regions is in the foundations stage: Governments, political activists, and grassroots groups are all attempting to win public approval, to motivate supporters, and to achieve specific political and social goals (Culbertson & Chen, 1996). The foundations stage represents the beginning of when groups recognize the value of strategic communication. Once that value is recognized, expansion begins.

Expansion

The expansion stage captures the growth of public relations practice to obtain positive attention for events, organizations, people, or policies through publicity and promotion. Organizations all over the world need to publicize and promote their positions, and this need fuels the expansion of public relations practices. This period of public relations history is usually marked by the specializations of publicity and press agentry. In the United States, from 1799 to 1899 public relations tactics and tools were extended into government and politics, entertainment and culture, activism and protest, and business and industry (Cutlip, 1995). American society witnessed the growth of public relations strategies and tactics. Many of these tactics are both illegal and unethical today. Unfortunately, when many people reflect on the status of public relations as a practice and a field of study, it is these kinds of public relations actions that first come to mind. Thus the field is still held accountable for the actions of this stage of development even though they are long past and no longer tolerated.

Many nations in the early stages of economic development are in the expansion phase of public relations development. According to Chen (1996), in China and in many postcommunist states (see Bentele & Peter, 1996; Vercic, Grunig, & Grunig, 1996) the publicity function of public relations is the norm. Practitioners attempt to gain media attention for their organizations, and their goal of press agentry focuses more on media coverage than on building relationships. Expansion is a necessary stage to reach higher levels of the practice because it sets the groundwork for public relations to develop as an institutionalized profession.

Institutionalization

The institutionalization stage reflects a time of increased sophistication and integration of public relations strategies and tactics throughout business, government, and other segments of society (Cutlip, 1995). Organizations need to meet new communication challenges, and this again fuels the inclusion of public relations practices in all aspects of organizational functioning. This period of public relations development is marked by two key developments: The first public relations agencies are established, and practitioners demonstrate more sophistication and integration of public relations strategies and tactics. This stage is marked by tremendous growth in public relations practice. Because industry often becomes convinced of the value of well-crafted promotion and publicity, public relations professionals gain more influence in organizations.

The growth of public relations agencies occurred in the United States in the latter half of the 20th century (for a summary, see Miller, 1998). Institutionalization has also been the case in other parts of the world, especially Western Europe, where public relations as an organizational communication function is fast becoming an invaluable tool for organizations as they adapt to the complexities of the European Union (Haug & Koppang, 1997). Major corporations, small businesses, and even nonprofit organizations also have institutionalized the public relations function in Europe. These societal practices pave the way for maturation of the field.

Maturation

The maturation stage captures the use of research and strategic planning. It is also the beginning of public relations management functions and processes. In the maturing field of public relations, technological advances will bring new media to the forefront of practice (Johnson, 1997). New technologies and the use of computer networks will set the groundwork for the global information revolution. As a field, public relations grows by meeting the challenges brought on by changing technology, advances in theory, and activist social movements that dramatically change the organization-public relationship (L. A. Grunig, 1992).

In the United States, by the mid-1960s public relations was coming into its own as a profession. Educational institutions were offering public relations courses through schools of journalism and mass communication. Books and journals on public relations tactics are now readily available. The Public Relations Society of America was founded in 1948, and professional organizations have been founded in many other nations around the world to improve the quality of public relations practice.

Organizations with established public relations programs will always continue to be concerned with publicity and promotion, but they are also moving beyond publicity to encompass strategic planning and research. In this stage, practitioners recognize their contributions to society and to the organizations they serve. Public relations counseling thus becomes recognized as vital expertise (J. E. Grunig, 1992). Today, in the maturation phase, academic education, in addition to experience, is a necessity for entry to the field. Thus one way to develop public relations is to establish the parameters for a professional practice and field of study. Standards for public relations education exist in diverse nations, including the United Kingdom (Hatfield, 1994) and the United Arab Emirates (Creedon, Al-Khaja, & Kruckeberg, 1995), among others (Pratt & Ogbondah, 1996). The next stage of historical development is also the beginning of the development of public relations as a social science.

Professionalization

The current stage of public relations development is that of professionalization. This stage reflects public relations practice for the 21st century as a complexity of management and technical functions focused on the building of strategic relationships for mutual benefit (J. E. Grunig, 1992). In this stage, practitioners and academics will together build upon the body of knowledge and work for the refinement of the practice. From the late 1980s through today, scholars have worked to explain how organizations can balance their interests with those of the communities around them (Kruckeberg & Starck, 1988). Organizations realize they can no longer dominate the public discourse as they had grown accustomed to doing. The goal of the profession, some scholars argue, is to develop public relations as communication management. Much of this research reflects the framework of two-way symmetrical communication (Grunig, 1976), which we discuss below in the section on major lines of research.

This overview of the historical development of public relations shows that the field has shaped, and been shaped by, a variety of societal factors. In the next section we outline the parameters of the academic area of public relations.

TODAY'S PUBLIC RELATIONS: PARAMETERS OF THE DISCIPLINE

Public relations scholarship examines the theory and practice of communication between organizations and key publics. Many different definitions of public relations have been offered, but it is generally accepted that public relations is strategic communication between an organization and its publics. Practitioners, the organizations in which they work, and the dynamics of organization-public relationships are the subjects of scholarly study in public relations. Practitioner roles include technicians who write public relations materials, managers who direct and counsel organizational communication efforts, and public relations agency members who span both of these role boundaries. Organizations that are the subjects of study include nonprofits, corporations, national governments, unions, and activist and social cause organizations.

The major framework that has guided public relations scholarship over the past decade has focused on symmetrical communication between organizations and publics (J. E. Grunig, 1989; L. A. Grunig, 1992; Grunig & Grunig, 1992; Grunig & Hunt, 1984). However, public relations researchers follow many diverse paths. A look at any conference program of the International Communication Association, the National Communication Association, or the Association of Educators in Journalism and Mass Communication reveals that public relations scholarship has examined such topics as theory development, crisis and risk communication, gender, technician and manager skills, communication with internal publics, the integrated marketing communication function of public relations, international practices and theory building, issues management, new technologies, activism, and social marketing.

The Public Relations Division is a relatively recent addition to the ICA—it gained divisional status in 1996—and many members had previously been involved in the Mass Communication and Organizational Communication Divisions. Members of the Public Relations Division include representatives from more than 20 nations, and many of the division's international members work in government positions. The field of public relations grew out of journalism and mass-media research, and in many parts of the world public relations is taught under the rubric of political science or journalism. However, in the past 15 years it has also been studied within a communication framework (see Van Slyke Turk &

Botan, 1999). The ICA Public Relations Division shares a focus on the formation, attitudes, and actions of publics with many other divisions. The work of division members encompasses ideas and theories from interpersonal communication, organizational communication, mass communication, political communication, international and development communication, and health communication. The relationships of the Public Relations Division with other divisions reflect the importance of organization-publics relationships and the mediated globalization of communication. Links between the Public Relations Division and other divisions of the ICA will no doubt develop further as advances in information technologies bring people together.

In public relations research there is an acceptance of systems theory as one organizing framework. Social science theories ground much of the research. Research has traditionally focused on the creators of organizational messages; however, as interpersonal theory, relationship building, and symbolic interactionism become more prevalent, public relations theory will become more public oriented. Indeed, there has been a movement to put the "public" back in public relations research (Karlberg, 1996; Ledingham & Bruning, 1998). Theories such as co-orientation theory (Broom, 1977; Johnson, 1989), persuasion and social learning theories (Bandura, 1977; McGuire, 1989), game theory (Murphy, 1989), and contingency theory (Cancel, Cameron, Sallot, & Mitrook, 1997) all contribute to public relations theory and research.

The conceptual links between the practice of public relations and scholarship in this field show that each area benefits from understanding the other. Public relations scholarship benefits when practitioners incorporate current theory and research into their actions. Similarly, public relations practices are improved when they are based on the most current theory and lines of research (Hazelton & Botan, 1989). In the next section we examine the lines of research within public relations that show the convergence of public relations practice with public relations scholarship.

MAJOR LINES OF RESEARCH

Generally, public relations scholars publish in journals such as *Public Relations Review, Journal of Public Relations Research,* and *Journalism & Mass Communication Quarterly.* In a recent bibliometric analysis, Robert Heath was identified as the most-published author, and the institutions with the greatest impacts on the field were identified as the University of Maryland, San Diego State University, the University of Houston, and the University of Georgia (Pasadeos, Renfro, & Hanily, 1999). Although there may be some debate about the major lines of research, topics of most interest for ICA members include symmetrical communication, public relations roles, issues management, negotiation, publics, international practices, and public relations and communications technology. We discuss each of these briefly below.

Public Relations and Two-Way Symmetrical Communication

Efforts to advance two-way symmetrical communication or models of public relations span a period of more than 20 years. Grunig (1976) first explored the communication behaviors of public relations practitioners. That study was successful at correlating types of organizations with the two types of public relations communication behaviors. The relationships in the data, however, did not fit a logical pattern that could be explained by two types of public relations communication behavior.

Grunig (1984) then reconceptualized the communication behaviors to result in four models of public relations. *One-way* versus *two-way* alludes to the *direction* of communication: One-way disseminates information, and two-way exchanges information. *Asymmetrical* versus *symmetrical* refers to the *purpose* of public relations as an unbalanced communication relationship between organizations and publics whereby organizations attempt to change publics. *Symmetrical* can also be used to describe a balanced organization-public communication relationship, wherein either the organization or the public can adjust the relationship. The direction and purpose of communication form the theoretical assumptions underlying this line of research.

Grunig and Hunt (1984) conceptualized four models as historical stages in the development of public relations practice in the United States: press agentry, public information, two-way asymmetrical, and two-way symmetrical. The press agentry model depicts public relations as the dissemination of information for propaganda purposes (one-way and asymmetrical). In the public information model, public relations is the dissemination of information, with truth being more important (one-way and asymmetrical). Public relations in the two-way asymmetrical model is the one-way dissemination of scientific-based information for persuasion (one-way and asymmetrical). The two-way symmetrical model characterizes public relations practice as the mutual exchange of information, between the organization and public, for understanding and adjustment of the organization-public relationship (two-way and symmetrical).

J. E. Grunig (1989) reformulated the assumptions of these four models as worldviews. The press agentry, public information, and two-way asymmetrical models were identified as craft and scientific versions that reflect the dominant worldview of public relations. The two-way symmetrical model has been represented as an emerging worldview of public relations practice and, according to Grunig (1992), is the only truly balanced model of communication between organizations and publics. Grunig and White (1992) have further explained the philosophical assumptions underlying the symmetrical worldview. Presuppositions of symmetrical communication include equality, autonomy, innovation, decentralization of management, responsibility, conflict resolution, and interest group liberalism (J. E. Grunig, 1992). These presuppositions constitute a normative model of effective two-way communication between organizations and publics. Dozier,

Grunig, and Grunig (1995) and Deatherage and Hazelton (1998) tested the worldviews and found that support exists for symmetrical to be a normative model of effective public relations.

Internationally, Grunig and Hunt's models continue to be taught and practiced as a framework for effective public relations. However, because Grunig and Hunt's models were developed by Americans to explain American practices, they may need to be modified if they are to describe fully all of the different international public relations practices. Progress has been made in the internationalization of the models of public relations. Two additions to the models of public relations include Sriramesh's (1992, 1996) personal influence model and Huang's (1990) cultural interpreter framework. These two new models capture the dynamics of public relations in high power distance nations that are in the early stages of economic and political development. One of the most important parts of the symmetrical framework is that it argues for the inclusion of public relations managers in the organizational leadership. How successful has public relations been in breaking into the top echelons of organizational decision making? The line of research concerning public relations roles explores this issue.

Public Relations Roles

One of the most fully developed areas of public relations research addresses practitioner roles and functions (Dozier & Broom, 1995; Lauzen, 1994). Broom and Smith (1979) and Broom (1982) first developed a schema for identifying public relations roles. After significant research, Dozier (1984) and Broom and Dozier (1986) further refined the conceptualization of public relations roles. In general, public relations professionals fall into one of two categories: technicians or managers. At the most basic level of analysis, public relations students are taught that technicians "provide technical services such as writing, editing, photography, media contacts, or production of publications," whereas public relations managers "plan and direct public relations programs" (Hunt & Grunig, 1994, p. 4).

Dozier (1992) has argued that roles research is useful for understanding the development of public relations because "roles are not only useful as descriptors of what practitioners do in organizations, they are powerful theoretical and empirical links between concepts in a model of the public relations function" (pp. 334-335). That is, the differentiated roles of public relations professional have traditionally served as the link between describing the practice of public relations and the intellectual development and advancement of the field. The roles of public relations technicians and managers, however, are not static, and many technician tasks may become part of the management function (Napoli, Taylor, & Powers, 1999). As Newsom, Turk, and Kruckeberg (1996) observe, "While most public relations practitioners accept the idea of there being distinct technician and manager roles due to a variety of activities that public relations incorporates, in reality public relations practitioners juggle the two roles simultaneously most of the time" (p. 20). Exciting recent research into public relations roles points to the emergence of an agency role that combines parts of the technician and manager roles (Toth, Serini, Wright, & Emig, 1998).

Internationally, public relations roles research offers a unique perspective on the development of the field in other nations. For instance, in Thailand, managers often perform tasks very much like those performed by technicians (Ekachai & Komolsevin, 1996). Regardless of the nation of practice, roles research shows the level of acceptance that public relations professionals experience in their organizations; it also shows the development of the profession. Why is it so important for practitioners to be accepted into the dominant coalitions in their organizations? Public relations as a strategic management function helps organizations to understand their environments more fully, and, as we show in the next subsection, issues management is a necessary part of successful relationship building with publics.

Public Relations and Issues Management

In 20 short years, issues management has emerged as a dynamic area of study in public relations (Heath, 1990, 1994, 1998; Heath & Nelson, 1986; Renfro, 1993). Private sector executives, practitioners, and scholars from diverse disciplines have advanced a body of literature that in 1990 included more than 240 articles, books, and featured topics essential to the practice of issues management (Heath & Cousino, 1990). Perhaps the easiest way to explain issues management is to elaborate on the two words that make up this term. An issue, as Crable and Vibbert (1985) note, is a question that is talked about in public. A policy is the answer to that question, or a way to manage it. Issues management is how organizations participate in and shape issue resolution.

Jones and Chase (1979) presented the first model of issues management as a proactive public relations venture to participate in the formation of public policy. Chase (1984) later refined and developed the issues management model. Generally, the Jones and Chase model integrated line and staff functions within a systems process for public issue and public policy management (see Jones & Chase, 1979, p. 9). Specifically grounded in systems theory and sensitivity to the environment, the model includes five distinct steps: issue identification, issue analysis, issue change strategy options, issue action program, and evaluation of results. The organization-public relationship is at the center of this line of research.

Research has looked at environmental scanning (Lauzen, 1995), the relationship between public relations and issues management (Gaunt & Ollenburger, 1995; Lauzen, 1997), uses of technology (Ramsey, 1993), and the mediation of organizational environments (Lauzen & Dozier, 1992, 1994). Heath (1997) reflects on and expands much of the research and theory about issues management in his book *Strategic Issues Management,* and this work, along with Lauzen's (1997), describes the link between public relations and issues management as most significant when organizations practice a two-way communication model of public relations.

The issues management literature demonstrates that research perspectives range from the systems approach to a strategic approach to a rhetorical orientation. The systems approach involves organizational environmental scanning, identification, and monitoring of issues. The strategic reduction of uncertainty approach emphasizes organizational action and decision-making behavior through strategic issues diagnosis. The rhetorical approach focuses on organizational participation in the public policy process through issues status management. Each of these approaches is regularly studied and practiced in public relations, and issues management is one of the areas of public relations that best show the convergence of scholarship with communication practice.

Public Relations as Negotiation

Research interest in public relations as negotiation was initially related to the advancement of the two-way symmetrical model of public relations. Grunig and Grunig (1992) present a review of theories of negotiation and conflict resolution in an attempt to generate support for the symmetrical model as both a normative and a positive model. These authors do not articulate a view of public relations as negotiation; rather, they "review theories of dispute resolution, negotiation, mediation, and conflict management . . . because of the similarities in the presuppositions of these theories and those of the symmetrical model" (p. 313). More recent research has examined negotiation tactics as they apply to public relations practice (Plowman, Briggs, & Huang, 2000).

Vasquez (1996) has conceptualized an issue development approach to public relations as negotiation based on the role and function of public relations professionals as organizational boundary spanners. Boundary spanners are representatives of the organization "whose activities place them at organization boundaries for the purpose of effecting transactions with the environment" (Adams, 1976, p. 1176). An issue development perspective on public relations as negotiation reconceptualizes public relations activities as attempts to negotiate the organization-public relationship through the construction of frames of information that define and redefine the relationship. The frames of information are conceptualized and constructed based on the issue development process of naming, blaming, and claiming, and may or may not include organizational use of arguments, cases, and multiple agenda items. Further, these frames of information contain explicit and implicit messages about organizational values, images, and issues. At the heart of the negotiation literature is the acceptance of the public as an important part of any public relations communication.

Publics in the Public Relations Process

There is a rich tradition of discussion about the formation of publics in the social sciences. John Dewey (1927) defines a public as a group of people who (a) face a similar problem, (b) recognize the problem exists, and (c) organize to do something about the problem. Two programs of research characterize the public relations research interest in publics. The first takes the approach that publics react to problems in their environments and then become active. Grunig (1976, 1978, 1982, 1983a, 1983b, 1987) has advanced a situational theory of publics. Situational theory defines eight publics that indicate when communication should be directed to a public based on the publics' information-processing and information-seeking behaviors. Situational theory provides for the precise identification and segmentation of a public based on a pattern of similar behaviors defined through independent and dependent variables: Problem recognition, constraint recognition, and level of involvement constitute the independent variables; information-seeking and information-processing behaviors constitute the dependent variables. Overall, Grunig's (1989; Grunig & Hunt, 1984) research has identified four enduring types of publics: An all-issue public is active on all issues, an apathetic public is inattentive to all issues, a single-issue public is active on one or a small set of issues that concern a portion of the population (e.g., save the whales), and a hot-issue public is active on those issues that involve nearly everyone (e.g., drunk driving, toxic waste).

The second program of research takes the approach that publics are active and cocreate issues in the environment. Vasquez (1993, 1994, 1995) argues for a *Homo narrans* paradigm for public relations by combining Bormann's symbolic convergence theory and Grunig's situational theory of publics. This paradigm attempts to understand how individuals first become and then function as a public, thus providing a communication-based explanation for the emergence of a public.

Vasquez (1993, 1994, 1995), extending Dewey, explains how a public comes into existence through a five-stage cycle of participation behaviors, activities, and processes unique to the dynamics of a public. As individuals progress through stages of the model, participation behaviors and communication processes change to indicate a different stage in the model. In the first stage, *formation*, a small set of individuals are concerned about an issue or problem that directly or indirectly affects them. These individuals then seek to establish *connections* between themselves and others affected by or interested in the issue. In essence, the issue is framed and reframed to gain the support of key individuals or groups and may include any concerns or subissues others seek to have addressed. This growing entity of concerned individuals attempts to generate mass *discussion* of the issue through widespread dissemination of information about the nature of the issue and proposed solutions. More and more people become involved in the issue through participation in the framing, reframing, and development of opposing viewpoints and solutions to the issue. The media also engage in framing and reframing activities around the group of concerned individuals and the issue. Media reports, however, dichotomize and polarize the frames and reflect an evolving explanation of the issue and proposed solution. Individual and media participation in the process of framing and reframing eventually evolves opposing viewpoints and solutions for the issue. Any individual interested in the issues can reach a *determination* to support or oppose a proposed solution to the issue that is consistent with the cases, arguments, and multiple agenda items that define the frame and viewpoint of the issue. As some form of action is taken on the issue, the issue is resolved and individuals turn their attention to other problems or concerns that affect them. In essence, the individuals and groups who make up the collective public of this particular issue *dissolve* to reformulate around a different problem that affects them.

Vasquez's model further explains the active and cocreative nature of individuals by accounting for participation and cocreation features at each stage of the model. Publics are diverse, and levels of public participation in and interest in social and business issues vary across the world. In the next subsection we look at the current status of international public relations and the role that public relations plays in building organization-public relationships throughout the world.

International Public Relations

International public relations research represents one of the fastest-growing areas of research in this field. Taylor (2000) found that more than 70 articles have been written on this topic in the past decade. This area is important because as new communication technologies are developed and the globalization of business increases, more and more public relations practitioners will need to be able to communicate with a wide array of international audiences (Epley, 1992). Public relations communication with international publics is quickly becoming a reality for small and large organizations alike.

The growth of public relations research in this area has been attributed to the need for organizations to alter or negotiate relationships with publics (Botan, 1992). Moreover, because of the profession's research skills, public relations serves as the eyes, ears, and voice of organizations. As organizations move into the global economy, practitioners need to adjust so that they can see, listen to, and speak to international publics. The internationalization of public relations is both an opportunity and a challenge for professionals as well as scholars.

With globalization, public relations professionals are operating in intercultural contexts, and this gives us an opportunity to extend theory and research beyond American public relations. Public relations as a strategic communication and management function can positively affect the developing nations of the world. Development communication (Newsom, Carrell, & Kruckeberg, 1993), nation building (Taylor, 1998; Taylor & Botan, 1997; VanLeuven, 1996), and public diplomacy (Kunczik, 1990; Signitzer & Coombs, 1992) all draw on public relations theory. But there are also challenges for the internationalization of public relations; these include dealing with issues of social culture, linguistic determinism, and media development, as well as questions of ethics.

The first and perhaps most important challenge lies in how public relations relates to the cultures of varying societies (Grunig, Grunig, Sriramesh, Huang, &

Lyra, 1995; Sriramesh, 1992, 1996). Sriramesh and White (1992) suggest that international public relations needs to reflect the cultural and societal norms of host nations. This will create public relations situations that are unique to each society. A second obstacle is language. Key public relations messages need to be checked and rechecked for their appropriateness for international audiences. Everyone remembers the Nova manufactured by Chevrolet and its demise in South America. It is only through research and cultural awareness that such a situation will not happen again. A third factor that will make practitioners rethink their assumptions about public relations is the level of media development in different nations. In many parts of the developing world, governments continue to dominate media ownership and content. Thus organizations may have to pay to have stories published or may have to work with less-than-credible media. This will change the dynamics of media relations. Finally, issues of ethics will continue to challenge public relations practitioners in the international arena. Cultural variation, different norms of conduct, and different levels of social and political development all will demand different approaches to practice.

Just as the influence of globalization and internationalization on public relations provides exciting opportunities, so do developments in the area of communication technology.

Public Relations and Communications Technology

The newest area of public relations research concerns the uses of communications technology. Mitra (1997) suggests that the Internet is becoming a place where new publics form out of the connecting of individuals who might otherwise never communicate. Thus the Internet may be a way for public relations practitioners to reach traditionally isolated or geographically distant publics. The important point to remember in any treatment of public relations and communications technology is that the use of such technology does not have to create distance between an organization and its publics. Internet communication, for example, can include the "personal touch" that makes public relations effective.

Public relations practitioners and scholars have expressed great interest in the World Wide Web (Coombs, 1998; Esrock & Leichty, 1998; Heath, 1998; Kent & Taylor, 1998; Mickey, 1998; Neff, 1998). From a functional perspective, organizational Web sites and home pages serve as outlets for news releases, as opportunities for research, and as tools for dissemination of organizational information (Johnson, 1997). From a tactical perspective, Web sites also offer opportunities for immediate response to organizational problems and crises. The Internet is one more communication medium for public relations practitioners to utilize in their communication with important publics. But, for all its public relations potential, it still remains underutilized by many organizations and underexamined by scholars as a tool for building organizational-public relationships.

How can public relations professionals use the World Wide Web and other new communication technologies to their full potential? One answer may lie in an understanding of dialogic communication (Kent, 1998-1999; Kent & Taylor, 1998). The creation of effective dialogic relationships with publics necessarily requires just that: dialogue. Without a dialogic loop in Webbed communication, Internet public relations becomes nothing more than a new monologic communication medium, or a new marketing tool. The Web allows public relations practitioners the opportunity to create dynamic and lasting relationships with publics, but doing so requires that they incorporate dialogic loops into Web pages and Webbed communication. Public relations has many opportunities to shape the organization-public relationship, and further research is needed to advance the field.

Areas of Future Research

The lines of research addressed above are the major areas of study in the field of public relations. However, several other areas influence the direction of the field and will shape public relations practice and scholarship in the 21st century. For example, public relations as a community-building function has become a valuable framework for understanding the roles that public relations can play in helping organizations to serve the communities in which they operate (Kruckeberg & Starck, 1988). Ethics in public relations will also continue to receive both scholarly and professional attention.

Several approaches characterize the likely directions of future research, including but not limited to co-orientation (e.g., Broom, 1977), advocacy (e.g. Heath, 1997), professionalism (e.g., Bovet, 1993), game theory (e.g., Murphy, 1989), corporate responsibility (e.g., K. A. Leeper, 1996), accommodation (e.g., R. V. Leeper, 1996), and contingency theory (e.g., Cancel et al., 1997). Topical areas for the new millennium will encompass the role of public relations in society and examine ethics in intercultural/international contexts.

The convergence of academic and practitioner interests is most notable in discussions of such topics as professionalism, education, accreditation, technology and globalization of information, the relationship of public relations to marketing, and the role of theory. These topics are fundamental in the relationship between scholars and practitioners. Challenges remain despite discussions between and among scholars and practitioners. These issues provide the biggest challenges for the public relations discipline to shed its emerging status and to advance scholarship further.

One of the major issues for scholars, educators, and professionals in public relations is that of gender. The consideration of gender and its impact on women public relations practitioners is an important aspect of the field currently receiving scholarly attention (Aldoory, 1998; Creedon, 1991; Grunig, 1995; Serini, Toth, Wright, & Emig, 1997, 1998). Research shows that women continue to fall behind their male counterparts in many areas of the field. There are fewer opportunities for women in the highly desirable area of management, and often women are relegated to performing technician roles, even when they believe they are acting as managers (Hon, Grunig, & Dozier 1992). In a study of 200 public relations managers, Napoli et al. (1999) found that female managers spent approximately 9% more time writing—a technician task—compared with their male counterparts. But the news is not all bad. Serini et al. (1997) found that male and female practitioners in their sample appeared to be willing to respect each other and "to engage in dialogue on the issues in ways that will result in collaboration and benefits for both" sexes (p. 116).

After conducting a bibliometric study of the past 5 years of public relations research, Pasadeos et al. (1999) have concluded that scholars should expand the topical diversity of scholarship. Public relations research has been concentrated on concerns with two-way symmetrical communication, practitioner roles and functions, and issues management; as Pasadeos et al. note, "It would help the field greatly if some young scholars were to break with the current mold and undertake more audience-centered research" (p. 48). This call to focus on the public in research is also needed in the areas of crisis communication management, risk communication, investor relations, and fund-raising. Specialty areas of public relations practice—such as strategic planning, activism, labor, image and identity, health care, and political, educational, and government public relations—are also areas ripe for increased research. The incorporation of interpersonal communication theory and research into public relations scholarship is emerging as a leading area for future research (Broom, Casey, & Ritchey, 1997; Ledingham & Bruning, 1998). All of the areas we have mentioned can provide researchers with opportunities for increased insights into how public relations functions to build relationships with key publics.

Further, more research needs to be conducted using qualitative techniques. Most of the research undertaken thus far in public relations has applied quantitative methods and techniques. Given the call for topical diversity, the discipline could also benefit from methodological diversity. Scholars interested in quantitative techniques should adhere to Morton and Lin's (1995) suggestion for more rigorous quantitative investigations. Equally important, if public relations is to achieve topical and methodological diversity in the new millennium, journal editors and reviewers will need to be more accepting of such scholarship.

METATHEORETICAL ASSUMPTIONS FOR THE NEW MILLENNIUM

Theory and research in public relations, when viewed as a whole, have expanded by extension and intension. Theory development is a constant process of testing and formulating sets of concepts believed to explain how things operate (Littlejohn, 1992). Theories grow by extension, "piece-by-piece, moving from an understanding of one bit of reality to an adjoining bit by adding new concepts to the old" (Littlejohn, 1992, p. 28), or by intension, "the process of developing an increasingly precise understanding of individual concepts" (p. 28). Collectively, a body of literature has been advanced, but a fundamental question remains: What are the metatheoretical assumptions guiding public relations research into the new millennium?

A clear understanding of the metatheoretical foundations of public relations is needed. Such an understanding is important if we are to identify the overarching or metatheoretical assumptions framing research and theory development. A metatheoretical discussion of public relations research is important and appropriate because research has tended to focus on the development of definitions, techniques, structures, and procedures as well as general and related concepts. Littlejohn (1992) refers to this level of analysis as the hypothetical level. The hypothetical level, however, is framed by the more abstract and general assumptions of the metatheoretical level (p. 30). Given the emerging nature of public relations as a distinct social science, the examination and discussion of metatheoretical assumptions is long overdue.

Three major themes guide metatheoretical assumptions: ontology, epistemology, and axiology. Ontology accounts for questions of existence or the nature of the phenomena researchers seek to know. Epistemology concerns questions of knowledge, or how we know what we claim to know. Axiology addresses questions of value. As Littlejohn (1992) notes, "Epistemology and ontology go hand-in-hand because our conception of knowledge depends in part on the nature of the knowable" (p. 32). The three themes are not distinct entities. When discussing one theme, the scholar must always examine the other two. Let us now look more closely at how these themes frame public relations as an emerging social science discipline.

Public relations research reflects at least eight assumptions—three ontological, three epistemological, and two axiological—that will guide research for the new millennium. We have identified these assumptions inductively, through survey of the research, as opposed to deductively.

Ontological Assumptions

Public relations is by all accounts an emerging social science field of study. The close and growing relationships between the Public Relations Division and other ICA divisions will work to expand public relations as a social science field of study. Indeed, public relations as a field of study exists because both scholars and practitioners seek to better understand how organizations communicate with internal and external publics.

Public relations research and practice are inextricably intertwined. Public relations is both an academic discipline and a professional practice. The maturing of professional public relations practice has provided for the scientific examination of roles, functions, processes, ethics, strategies, and organizational responses to issues. Public relations is an academic area of study because scholars also seek to understand and critique organization-public relationships. Open communication between those who study public relations and those who work in the field will strengthen both areas.

Public relations scholarship is moving conceptually from a mass communication foundation to a relationship-building orientation. With this conceptual move comes a new emphasis on understanding the communication dynamics of relationship building. Scholars can examine the roles of public relations practitioners in their relationships with organizational leaders, analyze the media's roles in shaping relationships, understand public reactions to organizational decisions, and study how language shapes relationships. Although there is considerable value in the past research traditions, the body of knowledge could benefit from the work of new researchers and the application of new research perspectives. Research will be strengthened if it can move away from an organization-centric model and focus on relationship building. As scholars focus more on relationships, public relations will become more valued as a framework for understanding and extending communication research.

Epistemological Assumptions

Public relations examines the relationships between organizations and publics. Organizations can include nonprofits, corporations, national governments, unions, and activist and social cause organizations. Analysis focuses on the boundary-spanning experiences, training, and competencies of practitioners in the field at all levels of responsibility.

Knowledge about public relations is gained through all research methods and techniques available. Research using focus groups, interviews, survey research, and experiments has shown that public relations scholars are working both to describe and to predict the development of organization-public relationships. There has been a preference for quantitative approaches, and there is a need for more rigorous quantitative investigations (Morton & Lin, 1995). However, as the field follows the critical turn of other academic areas, more qualitative research—including rhetorical, critical, and feminist methodologies—will add to the knowledge base. Increasingly, public relations education will play an integral role in advancing the discipline and practice.

Axiological Assumptions

Public relations research and practice make vital contributions to society. Society could not exist without the exchange and examination of ideas that occur through public relations practice. The history of the practice demonstrates its immense contribution to the development of the United States. Institutions and organizations of society have benefited from the opportunity to publicize, promote, conduct research, participate in collaborative decision making, and be counseled in their relationships with other key individuals, groups, and institutions. The need for public relations will continue to grow due to rapid developments in technology, innovation in business processes, and the need for people and organizations to adjust to change.

The value of public relations research, both to society and as an academic field of study, is that it examines the organization-public relationship from a variety of vantage points. Whether one assumes a two-way symmetrical, issues management, best practices, publics-centered, or some new approach, the process and practice of public relationship building are enhanced. It is our hope that organizations and institutions will become better citizens of society and that communication will bring us together in our differences.

Directions for Public Relations in the New Millennium

The directions that public relations research should take in the next millennium are clear. There is convergence between the scholarly area of public relations and the practice. Public relations needs to move beyond its traditional lines of research and move toward additional explanatory theoretical frameworks. Interpersonal communication may provide one such framework (Broom et al., 1997; Ledingham & Bruning, 1998). The education of future scholars should be one of the most pressing concerns for the field. New Ph.D.s with backgrounds in public relations practice and in other social sciences will strengthen public relations research. The topics of licensing and accreditation also need to be addressed, for both pragmatic and philosophical reasons.

New ideas are needed in the field to address the various needs of practitioners and scholars alike. Open communication between those who study public relations and those who work in it will strengthen both areas. The Public Relations Division will continue to advance theory and practice. With the ICA's emphasis on globalization and internationalization, public relations will continue to benefit and contribute to the future of communication scholarship. Because public relations scholarship focuses on the building of mutually beneficial relationships, the discipline is well positioned to lead the way toward an understanding of the complex relationships that will be created in the new millennium.

REFERENCES

Adams, J. S. (1976). The structure and dynamics of behavior in organizational boundary roles. In M. D. Dunnette (Ed.), *Handbook of industrial and organizational psychology* (pp. 1175-1199). Chicago: Rand McNally.

Aldoory, L. (1998). The language of leadership for female public relations professionals. *Journal of Public Relations Research, 10,* 73-101.

Bandura, A. (1977). *Social learning theory.* Englewood Cliffs, NJ: Prentice Hall.

Bentele, G., & Peter, G. M. (1996). Public relations in the German Democratic Republic and the new Federal German States. In H. M. Culbertson & N. Chen (Eds.), *International public relations: A comparative analysis* (pp. 349-365). Mahwah, NJ: Lawrence Erlbaum.

Botan, C. H. (1992). International public relations: Critique and reformulation. *Public Relations Review, 18,* 149-159.

Bovet, S. F. (1993). The burning question of ethics: The profession fights for better business practices. *Public Relations Journal, 49*(11), 24-25, 29.

Broom, G. M. (1977). Co-orientation measurements of public issues. *Public Relations Review, 3*(4), 110-119.

Broom, G. M. (1982). A comparison of sex roles in public relations. *Public Relations Review, 8*(3), 17-22.

Broom, G. M., Casey, S., & Ritchey, J. (1997). Toward a concept and theory of organization-public relationships. *Journal of Public Relations Research, 9,* 83-98.

Broom, G. M., & Dozier, D. M. (1986). Advancement for public relations role models. *Public Relations Review, 12*(1), 37-56.

Broom, G. M., & Smith, G. D. (1979). Testing practitioner's impact on clients. *Public Relations Review, 5*(3), 22-28.

Cancel, A. E., Cameron, G. T., Sallot, L. M., & Mitrook, M. (1997). It depends: A contingency theory of accommodation in public relations. *Journal of Public Relations Research, 9,* 31-63.

Chase, H. (1984). *Issues management: Origins of the future.* Stamford, CT: Issue Action.

Chen, N. (1996). Public relations in China: Introduction of an occupational field. In H. M. Culbertson & N. Chen (Eds.), *International public relations: A comparative analysis* (pp. 121-153). Mahwah, NJ: Lawrence Erlbaum.

Coombs, W. T. (1998). The Internet as potential equalizer: New leverage for confronting social responsibility. *Public Relations Review, 24,* 289-303.

Crable, R. E., & Vibbert, S. L. (1985). Managing issues and influencing public policy. *Public Relations Review, 11*(2), 3-16.

Creedon, P. (1991). Public relations and "women's work": Toward a feminist analysis of public relations roles. *Public Relations Research Annual, 3,* 67-84.

Creedon, P., Al-Khaja, M. A. W., & Kruckeberg, D. (1995). Women and public relations education and practice in the United Arab Emirates. *Public Relations Review, 21,* 59-76.

Culbertson, H. M., & Chen, N. (Eds.). (1996). *International public relations: A comparative analysis.* Mahwah, NJ: Lawrence Erlbaum.

Cutlip, S. M. (1994). *The unseen power: Public relations, a history.* Hillsdale, NJ: Lawrence Erlbaum.

Cutlip, S. M. (1995). *Public relations history from the 17th to the 20th century: The antecedents.* Mahwah, NJ: Lawrence Erlbaum.

Cutlip, S. M., Center, A. H., & Broom, G. M. (1999). *Effective public relations* (8th ed.). Upper Saddle River, NJ: Prentice Hall.

Deatherage, C. P., & Hazelton, V., Jr. (1998). Effects of organizational worldviews on the practice of public relations: A test of the theory of public relations excellence. *Journal of Public Relations Research, 10,* 57-71.

Dewey, J. (1927). *The public and its problems.* Chicago: Swallow.

Dozier, D. M. (1984). Program evaluation and roles of practitioners. *Public Relations Review, 10*(2), 13-21.

Dozier, D. M. (1992). The organizational roles of communication and public relations practitioners. In J. E. Grunig (Ed.), *Excellence in public relations and communication management* (pp. 327-356). Hillsdale, NJ: Lawrence Erlbaum.

Dozier, D. M., & Broom, G. M. (1995). Evolution of the manager's role in public relations practice. *Journal of Public Relations Research, 7,* 3-26.

Dozier, D. M., Grunig, J. E., & Grunig, L. A. (1995). *Manager's guide to excellence in communication management.* Mahwah, NJ: Lawrence Erlbaum.

Ekachai, D., & Komolsevin, R. (1996). Public relations in Thailand: Its functions and practitioners' roles. In H. M. Culbertson & N. Chen (Eds.), *International public relations: A comparative analysis* (pp. 155-170). Mahwah, NJ: Lawrence Erlbaum.

Epley, J. S. (1992). Public relations in the global village: An American perspective. *Public Relations Review, 18,* 109-116.

Esrock, S. L., & Leichty, G. B. (1998). Social responsibility and corporate Web pages: Self-presentation or agenda-setting. *Public Relations Review, 24,* 305-319.

Gaunt, P., & Ollenburger, J. (1995). Issues management revisited: A tool that deserves another look. *Public Relations Review, 21,* 199-210.

Grunig, J. E. (1976). Organizations and public relations: Testing a communication theory. *Journalism Monographs, 46.*

Grunig, J. E. (1978). Defining publics in public relations: The case of a suburban hospital. *Journalism Quarterly, 55,* 109-118.

Grunig, J. E. (1982). The message-attitude-behavior relationship: Communication behaviors of organizations. *Communication Research, 9,* 163-200.

Grunig, J. E. (1983a). Communication behaviors and attitudes of environmental publics: Two studies. *Journalism Monographs, 81.*

Grunig, J. E. (1983b). Washington reporter publics of corporate public affairs programs. *Journalism Quarterly, 60,* 603-615.

Grunig, J. E. (1984). Organizations, environments, and models of public relations. *Public Relations Research and Education, 1*(1), 6-29.

Grunig, J. E. (1987, May). *When active publics become activists: Extending a situational theory of publics.* Paper presented at the annual meeting of the International Communication Association, Montreal.

Grunig, J. E. (1989). Symmetrical presuppositions as a framework for public relations theory. In C. H. Botan & V. Hazelton, Jr. (Eds.), *Public relations theory* (pp. 17-44). Hillsdale, NJ: Lawrence Erlbaum.

Grunig, J. E. (Ed.). (1992). *Excellence in public relations and communication management.* Hillsdale, NJ: Lawrence Erlbaum.

Grunig, J. E., & Grunig, L. A. (1992). Models of public relations and communication. In J. E. Grunig (Ed.), *Excellence in public relations and communication management* (pp. 285-325). Hillsdale, NJ: Lawrence Erlbaum.

Grunig, J. E., Grunig, L. A., Sriramesh, K., Huang, Y. H., & Lyra, A. (1995). Models of public relations in an international setting. *Journal of Public Relations Research, 7,* 163-186.

Grunig, J. E., & Hunt, T. (1984). *Managing public relations.* New York: Holt, Rinehart & Winston.

Grunig, J. E., & White, J. (1992). The effects of worldview on public relations theory and practice. In J. E. Grunig (Ed.), *Excellence in public relations and communication management* (pp. 31-64). Hillsdale, NJ: Lawrence Erlbaum.

Grunig, L. A. (1992). Activism and public relations. In J. E. Grunig (Eds.), *Excellence in public relations and communication management* (pp. 494-510). Hillsdale, NJ: Lawrence Erlbaum.

Grunig, L. A. (1995). The consequence of culture for public relations: The case of women in the foreign service. *Journal of Public Relations Research, 7,* 139-161.

Hatfield, C. R. (1994). Public relations education in the United Kingdom. *Public Relations Review, 20,* 189-199.

Haug, M., & Koppang, H. (1997). Lobbying and public relations in a European context. *Public Relations Review, 23,* 233-247.

Hazelton, V., Jr., & Botan, C. H. (1989). The role of theory in public relations. In C. H. Botan & V. Hazelton, Jr. (Eds.), *Public relations theory* (pp. 3-15). Hillsdale, NJ: Lawrence Erlbaum.

Heath, R. L. (1990). Corporate issues management: Theoretical underpinnings and research foundations. In J. E. Grunig & L. A. Grunig (Eds.), *Public relations annual 2* (pp. 29-65). Hillsdale, NJ: Lawrence Erlbaum.

Heath, R. L. (1994, May). *Issues management: The unfinished agenda.* Paper presented at the annual meeting of the International Communication Association, Sydney.

Heath, R. L. (1997). *Strategic issues management: Organizations and public policy challenges.* Thousand Oaks, CA: Sage.

Heath, R. L. (1998). New communication technologies: An issues management point of view. *Public Relations Review, 24,* 273-288.

Heath, R. L., & Cousino, K. R. (1990). Issue management: End of first decade progress report. *Public Relations Review, 16*(1), 6-18.

Heath, R. L., & Nelson, R. A. (1986). *Issue management: Corporate public policy making in an information society.* Beverly Hills, CA: Sage.

Hon, L., Grunig, L. A., & Dozier, D. M. (1992). Women in public relations: Problems and opportunities. In J. E. Grunig (Ed.), *Excellence in public relations and communication management* (pp. 419-438). Hillsdale, NJ: Lawrence Erlbaum.

Huang, Y. H. (1990). *Risk communication, models of public relations, and anti-nuclear activism: A case study of nuclear power in Taiwan.* Unpublished master's thesis, University of Maryland, College Park.

Hunt, T., & Grunig, J. E. (1994). *Public relations techniques.* New York: Holt, Rinehart & Winston.

Johnson, D. J. (1989). The coorientation model and consultant roles. In C. H. Botan & V. Hazelton, Jr. (Eds.), *Public relations theory* (pp. 243-264). Hillsdale, NJ: Lawrence Erlbaum.

Johnson, M. A. (1997). Public relations and technology: Practitioner perspectives. *Journal of Public Relations Research, 9,* 213-236.

Jones, B. L., & Chase, W. H. (1979). Managing public policy issues. *Public Relations Review, 7*(2), 3-23.

Karlberg, M. (1996). Remembering the public in public relations research: From theoretical to operational symmetry. *Journal of Public Relations Research, 8,* 263-278.

Kent, M. L. (1998-1999). Does your Website attract or repel customers? *Public Relations Quarterly, 43*(2), 31-33.

Kent, M. L., & Taylor, M. (1998). Building dialogic relationships through the World Wide Web. *Public Relations Review, 24,* 321-334.

Kruckeberg, D., & Starck, K. (1988). *Public relations and community: A reconstructed theory.* New York: Praeger.

Kunczik, M. (1990). *Images of nations and international public relations.* Bonn, Germany: Friedrich-Ebert Stiftung.

Lauzen, M. M. (1994). Public relations practitioner role enactment in issue management. *Journalism Quarterly, 71,* 356-369.

Lauzen, M. M. (1995). Toward a model of environmental scanning. *Journal of Public Relations Research, 7,* 187-203.

Lauzen, M. M. (1997). Understanding the relation between public relations and issues management. *Journal of Public Relations Research, 9,* 65-82.

Lauzen, M. M., & Dozier, D. M. (1992). The missing link: The public relations manager role as mediator of organizational environments and power consequences for the function. *Journal of Public Relations Research, 4,* 205-220.

Lauzen, M. M., & Dozier, D. M. (1994). Issues management mediation of linkages between environmental complexity and management of the public relations function. *Journal of Public Relations Research, 6,* 163-184.

Ledingham, J., & Bruning, S. (1998). Relationship management in public relations: Dimensions of an organization-public relationship. *Public Relations Review, 24,* 55-65.

Leeper, K. A. (1996). Public relations ethics and communitarianism: A preliminary investigation. *Public Relations Review, 22,* 163-179.

Leeper, R. V. (1996). Moral objectivity, Jürgen Habermas' discourse ethics and public relations. *Public Relations Review, 22,* 133-150.

Littlejohn, S. W. (1992). *Theories of human communication* (4th ed.). Belmont, CA: Wadsworth.

McGuire, W. J. (1989). Theoretical foundations of campaigns. In R. E. Rice & C. K. Atkin (Eds.), *Public communication campaigns* (2nd ed., pp. 43-65). Newbury Park, CA: Sage.

Mickey, T. J. (1998). Selling the Internet: A cultural studies approach to public relations. *Public Relations Review, 24,* 335-319.

Miller, K. S. (1998). *The voice of business: Hill and Knowlton and postwar public relations.* Chapel Hill: University of North Carolina Press.

Mitra, A. (1997). Diasporic Web sites: Ingroup and outgroup discourse. *Critical Studies in Mass Communication, 14,* 158-181.

Morton L. P., & Lin, L. Y. (1995). Content and citation analysis of public relations review. *Public Relations Review, 21,* 337-349.

Murphy, P. (1989). Game theory. In C. H. Botan & V. Hazelton, Jr. (Eds.), *Public relations theory* (pp. 173-192). Hillsdale, NJ: Lawrence Erlbaum.

Napoli, P., Taylor, M., & Powers, G. (1999). The writing activities of public relations practitioners: Relationships between task and experience. *Public Relations Review, 25,* 369-380.

Neff, B. D. (1998). Harmonizing global relations: A speech act theory. *Public Relations Review, 24,* 351-376.

Newsom, D., Carrell, B., & Kruckeberg, D. (1993). *Development communication as a public relations campaign.* Paper presented at the meeting of the Association for the Advancement of Policy, Research, and Development in the Third World, Cairo.

Newsom, D., Turk, J., & Kruckeberg, D. (1996). *This is PR.* Belmont, CA: Wadsworth.

Pasadeos, Y. R., Renfro, R. B., & Hanily, M. L. (1999). Influential authors and works in public relations scholarly literature: A network of recent research. *Journal of Public Relations Research, 11,* 29-52.

Pimlott, J. A. R. (1951). *Public relations and American democracy.* Princeton, NJ: Princeton University Press.

Plowman, K. D., Briggs, W. G., & Huang, Y.-H. (2000). Public relations and conflict resolution. In R. L. Heath & G. M. Vasquez (Eds.), *Handbook of public relations.* Thousand Oaks, CA: Sage.

Pratt, C., & Ogbondah, C. W. (1996). International public relations education: U.S. issues and perceptions. In H. M. Culbertson & N. Chen (Eds.), *International public relations: A comparative analysis* (pp. 361-395). Mahwah, NJ: Lawrence Erlbaum.

Ramsey, S. A. (1993). Issues management and the use of technologies in public relations. *Public Relations Review, 19,* 261-275.

Renfro, W. L. (1993). *Issues management in strategic planning.* Westport, CT: Quorum.

Serini, S. A., Toth, E. L., Wright, D. K., & Emig, A. G. (1997). Watch for falling glass . . . : Women, men, and job satisfaction in public relations: A preliminary analysis. *Journal of Public Relations Research, 9,* 99-118.

Serini, S. A., Toth, E. L., Wright, D. K., & Emig, A. G. (1998). Power, gender, and public relations: Sexual harassment as a threat to the practice. *Journal of Public Relations Research, 10,* 193-218.

Signitzer, B. H., & Coombs, T. (1992). Public relations and public diplomacy: Conceptual convergences. *Public Relations Review, 18,* 137-147.

Sriramesh, K. (1992). Societal culture and public relations: Ethnographic evidence from India. *Public Relations Review, 18,* 201-211.

Sriramesh, K. (1996). Power distance and public relations: An ethnographic study of southern Indian organizations. In H. M. Culbertson & N. Chen (Eds.), *International public relations: A comparative analysis* (pp. 171-190). Mahwah, NJ: Lawrence Erlbaum.

Sriramesh, K., Kim, Y., & Takasaki, M. (1999). Public relations in three Asian cultures: An analysis. *Journal of Public Relations Research, 11,* 271-292.

Sriramesh, K., & White, J. (1992). Societal culture and public relations. In J. E. Grunig (Ed.), *Excellence in public relations and communication management* (pp. 597-616). Hillsdale, NJ: Lawrence Erlbaum.

Taylor, M. (1998). Nation building as strategic communication management: An analysis of campaign planner intent in Malaysia. In L. Lederman (Ed.), *Communication theory: A reader* (pp. 287-293). Dubuque, IA: Kendall Hunt.

Taylor, M. (2000). International public relations: Opportunities and challenges for the 21st century. In R. L. Heath & G. M. Vasquez (Eds.), *Handbook of public relations.* Thousand Oaks, CA: Sage.

Taylor, M., & Botan, C. H. (1997). Public relations campaigns for national development in the Pacific Rim: The case of public education in Malaysia. *Australian Journal of Communication, 24*(2), 115-130.

Toth, E. L., Serini, S. A., Wright, D. K., & Emig, A. G. (1998). Trends in public relations roles: 1990-1995. *Public Relations Review, 24,* 145-163.

VanLeuven, J. K. (1996). Public relations in Southeast Asia: From nation building campaigns to regional interdependency. In H. M. Culbertson & N. Chen (Eds.), *International public relations: A comparative analysis* (pp. 207-221). Mahwah, NJ: Lawrence Erlbaum.

Van Slyke Turk, J., & Botan, C. H. (Eds.). (1999). Education [Special issue]. *Public Relations Review, 25*(1).

Vasquez, G. M. (1993). A *Homo narrans* paradigm for public relations: Combining Bormann's symbolic convergence theory and Grunig's situational theory of publics. *Journal of Public Relations Research, 5,* 201-216.

Vasquez, G. M. (1994). Testing a communication theory-method-message-behavior complex for the investigation of publics. *Journal of Public Relations Research, 6,* 267-291.

Vasquez, G. M. (1995). *Negotiating public relationships: The co-creation of issues.* Unpublished doctoral dissertation, Purdue University.

Vasquez, G. M. (1996). Public relations as negotiation: An issue development perspective. *Journal of Public Relations Research, 8,* 57-77.

Vercic, D., Grunig, L. A., & Grunig, J. E. (1996). Global and specific principles of public relations: Evidence from Slovenia. In H. M. Culbertson & N. Chen (Eds.), *International public relations: A comparative analysis* (pp. 31-65). Mahwah, NJ: Lawrence Erlbaum.

Wilcox, D. L., Ault, P., & Agee, W. K. (1998). *Public relations: Strategies and tactics.* New York: HarperCollins.

CHAPTER CONTENTS

15 The Complexities of Feminism in Communication Scholarship Today

LINDA ALDOORY
University of Maryland

ELIZABETH L. TOTH
Syracuse University

This chapter describes directions for feminist scholarship in communication today, what these directions mean for the state of the art in feminist scholarship, and how research can be advanced to expand the understanding of feminism and communication. Nine streams of research are highlighted: historical and prediction essays, methodological and epistemological issues, knowledge and identity, media representations and political economy, the audience, interpersonal discourse and rhetoric, workplace issues, pedagogy and academia, and new technologies. The chapter concludes with specific suggestions for moving research toward accomplishing diverse methodology and improving women's lives.

D IVERSE opinions govern feminist scholarship in communication today. There are several ways to do research and to think about feminism, and most feminist scholars endorse the dialogue and complexities that these many voices spark. Our purpose in this chapter is to describe some current directions of feminist scholarship in communication, what these directions mean for the state of the art in feminist scholarship, and how this research can be advanced to expand our understanding of feminism and communication.

In 1913, Rebecca West defined feminism with the following statement: "I myself have never been able to find out precisely what feminism is: I only know that people call me a feminist whenever I express sentiments that differentiate me

AUTHORS' NOTE: We want to thank the members of the Feminist Scholarship Division who responded to our inquiries, because this chapter could not have been written without them. Special appreciation goes to Rashmi Luthra and Dafna Lemish, chairs of the division, for their valuable contributions to earlier drafts.

Correspondence: Linda Aldoory, Department of Communication, 2130 Skinner Building, University of Maryland, College Park, MD 20742-7635; e-mail la74@umail.umd.edu

Communication Yearbook 24, pp. 345-361

from a doormat" (West, 1913/1982). More than 80 years later, feminist scholars still have difficulty agreeing on any more than this as a definition of feminism. Many suggest that feminism is rooted in choice and self-determination and does not prescribe one "official" position (Foss, Foss, & Griffin, 1999). Others offer at the minimum a general understanding of what feminism is. For example, Liesbet van Zoonen (1994) states, "Gender and power, although both very much in debate, form the constituents of feminist theory" (p. 4). Angharad Valdivia (1995) defines feminism as "the theoretical study of women's oppression and the strategical and political ways that all of us, building on that theoretical and historical knowledge, can work to end that oppression" (p. 8). Many feminists have expanded feminism to include fighting against oppression of all people who are marginalized by a dominant culture, "including but not limited to people of color, people with disabilities, people of different ages and socioeconomic classes, and lesbians and gay men" (Foss et al., 1999, p. 2). Ramona Rush and Autumn Grubb-Swetnam (1996) define a feminist as "a person who believes in equal rights for everyone, including women, and when women are denied their rights, especially women" (p. 499).

The scholarship defined as feminist has many of the same complexities. Cirksena (1996) and many others, however, have offered general themes or principles that they say characterize feminist research. The more common themes include (a) explicit attention to inequitable power dimensions of gender relations; (b) discussions of gender along with other identities, such as race and class; (c) sensitivity to research participants' lives and ensuring diversity among participants (Foss & Ray, 1996); (d) critiquing and reconceptualizing androcentric methods and theory (Foss & Ray, 1996); (e) "action-oriented" research and findings linked to improving the status of women or women's everyday lives; and (f) giving research participants roles in the research design and process.

The goals of feminist research have also differed, usually according to the political and philosophical traditions from which the feminist researchers come: liberal, radical, Marxist, neo-Marxist, socialist. Added to these traditions are newer movements in ecofeminism, postcolonialism, and postmodernism, among others. These traditions, then, create many goals that have been elaborated by feminist scholars: equality and parity of work-related opportunities and status; complete transformation of dominant systems guiding work, family, media, and so on; women gaining power positions or separate domains of society; publishing within mainstream communication journals; and practical action research.

Some feminist researchers have argued that certain goals for U.S. white women in communication have been accomplished, and that these women have achieved some measure of equality, opportunities, and visibility in many professions. Feminist researchers often acknowledge these gains and pursue the study of them further. At the same time, however, researchers acknowledge that there are still significant gaps. Donna Allen, Ramona R. Rush, and Susan J. Kaufman (1996) assert: "So many of us still are kept in stages and cages of frustration, oppression, repression, depression, legislation, litigation, isolation, humiliation, mutilation, while waiting and hoping for far more than 'just a moment, please' of recognition"

(p. xi). Some feminist researchers and others sensitive to feminist research are beginning to work on these discrepancies by engaging in active research to transform the dominant norms. Angharad Valdivia (1995) writes, "A major additional lesson learned by dominant culture feminist scholars, or one that, as Haraway (1985) notes, they 'were forced kicking and screaming to notice' . . . , was that the term *women* applied to differently situated individuals" (p. 9). The number of published feminist works in communication addressing women of color, however, still lags significantly behind the number addressing white women. In addition, one member of the International Communication Associations's Feminist Scholarship Division (FSD) who was part of a listserv discussion about this chapter reminded us that "white" feminists from outside North America are also often ignored owing to the U.S. focus in communication research.

These complexities of feminism and the differing goals of feminist scholarship have meant that feminist scholars do not seek one overarching theory. Feminist scholarship addresses several communication theories in many different areas, such as mass communication, organizational communication, interpersonal communication, and public relations, to name only a few. What has developed within the community of feminist scholars, which includes the ICA's Feminist Scholarship Division, is support for communicating with many voices about differences. Our mapping of this terrain here, with the help of FSD members' comments on our preliminary ideas, includes some discussion of the directions in feminist research since 1996. We then address some current streams of research for communication scholars in other areas, for those who want to teach feminist studies and conduct further research, and for new graduate student feminist scholars.

DIRECTIONS FOR FEMINIST RESEARCH

The traditional questions of gender and power, as well as current concerns among feminists, have led to certain directions in current scholarship. We note a few of these directions—suggested by published research, convention papers, and FSD members responding to our call for feedback—below.[1]

- Feminist scholars have made a genuine effort to move in an international direction and also to incorporate more diversity in their research with regard to participants, designs, and processes. Although difficult to do, this includes examining multiple identities for researchers and research participants and the combined impacts of gender, sexuality, class, education, race, and so on.
- Feminist scholars are challenging mainstream theories through the construction of new theory from marginalized perspectives (Foss & Ray, 1996; Hegde, 1996). They are exploring the contributions of marginalized and often underrepresented voices to transform the boundaries of communication theory (Foss & Ray, 1996, p. 253).
- Although interdisciplinarity is still a contested issue, many feminist scholars agree that feminist research should cut across a variety of journals and a broad

range of communication disciplines. One FSD member explained, "Our theory building needs attention from scholars less familiar with feminist theory." Another member commented, "If FSD members present papers in every division of ICA, exposure to feminist perspectives in the field will increase. . . . feminist research in these divisions will undoubtedly demonstrate alternative ideas and methods to the 'standard' routine."

- Praxis and studies of everyday life have changed the process as well as the goals of many feminist studies. Researchers are looking toward benefiting the research participants themselves. As one FSD member told us: "I think that the overarching need is to move beyond description and to study everyday life. I am thinking of some case studies in feminist leadership in the academy, for example. We need to understand the realities of leadership and the compromise it entails."

- Several FSD members talked about trying to move beyond purely descriptive studies, commentary alone, or "empty rhetoric," as one member put it. Instead, the focus should be on producing studies addressing theory, context, causes, production, and meaning or impact of communication systems on women's lives.

SOME CURRENT STREAMS OF RESEARCH

Over the past 3 years, journal articles, conference papers, books, and book chapters by feminist scholars have included some streams of research that are relatively new and some that are more traditional and have defined feminist research from its beginnings. As the descriptions below attest, the research agenda remains broad and diverse.

Historical and Prediction Essays

Some scholars have examined and critiqued the history, current status, and future of feminist research in communication (Shields, 1997). For example, Annabelle Sreberny-Mohammadi (1996) outlines the contributions and status of women and women-centered media on an international level, focusing on the Southern Hemisphere. Other researchers have focused on the status of U.S. media and women of color (Dates & Stroman, 1996; Samuels, 1996). Jannette L. Dates and Carolyn A. Stroman (1996) examined the place of African American women in different industries of mass communication. They found few studies in this area, and most of these focused on portrayals of African American women, "like most of the research on African Americans" (p. 254). Dates and Stroman conclude that "African American women and mass communications is a fairly unexplored research topic" (p. 255).

Kathryn Cirksena (1996) conducted a study documenting and evaluating "the growth of scholarship on feminism, women and gender in communications" (p. 153). Looking at *Communication Abstracts* from 1983 to 1992, Cirksena found that the most common keyword descriptors for abstracts were "gender" and "sex roles" rather than "feminist" (p. 156). She asserts, "Although the amount of research on gender has increased in these 10 years, what this assessment suggests is that, compared with some other disciplines, communications remains relatively unaffected by the feminist intellectual revolution" (p. 158).

Methodological and Epistemological Issues

Methodological and epistemological issues are frequent topics for essays as well as for conference panels and personal discussions among feminists in communication. Whereas many authors have critiqued androcentric theory and method, some have examined the characteristics or criteria of feminist scholarship itself (Bulkeley, 1996; Einsiedel, 1996; Gaternby & Humphries, 1996; Novek, 1996; Rush, 1996a, 1996b). One such characteristic under current scrutiny is standpoint epistemology, the philosophy that all knowledge derives from a location and that recognition of this location creates less biased science (B. J. Allen, 1996; Mathison, 1997; Orbe, 1998). Other epistemological issues have included transnational and postcolonial feminist theory and the influence of globalization on research practices and theory building (Hegde, 1998; Shome, 1996). In addition, some researchers have presented the Afrocentric perspective on communication and theory building (B. J. Allen, 1996; Davis, 1998; Hutton, 1996). Frankie Hutton (1996) has used the Afrocentric model as a "foundation to analyze and explore the work of four archetypical African American female journalists" (p. 59). Olga Idriss Davis (1998) asserts, "Black feminism stands at the intersection of racism fostered by a white feminist agenda and sexism in black nationalism" (p. 78). Another site for questions of epistemology has been derived from environmental communication. JoAnn Valenti (1996, p. 41) asserts that public understanding of environmental literacy is a prerequisite of sustainability.

Ramona R. Rush (1996b) and others (e.g., Creedon, 1993, 1996) have called for complete transformations in epistemology and method. Rush suggests 10 tenets for what she terms "deeper communications" (p. 8). Among these tenets are that a theory and its research should be ecologically based, should be inclusive and thus diverse, should go beyond dualistic thinking, should basically be concerned about human spirituality and sexuality, should be healing and liberatory, should employ realistic frameworks, and should have a global civil society worldview with concern and respect for the information, communication, and integration of all citizens.

Knowledge and Identity

Several scholars have addressed women's self-identity, identity formation, and feminist consciousness. For example, a few authors have discussed the polarization of men and women, or private versus public spheres of life and the essentialist view that women are relegated to private functions whereas men control the public functions of our society (Bell, 1997; Griffin, 1996; Wood, 1998). Radha S. Hegde (1996) presents a feminist "rethinking" of personal agency and power from the standpoint of battered women in a shelter in southern India. Lisa A. Flores (1996) highlights Chicana feminists and their constructions of identity as feminists. She found that the Chicana feminists she studied resisted mainstream definitions for themselves and created an alternative discursive space. Davis (1998) illustrates how a black woman can locate self and violate the space of otherness through African American women's rhetorical tradition.

Most of the literature on knowledge and identity speaks to the feminine or to the woman, but in a special forum published in *Communication Theory,* the contributors discuss masculinity and the role of men in the construction of gender. Carole Spitzack (1998) introduces the forum by arguing that the feminine is often interrogated in relation to, or as compared to, a stable, monolithic notion of masculinity. She asserts that "such an imbalance not only endorses an agenda of unilateral change, thereby preserving the normative power of the masculine, but it also forecloses the need for sustained conversations in which gender is figured as a cultural production" (p. 141).

Media Representations and Political Economy

The majority of the work of feminist scholars has employed textual analyses of media images—such as music videos, magazines, and news coverage—in examinations of representations of race, gender, and sexuality (Andsager & Roe, 1999; Ashley & Olson, 1998; Bird, 1996; Clark & Hoover, 1997; Cloud, 1996; Danner & Walsh, 1999; Garner, Sterk, & Adams, 1998; Kinnick, 1998; Kitch, 1998; Liebes & Livingstone, 1998; Livingstone, 1996; O'Brien, 1996; Sklar, 1997; Sullivan, 1998; Triece, 1999; Vavrus, 1998; Xiao & Heisey, 1996). Marian Meyers (1996) analyzed news coverage in the *Washington Post* concerning the debate over the racial integration of the military ordered by President Truman in 1948. Her research focused on how racism and African Americans were portrayed and how the "pro-integration" stance of the newspaper challenged U.S. dominant ideology. Mia Consalvo (1998) examined racist and sexist frames found in news coverage of the domestic violence murder of a mail-order bride and how smaller minority presses broke out of the dominant frames.

Several textual studies have focused on the political economy of media, assessing ideology and media production through the examination of media images (Akhavan-Majid & Ramaprasad, 1998; Brown, 1997; Eisler, 1996; Fair, 1996; Luthra, 1999; Steeves, 1997). Lisa M. Cuklanz (1996, 1998), for example, has written about images of rape and how the images on television and in newspapers serve to maintain patriarchal norms. Janet M. Cramer (1998) has shown, through her examination of turn-of-the-century women's publications as evidence of sites of resistance, that our that U.S. dominant ideology perpetuates certain restrictive, oppressive frames for women. In *Gender Violence and the Press* (1997), H. Leslie

Steeves analyzes the press coverage that followed after 19 girls were murdered and more than 70 were raped by their male colleagues at St. Kizito Mixed Secondary School in Kenya. She concludes that expressions of feminist resistance were evident but were overwhelmed by patriarchal perspectives on rape, and that the efforts of individual journalists and women's organizations illustrate "the increased availability of alternative meanings for those who wanted them" (p. 99).

Carolyn M. Byerly and Catherine A. Warren (1996) are political economists who, instead of analyzing media content, studied the strategies of activist employees who produced content at 18 U.S. newspapers. These researchers situated their study "within the critical theory of media, particularly media hegemony related to gender, race and sexual orientation." They assert that their findings "begin to reframe news producers as subjects quite capable of actively engaging in struggles over the relations of power between themselves and those who manage them, and over meaning in their daily work lives and the news stories that they produce" (p. 1).

The Audience

Research has also examined audiences of media and effects of media images on certain people (Chang & Hitchon, 1997; Durham, 1996; Gray, 1996). Elizabeth Dodson Gray (1996) examined television's role in transforming attitudes toward domestic violence against women and children. Christine Kellow and Leslie Steeves (1998) investigated the role of government-controlled radio in the Rwandan genocide of 1994. They suggest that the radio messages may have helped incite the genocide in Rwanda. Sally J. McMillan and Debra Merskin (1996) found that higher levels of comfort by audience members with personal product advertising can influence media selection and advertising use.

Some researchers who have looked at audiences have used the cultural approach, in which they explored cultural determinants for interpretations of media texts. Scholars have often analyzed meaning making and constructions of self using soap operas (Scodari, 1998) and films (Cooper, 1999; Henke, Umble, & Smith, 1996). In their dissertation work, however, Tonja E. Olive (1996) and Linda Aldoory (1998b) used the cultural approach to examine health messages. Both explored how women from different racial, class, and sexual backgrounds made meaning of health messages from a variety of media channels.

Interpersonal Discourse and Rhetoric

One focus for feminist researchers in interpersonal communication has been the rhetorical strategies used or perceived by women (Berryman-Fink & Riley, 1997; Brookey, 1998; Campbell, 1998; Clair, Chapman, & Kunkel, 1996; Cloud, 1996; Downey, 1997; Flores, 1996; Foss, Griffin, & Foss, 1997; Garner et al., 1998; Gayle & Griffin, 1998; Hallstein, 1996; Hegde, 1996; Miller, 1997; Shugart,

1997; Steiner, 1997; Torrens, 1997; Triece, 1999; Wilkins, 1999; Wood, 1998). Celeste M. Condit (1997), for example, examined public persuasion tactics as a feminist art form that enables women to engage in collective action. Davis (1998) describes black women's rhetorical traditions in the United States and surmises that a black feminist approach celebrates the theoretical significance of the "ordinariness of everyday life" to reveal black women's ways of crafting identities within an oppressive reality (p. 77).

Sonja K. Foss, Karen A. Foss, and Cindy L. Griffin recently published *Feminist Rhetorical Theories* (1999), in which they detail the lives and work of nine feminists (including bell hooks, Gloria Anzaldúa, Cheris Kramarae, Trinh T. Minh-ha, and Paula Gunn Allen) who have developed rhetorical theories that are substantially different from traditional rhetorical theory. Foss and her colleagues write about these women, "They re-vision rhetoric and encourage scholars to rethink traditional constructs from new critical perspectives" (p. 1).

Workplace Issues

Some studies have centered specifically on organizational communication or on everyday practices by women in communication professions (Henry, 1998; Kassell, 1996; Mattson & Buzzanell, 1999; Pedelty, 1996; Reed, 1996; Rohlfing, 1996; Simpson, 1996). For example, Marlene G. Fine (1996) has developed a theoretical frame and a set of practices to guide organizations in creating culturally diverse workforces. Various feminist perspectives have been used also to study issues of leadership traits and processes (Aldoory, 1998a; Buzzanell et al., 1998), trends in public relations roles (Toth, Serini, Wright, & Emig, 1998; Zoch, Patterson, & Olson, 1997), and sexual harassment as a threat to effective public relations (Serini, Toth, Wright, & Emig, 1998).

Many of the researchers who have addressed workplace issues have focused on the roles of individuals and groups in the making of news (Byerly & Warren, 1996), the roles of sources (Zoch & Van Slyke Turk, 1998), and the role of the newsroom as a site for praxis (Durham, 1998a). For example, Erika Engstrom and Anthony J. Ferri (1998) surveyed female television news anchors and found that these women perceived physical appearance and the balancing of family and career as major challenges in their work.

Feminist research concerning workplace issues also includes work on a global understanding of women's roles in media professions (e.g., Toro, 1996). Florangel Rosario-Braid (1996) discusses Filipino women's impacts on newspapers and magazines in the Philippines. Fran P. Hosken (1996) details the historical development of Women's International Network (WIN) News. Frieda Werden (1996) describes the founding of WINGS, Women's International News Gathering Service. Sreberny-Mohammadi (1996) has written a summary article on global communication practices by women in which she maps out the contributions of some "new women-centered media" (p. 234).

Pedagogy and Academia

Some feminist scholars have examined pedagogy as a site that can connect theory and scholarship with our real lives as teachers (Bell, 1997; Dow, 1997). One of Lana Rakow's (1992) recent foci, for example, has been curriculum reform. B. Carol Eaton (1999) studied teachers themselves, both feminist and nonfeminist, and found that feminist professors continue to feel marginalized and feminists of color often feel separated by their white counterparts. Rashmi Luthra (1996) argues for the merging of feminist content and teaching strategies with development and international communication courses. Meenakshi Gigi Durham (1998b) has written about her strategies for "revolutionizing" teaching of magazine design. She argues that consciousness-raising must be connected to praxis, the act of teaching, if women are to combat the hegemonic constructions at work in media. Mercedes Lynn de Uriarte (1996) details how an alternative publication created by Latino students challenged the status quo on their campus.

New Technologies

For feminists, research into new technologies does not have a long history; most of this research so far has appeared in the form of conference papers and book chapters. Donna Allen (1996) has written about women and technology, explaining the link between increasing opportunities for democracy and increasing use and acquisition of communication technology by women. She argues that up until recently, only a few wealthy white men were able to use technology to reach the majority with their viewpoints. Today, although men still own the mass media, new and different communication technologies have allowed women and other "unheard people" to offer the public very different information (p. 325).

Barbara Warnick (1999), taking up the focus of women's participation on-line, argues that persuasive appeals aimed at getting women to come on-line have marginalized and excluded some women even as they invited them to participate. She found through rhetorical analysis that gateway Web sites and general-audience Internet trade books construct female audiences as late arrivals on a new frontier who are unprepared for a "hostile male-dominated environment" (p. 1).

Additional Streams?

After we shared the above list of research streams with the FSD membership, we received some significant feedback. One member, for example, suggested that we add a discussion of feminist research within performance studies, "especially given the growth of interest in topics such as performance/performativity and in communication phenomena such as personal narrative, performative writing, and performance art." A couple of other members were concerned about whether research involving women of color, lesbians, other marginalized groups, and global issues should be categorized as their own stream of research. As one explained: "Placing the work about women of color or marginalized groups into a separate category diminishes its integral nature to what is considered significant 'streams of research.' Highlighting these issues within the streams, on the other hand, offers equal space for the work." Another member, however, asserted, "One way to highlight, call special attention to and celebrate the scholarship of African American, Asian American, Latina, Native American women and those of international background would be to delineate several specific categories that do identify their work as reflections of important topics in feminist communication." We felt that isolating this work would only continue to set apart and marginalize the contributions of these perspectives. This debate around inclusivity is one of the most important and significant debates guiding feminist research today.

SUGGESTIONS FOR FUTURE RESEARCH

Since 1996, feminist research has emphasized descriptions of the media, rhetorical and discourse analyses and critiques, and essays on what constitutes feminism. In our review of the literature, we found few studies that incorporated the characteristics suggested for feminist scholarship—that is, collaboration, reflexivity, diversity, and praxis or social change. We also found that inclusion and a focus on everyday experiences of differently situated women were rare. Although most authors acknowledge that race, ethnicity, class, sexuality, age, and global issues intersect with gender, research participants have often been white, middle-class, heterosexual Western women. The feminist scholars of color interviewed by Eaton (1999) call this "hegemonic feminism," where race and class myopia create a focus on white women's issues in communication (p. 296). Some lessons learned from graduate students' research include practical tactics and methods for getting around barriers such as this myopia. Below are some of these students' suggestions, based on actual research they completed:

- Feminist researchers should make it a self-imposed requirement to avoid relying solely on convenience samples of college students and professional associations. At many universities, student populations are predominantly white, educated, middle- to upper-class, and female. Some communities or places researchers might consider when looking for participants include community colleges and trade schools, worship congregations, nonprofit organizations, chambers of commerce, bowling alleys, organized resident groups in housing projects, weekly farmers markets, and Internet user groups and listservs.
- When researchers are making contacts with prospective research participants, elements of power and trust become critical. Feminist scholars should reconsider their methods of recruiting and of conducting the research. For example, when doing focus groups, researchers could recruit co-recruiters and cofacilitators from the same communities as the participants and have them share in the responsibilities and feedback of the research.

- In quantitative research, feminist researchers should consider the confounding effects of the multiple identities of participants and include such elements as sexuality, race, country of origin, and education level as interacting variables.
- In conducting quantitative studies, feminist researchers should consider the true randomness of random samples. Even with random digit dialing techniques, which reduce the problem of unlisted phone numbers, some voices are not included because they do not have phones with which to communicate.
- At every stage of the research process, feminist researchers should consider their own impact as researchers. Allowing space to analyze their own identities and standpoints will inevitably help researchers to understand the partiality of all individuals' perspectives.
- Feminist researchers should ask for input from research participants and, more important, use it. Feminist scholars often share their findings with participants, but may not change or add anything as a result of participants' interpretations or comments. Participants are experts in their own experiences and can offer appropriate interpretations. There is a place for researcher interpretations and a place for respondents' interpretations, and both fulfill theory building within a feminist paradigm for scholarship.
- Feminist researchers should consider teaching as one site for liberation and feminist research. Eaton (1999) found that many of the feminist scholars she interviewed did not have any exposure as graduate students to feminist studies, or if they did, they learned about it as a distinct, separate approach to scholarship.
- Feminist researchers should get involved with feminist groups and women's networks. These can provide dozens of resources, including funding, workshops and training, publishing opportunities, campaigns and collective efforts for social change, data and information sources, and membership in safe and alternative communities.
- Feminist researchers should consider attaching the label *feminist* to all their research, lectures, and other presentations. Research identified as such may be criticized both by nonfeminists who consider the label unimportant or wrong and by feminists who do not consider the research feminist. However, the goal is to engage in this struggle so that more scholarship and discourse will be created and new opportunities will be given to future feminist communication scholarship.

CONCLUSIONS

Over the past 3 years, increasing numbers of articles have been published by feminists in mainstream communication journals. In addition, the journal *Women's Studies in Communication* publishes reports on research tackling such topics as global issues for women, everyday lives of marginalized women, and the political economy of media production. New streams of research have developed, such as studies involving new communication technologies, and we have a solid track record with research on more long-term concerns, such as media representations and our identity as feminists.

However, after looking at the past 3 years of research, we also agree with what Valdivia noted in 1995: Although most feminist scholars begin their work by acknowledging that race, ethnicity, class, sexuality, age, and global issues intersect with the topic of gender, they are still focusing primarily on white, middle-class, heterosexual, Western women (p. 9). Eaton (1999), who listened to several academic feminists of color, asserts that a "hegemonic feminism" controls the field of communication, where race and class myopia create a focus on white women's issues (p. 296). In particular, issues around class still remain unexplored. As Valdivia (1995) bluntly puts it, "We neither hear from nor about working-class women" (p. 10).

Some of the actions suggested earlier in this chapter may help feminist researchers in the future with such concerns as the absence of voices in research. In addition, the literature reviewed in this chapter may help graduate students to build a future as inclusive, feminist scholars. We all have a lot of work to do within the realm of feminist scholarship, however, as well as outside the boundaries of communication research. It is never satisfying to complete a summary chapter on feminist research, because we are consciously and continuously aware of leaving voices out and privileging others. This review does offer a glimpse, however, of the complexities and the directions of feminist research today. Feminist scholars communicate with many voices across difference. We encourage those who are interested in feminist research and those who will make up the new wave of feminist scholars to continue the dialogue, to consider new ways of thinking, to pick up where others have left off, and to produce feminist research for social justice and change.

NOTE

1. To help gather information and suggestions for this chapter, we requested input from FSD members through the division's listserv.

REFERENCES

Akhavan-Majid, R., & Ramaprasad, J. (1998). Framing and ideology: A comparative analysis of U.S. and Chinese newspaper coverage of the Fourth United Nations Conference on Women and NGO Forum. *Mass Communication and Society, 1*(3-4), 131-152.

Aldoory, L. (1998a). The language of leadership for female public relations professionals. *Journal of Public Relations Research, 10,* 73-101.

Aldoory, L. (1998b). *The need for meaningful health communications: Female audience interpretation analysis of mass media health messages.* Unpublished doctoral dissertation, Syracuse University.

Allen, B. J. (1996). Feminist standpoint theory: A black woman's (re)view of organization socialization. *Communication Studies, 47,* 257-271.

Allen, D. (1996). Women and technology: Transforming communication and democracy. In D. Allen, R. R. Rush, & S. J. Kaufman (Eds.), *Women transforming communications: Global intersections* (pp. 322-331). Thousand Oaks, CA: Sage.

Allen, D., Rush, R. R., & Kaufman, S. J. (1996). Introduction: Websters and spinsters. In D. Allen, R. R. Rush, & S. J. Kaufman (Eds.), *Women transforming communications: Global intersections.* Thousand Oaks, CA: Sage.

Andsager, J. L., & Roe, K. (1999). Country music video in country's year of the woman. *Journal of Communication, 49*(1), 69-82.

Ashley, L., & Olson, B. (1998). Constructing reality: Print media's framing of the women's movement, 1966 to 1986. *Journalism & Mass Communication Quarterly, 75,* 263-277.

Bell, E. (1997). Listen up. You have to: Voices from "Women and communication." *Western Journal of Communication, 61,* 89-100.

Berryman-Fink, C., & Riley, K. V. (1997). The effect of sex and orientation on perceptions in sexually harassing communication. *Women's Studies in Communication, 20,* 25-44.

Bird, S. E. (1996). CJ's revenge: Media, folklore, and the cultural construction of AIDS. *Critical Studies in Mass Communication, 13,* 44-58.

Brookey, R. A. (1998). Keeping a good wo/man down: Normalizing Deborah Sampson Gannett. *Communication Studies, 49,* 73-85.

Brown, M. E. (1997). Feminism and cultural politics: Television audiences and Hillary Rodham Clinton. *Political Communication, 14,* 255-270.

Bulkeley, C. C. (1996). Transforming faith in the First Amendment. In D. Allen, R. R. Rush, & S. J. Kaufman (Eds.), *Women transforming communications: Global intersections* (pp. 19-27). Thousand Oaks, CA: Sage.

Buzzanell, P., Ellingson, L., Silvio, C., Pasch, V., Dale, B., Mauro, G., Smith, E., Weir, N., & Martin, C. (1998). Leadership processes in alternative organizations: Invitational and dramaturgical leadership. *Electronic Journal of Communication, 8*(1).

Byerly, C. M., & Warren, C. A. (1996). At the margins of center: Organized protest in the newsroom. *Critical Studies in Mass Communication, 13,* 1-23.

Campbell, K. K. (1998). Inventing women: From Amaterasu to Virginia Woolf. *Women's Studies in Communication, 21,* 111-126.

Chang, C., & Hitchon, J. (1997). Mass media impact on voter response to women candidates: Theoretical development. *Communication Theory, 7,* 29-52.

Cirksena, K. (1996). Feminism after ferment: Ten years of gendered scholarship in communications. In D. Allen, R. R. Rush, & S. J. Kaufman (Eds.), *Women transforming communications: Global intersections* (pp. 153-160). Thousand Oaks, CA: Sage.

Clair, R. P., Chapman, P. A., & Kunkel, A. W. (1996). Narrative approaches to raising consciousness about sexual harassment: From research to pedagogy and back again. *Journal of Applied Communication Research, 24,* 241-259.

Clark, L. S., & Hoover, S. M. (1997). Controversy and cultural symbolism: Press relations and the formation of public discourse in the case of the RE-imagining event. *Critical Studies in Mass Communication, 14,* 310-331.

Cloud, D. L. (1996). Hegemony or concordance? The rhetoric of tokenism in "Oprah" Winfrey's rags-to-riches biography. *Critical Studies in Mass Communication, 13,* 115-137.

Condit, C. M. (1997). In praise of eloquent diversity: Gender and rhetoric as public persuasion. *Women's Studies in Communication, 20,* 91-116.

Consalvo, M. (1998). "3 shot dead in courthouse": Examining news coverage of domestic violence and mail-order brides. *Women's Studies in Communication, 21,* 188-211.

Cooper, B. (1999). The relevancy and gender identity in spectators' interpretations of *Thelma & Louise. Critical Studies in Mass Communication, 16,* 20-41.

Cramer, J. M. (1998). Woman as citizen: Race, class, and the discourse of women's citizenship, 1894-1909. *Journalism and Mass Communication Monographs, 165.*

Creedon, P. (Ed.). (1993). *Women in mass communication: Challenging gender values* (2nd ed.). Newbury Park, CA: Sage.

Creedon, P. (1996). The rib syndrome: Rebels, servants, and victims. In D. Allen, R. R. Rush, & S. J. Kaufman (Eds.), *Women transforming communications: Global intersections* (pp. 188-198). Thousand Oaks, CA: Sage.

Cuklanz, L. M. (1996). *Rape on trial: How the mass media construct legal reform and social change.* Philadelphia: University of Pennsylvania Press.

Cuklanz, L. M. (1998). The masculine ideal: Rape on prime-time television, 1976-1978. *Critical Studies in Mass Communication, 15,* 423-448.

Danner, L., & Walsh, S. (1999). "Radical" feminists and "bickering" women: Backlash in U.S. media coverage of the United Nations Fourth World Conference on Women. *Critical Studies in Mass Communication, 16,* 63-84.

Dates, J. L., & Stroman, C. A. (1996). African American women and mass communication research. In D. Allen, R. R. Rush, & S. J. Kaufman (Eds.), *Women transforming communications: Global intersections* (pp. 249-258). Thousand Oaks, CA: Sage.

Davis, O. I. (1998). A black woman as rhetorical critic: Validating self and violating the space of otherness. *Women's Studies in Communication, 21,* 77-89.

de Uriarte, M. L. (1996). Demonstrations in intellectual diversity: Applied theory to challenge campus press hegemony. In D. Allen, R. R. Rush, & S. J. Kaufman (Eds.), *Women transforming communications: Global intersections* (pp. 170-181). Thousand Oaks, CA: Sage.

Dow, B. J. (1997). Politicizing voice. *Western Journal of Communication, 61,* 243-251.

Downey, S. D. (1997). Rhetoric as balance: A dialectic feminist perspective. *Women's Studies in Communication, 20,* 137-150.

Durham, M. G. (1996, May). *A wrinkle in space: Articulating adolescent girls' resistance to patriarchal discourse to popular media.* Paper presented at the annual meeting of the International Communication Association, Chicago.

Durham, M. G. (1998a). On the relevance of standpoint epistemology to the practice of journalism: The case for "strong objectivity." *Communication Theory, 8,* 117-140.

Durham, M. G. (1998b). Revolutionizing the teaching of magazine design. *Journalism and Mass Communication Educator, 53*(1), 23-32.

Eaton, B. C. (1999). *The structure of social science revolutions: The unrealized potential of feminist scholarship in the field of mass communications.* Unpublished doctoral dissertation, Syracuse University.

Einsiedel, E. F. (1996). Action research: Implications for gender, development, and communications. In D. Allen, R. R. Rush, & S. J. Kaufman (Eds.), *Women transforming communications: Global intersections* (pp. 49-58). Thousand Oaks, CA: Sage.

Eisler, R. (1996). Communication, socialization, and domination: The replication of violence and the partnership alternative. In D. Allen, R. R. Rush, & S. J. Kaufman (Eds.), *Women transforming communications: Global intersections* (pp. 28-40). Thousand Oaks, CA: Sage.

Engstrom, E., & Ferri, A. J. (1998). From barriers to challenges: Career perceptions of women TV news anchors. *Journalism & Mass Communication Quarterly, 75,* 789-802.

Fair, J. E. (1996). The body politic, the bodies of women, and the politics of famine in U.S. television coverage of famine in the horn of Africa. *Journalism and Mass Communication Monographs, 158.*

Fine, M. G. (1996). Multicultural literacy: Communicating in culturally diverse organizations. In D. Allen, R. R. Rush, & S. J. Kaufman (Eds.), *Women transforming communications: Global intersections* (pp. 303-321). Thousand Oaks, CA: Sage.

Flores, L. A. (1996). Creating discursive space through a rhetoric of difference: Chicana feminists craft a homeland. *Quarterly Journal of Speech, 82,* 142-156.

Foss, K. A., Foss, S. K., & Griffin, C. L. (1999). *Feminist rhetorical theories.* Thousand Oaks, CA: Sage.

Foss, S. K., Griffin, C. L., & Foss, K. A. (1997). Transforming rhetoric through feminist reconstruction: A response to the gender diversity perspective. *Women's Studies in Communication, 20,* 117-135.

Foss, S. K., & Ray, E. B. (1996). Introduction: Theorizing communication from marginalized perspectives. *Communication Studies, 47,* 253-256.

Garner, A., Sterk, H. M., & Adams, S. (1998). Narrative analysis of sexual etiquette in teenage magazines. *Journal of Communication, 48*(4), 59-78.

Gaternby, B., & Humphries, M. (1996). Feminist commitments in organizational communication: Participatory action research as feminist praxis. *Australian Journal of Communication, 23*(2), 73-88.

Gayle, B. M., & Griffin, C. L. (1998). Mary Ashton Rice Livermore's relational feminist discourse: A rhetorically successful feminist model. *Women's Studies in Communication, 21,* 55-76.

Gray, E. D. (1996). Television's transformative role in courtroom justice for women and children. In D. Allen, R. R. Rush, & S. J. Kaufman (Eds.), *Women transforming communications: Global intersections* (pp. 273-279). Thousand Oaks, CA: Sage.

Griffin, C. L. (1996). The essentialist roots of the public sphere: A feminist critique. *Western Journal of Communication, 60,* 21-39.

Hallstein, D. L. O. (1996). Feminist assessment of emancipatory potential and Madonna's contradictory gender practices. *Quarterly Journal of Speech, 82,* 125-141.

Haraway, D. J. (1985). A manifesto for cyborgs: Science, technology, and socialist feminism in the 1980s. *Socialist Review, 80*(2), 65-102.

Hegde, R. S. (1996). Narratives of silence: Rethinking gender, agency, and power from the communication experiences of battered women in south India. *Communication Studies, 47,* 303-317.

Hegde, R. S. (1998). A view from elsewhere: Locating difference and the politics of representation from a transnational feminist perspective. *Communication Theory, 8,* 271-297.

Henke, J. B., Umble, D. Z., & Smith, N. J. (1996). Construction of the female self: Feminist readings of the Disney heroine. *Women's Studies in Communication, 19,* 229-249.

Henry, S. (1998). Dissonant notes of a retiring feminist: Doris E. Fleischman's later years. *Journal of Public Relations Research, 10,* 1-33.

Hosken, F. P. (1996). Women and international communication: The story of WIN News. In D. Allen, R. R. Rush, & S. J. Kaufman (Eds.), *Women transforming communications: Global intersections* (pp. 208-217). Thousand Oaks, CA: Sage.

Hutton, F. (1996). Afrocentric, archetypical perspectives: Four black female journalists. In D. Allen, R. R. Rush, & S. J. Kaufman (Eds.), *Women transforming communications: Global intersections* (pp. 59-72). Thousand Oaks, CA: Sage.

Kassell, P. (1996). The birth, success, death, and lasting influence of a feminist periodical: New directions for women (1972-1993-?). In D. Allen, R. R. Rush, & S. J. Kaufman (Eds.), *Women transforming communications: Global intersections* (pp. 199-207). Thousand Oaks, CA: Sage.

Kellow, C. L., & Steeves, H. L. (1998). The role of radio in the Rwandan genocide. *Journal of Communication, 48*(3), 107-128.

Kinnick, K. N. (1998). Gender bias in newspaper profiles of 1996 Olympic athletes: A content analysis of five major dailies. *Women's Studies in Communication, 21,* 212-236.

Kitch, C. (1998). The American woman series: Gender and class in the *Ladies' Home Journal,* 1897. *Journalism & Mass Communication Quarterly, 75,* 243-262.

Liebes, T., & Livingstone, S. (1998). European soap operas: The diversification of a genre. *European Journal of Communication, 13,* 147-180.

Livingstone, S. (1996). Television discussion and the public sphere: Conflicting discourses of the former Yugoslavia. *Political Communication, 13,* 259-280.

Luthra, R. (1996). International communications instruction with a focus on women. *Journalism and Mass Communication Educator, 50*(4), 42-51.

Luthra, R. (1999). The women's movement and the press in India: The construction of female foeticide as a social issue. *Women's Studies in Communication, 22,* 1-25.

Mathison, M. A. (1997). Complicity as epistemology: Reinscribing the historical categories of "woman" through standpoint feminism. *Communication Theory, 7,* 149-161.

Mattson, M., & Buzzanell, P. M. (1999). Traditional and feminist organizational communication ethical analyses of messages and issues surrounding an actual job loss case. *Journal of Applied Communication Research, 27,* 49-72.

McMillan, S. J., & Merskin, D. (1996, August). *Personal comfort and personal care products: A survey of women's dependency on advertising.* Paper presented at the annual meeting of the Association for Education in Journalism and Mass Communication, Anaheim, CA.

Meyers, M. (1996). Integrating the military: News coverage in the "Washington Post," 1948. *Howard Journal of Communications, 7,* 169-183.

Miller, S. (1997). The woven gender: Made for a woman, but stronger for a man. *Southern Communication Journal, 62,* 217-228.

Novek, E. M. (1996). Observation is only the beginning: A case study of a committed communication intervention. *Women's Studies in Communication, 19,* 77-92.

O'Brien, P. C. (1996). The happiest films on earth: A textual and contextual analysis of Walt Disney's *Cinderella* and *The Little Mermaid. Women's Studies in Communication, 19,* 156-183.

Olive, T. E. (1996). *Cultural and collective stories of health and illness: An analysis of women's stories and media representations of breast cancer.* Unpublished doctoral dissertation, University of South Florida.

Orbe, M. P. (1998). From the standpoint(s) of traditionally muted groups: Explicating a co-cultural communication theoretical model. *Communication Theory, 8,* 1-26.

Pedelty, M. (1996). The marginal majority: Women war correspondents in the Salvadoran Press Corps Association (SPCA). *Critical Studies in Mass Communication, 14,* 49-76.

Rakow, L. (1992). Preface. In L. Rakow (Ed.), *Women making meaning: New feminist directions in communication* (pp. 3-17). New York: Routledge.

Reed, B. S. (1996). Women at Hearst magazines: A case study of women in magazine publishing. In D. Allen, R. R. Rush, & S. J. Kaufman (Eds.), *Women transforming communications: Global intersections* (pp. 259-272). Thousand Oaks, CA: Sage.

Rohlfing, M. E. (1996). "Don't say nothin' bad about my baby": A re-evaluation of women's roles in the Brill Building era of early rock 'n' roll. *Critical Studies in Mass Communication, 13,* 93-114.

Rosario-Braid, F. (1996). Filipino women in communications: Breaking new ground. In D. Allen, R. R. Rush, & S. J. Kaufman (Eds.), *Women transforming communications: Global intersections* (pp. 280-289). Thousand Oaks, CA: Sage.

Rush, R. R. (1996a). A systemic commitment to women in the academy: Barriers, harassment prevent "being all that we can be." In D. Allen, R. R. Rush, & S. J. Kaufman (Eds.), *Women transforming communications: Global intersections* (pp. 144-152). Thousand Oaks, CA: Sage.

Rush, R. R. (1996b). Ten tenets for deeper communications: Transforming communications theory and research. In D. Allen, R. R. Rush, & S. J. Kaufman (Eds.), *Women transforming communications: Global intersections* (pp. 3-18). Thousand Oaks, CA: Sage.

Rush, R. R., & Grubb-Swetnam, A. (1996). Feminist approaches. In M. B. Salwen & D. W. Stacks (Eds.), *An integrated approach to communication theory and research.* Mahwah, NJ: Lawrence Erlbaum.

Samuels, A. J. (1996). Women, ethnic and language minorities, and mass media. In D. Allen, R. R. Rush, & S. J. Kaufman (Eds.), *Women transforming communications: Global intersections* (pp. 106-110). Thousand Oaks, CA: Sage.

Scodari, C. (1998). "No politics here": Age and gender in soap opera "cyberfandom." *Women's Studies in Communication, 21,* 168-187.

Serini, S. A., Toth, E. L., Wright, D. K., & Emig, A. G. (1998). Power, gender, and public relations: Sexual harassment as a threat to the practice. *Journal of Public Relations Research, 10,* 193-218.

Shields, V. R. (1997). Selling the sex that sells: Mapping the evolution of gender advertising research across three decades. In B. R. Burleson (Ed.), *Communication yearbook 20* (pp. 71-109). Thousand Oaks, CA: Sage.

Shome, R. (1996). Postcolonial interventions in the rhetorical canon: An "other" view. *Communication Theory, 6,* 40-60.

Shugart, H. A. (1997). Counterhegemonic acts: Appropriation as a feminist rhetorical strategy. *Quarterly Journal of Speech, 83,* 210-229.

Simpson, P. A. (1996). The Washington Press Club Foundation's Oral History Project: Getting women journalists to speak of themselves, for themselves, for herstory's sake. In D. Allen, R. R. Rush, & S. J. Kaufman (Eds.), *Women transforming communications: Global intersections* (pp. 290-302). Thousand Oaks, CA: Sage.

Sklar, A. (1997). (De)constructing the (information) highway: Discourse analysis of Canadian popular press. *Electronic Journal of Communication, 7*(4).

Spitzack, C. (1998). Theorizing masculinity across the field: An interdisciplinary conversation. *Communication Theory, 8,* 141-143.

Sreberny-Mohammadi, A. (1996). Women communicating globally: Mediating international feminism. In D. Allen, R. R. Rush, & S. J. Kaufman (Eds.), *Women transforming communications: Global intersections* (pp. 233-242). Thousand Oaks, CA: Sage.

Steeves, H. L. (1997). *Gender violence and the press: The St. Kizito story.* Athens: Ohio University, Center for International Studies.

Steiner, L. (1997). A feminist schema for analysis of ethical dilemmas. In F. L. Casmir (Ed.), *Ethics in intercultural and international communication.* Mahwah, NJ: Lawrence Erlbaum.

Sullivan, D. B. (1998). Images of a breakthrough woman candidate: Dianne Feinstein's 1990, 1992, and 1994 campaign television advertisements. *Women's Studies in Communication, 21,* 7-26.

Toro, M. S. (1996). Feminist international radio endeavor—FIRE. In D. Allen, R. R. Rush, & S. J. Kaufman (Eds.), *Women transforming communications: Global intersections* (pp. 226-232). Thousand Oaks, CA: Sage.

Torrens, K. M. (1997). All dressed up with no place to go: Rhetorical dimensions of the nineteenth century dress reform movement. *Women's Studies in Communication, 20,* 189-210.

Toth, E. L., Serini, S. A., Wright, D. K., & Emig, A. G. (1998). Trends in public relations roles: 1990-1995. *Public Relations Review, 24,* 145-163.

Triece, M. E. (1999). The practical true woman: Reconciling women and work in popular mail-order magazines, 1900-1920. *Critical Studies in Mass Communication, 16,* 42-62.

Valdivia, A. N. (1995). Feminist media studies in a global setting: Beyond binary contradictions and into multicultural spectrums. In A. N. Valdivia (Ed.), *Feminism, multiculturalism, and the media: Global diversities* (pp. 7-29). Thousand Oaks, CA: Sage.

Valenti, J. M. (1996). Environmental communication: A female-friendly process. In D. Allen, R. R. Rush, & S. J. Kaufman (Eds.), *Women transforming communications: Global intersections* (pp. 41-48). Thousand Oaks, CA: Sage.

van Zoonen, L. (1994). *Feminist media studies.* Thousand Oaks, CA: Sage.

Vavrus, M. (1998). Working the Senate from the outside in: The mediated construction of a feminist political campaign. *Critical Studies in Mass Communication, 15,* 213-235.

Warnick, B. (1999). Masculinizing the feminine: Inviting women on line ca. 1997. *Critical Studies in Mass Communication, 16,* 1-19.

Werden, F. (1996). The founding of WINGS (Women's International News Gathering Service): A story of feminist radio survival. In D. Allen, R. R. Rush, & S. J. Kaufman (Eds.), *Women transforming communications: Global intersections* (pp. 218-225). Thousand Oaks, CA: Sage.

West, R. (1982). *The young Rebecca: Writings of Rebecca West, 1911-17* (J. Marcus, Ed.). London: Macmillan.

Wilkins, K. G. (1999). Development discourse on gender and communication in strategies for social change. *Journal of Communication, 49*(1), 39-68.

Wood, J. T. (1998). Ethics, justice, and the "private sphere." *Women's Studies in Communication, 21,* 127-149.

Xiao, X., & Heisey, D. R. (1996). Liberationist populism in the Chinese film "Tian Xian Pei": A feminist critique. *Women's Studies in Communication, 19,* 313-333.

Zoch, L. M., Patterson, B. S., & Olson, D. L. (1997). The status of the school public relations practitioner: A statewide exploration. *Public Relations Review, 23,* 361-375.

Zoch, L. M., & Van Slyke Turk, J. (1998). Women making news: Gender as a variable in source selection and use. *Journalism & Mass Communication Quarterly, 75,* 762-775.

CHAPTER CONTENTS

16 Language and Social Interaction: Taking Stock and Looking Forward

ANN WEATHERALL
Victoria University of Wellington

CYNTHIA GALLOIS
JEFFERY PITTAM
University of Queensland

The Language and Social Interaction Division of the International Communication Association attracts a membership from a wide range of disciplines. The unifying concern of language and social interaction (LSI) researchers is to understand how communication works through the empirical study of everyday language use and talk in social interaction. This essay, along with Sanders, Fitch, and Pomerantz's contribution to this volume in Chapter 17, describes the distinctive features of LSI research. This chapter sketches four major approaches to the field: conversation analysis, ethnography of communication, discourse analysis, and language and social psychology. The present state of theory and research is considered under the broad headings of power and identity, central concerns of LSI researchers. The tensions that emerge as a result of the different perspectives and commitments of LSI scholars are considered, and a research agenda aimed at resolving these tensions is outlined.

AS a field, language and social interaction (LSI) research is concerned with exploring the details of human discourse and interaction. The primary focus of the Language and Social Interaction Division of the International Communication Association, as outlined in the divisional statement, is on interpersonal and group settings, either face-to-face or mediated (e.g., by telephone or computer). The simplicity of this statement belies the sophisticated theoretical and methodological approaches that characterize the research of the division's membership. LSI research is a multidisciplinary endeavor, as the special end-of-millennium issue of the journal *Research on Language and Social Interaction,* made up of short essays by members of the journal's editorial board, attests (see Tracy's,

Correspondence: Cynthia Gallois, School of Psychology, University of Queensland, St. Lucia, Qld., Australia 4072; e-mail c.gallois@mailbox.uq.edu.au

Communication Yearbook 24, pp. 363-383

1999, editorial comments on the field). Characteristic features of the LSI Division are the tensions that emerge and the debates that ensue when researchers with different disciplinary commitments engage in dialogue about, for example, what counts as context (Pomerantz, 1998).

The LSI Division, at each ICA conference, focuses on the work of a leading scholar in the area, and the field's breadth can be seen in the selections since 1993: Howard Giles, James Bradac, Emmanuel Schegloff, Robert Hopper, and Janet Bavelas. The various disciplinary affiliations of these leading scholars indicate the dynamism of the division. Of course, in examining any division of the ICA, one finds a range of research, theories, and methods. What is central and peripheral to a division is not static; it changes over time with changes in approaches to research and in response to which scholars are active in the division, what they desire for its future identity, and so forth. In addition, at any given time, members within a division have related but differing portraits of the division, depending on their intellectual perspectives, methodological commitments, and visions for the field. For LSI research, representatives of the division offer two essays with somewhat different perspectives. This one reflects our backgrounds in social psychology and sociolinguistics. The authors of the essay presented in the next chapter, Sanders, Fitch, and Pomerantz, are scholars from the traditions of ethnography of communication and conversation analysis, which have historically been at the center of the field. In this essay we put somewhat more emphasis on discourse analysis and language and social psychology, whereas Sanders et al. consider ethnography of communication and conversation analysis in more detail from their perspective.

That LSI as a research area does not easily admit to straightforward description is not to imply an absence of coherence. Within the LSI Division a central concern of research and theory involves how language and other expressive forms, especially nonverbal behavior, are structured within interactions to coordinate meaning and social action. In short, the aim is to understand how communication works. In this chapter we first consider what makes the LSI Division distinctive from other divisions within the International Communication Association. We also sketch out the main approaches taken by LSI scholars, concentrating on conversation analysis, ethnography of communication, variants of discourse analysis, and the wide variety of studies that go under the general rubric of language and social psychology. We attempt to characterize the present state of research and theory in these areas. In doing this, we frame the work under the broad headings of power and identity, which emerge as concerns for many scholars in LSI. We couch this discussion in the major contexts within which power and identity have been studied. Later in the essay, we point to tensions between the different approaches to the study of language and social interaction at the present time. These include debates about the appropriate types of texts to study (natural or partly/fully contrived), the roles and appropriateness of qualitative and quantitative methodologies, the priority of language or other social variables, and what counts as context in the interpretation of talk. Finally, we attempt to frame a research agenda aimed at resolving these tensions in the next century.

For those who wish to get a comprehensive idea of the perspectives represented in LSI research, we direct readers to the journals that publish the bulk of work in this area, including *Discourse and Society, Journal of Language and Social Psychology, Journal of Pragmatics, Language in Society, Research on Language and Social Interaction,* and *Semiotica.* Throughout this essay, we also refer to comprehensive reviews of each analytic approach.

THE DISTINCTIVENESS OF THE LSI DIVISION WITHIN THE ICA

No area within the International Communication Association has a monopoly on language; this crucial part of communication is central to all divisions and interest groups. Many divisions, including LSI, emphasize the combination of language and other components of communication, particularly nonverbal behavior, in interaction. In addition, the contexts of research do not neatly divide the LSI Division from other divisions. Arguably, the key distinctive feature of work within the LSI Division is its focus on the empirical analysis of *language behavior,* broadly construed. Bavelas, Hutchinson, Kenwood, and Matheson (1997) have suggested that face-to-face interaction should be considered the paradigm case for analyses of language and social interaction, whereas others have highlighted the importance of studying mediated talk, such as cellular telephone conversations, for revisiting what defines everyday social interaction (e.g., Katriel, 1999). Thus there has been from the start a strong focus on language *processes* and *practices* rather than language *effects.* Indeed, scholars using the framework of conversation analysis argue that the only way to discover the impact of communication is through close analysis of the details of interactions and the orientations that participants display in their talk (see Schegloff, 1997).

For researchers in the LSI Division, the stress has been on spoken words and on the structure and sequencing of interaction. Where nonverbal behavior has been studied (e.g., nonverbal markers of transition-relevant places in turn taking), this has usually been done as a complement to the analysis of the language text (see Bavelas, 1994; Fox, 1999). Currently, many researchers acknowledge the importance of studying language and nonverbal behavior together as a package. One example is the communication predicament model of aging, which proposes that nonverbal behavior functions together with linguistic manifestations of "secondary baby talk" in the construction of old-age identity (Fox & Giles, 1996; Hummert & Ryan, 1996).

LSI as a field has a strong focus on understanding from language use how talk-in-interaction simultaneously creates and re-creates concepts of interest to analysts, including context, identity, relationship quality, power relations, and prejudice. The primary focus is on language use as social practice, and thus on the ways in which language simultaneously shapes and is shaped by situations, social structures, and ideologies (see Fairclough, 1989; Fairclough & Wodak, 1997).

Researchers in popular and mass communication analyze language use, but their emphasis is on the characteristic features of the medium and the impacts these features have on the audience. Researchers in LSI may also examine language in the mass media—for example, in news interviews (Heritage & Roth, 1995) or soap operas (e.g., Weatherall, 1996). For these researchers, however, the analysis of media is focused on the language rather than on the impacts of the media.

Cultural variation in communicative practices is a central area of interest to LSI researchers (see Carbaugh, 1990). Issues of power, identity, and intergroup relations often emerge from LSI-inspired research (e.g., van Dijk, 1993; Wetherell & Potter, 1992). One example of such work is Hecht, Collier, and Ribeau's (1993) examination of the ways in which African American identity is expressed, negotiated, and reproduced in U.S. culture. Another is Katriel and Shenhar's (1990) analysis of how narrative accounts of Israeli settlement formed part of the communicative construction of that country's culture and politics.

Many of the texts studied by researchers in LSI are gathered from applied contexts, particularly in organizations and in health settings. The major distinguishing feature of LSI work is the empirical approach taken, rather than the content. The large body of work in LSI on conversations between health providers and patients, for example, focuses on the language used and the ways in which language creates and re-creates social relations in context (e.g., Pomerantz, Fehr, & Ende, 1997; Saunders, 1998). Conversation analysis has been an important empirical approach for examining relationship performance through the details of speech and nonverbal behavior. By contrast, researchers in other ICA divisions usually treat language as an independent variable whose effects on, for example, patient perceptions are studied. In the area of organizational communication, Gardner, Paulsen, Gallois, Callan, and Monaghan (in press) provide a discussion of the distinctions between an LSI approach and other approaches.

In summary, the distinctive quality of LSI research lies first in its emphasis on *language* as opposed to other forms of communication, although today most researchers in all areas of communication research consider language as a part of a total communication package. Second, the focus of LSI research is on *talk-in-interaction*. Finally, LSI scholars concentrate on the analysis of *process* rather than on effects or consequences. In the next section, we explore further the major approaches employed by LSI researchers.

MAJOR APPROACHES IN
LANGUAGE AND SOCIAL INTERACTION RESEARCH

There is no doubt that researchers in LSI form a multidisciplinary community, but the definitions of approaches that constitute that community differ. For example, Wieder (1999) suggests that the traditions primarily identified with LSI research are ethnomethodology, conversation analysis, microanalysis, and the ethnography of speaking. As our own disciplinary roots are in social psychology and sociolinguistics, rather than anthropology or sociology, we use a different set of categories: conversation analysis, ethnography of communication, discourse analysis, and language and social psychology. These categories are not exhaustive or mutually exclusive, but in our view they give a good representation of the diversity and flavor of research in LSI.

Conversation Analysis

Arising from an interest in the routine activities of everyday life, conversation analysis (CA) emerged from a larger ethnomethodological tradition, where language was recognized as sequencing social interaction and organizing social action (for overviews and edited collections, see Atkinson & Heritage, 1984; Nofsinger, 1991; Pomerantz & Fehr, 1997; Psathas, 1990; Sacks, 1992). Wetherell (1998) notes that a feature of CA that distinguishes it from other approaches to language and social interaction is that it resists imposing external social causes or internal psychological motivations onto the analysis of text. Instead, in CA interaction is analyzed "as the primordial site of the social—the immediate and proximate arena in which sociality is embodied and enacted, whatever else may be going on at so called 'macrosociological levels' " (Schegloff, 1999, p. 141).

The normative structures that have been identified as shaping social interaction and providing important vehicles for social action include turn taking, adjacency pairs, membership categorization devices, preference structure, openings, closings, and sequential relevance. These structures have been shown to organize interaction and social action, and they provide researchers with analytic wedges that can help them to understand the dynamics of different forms of social interaction. In both its development and its current application, CA has been an important approach for the analysis of organizational interaction (see Drew & Heritage, 1992; Wodak & Iedema, 1999). In addition, CA has informed analyses in a variety of contexts, ranging from Internet-mediated interaction (Fitch, 1999; Rintel & Pittam, 1997) to those involving refusing sex (Kitzinger & Frith, 1999). In Schegloff's (1999) view, CA's contribution to the future of LSI research lies in the application of its insights about conversational structures to interactional practices in settings not previously examined.

Ethnography of Communication

With disciplinary roots in anthropology, ethnographers of communication emphasize the influence of culture and social identity on ways of speaking and social life (see Fitch & Philipsen, 1995; Gumperz & Hymes, 1986; Ochs, 1993). The SPEAKING framework (see Hymes, 1974) provides a scheme for studying ways of speaking in particular communities. Ethnographers of communication usually gather data through participant observation and consultation with native speakers. This analytic approach contrasts with conversation analysis, and this contrast engenders some tension within the LSI community (Sanders, 1999; see also Sanders et al., Chapter 17, this volume).

Ethnographers of communication have described patterns of language in social interaction in many cultures, and their insights have been particularly influential in the study of cross-cultural communication. Ethnographic studies of speech communities have also highlighted how ways of speaking define social group boundaries within cultures (Carbaugh, 1996). Examples include Dollar and Zimmers's (1998) analysis of the communicative accomplishment of identity in U.S. street people and Philipsen's (1992) description of the patterns and functions of speech in a working-class area of Chicago.

Discourse Analysis

Describing the discourse-analytic approaches represented in LSI research is not a simple task. The diversity of discourse studies that LSI researchers may draw upon, ranging from detailed analyses of pragmatic structures and sociolinguistic markers to broad analyses of spoken texts, is evident in van Dijk's (1997a, 1997b) multidisciplinary introduction to the topic. Despite the breadth of work he presents, van Dijk misses some of the subtle distinctions among variants of discourse analysis that are important in LSI research. For example, within social psychology at least two forms of discourse analysis have been proposed (Burman & Parker, 1993). One style traces its theoretical roots to ethnomethodology, conversation analysis, and speech act theory (e.g., Edwards & Potter, 1992), whereas the other is more heavily influenced by Foucault and poststructural theory (e.g., Gavey, 1996). Within the LSI community, variants of the first form (sometimes called discursive social psychology), with an emphasis on the fine-grained analysis of the action orientation of social interaction, have been influential. A recent example of work influenced by this form of discourse analysis is Buttny's (1997) examination of the function of reported speech in racist talk. Research conducted by Coupland and his colleagues on age-identity marking in intergenerational interactions is another example of a related but more sociolinguistic variant (e.g., Coupland & Nussbaum, 1993). Finally, a variant that shares this common thread is Tracy's (1995) action-implicative discourse analysis, where identity and moral issues in interactional conduct are foregrounded. This approach is unique in that it proposes that discursive practices can be evaluated in terms of their communicative outcomes. Using it, Tracy and Tracy (1998) conducted a fine-grained analysis of emergency 911 telephone calls to assess the organizational structure of instances of rudeness or face attack.

More readily identifiable as a distinct form of discourse analysis within LSI research is critical discourse analysis (CDA; Fairclough & Wodak, 1997; Wodak, 1999). A central, but not unique, aspect of CDA is its emphasis on the analysis of language use and power. An important focus is how language, in spoken, written, or visual form in a variety of media, is ideologically shaped by the power relations in social institutions and in society as a whole (Fairclough, 1989). The political aspect of CDA is shared with the forms of discursive social psychology described above (Burman & Parker, 1993). Another variant of CDA can be found in van Dijk's (1993) work on discourse and racism, which explores the links among language, social cognition, social interaction, and social structure.

Language and Social Psychology

The fourth major approach that in our view contributes to the distinctiveness of LSI research is language and social psychology. Here, a community of scholars depart from their disciplinary colleagues within psychology by emphasizing the crucial role played by language and communication in interpersonal and intergroup phenomena. An important development in the past decade is that researchers in language and social psychology have responded to calls to study naturally occurring language (e.g., Gallois & Pittam, 1995) and thus have become increasingly involved with LSI.

The study of language attitudes has spanned the history of language and social psychology. The development of the matched guise technique in language attitude research spawned an "empirical avalanche" (Giles & Coupland, 1991) in which research described hearers' responses to a large number of language varieties. Bradac (1990) reviewed the research on language attitudes in impression formation and concluded that all levels of language, from phonology to syntax to pragmatics, have the potential to affect the impressions a speaker gives. An important implication of this generalization is that all levels of language may carry social information that is consequential for interaction and subsequent social action. Of course, one difficulty is in demonstrating the level of language that interactants are attending to as consequential. Communication accommodation theory (CAT) has emerged as a leading framework within language and social psychology for understanding how accent, conversational style, and style shifts are sociopsychologically motivated in social interaction (Gallois, Giles, Jones, Cargile, & Ota, 1995; Giles, Coupland, & Coupland, 1991). An important feature of CAT is that it attends to power and identity issues that are psychologically salient and that motivate communicative behaviors in social interaction. Indeed, as we show in the following sections, power and identity issues often emerge as important in the study of language and social interaction.

POWER, LANGUAGE, AND SOCIAL INTERACTION

An important thread in research on power and language can be traced back to feminist concerns about the relationships between language and women's position in society. An enduring claim has been that women tend to use a distinctive language style that makes their speech appear hesitating, ingratiating, and weak (Lakoff, 1990). Whether or not there is a language style distinctive to women, why it exists, whether it is powerless, and what defines it continue to be topics of debate in LSI research (Ochs 1992; Weatherall, 1998; Wodak, 1997).

Powerful and Powerless Language Styles

In some research in the language and social psychology tradition, questions about what constitutes powerful and powerless language have shifted away from the topic of gender and have begun to focus more on the features of speech that engender change and compliance (Ng & Bradac, 1993). The question of which features of language typify communicators who are perceived as effective and credible has generated considerable interest (Bradac, 1990). Related topics that have attracted the interest of LSI researchers include persuasive language and equivocation (e.g., Bavelas, Black, Chovil, & Mullett, 1990). Much of this research has been conducted using experimental and quasi-experimental studies to investigate the perception, evaluation, and impact of communicators using different styles (e.g., intensity, lexical diversity, and speech rate; see Ng & Bradac, 1993).

Research on powerful language in language and social psychology is often based on the assumptions that the constituents of powerful language can be reduced to an identifiable set of language features and that there is a stable relationship between a language form (e.g., tag questions) and its function (e.g., signaling uncertainty). Other researchers have questioned these assumptions, arguing that there is not necessarily a systematic relationship between form and function (Ochs, 1992). Beyond this, one form may separately or simultaneously have multiple functions, a point that was made early in the study of tag questions (e.g., Cameron, McAlinden, & O'Leary, 1988).

Conversation analysts have an alternative conception of power in talk. For them, language, power, and social action are interdependent, framed partially in terms of the normative structures in conversation to which participants orient. The idea of *preference* provides a good illustration (e.g., Pomerantz, 1984): An answer is the preferred response to a question, an acceptance is preferred for an invitation, and agreement is preferred for an assessment. Dispreferred responses demand more work, generally including at least some kind of account. Speakers thus exercise power when they achieve the preferred orientation to their speech.

A crucial point made by both conversation analysts and discursive social psychologists is that the function of linguistic forms is defined by the ways in which interlocutors orient to their use. For example, Edwards and Potter (1992) analyzed Oliver North's testimony during the Iran-Contra hearings. They argue that the high frequency of "powerless" speech features, such as tag questions and false starts, could be understood as a powerful strategy on North's part to hedge meaning, so that he could avoid being held to account in the future for anything that he said. The power of language thus lies in communicators' ability to utilize the linguistic resources available to them to achieve their interactive goals.

Sociostructural Norms, Cultural Resources, and Social Values

The idea that power in communication is not only a matter of language style has already been discussed. In part, power involves the everyday normative structures of conversations that function as resources for social actions (see Gallois, 1994). A further aspect of power in language is the ability of language to reflect and perpetuate cultural values and beliefs about social groups, a feature that has long been appreciated by feminist researchers working on gender bias in language (Lakoff, 1990; Wodak, 1997).

That language produces and reproduces dominant beliefs and ideologies is a central tenet of many forms of discourse analysis (Gavey, 1996; Parker, 1992; van Dijk, 1993; Wetherell & Potter, 1992; Wodak, 1997). Critical discourse analysts have been able to describe several linguistic devices, such as agent deletion and pluralization, that function to mask power (Fairclough, 1989), as have researchers in other approaches as well (Henley, Miller, & Beazley, 1995; Ng & Bradac, 1993). Across the broad range of approaches for studying the transmission of cultural norms, beliefs, and values, however, there are two substantial areas of concern related to the overt expression of power in language: sexism and racism.

Sexism

The idea that sexism is coded in language and is consequential for social interaction is not new (see Lakoff, 1990). Weatherall (1996) describes a typology of sexist language in which different aspects of language that had been identified as sexist are classified as ignoring (e.g., masculine generic language), defining (e.g., address practices and naming conventions), or deprecating women (e.g., terms for sexually active women). In a review of the literature examining the impact of sexist language, Falk and Mills (1996) conclude that there is overwhelming evidence that the use of these forms impairs the interpretation, comprehension, and recall of material.

Research in the 1990s tended to move away from isolating sexist language forms and testing their impacts toward a more discursive approach in which references about and to women are examined in an interactive context and the social consequences of those references are considered (e.g., Hopper & LeBaron, 1998). Influenced by discursive social psychology, Weatherall and Walton (in press) examined the metaphors that a speech community used to refer to sex and sexual experience. The metaphors used tended to highlight the violent and competitive aspects of sexual relations. Weatherall and Walton suggest that a conscious and strategic shift in the use of metaphoric constructions that highlight the caring, sharing, creative, and fun aspects of sex may help to transform current culturally dominant frameworks for understanding of sexual experience.

Racism

Discourse analysis (in all its variants) has also produced some important insights into how racism is reflected and reproduced in talk with and about others of similar or different ethnic origins. In a study of politicians' and laypersons' explanations of issues concerning race relations in New Zealand, Wetherell and Potter (1992) identified a set of linguistic repertoires that functioned as resources for explaining the (racist) status quo in seemingly palatable forms (see also van Dijk, 1993).

In a study influenced by the model of discourse as social action (Edwards & Potter, 1992), but using a CA-inspired method of analysis, Buttny (1997) considered the form and function of reported speech in discussion groups, occasioned by the researcher, about racial discrimination. Buttny argues that reported speech is a resource that speakers may use to represent assessments of others' actions in racial discrimination. Using a very similar methodological approach, Kleiner (1998) examined the structure and use of what he calls "pseudo-argument" in student conversations about race. Pseudo-arguments were constructed to simulate arguments against an absent antagonist and were used to validate speakers' beliefs and values.

Cultural beliefs and values are created and reflected in everyday talk. Identity is also constructed in discourse, and identity may influence the ways in which language is evaluated. Power and identity are often interdependent, in that power encourages particular constructions of identity. In the next section, we shift the emphasis from research primarily concerned with power to that in which identity is brought more into focus.

IDENTITY, LANGUAGE, AND SOCIAL INTERACTION

There is widespread agreement among LSI researchers that who we are, our personal and social identity, is fundamental to all social interaction (Pittam, 1999). Beyond this, however, there is little consensus on how to conceptualize identity and its relationship to language and social interaction (for discussions of the philosophical origins of debates about identity and its relevance to communication, see Harré, 1994; Shotter & Gergen, 1994).

From a language and social psychology perspective, identity forms part of the self-concept. An individual's personal and social identities are relatively stable as part of the self-concept, but at the cognitive and behavioral levels, different social identities may be more or less salient, depending on their contextual relevance. According to this approach, identity exists prior to language and is a motivating force behind language behavior. Language is treated as a marker of identity, and social interaction is viewed as a site where psychological distance, whether interpersonal or intergroup, is displayed and negotiated.

In stark contrast to this approach, scholars conducting conversation analysis treat identity as a local achievement displayed and constituted through the structural organization of social interaction and its demonstrated salience to participants. Aronsson (1998) suggests that a choreographic metaphor is appropriate for the CA approach to identity, because it highlights the dynamic and dialogic aspects where language and social interaction are constituent of identity. An illustration of the CA position on identity can be found in Heritage and Roth's (1995) study of question-answer sequences in news interviews. From a case-by-case analysis through to a quantitative summary, Heritage and Roth demonstrate that questioning is an activity that *constitutes* a news interview context. In addition, the ways participants orient to turn-type preallocation constitute their respective identities as interviewer and interviewee (see Nofsinger, 1995).

The conception of identity within discourse analysis lies somewhere between the positions described above. On the one hand, discourse analysts invoke social categories, such as gender or ethnicity, as if they exist independent of the interaction. On the other hand, they are reluctant to treat identities as if they are stable, coherent psychological phenomena. The analytic concern of discourse analysis is with how and why identities (or other social objects) are constructed and negotiated in conversation (see Antaki & Widdicome, 1998).

The construction of identity as something that is "beneath" language or as an "effect of" language is highlighted in recent research on the links between gender and language.

Gender and Identity

The question of whether gender affects ways of talking—and, if it does, how and why—can be understood as being predicated upon particular notions of identity. Thus the construct of "women's language" presupposes that there is some kind of shared nature of women (or men) that exists underneath language and is expressed through it, albeit in nuanced and context-dependent ways (see Wodak, 1997). This conception of a preexisting gender identity spans both sides of the debate about the best explanation of women's language (Cameron, 1996). Regardless of whether "genderlects" are due to the segregated subcultures of boys and girls (i.e., the difference position) or women's language derives from women's relatively powerless position (i.e., the dominance position), the underlying assumption about identity is that it preexists language.

Increasing dissatisfaction with the "now you see it, now you don't" character of gendered language styles in social interaction has led some commentators to propose a theoretical reformulation of the effects of gender on interaction (e.g., Bergvall, Bing, & Freed, 1996). This proposal reflects a shift away from what we have characterized as the language and social psychology construction of identity toward a position more compatible with conversation or discourse analysis, where gender is seen as socially constructed and negotiated in social interaction. In this way, the question shifts from how gender is reflected in language and social interaction to the ways in which speakers orient to "gender context" in the mundane interactions of life. For example, Hopper and LeBaron (1998) examined a sample of conversations in which gender was "noticed" by speakers during the interaction. These researchers argue that the frequency of gender marking in conversation provides a resource that increases the ease with which gender can be occasioned, thus providing a pervasive structural resource for extending gender relevance in a social interaction.

Other discourse-analytic approaches, particularly those influenced by the ethnography of communication, hold that language in social interaction can simultaneously reflect and construct gender identities. This more eclectic position has been proposed by Ochs (1992), who argues that although few features of language directly and exclusively index gender, linguistic features do index social meanings. Ochs suggests that it is the meanings associated with speech acts or social activities that become resources for the construction and negotiation of gender identities. Using this approach, Sheldon (1996) found that conflict talk in American children is indexed by gender, where confrontation and negotiation are associated with masculinity and femininity, respectively. These styles subsequently function as resources to occasion gender as a salient feature of an interaction or to accomplish a gendered version of the self in various social interactions.

Culture and Identity

In the area of culture, language, and social interaction, the different approaches to the study of identity also emerge, albeit in a slightly different way. For example, an explicit emphasis on culture and identity is rarely seen in CA approaches. An exception appears in comparative studies of interactive practices across speech communities, where many features (such as telephone openings) seem quite robust across languages (Hopper & Chen, 1996). As noted earlier, the relationships among culture, identity, and language practices are a definitive aspect of work in the ethnography of communication (Carbaugh, 1990, 1996; Philipsen, 1992). Discourse analysts often argue for the constructed nature of cultural identity and are concerned with the functions that different constructions of ethnic identity perform in talk (e.g., Wetherell & Potter, 1992).

According to the theoretical framework developed by Gumperz (1992), social categories such as ethnicity are communicatively produced through contextualization cues, such as prosody and formulaic expressions. These cues function to highlight the relational aspects of an exchange, which are essential for interpreting meaning and negotiating the smooth management of the interaction. Some researchers depart from Gumperz's position and argue that "passing" as an authentic member of an ethnic group requires more than performance of the appropriate conversational styles and conventions. For example, Tai (1996) found that Taiwanese residents in Japan who could "pass linguistically" were still characterized as "foreigners." Tai attributes this to Japanese exclusionary attitudes toward foreigners.

The idea that successful communication across cultural boundaries relies on negotiation of the correct performance or interpretation of contextualization cues has inspired much research in LSI. Petronio, Ellemers, Giles, and Gallois (1998) point to the analogies between negotiating interpersonal and intergroup boundaries in communication and note the subtle influence of context on decisions about managing boundaries. This research emphasizes understanding the interpersonal and intergroup forces that contribute to problematic communication. The assumption in language and social psychology that identity is prior to language holds true for ethnic as well as gender identity (see Gallois & Pittam, 1996).

Organizational Identity

Social interaction in various institutional contexts has attracted considerable contemporary interest from LSI researchers (Drew & Heritage, 1992; Wodak & Iedema, 1999). Research in conversation analysis has been particularly successful in developing a coherent, cumulative research program on organizational discourse (Heritage, 1999). One of the reasons for CA's success in the area is that talk-in-interaction is the primary medium through which institutional or professional identities are enacted, and it is how many practical work activities are achieved. Among their contributions, conversation analysts have documented how basic conversational structures, such as turn taking, person reference, and lexical choice, are adapted to particular contexts in order to produce identities on the one hand and to organize activities on the other (Hopper, 1995). For example, emergency telephone calls are structurally organized to identify and acknowledge a situation as an emergency, establish the request, extract the necessary information, give a response, and end the call. Through interactants' orientations to the relevance of the structure of the call, the activity at hand gets accomplished (Tracy & Tracy, 1998; Zimmerman, 1992).

Age and Identity

In the area of aging and ageism, discourse analysis and language and social psychology have been predominant (Coupland & Nussbaum, 1993; Hummert & Ryan, 1996). A discursive approach is particularly amenable to examining the construction of age identity, because age categories are inherently ambiguous. The ambiguity means that definitions and meanings of age are contextually sensitive and open to negotiation during interaction. For example, Williams, Coupland, Folwell, and Sparks (1997) found that young adults used media stereotypes of "Generation X" as resources to construct generation boundaries. Those constructions then triggered intergenerational comparisons that, in turn, constructed older people as being simultaneously overpowering, self-righteous, and objects of amusement.

Communication accommodation theory has been used as to explain how age stereotypes and age identity influence language behavior in intergenerational interactions (e.g., Williams & Giles, 1996). Young to old patronizing speech has been found to be consequential for the psychological and physical health of older adults (Hummert & Ryan, 1996). CAT predicts that this behavior is often motivated by a desire to reduce communicative distance between younger and older interlocutors. Stereotypes about the extent of old-age deficits mediate the younger actor's behavior, however, and may result in overaccommodation, which makes the communicative encounter unsatisfactory for the older person (Coupland & Nussbaum, 1993).

This brief and selective review of the various approaches to language and social interaction, and the research conducted using them on the central themes of power and identity, also highlights some of the tensions that are inherent in this area. In the next section, we attempt to make some key tensions explicit, the better to find a way of moving forward.

TENSIONS WITHIN LANGUAGE
AND SOCIAL INTERACTION RESEARCH

One of the exciting aspects of the LSI Division is that it brings together scholars from different disciplinary backgrounds. The multidisciplinary nature of the division presents intellectual challenges as members try to come to terms with unfamiliar theoretical frameworks, methodological approaches, and technical jargon. The diversity also engenders debates about the relative limitations and strengths of different paradigms. We describe below four areas of tension that color these debates at the present time, and that are likely to do so well into the 21st century.

Natural or Constructed Language

One criticism that has been voiced against research in language and social psychology in particular is that the language analyzed tends to be constructed by researchers for the purposes of the study. At its most contrived, this means that people may make pen-and-paper judgments about constructed (written) sentences or vignettes. In language attitude research, audio recordings of staged or semistaged speech are generally used as stimuli. Research may even be one step further removed from actual language use, for instance, in research that asks people to indicate how they felt about a conversation they remember having (see Potter & Wetherell, 1995).

It would be difficult to deny that the instances just described are anything but unnatural. Just because the research does not investigate spontaneous language does not mean it has nothing to contribute to an understanding of language and social interaction, however. For example, if you want to find out about people's experiences of particular types of conversations, there are few options other than to ask them. If you want to provide compelling evidence that accent influences person perception in consequential ways, an experimental design that controls for everything other than speech variety is a valid approach. Even so, endorsing the use of contrived language in some circumstances is not to deny that research using spontaneous, natural conversation is vital to our understanding of language and social life. Of course, "natural" language is itself problematic (Potter & Wetherell, 1995).

Researchers in language and social psychology have acknowledged the limitations of contrived examples and have endeavored to embrace more natural language in their research (Gallois & Pittam, 1995; Weatherall, 1998). Where natural language is not used, the challenge for these researchers is to demonstrate that the phenomena they study have practical significance; that is, that the patterns found in the controlled setting will map back onto natural language. Research that links naturally occurring language to the constructed language of experimental research produces a compelling story (e.g., Henley et al., 1995).

Description of Language

Related to the tension emerging from debates about the validity of studying language that is more or less natural is the issue of data description for the purpose of identifying regularities or exceptions. For researchers in language and social psychology who work with more natural language, this generally involves some kind of quantitative representation of the data. Language may be coded on the dimensions of interest (e.g., gender of interlocutors), then the features of concern (e.g., address forms) may be identified, counted, and analyzed statistically. Coding and categorizing linguistic forms has some difficulties associated with it that we will not detail here (see Cameron et al., 1988). A strength of this approach, however, is that well-established procedures exist to ensure that coding procedures are reliable and replicable.

Discourse analysis and ethnography also involve identifying patterns in language use. Unlike researchers working in language and social psychology, however, discourse analysts and ethnographers are not prepared to reduce the data into the relatively discrete and mutually exclusive categories necessary for statistical testing. This is because in natural language linguistic features or conversational extracts can have multiple interpretations or subtle shades of meaning that discrete coding categories fail to capture. Often, the research aim is to explicate the range of acceptable discourse rather than to pinpoint the most frequently occurring features or forms. Thus qualitative descriptions of the data are preferred. The strength of a qualitative approach is that it is sensitive to the multiple meanings, contradictions, and variability in the data. A problem with categorizing language flexibly and with attention to nuance, however, is that it is unlikely that two independent researchers will converge in their interpretations. It is not the case that "anything goes," but there is a clear need to establish criteria by which to evaluate this research.

The Role of Larger Social Variables

In contrast, conversation analysis involves a very rigorous empirical approach. Part of the rigor derives from a commitment to treating features of talk only as they are attended to by the participants in the interaction. For example, in principle, a CA approach to the study of gender will be restricted to instances of talk where gender is "noticed" and is clearly consequential in the structural organization of the interaction (Hopper & LeBaron, 1998). In CA, it is order at the local level, on a case-by-case basis, that provides information about the normative structures organizing the interaction (Schegloff, 1993). In this view, the confusion that can result when gender, for example, is assumed to have an influence on all interactions is evidenced by the speech styles literature. The "now you see them, now you don't" quality of gender differences in language style illustrates the danger of imposing categories on an interaction where the participants themselves may not perceive the categories as salient.

The imposition of broad categories on the data, as is done in discourse analysis and the language and social psychology approach, is motivated by a recognition that larger variables, such as dominant belief systems and social categories like class, have a pervasive influence on social behavior and are habitually used by participants to make sense of their worlds. The danger in imposing such categories on the data is that what is found may be no more than a reflection of the analysts' own interests. The tricky issue of what knowledge of the world should be imported into any interpretation of text is treated in depth by Schegloff (1997) and Wetherell (1998).

TAKING STOCK AND LOOKING FORWARD

Researchers working on language and social interaction, like their predecessors in related areas, have been successful in highlighting that social life is largely experienced through conversation. Language not only reflects the world, it structures social interaction, shapes understanding, and makes things happen. As we enter a new millennium, it is imperative that this field retain its strong commitment to the study of language processes as they occur in real interactions between people. In this final section, we point to some ways of doing this.

First, it is important to resolve the tensions described above, at least to the point that they do not interfere with progress in research and theory development. In 1995, Gallois and Pittam argued for a "let a hundred flowers bloom" approach to the treatment of natural language, although others (including Potter & Wetherell, 1995) argued that one position (their own) is far more likely than others to be fruitful for an understanding of social interaction. To some extent, the approach advocated by Gallois and Pittam has characterized the field as a whole. Too often, however, researchers taking different approaches have simply ignored each other. It is time for proponents of each approach to acknowledge the others. A number of the contributors to the special end-of-millennium issue of *Research on Language and Social Interaction* come to this same conclusion, and some of them have developed interesting ways to classify the range of research.

Even today, however, there is a tendency for advocates of one approach to describe the others in terms of out-group stereotypes rather than in terms of what is really being done (see Bradac, 1999; Potter, 1999). If one reads work from different paradigms closely and carefully, the similarities are striking. For example, conversation analysts, even though they emphasize local order, nevertheless sometimes do count and code (e.g., Heritage & Roth, 1995). In this way, they converge with language and social psychology researchers in the conclusions they draw. On the other hand, researchers in language and social psychology, even though they start from the premise that social categories exist prior to language, nevertheless acknowledge that identity emerges from and is negotiated through context. Indeed, recent versions of communication accommodation theory hold this as an essential assumption that colors the methodology that can be used and even the extent to which the theory can be tested in a traditional sense (Cargile, Giles, & Clément, 1995; Gallois et al., 1995; Gallois & Giles, 1998). Researchers must come to grips with these similarities as well as with the differences, and they must also understand that a pure application of one approach or another may blind them to important issues that can compromise the quality or generalizability of their results.

Second, it is time to integrate the various theories and approaches in the area. This process has already begun, as the borrowing from conversation analysis by discourse analysts and the use of quantitative methods by conversation analysts attest. The strengths and weaknesses of the approaches are largely complementary, so that there is considerable scope for developing this endeavor further. For example, it may be useful to analyze the same text from different approaches and using different theories in order to compare directly the insights gleaned from different approaches. Interestingly enough, the LSI Division's preconference before the 1999 ICA meetings did just this.

To say that there should be more integration is not to say that every researcher in LSI should try to use every approach. All researchers are inescapably influenced by their disciplinary training and the paradigms that formed them, and it may be too difficult for some to reach into the heart of another paradigm. Researchers need to be realistic about what they personally can do. What it does mean, however, is that scholars and teachers should exercise the same self-reflexivity that they demand of others. All should be explicit about the strengths and limitations of their own work and should be open to the capacity of other approaches to provide insights that their own approaches cannot. In this way, where a borrowing or mixing of methodologies is feasible, it can be more easily achieved.

Finally, there is great scope to apply the theories and methods in this area to new arenas of language and social interaction research. For example, the study of mediated communication in LSI is still new (Katriel, 1999; Rintel & Pittam, 1997); much of this research outside LSI is being conducted using the effects approach, rather than through the examination of language processes as they develop. This is a fascinating new area in which to watch the negotiation of power and identity, as conventions develop that do not exist or that are managed very differently in face-to-face, telephone, or written communication. To do this, however, researchers in LSI must break with the tradition of comparing everything with face-to-face interaction and must take account of the richness of mediated communication. This is especially important, as these new media are likely to become as ubiquitous as telephone conversation has been in the 20th century and as face-to-face interaction has been in the past. The aims and the methods of research in language and social interaction are ideally suited to this task.

REFERENCES

Antaki, C., & Widdicome, S. (Eds.). (1998). *Identities in talk.* London: Sage.

Aronsson, K. (1998). Identity-in-interaction and social choreography. *Research on Language and Social Interaction, 31,* 75-90.

Atkinson, J. M., & Heritage, J. (Eds.). (1984). *Structures of social action: Studies in conversation analysis.* Cambridge: Cambridge University Press.

Bavelas, J. B. (1994). Gestures as part of speech: Methodological implications. *Research on Language and Social Interaction, 27,* 201-222.

Bavelas, J. B., Black, A., Chovil, N., & Mullett, J. (1990). *Equivocal communication.* Newbury Park, CA: Sage.

Bavelas, J. B., Hutchinson, S., Kenwood, C., & Matheson, D. H. (1997, May). *Using face-to-face dialogue as a standard for other communication systems.* Paper presented at the annual meeting of the International Communication Association, Montreal.

Bergvall, V. L., Bing, J. M., & Freed, A. F. (Eds.). (1996). *Rethinking language and gender research: Theory and practice.* Harlow, England: Addison Wesley Longman.

Bradac, J. J. (1990). Language attitudes and impression formation. In H. Giles & W. P. Robinson (Eds.), *Handbook of language and social psychology* (pp. 387-412). Chichester: John Wiley.

Bradac, J. J. (1999). Language$_{1...n}$ and social interaction$_{1...n}$: Nature abhors uniformity. *Research on Language and Social Interaction, 32,* 11-20.

Burman, E., & Parker, I. (Eds.). (1993). *Discourse analytic research.* London: Routledge.

Buttny, R. (1997). Reported speech in talking race on campus. *Human Communication Research, 23,* 477-506.

Cameron, D. (1996). Rethinking language and gender studies. In S. Mills (Ed.), *Language and gender: Interdisciplinary perspectives* (pp. 31-44). Harlow, England: Longman.

Cameron, D., McAlinden, F., & O'Leary, K. (1988). Lakoff in context: The social and linguistic function of tag questions. In J. Coates & D. Cameron (Eds.), *Women in their speech communities* (pp. 31-53). London: Longman.

Carbaugh, D. (Ed.). (1990). *Cultural communication and intercultural contact.* Hillsdale, NJ: Lawrence Erlbaum.

Carbaugh, D. (1996). *Situating selves: The communication of social identities in American scenes.* Albany: State University of New York Press.

Cargile, A. C., Giles, H., & Clément, R. (1995). The role of language in ethnic conflict. In J. Gittler (Ed.), *Racial and ethnic conflict: Perspectives from the social disciplines* (pp. 189-208). Greenwich, CT: JAI.

Coupland, N., & Nussbaum, J. F. (1993). *Discourse and lifespan identity.* Newbury Park, CA: Sage.

Dollar, N. J., & Zimmers, B. G. (1998). Social identity and communicative boundaries. *Communication Research, 25,* 596-617.

Drew, P., & Heritage, J. (Eds.). (1992). *Talk at work: Interaction in institutional settings.* Cambridge: Cambridge University Press.

Edwards, D., & Potter, J. (1992). *Discursive psychology.* London: Sage.

Fairclough, N. (1989). *Language and power.* London: Longman.

Fairclough, N., & Wodak, R. (1997). Critical discourse analysis. In T. A. van Dijk (Ed.), *Discourse studies: A multidisciplinary introduction: Vol. 2. Discourse as social interaction* (pp. 258-284). Thousand Oaks, CA: Sage.

Falk, E., & Mills, J. (1996). Why sexist language affects persuasion: The role of homophily, intended audience, and offence. *Women and Language, 19,* 36-43.

Fitch, K. L. (1999). Pillow talk? *Research on Language and Social Interaction, 32,* 41-50.

Fitch, K. L., & Philipsen, G. (1995). Ethnography of speaking. In J. Verschuren, J. Ostman, & J. Blommaert (Eds.), *Handbook of pragmatics manual* (pp. 263-269). Amsterdam: John Benjamins.

Fox, B. (1999). Directions in research: Language in the body. *Research on Language and Social Interaction, 32,* 51-59.

Fox, S., & Giles, H. (1996). Interability communication: Evaluating patronizing encounters. *Journal of Language and Social Psychology, 15,* 265-290.

Gallois, C. (1994). Group membership, social rules, and power: A social-psychological perspective on emotional communication. *Journal of Pragmatics, 22,* 301-324.

Gallois, C., & Giles, H. (1998). Accommodating mutual influence in intergroup encounters. In M. T. Palmer & G. A. Barnett (Eds.), *Progress in communication sciences: Vol. 14. Mutual influence in interpersonal communication: Theory and research in cognition, affect, and behavior* (pp. 130-162). Stamford, CT: Ablex.

Gallois, C., Giles, H., Jones, E., Cargile, A. C., & Ota, H. (1995). Accommodating intercultural encounters: Elaborations and extensions. In R. L. Wiseman (Ed.), *Intercultural communication theory* (pp. 115-147). Thousand Oaks, CA: Sage.

Gallois, C., & Pittam, J. (1995). Social psychological approaches to using natural language texts. *Journal of Language and Social Psychology, 14,* 5-17.

Gallois, C., & Pittam, J. (1996). Communication attitudes and accommodation in Australia: A culturally-diverse English-dominant context. *International Journal of Psycholinguistics, 12,* 193-212.

Gardner, M. J., Paulsen, N., Gallois, C., Callan, V. J., & Monaghan, P. (in press). Organisations. In H. Giles & W. P. Robinson (Eds.), *Handbook of language and social psychology* (2nd ed.). London: John Wiley.

Gavey, N. (1996). Women's desire and sexual violence discourse. In S. Wilkinson (Ed.), *Feminist social psychologies: International perspectives* (pp. 51-65). Milton Keynes: Open University Press.

Giles, H., & Coupland, N. (1991). *Language: Contexts and consequences.* Pacific Grove, CA: Brooks/Cole.

Giles, H., Coupland, N., & Coupland, J. (1991). Accommodation theory: Communication, context, and consequence. In H. Giles, N. Coupland, & J. Coupland (Eds.), *Contexts of accommodation: Developments in applied sociolinguistics* (pp. 1-68). Cambridge: Cambridge University Press.

Gumperz, J. J. (1992). Contextualisation and understanding. In A. Duranti & C. Goodwin (Eds.), *Rethinking context* (pp. 229-252). Cambridge: Cambridge University Press.

Gumperz, J. J., & Hymes, D. (Eds.). (1986). *Directions in sociolinguistics: The ethnography of communication.* Oxford: Blackwell.

Harré, R. (1994). Is there still a problem about the self? In S. A. Deetz (Ed.), *Communication yearbook 17* (pp. 55-73). Thousand Oaks, CA: Sage.

Hecht, M. L., Collier, M. J., & Ribeau, S. A. (1993). *African American communication.* Newbury Park, CA: Sage.

Henley, N. M., Miller, M., & Beazley, J. A. (1995). Syntax, semantics and sexual violence: Agency and passive voice. *Journal of Language and Social Psychology, 14,* 60-84.

Heritage, J. (1999). Conversation analysis at the century's end: Practices of talk-in-interaction, their distributions, their outcomes. *Research on Language and Social Interaction, 32,* 69-76.

Heritage, J. C., & Roth, A.L. (1995). Grammar and institution: Questions and questioning in the broadcast news interview. *Research on Language and Social Interaction, 28,* 1-60.

Hopper, R. W. (1995). Studying conversational interaction in institutions. In B. R. Burleson (Ed.), *Communication yearbook 18* (pp. 371-380). Thousand Oaks, CA: Sage.

Hopper, R. W., & Chen, C.-H. (1996). Languages, cultures, relationships: Telephone openings in Taiwan. *Research on Language and Social Interaction, 29,* 291-313.

Hopper, R. W., & LeBaron, C. (1998). How gender creeps into talk. *Research on Language and Social Interaction, 31,* 59-74.

Hummert, M. L., & Ryan, E. B. (1996). Toward understanding variations in patronizing talk addressed to older adults: Psycholinguistic features of care and control. *International Journal of Psycholinguistics, 12,* 149-170.

Hymes, D. (1974). *Foundations in sociolinguistics: An ethnographic approach.* Philadelphia: University of Pennsylvania Press.

Katriel, T. (1999). Rethinking the terms of social interaction. *Research on Language and Social Interaction, 32,* 95-101.

Katriel, T., & Shenhar, A. (1990). Tower and stockade: Dialogic narration in Israeli settlement ethos. *Quarterly Journal of Speech, 76,* 359-380.

Kitzinger, C., & Frith, H. (1999). Just say no? The use of conversation analysis in developing a feminist perspective on sexual refusal. *Discourse and Society, 10,* 293-316.

Kleiner, B. (1998). The modern racist ideology and its reproduction in "pseudo-argument." *Discourse and Society, 9,* 187-216.

Lakoff, R. (1990). *Talking power: The politics of language in our lives.* New York: Basic Books.

Ng, S. H., & Bradac, J. J. (1993). *Power in language: Verbal communication and social influence.* Newbury Park, CA: Sage.

Nofsinger, R. E. (1991). *Everyday conversation.* Newbury Park, CA: Sage.

Nofsinger, R. E. (1995). Micromanaging expert talk: Hosts' contributions to televised computer product demonstrations. In B. R. Burleson (Ed.), *Communication yearbook 18* (pp. 345-370). Thousand Oaks, CA: Sage.

Ochs, E. (1992). Indexing gender. In A. Duranti & C. Goodwin (Eds.), *Rethinking context* (pp. 335-358). Cambridge: Cambridge University Press.

Ochs, E. (1993). Constructing social identity: A language socialization perspective. *Research on Language and Social Interaction, 26,* 287-306.

Parker, I. (1992). *Discourse dynamics: Critical analysis for social and individual psychology.* London: Routledge.

Petronio, S., Ellemers, N., Giles, H., & Gallois, C. (1998). (Mis)communicating across boundaries: Interpersonal and intergroup considerations. *Communication Research, 25,* 571-596.

Philipsen, G. (1992). *Speaking culturally.* Albany: State University of New York Press.

Pittam, J. (1999). The historical and emergent enactment of identity in language. *Research on Language and Social Interaction, 32,* 111-117.

Pomerantz, A. (1984). Agreeing and disagreeing with assessments: Some features of preferred and dispreferred turn shapes. In J. M. Atkinson & J. Heritage (Eds.), *Structures of social action: Studies in conversation analysis* (pp. 152-164). Cambridge: Cambridge University Press.

Pomerantz, A. (1998). Multiple interpretations of *context:* How useful are they? *Research on Language and Social Interaction, 31,* 123-132.

Pomerantz, A., & Fehr, B. J. (1997). Conversation analysis: An approach to the study of social action as sense-making practices. In T. A. van Dijk (Ed.), *Discourse studies: A multidisciplinary introduction: Vol. 2. Discourse as social interaction* (pp. 64-91). Thousand Oaks, CA: Sage.

Pomerantz, A., Fehr, B. J., & Ende, J. (1997). When supervising physicians see patients: Strategies used in difficult situations. *Human Communication Research, 23,* 589-615.

Potter, J. (1999). Beyond cognitivism. *Research on Language and Social Interaction, 32,* 119-128.

Potter, J., & Wetherell, M. (1995). Natural order: Why psychologists should study (a constructed version of) natural language and why they have not done so. *Journal of Language and Social Psychology, 14,* 216-222.

Psathas, G. (Ed.). (1990). *Interaction competence.* Washington, DC: University Press of America.

Rintel, S., & Pittam, J. (1997). Strangers in a strange land: Interaction management on Internet relay chat. *Human Communication Research, 23,* 507-534.

Sacks, H. (1992). *Lectures on conversation* (Vols. 1-2) (G. Jefferson, Ed.). Oxford: Blackwell.

Sanders, R. E. (1999). The impossibility of culturally contexted conversation analysis: On simultaneous, distinct types of pragmatic meaning. *Research on Language and Social Interaction, 32,* 129-140.

Saunders, P. A. (1998). "You're out of your mind!" Humor as a face-saving strategy during neuropsychological examinations. *Health Communication, 10,* 357-372.

Schegloff, E. A. (1993). Reflections of quantification in the study of conversation. *Research on Language and Social Interaction, 26,* 99-128.

Schegloff, E. A. (1997). Whose text? Whose context? *Discourse and Society, 8,* 165-187.

Schegloff, E. A. (1999). What next? Language and social interaction at the century's turn. *Research on Language and Social Interaction, 32,* 141-148.

Sheldon, A. (1996). You can be the baby brother but you aren't born yet: Preschool girl's negotiation for power and access in pretend play. *Research on Language and Social Interaction, 29,* 57-80.

Shotter, J., & Gergen, K. J. (1994). Social construction: Knowledge, self, others, and continuing the conversation. In S. A. Deetz (Ed.), *Communication yearbook 17* (pp. 3-33). Thousand Oaks, CA: Sage.

Tai, E. (1996). Passing as a native in social interaction: Taiwanese in a changing Japanese society. *Research on Language and Social Interaction, 29,* 97-124.

Tracy, K. (1995). Action-implicative discourse analysis. *Journal of Language and Social Psychology, 14,* 195-215.

Tracy, K. (1999). Research on language and social interaction in 1999: An introduction. *Research on Language and Social Interaction, 32,* 1-4.

Tracy, K., & Tracy, S. J. (1998). Rudeness at 911: Reconceptualizing face and face attack. *Human Communication Research, 25,* 225-251.

van Dijk, T. A. (1993). *Elite discourse and racism.* Newbury Park, CA: Sage.

van Dijk, T. A. (Ed.). (1997a). *Discourse studies: A multidisciplinary introduction: Vol. 1. Discourse as structure and process* Thousand Oaks, CA: Sage.

van Dijk, T. A. (Ed.). (1997b). *Discourse studies: A multidisciplinary introduction: Vol. 2. Discourse as social interaction.* Thousand Oaks, CA: Sage.

Weatherall, A. (1996). Language about women and men: An example from popular culture. *Journal of Language and Social Psychology, 15,* 59-75.

Weatherall, A. (1998). Re-visioning gender and language research. *Women and Language, 21,* 1-10.

Weatherall, A., & Walton, M. (in press). The metaphorical construction of sex. *British Journal of Social Psychology.*

Wetherell, M. (1998). Positioning and interpretative repertoires: Conversation analysis and post-structuralism in dialogue. *Discourse and Society, 9,* 387-412.

Wetherell, M., & Potter, J. (1992). *Mapping the language of racism: Discourse and the legitimation of exploitation.* London: Harvester/Wheatsheaf.

Wieder, D. L. (1999). Ethnomethodology, conversation analysis, microanalysis, and the ethnography of speaking (EM-CA-MA-ES): Resonances and basic issues. *Research on Language and Social Interaction, 32,* 163-171.

Williams, A., Coupland, J., Folwell, A., & Sparks, L. (1997). Talking about generation X: Defining them as they define themselves. *Journal of Language and Social Psychology, 16,* 251-277.

Williams, A., & Giles, H. (1996). Intergenerational conversations: Young adults' retrospective accounts. *Human Communication Research, 23,* 220-250.

Wodak, R. (Ed.). (1997). *Gender and discourse.* London: Sage.

Wodak, R. (1999). Critical discourse analysis at the end of the 20th century. *Research on Language and Social Interaction, 32,* 185-194.

Wodak, R., & Iedema, R. (1999). Discourse in organization. *Discourse and Society, 10,* 5-20.

Zimmerman, D. H. (1992). The interactional organization of calls for emergency assistance. In P. Drew & J. Heritage (Eds.), *Talk at work: Interaction in institutional settings* (pp. 418-469). Cambridge: Cambridge University Press.

CHAPTER CONTENTS

17 Core Research Traditions Within Language and Social Interaction

ROBERT E. SANDERS
University at Albany, State University of New York

KRISTINE L. FITCH
University of Iowa

ANITA POMERANTZ
University at Albany, State University of New York

Research undertaken by members of the Language and Social Interaction Division of the ICA addresses diverse topics, often topics of interest to scholars in other divisions as well. But it is not the topics that particular studies address that distinguish and coalesce work in language and social interaction (LSI); it is what these studies contribute directly or indirectly to helping us understand. Work within the core traditions of LSI research gives primary emphasis to the discursive practices through which persons construct or produce the realities of social life (e.g., action, relationship, community, identity, conflict or cooperation, organization, power). And a further, more basic, commonality underlying work in LSI is that it contributes to our understanding of what persons do, on what basis, to produce socially meaningful action and achieve (or fail to achieve) mutual understanding. Following an initial overview of LSI research and its main traditions in these basic terms, this essay gives more detailed attention to the goals, methods, and topics in the two most populous areas of LSI research: the ethnography of speaking and conversation analysis.

F ACED with the task of representing the concerns and current state of research within the Language and Social Interaction Division of the International Communication Association, Weatherall, Gallois, and Pittam write in Chapter 16 of this volume:

Wieder (1999) suggests that the traditions primarily identified with LSI research are ethnomethodology, conversation analysis, microanalysis, and the ethnography of

Correspondence: Robert E. Sanders, Department of Communication, BA 119, University at Albany, State University of New York, 1400 Washington Avenue, Albany, NY 12222; e-mail r.sanders@albany.edu

Communication Yearbook 24, pp. 385-408

speaking. As our own disciplinary roots are in social psychology and sociolinguistics, rather than anthropology or sociology, we use a different set of categories: conversation analysis, ethnography of communication, discourse analysis, and language and social psychology.

That they write to their strengths is fair enough, but how work in LSI is described cannot be simply a matter of preference. By recasting the component areas of LSI as they do, Weatherall and her colleagues succeed in capturing some issues and interests in LSI that might not otherwise have gotten due attention. At the same time, however, they end up with a somewhat different portrait of what LSI's essential concerns are from what one gets by foregrounding just the traditions that Wieder (1999) identifies—the same traditions that the LSI Division's mission statement names. Hence, in proceeding as they do, Weatherall et al. create a need for someone else to write a companion essay from perspectives that *do* foreground those traditions. That is what we seek to accomplish here. In writing this essay, we do not think of Weatherall and her coauthors as competitors or adversaries, but as colleagues. In fact, we think that the picture one gets from the two essays combined is better than what one would get from either essay alone.

We begin the first main section of the essay with a capsule definition of what, centrally, our subject matter is, including an exposition of the range and content of research topics in LSI. We then present thumbnail descriptions of the concerns of those core LSI traditions, coupled with discussion of their ties to other areas that Weatherall and her coauthors emphasize. We next present an overview of the relationship of work in the LSI Division to work in other divisions of the ICA. Along the way, we highlight points on which our divergence from Weatherall et al.'s thinking seems particularly significant. We then present two sections in which we discuss more extensively work in what we regard as LSI's two most populous traditions, the ethnography of communication, and conversation analysis and ethnomethodology. We close with a brief discussion of current trends and issues.

LANGUAGE AND SOCIAL INTERACTION RESEARCH

Definition and Focus

Researchers in the LSI Division address diverse topics, often topics of interest to scholars in other divisions as well. But there is a basic commonality across studies of these diverse topics that is distinctive of work in LSI. One way to state it is to say that work within LSI's core traditions gives primary emphasis to the discursive practices themselves through which persons construct or produce the realities of social life (e.g., action, relationship, community, identity, conflict or cooperation, organization, power). But this rests on another, more basic, commonality underlying work in LSI: The work contributes to our understanding of what persons do, on what basis, to produce socially meaningful action and achieve (or fail to achieve) mutual understanding.

To ground these statements of our core interest, it will help to cite the observation of ordinary language philosophers in the 1950s and 1960s (Austin, 1962; Grice, 1957, 1975; Searle, 1969; Wittgenstein, 1953) that what is meant and understood when something is said—its situated, social meaning—is often different from the literal, semantic meaning of the sentence itself. The upshot is that communicating—achieving mutual understanding—is problematic in that it is not automatically achieved as long as all parties speak and interpret according to the lexical and syntactic rules of a shared language. Something more, something more complicated, is required to achieve communication, and it comes primarily from the culture of which speaker and hearer are part and the interaction in which they are engaged. This line of thought dovetails with contemporaneous thinking in the 1950s to the early 1970s in anthropology and sociology about achieving and participating in community (especially in work by Hymes and Gumperz; see, e.g., Gumperz, 1971; Gumperz & Hymes, 1972; Hymes, 1972, 1974) and constructing the lived particulars of social life (most influentially at the time by Goffman, Garfinkel, and, increasingly, Sacks; see Garfinkel, 1967; Goffman, 1959; Sacks, 1992).

On that foundation, the great majority of work in LSI emphasizes the social basis of what persons interacting say and do. Whether the immediate topic is personal relationships, workplace practices, social influence, or conflict, work in the core traditions in LSI research focuses on the jointly produced, communal, and/or interactional basis of communication practices, not their individual, psychological basis.

Across diverse topics, then, research in LSI examines the performances of persons engaged in interaction in naturally occurring contexts, taking into account the components and internal organization of interactions and of language and other expressive modes (e.g., gestures, vocal inflections, bodily orientations, facial expressions, clothing, spatial positioning). This research is revealing about one or more of four interconnected matters: (a) what particulars of conduct and interaction are socially meaningful; (b) what the basis is, for instance, in interaction or in the community and its history and customs, for the social meaningfulness of such particulars; (c) how interactants use particulars of conduct and interaction in the moment to achieve socially meaningful actions and mutual understanding; and (d) how achieving socially meaningful actions and mutual understanding is interdependent with achieving social goals (e.g., interpersonal, organizational, or political goals). Obviously, we disagree with Weatherall et al.'s comment that "LSI as a research area does not easily admit to straightforward description."

Points of Divergence Between the Two Essays

To clarify further the conceptual and methodological foundations of work in LSI from our perspective, we want to qualify and supplement some of the details of Weatherall et al.'s description.

Subject Matter

Weatherall and her coauthors state that "the key distinctive feature of work within the LSI Division is its focus on the empirical analysis of *language behavior.*" To that we would say, "Yes—in a way." We would make the following three amendments:

1. We prefer to say our concern is with *actions* and *practices,* not *behavior.* Actions and practices are what people, as social beings, mutually engage in and can mutually recognize and cooperate in. The term *behavior* is associated historically with studies of the conduct of individuals as psychological beings, with reference to their personal motivations and internal states and processes.
2. It is not just *language* practices and actions that are of central interest. LSI researchers also have interests in other modes of communication (e.g., gestures, vocal inflections, bodily orientations, facial expressions, clothing, spatial positioning). Further, where Weatherall et al. say that the analysis of such phenomena is a "complement to the analysis of the language text," we think that this is in doubt (see Goodwin, 1981; Kendon, 1994).
3. LSI researchers are not interested only in *language* (and other modes of expression); they are interested equally, if not primarily, in *social interaction.* At minimum, work in LSI has an overriding interest in the interrelationship of language and social interaction, even if specific studies focus mainly on one or the other.

Research Goals and Data

Weatherall et al. say that "LSI as a field has a strong focus on understanding from language use how talk-in-interaction simultaneously creates and re-creates concepts of interest to analysts, including context, identity, relationship quality, power relations, and prejudice." This statement introduces a further, critical way in which our thinking may diverge from theirs, aside from their reference again to an interest in just "language" processes—at least, we would phrase the matter differently.

The aspect of Weatherall et al.'s statement that we find troubling is that it suggests that LSI researchers do not find "language processes" of interest in their own right, but only as symptoms of or instrumentalities for something else ("context, identity, relationship quality, power relations, and prejudice"). It is not that we disagree that there is interest in such matters among many LSI scholars, nor do we disagree that "language processes" (and other modes of expression) are revealing about and socially constructive of these matters. But this overlooks the fact that the distinction of LSI research is that it holds language (and other modes of expression) and social interaction as discursive/symbolic/social realities in their own right that merit analysis as such.

It might simplify matters if we just summarize what data are utilized in LSI research and why. Work in LSI relies on any data, qualitative or quantitative, obtained from direct observation of naturally occurring events, laboratory research, interviews, and logical or formal analysis, that shed light on what is socially meaningful to the people interacting and/or how it comes to be so. However, we hold any claims about what is meaningful, or how it comes to be so, as ultimately being accountable to (a) what people, as they interact within the full complexity of naturally occurring contexts, are observed actually to say and do, and visibly orient to and take account of; and (b) how the interacting people themselves understand and account for their discursive practices. This greatly favors field research, of course, but not exclusively. As Bavelas (1999) points out, laboratory settings can constitute naturally occurring, albeit controlled, contexts within which research participants interact. It is with reference to findings about what makes components of language and social interaction meaningful, and how they come to be so, that attention may be drawn to such matters as "context, identity, relationship quality, power relations, and prejudice."

Research Topics

Weatherall et al. give particular attention to what they identify as two significant themes or topics in LSI research: power and identity. This raises an interesting issue. We disagree with them for singling these out, and we think many other LSI scholars would also, but we do not think there would be a single or consistent reason within LSI research for disagreeing, and that turns out to be the point.

Note, first, in keeping with the discussion above of goals, that there are two distinct kinds of topics that work in LSI is about, sometimes both kinds simultaneously. One kind of topic concerns the materials of language (and other expressive forms) and of social interaction per se. These are topics having to do with codes, production or interpretation rules, recurrent interactional structures, forms of personal address, rituals and practices, meaning distinctions, and the like. The other kind of topic is what Weatherall et al. stress—personal, interpersonal, or social activities, states and qualities that are produced or constructed in language and social interaction. This latter kind of topic has to do with diverse matters involving not only power and identity, but personal relationships, social class, conflict, cognition, ethnicity, and social influence, to name a few.

In our view, the reality is this: Some work in LSI is about the first kind of topic, and some is about the second kind; there is a long and growing list of topics that resist consolidation under a few headings; and at the same time, for many researchers one or a few topics have primacy (but not the same ones). Hence, if one tried to get a handle on what work in LSI is about, and what the issues are, by surveying our topics, it would indeed be hard to arrive at a "straightforward description." But—as Weatherall et al. also contend—this does not reveal a failure of mission or coherence in LSI research. Given the core LSI research interest in the underpinnings of the communication process, it would be a failure of mission if work in LSI were *not* attentive to a broad array of phenomena and topics. As we have already discussed, it is not the topics that particular studies address that distinguish and coalesce work in LSI; it is what studies on diverse topics contribute directly or indirectly to helping us understand—the basis for, and means of, achieving socially meaningful actions and mutual understanding.

Three Main Research Traditions

The mission statement of ICA's Language and Social Interaction Division lists a number of component research areas: "language theory, linguistics, pragmatics, semiotics, sociolinguistics, ethnography of speaking, conversation analysis and related approaches to human social interaction." However, these can be reduced to three:

1. Language theory, linguistics, pragmatics, and semiotics have in common an interest in the production rules and interpretation rules of systems of expression, most prominently natural language.
2. Ethnography of communication and sociolinguistics have in common an interest in communal ways of speaking that for members of the community give particular meaning and utility to specific patterns of communication customs, practices, and rituals, as well as particular phrasings, topics, forms of address, directness, displays of distance or familiarity, and so on.
3. Conversation analysis and, more broadly, ethnomethodology have an interest in what particulars among the available materials of expression and interactional structure display—or are means for accomplishing—socially meaningful action by persons engaged in interaction.

Although we will not go into detail below about the work that has been done in LSI from within the first of the three core strands (language theory, linguistics, pragmatics, and semiotics), much has been done in those areas to establish what particulars of utterances—and of other forms of physical expression—bear on their social meaningfulness. This has been accompanied by solid theoretical work on the conventions and interpretation rules that enable people to interpret them reliably. For example, much work has been done that sheds light on how different phrasings of the "same" proposition can change what the utterance implicates regarding the speaker's perceptions and purposes. Yet, to be investigated systematically is what difference other elements make in this regard, such as the speaker's inflections, facial expressions and gestures, and bodily orientation, as well as such other visible details as the person's age and race, biological sex, clothing, and the physical setting.

From within the ethnography of communication and sociolinguistics frameworks, which we elaborate more fully below, patterned communication practices—and cultural understandings about communication itself as well as about personhood, relationships, institutions, and practices—are considered to be the basis for the social meaningfulness of various particulars of language use, rituals, and other expressive resources. For example, Philipsen's (1992) study of male role enactment in a blue-collar urban American neighborhood and Pratt and Wieder's

(1993) analysis of public speaking among Osage Indians both make clear that when and to whom one speaks, about what, whether in public or in private, are culturally meaningful choices that influence community members' judgments about one's social identity and worth.

From within the frameworks provided by ethnomethodology and conversation analysis, also elaborated below more fully, close attention has been given to the materials with which actions are performed, and their interactional positioning, which enables persons who are interacting to make themselves coherent and "predictable" to each other, materials that are thus socially meaningful as resources for achieving orderly, coordinated interaction. For example, Maynard (1997) shows that the delivery of news is organized in such a way that hearers can orient to whether good or bad news is coming and anticipate what it is.

To facilitate the integration of our essay with Weatherall et al.'s, we need to relate these three strands that we have identified as being central in LSI research to the two strands they name over and above the ones we have identified: "discourse analysis" and "language and social psychology."

Discourse analysis is a label with sufficiently diverse roots and applications that, in keeping with Weatherall et al.'s usage, it can serve as a broad, covering term. As such, it encompasses some of the work that we associate with "language and language pragmatics" as well as some work we associate with "conversation analysis" and even some work we associate with "sociolinguistics." However, in our experience, persons whose work is identifiable with reference to those narrower rubrics are likely to use them, and not to describe themselves as engaged in "discourse analysis."

On the other hand, "discourse analysis" does have a presence in LSI research with reference to three narrower senses of the term. Some researchers who identify their work as discourse analysis are concerned with how multiple sentences are made to markedly form a whole (for example, a narrative) and how discourse materials such as connectives, sequencing, and phrasing serve to display the interconnections and subordinations of the whole's parts. There is some overlap in this sense of discourse analysis with concerns in language pragmatics, semiotics, and conversation analysis. Other researchers who identify their work as discourse analysis are concerned with ways in which personal and societal values, ideologies, operational premises, and the like are tacitly encoded in, and validated and reinforced by, the way sentences are formed and interconnected as components of wholes. Discourse analysis in this second sense overlaps some work and interests in sociolinguistics and the ethnography of communication. A third group of researchers who identify their work as discourse analysis, discursive psychologists, are concerned with the ways in which processes that have traditionally been regarded as internal and mental, such as perception, attitude, memory, and self-concept, have their primary existence for self and others in the ways sentences are formed and interconnected within larger discourse structures.

Although the current version of the LSI Division's mission statement does not refer directly to "language and social psychology," scholars from within this area have been honored by the division's membership, and work in that area has been included in the division's conference programs and has occasionally been published in relevant journals. However, much work in language and social psychology emphasizes the individual, psychological basis of language behavior, whereas the emphasis in the three core traditions we have identified above is, as noted, on the jointly produced, communal, and/or interactional basis for social conduct. However, the phenomena of interest from both perspectives overlap considerably, and there is mutual benefit in having both perspectives at work within LSI research. It is useful in the course of emphasizing the communal and interactional basis of social conduct to be made aware of relevant details and overlooked phenomena that are attributable to psychological processes. We presume that this also works in reverse.

The LSI Division's Relation to Other ICA Divisions

From within the three core traditions we have described, coupled with discourse analysis and language and social psychology, some work can be found in LSI that overlaps at least some work in each of the other divisions of the International Communication Association. Overlap between the work undertaken by LSI Division scholars and that conducted by researchers in other divisions can run in either or both of two directions. In one direction, phenomena of interest to LSI researchers may also have been examined by scholars in other divisions. In the other direction, researchers in other divisions have interests in phenomena that have been examined by LSI Division members, or LSI researchers have developed methods of analysis that scholars in other divisions are interested in utilizing. The level of actual cross-fertilization between the LSI Division and other divisions varies, but there is potential for far more of it than currently takes place.

Below, we survey points of intersection between the work done by members of the LSI Division and that of members of some other divisions based on language in the divisions' mission statements. In addition to those discussed at greater length, we want first to mention briefly (along with quotations from their mission statements that pertain to matters of interest to LSI scholars as well) the Information Systems Division ("modeling and study of interaction"), the Health Communication Division ("provider-patient interaction"), the Political Communication Division ("the interplay of communication and politics, including the transactions that occur among citizens . . . and among officials within governments"), the Instruction and Developmental Communication Division ("communication related to any learning environment"), the Feminist Scholarship Division ("the relationship of gender and communication"), and the Visual Communication Interest Group ("technology and human interaction"). In addition to these, work in LSI most commonly draws on, and most directly cultivates common ground with, research conducted by members of the following divisions.

The Interpersonal Communication Division: "mutual influence, intergroup relations, communication rules and structure, form and function of conversation, effects of message variation and communicative competence." There is as much interest in these topics in LSI research as there is in interpersonal communication research. The main difference is one of emphasis, with interpersonal communication researchers concerned primarily with identifying the types and qualities of interrelationships, influences, and communication that occur between people on a personal level; the concern in LSI research is primarily the discursive practices (and their communal underpinnings) that produce or construct those interrelationships, influences, and communication.

The Organizational Communication Division: "negotiation and bargaining tactics, superior-subordinate communication, decision making, interviewing, assimilation processes, performance feedback, power and influence, and communication competency. At broader levels, members study communication climates and cultures." Here, too, there is as much attention to these topics in LSI research as in organizational communication research, and again the difference is one of emphasis. For organizational communication scholars, the emphasis is on identifying the types and qualities of various organizational processes and what role communication plays; for LSI researchers the emphasis again is on the discursive practices that produce or construct those organizational processes.

The Intercultural and Development Communication Division: "comparisons of different communication systems in different cultural, national or ethnic groups." Researchers in intercultural and development communication have an interest in both macro-level communication systems that are distinctive of cultural, national, or ethnic groups and micro-level or interpersonal communication practices distinctive of such groups. The latter are also of particular interest to LSI researchers, especially those concerned with the ethnography of communication and sociolinguistics. The main difference seems to be in methodological preferences, with intercultural and development communication researchers relying on aggregated data and statistical analysis, whereas LSI researchers rely on individual-level data and on qualitative and interpretive analysis.

The Philosophy of Communication Division: "cultural studies and postmodernism . . . semiotics and the philosophy of language . . . phenomenological and interpretive study of communication events." There is considerable common ground here, in that much work in LSI has roots in cultural studies, or semiotics, or the philosophy of language, and there are also interpretive studies of communication. Perhaps the differences can be summed up as follows: Members of the LSI Division are concerned with the empirical aspects of topics in which members of the Philosophy of Communication Division have epistemological, philosophical, or metatheoretical interest.

The only ICA divisions whose mission statements have not revealed overlaps with LSI scholarship are the Mass Communication, Popular Communication, and Public Relations Divisions. We nonetheless consider that there is some overlap between work in LSI and some of the work in each of these three divisions, but we will not claim it unilaterally.

THE ETHNOGRAPHY OF COMMUNICATION

Overview

Research in LSI that we put under the heading *ethnography of communication* concentrates on the study of culture as a system of meaning underlying social interaction. Work in this general area embraces somewhat distinct interests, however, with differing degrees of emphasis, most prominently an emphasis on social semiotics (Leeds-Hurwitz, 1993, 1995; Sigman, 1987) and an emphasis on cultural codes and ways of speaking. The latter interest was originated by Dell Hymes (1972) under the label "ethnography of speaking" and developed in the field of communication by Gerry Philipsen (1992). We focus here on this latter interest, which involves a model of language and social life the key tenets of which are as follows:

1. Social interaction is always interaction *somewhere*—that is, it is always situated within a symbolic code of meaning specific to a speech community.
2. Ways of speaking, like the codes of meaning that underlie them, vary across speech communities.
3. In every speech community there are ways of speaking that are valued and treated as sensible by virtue of their coherence with an underlying system of understanding.

As is obvious from these statements, this perspective on social interaction revolves around communities, ways of speaking, and codes of meaning. Speech communities, as defined by Hymes and as they are generally studied by ethnographers in LSI research, consist of groups of people who share at least one valued way of speaking. A "way of speaking" involves an interconnection between language and social life that is indexed by the mnemonic SPEAKING as follows: *s*etting, *p*articipants, *e*nds, *a*ct sequence, *k*ey, *i*nstrumentality, *n*orm, genre (Hymes, 1972). Contrary to the implication of this mnemonic that attention is given exclusively to verbal means of expression, the ethnography of communication encompasses studies of a wide variety of modes and instrumentalities of communication: written texts, music, language switching, rituals of everyday talk, sign language, museum displays, and so on.

To say that a group of people shares one or more valued ways of speaking is not to say that all members agree to an implicit system of values, that all engage in that way of speaking equally, or that there is never skepticism, resistance, or outright refusal to communicate in those ways. Rather, it means that certain ways of communicating and certain symbolic premises that support those ways as being reasonable and intelligible (and more morally significant evaluations, such as sacred or profane) are known to members of the group and are available as rhetorical resources for constructing meaning within the group. One may construct meaning by resisting and by protesting ignorance, just as one may facilitate understanding and connection by drawing on common codes of expression.

Methods, Data, and Challenges

Ethnographies of speaking from this tradition, reflecting its anthropological roots, typically rely on extended periods of intense interaction between the ethnographer and the group of people whose ways of speaking are the focus of interest, with the ethnographer acting either as a member or as a participant observer. Ethnographic reports most often focus on describing the ways of speaking themselves and the codes of meaning that they reveal, rather than on specifying boundaries or membership in any geographic or demographic sense.

Ethnographic methods most often used in work of this kind are participant observation, interviews, textual analysis, and analysis of video- or audio-recorded interactions. Methodological debates in the area tend to coincide, reasonably enough, with epistemological tensions. Those who favor traditional ethnographic practice acknowledge that any researcher who takes an active role in a cultural scene in order to study it can never be completely objective in his or her interpretations of that scene. Nonetheless, they stress the effort to be as systematic as possible in data collection practices and as unbiased as possible in data analysis procedures and in the reporting of findings.

Postmodern challenges to such research practices, however, raise the question of whether the presence of an ethnographer necessarily alters the interactions that are observed. They also question whether the "report" of cultural activities is ever more than the ethnographer's discovery of an order he or she was committed to finding before entering the field. They claim that conventions of social science writing create an illusion of objectivity that is unsustainable when ethnographic texts themselves are deconstructed. Finally, they contend that ethnographies committed to a neutral stance actually reinforce power imbalances by insisting on the cultural integrity of oppressive practices. Some traditional ethnographers have responded to these challenges by specifying in more detail the influence of members of the culture itself on deriving and reporting the findings; by studying cultures of which they themselves are members; by writing in more narrative, first-person styles that emphasize their own experiences of the research process and how those shaped the findings they report; and by bringing critical theory more explicitly to bear on their analyses of the cultural practices they study.

A quite different set of challenges to traditional reliance on field notes and interviews as primary sources of data for ethnographers has arisen from conversation analysis (CA). The publication in 1988 of Michael Moerman's *Talking Culture,* in which he argues for and illustrates how cultural values and premises can be traced through close attention to transcribed conversations, led to greater reliance among some ethnographers on tape-recorded or videotaped interactions and on transcription as part of the analytic process. A special issue of *Research on Language and Social Interaction* published in 1990-1991 includes varied explorations of connections between ethnography and CA (Hopper, 1990-1991). The two areas have been brought closer together by a number of conversation and discourse analysts' attempts to make their work "more ethnographic," which generally means increased attention to the institutional and/or social contexts of particular kinds of interactions. Although these attempts are not ethnographies in the sense of being first and foremost investigations of cultural codes, they do incorporate some of the ethnographic spirit of examining broader foundations for talk than the immediate interaction as part of the meaningfulness of a given moment of social interaction.

Samples of Ethnographic Research

A significant body of ethnographic work in LSI focuses on enactments of culture within a particular setting or scene, or on a group within such a scene. Lindsley (1999), for example, uses ethnographic data from a U.S.-owned assembly plant, or *maquiladora,* in Mexico as the basis for a model of problematic, communication-specific intercultural interaction. She describes how the macro context (a history of U.S. domination of Mexico reflected in everyday interactional practices), individuals' (in)competencies (monolingual U.S. managers who often know little about Mexican ways, compared with Mexican managers who are required to be bilingual and are presumed to be knowledgeable about U.S. cultural norms), and communication behavior (specifically, negotiation of cultural and organizational identities) interrelate and affect multilevel attributions of meaning in intercultural interaction. Basing this model on observation, interviews, and analysis of organizational documents offers a general framework for explaining problematic communication in intercultural communication settings grounded in rich particulars of one such situation.

Relatedly, Bucholtz (1999) describes a group of high school girls who reject the (supposedly shared) communal goal of their peers who seek to be "cool" in favor of celebrating their individual uniqueness, even to the point of seeming weird. Bucholtz notes the value placed by these "nerds" on showing intelligence, heard in their use of formal registers, word play that shows wide vocabulary and extensive knowledge, orientation to taking schoolwork seriously and doing well, and so forth. She proposes that "where other scholars tend to equate nerdiness with social death, . . . nerds in US high schools are not socially isolated misfits, but competent members of a distinctive and oppositionally defined community of practice"

(p. 211). Her argument centers on the concept of a community of practice, in contrast to the Hymesian notion of speech community; she proposes that a community of practice is a more fluidly defined entity constructed by the members themselves, rather than imposed on them by analysts as static social categories. We discuss this distinction more fully below in regard to significant issues facing LSI scholars.

A second category of work within the ethnography of communication tradition in LSI research focuses on one or more communicative activities specific to, and perhaps unique within, a group. An example of this type of work is Braithwaite's (1997) analysis of a ritual of legitimation in an organization of Vietnam veterans. The vets whom Braithwaite observed and interviewed described themselves as being able to talk to other vets in ways that were impossible around other people. They cited discursive resources they shared with other vets that were grounded in the common experience of having been in the armed forces in Vietnam, and encounters with attributions and associations about such experiences that other North Americans made. The creation and affirmation of shared identity as a legitimate member of the Vietnam vet community was accomplished through such discursive resources as coming home stories, stereotypes about Vietnam vets, and profound interest in, and a sense of being personally affected by, the Vietnam Veterans' Memorial, as well as by their subordination of personal uniqueness and difference to the communal identity of "being a vet." This sense of belonging and of being understood was a powerful source of meaning for the men in the organization as they juxtaposed their own complex experiences of the Vietnam War with those of other Americans who were never there. Studies of this kind highlight the specificity of communicative practices individuals use to construct their identities vis-à-vis their experiences, both shared and unique.

A third category of work within the ethnography of communication tradition focuses on a native term and the cluster of meanings that surrounds it in the community that generates it. Bloch (1998) examines the Israeli term *freier*, one translation of which is "sucker." The term is applied to people who have been made fools of by " 'an entity,' typically an entity greater than a mere individual, such as the 'System' " (p. 184). It is used quite often to describe Americans in Israel who steadfastly follow laws, rules, and codes of polite conduct rather than adapting to the more pioneer-spirited "everyone for him- or herself" approach to social life that Bloch says is characteristic of Israeli culture. Bloch offers detailed analysis of several dimensions of the meanings and uses of the term *freier:* that Americans, unlike other immigrant groups in Israel, tend to have left their country by choice rather than because of economic or political pressure; that Americans sometimes attempt to impose order on the Israeli social system by insisting that laws, rules, and conventions should be followed, even when they disadvantage the individual; that an apparent contradiction between a collectivist society and widespread willingness to act in ways that seem self-interested is more accurately seen as a culturally distinctive view of rules, their origin, and the importance of not taking everything "the System"—any system—says at face value. Although the starting point for Bloch's analysis is an ongoing circumstance of intercultural contact, U.S. immigrants in Israel, her primary focus is on the complex meanings that a single native term may index—a point elaborated on by Carbaugh (1989).

A final category (although this is not intended to represent an exhaustive list of the types of ethnographic work represented in LSI research) consists of studies of the cultural particulars of a presumably universal practice, either in comparative perspective or within the boundaries of a particular speech community. Among the practices most often examined in this category are narratives (e.g., Blum-Kulka, 1997; Schely-Newman, 1999), personal address (see Philipsen & Huspek, 1985), and directives (e.g., Blum-Kulka, House, & Kasper, 1989; Fitch, 1994; Tannen, 1981). In one study of this type, Goldsmith and Fitch (1997) examined advice among some middle-class Americans, operating within what might be the broadest interpretation of a speech community. Based on interviews about, and observations of, advice sequences in the eastern, western, and midwestern regions of the United States, Goldsmith and Fitch conclude that giving and getting advice poses three specific dilemmas for middle-class white Americans: Advice may be seen as helpful or as butting in; advice may be experienced as honest or as supportive, but the two come into conflict; and seeking and taking advice may enact respect and gratitude, although recipients reserve the right to make their decisions. The goal of this study, along with others in this category, is to show that practices that occur in every speech community nonetheless reflect unique patterns and characteristics as they enact community-specific systems of symbolic premises about people, relationships, and communicative activity.

A Current Issue

An issue at the heart of ethnographic studies in LSI is the definition of the groups of people, and their practices, that are the foci of investigation. The Hymesian notion of speech community is one that, although always widely invoked as a common premise of ethnographies of speaking, has been challenged and debated from the beginning. Defining a group of people in terms of the valued ways of speaking members presumably share invites a number of critiques. First, the goal of discovering shared ways of speaking creates the potential for researchers to overlook marginal peoples and practices in favor of those more likely to embody, and more able to articulate, the preferred patterns of communicative behavior. Similarly, researchers may ignore or downplay variation within the group and resistance to norms of speaking (and the likelihood that such norms, and shared values more generally, are likely to further the interests of some members of the group over others) in their effort to identify what unites and characterizes the group as a whole. Second, defining a group in terms of language use runs the risk of trivializing, or missing entirely, the material practices that create the group and its position vis-à-vis other social groups. Finally, there is some uneasiness that defining group boundaries in terms of language use is, in one sense, too fluid: Anyone who can communicate competently, according to the group's definition of competence, is arguably eligible for membership and need only refuse to communicate in those ways to call into question his or her membership in the group. On the other hand, because such definition of group boundaries is argued to be the researcher's claim, ethnographic descriptions of categories of persons and types of talk within communities are seen as too rigid and as imposed from outside the group (the clearest case being sociolinguistic markers of class, gender, and regional identity).

An alternative model of social interaction proposed to address these issues in more productive ways is that of communities of practice, or C of P (Eckert & McConnell-Ginet, 1992; Wenger, 1998; and many others). The main C of P idea is to view groups as aggregates of people who have in common that they engage in some practice or activity of importance. The practices or activities studied involve many aspects of social life beyond language and center on jointly negotiated enterprises (although the relationships may be conflictual as well as harmonious). This perspective, exemplified in the Bucholtz (1999) study cited above, emphasizes that membership in a community of practice is internally constructed rather than externally imposed as a matter of social or behavioral properties that one exhibits. Such a perspective makes it possible for researchers to focus on people's active engagement in resistance to, as well as reproduction of, arrangements of social identities in their communities, whether those identities are race, class, gender, or experientially based. Although much discussion contrasting the "community of practice" concept with the "speech community" concept has focused on Labov's notion of speech community, distinct in some significant ways from the Hymesian concept, there is much to suggest that fruitful contrasts remain to be drawn between these two positions on the fundamental unit of analysis in ethnographic research.

CONVERSATION ANALYSIS AND ETHNOMETHODOLOGY

Overview

The defining focus of conversation analysis and ethnomethodology is the study of the organization of meaningful conduct of people in society. Most broadly, conversation analysts and ethnomethodologists study how people accomplish their activities in interaction and make sense of the world around them. The core analytic objective is to illuminate how actions, roles, and identities are accomplished interactionally and how characterizations of events, objects, and people are produced and understood as intelligible and sensible.

The conversation-analytic and ethnomethodological research program rests on the following set of assumptions:

1. Persons in society engage in behavior that is intended to be understood, and is understood, to mean particular things. As such, the conduct of everyday life is sensible and meaningful and is produced to be so.

2. Persons in society produce and understand their own and others' conduct using shared procedures or methods. The aim of research is to explicate the shared methods that people use to produce and recognize their own and other people's conduct.

3. Conversation analysts and ethnomethodologists attempt to explicate the relevance of the parties to an interaction. This is a starting place quite different from that of research that uses investigator-stipulated theoretical and conceptual definitions of research questions.

The sense or meaning that people make of particular conduct depends upon the context in which the conduct is produced. Conversation analysts and ethnomethodologists use two senses of *context*. One involves the temporal organization of actions and interaction. The conduct of a person in interaction is shaped by what was just said or done and/or what can be anticipated to be said or done next. In important ways, the sense or intelligibility of an action is provided for by its location in an ongoing series of actions. A second sense of context involves the nature of the occasion, who is interacting with whom, when the interaction is taking place, and so on. Conversation analysts and ethnomethodologists regard these matters as crucial to the understanding and analysis of conduct, but they treat them as analytically problematic—that is, as not obvious and given. They argue that analysts' claims about the nature of the occasion, the identities of the participants, their roles, and so on must be shown to be relevant to the participants themselves. Furthermore, they maintain that not only do the participants' understandings of who, what, and where they are contribute to the production of their conduct and their understanding of it, but their conduct helps to constitute the identities, roles, and occasion that provide the context for the interaction.

Methods and Data

In studying the organization of meaningful conduct of people in society, conversation analysts and ethnomethodologists do not limit themselves to explicating talk alone. They analyze the embodied ways in which social actions are accomplished. This includes examining the sounds, gestures, and bodily movements that are employed in the course of interaction. They pay particular attention to the details of the temporal organization of, and the various contingencies that arise in, the unfolding development of action and interaction. Conversation analysis provides analytic tools for examining the moment-to-moment negotiations in which persons engage as they interact.

To summarize the aims of the research program, conversation analysts and ethnomethodologists examine the organization of actions and interaction; they consider how the packaging of actions and the timing and taking of turns provide for certain understandings of the actions performed and the matters talked about; and they consider how the ways the actions are accomplished implicate certain identities, roles, and/or relationships for the interactants.

The assumptions of this program of research carry methodological implications for the types of interactions studied and the forms of data collected and analyzed. Conversation analysts and ethnomethodologists may study any sort of interaction, from chats between friends to consultations with physicians, from job interviews to broadcast news commentaries, from political speeches and debates to orchestra rehearsals. In each case, the researcher is interested in explicating the methods or procedures people employ to conduct particular activities. Regardless of the site for collecting data, conversation analysts and ethnomethodologists strongly prefer to work with recorded instances of talk-in-interaction. They have shown that certain features of the details of actions in interaction are not recoverable without the use of audio and video recordings.

Samples of Conversation-Analytic Research

To provide the reader with a sense of the range of studies that conversation analysts conduct, we offer examples of different kinds of studies that fall within this tradition: (a) studies that isolate a discourse form and analyze its uses; (b) studies that analyze the practices for performing particular conversational activities; (c) studies that examine the dynamics of engagement/disengagement; (d) studies that reveal the collaborative nature of matters that seem, at first glance, to be unilateral; and (e) studies that show how interactional practices of a group relate to the group's culture and/or are partially constitutive of the group's culture.

Analysis of the uses of a particular discourse item or form. Holt (1996) collected instances of speakers offering direct quotations or direct reported speech in the course of telling a story, making an argument, reporting a problem, and other activities. Her project was to identify when and where speakers offer direct reported speech and, more important, the functions served by packaging a report as direct reported speech rather than as a paraphrased report. Holt found that one of the important features of a speaker's giving direct reported speech is that it provides the audience with evidence about the other's vocal forms and attitudes from which they can draw certain conclusions without the speaker's articulating those conclusions.

Practices for accomplishing a particular conversational activity. Drew (1998) analyzed some practices or methods through which interactants complain to co-interactants about third parties. Three features of these types of complaints are that (a) they are produced with clearly bounded beginnings and ends, (b) they contain an explicit formulation of the transgression, and (c) there is an overt expression of moral indignation about what the third party has done. Drawing on complaint data, Drew illustrates that the moral reprehensibility of conduct is constituted through reasoning that is tied to discursive practices.

The dynamics of engagement and disengagement. Szymanski (1999) explored how members of small work groups use audible and visible actions to coordinate conversational interaction. She describes the methods by which participants make relevant a lapse in their talking and methods by which they reengage in turn-by-turn talk after a lapse. For reengaging talk, individuals do two things: They set the stage for reengagement, and they produce talk that initiates the reengagement. Participants make relevant a place for reengaging talk by discontinuing individual work or by producing physical movements that show availability. The types of conversational actions used for reengagement talk include participants' posing questions arising from their activity on a common task, offering comments on things that exist or are happening around them, and making noteworthy comments on their own work.

The collaborative nature of apparently unilateral discursive activities. Psychotherapy sometimes is viewed as an interaction in which the therapist is key to bringing about change in the client. By offering certain interpretations of the client's reports, the therapist purportedly has the power to lead the client to see and act differently. Buttny's (1996) research shows how therapy involves collaborative interaction in which both the therapist and the client influence the set of interpretations that becomes ratified. Buttny studied how therapist and client interactionally coconstruct a version of the client's problems during an initial therapy consultation. He demonstrates how the therapist draws on the client's understanding or assessment of the therapist's version as a resource for bringing the focus back to the therapeutic position.

Interactional practices, relationships, and culture. Hopper and Chen's (1996) research on telephone openings in Taiwan shows how the ways in which people greet each other both display and accomplish their cultural memberships and their state of interpersonal relationship. In some communities in the United States, persons open their telephone calls to friends and acquaintances by providing the telephone answerer only a voice sample in the greeting as the basis on which the answerer should attempt to recognize the caller's identity. Schegloff has labeled this principle "oversuppose and undertell." Hopper and Chen show that Taiwanese callers in similar circumstances exhibit a more conservative gambit, using a principle that Hopper and Chen label "undersuppose and undergreet." This principle prescribes the choosing of greeting tokens so that any error made in relationship estimation will be made in the direction of greater formality or distance.

Current Issues

Three significant issues are likely to be part of the future directions of conversation-analytic and ethnomethodological work. All of these issues are discussed in essays included in a recent special issue of *Research on Language and Social*

Interaction titled "Language and Social Interaction at the Century's Turn" (1999). The first concerns the scope of the claims of conversation-analytic studies, the second involves the benefits and tensions of borrowing concepts and methods from closely related approaches, and the third has to do with the use of a variety of sampling and quantitative methods to address questions about the distribution and efficacy of specified interactional practices.

One trend that has been taking place over recent years is that researchers increasingly are defining their projects as analyses of practices that are specific to an organization, profession, or work site rather than analyses of practices that operate more generally across contexts. A concern expressed by Schegloff (1999) is that if the field of conversation analysis is dominated by studies in which findings apply only to particular organizations, groups, or cultures, the program of research will stagnate: "Either there is stagnation or we advance, and advance requires moving our analytic resources beyond what has already been achieved, within a frame of respect for past achievements that deserve it" (pp. 145-146). Researchers sometimes choose to limit the scope of their findings based on the audience's needs and/or on methodological grounds. On pragmatic grounds, one's target audience may be interested in findings pertaining to an organization or group rather than generic features of interactional organization. On methodological grounds, the data upon which the findings rest may be limited in number or sampling method such that the researcher hesitates to generalize.

In sorting out the scope of a project, it is important for the researcher to appreciate the relationship between of the scope of his or her claims and the research questions that direct the researcher's choices of what to analyze. Schegloff offers a list of issues that researchers doing limited studies neglect to address:

> Increasingly (though not exclusively), those who describe what happens in a particular setting and how the parties do what they do, do *not* go on to ask how this relates to other forms that the activity in question can take, to how such things are done in other contexts (and how the notion "such things" is properly formulated for *their* inquiry), to how the doing of the target activity figures in the panoply of their activities and orders of activity that are also ongoing, and to how what has just been described can help us to broaden our understanding of the whole *domain* of practices of which it is a part. (p. 144)

If researchers have good reasons for basing their studies on interaction in particular settings, those studies can have implications that go beyond the settings. Researchers can ensure the breadth of their studies by posing questions that relate their work to other aspects of interaction in their particular contexts and to interaction in other contexts.

A second issue facing conversation analysis and ethnomethodology involves the consequences of attempts to combine these methods with other approaches that have similar assumptive bases. As noted above, Wieder (1999) identifies four research traditions within LSI scholarship that have related assumptions, backgrounds, and conceptual roots: ethnomethodology, conversation analysis, microanalysis, and ethnography of speaking. Some of the resonances and comparabilities making up the common ground are as follows: (a) Overlapping sets of social interactional concepts are employed; (b) the entities referred to by the concepts come about by virtue of the participants' engagement with one another; (c) the ecology of the setting is always relevant; (d) the visible, accountable phenomena of communicating, along with their circumstances and contexts, are the primary thematic phenomena; (e) interaction in its context is the unit of analysis or field of analysis; (f) there is an interest in explaining and understanding social interactions by locating them within, and as a coherent aspect of, a structural configuration or contexture; (g) interactional phenomena are viewed as things for direct observation; and (h) the concepts of convention, norm, rule, and instruction play a central role as topics and objects for description and analysis.

Given such resonances and comparabilities, Wieder (1999) suggests that responsible reflective appropriation of the concepts and strategies of one of these traditions by another opens up rich possibilities:

> The appropriation of one EM-CA-MA-ES stream's methods of object location or phenomena discovery and the conceptual consequences of situating the other's objects within one's own scheme is a potential source of increasing that scheme's scope as well as a source of theoretical stimulation. (pp. 168-169)

Wieder forecasts that future studies might be an ensemble of EM-CA-MA-ES-based ethnographies of interaction. He suggests that using the other traditions' concepts and methods reflectively would be a way to interrogate the assumptive ground of conceptual schemes.

A third issue facing conversation analysis involves whether CA research can be used to answer questions that are central to most applied research projects. Although many of the conversation-analytic studies to date have analyzed conversational organization and practices, they have not attempted to determine the distribution of use of those practices within the population or made claims about the efficacy of the use of some strategies over others. Heritage (1999) makes an argument that conversation analysts can do their studies in ways that will permit them to make claims about distributions and outcomes:

> Granted that particular interactional practices are available to be deployed, who deploys them, when and where, and with what consequences or outcomes? Such questions can be meaningfully raised for data in which environments are broadly standardized, and participants have choices among actions that are analytically well understood. (p. 71)

Heritage argues that the primary prerequisite of answering questions of distributions and outcomes is mastery of conversation-analytic research techniques and findings. Then, in addition to conversation-analytic methods, researchers would need to know more traditional social scientific research methods, including sampling and statistical analysis techniques. Although Heritage predicts that more quantitative analyses will be included in future CA studies, he also advises that the path for those who are "applied" will not be an easy one.

CONCLUSION: LSI ISSUES AND TRENDS

There has been a shift in LSI research away from relatively insular groups of scholars working side by side, assuming that their respective results will meld. The recent trend at conventions, and sometimes in journals, has been toward discussion about the interconnections and boundaries of different research areas. In fact, this essay and that presented in Chapter 16 by Weatherall et al. constitute a good example of just such dialogue and some relevant issues. There are others—we cite below two of the more prominent ones.

There is currently some discussion within LSI research based on differences in the analytic methods and descriptive resources relied upon by ethnographers and conversation analysts. For ethnographers, the question is for what reasons and to what extent a close examination of the particulars of interactions becomes productive as evidence about culture and its discursive practices. For conversation analysts and discourse analysts, the question is whether and how to use informants' accounts to supplement, complement, or illuminate analyses of interactional conduct. There has been some movement toward greater common ground methodologically as a result, but disagreements are still common about whether particular studies give too much or too little attention to the specifics of interaction or to informants' accounts. For those who do conversation analysis, the issue is whether the data they utilize will uphold analytic rigor and sustain a focus on interactional phenomena. For those who do ethnography, the issue is whether standards in LSI research for assessing the quality and adequacy of evidence will be sufficiently pluralistic to be duly supportive of ethnographers' working practices and goals. At the same time, there is a new urgency about addressing these issues within LSI research because of recent ferment among ethnographers themselves about their goals and methods. The formation of a new Ethnography Division in the National Communication Association has been the basis for some discussion (mainly informal so far) of what might distinguish work in the ethnographic tradition that has been central to LSI research from that which is more readily encompassed within this new division. Although the new division is founded on a premise of openness to ethnographic work of all kinds, its founders are best known for work that focuses attention on the experiences of the researchers themselves, and one of the stated goals of the group is to give voice to alternative forms of writing (see Banks & Banks, 1998; Bochner & Ellis, 1995; Brettel, 1993; Ellis, 1996; Richardson, 1995; Van Maanen, 1995; Wolf, 1992).

A second area of discussion involves growing attention among LSI scholars to nonlinguistic, especially "visible," modes of communication (gesture and facial expression, gaze, spatial organization, body torque, concurrent physical activity, and so on, and their interplay with each other, with what is being said, and with the social and physical activity taking place). There are potential ramifications for the work in most of LSI's main research areas. Moerman (1990-1991) captures what is at stake, what adjustments in our work are becoming necessary, when he points out that when people come together, it is often not just to talk, but to engage in activities in which talk is only one of the resources on which they rely to engage in and coordinate effort in those activities. This view brings semiotics as a distinct perspective increasingly to the fore and forces us to problematize whether language should be analytically at the center in studies of interaction. Coupled with this, Goodwin (1981), Bavelas (1990, 1994), Kendon (1994), Streeck (1994), and Schegloff (1998), among others, have given close attention to the organization and internal logic of visible acts in their own right and how they are both a separate modality of interaction and a component of social interaction along with language. This work coincides with, perhaps has been fueled by, the emergence of new technologies for recording, microanalyzing, and presenting reports on visible practices and actions. This in turn is bringing some researchers up against the limitations of traditional forms of publication, with their dependence on text and static images. In response to such concerns, Jarmon (1996) published her dissertation as a computer-readable compact disk to exhibit dynamic images.

In our view, work being done in LSI has a vitality and momentum, and a felt kinship, across the several component traditions and diverse research topics that LSI research comprises. We attribute this to the underlying commonalities we cited at the beginning: an interest in the discursive practices that constitute the realities of social life and in the achievement of socially meaningful action and shared understanding.

REFERENCES

Austin, J. (1962). *How to do things with words.* New York: Oxford University Press.

Banks, A., & Banks, S. (Eds.). (1998). *Fiction and social research: By ice or fire.* Walnut Creek, CA: AltaMira.

Bavelas, J. B. (1990). Behaving and communicating: A reply to Motley. *Western Journal of Speech Communication, 54,* 593-602.

Bavelas, J. B. (1994). Gestures as part of speech: Methodological implications. *Research on Language and Social Interaction, 27,* 201-222.

Bavelas, J. B. (1999, May). *Is there a place for social psychology in LSI?* Paper presented at the annual meeting of the International Communication Association, San Francisco.

Bloch, L.-R. (1998). Communicating as an American immigrant in Israel: The *freier* phenomenon and the pursuit of an alternative value system. *Research on Language and Social Interaction, 31,* 177-208.

Blum-Kulka, S. (1997). *Dinner talk: Cultural patterns of sociability and socialization in family discourse.* Mahwah, NJ: Lawrence Erlbaum.

Blum-Kulka, S., House, J., & Kasper, G. (1989). *Cross-cultural pragmatics: Requests and apologies.* Norwood, NJ: Ablex.

Bochner, A., & Ellis, C. (1995). Telling and living: Narrative co-construction and the practices of interpersonal relationships. In W. Leeds-Hurwitz (Ed.), *Social approaches to communication* (pp. 201-216). New York: Guilford.

Braithwaite, C. (1997). "Were you there?" A ritual of legitimacy among Vietnam vets. *Western Journal of Communication, 61,* 423-447.

Brettell, C. B. (Ed.). (1993). *When they read what we write: The politics of ethnography.* Westport, CT: Bergin & Garvey.

Bucholtz, M. (1999). "Why be normal?" Language and identity practices in a community of nerd girls. *Language in Society, 28,* 203-224.

Buttny, R. (1996). Clients' and therapists' joint construction of the clients' problems. *Research on Language and Social Interaction, 29,* 125-153.

Carbaugh, D. (1989). Fifty terms for talk: A cross-cultural study. In S. Ting-Toomey & F. Korzenny (Eds.), *Language, culture, and communication: Current directions* (pp. 93-120). Newbury Park, CA: Sage.

Drew, P. (1998). Complaints about transgressions and misconduct. *Research on Language and Social Interaction, 31,* 295-325.

Eckert, P., & McConnell-Ginet, S. (1992). Think practically and look locally: Language and gender as community-based practice. *Annual Review of Anthropology, 21,* 461-490.

Ellis, C. (1996). *Composing ethnography: Alternative forms of qualitative writing.* Walnut Creek, CA: AltaMira.

Fitch, K. (1994). A cross-cultural study of directive sequences and some implications for compliance-gaining research. *Communication Monographs, 61,* 185-209.

Garfinkel, H. (1967). *Studies in ethnomethodology.* Englewood Cliffs, NJ: Prentice Hall.

Goffman, E. (1959). *The presentation of self in everyday life.* Garden City, NY: Doubleday.

Goldsmith, D., & Fitch, K. (1997). The normative context of advice as social support. *Human Communication Research, 23,* 454-476.

Goodwin, C. (1981). *Conversational organization: Interaction between speakers and hearers.* New York: Academic Press.

Grice, H. P. (1957). Meaning. *Philosophical Review, 66,* 377-388.

Grice, H. P. (1975). Logic and conversation. In P. Cole & J. L. Morgan (Eds.), *Syntax and semantics 3: Speech acts* (pp. 41-58). New York: Academic Press.

Gumperz, J. J. (1971). *Language in social groups.* Stanford, CA: Stanford University Press.

Gumperz, J. J., & Hymes, D. (Eds.). (1972). *Directions in sociolinguistics: The ethnography of communication.* New York: Holt, Rinehart & Winston.

Heritage, J. (1999). Conversation analysis at century's end: Practices of talk-in-interaction, their distributions, and their outcomes. *Research on Language and Social Interaction, 32,* 69-76.

Holt, E. (1996). Reporting on talk: The use of direct reported speech in conversation. *Research on Language and Social Interaction, 29,* 219-245.

Hopper, R. W. (Ed.). (1990-1991). Ethnography and conversation analysis [Special section]. *Research on Language and Social Interaction, 24*(2).

Hopper, R. W., & Chen, C.-H. (1996). Languages, cultures, relationships: Telephone openings in Taiwan. *Research on Language and Social Interaction, 29,* 291-313.

Hymes, D. (1972). Models of the interaction of language and social life. In J. J. Gumperz & D. Hymes (Eds.), *Directions in sociolinguistics: The ethnography of communication* (pp. 35-71). New York: Holt, Rinehart & Winston.

Hymes, D. (1974). *Foundations of sociolinguistics: An ethnographic approach.* Philadelphia: University of Pennsylvania Press.

Jarmon, L. H. (1996). *An ecology of embodied interaction: Turn-taking and interactional syntax in face-to-face encounters.* Unpublished doctoral dissertation, University of Texas, Austin.

Kendon, A. (Ed.). (1994). Gesture and understanding in social interaction [Special issue]. *Research on Language and Social Interaction, 27*(3).

Language and social interaction at the century's turn [Special issue]. *Research on Language and Social Interaction, 32*(1-2).

Leeds-Hurwitz, W. (1993). *Semiotics and communication: Signs, codes, cultures.* Hillsdale, NJ: Lawrence Erlbaum.

Leeds-Hurwitz, W. (Ed.). (1995). *Social approaches to communication.* New York: Guilford.

Lindsley, S. L. (1999). A layered model of problematic intercultural communication in US-owned maquiladoras in Mexico. *Communication Monographs, 66,* 145-167.

Maynard, D. W. (1997). The news delivery sequence: Bad news and good news in conversational interaction. *Research on Language and Social Interaction, 30,* 93-130.

Moerman, M. (1988). *Talking culture: Ethnography and conversation analysis.* Cambridge: Cambridge University Press.

Moerman, M. (1990-1991). Exploring talk and interaction. *Research on Language and Social Interaction, 24,* 173-187.

Philipsen, G. (1992). *Speaking culturally.* Albany: State University of New York Press.

Philipsen, G., & Huspek, M. (1985). A bibliography of sociolinguistic studies of personal address. *Anthropological Linguistics, 27,* 94-101.

Pratt, S., & Wieder, D. L. (1993). The case of *saying a few words* and *talking for another* among the Osage people: "Public speaking" as an object of ethnography. *Research on Language and Social Interaction, 26,* 353-408.

Richardson, L. (1995). Narrative and sociology. In J. Van Maanen (Ed.), *Representation in ethnography* (pp. 198-221). Thousand Oaks, CA: Sage.

Sacks, H. (1992). *Lectures on conversation* (2 vols.) (G. Jefferson, Ed.). Oxford: Blackwell.

Schegloff, E. A. (1998). Body torque. *Social Research, 65,* 535-596.

Schegloff, E. A. (1999). What next? Language and social interaction study at the century's turn. *Research on Language and Social Interaction, 32,* 141-148.

Schely-Newman, E. (1999). Mothers know best: Constructing meaning in a narrative event. *Quarterly Journal of Speech, 85,* 285-302.

Searle, J. R. (1969). *Speech acts: An essay in the philosophy of language.* London: Cambridge University Press.

Sigman, S. J. (1987). *A perspective on social communication.* Lexington, MA: Lexington.

Streeck, J. (1994). Gesture as communication II: The audience as co-author. *Research on Language and Social Interaction, 27,* 239-267.

Szymanski, M. H. (1999). Re-engaging and dis-engaging talk in activity. *Language in Society, 28,* 1-23.

Tannen, D. (1981). New York Jewish conversational style. *International Journal of the Sociology of Language, 30,* 133-149.

Van Maanen, J. (Ed.). (1995). *Representation in ethnography.* Thousand Oaks, CA: Sage.

Wenger, E. (1998). *Communities of practice.* New York: Cambridge University Press.

Wieder, D. L. (1999). Ethnomethodology, conversation analysis, microanalysis and the ethnography of speaking (EM-CA-MA-ES): Resonances and basic issues. *Research on Language and Social Interaction, 32,* 163-171.

Wittgenstein, L. (1953). *Philosophical investigations.* Oxford: Blackwell.

Wolf, M. A. (1992). *A thrice-told tale: Feminism, postmodernism, and ethnographic responsibility.* Stanford, CA: Stanford University Press.

CHAPTER CONTENTS

18 Underestimating Our Own Weight? The Scope and Impact of Communication Research on Public Policy

DALE KUNKEL
WENDY JO MAYNARD FARINOLA
University of California, Santa Barbara

This chapter examines the scope and impact of communication research on public policy, with attention to three broad areas: mass communication, interpersonal communication, and organizational communication. In their review of research on mass communication, the authors focus on the topics of children and television violence and the effects of viewing pornography. In their discussion of research on interpersonal communication, they review research in health risk behaviors, hate speech, and crisis communication. They then address two areas of research in organizational communication: sexual harassment and privacy in the workplace. After a brief discussion of the breadth of communication policy research, the authors conclude with some observations on prospects for the future of this field.

S CHOLARLY assessment of the state of the field of communication research has often reflected a self-critical view. Among the most frequently cited complaints are three in particular. First is the inability of the field to define itself and establish central theories that unite its disparate elements:

> There is no predominant method and no central paradigm. . . . Communication eludes the concept of boundary. (Comstock, 1983, pp. 42-43)

> What communication theory should look like, what it is for, the boundaries and internal divisions of the field, how communication research should be conducted, . . . all must be regarded as open questions at the present time. (Craig, 1993, p. 26)

Correspondence: Dale Kunkel, Department of Communication, University of California, Santa Barbara, CA 93106; e-mail kunkel@sscf.ucsb.edu

Communication Yearbook 24, pp. 411-431

Second is the lack of recognition from the outside world, including other academic disciplines:

> Much of the output . . . has little influence upon scholars in fields outside of communication who are studying media or communication issues. (Dennis, 1993, p. xii)

> Not only are the most cited books on topics relevant to communication rarely written by those formally in the field, but these works cite few, if any, who are. (Beniger, 1993, p. 18)

And third is the failure of communication research to produce meaningful findings that lead to "real-world" influence:

> Much of the field has been insular, disconnected, and often invisible. (Noam, 1993, p. 204)

> Policy makers in business and government who are open to intelligence from all sources have little contact with communication research generated by those in the universities. (Dennis, 1993, p. xii)

Such criticisms have emerged in virtually every major collection of "state-of-the-art" essays about communication research over the past several decades.

In the realm of communication law and policy, many observers reflect similarly negative views in sizing up the impact of communication research. Noam (1993) asserts that communication research has been "largely absent" in the shaping of policy, or at best has played only a "minor role" (pp. 199-200). Mueller (1995) notes that "the closer we get to ideas which have shaped public policy, the more communication scholarship recedes from the picture" (p. 459). Wartella (1993, p. 137) interprets the historical record to argue that although communication research can make a difference in children's media, it usually does not.

In this essay, we seek to challenge the prevailing view of communication research as ineffectual if not absent entirely from the public policy landscape. Moreover, in the process of making our case that communication research has yielded substantial contributions in the policy domain, we also make another potentially controversial assertion: Communication research that informs or influences public policy can be found across much of the full range of subdivisions of the field, reaching far beyond the realms of mass-media and technology studies that have more traditionally been associated with policy linkages.

It is our position that communication policy research is a vital element of the field that is contributing significant knowledge to help inform and influence public policy, despite persistent concern to the contrary. In support of this view, we will identify research across a diverse range of subdivisions in the field that has played an important role in shaping policy debates, if not outcomes.

Before proceeding with our evidence, we must first underscore that we conceptualize and define communication policy research in broad terms. In the past, this label has generally been applied to the work of those who study the policy-making process or who examine the patterns and trends in communication policy over the years. In other words, communication policy research has been commonly understood as research *about* communication policy. Furthermore, the term *communication policy* has been linked in the minds of many observers principally with the area of electronic mass-media regulation. Books of all kinds within the realm of mass communication processes and effects regularly include sections devoted to "policy implications," whereas those devoted to other aspects of the field, such as interpersonal or organizational communication, typically eschew such considerations.

Our view contrasts with this narrow perspective. We assert that the defining characteristic of communication policy research is not simply that a study examines, or is *about,* the communication policy-making process; rather, communication policy research may include studies with findings that *inform* communication policy makers about important issues under their purview. From this perspective, one can see that communication policy research may encompass virtually any subdivision or interest area within the field. Interpersonal researchers may examine factors that contribute to child abuse, violence in the family, or other social problems with their roots in human interaction. Those who study information systems and/or communication technologies might offer insights on privacy issues associated with the growing prominence of electronic networks. Obvious ties to policy concerns also emerge in the areas of organizational, health, and political communication, and this list can hardly be considered exhaustive. The essential ingredients in the mix are that the nature of the knowledge produced has important implications for social policy concerns and that policy makers recognize it as possessing high credibility.

To summarize, we believe that the field of communication encompasses a broad array of topic areas that produce studies with important policy implications. Policy-related communication research can thus be characterized as a rather decentralized collection of research efforts that have their conceptual roots in widely dispersed, domain-specific areas throughout the entire realm of study of communication phenomena. The common bond is their ability to provide useful information related to public policy concerns, whether the research in question is broad and theoretical in nature or narrow and applied, as is found in many problem-centered studies.

Given this foundation, we now turn to the task of supporting our position by reviewing a broad range of communication research that has informed and/or influenced public policy.[1] We begin by considering some examples related to mass communication, the area of research with which we are most familiar.

MASS COMMUNICATION

Two issues in mass communication—the effects of television violence on children, and the effects of exposure to pornographic media—provide useful case studies in which our field has produced significant research findings that have made noteworthy contributions to the policy agenda.

Children and Television Violence

The most long-standing concern in the realm of children and television involves the impact of violent portrayals on young viewers. A prominent psychologist, Albert Bandura, played a pivotal role in the 1960s by first linking children's exposure to media violence with subsequent aggressive behaviors (Bandura, 1965; Bandura, Ross, & Ross, 1961, 1963). Other psychologists, such as Leonard Berkowitz (1964, 1986), Leonard Eron (1986; Eron, Huesmann, Lefkowitz, & Walder, 1972), and Rowell Huesmann (1982; Huesmann & Eron, 1986), followed and have since devoted decades to their efforts to study the effects of televised violence. Yet despite the field of psychology's high profile here, researchers from the field of communication have provided at least equivalent contributions to knowledge in this area, and arguably have even dominated their peers in psychology and other disciplines.

Two research collections are widely recognized as benchmarks in this area: the 1972 U.S. surgeon general's report on television violence (Surgeon General's Scientific Advisory Commission on Television and Social Behavior, 1972) and the "surgeon general's update" later produced by the National Institute of Mental Health (Pearl, Bouthilet, & Lazar, 1982). Of the 52 authors who contributed to the 1972 surgeon general's report, a plurality of 23 were housed in communication programs at major universities, compared with 10 from psychology and 19 from all other fields. Similarly, the NIMH report features 30 individual contributions, of which 14 had first or sole authors aligned with the field of communication, compared with only 8 for psychology and 8 from other fields. Particularly prominent within the field of communication is George Gerbner's research on the cultivation effects of television violence (Gerbner & Gross, 1976; Gerbner, Gross, Morgan, & Signorielli, 1986), which was cited frequently by policy makers throughout the 1970s and 1980s.

These two research collections are arguably the most widely cited and influential pieces of evidence produced regarding the issue of television violence, and in both cases the field of communication established a dominant presence. Whenever the issue of televised violence is debated in the policy arena, these projects tend to form the nucleus of the relevant empirical support. What is most interesting, however, is that the field of communication has received essentially no credit or acknowledgment for its contributions in this realm.

When both of the above-noted TV violence reports were published, it was psychology that succeeded in stealing the thunder. Shortly after the NIMH report was published, a special section of *American Psychologist* (July 1983), the flagship journal of the American Psychological Association, reviewed the major findings of the research, reprinting some key passages and presenting reactions from a U.S. senator and a leading broadcast industry executive. In introducing the section, Singer (1983) noted "the invited articles represent only a small fraction of those psychologists currently involved in television research" (p. 816). Nowhere throughout the issue was there any mention of the contributions from communication, despite a sharp focus at times on media institution issues that might help explain the prevalence of violence in entertainment television content, an issue arguably closer to the heart of the field of communication than to psychology. We do not mean to argue here that psychology should not receive credit for its policy contributions; rather, we wish to ask why communication does not seek or obtain similar recognition for at least equivalent contributions.

More recently, Congress enacted legislation in 1996 that led to the V-chip television ratings and blocking capability (Price, 1998). In this realm, communication research has played an influential role in two distinct aspects of policy development. Although a strong scientific consensus had already emerged by the 1990s that television violence contributes to psychological harm in child viewers (American Medical Association, 1996; American Psychological Association, 1993; National Academy of Sciences, 1993), a new study of violence on television conducted jointly at four of the leading communication programs in the country served as a catalyst for congressional approval of the V-chip proposal. That joint project, known as the National Television Violence Study (NTVS; Wilson et al., 1997), issued its first of three annual reports in January 1996 on the risks posed by violence on television, criticizing the industry sharply for glamorizing and/or sanitizing most violent portrayals, both of which tend to enhance the risk of harmful effects. Within a matter of days, criticism of TV violence found its way into President Clinton's State of the Union Address, and within a matter of weeks, Congress approved the V-chip proposal (Zoglin, 1996). Congressman Edward Markey (1996), the leading proponent of the V-chip, identified the NTVS report as a principal catalyst for congressional approval of this new policy.

Once the V-chip law was passed, the television industry faced the task of devising a system of ratings to categorize programs for potential blocking by parents. Although academic experts strongly recommended and parents strongly preferred a system of content-based ratings, the industry instead elected to employ a set of age-based advisory categories for use with the V-chip blocking technology (Cantor, 1998; Gruenwald, 1997). A major controversy ensued about the adequacy of the program rating categories, and the debate was powerfully informed by the NTVS research conducted at the University of Wisconsin regarding children's reactions to various age and content program ratings (Cantor & Harrison, 1997). The data made clear that content ratings (e.g., "contains violent content") do not increase children's interest in programs, whereas age-based advisories (e.g., "parental discretion advised") do. Thus age-based ratings pose the risk of creating a boomerang effect by attracting children's attention to the very programs the rating system indicates pose some cause for concern.

Based on this evidence, criticism of the age-based ratings approach was pursued by communication researchers not only in academic circles, but also in opinion columns in the nation's leading newspapers, including the *New York Times* (Kunkel, 1996) and *Washington Post* (Cantor, 1996). A congressional hearing ensued (U.S. Senate, 1997), and shortly thereafter the V-chip ratings framework was amended to incorporate content-specific categories that complement the age-based advisory ratings (Farhi, 1997). Here again, research played a pivotal role in shaping debate about the implementation of the V-chip rating categories, leading to a revision of the rating system that was clearly influenced by the relevant empirical evidence produced by communication researchers.

The Effects of Viewing Pornography

Although the topic has received somewhat less attention in recent years, U.S. policy makers have long maintained an interest in the relationship between exposure to sexually explicit media content and subsequent antisocial behavior. In the 1980s, scientific research conducted by communication scholars gained center stage in the policy debate surrounding the issue of restricting sexually explicit pornographic materials (Showers, 1994). In order for the government to regulate pornography, a case must be established that exposure to such content generates some harm to society. In legal terms, this represents a "compelling governmental interest," a necessary element to overcome First Amendment protections that would otherwise prohibit any media content regulation.

In 1986, the attorney general of the United States established a national commission on pornography that studied and published a major report on the relationship between pornography and antisocial behavior (U.S. Attorney General's Commission on Pornography, 1986). The recommendations in the report, which include a range of proposed restrictions on the production and distribution of pornographic materials, stemmed from the commission's interpretation of the social science evidence as demonstrating "harmful" effects from exposure to pornography. As the report makes clear, the "conclusions rest on findings from the social sciences . . . to a significant extent" (p. 322).

The commission's interpretation of the scientific data was sharply challenged by many in the field (Linz, Donnerstein, & Penrod, 1987; Paletz, 1988). Indeed, the debate among scholars regarding the evidence of harmful effects from exposure to explicit sexual materials has been quite robust. Leading researchers have at times disagreed strongly with one another regarding interpretations of the scientific evidence, as demonstrated by three different colloquy exchanges published in the *Journal of Communication* between 1986 and 1988 (winter 1986, pp. 174-188; summer 1987, pp. 185-192; spring 1988, pp. 180-192). Throughout all of the controversy, communication researchers have been among the most prominent experts involved in the debate.

The primary academic research cited by the Attorney General's Commission on Pornography came from four senior scholars housed in communication programs: Jennings Bryant, Edward Donnerstein, Neil Malamuth, and Dolf Zillmann. In addition, Edna Einsiedel, a researcher with a Ph.D. in mass communication from Indiana University, served as the commission's staff social scientist and was responsible for drafting the research sections of the commission's final report. After completing that work, Einsiedel (1988) later offered her own independent analysis of the empirical evidence on pornography effects and the difficulties that policy makers have encountered in trying to apply it in their work.

The ultimate outcome of the report of the Attorney General's Commission on Pornography was essentially no shift at all in the law's fundamental treatment of sexually explicit material. In the absence of a clear scientific consensus about the possible harmful effects of such material, an adequate base of political support could not be established to implement the commission's recommendations (Wilcox, 1987; Zillmann, 1989). Yet a major national policy debate that stretched over a period of several years had been engaged, and clearly the center of that tempest involved evidence that had been generated by leaders in the field of communication research.

The topic areas of research and policy linkage that we have explored above fall within the domain of mass communication, a realm in which the application of communication research to public policy has been well acknowledged in the past (Anderson, Meyer, & Hexamer, 1982; Comstock, 1976). Certainly there are many other areas and examples that we could cite here, but we have established our case effectively for mass communication. Thus we turn now to a different research context, that of interpersonal communication, to consider some of the policy applications of studies in that realm.

INTERPERSONAL COMMUNICATION

We have identified three distinct and diverse areas of interpersonal research that hold clear and strong linkages to public policy concerns: studies of health risk behaviors, hate speech, and crisis communication involving public service agencies.

Health Risk Behaviors

Perhaps the most abundant collection of research with policy linkages in the realm of interpersonal communication involves the study of risk-related behaviors with public health and safety implications (Rice & Atkin, 1994). A wide range of behaviorally based health problems pose significant costs for most countries around the world. These problem areas include smoking, drug abuse, drunk driving, teen pregnancy, and transmission of AIDS/STDs. Public policy makers are interested in identifying effective strategies to increase people's understanding of the harms that are associated with these health issues as well as in learning which tactics hold the greatest potential to alter the "risky" behaviors that contribute to them. Obviously, communication processes are centrally implicated in the accomplishment of both these goals.

Although the study of public health communication campaigns may involve mass communication channels, such research is conceptually grounded in the interpersonal realm, where persuasion research has historically been centered (Burgoon, 1989; Burgoon & Bettinghaus, 1980; Dillard, 1993). Interpersonal research addressing health communication encompasses all aspects of the communicative process, including source, message, channel, and audience characteristics.

The sheer volume of research in the area of health communication has allowed scholars to refine and develop theoretical propositions regarding the contexts in which varying persuasive strategies are most effective in altering health- related behaviors. Indeed, matching appropriate message strategies with knowledge about target audience characteristics has been a primary goal of communication researchers who seek to design and/or evaluate the effectiveness of health information campaigns or interventions (Schooler, Chaffee, Flora, & Roser, 1998).

One of the most widely used persuasive strategies in this realm is the fear appeal (Hale & Dillard, 1995; Witte, 1992a, 1998). Fear appeals seek to motivate the message receiver to change behavioral patterns that pose health risks by convincing the individual that he or she is susceptible to a particular threat. Research indicates that fear appeals tend to work best when the target audience has a strong sense of personal efficacy in controlling the relevant behavior and is therefore capable of performing the recommended response (Rogers, 1975, 1983; Witte, 1992b, 1998). Fear appeals have been employed effectively in campaigns promoting AIDS prevention (Nowak & Siska, 1995; Sheer & Cline, 1994), cessation of cigarette smoking (McAlister, Ramirez, Galavotti, & Gallion, 1989), and sun safety (Buller, Borland, & Burgoon, 1998; Parrott, Monahan, Ainsworth, & Steiner, 1998).

In other contexts, however, positive affect appeals may hold a higher probability of success in accomplishing intended effects in certain target audiences (Batra & Stayman, 1990; Monahan, 1995). Positive appeals work best when the target audience is unfamiliar with the topic to be addressed; in contrast, when the audience already holds a negative attitude toward the behavior in question, positive affect is unlikely to overcome any strongly held negative feelings (Monahan, 1995). Positive affect messages have enjoyed some degree of success in antidrug campaigns, such as "Just Say No" and "Be Smart—Don't Start" (Donahew, Sypher, & Bukowski, 1991).

Numerous other persuasive strategies have been studied, as have a broad range of audience-related mediating variables such as age-based developmental differences (Austin, 1995), cultural sensitivities (Witte & Morrison, 1995), and the target's motives for attending to the message (Parrott, 1995). It is impossible for us to review here the full breadth of research contributions in this realm, but it is clear that communication research has played a significant role in informing and influencing the shape of public health communication campaigns worldwide across a diverse range of issues and topics. Such campaigns are among the most visible types of public policy initiatives for governments around the globe.

Hate Speech

Another distinct area of interpersonal research with strong policy implications involves the study of hate speech. *Hate speech* is an encompassing, generic term that has come to refer to verbal attacks based on race, ethnicity, religion, or sexual orientation (Smolla, 1993). During the 1990s, policy makers increasingly pursued efforts to curb hate speech (Calvert, 1997), although not all such efforts have been upheld as constitutional in the United States (*Doe v. University of Michigan,* 1989).

In the United States, the First Amendment's guarantee of freedom of speech poses a potential challenge to the constitutionality of laws and policies against hate speech. In interpreting and applying the First Amendment, however, the U.S. courts have never embraced an absolutist perspective; rather, they have employed a balancing test in which they weigh the interests of the government in restricting the speech in question with the individual's and society's interest in free expression (Carter, Franklin, & Wright, 1996). A central factor in shaping a court's judgment in such balancing tests is the evidence of harm that can be linked to the proscribed content. Thus studies that examine who may be harmed, in what ways, and by what types of hate speech content may provide influential if not critical evidence for this area of law.

In recent years, communication scholars have begun to address these issues from a broad range of perspectives, including both critical cultural analysis and empirical quantitative approaches. Calvert (1997) has applied two theoretical frames derived from Carey (1989) that have led him to examine both direct, immediate impacts on the specific targets of hate speech and the long-term, cumulative implications for society's treatment of subordinated minority groups. Calvert concludes that courts are likely to consider only the direct and immediate impacts of hate speech, and he draws important parallels between the probable harms of hate speech and the harms that courts have previously accepted as adequate evidence to justify some limitations on First Amendment freedoms.

Calvert's arguments set the stage for more definitive empirical investigation, and such studies have now begun to emerge. Leets and Giles (1997) have applied social scientific methodology to an examination of the impact of strong, direct racist speech targeting ethnic minorities. These researchers present self-report evidence of psychological pain that is "hard to endure" (p. 289) for members of a group targeted by hate speech. Indeed, the subjects in one of their experiments rated the emotional distress associated with a loss of dignity from hate speech remarks to be more difficult to bear than physical pain.

The same investigators have also examined how the attribution of harm is influenced by variables such as group membership, message severity, message explicitness, and the medium of expression (Leets, 1999; Leets & Giles, 1997; Leets,

Giles, & Noels, 1999). Their approach allows them to develop theory in this area of effects while at the same time gathering evidence that has significant policy implications.

Evidence from communication researchers assessing the harmfulness of hate speech seems likely to play an important role in shaping the future of law and policy in this realm, both in the United States and abroad. Downing (1999) notes that although other countries do not face the First Amendment dilemma that is unique to the United States, they nonetheless face the same normative issues associated with hate speech policy in the United States, that of protecting subordinated minority groups from extremist attacks. Indeed, it may turn out that research documenting the harmfulness of hate speech could have stronger policy impact outside the United States, particularly in those countries that lack strong freedom of speech guarantees such as are found in the First Amendment of the U.S. Constitution.

Crisis Communication

Our third example in the realm of interpersonal communication involves the study of crisis communications—more specifically, 911 emergency call taking. The most common means by which people in the United States report emergencies to public authorities is via the 911 telephone system. Public safety operators who field 911 calls must make split-second decisions about the resources to dispatch in response to each call. The operators have a critical need for information on which to base their decisions, yet they must obtain that information from people who are often distraught, panicked, or hysterical. Effective communication strategies under such stressful conditions can literally mean the difference between life and death in many cases.

Communication researchers have studied audiotape recordings of emergency phone calls to identify effective as well as dysfunctional interaction strategies for call takers (Tracy, 1997; Zimmerman, 1984, 1992). It is well established that in everyday interaction, most people are polite and adhere to informal communication rules that assist one another in maintaining the respect of the other party, often known as "saving face" (Brown & Levinson, 1987; Goffman, 1955). Rudeness or other personal attacks are typically avoided, except when contextual factors instigate stress or anxiety that overcomes the normal "traffic rules" of social interaction. Yet, given the inherently stressful nature of emergency calls, face attacks are a relatively common aspect of conversation encountered by 911 emergency operators.

Emergency call takers face a unique occupational hazard from being forced to indulge face attacks (e.g., "What's wrong with you? Why haven't you gotten someone here to help me yet?") on a regular basis without responding in aggressive fashion. This situation may lead to significant stress and emotional suffering (S. J. Tracy & K. Tracy, 1998). When such reactions become strong enough, call takers may respond to emergency callers with their own face attacks in an effort to reassert their authority and control of the situation (K. Tracy & S. J. Tracy, 1998).

When this occurs, the escalation of attacks on both sides may quickly render the conversation dysfunctional, potentially impeding a critically important exchange of information.

The findings of communication research in the realm of emergency call taking have some compelling policy implications. Studies in this area have provided solid, theoretically grounded principles that can help call takers and their supervisors to recognize problematic approaches to emergency call conversations as well as identify strategies for call takers that are most likely to prove effective when they are dealing with distraught and/or panicked callers.

Clearly, the public service organizations that handle emergency calls have gained significant insight about optimal approaches for communicating effectively with citizens in crisis. By establishing research-based policies and procedures for call taking that maximize effective communication under the most difficult of circumstances, emergency service providers have improved their performance in responding to crisis situations. The knowledge generated by research in this area may also be applied in other occupational settings that involve high-stress communication environments, such as hospital emergency rooms and air traffic control towers.

To summarize our evidence in the interpersonal realm, we have identified three very distinct topic areas in which communication research has provided meaningful public policy contributions. Research has long played an active and central role in shaping public health campaigns in many countries around the globe. Two additional topics, the study of hate speech and of public safety crisis communication strategies, represent more-recent additions to the field's policy research agenda. Collectively, these three topics demonstrate the breadth of communication research in the interpersonal domain that holds important policy implications.

ORGANIZATIONAL COMMUNICATION

Finally, we turn our attention to organizational communication. This area of study considers the formal and informal communication patterns that exist within a defined group or organization and examines how these communication processes affect a wide range of dependent variables, including employee satisfaction and organizational productivity, among many other outcomes. In this realm, we will consider two topics in which communication research has contributed important evidence to inform public policy: sexual harassment and privacy in the workplace.

Sexual Harassment

Legal scholar Catharine MacKinnon (1979) provided the seminal argument that women who are sexually harassed in the workplace suffer disadvantages compared with other workers and therefore experience a form of discrimination that violates equal employment opportunities guaranteed by existing law. From this perspective, victims of harassment should be afforded the same legal protection as that available to victims of sex discrimination under Title VII of the 1964 Civil Rights Act (Gutek, 1997).

This argument was subsequently adopted and implemented as public policy in the United States by the Equal Employment Opportunity Commission (1980). Under present law, unwelcome sexual advances, requests for sexual favors, and any other verbal or physical conduct of a sexual nature constitute sexual harassment when their acceptance or rejection influences employment or academic advancement decisions, or when they serve to create a hostile or offensive working or academic environment. Although few other countries have implemented legal protections comparable to those afforded women in the United States, research suggests that harassment in the workplace and in educational institutions is widespread around the world (Barak, 1997).

The communication discipline is a particularly appropriate site for research about sexual harassment because such behavior involves message sending and receiving (Gilsdorf, 1990; Keyton, 1996). As Wood (1993) notes:

> Whatever else sexual harassment may entail . . . it is undeniably a communication issue. . . . First, the existence and meaning of sexual harassment are constructed symbolically both through culturally formed and legitimated definitions and through the processes whereby individuals interpret experiences. Second, sexual harassment and the responses to it are enacted through communication. (p. 10)

Most cases of sexual harassment involve opposite-sex dyads; that is, a male and female interacting with each other. Therefore, a highly salient aspect of communication research involves the examination of gender differences in perceiving and defining what constitutes sexual harassment (Booth-Butterfield, 1989; Gutek & O'Connor, 1995; Jansma, 1996; Saal, 1996). Evidence from such research can lead to insights that are potentially valuable for reconciling conflicting accounts of interactions—for example, cases in which one party perceives harassment and the other claims no harassing intent.

Furthermore, research that seeks to provide theoretical explanations for sexual harassment must encompass not only individual psychosocial factors involving the genders but the role of the organizational context in which the behavior occurs (Booth-Butterfield, 1986). Just as there are differences in individuals' attitudes toward and responses to harassment, there are differing levels of organizational awareness of, tolerance for, and reactions to the occurrence of sexual harassment (Keyton, 1996). For example, research has consistently indicated that harassing behavior is significantly underreported, typically because of victims' fear of humiliation, reprisals, or lack of support from authorities in the organization (Dunwoody-Miller & Gutek, 1985; Gutek & Koss, 1993). Thus it seems clear that organizational climate may play a significant role in the identification as well as the amelioration of sexual harassment.

Communication research not only contributes to the understanding of how and why sexual harassment occurs, it also offers important contributions in terms of shaping strategies to reduce such actions. Berryman-Fink (1993) suggests training that explores differences in male-female communication styles. Bingham (1991) proposes multistep strategies to promote consciousness-raising and appropriate responses to potentially harassing behavior. These and other related studies in this area have helped to inform organizations about how best to sensitize employees in an effort to reduce occurrences of sexual harassment.

In sum, because sexual harassment occurs within organizational settings, many of its aspects can be analyzed through the lens of organizational communication theory and research. Evidence produced by the field of communication holds significant implications for policy makers whose goal is to combat sexual harassment. Communication research has not only helped to explain how and why harassing behavior occurs, it has provided findings that serve to inform efforts to limit the occurrence of such behavior.

Privacy in the Workplace

Workplace privacy is another organizational issue that emerged on the public policy agenda during the 1980s. During that period, many businesses began to question the medical status of job applicants and/or employees, to implement employee drug testing, and to pursue videotape surveillance in the workplace environment (Sculnick, 1989). Burgoon (1982) has proposed four types of privacy considerations: physical, psychological, social, and informational. Judgments about what actions are considered invasive are dependent upon many situational considerations, including the type of privacy concerns involved and the nature of the employee-employer relationship (Burgoon, Buller, & Woodall, 1989).

As technological innovations have provided increasing opportunities for employers to surveil and/or independently evaluate their employees' actions and assertions, policy makers have sought to find the proper balance between the rights of these two groups. The U.S. Congress has enacted legislation to prohibit mandatory polygraph testing and to protect against surreptitious wiretapping (U.S. Congress, 1987), yet this topic area remains highly controversial as the appropriate legal boundaries are negotiated in this realm.

Communication research has examined how workers react to various types of privacy-threatening techniques in the workplace. Botan (1996) examined the effects of panoptic electronic surveillance in an organization. A panopticon is a physical setting (e.g., prison, workhouse, school, medical facility) in which all parts of the interior are visible from a single point, with occupants always potentially exposed to observation yet unable to know exactly when they are or are not being observed. Botan found that the greater the potential for workplace surveillance, the greater the probability of a number of negative outcomes for the organization, including reduced employee self-esteem and job performance. Similarly, other researchers have reported adverse outcomes in job satisfaction and performance associated with varying types of intrusive actions by employers (LePoire, Burgoon, & Parrott, 1992; Parrott, Burgoon, Burgoon, & LePoire, 1989).

One consequence of this pattern of findings seems to be that organizations are less anxious to pursue privacy-threatening techniques in the workplace and more willing to acquiesce to public policies that restrict employers' rights in this realm (Botan, 1996). In the absence of any data documenting the negative outcomes for organizations of many invasive techniques for monitoring their employees, one might well expect to see a somewhat different policy framework, as employers would likely push more aggressively for further intrusions on employee privacy in order to better promote their own self-interests.

In sum, our analysis indicates that organizational communication research represents yet another distinct area in the field that has contributed evidence with some palpable policy implications. The topics of sexual harassment and privacy in the workplace are both areas in which the achievement of public policy goals has been supported by studies that help us better understand the nature of these problems and the implications of various efforts to solve them.

THE BREADTH OF COMMUNICATION POLICY RESEARCH

The evidence we have presented in this chapter establishes clearly that there is highly credible work produced within communication research that contributes in varying ways to major public policy debates, decisions, and related responses. Across all three subdivisions of the field discussed above—mass, interpersonal, and organizational—communication researchers have made noteworthy contributions that inform and influence many public policy concerns.

How well have we made our case that communication policy research can be found broadly across the field's disparate interests? The three areas of the field that we have chosen to consider were selected judiciously. These areas arguably represent the widest range of "levels of analysis" within the field of communication. Paisley (1984) has observed that academic fields may be defined either by a central focus on a single level of analysis, which is then applied across a wide range of variables of interest (e.g., psychology's focus on the individual), or by a central focus on a single variable, which is then applied across a wide range of levels of analysis (e.g., political science). From this perspective, communication is a "variable" rather than a "level" field. Its focus is on the production, distribution, interpretation, and impact of messages, albeit across many distinct levels of analysis.

By demonstrating policy applications of research across the full range of levels in the field of communication, we believe we have made the strongest possible case in support of our breadth assertion. With that said, we are confident that other distinct areas of the field that are not easily subsumed by these levels, such as the study of communication technology, also contribute actively and meaningfully to the public policy agenda.

Citing communication technology as yet another example of an area of study within the field that holds strong policy implications underscores the novelty of the means by which communication as a field has been subdivided into specialty areas. Some divisions, such as mass, interpersonal, and organizational, reflect levels; others, such as political, health, and technology, represent variables. If one conceptualizes levels and variables as a two-dimensional matrix, it is inevitable that these differing subdivisions of the field will experience some overlap. Thus it is arguably the case that some of the variable subdivisions, such as technology and health communication in particular, may comprise the strongest concentration of policy-relevant research across the field as a whole. It must be recognized, however, that the construct of "policy-related research" functions as a variable that can be applied across both other levels and other variables used for framing and/or defining the field. This brings us full circle back to our original assertion: Communication research that informs or influences public policy can be found across much of the full range of subdivisions of the field. Communication policy research certainly cannot be characterized as an isolated area of the field in and of itself; rather, it overlaps with various distinct topic areas of study that hold policy implications.

PROSPECTS FOR THE FUTURE

If we are correct in our assertion that the field of communication has made significant contributions to policy, the question then follows: Why does it seem that communication receives scant recognition or credit from both the policy community and society at large? Despite the active role of communication research in contributing to policy debates, we believe that the field fails to receive its due in terms of public recognition because of the lack of any clear identity, or, as Wartella (1993) puts it, the lack of a "public face." Furthermore, we attribute this shortcoming to three primary factors: the absence of any common body of theory or knowledge that defines communication for those outside the field, the diversity of approaches to inquiry practiced in the field, and the lack of any professionally based infrastructure to serve as a liaison between the field and leading social institutions as well as the public as a whole.

Across all of the programs in the academy labeled as communication, conspicuously absent is any shared "core" curriculum or body of knowledge, a situation that does little to clarify confusion about our identity among colleagues in other disciplines. Communication as a field means different things to different people. At many schools, communication study emphasizes practical skills training in media-related areas, such as journalism, advertising, and public relations. At others, the orientation is grounded in theory and research, with students receiving about the same degree of direct vocational preparation that they would encounter as English or sociology majors—which is to say, not much at all.

Even in those communication programs that emphasize a theoretical perspective, a wide range of methodological approaches to inquiry are typically employed, from empirical social science to more humanistic perspectives such as cultural studies and media aesthetics. Although this diversity arguably has its merits, it almost certainly contributes to the amorphous image the field projects to the outside world.

Finally, the field of communication has yet to propagate any professional association that plays an active role in representing research produced by the field to the policy community. Notwithstanding this void, communication research has clearly contributed a wealth of evidence that has shaped policy debates and outcomes, as we have demonstrated in this chapter. The problem is not that our research fails to reach the policy arena; rather, it reaches the policy arena but the field receives no credit because the underlying source remains unrecognized.

As a group, we as communication researchers may be too easily resigned to the belief that the field of communication is not big enough or cohesive enough or that we are not clear enough about what we do to compete for attention and resources with other major disciplines. Yet such a view is at odds with the research contributions we have chronicled above. From our perspective, the field of communication has among its strengths a broad range of policy-oriented research accomplishments. As the field matures and develops a stronger identity with external audiences, this base of policy-related studies holds the potential to play an important role in defining communication research as an academic discipline.

NOTE

1. For purposes of this essay, *public policy* refers to the formal actions taken by government bodies, including the process of making the law as well as executing it (Kelman, 1987).

REFERENCES

American Medical Association. (1996). *Physician guide to media violence.* Chicago: Author.
American Psychological Association. (1993). *Violence and youth: Psychology's response.* Washington, DC: Author.
Anderson, J. A., Meyer, T. P., & Hexamer, A. (1982). An examination of the assumptions underlying telecommunications social policies treating children as a specialized audience. In M. Burgoon (Ed.), *Communication yearbook 5* (pp. 369-384). New Brunswick, NJ: Transaction.
Austin, E. W. (1995). Reaching young audiences: Developmental considerations in designing health messages. In E. Maibach & R. L. Parrott (Eds.), *Designing health messages: Approaches from communication theory and public health practice* (pp. 114-144). Thousand Oaks, CA: Sage.
Bandura, A. (1965). Influence of models' reinforcement contingencies on the acquisition of imitative responses. *Journal of Personality and Social Psychology, 1,* 589-595.
Bandura, A., Ross, D., & Ross, S. A. (1961). Transmission of aggression through imitation of aggressive models. *Journal of Abnormal and Social Psychology, 63,* 575-582.

Bandura, A., Ross, D., & Ross, S. A. (1963). Imitation of film-mediated aggressive models. *Journal of Abnormal and Social Psychology, 66,* 3-11.

Barak, A. (1997). Cross-cultural perspectives on sexual harassment. In W. O'Donohue (Ed.), *Sexual harassment: Theory, research, and treatment* (pp. 263-300). Boston: Allyn & Bacon.

Batra, R., & Stayman, D. M. (1990). The role of mood in advertising effectiveness. *Journal of Consumer Research, 17,* 203-214.

Beniger, J. R. (1993). Communication: Embrace the subject, not the field. *Journal of Communication, 43*(3), 18-25.

Berkowitz, L. (1964). The effects of observing violence. *Scientific American, 21*(2), 35-41.

Berkowitz, L. (1986). Situational influences on reactions to observed violence. *Journal of Social Issues, 42*(3), 91-106.

Berryman-Fink, C. (1993). Preventing sexual harassment through male-female communication training. In G. L. Kreps (Ed.), *Sexual harassment: Communication implications* (pp. 267-280). Cresskill, NJ: Hampton.

Bingham, S. G. (1991). Communication strategies for managing sexual harassment in organizations: Understanding message options and their effects. *Journal of Applied Communication Research, 19,* 88-115.

Booth-Butterfield, M. (1986). Recognizing and communicating in harassment-prone organizational climates. *Women's Studies in Communication, 9,* 42-51.

Booth-Butterfield, M. (1989). Perception of harassing communication as a function of locus of control, work force participation, and gender. *Communication Quarterly, 37,* 262-275.

Botan, C. (1996). Communication work and electronic surveillance: A model for predicting panoptic effects. *Communication Monographs, 63,* 293-313.

Brown, P., & Levinson, S. C. (1987). *Universals in language usage: Politeness phenomena.* Cambridge: Cambridge University Press.

Buller, D. B., Borland, R., & Burgoon, M. (1998). Impact of behavioral intention on effectiveness of message features: Evidence from the Family Sun Safety Project. *Human Communication Research, 24,* 433-453.

Burgoon, J. K. (1982). Privacy and communication. In M. Burgoon (Ed.), *Communication yearbook 6* (pp. 206-249). Beverly Hills, CA: Sage.

Burgoon, J. K., Buller, D. B., & Woodall, G. W. (1989). *Nonverbal communication: The unspoken dialogue.* New York: Harper & Row.

Burgoon, M. (1989). The effects of message variables on opinion and attitude change. In J. Bradac (Ed.), *Messages in communication science: Contemporary approaches to the study of effects* (pp. 129-164). Newbury Park, CA: Sage.

Burgoon, M., & Bettinghaus, E. P. (1980). Persuasive message strategies. In M. E. Roloff & G. R. Miller (Eds.), *Persuasion: New directions in theory and research* (pp. 141-169). Beverly Hills, CA: Sage.

Calvert, C. (1997). Hate speech and its harms: A communication theory perspective. *Journal of Communication, 47*(1), 4-19.

Cantor, J. (1996, December 30). The V-chip debate: Unsuitable for kids doesn't mean unsuitable to be seen. *Washington Post,* p. A11.

Cantor, J. (1998). Ratings for program content: The role of research findings. *Annals of the American Academy of Political and Social Science, 557,* 54-69.

Cantor, J., & Harrison, K. (1997). Ratings and advisories for television programming. In *National Television Violence Study* (Vol. 1). Thousand Oaks, CA: Sage.

Carey, J. W. (1989). *Communication as culture: Essays on media and society.* Winchester, MA: Unwin Hyman.

Carter, T. B., Franklin, M. A., & Wright, J. B. (1996). *The First Amendment and the fifth estate: Regulation of electronic mass media.* Westbury, NY: Foundation.

Comstock, G. (1976). The role of social and behavioral science in policymaking for television. *Journal of Social Issues, 32*(4), 157-178.

Comstock, G. (1983). The legacy of the past. *Journal of Communication, 33*(3), 42-50.

Craig, R. T. (1993). Why are there so many communication theories? *Journal of Communication, 43*(3), 26-33.

Dennis, E. E. (1993). Foreword. In P. Gaunt (Ed.), *Beyond agendas: New directions in communication research* (pp. xi-xii). Westport, CT: Greenwood.

Dillard, J. P. (1993). Persuasion past and present: Attitudes aren't what they used to be. *Communication Monographs, 60,* 90-97.

Doe v. University of Michigan, 721 F. Supp. 852 (E.D. Mich. 1989).

Donahew, L., Sypher, H., & Bukowski, W. (1991). *Persuasive communication and drug abuse prevention.* Hillsdale, NJ: Lawrence Erlbaum.

Downing, J. D. H. (1999). "Hate speech" and "First Amendment absolutism" discourses in the U.S. *Discourse and Society, 10,* 175-189.

Dunwoody-Miller, V., & Gutek, B. A. (1985). *Sexual harassment in the state workforce: Results of a survey* (SHE Project Report). Sacramento: California Commission on the Status of Women, Sexual Harassment in Employment Project.

Einsiedel, E. F. (1988). The British, Canadian, and U.S. pornography commissions and their use of social science research. *Journal of Communication, 38*(2), 108-121.

Equal Employment Opportunity Commission. (1980). Discrimination because of sex under Title VII of the 1964 Civil Rights Act as amended: Adoption of interim guidelines—sexual harassment. *Federal Register, 45,* 25025-25026.

Eron, L. D. (1986). Interventions to mitigate the psychological effects of media violence on aggressive behavior. *Journal of Social Issues, 42*(3), 155-169.

Eron, L. D., Huesmann, L. R., Lefkowitz, M., & Walder, L. (1972). Does television violence cause aggression? *American Psychologist, 27,* 253-263.

Farhi, P. (1997, July 10). TV ratings agreement reached. *Washington Post,* p. A1.

Gerbner, G., & Gross, L. (1976). Living with television: The Violence Profile. *Journal of Communication, 26*(2), 172-199.

Gerbner, G., Gross, L., Morgan, M., & Signorielli, N. (1986). Living with television: The dynamics of the cultivation process. In J. Bryant & D. Zillmann (Eds.), *Perspectives on media effects* (pp. 17-40). Hillsdale, NJ: Lawrence Erlbaum.

Gilsdorf, J. W. (1990). Sexual harassment as a liability issue in communication. *Bulletin of the Association for Business Communication, 53*(3), 68-75.

Goffman, E. (1955). On facework: An analysis of ritual elements in social interaction. *Psychiatry, 18,* 213-231.

Gruenwald, J. (1997, February 15). Critics say TV ratings system doesn't tell the whole story. *Congressional Quarterly, 55,* 424-425.

Gutek, B. A. (1997). Sexual harassment policy initiatives. In W. O'Donohue (Ed.), *Sexual harassment: Theory, research, and treatment* (pp. 185-198). Boston: Allyn & Bacon.

Gutek, B. A., & Koss, M. P. (1993). Changed women and changed organizations: Consequences of and coping with sexual harassment. *Journal of Vocational Behavior, 42,* 28-48.

Gutek, B. A., & O'Connor, M. (1995). The empirical basis for the reasonable woman standard. *Journal of Social Issues, 51*(1), 151-166.

Hale, J. L., & Dillard, J. P. (1995). Fear appeals in health promotion campaigns: Too much, too little, or just right? In E. Maibach & R. L. Parrott (Eds.), *Designing health messages: Approaches from communication theory and public health practice* (pp. 65-80). Thousand Oaks, CA: Sage.

Huesmann, L. R. (1982). Television violence and aggressive behavior. In D. Pearl, L. Bouthilet, & J. Lazar (Eds.), *Television and behavior: Ten years of scientific inquiry and implications for the eighties: Vol. 2. Technical reviews* (pp. 126-137). Washington, DC: Government Printing Office.

Huesmann, L. R., & Eron, L. D. (Eds.). (1986). *Television and the aggressive child: A cross-national comparison.* Hillsdale, NJ: Lawrence Erlbaum.

Jansma, L. (1996). *The effectiveness of assertive communication as an intervention strategy for unintentional sexual harassment: A review and critique of sexual harassment research, a theoretical re-*

formulation with communication implications, and three empirical studies. Unpublished doctoral dissertation, University of California, Santa Barbara.

Kelman, S. (1987). *Making public policy: A hopeful view of American government.* New York: Basic Books.

Keyton, J. (1996). Sexual harassment: A multidisciplinary synthesis and critique. In B. R. Burleson (Ed.), *Communication yearbook 19* (pp. 93-155). Thousand Oaks, CA: Sage.

Kunkel, D. (1996, December 14). TV industry tunes out families. *New York Times,* p. A21.

Leets, L. (1999, May). *When words wound: Another look at racist speech.* Paper presented at the annual meeting of the International Communication Association, San Francisco.

Leets, L., & Giles, H. (1997). Words as weapons—when do they wound? Investigations of harmful speech. *Human Communication Research, 24,* 260-301.

Leets, L., Giles, H., & Noels, K. (1999). Attributing harm to racist speech. *Journal of Multilingual and Multicultural Development, 20,* 209-215.

LePoire, B. A., Burgoon, J. K., & Parrott, R. L. (1992). Status and privacy restoring communication in the workplace. *Journal of Applied Communication Research, 20,* 419-436.

Linz, D., Donnerstein, E., & Penrod, S. (1987). The findings and recommendations of the Attorney General's Commission on Pornography: Do the psychological facts fit the political fury? *American Psychologist, 42,* 946-953.

MacKinnon, C. (1979). *Sexual harassment of working women.* New Haven, CT: Yale University Press.

Markey, E. (1996, March). It takes a v-Chip [On-line]. Available Internet: http://www.house.gov/markey/chip.htm

McAlister, A., Ramirez, A. G., Galavotti, C., & Gallion, K. J. (1989). Antismoking campaigns: Progress in the application of social learning theory. In R. E. Rice & C. K. Atkin (Eds.), *Public communication campaigns* (2nd ed., pp. 291-307). Newbury Park, CA: Sage.

Monahan, J. L. (1995). Thinking positively: Using positive affect when designing health messages. In E. Maibach & R. L. Parrott (Eds.), *Designing health messages: Approaches from communication theory and public health practice* (pp. 81-98). Thousand Oaks, CA: Sage.

Mueller, M. (1995). Why communications policy is passing "mass communication" by: Political economy as the missing link. *Critical Studies in Mass Communication, 12,* 457-472.

National Academy of Sciences. (1993). *Understanding and preventing violence.* Washington, DC: National Academy Press.

Noam, E. (1993). Reconnecting communications studies with communications policy. *Journal of Communication, 43*(3), 199-206.

Nowak, G. J., & Siska, M. J. (1995). Using research to inform campaign development and message design: Examples from the "America responds to AIDS campaign." In E. Maibach & R. L. Parrott (Eds.), *Designing health messages: Approaches from communication theory and public health practice* (pp. 169-185). Thousand Oaks, CA: Sage.

Paisley, W. J. (1984). Communication in the communication sciences. In B. Dervin & M. J. Voigt (Eds.), *Progress in communication sciences* (Vol. 5, pp. 1-43). Norwood, NJ: Ablex.

Paletz, D. (1988). Pornography, politics, and the press: The U.S. Attorney General's Commission on Pornography. *Journal of Communication, 38*(2), 122-136.

Parrott, R. L. (1995). Motivation to attend to health messages: Presentation of content and linguistic considerations. In E. Maibach & R. L. Parrott (Eds.), *Designing health messages: Approaches from communication theory and public health practice* (pp. 7-23). Thousand Oaks, CA: Sage.

Parrott, R. L., Burgoon, J. K., Burgoon, M., & LePoire, B. A. (1989). Privacy in the physician-patient relationship: More than a matter of confidentiality. *Social Science and Medicine, 29,* 1381-1385.

Parrott, R. L., Monahan, J., Ainsworth, S., & Steiner, C. (1998). Communicating to farmers about skin cancer: The behavior adaptation model. *Human Communication Research, 24,* 386-409.

Pearl, D., Bouthilet, L., & Lazar, J. (Eds.). (1982). *Television and behavior: Ten years of scientific progress and implications for the eighties: Vol. 1. Summary report.* Washington, DC: Government Printing Office.

Price, M. (1998). *The V-chip debate.* Mahwah, NJ: Lawrence Erlbaum.

Rice, R. E., & Atkin, C. K. (1994). Principles of successful public communication campaigns. In J. Bryant & D. Zillmann (Eds.), *Media effects: Advances in theory and research* (pp. 365-387). Hillsdale, NJ: Lawrence Erlbaum.

Rogers, R. W. (1975). A protection motivation theory of fear appeals and attitude change. *Journal of Psychology, 91,* 93-114.

Rogers, R. W. (1983). Cognitive and physiological processes in fear appeals and attitude change: A revised theory of protection motivation. In J. T. Cacioppo & R. E. Petty (Eds.), *Social psychophysiology* (pp. 153-176). New York: Guilford.

Saal, F. E. (1996). Men's misperceptions of women's interpersonal behaviors and sexual harassment. In M. Stockdale (Ed.), *Sexual harassment in the workplace: Perspectives, frontiers, and response strategies* (pp. 67-84). Thousand Oaks, CA: Sage.

Schooler, C., Chaffee, S. H., Flora, J. A., & Roser, C. (1998). Health campaign channels: Tradeoffs among reach, specificity, and impact. *Human Communication Research, 24,* 410-432.

Sculnick, M. W. (1989). Two recent drug-testing cases portend new limits on employees' privacy expectations in those organizations that deal with the health and safety of the public: Skinner and Raab decisions. *Employment Relations Today, 16,* 141-146.

Sheer, V. C., & Cline, R. J. (1994). The development and validation of a model explaining sexual behavior among college students: Implications for AIDS communications campaigns. *Human Communication Research, 21,* 280-304.

Showers, R. (1994). Research, public policy, and law: Combination for change. In D. Zillmann, J. Bryant, & A. Huston (Eds.), *Media, children, and the family: Social scientific, psychodynamic, and clinical perspectives.* Hillsdale, NJ: Lawrence Erlbaum.

Singer, D. (1983). A time to reexamine the role of television in our lives. *American Psychologist, 38,* 815-816.

Smolla, R. (1993). *Free speech in an open society.* New York: Alfred A. Knopf.

Surgeon General's Scientific Advisory Commission on Television and Social Behavior. (1972). *Television and growing up: The impact of televised violence* (Report to the Surgeon General, U.S. Public Health Service). Washington, DC: Government Printing Office.

Tracy, K. (1997). Interactional trouble in emergency service requests: A problem of frames. *Research on Language and Social Interaction, 30,* 315-343.

Tracy, K., & Tracy, S. J. (1998). Rudeness at 911: Reconceptualizing face and face attack. *Human Communication Research, 25,* 225-251.

Tracy, S. J., & Tracy, K. (1998). Emotion labor at 911: A case study and theoretical critique. *Journal of Applied Communication Research, 26,* 390-411.

U.S. Attorney General's Commission on Pornography. (1986). *Final report* (2 vols.). Washington, DC: U.S. Department of Justice.

U.S. Congress, Office of Technology Assessment. (1987). *The electronic supervisor: New technology, new tensions* (Publication No. OTA-CIT-333). Washington, DC: Government Printing Office.

U.S. Senate, Committee on Commerce, Science, and Transportation. (1997, February 27). *Hearing on television rating system* (Document No. 105157). Washington, DC: Government Printing Office.

Wartella, E. (1993). Communication research on children and public policy. In P. Gaunt (Ed.), *Beyond agendas: New directions in communication research* (pp. 137-148). Westport, CT: Greenwood.

Wilcox, B. L. (1987). Pornography, social science, and politics: When research and ideology collide. *American Psychologist, 42,* 941-943.

Wilson, B., Kunkel, D., Linz, D., Potter, W. J., Donnerstein, E., Smith, S., Blumenthal, E., & Gray, T. (1997). Violence in television programming overall: University of California Santa Barbara study. In *National Television Violence Study* (Vol. 1). Thousand Oaks, CA: Sage.

Witte, K. (1992a). Putting the fear back into fear appeals: Reconciling the literature. *Communication Monographs, 59,* 329-349.

Witte, K. (1992b). The role of threat and efficacy in AIDS prevention. *International Quarterly of Community Health Education, 12,* 225-249.

Witte, K. (1998). Fear as motivator, fear as inhibitor: Using the extended parallel process model to explain fear appeal successes and failures. In P. A. Andersen & L. K. Guerrero (Eds.), *Handbook of communication and emotion: Research, theory, applications, and contexts* (pp. 423-450). New York: Academic Press.

Witte, K., & Morrison, K. (1995). Intercultural and cross-cultural health communication: Understanding people and motivating healthy behaviors. In R. L. Wiseman (Ed.), *Intercultural communication theory* (pp. 216-246). Thousand Oaks, CA: Sage.

Wood, J. T. (1993). Naming and interpreting sexual harassment: A conceptual framework for scholarship. In G. L. Kreps (Ed.), *Sexual harassment: Communication implications* (pp.9-26). Cresskill, NJ: Hampton.

Zillmann, D. (1989). Pornography research and public policy. In D. Zillmann & J. Bryant (Eds.), *Pornography: Research advances and policy considerations* (pp. 387-405). Hillsdale, NJ: Lawrence Erlbaum.

Zimmerman, D. H. (1984). Talk and its occasion: The case of calling the policy. In D. Schiffrin (Ed.), *Meaning, form, and use in context* (pp. 210-228). Washington, DC: Georgetown University Press.

Zimmerman, D. H. (1992). The interactional organization of calls for emergency assistance. In P. Drew & J. Heritage (Eds.), *Talk at work* (pp. 418-469). Cambridge: Cambridge University Press.

Zoglin, R. (1996, February 19). Chips ahoy. *Time,* pp. 58-61.

CHAPTER CONTENTS

19 Camera as Witness, Image as Sign: The Study of Visual Communication in Communication Research

MICHAEL GRIFFIN
Macalester College

This chapter summarizes the state of the study of visual communication in communication research. The author outlines major themes and theories characterizing the study of visual communication and concludes by isolating key issues and current trends in the field.

G IVEN the daunting, and perhaps unrealistic, task of adequately character-izing the interdisciplinary terrain of visual communication studies, it is necessary that I begin this essay with a caveat. A truly comprehensive overview of the traditions of visual communication study would be impossible even in a book-length treatment. The study of visual communication comprises such wide-reaching and voluminous literatures as art history; the philosophy of art and aesthetics; semiotics; cinema studies; television and mass-media studies; the history and theory of photography; the history and theory of graphic design and typography; the study of word-image relationships in literary, aesthetic, and rhetorical theory; the development and use of charts, diagrams, cartography, and questions of geographic visualization (images of place and space); the physiology and psychology of visual perception; the impact of new visual technologies (including the impact of digitization and the construction of "virtual realities"); growing concerns with the concept and/or acquisition of "visual literacy"; and the boundless social and cultural issues embedded in practices of visual representation. Amid such an eclectic field no consensus has emerged regarding canonical texts. Even the concept of "imagery" itself seems to have no clear boundaries, encompassing concepts of the image that extend from the perceptual process through the mental reproduction of perceptions in eidetic imagery, dreams, and

Correspondence: Michael Griffin, Department of Communication, Macalester College, 1600 Grand Ave., St. Paul, MN 55105; e-mail griffin@macalester.edu

Communication Yearbook 24, pp. 433-463

433

memory to the realms of abstract symbols and ideas by which we mentally map experience and the physical creation of pictures and visual media. Consequently, the study of imagery is as integral to the study of language, cognition, psychoanalysis, and ethology as it is to the study of pictorial or graphic representation.

Here I attempt to address a few key themes and theories within the limits of a single chapter. In doing so, I remain necessarily selective and incomplete. No doubt many readers will find fault with chosen emphases and inevitable omissions. To those readers I offer my apologies. It is my hope that critical consideration of this survey will encourage others to address gaps in my treatment.

For purposes of manageability, I have chosen to focus this discussion on the study of *pictures* rather than on the broader concept of *the visual,* and with a bent toward the study of 20th-century mass communication media rather than the larger history of art and visual representation.[1] The choice to concentrate on the pictorial directs the emphasis toward the production and interpretation of communication media and avoids the insurmountable problem of addressing a diffuse and boundless range of the visual. The focus on recent history reflects the concern for contemporary media and cultural environments that is such a prominent part of communication studies.

In this context the study of visual communication as an institutional interest area has grown primarily in response to perceived gaps in the more widely established field of mass communication research. The relationship to mass communication may not be readily apparent, for visual communication study did not emerge within established traditions of mass communication research, nor was it bound by the same theoretical or methodological paradigms. Yet the study of visual communication (as opposed to the study of art, art history, design, or architecture) has been defined in relation to the mechanical reproduction of imagery that has characterized modern mass media (Benjamin, 1936/1969; Berger, 1972; Ivins, 1953).

Those intrigued by the role and influence of visual imagery in mass-circulation publications, television, and the entire range of commercial advertising have often been disappointed by the lack of attention given to pictures in established traditions of mass communication research. None of the prominent strains of mass communication research—public opinion and attitude research, social psychological studies of behavior and cognition, experimental studies of media exposure, marketing research, correlational studies of media effects, content analysis, studies of media uses and gratifications, agenda-setting research, or sociologies of media organizations and media production—has routinely incorporated the analysis of visual forms and their role in communication processes.[2] Even studies of political communication, where one might expect a keen interest in the role of visual images, focus overwhelmingly on rhetorical strategies, issue framing, and concern for the tactical effects of linguistic symbols and slogans, and lack sustained attention to the contributions of the visual. A 1990 survey of political communication literature, for example, found that only 5 out of more than 600 articles and studies actually examined the concrete visual components of televised election coverage and advertising, and that when the term *image* was used, it most often referred to conceptual interpretations of the public ethos of political candidates rather than specific concrete visual attributes of media presentations (Johnston, 1990).[3]

Against this background, the growing interest in visual communication throughout the 1970s and 1980s was often perceived as a corrective response. The increasingly ubiquitous visual appeals of advertising, both commercial and political, and the alarming number of hours most people spent watching television had certainly made media researchers aware of the potential impacts of images and triggered some interest in including visual analysis in their work. Yet few examples of research specifically focused on the visual mode could be found in the mass communication literature, and those hoping to pursue such research needed to look beyond the boundaries of communication scholarship for theories, templates, and inspiration. Often, this meant foraging purposefully among literatures institutionally separated from communication: aesthetics, anthropology, art history, graphic design, electronic and video arts, film theory and history, the philosophy of perception and knowledge, literary theory, linguistics, semiology. Sometimes it meant opening doors to those developments within communication more attentive to the impacts of images: to feminist scholars and others interested in gender portrayals (Kaplan, 1983; Tuchman, Daniels, & Benet, 1978), to those concerned with representations of homosexuality (Dyer, 1977, 1993; Gross, 1988, 1989), to those concerned with the stereotyping of various racial, cultural, and social groups (Craig, 1991; Gerbner et al., 1980; Lester, 1996; Miller, 1978; Shaheen, 1988; Turow, 1978). And sometimes it meant reframing or redefining entrenched areas of professional and technical training: in film and video production, photography and photojournalism, broadcast journalism, and typography and publication design (Barnhurst, 1991).

By the 1980s, this trend led to movements within academic communication associations to provide expanded forums for visual communication research presentations. In the International Communication Association, nondivisional paper sessions were organized around visual communication themes, eventually leading to the establishment of a Visual Communication Interest Group. In the Association for Education in Journalism and Mass Communication, attempts were made to encourage the presentation of scholarly research in the Visual Communication Division, a division previously focused almost exclusively on professional training in graphic design and photojournalism.[4] In the Speech Communication Association, an interest group on "visual literacy" was formed. These developments have continued to influence, albeit unevenly, the place of visual communication studies within the larger field of communication research. However, primary sources of new theory and new research have continued to originate from outside these institutional parameters. In the remaining pages I will attempt to chart some of the major influences in the intellectual history of visual communication studies that led it to be identified as a distinct subfield within communication research.

HISTORY AND THEORY

The rise of contemporary visual communication studies was, of course, preceded by centuries of thought and writing concerning the arts and the visual image. Yet the last decades of the 20th century saw a renewed philosophical concern with the visual that Mitchell (1994), following Rorty's (1979) notion of "the linguistic turn," has called "the pictorial turn." Mitchell argues that although "the problem of pictorial representation has always been with us, it presses inescapably now, and with an unprecedented force, on every level of culture, from the most refined philosophical speculations to the most vulgar productions of the mass media" (p. 16).

> The simplest way to put this is to say that, in what is often characterized as an age of "spectacle" (Debord), "surveillance" (Foucault), and all-pervasive image-making, we still do not know exactly what pictures are, what their relation to language is, how they operate on observers and on the world, how their history is to be understood, and what is to be done with or about them. (p. 13)

Most immediately pertinent to my discussion at this point is the extensive body of literature exploring the ontology and epistemology of photography and the cinema, the foundations of contemporary lens-based media. Writings on photography since the middle of the 19th century have continually explored, and revisited, the nature of the photographic image as art versus science, pictorial expression versus mechanical record, trace versus transformation (Goldberg, 1988; Sontag, 1977; Trachtenberg, 1980). Meanwhile, the practice of photography has been dogged by the ongoing contradictions between the craft of picture making and the status of photographs as "reflections of the real" (Bolton, 1989; Brennen & Hardt, 1999; Griffin, 1995; Schwartz, 1992). Similarly, the extensive literature of film theory, going back at least to the treatises of Lindsay (1916), Munsterberg (1916/1970), Pudovkin (1926/1954), Eisenstein (1942, 1949), and Arnheim (1932/1957), has struggled with the nature of cinema and its proper aesthetic and communicational development. A wellspring of analytic concepts regarding the composition and juxtaposition of images have been applied to sophisticated analyses of mise-en-scène (the construction of the shot) and montage (the structuring of sequences of shots through editing). The synthesis of realist theories of mise-en-scène, formalist theories of montage, and structural theories of narrative in the work of Jean Mitry (1963, 1965, 1972) and the subsequent application of linguistically based semiotic theory to cinema by Christian Metz (1974) pushed film analysis into new territories of narrative and syntactic exegesis in the attempt to identify a "language of film." We are still looking.

Film Studies

Film theory is such an important foundation for the development of visual communication studies that one is tempted to say that all contemporary visual media studies can be described as the application of concepts from film theory to other forms of media. However, because film theory is a body of concepts and tools borrowed from the study of art, psychology, sociology, language, and literature, and work in visual communication has often returned to these various sources for new applications to photography, design, electronic imaging, and virtual reality, it would be more accurate to say that film theory established central theoretical parameters of debate that still shape visual communication research. These parameters primarily involve the distinction between formative and realist theories (Andrew, 1976, 1984), a key issue discussed below, but also involve questions concerning the scope and centrality of narrative, an issue that has preoccupied the philosophy of representation across numerous fields (Clifford, 1988; Fisher, 1985, 1987, 1989; Marcus & Fischer, 1986; Ricouer, 1980; Rorty, 1979; Rosaldo, 1989; White, 1987).

Formative theories treat cinematic presentations as wholly constructed visual expressions, or rhetoric, and seek to build schematic explanations for the semantic and syntactic capacity and operation of the medium. Realist theories argue that there is a natural relationship between life and image. They assert that photographic motion pictures inherently mimic everyday perception and, moreover, that the goal for filmmakers should be to employ that essential capacity to create the most realistic possible simulations of actual experience. All film students learn about the concepts of film art posited by early formalists such as Munsterberg, Arnheim, Kuleshov, Pudovkin, Eisenstein, and Balazs and countered by realists such as Bazin (1967) and Kracauer (1960). Many aspects of this theoretical opposition have reemerged repeatedly as visual communication studies has come to encompass parallel issues in television, photojournalism, news, advertising, and most recently digital image creation and manipulation.

The heart of the matter, and arguably *the* central question of all visual communication study, is the precise status of the image as a copy or analogue. As Andrew (1976) writes of the work of Bazin and Mitry, "Bazin spent his life discussing the importance of the 'snugness' with which the filmic analogue fits the world, whereas Mitry has spent his life investigating the crucial differences which keep this asymptote forever distinct from the world it runs beside and so faithfully mirrors" (p. 190). Historically, film and photographic theory and criticism were absorbed with these questions as they pertained to the properties of the image-text itself. As I will discuss at a later point, visual communication studies turned the question toward the manner in which images are utilized and interpreted by media production institutions and viewing audiences.

The key point here, to be revisited throughout this essay, is that the study of pictures brought into even greater relief questions of reflection and construction in human representation. And although these issues are not confined to modern visual media, and perhaps are questions that cannot be asked of pictures as if they were a purely visual medium, somehow outside of intertextual contexts, they have become defining issues for visual communication study in an era of constant photographic reproduction, when it is so often taken for granted that visual media

technologically mimic reality.[5] Various technical advances have seemed to provide an inexorable progression toward ever more convincing re-creations of the
"real world" and have consistently raised the ante on illusion and simulation. Yet
film theory has persistently directed attention toward the processes of constructing
visual representations, constantly reminding us of the inherent tension between
the craft of picture making and the perception of pictures as records. Against the
commonsense assumptions so often made that visual media give us a window on
the world from which to witness "reality," film theory from the beginning has
interrogated the ways in which such "windows" are created and structured to
shape our view. Even in the practice of documentary film, theorists such as
Nichols (1991) show us the patterns or "modes" of representational strategy that
make each documentary a formal and rhetorical articulation. Writers on still photography, perhaps ironically, followed the development of film theory in fully theorizing the ontology of the photograph, but in the past 50 years have also contributed an extensive literature on the relationships of photo images to their subjects
(see Barthes, 1977, 1981; Berger, 1980; Burgin, 1982; Eco, 1986; Sontag, 1977;
Sekula, 1975; Tagg, 1988).

The fact that film studies provided an important stock of conceptual tools for the
study of pictorial communication of all types was not lost on communication
scholars who hoped to better understand the growing prominence of visual mass
media in postindustrial society. British cultural studies also borrowed freely from
film studies (much of it centered on the British Film Institute and its sponsored
book and journal publications), and the resulting sensitivity to the culturally constructed nature of visual representation in much cultural studies work made it
attractive to visual communication scholars in the United States. Writings on
visual media by such British and Australian cultural critics and scholars as John
Berger (1972), Raymond Williams (1974), Laura Mulvey (1975/1989), Richard
Dyer (1977), Judith Williamson (1978), Dick Hebdige (1979), and John Fiske and
John Hartley (1978) drew the attention of those tuned in to what the British
increasingly called *lens theory*. The influence of this brand of cultural studies on
the American scene fueled a nascent interest in semiotic analysis and the interpretation of media texts, and it was not a far leap to imagine the incorporation of visual
analysis into studies of representation, meaning, and ideology.[6] Moreover, the
fast-growing popularity of cultural studies often helped to open up additional cur-
ricular space for addressing the nature of visual symbol systems and processes of
meaning construction. A convergence of interest in the study of photographically
mediated culture was building from several directions, including anthropology,
sociology, and the psychology of art.

The Psychology of Art and Visual Representation

Alongside film theory, another literature that contributed significantly to discussions of the ontology of the image lies at the intersection of aesthetics, art history, and the psychology of visual perception. The work of E. H. Gombrich serves

to represent the essential themes of this tradition, although its roots lie in the earlier work of Panofsky (1924/1991) and others. In his highly influential book *Art and Illusion: A Study in the Psychology of Pictorial Representation,* Gombrich (1960) makes a powerful case for the conventionality of schemes for visual representation. Using an eminent art historian's knowledge of the traditions of Western art, and particularly the development of linear perspective in Renaissance art, he argues that picture forms of all kinds are conventionally constructed according to learned schemata, not copied from nature. Building from the idea that perceptual gestalts are not necessarily innate but are often learned (a concept fully developed in the perceptual research of Gregory, 1966, 1970), Gombrich argues that perceptions of visual representations in art operate by means of gestalts that are culturally based and that, in this sense, pictures are *read* based on prior knowledge of cultural conventions.[7]

Gombrich develops the metaphor of "reading images" in his article "The Visual Image," written for *Scientific American* in 1972. Here he reiterates the ways in which images are intertwined with cultural systems of language and function and depend upon "code, caption, and context" for understanding. Pictures rarely stand alone, and rarely communicate unambiguously when they do. The mutual support of language and image facilitates memory and interpretation, making visual communication (as distinct from artistic expression) possible. Without using the same structuralist paradigm or terminology, Gombrich comes very close to reproducing the semiological notions of icon, index, and symbol in his analysis, concepts originally found in the work of Peirce (1931). Gombrich and others have found these distinctions to be as useful when applied to images as when applied to language: the iconic aspects being those that signify by resemblance, the indexical by causal relation, and the symbolic by arbitrary and conventional agreement. Most images seem to combine all three qualities of signification in some measure, although it is most often the iconic prevalence and/or limits of images that preoccupy scholars of the visual, the iconic being that which most clearly distinguishes visual signs from lexical, mathematical, musical, and sociogestural (Gross, 1974a).

Gombrich cites the pictorial plaque placed on the side of the *Pioneer* space probe as a prime example of the naïveté with which even highly educated people assume that pictures communicate naturally and directly, without prior knowledge of the message system. The plaque was designed by NASA scientists as a universal greeting, "on the off chance that somewhere on the way it is intercepted by intelligent scientifically educated beings" (NASA press release). Breaking down each part of the pictorial greeting, Gombrich (1972) points out that outside of certain culturally specific conventions of abstract line drawing, perspective, foreshortening, and symbols, such as an arrow showing direction of flight and a hand waving to indicate "hello" (all uniquely specific to a tradition of Western art practiced in only particular regions of Earth), this configuration of lines looks "like nothing on earth." Without prior knowledge of the particular Anglo-American use of symbols and visual forms, Gombrich writes, "our 'scientifically educated' fellow creatures in space might be forgiven if they saw the figures as wire constructs with loose bits and pieces hovering weightlessly in between" (p. 92). Indeed, given the collection of highly conventionalized drawings and symbols that make up this plaque, it would be a miracle if many people on Earth, much less from other worlds, were able to decipher the message clearly. Yet the fact that it is *visual* seems to have masked this realization from its creators.

Although a substantial body of research by perceptual psychologists (Gibson, 1982; Hochberg, 1978, 1983, 1984; Kennedy, 1984; Marr, 1982) contradicts Gombrich's suggestion that visual apprehension is culturally learned—providing evidence instead that visual perception is a natural, hard-wired set of sensory, neurological, and perceptual processes—the impact of Gombrich's analysis has still been enormous. His writings provide a strong case "against the equation of art and communication" (Gombrich, 1972, p. 92) and help to lay a basis for the study of visual communication as distinct from the study of art. They also demonstrate that we need to understand the history of art, and the various traditions of depiction and symbolization that have influenced visual practices, before we can hope to explain the role of visual communication in modern media systems. Together with film theory, semiotics, the social history of art, and anthropological concerns with art and visual representation, the psychology of visual representation has contributed to an eclectic body of theory and research on which communication scholars began to draw for conceptualizing approaches to visual communication analysis.

Word and Image: Extratextual and Intertextual Influences

Other strains in the history of art and aesthetics that have contributed heavily to contemporary thinking about visual communication include the social history of art and aesthetic theories regarding the relationship between pictures and language. The social history of art, particularly in the work of writers such as Svetlana Alpers (1983), Michael Baxandall (1972, 1985), and Michael Fried (1980), offers models for investigating relationships between the production of images and the social contexts of their sponsorship, use, and interpretation. Alpers has explored the relationship of picture making to description, from the ekphrastic tradition of the Sophists, in which they used the subject matter of paintings as jumping-off points for discursive monologues and storytelling—a model, she argues, for Vasari's famous descriptions of Renaissance paintings (Alpers, 1960)—to the 17th-century tradition of Dutch painting, when Northern European painters broke with the narrative tradition of Italian painting to create a new "descriptive pictorial mode."

Baxandall's (1972) study of painting and experience in 15th-century Italy provides a prime historical example of what Gross (1974b) calls "doing the ethnography of visual communication." It demonstrates how patronage and contractual obligations, on the one hand, and viewer expectations and understandings of convention, on the other, combined to make of painting a currency of social communication, a socially shared system of conventions from which viewers could infer the social status and wealth of the patron; the ecclesiastical and religious functions of the picture; the theological, elemental, and even astrological messages encoded in colors, forms, and symbols; and the institutional ends to which paintings were attached. Becker's *Art Worlds* (1982) applies a similar approach to 20th-century social worlds of artistic production, with specific attention paid to painting and photography, among other arts. Gross's edited volume *On the Margins of Art Worlds* (1995) follows in this vein; it contains a collection of studies explicitly devoted to the social definitions and boundaries that have emerged among worlds of visual art and communication. I will explore the importance of the sociology and anthropology of visual communication further in the next section.

Related to these extratextual studies of visual communication practice and meaning is a long history of attention to the intertextual relationships between word and image. Whether in studies of the relationship between religious painting and scripture, pictures and narrative, or attempts to pursue the study of *iconology* (the general field of images and their relation to discourse), the existence of pictures within larger multitextual contexts has led to several rich traditions of scholarship. Here the dispersed boundaries of visual communication studies become especially apparent. The coherence of visual communication studies as a field diffuses into myriad strains of philosophy, literary theory, linguistics, cultural theory, art history, and media studies— concerns with the subject/spectator (the look, the gaze, the glance, observation, surveillance, and visual pleasure) and with the interpreter/reader (decipherment, decoding, visual experience, "visual literacy," or "visual culture") running through numerous disciplines and theories, from Panofsky (1939, 1924/1991) to Deleuze (1986, 1988, 1989).

It is impossible for me to survey (or even briefly catalog) this expansive literature on "scopic regimes" and the myriad historical attempts to investigate the interactions of verbal and visual representation in the study of the "Sister Arts" —painting and literature, *ut pictura poesis, icon* and *logos,* image/text, languages of art, semiotics—all attempts to treat representation and discourse in one master theory of pictures or science of representation. For those interested in a detailed and erudite exploration of these traditions and their relevance to our contemporary "culture of images," "society of the spectacle," or "world of semblances and simulacra," I recommend the companion books of W. J. T. Mitchell, *Iconology: Image, Text, Ideology* (1986) and *Picture Theory: Essays on Verbal and Visual Representation* (1994). Those interested in an extensive and provocative history of 20th-century French philosophy's attempt to explain (and subjugate?) the visual within structuralist and poststructuralist theory should see Martin Jay's *Downcast Eyes: The Denigration of Vision in Twentieth-Century French Thought* (1993).

Unable to give more than a passing nod to the vast traditions of image/text theory in philosophy and the arts in so brief a précis, I will turn instead to a development that played a central role in the growth of visual communication study within the universe of International Communication Association research and activities, the growth of social communicational studies of picture making and reception in the "anthropology of visual communication."

THE ANTHROPOLOGY (AND SOCIOLOGY)
OF VISUAL COMMUNICATION

Research that came to be identified under the label of anthropology of visual communication emerged in the 1960s and 1970s largely in association with the work of Sol Worth, Jay Ruby, Richard Chalfen, Larry Gross, Howard S. Becker, and their students. It was carried forward by scholars particularly interested in the cultural codes and social contexts of image making within particular communities, subcultures, and social groups. This movement was influenced by work in the psychology of art and representation, film theory, semiotics, and the social history of art. For example, attempts to assess and compare the types of psychological schemata suggested by Gombrich in image making and image interpretation across different cultures suggested that processes of visual communication are not universal and need to be explored within specific sociocultural settings. Hudson (1960), Deregowski (1968, 1973), and Cook (1981) compared perceptions of depth perspective in pictures, and susceptibility to visual illusions grounded in expectations of linear perspective (such as the Ponzo illusion), across Western and non-Western cultures. Hudson found a sharp difference in perceptions of conventional two-dimensional depth cues between subjects with formal Western schooling and those without. Deregowski found that people in Western cultures, where the use of linear perspective is common and normative, were much more susceptible to such illusions than were people for whom linear perspective is not a naturalized expectation. Cook found much smaller differences among groups, seemingly providing evidence contradictory to that found by Hudson and Deregowski. There is also a history of anecdotal reports suggesting that people in parts of the world isolated from industrial culture find photographic images confounding and need to go through a process of learning to decipher the relationships between two-dimensional shapes and tones and three-dimensional referents before they can more readily "read" the appearances of photographic prints. Messaris (1994, pp. 60-70) reviews this research on cultural differences in pictorial construction and perception and suggests that the empirical evidence on this question does not, in fact, support the idea that pictorial apprehension is a learned cultural skill. He asserts that the position posited by philosopher Nelson Goodman in *Languages of Art* (1976), that all forms of representation (visual, lexical, musical, architectural, and kinesthetic) require an understanding of symbolic conventions and codes that must be culturally learned, is overstated and contradicted by evidence on visual perception. Nevertheless, the idea that people raised in different cultures may see and picture the world differently provided a stimulus for expanding social research in visual communication, and Messaris readily concedes that whether or not basic pictorial apprehension is more natural than many cultural theorists believe, interpretations of meaning in pictures remain heavily dependent on cultural experience and convention.

The anthropology of visual communication was also heavily influenced by new approaches to the study of linguistics, not only by structuralist tendencies and the semiological theories and methods that structural linguistics engendered, but in particular by the rise of soiolinguistics in the work of Hymes (1964, 1967), Labov (1966), Bernstein (1971), and others. Sociolinguists had begun to examine the differing uses of language across subcultures, social classes, and ethnic groups and provided exemplars for the similar study of visual "languages" in varying social contexts. A key figure in adapting these influences to the study of visual communication was Sol Worth. *Studying Visual Communication* (1981c), a collection of Worth's writings edited posthumously by his colleague and coauthor Larry Gross, is perhaps the best starting point for those interested in gaining a sense of the origins of the field of visual communication research.

"The central thread that runs through Worth's research and writings is the question of how meaning is communicated through visual images" (Gross, 1981, p. 1). Initially, Worth was fascinated by novice filmmaking, particularly what he called the "bio-documentary" films made by his students, as manifestations of individually subjective, psychological issues. Before long, however, he began to shift the focus of his attention to the nature of film as cultural communication, both as a reflection of the worldviews, values, and concerns of a filmmaker's cultural group and as a reflection of the codes and conventions of image making and film construction shared by that group—agreements about the status of sign-events, syntax rules, rules by which we make inferences from sequences of signs.

These interests led to the landmark Navajo Filmmakers Project, in which Worth collaborated with anthropologist John Adair and graduate assistant Richard Chalfen to train Navajo students in Arizona to make 16mm films and then screened and studied their film products, not as records *about* their culture, but as examples *of* Navajo culture, "reflecting the value systems, coding patterns, and cognitive processes of the maker" (Worth, 1972/1981d, p. 104). Worth and Adair (1972) reasoned that studying the filmmaking products of the Navajo, rather than making films about them, "would come closer to capturing *his* vision of *his* world" (p. 15). But they were interested in the degree to which such visual creation would, in fact, exhibit culturally specific versus pancultural attributes.

Can anyone make movies? Can anyone understand a movie? How do you learn? What do you learn? We will be discussing two things that are inseparable but nevertheless slightly different. One is the study of images themselves in their cultural context, under the variety of constraints that culture and its technology impose. The other is the study of the way the human mind in general—panculturally—deals with images. The first would ask why a particular person, in a particular culture, in a particular situation, made a particular image or interpreted it in a particular way. The second would seek to learn how these particular ways are related to ways that all men use when they try to make sense of pictures. (Worth & Adair, 1972, p. 15)

The Navajo films (now in the collection of the Museum of Modern Art in New York) and the published results of the project, including the book *Through Navajo Eyes: An Exploration in Film Communication and Anthropology* (Worth & Adair, 1972), were praised by such commentators as Margaret Mead (1977) as a "break-through in cross-cultural communications" (p. 67). Inspired by anthropological and symbolic interactionist concerns with the issues and problems of social repre-sentation, *Through Navajo Eyes* came to be a seminal work for communication scholars who increasingly questioned the use of film and photography as objective recording tools. Worth and Adair directly challenged the established use of docu-mentary film and photography as data collection tools for social scientists, arguing that such taken-for-granted uses of mechanical devices for "objective" representa-tion are seriously problematic. Here, and in later writings and lectures, Worth vig-orously argued that filmed "records" of other cultures are more likely to reflect the perspectives and priorities of the filmmaker, and his or her own cultural back-ground, than to penetrate and reveal the culture and worldview of the people in front of the camera.

Worth's observations were met with annoyance and defensiveness by many in the documentary film world, but they were echoed by other anthropologists, such as Jay Ruby, whose numerous articles throughout the 1970s also questioned the naive use of film and photography in ethnographic and social science research (see Ruby, 1981). Ruby's edited collection *A Crack in the Mirror: Reflexive Perspec-tives in Anthropology* (1982) recapitulates this critical groundswell and carries it from anthropology's use of visual media to questions of written and narrative rep-resentation. It is no coincidence, I believe, that the "crisis of representation" in anthropology that struck in the 1980s with such critiques of anthropological reporting and representation as Marcus and Fischer's *Anthropology as Cultural Critique: An Experimental Moment in the Human Sciences* (1986), Clifford and Marcus's edited volume *Writing Culture: The Poetics and Politics of Ethnogra-phy* (1986), Clifford's *The Predicament of Culture: Twentieth-Century Ethnogra-phy, Literature, and Art* (1988), and Rosaldo's *Culture and Truth: The Remaking of Social Analysis* (1989) were preceded by challenges to the neutrality of visual technology and its use in representations of culture.

This critique of documentary practice led Worth (1980) to propose "a shift from visual anthropology to the anthropology of visual communication," suggesting the need to abandon taken-for-granted assumptions about the capacity of film and photography to portray culture from the outside. Instead, Worth suggested, it would be better to study the forms and uses given to visual media by the members of different cultures and social groups themselves. He vigorously distinguished this work from traditional "visual anthropology," much of which he considered naive and unreflective in its reliance on photographic records *about* culture, and increasingly became identified with the alternative of studying all forms of visual communication as examples *of* culture, to be analyzed for the patterns of culture that they reveal.

The Navajo Film Project inspired a stream of subsequent research on visual media as coded cultural texts, keys to cultural concepts and symbolic systems. Worth's idea of an "anthropology of visual communication" dovetailed with the work of many of his students and colleagues as well as other scholars working along cognate trajectories, leaving a fruitful legacy. These included, among other related research, groundbreaking studies of family photography and home moviemaking (Chalfen, 1975, 1987; Musello, 1980); explorations of the nature and limits of documentary representation (Feld, 1985; Linton, 1992; Ruby, 1975, 1982; Ruby & Taureg, 1987); the study of pictorial perception, learning, and inter-pretation (Custen, 1982; Messaris, 1982; Messaris & Gross, 1977; Messaris & Pallenik, 1977; Worth & Gross, 1974/1981); the socialization of children to visual forms (Eadie, Sutton-Smith, & Griffin, 1983; Griffin, 1985; Messaris & Sarett, 1981; Pallenik, 1976); the nature of visual rhetoric and persuasion and questions of visual literacy (Carey, 1974; Linton, 1982; Messaris, 1994, 1997; Worth, 1969/1981a, 1975/1981b); the history of institutionalized standards and practices in picture making and use, both professional and amateur (Becker, 1985; Griffin, 1992a, 1995; Hardt, 1989, 1996; Hardt & Ohrn, 1981; Schiller, 1981; Schwartz, 1992; Worth & Ruby, 1977/1981); the study of social worlds of visual production and legitimation, from art to advertising to news (Becker, 1974a, 1974b, 1982; Gross, 1995; Rosenblum, 1978; Schwartz & Griffin, 1987; Tuchman, 1978); and the ethics of visual representation (Gross, Katz, & Ruby, 1988).

A key theoretical path involved what Worth and Gross (1974/1981) called "interpretive strategies," an approach to the study of communication events that they first fully articulated in an article titled "Symbolic Strategies." In this article they clarified a set of important conceptual distinctions: first, between *sign-events,* events that provoke interpretive responses, and *nonsign-events,* events that we ignore or code "transparently"; second, between *natural* sign-events and those they called *symbolic.* Natural sign-events are those for which we assume a natural cause rather than an intended meaning. For example, a tree bending in the wind may be interpreted as a sign of an approaching storm, but we usually do not assume that the tree has been bent by someone intentionally to convey a message to us. Therefore, the tree bending in the wind would be a *natural* sign-event. This could change if the observer happened to believe that a supernatural entity was intention-ally bending the tree to convey a message. A painting of a tree bending in the wind, on the other hand, would more likely be seen by a viewer as a *symbolic* sign-event, a picture painted by an "author" with an intention to convey some meaning or emo-tion. When we assume intention we look for some purposeful order, pattern, or sequence and rely upon some shared system of rules of implication and inference. That is, when we assume implicative intent we assume that we are meant to infer meaning, and if we feel justified in investing some attention to the event, we may even go beyond simple awareness of the presence of order or pattern and recognize structural relationships among elements. Structural recognition allows for even higher levels of inference, including the interpretation of tropes, narrative structure, and variations on a theme.

Worth and Gross (1974/1981) described the interpretation of natural sign-events as *attribution;* we simply *attribute existence* to these events and respond according to our familiarity with related life experiences. For instance, upon seeing the tree bending in the wind we might decide to take an umbrella with us on our walk. Worth and Gross described the interpretation of symbolic events as *inference;* we assume that an author/creator intends to imply a meaning, so we attempt to infer one. When viewing the painting of a tree bending in the wind we may look for details of subject matter that the painter has chosen to include in the frame (or even notice that he or she has chosen to leave something out). We may pay attention to the perspective of the canvas, the colors employed, the technique of rendering. At the most complex levels of inference we may look for stylistic conventions that place the painting within a particular era, or a particular school of work, and draw conclusions about intent based upon prior knowledge of the concerns of painters employing those conventions and structures.

Worth and Gross, and others, found the attribution/inference distinction useful, not because sign-events are stable and can be categorically sorted into one type or another, but because they describe shifting interpretive strategies on the part of the observer/audience. An event that might be treated as natural by a viewer in one situation might be treated as symbolic by a different viewer (or the same viewer) in another instance. Of particular interest are the examples that Worth and Gross called "ambiguous," when the stance of the interpreter shifts between attribution and inference, or among levels of complexity in appreciation. This is especially common with photographs or film, and the attribution/inference paradigm is perhaps most interesting when photographically mediated events are at issue. It is then that we are most likely to slip into strategies of attribution, even as sophisticated levels of inference are most needed to negotiate the complex worlds of media representation and potential manipulation.

Worth addresses one aspect of the ambiguity in his article "Pictures Can't Say Ain't" (1975/1981b), where he attempts to clarify the specific types of *implication/inference,* or *articulation/interpretation,* that are possible given the nature of visual forms. Here he is particularly interested in the differences between what pictures and language can do with regard to propositions, negation, conditionals, counterfactuals, past-future tenses, interrogatives, correspondence, evidence, and other forms of logical syntax. As in many of his writings, he attempts to link semiotic concerns for the systemic properties of form and syntax in pictorial construction and the social anthropologist's concern with the processes of reception, interpretation, and use within specific sociocultural contexts. A point he emphasizes again and again is the inadequacy of the "reflection hypothesis" or correspondence theory that pictures operate by simple, direct resemblance to "reality." Echoing Gombrich, he reiterates that the nature of pictorial "realism" is not visual correspondence with "reality," but rather visual correspondence to recognized cultural conventions of representation:

I have briefly outlined earlier why I think the notion of matching to the real world is insufficient to explain how pictures mean. Now I can say that I don't believe this is what one matches pictures to at all. Correspondence, if it makes any sense as a concept, is not correspondence to "reality," but rather correspondence to conventions, rules, forms, and structures for structuring the world around us. What we use as a standard for correspondence is our knowledge of *how people make pictures*—pictorial structures—how they made them in the past, how they make them now, and how they will make them for various purposes in various contexts. We do not use as our standard of correspondence *how the world is made.* (Worth, 1975/1981b, p. 181)

Gross (1981) later addressed the issue in a similar way:

The tendency to see films as objective records of events rather than as a filmmaker's statement about events derives from a confusion of interpretive strategies. Worth had attacked the naivete of many anthropologists and others who were filmically unsophisticated, who assumed that filmed events could be uncritically interpreted as "natural." What such viewers fail to understand is that *all* mediated events are to some extent symbolic. The mediating agent always makes decisions—about what to shoot (and consequently, what not to shoot), and how; and having shot, about how to edit the footage (one rarely sees raw footage); and finally, about when, where, and how to exhibit the edited film.

A sophisticated viewer will recognize that the persons, objects, and events in a film are there, at least in part, because the filmmaker included them intentionally; that the sequence of events in the film has been ordered by the filmmaker's intention to say something by putting them in that order (which may not be the order they actually occurred in); and that the overall structure of the film reflects the filmmaker's intention, and ability, to use implicational conventions in order to communicate to viewers competent to draw the appropriate inferences. (p. 29)

By the time of the posthumous publication of Worth's *Studying Visual Communication* in 1981, then, the issue of conventionality and the exploration of properties of the visual mode with regard to the natural and the symbolic were firmly established as a central axis of visual communication theory and research. The decade of the 1980s saw an even broader range of scholars and institutional agendas take up issues in visual communication, culminating in the rising prominence of visual communication as a formalized subfield of communication research.

INTERDISCIPLINARY CROSSCURRENTS

Although it would clearly be an overstatement to credit Worth's legacy alone with the emergence of visual communication as a subfield within American communication research, it is equally clear that by the mid-1970s, Worth and Gross and their students had made the Annenberg School for Communication at the University of Pennsylvania one of the few key centers for the interdisciplinary cross-currents that came to define visual communication as a recognized area of study. Interest in Worth's notion of an anthropology of visual communication grew and became an important impetus fostering the growth of visual communication studies in general. The journal *Studies in the Anthropology of Visual Communication,* started by Worth and Ruby in 1974 and housed at Penn, provided a forum for the publication of work on society and photography and social worlds of art production by such noted scholars as sociologist Howard S. Becker at Northwestern, studies of the history of photojournalism and the rise of a photojournalistic profession by Hanno Hardt and Karen Becker at Iowa, work on aesthetic and symbolic education by Howard Gardner and David Perkins of Harvard Project Zero, ethnographic studies of photography and film by Jay Ruby and Richard Chalfen at Temple, reviews of children's filmmaking programs in New York by Brian Sutton-Smith at Columbia, and studies of visual and symbolic interpretation by Worth, Gross, and their students (Gross, 1985). Few are aware that Erving Goffman's book *Gender Advertisements* (1979), still considered a foundation study of patterns of gender portrayal in American advertising, was first published as a special issue of *Studies in the Anthropology of Visual Communication* in fall 1976.

After Worth's untimely death, Gross and Ruby responded to the growing interdisciplinary interest in visual communication issues by changing the name of the journal to *Studies in Visual Communication.* In keeping with its new name, the journal published contributions from an even wider range of disciplinary sources, representing the new critical histories of photography, work on the visual languages of science and cartography, research on caricature and political cartoons, essays on public art, new interpretations of the documentary tradition in photography and film, and a greater emphasis on television and media events. For a time, *Studies in Visual Communication* provided impressive evidence that scholarly attention to visual imagery was growing across the social sciences and humanities. It was a rigorous, well-edited scholarly journal with an internationally eminent editorial board and funding (for a time) that allowed for high-quality printing and picture reproduction on large-format, quality-weight glossy paper. This was a high time for visual scholars, knowing that there was a place for them to publish work complete with high-quality picture reproductions. *Studies,* as it was commonly called, not only represented the expansion of this active research area but set the standard for what a visual communication journal could be. Unfortunately, in 1985 the journal lost its funding subsidy and ceased publication. There have been repeated attempts to institute a new journal to take its place. In fact, the organization of a Visual Communication Interest Group in the International Communication Association was an outgrowth of discussions about the possibility of a new journal.

Looking back, it is interesting to note the way that the emerging field of visual communication research resonated with long-standing historical issues in film and photography and paralleled emerging interests in schools of art and journalism. As noted earlier, film theory has long been marked by a rift between the "realists" and the "formative" theorists and filmmakers; those who believe that the ultimate goal of cinema is to create more and more convincing reproductions of natural perception versus those who consider the cinema a new medium for the construction (through camera and editing techniques) of entirely new modes of perceiving the world and commenting upon it. As tools for exploring interpretive strategies, the concepts of attribution and inference echo that history. In photography, the 20th century saw a long competition between those for whom the camera represents a "window" and those who consider it a "mirror." In his 1970s retrospective of American photography at the Museum of Modern Art, John Szarkowski (1978) uses just this metaphor to describe predominant approaches to photo work before and after 1960. Increasingly, he argues, photographers have abandoned the idea of photography as a window on reality and have come to embrace the camera as a reflexive tool, a means of mirroring the photographer's own feelings or worldview. Worth's challenge to the documentary tradition in the human sciences paralleled the shift occurring in critical writings on art photography during the same period.

By the 1980s, traditional notions of visual media were being reevaluated across programs of art, communication, and journalism. A few journalism schools attempted to recast their photojournalism and publication graphics tracks into more integrated and multidisciplinary visual communication curricula. Communication scholars increasingly pointed out that, given the pervasively visual nature of contemporary mass media, it was no longer tenable to study mass communication separately from visual communication (Griffin, 1991, 1992b), and that even a medium such as the newspaper needs to be understood as an inherently visual phenomenon (Barnhurst, 1991, 1994). Although most programs of journalism and mass communication continued to treat photojournalism, publication graphics, and video production as little more than ancillary technical support designed to enhance the delivery of written reports, a few schools actually began to integrate a concern for the contributions of the visual throughout the professional and research curriculum. Concepts from visual anthropology and sociology, the history of film and photography, and the history of printing and publication design slowly and haltingly began to show up in core introductions to mass communication and in graduate proseminars on mass communication research.

The rise of visual communication studies, therefore, was also advanced by the creeping realization within traditional mass communication programs that all media of mass communication had become increasingly (and sometimes exclusively) reliant on visual imagery for their presentations of entertainment, public ceremonies and spectacles, news reporting, and advertising of all sorts, and that mass communication research and professional training could no longer legitimately ignore questions of visual communication. It was in this context that the momentum for a Visual Communication Interest Group within the ICA began to build.

AN INSTITUTIONAL INFRASTRUCTURE

The first signs of the growing presence of visual communication scholarship within the International Communication Association occurred in the early 1980s in the form of "nondivisional" paper sessions organized around visual communication themes.[8] These sessions were distinctive for their particular attention to the *forms* of representation created by the intersection of aesthetic and pictorial traditions, shifting industrial uses of visual media, and evolving visual media technologies. To many it seemed that the movement toward visual communication studies in fact best fulfilled cultural studies pioneer Raymond Williams's exhortation to focus attention on the *forms and practices* of media production and representation.

These developments were not exclusive to the ICA but were occurring widely across various networks of communication researchers and were reflected in the short-lived success of the journal *Studies in Visual Communication* and the establishment of several thematic conferences on visual communication throughout the 1980s.[9] These included the International Conference on Visual Communication held in Philadelphia in 1985,[10] an annual Visual Communication Conference that began to be held each year at sites in the western United States, and a conference on the theme of "Visible Evidence: Strategies and Practice in Documentary Film and Video," with periodic meetings in the United States and Europe. The concerns of these meetings overlapped to varying degrees with those of the International Visual Sociology Association, sponsor of a journal begun in 1986 called *Visual Sociology,* and the International Society for Visual Anthropology, sponsor of the journal *Visual Anthropology.* At the same time, at least two different networks of psychology, education, and communication scholars, one organized as the International Visual Literacy Association and another more recently organized as an interest group within the Speech Communication Association, have institutionalized an ongoing "visual literacy" movement responsible for frequent conferences on visual literacy and media literacy training.

The early 1990s saw a renewed effort to bring about a genuine integration of visual communication studies with mass communication research. In 1991, Barnhurst edited a special issue of *Journalism Educator* that presented a group of articles addressing the prominent role played by pictures and visual design in journalistic reporting and representation, and the glaring need for greater attention to visual communication as a central issue in journalism curricula. Barnhurst continued his efforts to integrate visual communication scholarship into journalism education with his 1994 book *Seeing the Newspaper.* In 1992, a long-planned double issue of *Communication* appeared on the topic of visual communication studies and mass communication research (Griffin, 1992b). In this special double issue, contributors explored topics ranging from the roots of mass communication research in early motion picture studies (Jowett, 1992) to the movement of advertising toward a central reliance on image association (Craig, 1992), the inherent tension in photojournalism and television news between accepted myths of unfettered realism and the actual artifice of routine image construction (Banks, 1992; Griffin, 1992a; Linton, 1992; Perlmutter, 1992; Schwartz, 1992), specific techniques of visual metaphor (Kaplan, 1992), and the potential practices of visual manipulation (Messaris, 1992). The following year, a modest research journal, *Visual Communication Quarterly,* was launched by journalism and mass communication scholars as an insert in the National Press Photographers Association magazine with a primary goal to share relevant academic research with practicing professional photojournalists.

The desire to resurrect a more substantial scholarly journal modeled after *Studies in Visual Communication* was part of the reason for a meeting of visual communication scholars held at the 1993 ICA conference in Washington, D.C. At this meeting the Visual Communication Interest Group was launched. Since then, the group has continued to grow (roughly tripling in membership) as visual communication has continued to receive increasing scholarly attention.

KEY ISSUES AND CURRENT TRENDS: THE STATE OF THE FIELD

The key issues for visual communication as we enter a new millennium are surprisingly similar to those of 25 years ago. The major difference is that greater attention is being paid to these issues within communication research itself, and the application of these ideas is being made across an even greater diversity of media forms and technologies, including digital ones. Several books in the past decade have adeptly summarized and recapitulated the major issues and problems of visual communication research at the end of the 20th century. Reference to these books provides a useful map for summarizing visual communication studies at the beginning of the 21st century.

In *Visual Literacy: Image, Mind, Reality* (1994), Messaris provides a sophisticated book-length review and analysis of issues of picture perception and apprehension, drawing on a broad range of research in the psychology of perception, film analysis, cognitive theories of spatial learning and intelligence, and theories of interpretive strategies. The book has been widely cited, for Messaris has laid out anew the chief ontological and epistemological questions concerning the distinctive status of images as communicative signs and challenged the prevailing opinion among contemporary scholars that visual communication is as much a matter of symbolic convention as are language and other sign systems. Taking a fresh look at the degree to which pictures communicate as "natural" analogues of human visual perception, and therefore veridical copies of our everyday visual impressions of the physical world, Messaris calls into question the extent to which visual apprehension relies upon learned cultural conventions or media-specific schemata for representation. While never claiming that convention plays no part in the process of visual perception, and recognizing the empirical evidence for clear cultural differences in such areas as linear perspective, he concludes that there is a preponderance of evidence to suggest that the iconic qualities of pictures do seem to mimic aspects of natural human perception, providing many of the same visual and informational cues as real-world visual experience. Furthermore, many aspects of pictorial structure or visual syntax in still and moving images (discerning figure-ground relationships and movements, for example, or inferring depth from occlusion) seem to be shared across cultures. "Although the particular physical environment of one's culture may make one more or less sensitive to certain visual cues, a base-level set of common perceptual processes is the shared property of all people" (p. 171).

Messaris's position is an extremely important one, for although he in no way argues for a return to a naive acceptance of the objective recording capacities of photographic media (quite the opposite), he does challenge what he considers the "extreme" position regarding conventionality of theorists such as Nelson Goodman. Goodman (1976) argues that because the correspondence of pictures to their referents follows no consistent rules, the connections between pictures and the things they represent are just as arbitrary as language; we see pictures as resembling "reality" not because they actually do in any physical or natural sense, but because they conform to the expectations of realistic rendering that we have learned and have been culturally conditioned to accept. Because many visual scholars, following Gombrich, have come to accept theories of conventionality that are sympathetic to Goodman's position, Messaris has been seen as something of an iconoclast. Yet what he has done is to remind us that the kinds of questions asked by Sol Worth decades ago have not been settled. His work echoes Worth's (1975/1981b) stated goal: "I should like to begin an exploration into how, and what kinds of things pictures mean . . . and how the way that pictures mean differs from the way such things as 'words' or 'languages' mean" (p. 162). And by eschewing the comfort of accepted wisdom concerning visual convention, Messaris meticulously demonstrates that relationships between the natural (and perhaps universal) characteristics of human image perception and the culture-bound aspects of representational schemata and connotative discernment are complex, ambiguous, and still at the heart of visual communication studies.

Following his treatise on the nature of images and visual literacy, Messaris turned to the cultural power of visual media, whose fleeting images mimic so convincingly the appearances of real life. In *Visual Persuasion: The Role of Images in Advertising* (1997), he argues that precisely because pictures enjoy such a close resemblance to real-world visual cues, they have a power to influence, persuade, or convince that goes beyond noniconic symbol systems. He outlines and examines the various means by which images operate to propose, persuade, and convince, providing a map for future research on visual influence. He explores three major strategies by which images are employed and in terms of which images demand further investigation: employing the iconic qualities of images to *simulate reality,* employing images as *evidence,* and employing reproduction, editing, and juxtaposition to construct *implied propositions.* These three categories of image use, and their intersections, suggest key areas of ongoing research that help to define the current parameters of visual communication studies.

Another recent book that provides an almost encyclopedic review of current issues in visual communication is Barry's *Visual Intelligence: Perception, Image, and Manipulation in Visual Communication* (1997). Not as iconoclastic as Messaris in her challenge of culturalist theories of visual perception, Barry explores many of the same issues surrounding perception and "visual common sense" and critically relates the myriad theories of vision and imagery that underlie the role and power of pictures in film, video, advertising, politics, and propaganda. Published 2 years before the school shootings in Littleton, Colorado, *Visual Intelligence* ends with a prescient discussion of the special power of imagery in the "new violence" of contemporary media and a call for heightened awareness about the potential dangers of a media-fueled culture of violence among the young.

Barthes (1977) has written that photography, "by virtue of its absolutely analogical nature, seems to constitute a message without a code" (pp. 42-43). The power of images to simulate reality, based on many of the properties of nonconventionality that Messaris explores and analyzes, sidesteps traditional rhetorical concerns with truth, falsity, and logical consistency. Instead, images simply imply existence; the subject matter of images just *is.* This quality not only lends itself to the proliferation of pseudoevents (Boorstin, 1961), and the ever-new developments and consequences of virtual realities (Barrett & Redmond, 1995; Heim, 1998), but makes of images a kind of automatic evidence that is rarely questioned. Therefore, the ontological questions regarding the status of images as simulated reality blur together with epistemological questions concerning the validity of images as evidence.

These compounded theoretical issues continually reemerge in nearly every area of visual communication studies. Recent studies of documentary representation (Corner, 1986, 1996; Nichols, 1991; Winston, 1995) have identified different "modes of representation" (or simulated reality) that take on the role of evidence, and consequently rhetorical proposition, in different ways. The expository mode, the observational mode, the interactive mode, and the reflexive mode—useful analytic categories for studying the historical evolution of documentary representation—are often confounded, however, by the "blurred boundaries" of "reality TV," infotainment, and fictional nonfiction that dominate postmodern television (Nichols, 1994). A great, but still largely unmet, challenge for visual communication scholars is to scan, chart, and interrogate the various levels at which images seem to operate: as evidence in visual rhetoric, as simulated reality bolstering and legitimating the presence and status of media operations themselves, as abstract symbols and textual indices, and as "stylistic excess"—the self-conscious performance of style (Caldwell, 1995). Visual style itself, apart from content-related denotation, connotation, and allusion, can be a powerful index of culture—subcultures, professional cultures, political cultures, commercial fashion. Initial forays suggest that scrutinizing visual forms of simulated "reality" can tell us a great deal about the nature of media rhetoric, the limits of veridical representation, and the self-conscious performance of style in newspapers (Barnhurst, 1994), photojournalism (Schwartz, 1992), TV news (Ericson, 1998; Ericson, Baranek, & Chan, 1987; Glasgow University Media Group, 1980; Griffin, 1992a; Hartley, 1982,

1992a, 1992b; Vidal-Beneyto & Dahlgren, 1987), and the various hybrid forms of infotainment, docudrama, reality TV, and simulated reality (Caldwell, 1995; Corner, 1995; Messaris, 1997; Nichols, 1994). These issues are perhaps more significant than ever for the processes of "remediation" that characterize "new" digital media and the emphases on "transparent immediacy" and "hypermediacy" that distinguish digital visualization (Bolter & Grusin, 1999).

Visual communication research, more than anything else, has been a path into the examination of the specific *forms* of our increasingly visual media surround. In the early stages of mass communication research, Lang and Lang (1953) reported on the "unique perspective of television and its effect." The heart of their study was a comparison of the televised coverage of Chicago's MacArthur Day parade to the reported observations and experiences of informants on the scene—a comparison that found the representation of the parade on television, the "TV reality," to be very different from, even contradictory to, the "reality" seen and experienced by those attending the event. Lang and Lang concluded that television's need to create a coherent presentational structure from separate, fragmented, and often only indirectly related scenes and activities resulted in a "televisual perspective" or televisual *form* specific to the nature and workings of that medium. Unfortunately, this fascinating line of research never took hold in mainstream mass communication research.[11] It was only decades later that visual communication studies provided an impetus to return to such analysis of media forms.

Two important books published in the 1990s revisit this concern with form as part of a heightened awareness of the visual. Corner's *Television Form and Public Address* (1995) suggests that only through the study of the specific visual forms of television, and not simply its most apparent content, will we come to understand more fully the rhetoric and influence of TV as our major forum of public address. Like Messaris, Corner sees the propositions and influence of television to reside in the nature of its simulated reality, its modes of depiction, and its presentational formats. This is not a return to a McLuhanesque essentialism regarding media technology; rather, it is a recognition (following Raymond Williams) that the historically and culturally specific forms of television that have evolved in particular industrial and commercial systems inexorably shape and delimit the nature of television discourse.

In *Televisuality: Style, Crisis, and Authority in American Television,* Caldwell (1995) revisits Lang and Lang's notion of televisuality in an even more explicit technical/aesthetic manner and finds an even greater gulf than they did between presentational styles and connections to external referents. Caldwell comprehensively describes a solipsistic universe of stylistic excess in which aesthetic performance dominates a self-referential world. Partly for economic reasons (the desire to cut costs on locations and sets), television producers increasingly create "virtual worlds of excessive videographics" in place of the realist style of conventional production techniques (pp. 77-78). This is an issue of particular concern to visual communication researchers as we proceed into an era of increasingly convincing virtual realism on the one hand and the increasingly solipsistic textualization of images in cyberspace on the other. More and more visual practices are moving away from the ideal that visual media can and should explore and reveal our social and natural environment and toward self-contained visual lexicons that reduce all visual elements to characters in digital texts. It is as if we seek to follow French structuralist philosophy to its logical conclusion, taming the autonomy and power of images and making them subservient to textual interpretation (Jay, 1993). It is not just what we *can* do with new digital technologies of manipulation (Mitchell, 1992), but to what purposes we seek to use the production of images in a postphotographic age (Lister, 1995).

All of which reminds us of the importance of studying not just images themselves but the social worlds out of which they are produced and in which they are received and used (Becker, 1982; Worth, 1981c). As the various essays in Gross's *On the Margins of Art Worlds* (1995) illustrate, cultural production is always implicated in the communication and reproduction of social distinction, historical memory, and cultural identity (see also Bourdieu, 1984, 1965/1990). Recently, an increasing number of studies have turned their attention to the role of visual images in the maintenance of collective memory, historical mythology, and "cultures of vision" (Brennen & Hardt, 1999; Burnett, 1995; Perlmutter, 1992, 1999; Zelizer, 1992, 1998). The entire movement of the past quarter century toward new, "critical" histories of photography has largely been an attempt to replace the concept of photographs as mechanical artifacts of reality with that of photographs as expressions of cultural vision (Bolton, 1989; Sekula, 1975).

Now, at the beginning of a new millennium, we struggle with the new challenge of relating some sense of a natural world with the artifice of cyberspace and interactive design. Postmodern theorists have long since thrown in the towel on referentiality, but it is still very unclear where we go "after photography." Are we destined to abandon the analogical project of realist exploration and resign ourselves to digitally generated symbols? Interestingly, at the same time that some are concerned with the "postlinguistic, postsemiotic rediscovery of the picture," not as naive mimesis but as "a complex interplay between visuality, apparatus, institutions, discourse, bodies, and figurality" (Mitchell, 1994, p. 16), the more mundane world of daily media production and consumption continues to subscribe to a relatively simple correspondence theory of representation. The relationships of visual representations to either external or intertextual references may often seem ambiguous, but the "reality" of such representations tends to be assumed nonetheless, by both producers and spectators. The central common tasks, then, that still confront, and help to define, visual communication scholarship are to explore and discern the precise ontological and epistemological status of visual media representations, to clarify the processes of viewer reception and interpretation, and to analyze the social and cultural ramifications of the peculiar properties of the visual in contemporary media.

Finally, in that emerging condition often referred to as the "global media environment" visual images have become a new sort of transnational cultural currency—*not* the "universal language" that promoters such as Eastman Kodak Company claimed for photography earlier in the century, but a currency of media control and power, indices of the predominant cultural visions of predominant media industries. Western ideals of feminine and masculine appeal, for example, have proliferated around the world in commercial and entertainment portrayals, making the peculiar look of Western fashion models a kind of global standard of beauty and sexual glamour (Griffin, Viswanath, & Schwartz, 1994). Similarly, the visual forms of news, entertainment, and cyberlandscape that have rapidly diffused globally seem to reconfirm Tunstall's (1977) observation that "the media are American" (see also Nordenstreng & Griffin, 1999). So it was that at the recent ICA meeting in San Francisco, sessions of the Visual Communication Interest Group included panels titled "Perceptual-Cognitive Approaches to Visual Communication Research," "Theorizing Visual Culture," "Social Experience and Visual Culture," "Realism, Narrative and the Image," "Photography, Imagination and Discourse," "Cultures of Graphic Design," and "Visual Form/Content Across Cultures."

NOTES

1. I use the term *picture* here in a sense that is similar to the Albertian definition of a picture noted by Alpers (1983): "a framed surface or pane situated at a certain distance from a viewer who looks through it at a second or substitute world" (p. xix). I do not, however, wish to limit my definition to a strictly Renaissance model of picture making; rather, I would include all types of visual image making that address viewers in a picturelike manner.

2. As in any such generalization there are, of course, exceptions. Tuchman's *Making News* (1978), for instance, is a well-known sociological study of news production that does, in fact, devote a chapter to visual representation. However, such examples are, indeed, rare in the mass communication literature.

3. I have addressed this issue in previous work (see Griffin & Kagan, 1996). Consciousness of the importance of visual images in political communication expanded greatly in the wake of the Reagan presidency, when such Reagan advisers as Michael Deaver averred that the control and manipulation of images overpowered anything that the public heard or read (Adatto, 1993; Deaver, 1987). Following the 1988 campaign, prominent political rhetoricians, such as Kathleen Hall Jamieson (1992), began for the first time to call explicitly for the *visual* analysis of political spots and contemporary political discourse.

4. See the special issue of *Journalism Educator* on visual communication study and teaching edited by Kevin Barnhurst (1991).

5. These issues relate as well to spatial and temporal constructs in literature and the earlier plastic arts, and were raised by writers at least as early as the 18th century (see the treatment of Lessing's *Laokoon* in Mitchell, 1986, pp. 95-115).

6. An early example of the incorporation of visual analysis in the study of representation and ideology is Stuart Hall's essay "The Determinations of News Photographs" (1973), in which Hall attempts to apply cultural and ideological analysis derived from studies of popular culture conducted at the Centre for Contemporary Cultural Studies at the University of Birmingham to news photographs in order to demonstrate how pictures enhance and frame the ideological positions of accompanying linguistic text. In the mid-1970s, the Glasgow University Media Group (1976, 1980) carried out some of the first detailed visual analyses of television news in order to expose the ideological nature of BBC reporting on industrial labor disputes. Although the Media Group has

been criticized for the assumptions of scientific objectivity that underpin their analyses of news "bias," these studies represent a new level of rigor in their employment of concrete visual analysis.

7. For comprehensive reviews of psychological theories of visual perception and controversies surrounding the nature of images and visual apprehension, see Messaris's *Visual Literacy* (1994) and Barry's *Visual Intelligence* (1997).

8. Messaris was instrumental in organizing some of the earliest of these visual communication sessions.

9. As I have noted, the tenure of the unique and impressive *Studies in Visual Communication* was unfortunately short-lived; an end to funding support forced the journal to cease publication after 1985.

10. A book of the proceedings, *Visual Explorations of the World* (Ruby & Taureg, 1987), subsequently appeared.

11. Almost 40 years later, mass communication and political communication theorist Doris Graber (1990, p. 134) explicitly bemoaned the fact that the visual elements of such important media genres as television news had not received much attention.

REFERENCES

Adatto, K. (1993). *Picture perfect: The art and artifice of public image making.* New York: Basic Books.

Alpers, S. (1960). Ekphrasis and aesthetic attitudes in Vasari's lives. *Journal of the Warburg-Courtald Institute, 23,* 190-215.

Alpers, S. (1983). *The art of describing: Dutch art in the seventeenth century.* Chicago: University of Chicago Press.

Andrew, D. (1976). *The major film theories.* New York: Oxford University Press.

Andrew, D. (1984). *Concepts in film theory.* New York: Oxford University Press.

Arnheim, R. (1957). *Film as art.* Berkeley: University of California Press. (Original work published 1932)

Banks, A. (1992). Frontstage/backstage: Loss of control in real-time coverage of the war in the Gulf. *Communication, 13*(2), 111-119.

Barnhurst, K. G. (Ed.). (1991). Visual communication study and teaching [Special issue]. *Journalism Educator, 46*(1).

Barnhurst, K. G. (1994). *Seeing the newspaper.* New York: St. Martin's.

Barrett, E., & Redmond, M. (Eds.). (1995). *Contextual media: Multimedia and interpretation.* Cambridge: MIT Press.

Barry, A. M. (1997). *Visual intelligence: Perception, image, and manipulation in visual communication.* Albany: State University of New York Press.

Barthes, R. (1977). The rhetoric of the image. In R. Barthes, *Image-music-text* (pp. 32-51). New York: Noonday.

Barthes, R. (1981). *Camera lucida: Reflections on photography* (R. Howard, Trans.). New York: Hill & Wang.

Baxandall, M. (1972). *Painting and experience in fifteenth century Italy.* New York: Oxford University Press.

Baxandall, M. (1985). *Patterns of intention: On the historical explanation of pictures.* New Haven, CT: Yale University Press.

Bazin, A. (1967). *What is cinema?* (H. Gray, Trans.). Berkeley: University of California Press.

Becker, H. S. (1974a). Art as collective action. *American Sociological Review, 39,* 767-776.

Becker, H. S. (1974b). Photography and society. *Studies in the Anthropology of Visual Communication, 1,* 3-26.

Becker, H. S. (1982). *Art worlds.* Berkeley: University of California Press.

Becker, K. E. (1985). Forming a profession. *Studies in Visual Communication, 11*(2), 44-60.

Benjamin, W. (1969). The work of art in the age of mechanical reproduction. In W. Benjamin, *Illuminations* (H. Arendt, Ed.; H. Zohn, Trans.) (pp. 217-251). New York: Schocken. (Original work published 1936)

Berger, J. (1972). *Ways of seeing.* New York: Penguin.

Berger, J. (1980). Uses of photography. In J. Berger, *About looking* (pp. 48-63). New York: Pantheon.

Bernstein, B. (1971). *Class, codes and control* (Vol. 1). London: Paladin.

Bolter, J. D., & Grusin, R. (1999). *Remediation: Understanding new media.* Cambridge: MIT Press.

Bolton, R. (Ed.). (1989). *The contest of meaning: Critical histories of photography.* Cambridge: MIT Press.

Boorstin, D. J. (1961). *The image: A guide to pseudo-events in America.* New York: Atheneum.

Bourdieu, P. (1984). *Distinction* (R. Nice, Trans.). Cambridge, MA: Harvard University Press.

Bourdieu, P. (1990). *Photography: A middle-brow art.* Stanford, CA: Stanford University Press. (Original work published 1965)

Brennen, B., & Hardt, H. (Eds.). (1999). *Picturing the past: Media, history and photography.* Urbana: University of Illinois Press.

Burgin, V. (Ed.). (1982). *Thinking photography.* New York: Macmillan.

Burnett, R. (1995). *Cultures of vision: Images, media, and the imaginary.* Bloomington: Indiana University Press.

Caldwell, J. T. (1995). *Televisuality: Style, crisis, and authority in American television.* New Brunswick, NJ: Rutgers University Press.

Carey, J. (1974). Temporal and spatial transitions in American fiction films. *Studies in the Anthropology of Visual Communication, 1,* 27-34.

Chalfen, R. (1975). Cinema naivete: A study of home moviemaking as visual communication. *Studies in the Anthropology of Visual Communication, 2,* 87-103.

Chalfen, R. (1987). *Snapshot versions of life.* Bowling Green, OH: Bowling Green University Press.

Clifford, J. (1988). *The predicament of culture: Twentieth-century ethnography, literature, and art.* Cambridge, MA: Harvard University Press.

Clifford, J., & Marcus, G. E. (Eds.). (1986). *Writing culture: The poetics and politics of ethnography.* Berkeley: University of California Press.

Cook, B. L. (1981). *Understanding pictures in Papua New Guinea.* Elgin, IL: David C. Cook Foundation.

Corner, J. (Ed.). (1986). *Documentary and the mass media.* London: Edward Arnold.

Corner, J. (1995). *Television form and public address.* London: Edward Arnold.

Corner, J. (1996). *The art of record: A critical introduction to documentary.* New York: Manchester University Press.

Craig, R. L. (1991). Designing ethnicity: The ideology of images. *Design Issues, 7*(2), 34-42.

Craig, R. L. (1992). Advertising as visual communication. *Communication, 13*(3), 165-179.

Custen, G. (1982). Talking about film. In S. Thomas (Ed.), *Film/culture: Explorations of cinema in its social context* (pp. 237-246). Metuchen, NJ: Scarecrow.

Deaver, M. (1987). *Behind the scenes.* New York: William Morrow.

Deleuze, G. (1986). *Cinema 1: The movement-image* (H. Tomlinson & B. Habberjam, Trans.). Minneapolis: University of Minnesota Press.

Deleuze, G. (1988). *Foucault.* Minneapolis: University of Minnesota Press.

Deleuze, G. (1989). *Cinema 2: The time-image* (H. Tomlinson & R. Galeta, Trans.). Minneapolis: University of Minnesota Press.

Deregowski, J. B. (1968). Difficulties in pictorial depth perception in Africa. *British Journal of Psychology, 59,* 195-204.

Deregowski, J. B. (1973). Illusion and culture. In R. L. Gregory & E. H. Gombrich (Eds.), *Illusion in nature and culture* (pp. 160-191). New York: Scribner.

Dyer, R. (1977). *Now you see it: Studies in lesbian and gay film.* London: Routledge.

Dyer, R. (1993). *The matter of images: Essays on representations.* London: Routledge.

Eadie, F., Sutton-Smith, B., & Griffin, M. (1983). Filmmaking by "young filmmakers." *Studies in Visual Communication, 9*(4), 65-75.

Eco, U. (1986). A photograph. In U. Eco, *Travels in hyperreality* (J. Radziewicz, Ed.; W. Weaver, Trans.) (pp. 213-217). New York: Harcourt Brace Jovanovich.

Eisenstein, S. M. (1942). *Film sense* (J. Leyda, Ed. & Trans.). New York: Harcourt Brace.

Eisenstein, S. M. (1949). *Film form: Essays in film theory* (J. Leyda, Ed. & Trans.). New York: Harcourt Brace.

Ericson, R. (1998). How journalists visualize fact. *Annals of the American Academy of Political and Social Science, 560,* 83-95.

Ericson, R., Baranek, P., & Chan, J. (1987). *Visualizing deviance: A study of news organization.* Milton Keynes: Open University Press.

Feld, S. (Ed.). (1985). *Chronicle of a summer* [Special issue]. *Studies in Visual Communication, 11*(1).

Fisher, W. R. (1985). The narrative paradigm: In the beginning. *Journal of Communication, 35*(4), 74-89.

Fisher, W. R. (1987). *Human communication as narration: Toward a philosophy of reason, value and action.* Columbia: University of South Carolina Press.

Fisher, W. R. (1989). Clarifying the narrative paradigm. *Communication Monographs, 56,* 55-58.

Fiske, J., & Hartley, J. (1978). *Reading television.* London: Methuen.

Fried, M. (1980). *Absorption and theatricality: Painting and the beholder in the age of Diderot.* Berkeley: University of California Press.

Gerbner, G., Gross, L., Morgan, M., & Signorielli, N. (1980). Aging with television: Images on television and conceptions of social reality. *Journal of Communication, 30*(1), 37-47.

Gibson, J. J. (1982). *Reasons for realism: Selected essays of James J. Gibson* (E. Reed & R. Jones, Eds.). Hillsdale, NJ: Lawrence Erlbaum.

Glasgow University Media Group. (1976). *Bad news.* London: Routledge.

Glasgow University Media Group. (1980). *More bad news.* London: Routledge.

Goffman, E. (1979). *Gender advertisements.* Cambridge, MA: Harvard University Press.

Goldberg, V. (Ed.). (1988). *Photography in print: Writings from 1816 to the present.* Albuquerque: University of New Mexico Press.

Gombrich, E. H. (1960). *Art and illusion: A study in the psychology of pictorial representation.* Princeton, NJ: Princeton University Press.

Gombrich, E. H. (1972). The visual image. *Scientific American, 227*(3), 82-96.

Goodman, N. (1976). *Languages of art: An approach to a theory of symbols* (2nd ed.). Indianapolis: Bobbs-Merrill.

Graber, D. A. (1990). Seeing is remembering: How visuals contribute to learning from television news. *Journal of Communication, 40*(3), 134-155.

Gregory, R. L. (1966). *Eye and brain: The psychology of seeing.* Princeton, NJ: Princeton University Press.

Gregory, R. L. (1970). *The intelligent eye.* New York: McGraw-Hill.

Griffin, M. (1985). What young filmmakers learn from television: A study of structure in films made by children. *Journal of Broadcasting & Electronic Media, 29,* 79-92.

Griffin, M. (1991). Defining visual communication for a multi-media world. *Journalism Educator, 46*(1), 9-15.

Griffin, M. (1992a). Looking at TV news: Strategies for research. *Communication, 13*(2), 121-141.

Griffin, M. (Ed.). (1992b). Visual communication studies in mass media research: Parts I and II [Special double issue]. *Communication, 13*(2-3).

Griffin, M. (1995). Between art and industry: Amateur photography and middlebrow culture. In L. Gross (Ed.), *On the margins of art worlds* (pp. 183-205). Boulder, CO: Westview.

Griffin, M., & Kagan, S. (1996). Picturing culture in political spots: 1992 campaigns in Israel and the U.S. *Political Communication, 13,* 43-61.

Griffin, M., Viswanath, K., & Schwartz, D. (1994). Gender advertising in the U.S. and India: Exporting cultural stereotypes. *Media, Culture & Society, 16,* 487-507.

Gross, L. (1974a). Modes of communication and the acquisition of symbolic competence. In D. R. Olson (Ed.), *Media and symbols: The forms of expression, communication, and education* (pp. 56-80). Chicago: University of Chicago Press.

Gross, L. (1974b). Art history as ethnography and as social analysis: A review essay. *Studies in the Anthropology of Visual Communication, 1*(1), 51-56.

Gross, L. (1981). Introduction. In S. Worth, *Studying visual communication* (L. Gross, Ed.) (pp. 1-35). Philadelphia: University of Pennsylvania Press.

Gross, L. (1985). Life versus art: The interpretation of visual narratives. *Studies in Visual Communication, 11*(4), 2-11.

Gross, L. (1988). The ethics of (mis)representation. In L. Gross, J. S. Katz, & J. Ruby (Eds.), *Image ethics* (pp. 188-202). New York: Oxford University Press.

Gross, L. (1989). Out of the mainstream: Sexual minorities and the mass media. In E. Seiter, H. Borcher, G. Kreutzner, & E. M. Warth (Eds.), *Remote control: Television, audiences and cultural power* (pp. 130-149). London: Routledge.

Gross, L. (Ed.). (1995). *On the margins of art worlds.* Boulder, CO: Westview.

Gross, L., Katz, J. S., & Ruby, J. (Eds.). (1988). *Image ethics.* New York: Oxford University Press.

Hall, S. (1973). The determinations of news photographs. In S. Cohen & J. Young (Eds.), *The manufacture of news: Social problems, deviance, and the mass media* (pp. 226-243). Beverly Hills, CA: Sage.

Hardt, H. (1989). Pictures for the masses: Photography and the rise of popular magazines in Weimar Germany. *Journal of Communication Inquiry, 13*(1), 7-29.

Hardt, H. (1996). The site of reality: Constructing photojournalism in Weimar Germany. *Communication Review, 1,* 373-402.

Hardt, H., & Ohrn, K. (1981). The eyes of the proletariat: The worker-photography movement in Weimar Germany. *Studies in Visual Communication, 7*(4), 72-83.

Hartley, J. (1982). *Understanding news.* New York: Methuen.

Hartley, J. (1992a). *The politics of pictures.* New York: Routledge.

Hartley, J. (1992b). *Tele-ology: Studies in television.* New York: Routledge.

Hebdige, D. (1979). *Subculture: The meaning of style.* London: Methuen.

Heim, M. (1998). *Virtual realism.* New York: Oxford University Press.

Hochberg, J. E. (1978). *Perception* (2nd ed.). Englewood Cliffs, NJ: Prentice Hall.

Hochberg, J. E. (1983, March). Pictorial functions in perception. *Art Education,* pp. 15-18.

Hochberg, J. E. (1984). The perception of pictorial representations. *Social Research, 51,* 841-862.

Hudson, W. (1960). Pictorial depth perception in sub-cultural groups in Africa. *Journal of Social Psychology, 52,* 183-208.

Hymes, D. (1964). Toward ethnographies of communication. In J. J. Gumperz & D. Hymes (Eds.), The ethnography of communication [Special publication]. *American Anthropologist, 66*(6, Pt. 2).

Hymes, D. (1967). Why linguistics needs the sociologist. *Journal of Social Research, 34*(4).

Ivins, W., Jr. (1953). *Prints and visual communication.* Cambridge: MIT Press.

Jamieson, K. H. (1992). *Dirty politics: Deception, distraction, and democracy.* New York: Oxford University Press.

Jay, M. (1993). *Downcast eyes: The denigration of vision in twentieth-century French thought.* Berkeley: University of California Press.

Johnston, A. (1990). Trends in political communication: A selective review of research in the 1980s. In D. L. Swanson & D. Nimmo (Eds.), *New directions in political communication* (pp. 329-362). Newbury Park, CA: Sage.

Jowett, G. (1992). Social science as a weapon: The origins of the Payne Fund Studies, 1926-1929. *Communication, 13*(2), 211-225.

Kaplan, E. A. (Ed.). (1983). *Regarding television: Critical approaches—an anthology.* Frederick, MD: University Publications of America.

Kaplan, S. J. (1992). A conceptual analysis of form and content in visual metaphors. *Communication, 13*(3), 197-209.

Kennedy, J. M. (1984). How minds use pictures. *Social Research, 51,* 885-904.

Kracauer, S. (1960). *Theory of film.* New York: Oxford University Press.

Labov, W. (1966). *The social stratification of English in New York City.* Washington, DC: Center for Applied Linguistics.

Lang, K., & Lang, G. (1953). The unique perspective of television and its effect: A pilot study. *American Sociological Review, 18,* 3-12.

Lester, P. M. (Ed.). (1996). *Images that injure.* New York: Praeger.

Lindsay, V. (1916). *The art of the moving picture.* New York: Macmillan.

Linton, J. M. (1982). The nature of the viewing experience: The missing link in the effects equation. In S. Thomas (Ed.), *Film/culture: Explorations of cinema in its social context* (pp. 184-194). Metuchen, NJ: Scarecrow.

Linton, J. M. (1992). Documentary film research's unrealized potential in the communication field. *Communication, 13*(2), 85-93.

Lister, M. (Ed.). (1995). *The photographic image in digital culture.* London: Routledge.

Marcus, G. E., & Fischer, M. M. J. (1986). *Anthropology as cultural critique: An experimental moment in the human sciences.* Chicago: University of Chicago Press.

Marr, D. (1982). *Vision: A computational investigation into the human representation and processing of visual information.* New York: W. H. Freeman.

Mead, M. (1977). The contribution of Sol Worth to anthropology. *Studies in the Anthropology of Visual Communication, 4,* 67.

Messaris, P. (1982). To what extent does one have to learn to interpret movies? In S. Thomas (Ed.), *Film/culture: Explorations of cinema in its social context* (pp. 168-183). Metuchen, NJ: Scarecrow.

Messaris, P. (1992). Visual manipulation: Visual means of affecting responses to images. *Communication, 13*(3), 181-195.

Messaris, P. (1994). *Visual literacy: Image, mind, reality.* Boulder, CO: Westview.

Messaris, P. (1997). *Visual persuasion: The role of images in advertising.* Thousand Oaks, CA: Sage.

Messaris, P., & Gross, L. (1977). Interpretations of a photographic narrative by viewers in four age groups. *Studies in the Anthropology of Visual Communication, 4,* 99-111.

Messaris, P., & Pallenik, M. (1977). Attribution and inference in the interpretation of candid and staged film events. *Studies in the Anthropology of Visual Communication, 4,* 51-58.

Messaris, P., & Sarett, C. (1981). On the consequences of television-related parent-child interactions. *Human Communication Research, 7,* 226-244.

Metz, C. (1974). *Film language.* New York: Oxford University Press.

Miller, R. M. (1978). *Ethnic images in American film and television.* Philadelphia: Balch Institute.

Mitchell, W. J. (1992). *The reconfigured eye: Visual truth in the post-photographic era.* Cambridge: MIT Press.

Mitchell, W. J. T. (1986). *Iconology: Image, text, ideology.* Chicago: University of Chicago Press.

Mitchell, W. J. T. (1994). *Picture theory: Essays on verbal and visual representation.* Chicago: University of Chicago Press.

Mitry, J. (1963). *Esthetique et psychologie du cinema* (Vol. 1). Paris: Paris Editions Universitaires.

Mitry, J. (1965). *Esthetique et psychologie du cinema* (Vol. 2). Paris: Paris Editions Universitaires.

Mitry, J. (1972). *Le mot et l'image.* Paris: Edition du Signe.

Mulvey, L. (1989). Visual pleasure and narrative cinema. In L. Mulvey, *Visual and other pleasures* (pp. 14-26). Bloomington: Indiana University Press. (Original work published 1975)

Munsterberg, H. (1970). *The film: A psychological study.* New York: Dover. (Original work published 1916)

Musello, C. (1980). Studying the home-mode: An exploration of family photography and visual communication. *Studies in Visual Communication, 6*(1), 23-42.

Nichols, B. (1991). *Representing reality: Issues and concepts in documentary.* Bloomington: Indiana University Press.

Nichols, B. (1994). *Blurred boundaries: Questions of meaning in contemporary culture.* Bloomington: Indiana University Press.

Nordenstreng, K., & Griffin, M. (Eds.). (1999). *International media monitoring.* Cresskill, NJ: Hampton.
Pallenik, M. (1976). A gunman in town! Children interpret a comic book. *Studies in the Anthropology of Visual Communication, 3,* 38-51.
Panofsky, E. (1939). *Studies in iconology.* Oxford: Oxford University Press.
Panofsky, E. (1991). *Perspective as symbolic form* (C. S. Wood, Trans.). New York: Zone. (Original work published 1924)
Peirce, C. S. (1931). *Collected papers.* Cambridge, MA: Harvard University Press.
Perlmutter, D. D. (1992). The vision of war in high school social science textbooks. *Communication, 13*(2), 143-160.
Perlmutter, D. D. (1999). *Visions of war: Picturing warfare from the Stone Age to the Cyber Age.* New York: St. Martin's.
Pudovkin, V. I. (1954). *Film technique and film acting* (I. Montagu, Trans.). London: Vision. (Original work published 1926)
Ricouer, P. (1980). Narrative time. *Critical Inquiry, 7,* 151-183.
Rorty, R. (1979). *Philosophy and the mirror of nature.* Princeton, NJ: Princeton University Press.
Rosaldo, R. (1989). *Culture and truth: The remaking of social analysis.* Boston: Beacon.
Rosenblum, B. (1978). *Photographers at work.* New York: Holmes & Meier.
Ruby, J. (1975). Is ethnographic film a film ethnography? *Studies in the Anthropology of Visual Communication, 2,* 104-111.
Ruby, J. (1981). Seeing through pictures: The anthropology of photography. *Camera Lucida, 3,* 20-33.
Ruby, J. (Ed.). (1982). *A crack in the mirror: Reflexive perspectives in anthropology.* Philadelphia: University of Pennsylvania Press.
Ruby, J., & Taureg, M. (Eds.). (1987). *Visual explorations of the world.* Aachen, Germany: Edition Heredot, Rader Verlag.
Schiller, D. (1981). *Objectivity and the news: The public and the rise of commercial journalism.* Philadelphia: University of Pennsylvania Press.
Schwartz, D. (1992). To tell the truth: Codes of objectivity in photojournalism. *Communication, 13*(2), 95-109.
Schwartz, D., & Griffin, M. (1987). Amateur photography: The organizational maintenance of an aesthetic code. In T. Lindlof (Ed.), *Natural audiences: Qualitative research of media uses and effects* (pp. 198-224). Norwood, NJ: Ablex.
Sekula, A. (1975, January). On the invention of photographic meaning. *Art Forum,* pp. 37-45.
Shaheen, J. G. (1988). Perspectives on the television Arab. In L. Gross, J. S. Katz, & J. Ruby (Eds.), *Image ethics* (pp. 203-219). New York: Oxford University Press.
Sontag, S. (1977). *On photography.* New York: Farrar, Straus & Giroux.
Szarkowski, J. (1978). *Mirrors and windows: American photography since 1960.* New York: Museum of Modern Art.
Tagg, J. (1988). *The burden of representation: Essays on photographies and histories.* London: Macmillan.
Trachtenberg, A. (Ed.). (1980). *Classic essays on photography.* New Haven, CT: Leete's Island.
Tuchman, G. (1978). Representation and the news narrative. In G. Tuchman, *Making news: A study in the construction of reality.* New York: Free Press.
Tuchman, G., Daniels, A. K., & Benet, J. (Eds.). (1978). *Hearth and home: Images of women in the mass media.* New York: Oxford University Press.
Tunstall, J. (1977). *The media are American.* New York: Columbia University Press.
Turow, J. (1978). Casting for TV parts: The anatomy of social typing. *Journal of Communication, 28*(2), 19-24.
Vidal-Beneyto, J., & Dahlgren, P. (1987). *The focused screen.* Strasbourg, France: Council of Europe.
White, H. (1987). *The content of the form: Narrative discourse and historical representation.* Baltimore: Johns Hopkins University Press.

Williams, R. (1974). *Television: Technology and cultural form.* London: Fontana/Collins.

Williamson, J. (1978). *Decoding advertisements.* London: Marion Boyars.

Winston, B. (1995). *Claiming the real: The documentary film revisited.* London: British Film Institute.

Worth, S. (1980). Margaret Mead and the shift from "visual anthropology" to the "anthropology of visual communication." *Studies in Visual Communication, 6*(1), 15-22.

Worth, S. (1981a). The development of a semiotic of film. In S. Worth, *Studying visual communication* (L. Gross, Ed.) (pp. 36-73). Philadelphia: University of Pennsylvania Press. (Reprinted from *Semiotica,* 1969, *1,* 282-321)

Worth, S. (1981b). Pictures can't say ain't. In S. Worth, *Studying visual communication* (L. Gross, Ed.) (pp. 162-184). Philadelphia: University of Pennsylvania Press. (Reprinted from *Versus,* 1975, *12,* 85-108)

Worth, S. (1981c). *Studying visual communication* (L. Gross, Ed.). Philadelphia: University of Pennsylvania Press.

Worth, S. (1981d). Toward an anthropological politics of symbolic forms. In S. Worth, *Studying visual communication* (L. Gross, Ed.) (pp. 85-107). Philadelphia: University of Pennsylvania Press. (Reprinted from *Reinventing anthropology,* by D. Hymes, Ed., 1972, New York: Pantheon)

Worth, S., & Adair, J. (1972). *Through Navajo eyes: An exploration in film communication and anthropology.* Bloomington: Indiana University Press.

Worth, S., & Gross, L. (1981). Symbolic strategies. In S. Worth, *Studying visual communication* (L. Gross, Ed.) (pp. 134-147). Philadelphia: University of Pennsylvania Press. (Reprinted from *Journal of Communication,* 1974, *24*[4], 27-39)

Worth, S., & Ruby, J. (1981). An American community's socialization to pictures: An ethnography of visual communication (a preproposal). In S. Worth, *Studying visual communication* (L. Gross, Ed.) (pp. 200-203). Philadelphia: University of Pennsylvania Press. (Original work written 1977)

Zelizer, B. (1992). *Covering the body: The Kennedy assassination, the media, and the shaping of collective memory.* Chicago: University of Chicago Press.

Zelizer, B. (1998). *Remembering to forget: Holocaust memory through the camera's eye.* Chicago: University of Chicago Press.

CHAPTER CONTENTS

20 Queer Communication Studies

LISA HENDERSON
University of Massachusetts

This essay charts the development of gay, lesbian, bisexual, and transgender studies—sometimes called queer studies—in communication since the early 1980s. It considers the intellectual and political stakes in a project closely connected to movements for sexual liberation and also describes the shifting significance of such terms as *gay* and *queer* and the people and practices they signify. The analysis combines theories of subjectivity with questions about sexual representation in public and private, opening (and closing) with commentary on the social meanings and hierarchies of sexual difference.

INTELLECTUAL PLACEMENT, INTELLECTUAL STAKES

Now is a good time to take stock of queer communication studies. From relative invisibility, queer studies in communication is acquiring a second and in some places a third generation of graduate student scholars and enjoying at least moderate regard among academics who are not centrally involved in the cultural study of sex. The subfield can now claim a powerful interdisciplinary literature, regular interest among graduate program applicants, routine discussion of sexual difference in undergraduate and graduate communication courses, a growing number of openly gay and lesbian scholars (and a smaller number of bisexual and transgender ones) working on both queer and nonqueer topics, and institutional forums for lesbian, gay, bisexual, and transgender scholarship in the National Communication Association and the International Communication Association, the two dominant professional associations for communication scholars in the United States.

AUTHOR'S NOTE: My thanks to Dean Glen Gordon, College of Social and Behavioral Sciences, University of Massachusetts, for funds for research assistance; also to James Allan, John N. Erni, Larry Gross, William Gudykunst, and two anonymous reviewers for their readings and editorial assistance; to Janice Irvine (convener) and members of the Sexuality Studies Reading Group at the Five College Women's Studies Research Center, Mount Holyoke College; and especially to Lynn Comella for her careful research assistance and insightful responses.

Correspondence: Lisa Henderson, Department of Communication, University of Massachusetts, Amherst, MA 01003; e-mail lhender@comm.umass.edu

Communication Yearbook 24, pp. 465-484

Such developments come from a range of motives and energy sources. Like other disciplines in the social sciences and humanities, queer studies in communication has emerged in the context of activist momentum for civil rights and sexual liberation for erotic minorities. Although these struggles are far from over, and although gains are limited by region and live in the perpetual shadow of retrenchment, real progress has been made in such areas as employment protection and sociopolitical recognition. Not surprisingly, many of those historically involved in gay and queer movements have been intellectuals, some of them academically trained and employed. With activist courage, a handful of faculty members introduced undergraduate communication courses in gay studies as early as 1980, usually with "special topic" designations and such titles as "Communication and Human Sexuality" and "Sexual Minorities and the Media." At that point, much of the literature that could be assigned had been written by nonacademic intellectuals and published in the nonacademic press. Although this is no longer true, activist thought and writing remain fundamental to queer studies in communication, alongside the more rarefied vernaculars of queer theory; see, for example, Gross and Woods's (1999) recent collection, *The Columbia Reader on Lesbians and Gay Men in Media, Society, and Politics.* Many of the students and teachers involved, moreover, have routinely committed a part of their intellectual labor to consciously political gestures both on campus and off.

In such a milieu, perhaps it is not surprising that a shifting emphasis (sometimes a tension) emerges between a liberatory impulse and the more traditional canons of academic investigation and detachment, an emphasis characteristic of the broader project of cultural studies and the longer-standing fields of feminist, labor, and critical race studies. Queer studies scholars, then, like their colleagues in those related fields, take on urgent political questions and strategies alongside a sustained theoretical inquiry not so readily incorporated into political action. Although such mandates may seem contradictory or at best parallel (coexisting but never intersecting in time and space), in this essay I want to take a more promising view. Rather than seeing discontinuities only as sources of antagonism or betrayal among divided groups of academics and activists (which indeed they can be), I imagine them instead as producing multiple points of intellectual intervention and possibility whose political qualities must be thought through at each juncture and whose outcomes cannot be confidently predicted or predetermined. From this perspective, to paraphrase Stuart Hall (1990), queer communication studies offers the possibility of transformation without guarantees.

For some readers, these introductory remarks may leave the impression that if personal histories, political commitments, and intellectual inquiry are so tightly bound in queer communication studies, then surely only lesbian, gay, bisexual, and transgender scholars have a place in the field. Although I think such a reaction is understandable, I want to challenge it on important intellectual grounds. Although the project of gay studies is certainly connected to the presence of queer scholars and students in communication, this is a historical and institutional relationship, not an epistemologically necessary one; interventions, therefore, are possible by knowledgeable people from many positions. Queers, I would say, have neither the privilege nor the burden of exclusive attention to queer studies. What we do have, perhaps, is a transparent attraction to a scene where queer desire mobilizes rather than abjects. This, then, raises a question: Why and how might nonqueer people take on such a project? This is not my particular question to answer, except to suggest that thinking about it as clear-sightedly as possible is an important part of the project itself.

Institutional formation aside, one need not be queer to recognize the structuring conditions of sexual difference and hierarchy or the socially consuming character of sexual practice, confession, normativity, representation, and hypocrisy. Why, for example, are geneticists and nonscientists alike boarding the bandwagon of genetic diagnosis of "gender identity disorder"? Why did it take the Clinton administration 63 pages to summarize the legal entitlements and benefits of heterosexual marriage in preparation for Clinton's stunning (if underreported) signing of the Defense of Marriage Act in 1996 (General Accounting Office, 1997)? Why do same-sex sexual relations remain illegal in 20 U.S. states? Why is homophobia still the most lucrative fund-raising platform for the religious Right? Why was Matthew Shepard fair game for murderous young men in Wyoming, and why did so many nongay people express shock at his death as though such brutality hadn't happened a thousand times before? Why have a handful of gay- and drag-themed films enjoyed unprecedented popularity in the past 5 years? How could the figure of the African American mother on welfare still be relied on in the recent justification of welfare "reform"? How, finally, are Bill Clinton's sexual "indiscretions" recuperable when Joycelyn Elders's recognition of childhood masturbation is grounds for involuntary resignation from her post as surgeon general, a post to which she was appointed by Clinton himself?

This short and exhortatory list illustrates an important insight in sexuality studies of the last 20 years, an insight that comes from community historians (e.g., Katz, 1976, 1992; Weeks, 1989), feminist theory (e.g., Rubin, 1993), and the historical philosophy of Michel Foucault (1978): Despite the popular claim that the Western history of sex is a history of repression, in fact there has never been a greater proliferation of sexual discourse than in the modern West. In religion and science, sexual truth and confession came to stand for truth and redemption themselves, and sexual norms were produced in virtually all disciplines and forms of social regulation. This, says Foucault, is the contradictory effect of sexualized regimes of knowledge: not to suppress (in the sense of banishing) but to aggressively *regulate* the body and its pleasures.

Such insights were at the core of what came to be identified in the 1980s as the "social constructionist" school of sexual theory. Recognition—and denaturalization—of the social organization of sexual desire and practice (with no resolution of the issue of where different forms of desire come from "in the first instance") gave rise to an active, interdisciplinary subfield of sexuality studies across history (e.g., D'Emilio, 1992; Peiss & Simmons, 1989), women's studies (e.g., Kennedy & Davis, 1994; Martin, 1994; Nestle, 1987), English and literary studies (e.g.,

Sedgwick, 1993), anthropology (e.g., Vance, 1991), sociology (e.g., Seidman, 1996), and communication (e.g., Chesebro, 1981; Fejes & Petrich, 1993; Ringer, 1994). How, scholars asked, has sexuality been pressed into discourse at different times and in different places, and what have been the sexual and *non*sexual consequences of such discursive production?

These questions acquire particular vigor in communication, given the field's central concern with human symbolic behavior in social, cultural, and historical context. As I have suggested, then, all communication scholars have a potential stake in the analysis of sexual practice, discourse, difference, and hierarchy, because sexual dominance and normativity are no less discursively organized (although they may be less conspicuously marked) than are sexual nondominance and nonconformism. This is not to equalize their significance or level their differences, but to recognize the mutual constitution of gay and straight, normal and pathological, dominant and nondominant. It is also to argue against imagining gay, lesbian, bisexual, and transgender studies at the margins of the field, an interesting sideline for those who need that kind of thing.

With the foregoing ideas and concerns in mind, my intention for the remainder of this essay is to write about queer studies in communication while also conveying nonqueer relevance. This is not to broaden the topic, as it is not narrow, but to invite all readers to consider their places in such a line of investigation. As well, I explore sexual definition and subjectivity, and the place of communicative practice in both, and theorize sexual representation in public and private. Throughout this review, moreover, I argue that it is crucial to keep the sex in "sexual difference"—to not desexualize the analysis in deference to more traditional academic discourses.

QUEER DEFINITION AND SUBJECTIVITY

Single white fem, early 40s, bottom/switch, seeks soft boy butch for love and transgression. No queer kids, baby dykes, lesbianfeminists, androgynes or daddies, please!

What's in a name? For many, enough to make a difference in how one gets through the day or night, let alone whether one responds to a personal ad like the one above. By my reading, the author is a morphological woman (probably designated a "girl" at birth), early middle-aged, of predominantly European descent, feminine in a lesbian kind of way but not straight looking, who desires sexual surrender but also to dominate another woman who is boyishly masculine in appearance and sensibility, who offers visible tenderness, and who will join the author in both the movement for political justice and as many nonprocreative, nonmarital, nondominant ways of having sex as she and her ideal respondent(s) can figure out.

There is no law, of course, against answering an ad that does not describe you, but there is efficiency and pleasure when such a gesture produces a match, an efficiency that requires knowledge and recognition from both author and reader. But because the terms of the ad—like all terms in human discourse—are socioculturally and historically situated, they are likely to carry a range of meanings among different speakers and thus are also likely to produce different reactions. Although the difference between daddies and boys, for example, may be perfectly apparent to the dyke who wants one but not the other, to someone else this can be a matter of considerable interpretive slippage. Different reactions, in other words, will locate different investments in time, place, and position among parties to the exchange—a familiar enough claim among communication scholars.

What is less generally familiar, however, is the weight of this claim for sexual definition and subjectivity, in queer contexts and the dominant mainstream. How, for example, are sexual identification and difference produced and expressed in situated communicative acts? What range of sexual differences (whether, say, "gay versus straight" or "daddy versus boy") marks an encounter, a relationship, a community, or a nation, and how traversable are those borders for different kinds of sexual subjects or citizens? Finally, what responses to sexual difference are routinely mobilized and with what consequences? For whom is the contrast between daddy and boy a source of personal interest and urgency (Where can I find a date? A friend? A sexual compatriot?) or, alternately, a source of contempt (That's not normal!)?

These are empirical questions about communicative circuits of sexual identification and value that can be explored at the most intimate and the most institutional levels of social life. If my lover rejects my sociosexual practices, that is one kind of loss with one set remedies, and if my mother rejects them, that is a second kind. If, on the other hand, my practices are rejected by my employer, an immigration official, or the family court judge reviewing my parental fitness in a custody dispute, these are new categories of loss that the earlier remedies cannot address (see Butler, 1997). Thus in communication research, the idioms of sexual identification bear analysis in relation to their material circumstances and effects. Such an approach to gay, lesbian, bisexual, and transgender studies in communication thus rewrites theories of ideology, introducing sexuality as a terrain (if never an isolated one) of symbolic and ideological struggle.

This approach, however, does not address a deeper epistemological significance in recent sexual inquiry, and here it is worth distinguishing the clustered terms *gay, lesbian, bisexual,* and *transgender* from the at once more partial and more inclusive term *queer.* For many scholars and activists, the former terms signify an expanding inventory of forms of sexual difference, available to researchers as already coherent variables and to policy makers and community organizers as stable social groups. *Queer,* in contrast, works in at least two ways: (a) as a cover term for all manner of sexual nonconformity and (b) to signify a kind of categorical slippage in which sexual difference cannot be pinned down and thus that makes room for sociosexual *in*determinacy as well as structure. For some, this latter meaning is a politically charged and energizing reconceptualization, whereas for others its very instability leaves it ethically bereft. We can therefore use the status of the term *queer* to consider the practice and stakes of sexual definition more generally, and also to challenge social theory with the at once giddy and baffling ambiguity of desire.[1]

Among scholars of rhetoric, for example, essays by Margaret Morrison (1992) and James W. Chesebro (1997) offer strikingly different responses to the indeterminacy of gay, lesbian, and queer expression and selfhood. For Morrison, there is a fruitful disruption under way, a postmodern rhetorical crisis in signifying the contingencies of selfhood. Gone is the presumption of coherence in a binary system of gender and sexual opposition. Amid new scientific and symbolic technologies of gender and sexual assignment, the lines between male and female and gay and straight are wrenched from the stabilizing fiction of nature into flourishing, corporeal rhetorics of desire that put into play "a kind of linguistic music that so confuses the Symbolic's binary-based systems that we are forced to begin to think differently" (Morrison, 1992, p. 13).

In Morrison's (1992) effervescent prose, linguistic excess encodes both the force and nuance of desire, which is "cathected in multiple forms and [yet] still exceed[s] form" (p. 17). For Morrison, desire is loopy, recursive, as intractable as a wave on the beach. As it becomes the object and agent of rhetoric, moreover, this intractability is a wonderful thing, potentially blasting us out of a complacency that cannot get beyond numbing replacements of one kind of "definitional border" (straight) with another (gay).

In charting gender indeterminacy, Morrison responds to the influential work of Judith Butler, who, in the early 1990s, brought together speech act theory and Esther Newton's (1979) anthropological study of drag culture to theorize gender difference as performance. Morrison's meditation on her adolescent status as tomboy illustrates Butler's (1990) idea that gender performance is "a copy for which there is no original." But despite the absence of a necessary foundation for gender difference, a cultural regime of binary gender opposition nonetheless enacts its power:

> Though I came into this world as a biological female, sometime after I entered language, I began to perform more and more as a "boy" who imitated the way "his" Dad walked and talked and gestured, how he tied his boots, rolled his shoulders, fed the cows. The acceptable term for "me" was "tomboy." My tomboyishness was cute, and family and friends alike encouraged it—that is, until I was eleven or so years old. . . . The biological female performing as "boy" copying "man" was no longer cute but "troubling" and eventually even called for consultations with a number of shrinks, too often the regime's chiefs of police. . . . It wasn't just that I was a "girl" performing "boyishly" or that I had teenage crushes on girls (I also had crushes on boys). It didn't matter that the performances I had learned were copies of gestures and expressions and body movements from a Dad who had probably copied his gestures and expressions from both his Mom and his Dad or, confusing matters still more, that I probably copied my Mom's performances of her copies of her own father's and mother's gender-performing-copies. The "trouble" was that what "I" appeared to be in my various performances apparently did not assimilate itself to a normalizing representation of

"straight young woman"—and perhaps not to "gay young woman" either. But the latter representation was not available to me in any case, for "lesbian" simply was not an "option" introduced into my world until late in my adolescence. (Morrison, 1992, pp. 17-18)

From Morrison's account of her own sexual and gender noncompliance, a view of the ordering power of language emerges, harnessed to parental and community approval and control. But, says Morrison, it is precisely in recognition of this power that a *re*ordering effect can potentially be produced, in a new context or different set of possibilities (such as the "lesbian" option that came to Morrison late in her adolescence, under social conditions she does not describe). Thus Morrison, like other queer theorists, invests in "queer" as a linguistic marker of sexual and gender openness, refusal, becoming, even uncertainty. Impatient caricatures notwithstanding, the playful quality in queer sensibility does not represent a failure to recognize sex-gender regimes. It understands them all too well and seeks to upend them with styles of language and "styles of flesh" (p. 18).

In "Ethical Communication and Sexual Orientation," Chesebro (1997) reveals profound inconsistency in the history of sexual classification, an inconsistency that, he finds, undermines the possibility of a set of values regulating gay and lesbian speech, a lesbian and gay communication ethic. According to Chesebro, since the 19th century, through Freud and later through Alfred Kinsey's reports on male and female sexualities, definitions of homosexuality from behavioral, psychological, anatomical, and genetic experts have borne considerable diversity and contradiction. In the contemporary United States, moreover, an already divided public (i.e., nongay) opinion on the normalcy and acceptability of homosexuality has been further complicated by the AIDS crisis, leaving gay and lesbian people *disoriented* as a social unit, with precious few external supports for developing their own "social identity, a sense of [their] own cultural integrity, and a sense of [their] own history and future" (Chesebro, 1997, p. 132). In the absence of coherence, Chesebro argues, a communicative ethic is unlikely to evolve.

Throughout Chesebro's essay, I read an overwhelming sense of loss and dispiritedness about the incoherence of gay and lesbian social identity. There is no foundation, he argues, no clear "locus of commitment" (Chesebro, 1997, p. 138, quoting Darsey) among lesbians and gay men, most of whom promote a rhetoric of diversity and difference within their ranks. At one level, then, Chesebro's lament is worlds apart from Morrison's relief and excitement in disrupting normative conceptions of sex and gender. But it is precisely from this apparent incoherence that Chesebro begins to wrestle an emergent lesbian and gay communication ethic after all, formed around the mixed definitions of the term *gay,* around *tolerance* (both tolerance for ourselves as "deviating from the norm" and the refusal to tolerate inhumane conditions), around desire (erotic desire and the desire for community through erotic attachment), and around paradox (in which *homosexual ethics* is not already a contradiction in terms). To these framing concepts, Chesebro adds the openness of sex-gender definition in gay and lesbian communities, in which "the mix of masculine and feminine characteristics provides an opportunity to increase the range and kinds of strategies available for defining and responding to one's self, others and circumstances" (p. 141). Although Chesebro never uses the terms *transgender* and *queer,* in his final paragraphs what I would call a queer sensibility surfaces, embracing lesbian and gay indeterminacy against the grain of a normative coherence.

A comparison of Morrison's and Chesebro's essays suggests that in different ways and with varying degrees of comfort, queer people negotiate sexual life and identification in an ongoing state of what Cory Young (1999), citing C. E. Morris, has named "critical liminality," a social and psychic borderland that calls for different sensibilities in different times and places. Sometimes, firm boundaries of self-definition offer the greatest security against the institutional fallout of compulsory heterosexuality. An affirmative lesbianism, for example, may be a great source of social and erotic energy for facing heterocentric indifference or hostility. On the other hand, that same fixity may be disorienting, at times leaving a person too little room to maneuver amid prescriptive alternatives to compulsory heterosexuality (too little room, for example, to explore such variations in female masculinity as the erotic distinction between "daddy" and "boy").

In offering these contrasts, I am not recommending one set of responses ("dyke and proud") over another ("queer and open"), but asking communication researchers to consider how lesbian, gay, bisexual, transgender, and queer people articulate and rearticulate their desires and their senses of self in relation to multiple others and multiple circumstances, how they (or we) cope with shifts in sexual subjectivity. Such questions are now posed by specialists in rhetoric (e.g., Slagle, 1995), language and social interaction (e.g., Brouwer, 1998; Corey, 1996; Johnson, 1995), and cultural studies (e.g., Woods, 1993). By taking on the peculiarly *queer* conditions of identification, they recognize every assertion of coherence as an ongoing signifying effect, and thus also begin to denaturalize that other powerful invention—heterosexuality. Although it may no longer feel like a sexual revolution is afoot, for some of us the cultural transparency of straightness is gone for good.[2] And, at least in principle, so is the scholarly worldview in which the complexities of social and cultural position can ever be fixed by singular tags—such as *gay*—that are themselves born of contradictory and contextual impulses and that are mediated, always, by other terms and conditions of difference. To make sense, for example, of the phrase *Asian gay male* is to take on the reciprocal production of ethnicity, sexuality, and gender, not as discrete items on a menu of cultural choices, but as a set of discursive filters and possibilities, each category a mode of expressing and limiting the others (Nakayama, 1994). None of them, moreover, bears a priori value in the hierarchy of cultural identification. Thus for many authors in gay and queer studies (e.g., Chua, 1995; Nero, 1991), an appeal to unitary "positive images" of nondominant identifications—sexual, racial, economic, and otherwise—has joined normative heterosexuality on the remainder table of naturalized social categories.

SEXUAL REPRESENTATION

Recently, I arrived at a gay political rally in western Massachusetts just in time to hear an organizer ask participants to write or call their state representatives to demand that they support a number of pro-gay initiatives in the State House. "Who's our rep?" asked a young lesbian standing nearby. "Ellen DeGeneres," answered the young woman beside her. Some of us snickered. Ronald Reagan and Jesse Ventura notwithstanding, the prospect of *queer* political representation emerging from the ranks of Hollywood celebrity seemed a little unlikely. Or did it?

I describe this scene to point out that the conditions of queer enfranchisement are closely tied to both the political and symbolic meanings of representation. As a social resource, representation occurs in the legislative context occupied by elected officials *and* in the media-industrial one occupied by DeGeneres. We commonly recognize, moreover, that influence in the former requires presence in the latter. Perhaps, then, our bemusement at the rally recognized the truth of the young woman's response, her witty elision of "state rep" and "Ellen DeGeneres."

The political and symbolic meanings of representation reverberate in media scholarship on lesbian, gay, bisexual, transgender, and queer images. Sometimes the links between them are explicit and direct, for example, in the rhetoric of gay movements (e.g., Darsey, 1991) and countermovements (e.g., Moritz, 1995) or the news coverage (and thus the sociopolitical salience) of queer political events. How many front-page column inches did major metropolitan dailies devote to coverage of the marches on Washington for lesbian and gay (and, later, bisexual and transgender) rights in 1979, 1987, and then in 1993? Such an empirical question presumes the political and symbolic importance of visibility beyond the space-time of the event itself—to participants, to queer readers at a distance, and to the many nongay readers unaware of the movements and agendas of gay people, especially in 1979 (Aday, 1996).

In the dominant commercial media, queer representation is obstructed by the chronic and sometimes cynical appeal to nonqueer audiences, most of whom, executives believe, tolerate queer life only to the extent that it flatters their sense of cultural "diversity." (It is in this context, for example, that we get the familiar trope of the wacky but lovable gay neighbor in an otherwise straight environment.) Despite a recent increase in the frequency of queer characters and appearances in fiction and some nonfiction genres, producers still recuperate queerness to straight prejudice or discomfort in the name of ratings, business, or journalistic objectivity. Robert Jensen (1996), for example, interviewed 12 newspaper editors on the question of whether or not they would run wedding announcements for same-sex marriages in their papers. Although most said yes (Jensen having deliberately sought out editors in whose papers such announcements had appeared), none said so unself-consciously or suggested that this is simply the right or equitable thing to do. Most of the editors, including those who had rejected and those who had accepted such announcements, offered arcane definitions and standards for whether such ceremonies were "official" and thus whether announcements of the ceremonies warranted publication. All but one, moreover, framed their responses in terms of protecting journalistic objectivity as a socially detached professional standard and were unwilling to take seriously the idea that such a standard was itself ensconced in institutional structure and dominant ideology. Jensen's work thus reminds us of the deep imbrication of institutional and personal life (newspaper editors mediating public recognition of personal relationships) and, indeed, of the always already public quality of such unions—straight, gay, or otherwise—despite heterocentric disavowals of interest in "what people do in private."

In queer scholarship, investigation of the public-private link (and likewise the political and symbolic meanings of representation) arises from the particular value of visibility to queer people, most of whose lives (and most of whose histories) have been bound by obsessive and often coercive concealment, and whose rhetorics and strategies of liberation have therefore been rooted in "coming out." Thus, for example, the ethical debates in the late 1980s and early 1990s about "outing" public figures as gay or lesbian had a long history, one that had gone unrecognized by those who dismissed the discussion as a skirmish among self-promoting gay activists. Larry Gross has composed and theorized this history in *Contested Closets: The Politics and Ethics of Outing* (1993). In the first part of the volume, Gross tracks public scandals of homosexual disclosure since the mid-19th century, takes to task the modern press for actively and hypocritically closeting gay and lesbian officials and celebrities (despite alleged commitments to investigation and free expression), and analyzes the sociohistorical relationship between sexual identity disclosure and community formation among erotic minorities. In the second part of the book, Gross collects a substantial number of original articles on outing from the gay and lesbian independent press, material that might otherwise have been lost or closeted by the vicissitudes of publishing, archiving, and indexing.[3]

In commercial entertainment media, the recent viability of gay and lesbian (more so than bisexual and transgender) themes is attributable both to increases in overall sociopolitical recognition and to the emergence of an arguably coherent queer "niche market." These developments are encouraged and monitored by such lobbying organizations as the Gay and Lesbian Alliance Against Defamation and brokered by a small but growing number of openly gay producers, writers, and executives in mainstream media organizations, as Marguerite Moritz (1989) points out in the case of lesbian characters on prime-time television, beginning in the mid-1980s. Here, too, however, queer characters are usually isolated in straight (and heterocentric) environments and are still used dramatically to gauge the generosity, confusion, or hostility of straight leads responding to queer family members and colleagues. It remains rare, in the year 2000, for fictional genres in the commercial mainstreams of television and cinema to portray lesbian, gay, bisexual, and transgender characters as fully human, contradictory, or politically conscious members of both queer and nonqueer communities (Gross, 1996; Sender, 1998).

Although such a conclusion is accurate, it does not articulate the complexities and possibilities of recent media attention to queer and related discourses. Two contexts that reveal such complexities are daytime talk television and media coverage of the AIDS epidemic. In *Freaks Talk Back: Tabloid Talk Shows and Sexual Nonconformity,* Joshua Gamson (1998) takes the view that television programs such as *The Jerry Springer Show* and *Sally Jessy Raphael* are more than the volatile freak performances many critics denounce them for being; they are also a forum for alternative sources of authority on queer life and nondominant gender and erotic practice. Rather than the usual panel of sober, heterocentric, and neoliberal professional experts, Gamson argues, tabloid television makes available—to viewers, studio audiences, and on-camera guests—a vocal and visual carnival of cultural refusal. The genre's occasions of argumentativeness and near violence, moreover, express real conflicts and frustrations muted elsewhere by a repressive civility. Not all members of the social groups featured on *Jerry Springer* and *Sally Jessy* (e.g., young people, poor people, sexual outsiders, and communities of color) will watch or like the programs, nor does Gamson expect the genre to finally be embraced by most cultural arbiters. His analysis reveals, however, some irreducible contradictions in tabloid programming and the paradox of queer visibility, contradictions that cannot be explained away with traditional appeals to cultural quality or traditional alarms about antisocial media influence.

In *Unstable Frontiers: Technomedicine and the Cultural Politics of "Curing" AIDS,* John Nguyet Erni (1994) deconstructs the co-occurring claims that "there is no cure for AIDS" and "a cure for AIDS is possible in time." The mobilizations of and challenges to both propositions—in medical, scientific, media, and activist discourses—generate the "unstable frontiers" of Erni's title. Like Gamson, Erni resists simple assessments of media images and political valence in favor of locating and clarifying the conjuncture of medical authority, political action, and the sexualized body. Also like Gamson, Erni reflects on his own discursive practice, where academic critique is itself a symbolic genre with its own codes and stakes. This is not to produce an infinite regress of metacommentary, but to ask what the real opportunities and consequences are of certain kinds of analytic juxtaposition and, with them, certain kinds of symbolic exclusion. As Morrison's (1992) work on queer rhetorics argues, such a consciously *de*stabilizing approach is at the postmodern heart of "queer" (in contrast to "lesbian, gay, bisexual, and transgender") theorizing.

As I pointed out earlier, the language of queerness has come to signify not just sexuality at the margins but also a contradictory tension in dominant sexual discourses, where the repudiation of nonnormative sexual life is indeed a condition of normative sexual formation and where the illicit character of sexual perversion sustains the seductive value of sex itself. Normalcy, in other words, needs perversion to know itself, and perversion is a big part of what makes sex sexy. In media studies, critics have read this generative quality of queerness—this infusion of homoerotic desire animating non- or even antihomoerotic images and narratives—in a variety of ways: as a structural condition of modern representation (e.g., Sedgwick, 1993), as a conscious in-joke that only barely conceals the queer lives of those who produced the images in the first place (e.g., Mayne, 1991), as a kind of fissure or leakage in institutional attempts to suppress queer identification in cultural production (e.g., Custen, 1992), and, finally, as a quality of the relationship between text and reader. This last gesture refers to a queer interpretive strategy that is sometimes conscious and politically resistive ("Batman and Robin are lovers!") but can also be a less conscious, less specific, but no less intriguing "otherness" that sometimes attaches to both "nonqueer" texts and nonqueer readers. Against the protests of those students and other detractors who insist that such "queer readings" are a stretch (and who would perhaps prefer that Kirk and Spock or Cagney and Lacey *not* be read as lovers), critics have explored the symbolic patterns that justify such readings—not necessarily as the conscious intentions of producers (although sometimes producers' intentions are indeed conscious) but as culturally relevant to the dense mix of texts, audiences, and symbolic practices that prevail in a given place and time. Alexander Doty (1995) has been among the most attentive interpreters of queer readings, and my own work on the popular reception of Madonna's video "Justify My Love" offers another example (Henderson, 1993).

Both Doty and I consider the mobilizing pleasures of queer readings, but there is also a not-so-pleasurable flip side. In a recent essay on media coverage of the Michael Jackson sex scandal, Erni (1998) connects queer figuration in the media to the brutal equation of male homoeroticism and child sexual abuse. How, Erni asks, might a queer critic queerly deconstruct Jackson's partial refusals of sexual and racial categorization, his engagements with children, and the mainstream media's implicit reproduction of the "gay = molester" logic without also appearing to trivialize the real threat of child sexual abuse? In a public culture that so often demands sexual disavowal as a condition of social legitimacy—a trade-off especially familiar to women, queers, nondominant racial groups, and young people—Erni offers an important reading of how media images of a suspect queerness are used both to make money (with a high-stakes media scandal) and to reassert the regulatory power of normative (hetero)sexuality. Here, too, the political stakes of queer readings come center stage, alongside the reciprocal mediations of sexuality, gender, race, and wealth, in the police investigation of Jackson himself and the cultural interrogation of his public persona.

As cultural critics producing queer readings, Doty, Erni, and I stand in for a more general queer audience. Although this is partly true for all critics and their readers, it is particularly true in queer studies, where most authors are themselves gay, lesbian, bisexual, or transgender and thus form their critical responses through professional vernaculars and as members of queer communities. Fewer studies exist of queer-identified audiences who are *not* also professional critics, although queer reception research has been under way for some time. For example, Richard Dyer (1986) solicited correspondence from gay men who had come of age in the 1950s and 1960s as Judy Garland fans, requesting that they reflect upon their attraction to Garland and her emergence as a gay cultural icon. Most of the men responded to Garland's layered identifications as evocative of their own; she was the girl next door but with a secret pain, a woman who prevailed against the grain of her own emotional trauma and who was a plucky but conventionally unglamorous performer in the glamour mill of classical Hollywood. Garland was a survivor, and as survivors themselves in the preliberation era, her gay fans loved her for it.

Adopting a range of research practices, other authors have more recently addressed gay, lesbian, bisexual, and transgender audiences. Henry Jenkins (1995), long in close ethnographic contact with *Star Trek* fan communities, has written about the organized network of Gaylaxians, fans of the original *Star Trek* television series and its multiple sequels and spin-offs in cinema and on television. Like other Trekkers, Gaylaxians are active both as a fan community (meeting, writing, and singing about a universe of spectacular characters and relationships developed from the original *Star Trek* cast) and as a grassroots lobbying group (in the case of the Gaylaxians, taking commercial producers to task for their reluctance to address homoerotic desire in the "alternative" world of *Star Trek*).

In an informative survey of audience responses to television characters who are both gay and black, Essex Hemphill (1995) joined a number of television watchers in BJP's, a lesbian-owned black entertainment complex in West Philadelphia, to talk about a "Men on Film" skit that aired on the comedy/variety program *In Living Color.* Hemphill was curious about how patrons saw (and whether they identified with) the caricatured snapping and dishing of the two "Men on . . ." queens. In addition to the responses of BJP's patrons, Hemphill reports those of local activists, writers, and filmmakers. What emerges from Hemphill's explorations is a range of pleasures and ambivalences in responses to "Men on Film." On the one hand, audience members enjoyed the precision of the actors' performances and the irreverence of the parody overall (in this and other *In Living Color* sketches). On the other, many were wary of the cultural vacuum into which "Men on . . ." would arrive for most nongay viewers, and thus how the skit might come to *stand for* black gay male sexuality in dominant social contexts (including the heterosexual mainstream of black communities)—as buffoonish, ineffectual, and misogynist. Although the artists and professional critics were more likely than the BJP's patrons and proprietors to express such ambivalence, all the respondents quoted received "Men on . . ." *as* parody, finding that such a form allows the space for pleasure in what might otherwise have been seen as a hostile, reductive stereotype. But, according to some speakers, precisely that space was also a source of discomfort because it closed down critical reaction (under the protective guise of humor) rather than opening it up. Thus, addressing variation within a black gay cultural locale, Hemphill's work cautiously affirms the perspective in audience studies that recognizes the conscious and critical potential of popular audiences and popular practices, especially in nondominant communities.

Katherine Sender (1999) convened focus groups across self-selected gender and sexual identifications to consider whether gay, lesbian, bisexual, and nongay readers respond differently to "gay window advertisements," those ads carefully coded to appeal to queer consumers while remaining unremarkable to heterosexuals. It is noteworthy that Sender found no necessary correspondence between the sexual identifications of readers and readings; although most queer readings (e.g., interpreting style cues to mean that certain models are lesbian or gay or projecting erotic relationships between models of the same gender) were produced by gay, lesbian, and bisexual respondents, not all were, nor did gay respondents consistently offer gay readings. Thus Sender's findings realign concepts in reception theory, tracking disjunctures between reading position and actual readings in the domain of a gendered sexual subjectivity. In advertising responses, queerness does belong to queers, but not only, and not all queer readers claim it in any obvious way. Sender also recognizes the ways in which nondominant readings are not, as previously suggested, necessarily resistive. They are subtextual, not consistently available to everyone but also not necessarily unintended or undesired by producers. Her findings also contribute, finally, to a critique of cultural appropriation—the commercial deployment of gayness in a consumer culture where "gay" means male, white, attractive, healthy, affluent, and apolitical, but also where some sexual outsiders find themselves "strangely grateful" for the market recognition, despite its limiting and politically detached terms (Sender, 1999, p. 192; see also Badgett, 1997; Bronski, 1984; Clark, 1993; Schulman, 1998).

It should be noted that Dyer's, Jenkins's, and Sender's queer audience research is related to the consumption of cultural materials produced in and by the commercial mainstream, whether of cinema and popular music (Garland), television and cinema (*Star Trek*), or national brand advertisements in mainstream glossies. Such a repertoire obscures the independent sector of queer cultural production, whose producers (like many of those in the dominant mainstream) *also* come from the ranks of queer communities, but openly so, and whose work is intended, first, for queer fans (see Bad Object Choices, 1991; Gever, Greyson, & Parmar, 1993). From the queer independent sector, in other words, come cultural texts made by, about, and for queer audiences. In this context, the demand to reconcile queer characters to dominant sensibility is at least interrupted, if not banished, and although the aesthetic preferences and cultural commitments of producers may not always mirror those of queer-identified audiences (see Rich, 1999), subcultural codes can be traded without didactic explanation (Henderson, 1999). In the potential identification between queer audiences and designated "queer" texts, historical exclusion becomes cachet, and thus representation becomes a cultural resource or form of power. It is not quite the same power as naturalization or the luxury of unself-consciousness enjoyed by nongay viewers of heteronormative texts, but a different kind, a conscious hailing that signifies agency as the flip side of subjection. Depending on the genre, such texts may also be exported to nongay or "crossover" audiences—especially plausible with queer rewritings of comic forms, such as the lesbian romantic comedy *Go Fish* (Henderson, 1999). But a different political dimension of agency arises in the independent documentation of rage, loss, rupture and injustice, and here documentary film practice offers important examples, such as Arthur Dong's *Licensed to Kill,* about the homophobic murder of gay men, Susan Muska and Gréta Olafsdóttir's *The Brandon Teena Story,* about the murder of a transgender teenager and his friends in the U.S. Midwest, and the vast array of AIDS activist film- and videomaking, best chronicled and interpreted by Alexandra Juhasz (1995).

But the parallel universes of mainstream and queer expression do intersect, sometimes below the threshold of straight perception (e.g., *Laverne & Shirley*), sometimes inciting political opportunism (e.g., debates about National Endowment for the Arts funding to galleries exhibiting the work of Robert Mapplethorpe), other times with effervescent controversy (Madonna's video *Vogue*) or exaltation (*Paris Is Burning*), and still other times with a fond but tempering pluralism that declares, as if not everyone were quite convinced, that "gays are people too" (*In & Out*).[4] In this encounter, queer sex is usually the cultural deal maker *and* deal breaker, why queerness is both so crucial to and so reviled in dominant discourses of human identification. This is a condition made clear in recent communication scholarship by on-line and personal responses to the publication of Frederick C. Corey and Thomas K. Nakayama's "Sextext" in *Text and Performance Quarterly* (1997). Corey and Nakayama originally presented "Sextext" at the first program of the Gay, Lesbian, and Bisexual Studies Interest Group at the 1995 ICA meetings in Albuquerque, New Mexico, where it was received as a witty, multigenre piece of fictional autoethnography and cultural criticism. Most important, for many of us in the audience, "Sextext" was about sex, using a fantasy of participation in the making of gay porn as the site of expression and reflection for two queer critics, a place where theory and desire might meet and combust rather than languish in conventional oppositions between mind and body, public and private, thinker and tramp. "I cruise theories," the authors begin. Reflecting on the contradictions of *teaching* theories of desire in the college classroom, they go on:

> The source of my frustration was not in the students, but in my own inability to articulate the dialectics of desire. I have been trained in the academy as a textual critic. I could see an advertisement and know, intuitively, the many layers of coding contained within and expressed through the images. I could not, however, find the words to communicate what I knew. Teaching was depressing. I felt inadequate.

> From my own experience, I knew the futility of trying to nail sexuality. I engaged in intimate and repeated same-sex activities with many men on the studio set, but I was surprised when some of them declared themselves heterosexual. My first experience with this phenomenon happened with another actor, Cliff. In the scene, we were construction workers wrapping up a long day's work. We splashed our bodies with baby oil to capture the chesty glisten of a hard day's work, and Cliff could not wait for the shot to begin. His cock bulged in his jeans, and he massaged himself to near explosion. . . . "Take it," the director said, and we cut loose. Cliff's nine inches surged forward and made each button of the jeans more impossible to release than the one before. Cliff gasped and moaned with each new button, and when I released the final button, I devoured Cliff. The head of his cock rocked deep into my throat. (Corey & Nakayama, 1997, p. 62)

As a communication scholar who, like Corey and Nakayama, has also written and taught about pornography, I recognized the dilemma of the "Sextext" protagonist—the rank inadequacy of available theoretical vernaculars for registering sexual desire. On the one hand, this can be a good thing, a form of protection for the precious specificities of sex *and* theory. On the other, for me, it also spoke to the anxious border guarding of academic life, particularly around sex, and for that reason I loved Corey and Nakayama's brazenness. I especially appreciated their courage as responses to "Sextext" rolled in on CRT-Net (Communication Research and Theory), the on-line listserv for interested communication scholars. What struck me is that whereas "Sextext" had clearly generated more discussion than any other single piece of communication scholarship, in all but a handful of responses, *no one mentioned sex.* Debates ensued about the blurred lines of truth claims and fiction in academic discourse and about editorial policy at *Text and Performance Quarterly.* But only rarely (in 7 of 100 cases, by my count) did scholars address the sexual content of Corey and Nakayama's work, and even then they did so indirectly—for example, defending the authors' academic freedom to write explicitly about sexual matters. Where, I wondered, was some reflection or at least acknowledgment of the questions Corey and Nakayama had raised—desire and its intractability, the contradictions of making pornography into academic work, the risk and pleasure of putting one's scholarly self on the line as desiring subject—where were they? The thundering sexual silences in the CRT-Net dialogue were themselves testimony to the cultural truth of Corey and Nakayama's work; sex, and perhaps especially a queer sexual voice, did not yet have a place in the critical discourse of communication scholars.[5]

CONCLUSION

The point of such a conclusion, however, is neither to dismiss the dialogue that *did* occur in response to "Sextext" nor to scold the field for conspiratorial inattention to sexuality. I would prefer, instead, to argue for the ways in which a communication scholarship attentive to sexual practices, discourses, and hierarchies can contribute to what sociologist Steven Seidman (1996) has called "sexual-political autonomy in a democratic culture of sexual difference" (p. 18). I am not naive enough to believe that all moments of intellectual inquiry have counterpart outcomes in sexual politics, or that political effect should become the singular litmus test for adequate or innovative scholarship. Drawing on Foucault's work, moreover, I am wary of most attempts, including queer ones, to regulate sexuality further for the projected good of the social body, to instill in sexual citizens new practices of self-surveillance and new regimens of sexual shame and exclusion (see Patton, 1996; Probyn, 1995). As critic, scholar, and teacher in communication, however, and as an active contributor to the Gay, Lesbian, Bisexual, and Transgender Studies Interest Group of the ICA, I recognize both the social force of symbolic practice and the survival value of desire, and seek riskier, more thoughtful exploration of the link between the two.

In selectively charting such intellectual territory in this essay, I have, inevitably, excluded developing topics and forms of investigation in communication research, and thus conclude with a list of suggestions and sources for readers and future researchers. Among the areas of sexual identification and cultural practice that I have not addressed are gay music scenes (e.g., Dyer, 1992), changing modes of sexual identification and affiliation among young queer people (e.g., Kielwasser & Wolf, 1992), the social class conditions of queer expression (e.g., Raffo, 1997), transgender and transsexual subjectivity (e.g., Califia, 1997; Prosser, 1998), and the range of gay, lesbian, bisexual, transgender, and queer communication scholarship arising in non-U.S. and non-English-language contexts (e.g., Erni & Spires, 1999; Miller, 1997; Valentine, 1997). I invite scholars to engage the researchers conducting such work and their questions; to continue to develop the repertoire of concrete research on sexual identification, expression, pleasure, and regulation in living populations and social institutions; and, finally, to queer their own sensibilities toward a more nuanced recognition of the place of communicative practice in human sexual life.

NOTES

1. The exploration of sexual indeterminacy and performance is sometimes the marker of "queer studies," an arguably postmodern approach to scholarship that stands in contrast to "lesbian, gay, bisexual, and transgender studies." This second approach locates gay, lesbian, and bisexual people as bounded groups with fairly stable sexual identifications. As an author who has participated in both approaches, I acknowledge the distinction here and elsewhere in this essay, although I resist enforcing it. For a deeper discussion, see Erni (1996).

2. See Sedgwick (1993) on the competing claims of a "universalizing" versus a "minoritizing" view of gayness, each of which produces a somewhat different characterization of heterosexuality. Also, for a history and critique of "heterosexuality" as a naturalized social category, see Katz (1992).

3. For additional accounts of the history of the gay and lesbian press and of gay and lesbian coverage in the dominant press, see Streitmatter (1995) and Alwood (1996), respectively.

4. On *Laverne & Shirley,* see Doty (1995); on Mapplethorpe, see Vance (1989); on Madonna's *Vogue,* see Patton (1993); and on *Paris Is Burning,* see Hemphill (1992).

5. There is, however, a communication literature on queer pornography (written, not surprisingly, by openly gay and queer authors). For example, see Nero (1992), Henderson (1991), and Conway (1998).

REFERENCES

Aday, S. (1996, May). *Invisible ink: Visibility and marginality in news coverage of gays and lesbians from 1980 through 1994.* Paper presented at the annual meeting of the International Communication Association, Chicago.

Alwood, E. (1996). *Straight news: Gays, lesbians, and the news media.* New York: Columbia University Press.

Bad Object Choices. (Ed.). (1991). *How do I look? Queer film and video.* Seattle, WA: Bay.

Badgett, M. V. L. (1997). Beyond biased samples: Challenging the myths on the economic status of lesbians and gay men. In A. Gluckman & B. Reed (Eds.), *Homo economics: Capitalism, community, and lesbian and gay life* (pp. 65-71). New York: Routledge.

Bronski, M. (1984). *Culture clash: The making of gay sensibility.* Boston: South End.
Brouwer, D. (1998). The precarious visibility politics of self-stigmatization: The case of HIV/AIDS tattoos. *Text and Performance Quarterly, 18,* 114-136.
Butler, J. (1990). *Gender trouble: Feminism and the subversion of identity.* New York: Routledge.
Butler, J. (1997). Merely cultural. *Social Text, 52-53,* 265-277.
Califia, P. (1997). *Sex changes: The politics of transgenderism.* San Francisco: Cleis.
Chesebro, J. W. (Ed.). (1981). *Gayspeak: Gay male and lesbian communication.* New York: Pilgrim.
Chesebro, J. W. (1997). Ethical communication and sexual orientation. In J. M. Makau & R. C. Arnett (Eds.), *Communication ethics in an age of diversity* (pp. 126-151). Chicago: University of Chicago Press.
Chua, L. (1995). The postmodern ethnic brunch: Devouring difference. In N. Blake, L. Rinder, & A. Scholder (Eds.), *In a different light: Visual culture, sexual identity, queer practice* (pp. 253-262). San Francisco: City Lights.
Clark, D. (1993). Commodity lesbianism. In H. Abelove, M. A. Barale, & D. M. Halperin (Eds.), *The lesbian and gay studies reader* (pp. 186-201). New York: Routledge.
Conway, M. T. (1998, Fall). Inhabiting the phallus: Reading *Safe is desire. Camera Obscura,* pp. 133-161.
Corey, F. C. (1996). Performing sexualities in an Irish pub. *Text and Performance Quarterly, 16,* 146-160.
Corey, F. C., & Nakayama, T. K. (1997). Sextext. *Text and Performance Quarterly, 17,* 58-68.
Custen, G. (1992). *Bio/pics: How Hollywood constructed public history.* New Brunswick, NJ: Rutgers University Press.
Darsey, J. (1991). From "gay is good" to the scourge of AIDS: The evolution of gay liberation rhetoric, 1977-1990. *Communication Studies, 42,* 43-66.
D'Emilio, J. (1992). Gay and lesbian studies: New kids on the block. In J. D'Emilio, *Making trouble: Essays on gay history, politics, and the university* (pp. 160-175). New York: Routledge.
Doty, A. (1995). There's something queer here. In C. K. Creekmur & A. Doty (Eds.), *Out in culture: Gay, lesbian, and queer essays on popular culture* (pp. 71-90). Durham, NC: Duke University Press.
Dyer, R. (1986). *Heavenly bodies: Film stars and society.* New York: St. Martin's.
Dyer, R. (1992). In defense of disco. In R. Dyer, *Only entertainment* (pp. 149-158). New York: Routledge.
Erni, J. N. (1994). *Unstable frontiers: Technomedicine and the cultural politics of "curing" AIDS.* Minneapolis: University of Minnesota Press.
Erni, J. N. (1996). Eternal excesses: Toward a queer mode of articulation in social theory. *American Literary History, 8,* 566-581.
Erni, J. N. (1998). Queer figurations in the media: Critical reflections on the Michael Jackson sex scandal. *Critical Studies in Mass Communication, 18,* 158-180.
Erni, J. N., & Spires, A. J. (1999). *Glossy subjects: G&L magazine and gay, lesbian, and tongzhi cultural visibility in Taiwan.* Manuscript submitted for publication.
Fejes, F., & Petrich, K. (1993). Invisibility, homophobia and heterosexism: Lesbians, gays and the media. *Critical Studies in Mass Communication, 10,* 396-422.
Foucault, M. (1978). *The history of sexuality: Vol. 1. An introduction* (R. Hurley, Trans.). New York: Pantheon.
Gamson, J. (1998). *Freaks talk back: Tabloid talk shows and sexual nonconformity.* Chicago: University of Chicago Press.
General Accounting Office. (1997). Defense of Marriage Act (Letter Report, 01/31/97, GAO/OGC-97-16). Washington, DC: Government Printing Office.
Gever, M., Greyson, J., & Parmar, P. (Eds.). (1993). *Queer looks: Perspectives on lesbian and gay film and video.* New York: Routledge.
Gross, L. (1993). *Contested closets: The politics and ethics of outing.* Minneapolis: University of Minnesota Press.

Gross, L. (1996). Don't ask, don't tell: Lesbian and gay people in the media. In P. M. Lester (Ed.), *Images that injure: Pictorial stereotypes in the media* (pp. 149-159). Westport, CT: Praeger.

Gross, L., & Woods, J. D. (Eds.). (1999). *The Columbia reader on lesbians and gay men in media, society, and politics.* New York: Columbia University Press.

Hall, S. (1990). The meaning of new times. In S. Hall & M. Jacques (Eds.), *New times: The changing face of politics in the 1990s* (pp. 116-134). London: Verso.

Hemphill, E. (1992). To be real. In E. Hemphill, *Ceremonies: Prose and poetry* (pp. 111-121). New York: Plums.

Hemphill, E. (1995). *In Living Color:* Toms, coons, mammies, faggots and bucks. In C. K. Creekmur & A. Doty (Eds.), *Out in culture: Gay, lesbian, and queer essays on popular culture* (pp. 389-401). Durham, NC: Duke University Press.

Henderson, L. (1991). Lesbian pornography: Cultural transgression and sexual demystification. In S. Munt (Ed.), *New lesbian criticism: Literary and cultural perspectives* (pp. 173-191). New York: Columbia University Press.

Henderson, L. (1993). Justify our love: Madonna and the politics of queer sex. In C. Schwichtenberg (Ed.), *The Madonna connection: Representational politics, subcultural identities, and cultural theory* (pp. 107-128). Boulder, CO: Westview.

Henderson, L. (1999). Simple pleasures: Lesbian community and *Go Fish. Signs, 5*(1), 34-64.

Jenkins, H. (1995). "Out of the closet and into the universe": Queers and *Star Trek.* In J. Tulloch & H. Jenkins, *Science fiction audiences: Watching Doctor Who and Star Trek* (pp. 237-265). New York: Routledge.

Jensen, R. (1996). The politics and ethics of lesbian and gay "wedding" announcements in newspapers. *Howard Journal of Communications, 7,* 13-28.

Johnson, P. (1995). SNAP! culture: A different kind of "reading." *Text and Performance Quarterly, 15,* 122-142.

Juhasz, A. (1995). *AIDS TV: Identity, community, and alternative video.* Durham, NC: Duke University Press.

Katz, J. N. (1976). *Gay American history.* New York: Thomas Crowell.

Katz, J. N. (1992). *The invention of heterosexuality.* New York: Dutton.

Kennedy, E. L., & Davis, M. D. (1994). *Boots of leather, slippers of gold: The history of a lesbian community.* New York: Penguin.

Kielwasser, A. P., & Wolf, M. A. (1992). Mainstream television, adolescent homosexuality, and significant silence. *Critical Studies in Mass Communication, 9,* 350-373.

Martin, B. (1994). Sexualities without genders and other queer utopias. *Diacritics, 24*(2-3), 104-121.

Mayne, J. (1991). Lesbian looks: Dorothy Arzner and female authorship. In Bad Object Choices (Ed.), *How do I look? Queer film and video* (pp. 103-143). Seattle, WA: Bay.

Miller, S. D. (1997). The *Reunion* of history and popular culture: Japan "comes out" on TV. *Journal of Popular Culture, 31*(2), 161-175.

Moritz, M. J. (1989). American television discovers gay women: The changing context of programming decisions at the networks. *Journal of Communication Inquiry, 13*(2), 62-78.

Moritz, M. J. (1995). The gay agenda: Marketing hate speech to mainstream media. In R. K. Whillock & D. Slayden (Eds.), *Hate speech* (pp. 55-79). Thousand Oaks, CA: Sage.

Morrison, M. (1992). Laughing with queers in my eyes: Proposing queer rhetorics and introducing a queer issue. *Pre/Text, 13*(3-4), 11-36.

Nakayama, T. K. (1994). Show/down time: "Race," gender, sexuality, and popular culture. *Critical Studies in Mass Communication, 11,* 162-179.

Nero, C. I. (1991). Toward a black gay aesthetic: Signifying in contemporary black gay literature. In E. Hemphill (Ed.), *Brother to brother: New writings by black gay men* (pp. 229-252). Boston: Alyson.

Nero, C. I. (1992). Free speech or hate speech: Pornography and its means of production. *Law and Sexuality: A Review of Lesbian and Gay Legal Issues, 2,* 3-9.

Nestle, J. (1987). *A restricted country.* Ithaca, NY: Firebrand.

Newton, E. (1979). *Mother camp: Female impersonators in America.* Chicago: University of Chicago Press.

Patton, C. (1993). Embodying subaltern memory: Kinesthesia and the problematics of gender and race. In C. Schwichtenberg (Ed.), *The Madonna connection: Representational politics, subcultural identities, and cultural theory* (pp. 81-106). Boulder, CO: Westview.

Patton, C. (1996). *Fatal advice: How safe-sex education went wrong.* Durham, NC: Duke University Press.

Peiss, K., & Simmons, C. (1989). Passion and power: An introduction. In K. Peiss & C. Simmons (Eds.), *Passion and power: Sexuality in history (pp. 3-13). Philadelphia: Temple University Press.*

Probyn, E. (1995). The outside of queer cultural studies. *University of Toronto Quarterly, 64,* 536-546.

Prosser, J. (1998). *Second skins: The body narratives of transsexuality.* New York: Columbia University Press.

Raffo, S. (Ed.). (1997). *Queerly classed: Gay men and lesbians write about class.* Boston: South End.

Rich, B. R. (1999). Collision, catastrophe, celebration: The relationship between gay and lesbian film festivals and their publics. *Gay and Lesbian Quarterly, 5*(1), 79-84.

Ringer, R. J. (Ed.). (1994). *Queer words, queer images: Communication and the construction of homosexuality.* New York: New York University Press.

Rubin, G. (1993). Thinking sex: Notes toward a radical theory of the politics of sexuality. In H. Abelove, M. A. Barale, & D. M. Halperin (Eds.), *The lesbian and gay studies reader* (pp. 3-44). New York: Routledge.

Schulman, S. (1998). *Stagestruck: Theatre, AIDS, and the marketing of gay America.* Durham, NC: Duke University Press.

Sedgwick, E. K. (1993). Epistemology of the closet. In H. Abelove, M. A. Barale, & D. M. Halperin (Eds.), *The lesbian and gay studies reader* (pp. 45-61). New York: Routledge.

Seidman, S. (1996). Introduction. In S. Seidman (Ed.), *Queer theory/sociology* (pp. 1-29). Cambridge, MA: Blackwell.

Sender, K. (Producer/Director). (1998). *Off the straight and narrow: Lesbians, gays and bisexuals on television* [Videotape]. Northampton, MA: Media Education Foundation.

Sender, K. (1999). Selling sexual subjectivities: Audiences respond to gay window advertising. *Critical Studies in Mass Communication, 16,* 172-196.

Slagle, R. A. (1995). In defense of queer nation: From identity politics to a politics of difference. *Western Journal of Communication, 59,* 85-102.

Streitmatter, R. (1995). *Unspeakable: The rise of the gay and lesbian press in America.* London: Faber & Faber.

Valentine, J. (1997). Skirting and suiting stereotypes: Representations of marginalized sexualities in Japan. *Theory, Culture & Society, 14*(3), 57-85.

Vance, C. (1989, September). The war on culture, *Art in America,* pp. 39-45.

Vance, C. (1991). Anthropology rediscovers sexuality: A theoretical comment. *Social Science and Medicine, 33,* 875-884.

Weeks, J. (1989). Inverts, perverts and Mary-Annes: Male prostitution and the regulation of homosexuality in England in the nineteenth and early twentieth centuries. In M. B. Duberman, M. Vicinus, & G. Chauncey (Eds.), *Hidden from history: Reclaiming the gay and lesbian past* (pp. 195-211). New York: New American Library.

Woods, J. D. (1993). *The corporate closet: The professional lives of gay men in America.* New York: Free Press.

Young, C. (1999, May). *Queer theory meets rhetorical criticism.* Paper presented at the annual meeting of the International Communication Association, San Francisco.

Author Index

Subject Index

ABOUT THE EDITOR

WILLIAM B. GUDYKUNST is Professor of Speech Communication and a member of the Asian American Studies Program faculty at California State University, Fullerton. His work focuses on developing a theory of interpersonal and intergroup effectiveness that can be applied to improving the quality of communication. He is the author or coauthor of *Asian American Ethnicity and Communication* (in press), *Bridging Differences: Effective Intergroup Communication* (third edition, 1998), *Communicating With Strangers: An Approach to Intercultural Communication* (with Y. Y. Kim; third edition, 1997), and *Bridging Japanese/ North American Differences* (with T. Nishida; 1994), among others. He also has edited or coedited *Intergroup Communication, Handbook of International and Intercultural Communication* (with B. Mody; third edition, in press), *Theories in Intercultural Communication* (with Y. Y. Kim; 1988), and *Communication in Personal Relationships Across Cultures* (with S. Ting-Toomey and T. Nishida; 1996), among others. He is a Fellow of the International Communication Association.

ABOUT THE CONTRIBUTORS

LINDA ALDOORY is Assistant Professor of Communication at the University of Maryland. She has published in the *Journal of Public Relations Research* and is coeditor of *The Gender Challenge to Media: Diverse Voices From the Field.* Her dissertation work focused on women's perceptions of mass-media health messages.

LEFKI ANASTASIOU is a doctoral candidate in the Department of Communication Studies at Northwestern University. She received her B.A. in communication and psychology from the State University of New York at Buffalo and her M.A. in communication studies from Northwestern University. Her research interests include interpersonal influence, interpersonal conflict, and bargaining and negotiation.

SANDRA BRAMAN is Associate Professor and holder of the Reese Phifer Chair in the Department of Telecommunications and Film at the University of Alabama. She specializes in the macro-level effects of the use of new information and communication technologies and their policy implications. She is coeditor of *Globalization, Communication, and Transnational Civil Society* (1996). Her research has been published in *Journal of Communication, Telecommunication Policy, Journalism Quarterly, Gazette, Media Development,* and *Media, Culture & Society,* among others.

ERIK P. BUCY is Assistant Professor in the Department of Telecommunications at Indiana University at Bloomington. His research interests focus on political communication and the impact of new communication technologies. A former journalist and press secretary, he has published in *Communication Yearbook 22,* the *Journal of Communication,* and the *Journal of Broadcasting,* among others.

GEORGE CHENEY is Professor of Communication Studies at the University of Montana–Missoula. Also, he is an Adjunct Professor of Management Communication at the University of Waikato in New Zealand. He has published extensively on organizational identity, power, corporate public discourse, workplace democracy, and business ethics. His most recent book is *Values at Work: Employee Participation Meets Market Place Pressure at Mondragón* (1999). He is a past Chair of the Organizational Communication Division of the International Communication Association and is coeditor (with George A. Barnett) of the research annual *Organizational Communication: Emerging Perspectives.*

NOSHIR S. CONTRACTOR is Associate Professor of Speech Communication and Psychology at the University of Illinois at Urbana-Champaign. His research interests include applications of systems theory to communication and the role of emergent communication and knowledge networks in organizations. His articles have appeared in *Decision Science, Organization Science, Social Psychology Quarterly, Human Communication Research, Journal of Broadcasting and Electronic Media,* and *Management Communication Quarterly.*

STANLEY A. DEETZ is Professor of Communication at the University of Colorado at Boulder. He is coauthor of *Leading Organizations Through Transition: Communication and Cultural Change* (2000) and *Doing Critical Management Research* (2000) and author of *Transforming Communication, Transforming Business: Building Responsive and Responsible Workplaces* (1995) and *Democracy in Communication and the Politics of Everyday Life* (1992), as well as editor or author of eight other books. He has published nearly 100 essays in scholarly journals and books regarding stakeholder representation, decision making, culture, and communication in corporate organization and has lectured widely in the United States and Europe. He is a Fellow of the International Communication Association and served as ICA President in 1996-1997.

JO ELLEN FAIR is Associate Professor in the School of Journalism and Mass Communication and Director of the African Studies Program at the University of Wisconsin–Madison. Her research explores how and why mass media are central to the production of knowledge in their description, classification, and labeling of events, issues, countries, and cultures, particularly within the African context.

WENDY JO MAYNARD FARINOLA is a doctoral candidate in communication at the University of California, Santa Barbara. Her research interests include mass-media effects, mass-media and new media policy, and the uses and effects of new media technologies.

T. ANDREW FINN is Associate Professor in the Department of Communications at George Mason University. His research interests focus on the channel characteristics and organizational implications of new media technologies.

KRISTINE L. FITCH is Associate Professor of Communication Studies at the University of Iowa. She has served as Chair of the Language and Social Interaction Division of the National Communication Association and on the editorial board of *Research on Language and Social Interaction.* She has published on the topics of personal relationships and persuasion from a cultural perspective.

ANDREW J. FLANAGIN is Assistant Professor of Communication at the University of California, Santa Barbara. His research focuses on the social impacts of advanced communication and information technologies, particularly inter- and intraorganizational patterns of communication and information sharing supported by technological systems. His research has appeared in *Human Communication*

Research, Organization Science, Communication Theory, and *Critical Studies in Mass Communication.*

WOLFGANG FRINDTE is founder and Head of the Communications Psychology Department at Friedrich-Schiller-Universität Institute of Psychology. He is principal investigator for several major research projects on distance education in the European Union.

CYNTHIA GALLOIS is Professor of Psychology and President of the Academic Board at the University of Queensland in Australia. Her research focuses on the role of social identity and prejudice in organizational, cross-cultural, and cross-gender communication, as well as the impact of identity on communication about sexual orientation, safe sex, and HIV/AIDS. She has served as editor of *Human Communication Research* and is the immediate past president of the Australian Society of Social Psychologists.

RICHARD A. GERSHON is Associate Professor of Telecommunications Management in the Department of Communication at Western Michigan University. His research interests include telecommunications management and business strategy. He is the author of *The Transnational Media Corporation: Global Messages and Free Market Competition,* named the 1998 book of the year by the U.S. National Cable Television Museum.

MICHAEL GRIFFIN is a Visiting Professor at Macalester College and the University of St. Thomas in St. Paul, Minnesota. In 1995-1996, he was an Annenberg Postdoctoral Fellow at the University of Pennsylvania. He has published in the areas of visual communication, media and culture, and international media. His most recent work is *International Media Monitoring* (coedited with K. Nordenstreng; 1999). He has served as Research Chair of the Visual Communication Interest Group of the International Communication Association.

MARK A. HAMILTON is Associate Professor of Communication Sciences at the University of Connecticut. He is currently Chair of the Information Systems Division of the International Communication Association, and he is a past Chair of the Intrapersonal and Social Cognitive Division of the National Communication Association. His research focuses on the processes through which messages affect audiences' beliefs, attitudes, and behaviors, as well as their evaluations of the message source. His research has appeared in *Communication Monographs, Human Communication Research, Communication Theory, Journal of Language and Social Psychology, Journal of Behavioral Medicine,* and *Perceptual and Motor Skills.*

PAUL M. HARIDAKIS is Assistant Professor in the School of Communication Studies at Kent State University. His research interests include media effects and media policy. His research has appeared in the *Journal of Media Ethics.*

CAROLINE HAYTHORNTHWAITE is Assistant Professor in the Graduate School of Library and Information Science at the University of Illinois, Urbana-Champaign. Her research addresses problems of information exchange and community development in computer-mediated environments. Her recent work examines the social networks of computer-supported distributed learners and knowledge coconstruction in distributed scientific teams.

LISA HENDERSON is Associate Professor of Communication at the University of Massachusetts, Amherst. From 1994 to 1999, she was Cochair of the Gay, Lesbian, Bisexual, and Transgender Studies Interest Group of the International Communication Association. Among her recent publications are "Simple Pleasures: Lesbian Community and *Go Fish*" (in *Signs,* 1999) and "*Storyline* and the Multicultural Middlebrow: Reading Women's Culture on National Public Radio" (in *Critical Studies in Mass Communication,* 1999). Her work in progress includes essays on queer canon formation and the queerness of televised sport, as well as a longer project on the cultural production of class difference and hierarchy.

PATRICIA KEARNEY is Professor of Communication Studies and Codirector of the Hauth Center for Communication Skills at California State University, Long Beach. Her research focuses on communication in the instructional process. She has written three books and more than 50 research articles, chapters, and research reports.

YOUNG YUN KIM is Professor of Communication at the University of Oklahoma. Her research addresses issues of communication in cross-cultural adaptation of immigrants and sojourners, multicultural organizations, and domestic interethnic relations. Her research has appeared in *Communication Yearbook, Human Communication Research, International Journal of Intercultural Relations,* and the *International and Intercultural Communication Annual.* Her books include *Communication and Cross-Cultural Adaptation* (1988), *Theories in Intercultural Communication* (with W. B. Gudykunst; 1988), *Communicating With Strangers: An Approach to Intercultural Communication* (with W. B. Gudykunst; third edition, 1997), and *Becoming Intercultural* (in press).

THOMAS KÖHLER studies psychology and sociology at Friedrich-Schiller-Universität (FSU) and at Swarthmore College. He is a Research Associate in the Department of Social Psychology and the Communications Psychology Department at FSU.

GARY L. KREPS is Chief of the Health Communication and Informatics Research Branch of the National Cancer Institute's Behavioral Research Program,

Division of Cancer Control and Population Sciences. He has written widely about health communication issues in many books, articles, and chapters. He received the Gerald M. Phillips Award for Distinguished Applied Communication Scholarship from the National Communication Association in 1998, and the 2000 Outstanding Health Communication Scholar Award from NCA and ICA.

DALE KUNKEL is Professor of Communication at the University of California, Santa Barbara. His research examines children and media topics, with an emphasis on public policy concerns. He was a principal investigator on the National Television Violence Study, and he has recently completed studies of the V-chip ratings and of sexual socialization messages on television, both funded by the Kaiser Family Foundation.

ANNIE LANG is Professor of Telecommunications and a member of the Cognitive Science Faculty at Indiana University at Bloomington. Her research interests include cognitive processing of mediated and unmediated messages, and physiological and emotional responses to media. Her recent publications have appeared in the *Journal of Communication, Journal of Broadcasting & Electronic Media. Communication Yearbook, Communication Research,* and *Media Psychology.* She is a former Chair of the Information Systems Division of the International Communication Association.

LEAH A. LIEVROUW is Associate Professor in the Department of Information Studies at the University of California, Los Angeles, and is affiliated with UCLA's Communication Studies Program. Her research focuses on the social and cultural changes associated with information and communication technologies and the relationship between new technologies and knowledge. She is coeditor of *The Handbook of New Media.*

ED McLUSKIE is a founding member of the Philosophy of Communication Division and a life member of the International Communication Association. His work has appeared in *Communication Yearbook, Journal of Communication,* and *Journal of Communication Inquiry.* He was a senior Fulbright Professor at the University of Vienna in 1997, where he conducted seminars on Frankfurt critical theory and American pragmatism as bases for developing theory in the study of communication.

J MICHEL METZ is Assistant Professor at the University of Central Florida. His research interests include computer-mediated communication, complexity theory, and technological ethnography.

JEFFERY PITTAM is a Reader in Communication Studies at the University of Queensland in Australia. He has published three books, including *Voice and Social Interaction* (1994), and more than 50 research articles and chapters in the area of intergroup communication, language and group membership, and discourse and identity. He is currently on the editorial board of *Research on Language and Social Interaction.*

TIMOTHY G. PLAX is Professor of Communication Studies at California State University, Long Beach. His programs of research focus on social influence and communication in instruction and training. He has written three introductory textbooks and more than 100 research articles, chapters, and research reports. He is a recipient of the 1998-1999 CSULB Distinguished Faculty Research and Creative Activity Award and the CSULB Associated Students Presidential Award.

ANITA POMERANTZ is Associate Professor of Communication at the University at Albany, State University of New York. She has served as Chair of the Language and Social Interaction Divisions of the National Communication Association and the International Communication Association, and on the editorial board of *Research on Language and Social Interaction.* Using audio- and videotapes of interaction, she analyzes the knowledge and reasoning processes employed in face-to-face interaction.

LINDA L. PUTNAM is Professor of Organizational Communication in the Department of Speech Communication at Texas A&M University. Her current research interests include negotiation and organizational conflict, metaphors of organizational communication, and language analysis in organizations. She is coeditor of the *Handbook of Organizational Communication: Advances in Theory, Research, and Methods* (2000), *Communication and Negotiation* (1992), *Handbook of Organizational Communication* (1987), and *Communication and Organizations: An Interpretive Approach* (1983). She has published more than 100 articles and book chapters in the areas of organizational communication, conflict management, negotiation, and organizational studies. She is the recipient of the 1993 Charles H. Woolbert Research Award for innovative research in communication and the 1999 Distinguished Scholar Award from the National Communication Association. She is a Fellow of the International Communication Association and Past President of the ICA and of the International Association for Conflict Management.

MICHAEL E. ROLOFF is Professor in the Department of Communication Studies at Northwestern University. His research interests include interpersonal conflict, persuasion, and bargaining. He is the immediate past editor of *Communication Yearbook* and is the current editor of *Communication Research.* He has published in *Human Communication Research, Personal Relationships,* and *Communication Monographs.*

ALAN M. RUBIN is Professor and Interim Director in the School of Communication Studies at Kent State University, where he also serves as Director of the

Communication Research Center. His research interests include media uses and effects, and the interface of personal and mediated communication. His current projects include uses of newer communication technologies and the role of aggression in television talk-show viewing. He is immediate past editor of the *Journal of Communication* and a past editor of the *Journal of Broadcasting & Electronic Media.*

ROBERT E. SANDERS is Professor and Chair of the Department of Communication and an affiliate member of the Program in Linguistics and Cognitive Science at the University at Albany, State University of New York. He has chaired the Language and Social Interaction Divisions of the National Communication Association and the International Communication Association, and was editor of *Research on Language and Social Interaction* from 1988 to 1998. He has published theoretical and empirical studies on "neo-rhetorical" participation in social interaction, recently on such topics as the enactment of role identities, relationship formation, compliance seeking, and children's methods of averting conflict.

DAVID R. SEIBOLD is Professor and Chair of the Department of Communication at the University of California, Santa Barbara. Author of nearly 100 publications on organizational communication, group decision making, and interpersonal influence, he has received numerous research and teaching awards. He is the immediate past editor of the *Journal of Applied Communication Research.* He has served as Chair of the Interpersonal and Small Group Division of the National Communication Association and is immediate past Chair of the Organizational Communication Division of the International Communication Association.

HEMANT SHAH is Associate Professor in the School of Journalism and Mass Communication and Director of the Asian American Studies Program at the University of Wisconsin–Madison. His research focuses on the role of journalism in social and economic development and on media depictions of minority groups. His research has been published in *Communication Review, Communication Theory, Critical Studies in Mass Communication, Journalism Monographs, Journalism Quarterly,* and *Media Asia,* among others.

MICHAEL A. SHAPIRO is Associate Professor of Communication at Cornell University. His research interests include the mental processing of communication, particularly as it relates to social reality, risk communication, and attitude. His recent research has appeared in *Journal of Communication, Communication Research, Journalism Quarterly,* and *Communication Yearbook.* He is a past Chair of the Information System Division of the International Communication Association and a former head of the Communication Theory and Methodology Division of the Association for Education in Journalism and Mass Communication.

S. SHYAM SUNDAR is Assistant Professor and Director of the Media Effects Research Laboratory in the College of Communications at Pennsylvania State University. His research investigates psychological aspects of technological features in on-line interaction from a media-effects perspective.

DAVID L. SWANSON is Professor and Head of the Department of Speech Communication, University of Illinois at Urbana-Champaign, and editor of *Political Communication*. His research concerning politics and the media has been published in numerous journals and volumes in the United States and abroad, where his work has been published in Spanish, Greek, Italian, and Japanese translations. His major works are *Politics, Media, and Modern Democracy* (with P. Mancini; 1996) and *New Directions in Political Communication* (with D. Nimmo; 1990). He is a former Chair of the Political Communication Division of the International Communication Association and the Rhetorical and Communication Theory Division of the National Communication Association.

JAMES R. TAYLOR is Emeritus Professor of Communication at the University of Montreal. He is coauthor of two books currently in press: *The Emergent Organization: Communication as Its Site and Surface* (with Van Every) and *The Computerization of Work* (with Groleau, Heaton, and Van Every). His earlier books include *Rethinking the Theory of Organizational Communication* (with Van Every) and *The Vulnerable Fortress: Organization and Management in the Information Age.*

MAUREEN TAYLOR is Assistant Professor of Communication at Rutgers University. She conducts research on international public relations, issues management, and communication in the nation-building process. Her research has been published in *Public Relations Research* and *Public Relations Review.*

ELIZABETH L. TOTH is Associate Dean for Academic Affairs and Professor of Public Relations at the S. I. Newhouse School of Public Communication at Syracuse University. She has published more than 50 articles, book chapters, and papers. Her coedited book *Rhetorical and Critical Approaches to Public Relations* won the National Communication Association PRIDE Award. She is also coeditor of *The Gender Challenge to the Media: Diverse Voices From the Field* and coauthor of *Women and Public Relations.* She received the 1998 Institute for Public Relations Pathfinder Award for her research on gender issues and public relations.

GABRIEL M. VASQUEZ is Assistant Professor of Communication at the University of Houston. His research focuses on public relations, issues management, and campaign management. He received the Outstanding Dissertation Award from the Public Relations Division of the International Communication Association in 1995.

JENNIFER H. WALDECK is Assistant Professor in Communication Studies at the University of Kansas. Her research interests include socialization in organizational and instructional contexts, communication technology use and assessment, and the use of quantitative research methods. She has presented her work at numerous professional conferences and has published in several journals. She serves on the editorial board of the National Communication Association's Committee on Assessment and Testing.

ANN WEATHERALL is Lecturer in the School of Psychology at Victoria University of Wellington, New Zealand. Her research interests are in feminist psychology and the social psychology of language and communication. She has published in a variety of journals, including *Human Communication Research* and *Journal of Language and Social Psychology*. She is currently working on a book titled *Women, Language, and Psychology*.

BARBIE ZELIZER is the Raymond Williams Term Chair and Associate Professor of Communication at the University of Pennsylvania's Annenberg School for Communication. Her most recent book, *Remembering to Forget: Holocaust Memory Through the Camera's Eye* (1998), won the Best Book Award from the International Communication Association, the Diamond Book Award from the National Communication Association, and the Bruno Brand Tolerance Book Award from the Simon Weisenthal Center. A Guggenheim Fellow, she has published widely on journalism as cultural practice and collective memory. Her media criticism has appeared in *The Nation* and *The Jim Lehrer News Hour*.